Elderly Client Handbook

FIFTH EDITION

Other titles available from Law Society Publishing:

Age Discrimination: A Guide to the New Law
General Editor: Shaman Kapoor

Assessment of Mental Capacity: A Practical Guide for Doctors and Lawyers (4th edn)
The British Medical Association and the Law Society

Inheritance Act Claims
Tracey Angus, Anna Clarke, Paul Hewitt and Penelope Reed

Lasting Powers of Attorney: A Practical Guide (2nd edn)
Craig Ward

Probate Practitioner's Handbook (7th edn)
General Editor: Lesley King

Trust Practitioner's Handbook (2nd edn)
Gill Steel with contributions by Robert Mowbray and Charles Christian

Will Draftsman's Handbook (9th edn)
Robin Riddett, Lesley King and Peter Gausden

Titles from Law Society Publishing can be ordered from all good bookshops or direct (telephone 0870 850 1422, email **lawsociety@prolog.uk.com** or visit our online shop at **www.lawsociety.org.uk/bookshop**).

ELDERLY CLIENT HANDBOOK

FIFTH EDITION

General Editor: Caroline Bielanska

The Law Society

Crown copyright material is reproduced with the permission of the Controller of Her Majesty's Stationery Office.

ISBN-13: 978-1-78446-022-8

Published in 2016 by the Law Society
113 Chancery Lane, London WC2A 1PL

Typeset by Columns Design XML Ltd, Reading
Printed by CPI Antony Rowe, Chippenham, Wilts

The paper used for the text pages of this book is FSC® certified. FSC (the Forest Stewardship Council®) is an international network to promote responsible management of the world's forests.

FSC
www.fsc.org
MIX
Paper from
responsible sources
FSC® C013604

Contents

CONTENTS

Foreword to the fifth edition

In 1962 I was fortunate to be taught Family Law by Professor Bromley (then senior lecturer) at Manchester University and I still treasure the second edition of his book on the subject. Until the first edition was published in 1957 this was not a discrete field of law, yet it is now part of most degree courses and professional examinations and there are separate family courts. Little did I think when this handbook was first published in 1994 that I was following in his footsteps by formulating elder law, and that some two decades later I would be writing a foreword to the fifth edition.

It was so much simpler then, and having been a solicitor in general practice I was able write the whole book on my own with the assistance of colleagues on the Law Society's mental health and disability committee, of which I was then a member. The social and legal climate has changed almost unrecognisably in the intervening years, with books on many new relevant topics: community care, healthcare, human rights, equality (including disability discrimination), civil partnerships, data protection and elder abuse, quite apart from a comprehensive mental capacity jurisdiction and the new Court of Protection. It is no longer feasible for one author to cover the entire topic and that there are 16 contributors to this edition highlights the specialisms that have developed. I can think of no one better equipped than Caroline Bielanska to coordinate the work as general editor. In her preface she draws attention to the role of the legal practitioner in this growing market and although, as she states, 'little remains of the original material', the structure has survived surprisingly well.

Despite the threat to traditional publishing by the internet, which has revolutionised access to the law, there remains room for a handbook of this nature. Statutory material may be found through a Google search and law reports are freely available on Bailii, but the busy practitioner needs an overview and guidance on practical issues. That has always been the purpose of this handbook. The elderly client practice is now recognised. The unmet need that I originally perceived has become a reality, the breadth of that need is increasing and this latest edition should go some way towards assisting the legal profession to tackle its important role. That now extends to the new mental capacity jurisdiction, the success of which depends upon the lawyers and other professionals involved. I urge you all to be pragmatic rather than too legalistic. Now that I am potentially an elderly client, I find myself desiring solutions rather than looking for problems. Life is too short!

Gordon R. Ashton OBE, LLB (Hons)
Retired District Judge and Nominated Judge of the Court of Protection
January 2016

Preface to the fifth edition

The word 'elderly' is not always a helpful label to identify a person or group, as there is no widely accepted age when a person becomes elderly. Before the introduction of the welfare state, when life expectancy was under 70 years of age, it may have been easier to identify those who lived beyond the average life expectancy as being 'elderly' or, by borrowing terminology from the National Assistance Act 1948, to identify certain people as 'aged'. More recently, there has been a trend to use the terms 'senior', 'elder' or even 'very elderly', but it is the word 'elderly' which still resonates with clients and their families and, when they seek legal advice and assistance, they have usually decided that this term is applicable to them or one of their family.

In 2009 there were more than 12 million people over retirement age (then 60 for women and 65 for men) in the United Kingdom. Both the number of retired people, and the percentage of the population comprising this group, have steadily increased over the last 60 years. It is expected that these upward trends will continue as the post-war baby boomers grow older. The change in population is even more pronounced when considering those over 85 years of age. In 1984 there were 650,000 people over 85, but 30 years later, it is estimated that nearly one in five people currently in the United Kingdom will live to see their 100th birthday.

As the number of elderly people increases, so will their needs. Forty per cent of all people aged 65 and over have a limiting, long-standing illness. It is estimated that one person in five will at some stage suffer from dementia or require nursing care. The ageing population and increased prevalence of long-term conditions have a significant impact on health and social care and it is thought this will require additional expenditure of £5 billion by 2018.

Although an elderly client is no different from a younger client, in so far as they buy and sell homes, make wills or get divorced, there are specific problems commonly encountered by the elderly which may cause them to seek legal advice. For example, a decline in a client's physical and/or mental ability may have a substantial and long-term adverse effect on his or her ability to carry out day-to-day activities, prompting the need to plan ahead or deal with the immediate consequences of their situation.

The advice, and the way it is provided, have to be adapted to take into account the client's circumstances. Changes to professional best practice, legislation and case law serve as a constant reminder that clients with physical and/or mental difficulties can be more vulnerable to abuse, fraud, manipulation, exploitation and poor decision-making. Advisers of elderly clients need to be alert to these risks, but also supportive of individual clients, so that they retain autonomy over their lives as much and for as long as possible.

Elderly clients are arguably becoming more litigious and demanding, and their needs increasingly complex. To serve these needs, advisers often have to navigate their way through an ever deepening bureaucracy associated with health and social care services. Families are smaller and more fragmented than in the past, and many older people become isolated. Some elderly clients may be asset rich, but cash poor because, for example, they have benefited from the rise in property values but have limited investments and savings.

How do elderly clients who want to continue to live in their own homes utilise that wealth if the asset cannot be realised? The desire to reduce or eliminate the tax burden often conflicts with the desire to reduce what they may pay for their social care, so that more can be passed to the next generation. Those who need care and support must also plan and manage their financial affairs to ensure that their care is sustainable for the remainder of their life.

The elderly client adviser is expected to balance these competing demands, taking into account wide-ranging legal and practical issues. This involves examining the value of the client's estate, the nature of the client's assets, the effects of care costs and inheritance tax, the dynamics of their family and other important relationships, lifetime gifts, their expectations and their life expectancy. Critically, the adviser must also consider whether the client has the requisite mental capacity and whether the client is being unduly influenced by others.

The scope of the advice needed can be very broad – almost taking us back to the days when all solicitors were generalists, looking after the whole range of the client's needs, but at the same time having in-depth specialist knowledge. The relationship with a client may continue over a long period. What may start out as advice about a will can evolve into lasting powers of attorney or a deputyship, advance decisions, welfare benefits, property ownership, care needs, housing needs, litigation, contracts, employment, insurance and a multitude of other areas of law. The interaction between different areas needs to be recognised, understood and advised upon. Some areas of law applicable to elderly clients also apply to younger disabled people, whose needs may be different but to whom the same legal principles are applied.

Since the last edition of this work was published in 2010, all public services have been subject to austerity measures, requiring public bodies to cut their outgoings by reducing staff and overheads, thus restricting what services are provided and in what ways. This has created inevitable delays in responses and limits on delivery from bodies such as HMRC, the Court of Protection, the DWP, the NHS and local authorities, leaving clients at risk of a lack of care provision or lack of money. The 'digitalisation agenda' is pushing more people to access information and apply for services online, such as applying for a benefit or making a lasting power of attorney. People are being encouraged to 'do it themselves'. This may pose a risk to some elderly clients as they may be more likely to make an error in the process or in their decision. Navigating the fragmented and complex systems of public bodies is not for the faint hearted. Clients who obtain impartial and comprehensive legal advice and assistance are best placed to find solutions to inadequate state delivery, protecting themselves and/or their estate. To some extent, then, the lawyers who serve these clients are empowering the disempowered.

The austerity measures are dovetailed with social care reform in the Care Act 2014, which came into force on 1 April 2015 in England and the Social Services and Well-being (Wales) Act 2014, which comes into force on 6 April 2016. Welfare benefits are, likewise, going through incremental reform, following the introduction of the Welfare Reform Act 2012. Reform has also been seen in the regulation of care, following numerous reports of abuse and neglect, including those occurring at Winterbourne and Stafford hospitals.

Following the House of Lords Select Committee's post-legislative scrutiny of the Mental Capacity Act 2005 and the General Comments made by the Committee of the United Nations Convention on the Rights of People with Disabilities, our mental capacity legislation is under review, with planned changes to court rules, safeguards for deprivation of liberty and the government considering whether the core legislation is compatible with the Convention rights. There have also been recent changes to the prescribed forms for lasting powers of attorney in an attempt to make it easier for people to register effective powers. These developments and the plethora of case law from the Court of Protection mean that advisers of elderly clients need up-to-date resources to support them in their role.

This book provides an overview of the law and practice relating to the needs of the elderly client, which will give readers useful summaries of subjects within their expertise, and accessible introductions to the areas of law less familiar to them. Although this approach precludes detailed exposition of the law and practice in every area covered by the book, practitioners will still find coverage of all the main issues affecting elderly clients and, where appropriate, references to more detailed sources. There are also practical reminders, tips, and explanations of the relevant professional and ethical guidance, which will improve the adviser's ability to combine the application of an up-to-date risk analysis with a concern for their clients' welfare and best interests.

One of the hardest tasks in editing and writing a book of this nature is deciding what should be left out, particularly as law constantly changes. Fortunately, this book is not alone in serving the needs of elderly client advisers. There are a growing number of specialist texts and online information products which fill the gaps when more specialist information is required, such as updated statutory material, case summaries and time-saving precedents.

I appreciate the continued involvement of retired District Judge Gordon Ashton, who wrote the first edition of this book in 1995 and revised the second edition with Anne Edis. Little remains of the original material, although his concept shines through 20 years later. I am indebted to him for sowing the seed of the need to establish a group which specialised in advising elderly clients: this seed grew into what is now Solicitors for the Elderly, in conjunction with which this work is being published. As a founding member and its former chair and chief executive, it is with great pride that I see how the organisation has flourished to be highly valued by its members and highly regarded by those with whom it engages. Long may it continue!

All the contributors to this book are busy practitioners and to my amazement have found the time and energy to produce such excellent material – they deserve praise for their efforts. For each contributor there are families and work colleagues shouldering the burden of home and work life, to enable the delivery of chapters and without them it would impossible to complete this Handbook. I am grateful to my husband, Gurp and my children, Max and Maya, for allowing me the space to write and edit this work and forgiving me for neglecting them.

The law is as stated on 1 October 2015.

Caroline Bielanska
October 2015

Notes on contributors

Julia Abrey is a solicitor and partner in Withers LLP in London specialising in elder law and Court of Protection matters. Julia is head of Withers' multi-jurisdictional elder law team and has a particular interest in international and cross-border mental capacity issues and is chair of STEP's cross-border Mental Capacity Special Interest Group. A contributor to a number of books, most recently *The International Protection of Adults* (Oxford University Press, 2015), Julia is an editor of and contributor to *Tolley's Finance and Law for the Older Client* (LexisNexis) and editorial board member of *Elder Law Journal* (Jordan Publishing). She is also one of the two UK members of the US National Academy of Elder Law Attorneys Inc. and a past chair of Solicitors for the Elderly. Julia features as a leading Court of Protection practitioner in *Legal 500*, *Chambers UK*, and the Citywealth *Leaders List* and *Powerwomen* listings, and is the STEP Trusted Advisor of the Year 2015/16.

Caroline Bielanska is a solicitor, mediator and former chief executive of Solicitors for the Elderly, an organisation she helped to found in 1999, and a member of STEP. She lectures regularly for a number of leading CPD providers and provides consultancy for law firms on an independent basis. She is the editor and principal contributor to *Elderly Clients: A Precedent Manual*, 5th edn (Jordan Publishing, 2016), author of *Elderly People and the Law*, 2nd edn (Jordan Publishing, 2014) and *Health and Social Care Handbook* (Law Society, 2006) and a contributor to a range of books, journals and loose leafs including *Heywood and Massey's Court of Protection Practice* (Sweet & Maxwell) and *Elder Law Journal* (Jordan Publishing). She sits on the Court of Protection Users' Group and is a member of the Court of Protection's Rules Review Committee, recommending changes to the court rules, practice directions and forms.

Serdar Celebi is a housing and community care solicitor at Cambridge House Law Centre and his cases have been reported in *Legal Action* (Legal Action Group) and the *Housing Law Casebook*, 6th edn (LAG, 2015).

Caroline Coats is a notary public, lecturer and writer with over 25 years' experience in private client work. Specialising in the legal issues of most concern to the elderly and disabled, she set up her own practice in 2003. She is a member of STEP and a regional coordinator for Solicitors for the Elderly as well as a trustee for various charities over the years. While involved with the Department of Health Common Assessment for Adults pilot, she drafted and developed an Advance Care Plan subsequently utilised nationwide, the latest version being accessed on **www.sayitonce.com** (the legacy website of the pilot).

Hugh Cumber is a barrister at 5 Stone Buildings. He has a traditional chancery practice and practises in the Court of Protection with a particular focus on property and affairs. He regularly contributes case notes and other commentary to the *Elder Law Journal* (Jordan Publishing). Between 2014 and 2015 he acted as judicial assistant to Lord Neuberger, president of the Supreme Court. He is a member of the Chancery Bar Association.

Imogen Davies is is a professional support lawyer at Withers LLP in London. She is an English law qualified solicitor, member of STEP (and has the STEP Advanced Certificate in Will Preparation) and is a member of the Law Society of England and Wales' capital taxes sub-committee. She has contributed to *McCutcheon on Inheritance Tax*, 6th edition (Sweet and Maxwell, 2013), the looseleafs *Practical Trust Precedents* and *Practical Will Precedents* (Sweet and Maxwell), and *Tax Planning for Farm and Land Diversification*, 3rd edition (Bloomsbury Professional, 2011).

David Foster is a partner in the firm of Foster & Foster in Enfield in London which currently specialises in social welfare law. Since 1980 he has worked in law centres and in private practice specialising in housing law. He is a founder member of the Housing Law Practitioners Association and was the first Law Society council member for housing law and a member of its housing law committee.

Sheree Green is a senior associate and the Court of Protection lead at Anthony Collins Solicitors. She is a member of the Law Society's mental health and disability committee and of the ad hoc Court of Protection rules committee, a regional co-ordinator for Solicitors for the Elderly and a Law Society accredited mental health specialist. Sheree is a contributor to the Law Society/BMA *Assessment of Mental Capacity*, 4th edn (Law Society, 2015) and the Law Society's Meeting the Needs of Vulnerable Clients Practice Note. She specialises in mental health and mental capacity matters and has been appointed by the Office of the Public Guardian to their panel of professional deputies.

Amanda King-Jones has been a partner of Thomas Eggar which is a trading style of Irwin Mitchell LLP since 1987 specialising in probate and the affairs of the elderly. She is co-author of the *Probate Practice Manual* (Sweet & Maxwell). She is a member of STEP and Solicitors for the Elderly, and an Office of the Public Guardian panel deputy.

Julia Krish is a barrister at Garden Court Chambers. She is a criminal practitioner and specialises in representing mentally disordered and vulnerable defendants, including the elderly. Since 2003 she has sat as a part-time judge in the Mental Health Tribunal. She is the co-author of *Advising Mentally Disordered Offenders*, 2nd edn (Law Society, 2009). For many years she has also provided training to both lawyers and doctors on criminal law and practice, and in particular on the interface between criminal law and mental disorder.

Susan Lowe is a solicitor with over 20 years' experience in private client work. She is a full member of Solicitors For the Elderly and set up her own practice in 2006. Her specialism is general private client work and the core work of the practice; her role as a Court of Protection deputy for over 30 individuals has involved dealing with financial and psychological abuse and families in conflict. Susan is a former member of the Court of Protection panel of deputies of last resort. Other activities include trusteeship of the charity in the village where Susan lives and providing 'drop-in' services at several assisted living facilities in her local area.

Cate Searle is a community care law solicitor who co-founded her Brighton-based firm, Martin Searle Solicitors, in 2004. Cate has a background in health and social care work and a degree in Developmental Psychology. She has many years' experience of representing clients who have disabilities, mental health problems or caring responsibilities across a range of legal issues, including Court of Protection litigation, safeguarding and NHS Continuing Healthcare. She also runs training seminars for private and elderly client solicitors across England.

Stewart Stretton-Hill is a senior associate with Thomas Eggar which is a trading style of Irwin Mitchell LLP. He qualified as a personal injury specialist in 2000 and acted on high value clinical negligence claims for children who sustained brain damage as a result of injury at birth. In 2007 he switched to private client specialising in advising on Court of Protection applications, powers of attorney and matters affecting elderly and vulnerable clients. Stewart is a member of STEP, Solicitors for the Elderly, and the Law Society Probate Section and is chairman of the firm's internal elderly and vulnerable client technical committee.

Joanna Sulek is qualified as a barrister and was a member of Mind's legal unit for almost twenty years, where she contributed extensively to training and publications on mental health law, mental health tribunals, disability discrimination legislation and other areas of law. She also contributed to Mind's work on legal advice, policy and casework. Prior to joining Mind, she was a lecturer in medical law, mental health and capacity law, and property and trusts, having previously worked as a Law Commission research assistant as well as in local government and the NHS. She has been a member of the Office of the Public Guardian consultative forum and the Official Solicitor and Public Trustee user group.

Martin Terrell is a partner in the firm of Thomson Snell & Passmore in Tunbridge Wells and a former director of Solicitors for the Elderly. He is author of *A Practitioner's Guide to the Court of Protection*, 3rd edn (Bloomsbury Professional, 2009) and a contributor to *Heywood & Massey: Court of Protection Practice* (Sweet & Maxwell), *Finance and Law for the Older Client* (Lexis Nexis) and *Court of Protection Practice 2010* (Jordan Publishing).

Gary Vaux manages a money advice and welfare rights service for a large county council. He is also a freelance trainer, author and consultant on social security matters, working with a range of voluntary and statutory organisations such as Chartered Institute of Housing, National Housing Federation, London Advice Services Alliance, Child Poverty Action Group, Fostering Network, Solicitors for the Elderly, Family Rights Group and many others. He chairs the social security advisers group for the Local Government Association and is a member of the DWP's Policy and Strategy Forum and the Operational Stakeholders Group. His particular interest is in those areas where social security and social care policies and practices intersect – and frequently collide.

Table of cases

Table of statutes

Table of statutory instruments

Table of international instruments

Abbreviations

1990 Act	National Health Service and Community Care Act 1990
2007 Regulations	Lasting Powers of Attorney, Enduring Powers of Attorney and Public Guardian Regulations 2007, SI 2007/1253
2009 Regulations	Lasting Powers of Attorney, Enduring Powers of Attorney and Public Guardian (Amendment) Regulations 2009, SI 2009/1884
2014 Regulations	Health and Social Care Act 2008 (Regulated Activities) Regulations 2014, SI 2014/2936
2015 Regulations	Lasting Powers of Attorney, Enduring Powers of Attorney and Public Guardian (Amendment) Regulations 2015, SI 2015/899
AA	attendance allowance
A&E	accident and emergency
ACAS	Advisory, Conciliation and Arbitration Service
ADR	alternative dispute resolution
ALMO	arm's length management organisation
AMHP	approved mental health professional
AP	authorised party
ATE	after the event
AVCs	additional voluntary contributions
BDRA 1953	Births and Deaths Registration Act 1953
BSL	British Sign Language
CA 2014	Care Act 2014
CaFA 2014	Children and Families Act 2014
CAO	child arrangements order
CCG	clinical commissioning group
CGT	capital gains tax
CIS	collective investment scheme
CJA 2003	Criminal Justice Act 2003
CJA 2009	Coroners and Justice Act 2009
COFA	Compliance Officer for Finance and Administration
COLP	Compliance Officer for Legal Practice
COPR	Court of Protection Rules 2007, SI 2007/1744
CPR	Civil Procedure Rules 1998, SI 1998/3132

CPS	Crown Prosecution Service
CQC	Care Quality Commission
CRAG	Charging for Residential Accommodation Guide
CRB	Criminal Records Bureau
CRPD	Convention on the Rights of Persons with Disabilities
CRU	Compensation Recovery Unit
CSCI	Commission for Social Care Inspection
CSSG	Care and Support Statutory Guidance
CSSIW	Care and Social Services Inspectorate for Wales
CTO	community treatment order
DBS	Disclosure and Barring Service
DLA	disability living allowance
DOLS	deprivation of liberty safeguards
DVLA	Driver and Vehicle Licensing Agency
DWP	Department for Work and Pensions
EA 2010	Equality Act 2010
ECT	electroconvulsive therapy
ELI	employer's liability insurance
EPA	enduring power of attorney
FCA	Financial Conduct Authority
FP(A)R	Family Procedure (Adoption) Rules 2005, SI 2005/2795
FPR	Family Procedure Rules 2010, SI 2010/2955
FSAVCs	free-standing AVCs
FSMA 2000	Financial Services and Markets Act 2000
GP	general practitioner
HASSASSA 1983	Health and Social Services and Social Security Adjudications Act 1983
HB	Health Board
HIAs	home improvement agencies
HMCTS	HM Courts and Tribunals Service
HMRC	HM Revenue and Customs
HSO	Health Service Ombudsman
HWB	health and wellbeing board
ICAS	Independent Complaints Advocacy Service
ICO	Information Commissioner's Office
IFA	independent financial adviser
IHT	inheritance tax
ILF	Independent Living Fund
IMCA	independent mental incapacity advocate
IMHA	independent mental health advocate
Inquests Rules	Coroners (Inquests) Rules 2013, SI 2013/1616
Investigations Regs	Coronors (Investigations) Regulations 2013, SI 2013/1629
IR	Insolvency Rules 1986, SI 1986/1925
IRP	independent review panel

ISA	Individual Savings Account
LASPO	Legal Aid, Sentencing and Punishment of Offenders Act 2012
LPA	lasting power of attorney
LPAHW	lasting power of attorney for health and welfare
LVT	Leasehold Valuation Tribunal
MatCA 1973	Matrimonial Causes Act 1973
MCA 2005	Mental Capacity Act 2005
MCCD	medical certificate of cause of death
MDT	multidisciplinary team
MHA 1983	Mental Health Act 1983
MHF	Mental Health Foundation
MIAM	mediation, information and assessment meeting
NCB	National Commissioning Board
NI	national insurance
NICE	National Institute for Health and Care Excellence
NHSBT	NHS Blood and Transplant
OPG	Office of the Public Guardian
PACE	Police and Criminal Evidence Act 1984
PALS	Patient Advice and Liaison Service
PD	Practice Direction
PDA 2013	Presumption of Death Act 2013
PEA	personal expenses allowance
PET	potentially exempt transfer
PIP	personal independence payment
RAO 2001	Financial Services and Markets Act 2000 (Regulated Activities) Order 2001, SI 2001/544
RC	responsible clinician
RMP	registered medical practitioner
RNIB	Royal National Institute of Blind People
RNID	Royal National Institute for Deaf People
S2P	State Second Pension
SALT	speech and language therapist
SAR	subject access request
SCIE	Social Care Institute for Excellence
SERPS	State Earnings Related Pension Scheme
SOAD	second opinion appointed doctor
SRA	Solicitors Regulation Authority
SSCS	Social Security and Child Support
SSWB(W)A	Social Services and Well-being (Wales) Act 2014
STEP	Society of Trust and Estate Practitioners
TDA 1999	Trustee Delegation Act 1999
TSA	Tenant Services Authority

TUPE	Transfer of Undertakings (Protection of Employment) Regulations 2006, SI 2006/246
UFSAMC	*Unified and Fair System for Assessing and Managing Care*
W3C	World Wide Web Consortium
WIQS	Wills and Inheritance Quality Scheme
YJCEA 1999	Youth Justice and Criminal Evidence Act 1999

PART A

The legal framework

CHAPTER 1

Capacity and best interests decision-making

Sheree Green

1.1 THE IMPORTANCE OF DETERMINING CAPACITY

It is a key principle of the law that every adult has the right to make his or her own decisions and is assumed to have the capacity (ability) to do so unless it is proved otherwise. In relation to older clients, the client's capacity to make a particular decision or carry out a legal transaction may be questioned either at the time the decision needs to be made or retrospectively (e.g. after the client has died). It is therefore important that solicitors who act for older clients must be able to recognise and cope with the legal implications of lack of capacity.

The Mental Capacity Act (MCA) 2005, supported by the accompanying MCA 2005 Code of Practice, provides the legal framework for the making of decisions on behalf of adults in England and Wales who may not have the requisite capacity to make a specific decision for themselves.

Solicitors and all other professionals working with adults who may lack capacity to make decisions for themselves need to be familiar with the principles behind MCA 2005 and the main provisions of the Act and must have regard to the MCA 2005 Code of Practice.

1.1.1 The Mental Capacity Act 2005

MCA 2005 confirms the previous common law position that capacity is function specific, relating to each particular decision at the time the decision needs to be made. The Act includes provisions to promote and encourage autonomy by ensuring that people are given all appropriate help and support to enable them to make their own decisions where possible, extending arrangements for people to prepare in advance for future lack of capacity and maximising their participation in any decision-making process.

MCA 2005 defines what it means to 'lack capacity', and integrates the jurisdiction for the making of personal welfare decisions, healthcare decisions and financial decisions on behalf of people lacking capacity to make such decisions.

1.2 TERMINOLOGY

1.2.1 Labels

In relation to mental capacity, terms with distinct meanings may be applied as labels, sometimes inappropriately.

The Mental Health Foundation (MHF) acknowledges that a variety of terms are used to describe people with mental health problems, some of which have negative connotations. Other definitions have been devised by people with mental health problems to change public perceptions and challenge stigma and discrimination.

The MHF sets out a number of frequently used terms:

- **People with mental health problems.** A broad definition used by a range of agencies. Emphasises and acknowledges that the person is a person first, not a psychiatric diagnosis, and that many people experience mental distress and this may be a 'problem', not necessarily an illness.
- **People with experience of mental and emotional distress.** An even broader definition than above that aims to be as inclusive as possible, and focuses on the experience itself rather than using the concept of 'problem' as a label.
- **People with a mental illness.** This is a narrower definition and is often used by psychological and psychiatric services. By placing the emphasis on the term 'illness', it acknowledges the need for medical treatment.

Disability

The Convention on the Rights of Persons with Disabilities (CRPD) is an international treaty that was passed by the United Nations in 2006 and ratified by the UK in 2009. The CRPD protects the rights and promotes equality of persons with disabilities. It uses a social model of disability and defines disability as including 'those who have long-term physical, mental, intellectual or sensory impairments which in interaction with various barriers may hinder their full and effective participation in society on an equal basis with others'.

1.2.2 Definitions

Capacity

Capacity refers to a person's ability to do something and, in a legal context, it refers to a person's ability to perform a specific juristic act (such as making a will, a gift, a contract or a power of attorney), which may have consequences for the person, or for other people.

4

Incapacity

Incapacity, or the inability to enter into a transaction, is either imposed by the law for policy reasons (e.g. in relation to children under 16 years) or arises by reason of 'an impairment of, or a disturbance in the functioning of, the mind or brain', according to MCA 2005. For an adult, it is not correct to say that the person 'lacks capacity' generally. Instead, a person may be deemed to lack capacity to make a specific decision at a particular moment in time. The adult may lack mental capacity to make one decision but possess capacity to make another decision; likewise, a person may have a mental disorder and be detained for treatment under the Mental Health Act 1983 but still have capacity to make decisions.

Lack of capacity: MCA 2005 definition

The statutory definition and test of capacity under MCA 2005 are described at **1.5.1**.

1.2.3 Vulnerability and adults at risk

Particular difficulties arise in relation to individuals who require assistance or support from others in order to make decisions. Although they may be able to make the decision in question if the relevant information is explained to them in a simple and straightforward manner, they are reliant on the person providing the information to be both honest and balanced. They are therefore potentially vulnerable to the risks of undue influence, bad advice or even the malign intent of others. See *Finsbury Park Mortgage Funding Ltd* v. *Ronald Burrows and Pegram Heron* LTL 3.5.02, where it was held solicitors owed a duty of care to a vulnerable older man to ensure he knew what he was doing. See also *Hammond* v. *Osborn* [2002] EWCA Civ 885 concerning undue influence of a vulnerable person by a carer.

If someone does not lack capacity to make a particular decision within the meaning of MCA 2005, but does fall within this category of vulnerable people, then no one can lawfully step in and make the decision for the person. However, the person's potential vulnerability may trigger the local authority's safeguarding duties for adults at risk under s.42(2) of the Care Act 2014 in England or s.126 of the Social Services and Well-being (Wales) Act 2014 to make enquiries. Where necessary, their case may be considered by the High Court in the exercise of its inherent jurisdiction. The definition of vulnerability is not straightforward, however. In *Re SA (Vulnerable Adult with Capacity: Marriage)* [2005] EWHC 2942 (Fam), Munby J made the following observations:

> [77] ... the authorities to which I have referred demonstrate that the inherent jurisdiction can be exercised in relation to a vulnerable adult who, even if not incapacitated by mental disorder or mental illness, is, or is reasonably believed to be, either (i) under constraint or (ii) subject to coercion or undue influence or (iii) for some other reason deprived of the capacity to make the relevant decision, or disabled from making a free choice, or incapacitated or disabled from giving or expressing a real and genuine consent.

...

[82] In the context of the inherent jurisdiction I would treat as a vulnerable adult someone who, whether or not mentally incapacitated, and whether or not suffering from any mental illness or mental disorder, is or may be unable to take care of him or herself, or unable to protect him or herself against significant harm or exploitation, or who is deaf, blind or dumb, or who is substantially handicapped by illness, injury or congenital deformity. This, I emphasise, is not and is not intended to be a definition. It is descriptive, not definitive; indicative rather than prescriptive.

The Court of Appeal confirmed in *Re L (Vulnerable Adults with Capacity: Court's Jurisdiction)* [2012] EWCA Civ 253 that the inherent jurisdiction of the High Court survives to act as a 'great safety net' to offer protection to vulnerable adults who are not deemed to 'lack capacity' according to the provisions of MCA 2005.

1.3 PRESUMPTIONS

1.3.1 Presumption of capacity

MCA 2005 (s.1(2)) has confirmed in statute the former common law presumption that an adult has capacity (although this presumption may be rebutted by a specific finding of lack of capacity).

It is important to note:

- If an act and the manner in which it was carried out are rational, there is a strong presumption that the individual was mentally capable at the time of the act.
- Eccentricity of behaviour or making an unwise decision is not necessarily a sign of lack of capacity (MCA 2005, s.1(4)) and care should be exercised before any such assumption is made.

1.3.2 Presumption of continuance

Before MCA 2005 came into effect, it was considered that, following a finding of incapacity:

- if a person was proved incapable of entering into contracts generally, the law presumed such condition to continue until it was shown to have ceased, although a lucid interval may still be proved;
- the longer the time that had elapsed since an act which it was sought to challenge or set aside on grounds of incapacity, the stronger the evidence required to do so would need to be.

Under MCA 2005, the legal approach to capacity requires issue-specific and time-specific assessment. As MCA 2005 has confirmed the importance of promoting and enabling autonomous decision-making, it is unlikely that the pre-MCA presumption of continuity would be upheld by the courts. Further, art.12 of the

CRPD requires the recognition of 'the right of people with disabilities to enjoy legal capacity on an equal basis with others in all aspects of life'. Any presumption of continuance would appear to be at odds with this.

1.3.3 Burden of proof

The presumption of capacity is relevant to the burden of proof. The burden of proof operates on the usual principle that the person who alleges rather than denies something has to prove his or her case. In cases involving incapacity, the onus is on the person who alleges that an individual lacks capacity to make a particular decision to produce the evidence necessary to rebut the presumption of capacity. The standard of proof is the usual standard in civil proceedings, the 'balance of probabilities' (MCA 2005, s.2(4)), rather than the higher standard of 'beyond reasonable doubt' which applies in criminal proceedings.

1.4 ASSESSMENT OF CAPACITY

The law adopts a functional approach – that capacity must be assessed in relation to the particular decision an individual purports to make at the time the decision needs to be made. The legal capacity required for each decision will depend on the complexity of the information relevant to the decision and the particular legal test of capacity (if one exists) to be applied.

Most individuals have some level of capacity and this should be identified and respected, so:

- legal definitions of mental capacity differ for different purposes;
- the severity of the test and means of assessment may depend upon the nature and implications of the particular decision.

Helpful guidance is given in *Assessment of Mental Capacity: A Practical Guide for Doctors and Lawyers* (BMA and Law Society, 4th edn, 2015).

1.4.1 Approaches

MCA 2005 confirms that in relation to decisions covered by the Act's provisions, the appropriate test is based on understanding an explanation of information relevant to the decision in question. However, common law tests of capacity may require additional considerations – for example, in relation to testamentary capacity, where other qualities such as memory, judgment and the ability to reason play an important role.

In specific circumstances, the outcome of a proposed decision may raise doubts regarding a person's capacity, and so result in a test of capacity being applied, e.g.:

7

- an elderly client instructs you to sell her substantial house for £900;
- a widow decides to go and live with her 'husband'.

However, just the facts of being very old or in a nursing home, or even making decisions that others would regard as unwise or eccentric, do not necessarily imply a lack of capacity.

Appearances

It is important to be alert to the risk of being misled by appearances or outward manifestations, when considering whether the client has capacity to make a particular decision. Note that:

- you must recognise the difference between ability and capacity, as it is not unusual for communication difficulties to disguise mental capacity;
- conversely, a person may be apparently capable but yet unable to understand something due to the complexity of the subject matter or the manner in which it is explained;
- appearance or condition (perhaps the consequence of physical illness or disabilities) or some aspect of a person's behaviour can create an impression of mental incapacity which is not justified – MCA 2005 (s.2(3)) confirms that such unjustified assumptions or prejudices cannot alone establish a lack of capacity;
- conversely, the absence of physical characteristics may disguise an underlying mental health problem or learning disability which could affect capacity;
- observance of the conventions of society can disguise lack of capacity, for example when a person has dementia and demonstrates a learnt behaviour pattern.

1.4.2 When capacity may need to be assessed

Doubts as to the mental capacity of a client may arise for many reasons:

- the client's circumstances (e.g. in a nursing home);
- what you have been told in advance (e.g. by family, nurses or doctors);
- your own observations (e.g. how the client looks and behaves);
- what the client says (e.g. a widow insists that her husband is still alive or proposes an irrational gift);
- the outcome of the client's decisions (e.g. to do impossible things);
- previous knowledge of the client.

It is essential for practitioners to take the trouble to investigate any of these indications, and ensure that the correct test of capacity is applied and any advice takes account of the client's circumstances. Much of the guidance that follows may be seen as 'best practice' and what can actually be done may be limited by time factors and costs, but once solicitors are involved, their professional duty to the client must be an overriding factor in all circumstances. Remember that:

- anyone acting in a professional role in relation to someone who may lack capacity must act in accordance with MCA 2005, having regard to the guidance in the MCA 2005 Code of Practice (see in particular, Chapter 4 of the Code);
- there is a presumption of capacity;
- while the MCA 2005 test of capacity will apply in relation to financial, health and welfare decisions covered by the Act's provisions, other tests apply for different purposes – so make sure you apply the appropriate test (see **1.5**);
- capacity is a question of fact and your opinion may be as good as that of others;
- the conclusion should be reached 'on the balance of probabilities' – you do not need to be satisfied beyond reasonable doubt;
- carers (lay or professional) may have had more experience than you of the person being assessed, so be wary if your conclusions are seriously at variance with theirs;
- capacity is a legal test, which may be informed by medical advice – your judgment will be very important;
- you should be alert to any conflict of interest when others are expressing their view; and
- if in doubt, you should obtain expert medical advice.

1.4.3 Who should assess capacity

The question of who should assess capacity will depend on the particular decision to be made. For most day-to-day decisions, the carer most directly involved with the person needing support at the time the decision has to be made should assess their capacity to make the decision in question. Where a legal transaction is involved, such as making a will or lasting power of attorney (LPA), the solicitor handling the transaction will need to be satisfied that the client has the required capacity, taking account of the views of carers or relatives where appropriate (bearing in mind the duty of confidentiality, see **2.5.2**) and perhaps assisted by an opinion from a doctor. Where consent to medical treatment or examination is required, the doctor or healthcare professional proposing the treatment should decide whether the patient has capacity to consent. Ultimately, if a person's capacity to do something is disputed, it is a question for a court, usually the Court of Protection, to decide.

When making assessments, different professionals may take into account different criteria:

- the medical profession is concerned with diagnosis, prognosis and medical treatment;
- care workers assess people according to their degree of independence which involves consideration of levels of competence in performing skills such as eating, dressing, communication and social skills;

- the lawyer is concerned with legal capacity, namely whether the individual is capable of making a reasoned and informed decision (in accordance with the relevant test of capacity) and is able to communicate that decision.

This should be borne in mind when seeking opinions about capacity. A multi-disciplinary approach is usually best when assessing capacity in difficult or disputed cases, and the assessment should not then be left entirely to a doctor. The role of the solicitor is crucial at the outset in ensuring that the doctor has the right information to make an informed assessment. The doctor needs to know the decision or purpose for which capacity is required, the legal test involved and any relevant background information. It is no use asking the doctor if a particular client can make a will. The doctor needs to have some indication of the extent of the client's property and the claims he should give effect to (see **1.5.3**). A consultant who has never met the client before may need more information than a GP who has known the client for many years.

Clear and concise letters of instruction to fellow professionals will help to set the requisite criteria needed by the lawyer. See *Assessment of Mental Capacity: A Practical Guide for Doctors and Lawyers* (BMA and Law Society, 4th edn, 2015).

When medical evidence should be obtained: the golden rule

The Court of Appeal has confirmed that in almost every case where a court is required to make a decision as to capacity, it will need medical evidence to guide it (*Masterman-Lister* v. *Brutton & Co and Jewell and Home Counties Dairies* [2002] EWCA Civ 1889 at para.[54]), although this will not necessarily be given greater weight than other relevant evidence (see *Richmond* v. *Richmond* (1914) 111 LT 273; *Birkin* v. *Wing* (1890) 63 LT 80). In *Hawes* v. *Burgess* [2013] EWCA Civ 74, the judge expressed concern that the medical expert had neither met nor examined the deceased, and as such he was not willing to accept the medical evidence on capacity in preference to the evidence of an experienced and independent solicitor who had met and taken instructions from the client.

Obtaining medical evidence about a person's capacity is sometimes required by the law (e.g. when an application is made to the Court of Protection – see **4.7**), while in other cases, it is merely desirable or a matter of good practice. There are particular circumstances, however, where the courts have advised that a doctor should witness a person's signature, thereby providing medical evidence as to the person's capacity. In *Kenward* v. *Adams* (1975) *The Times*, 29 November Templeman J set out what he called 'the golden if tactless rule' that, where a will has been drawn up for an elderly person or for someone who is seriously ill, it should be witnessed or approved by a medical practitioner, who should make a formal assessment of capacity and fully record the examination and findings. The need to observe this 'golden rule' was restated in: *Re Simpson (Deceased), Schaniel* v. *Simpson* (1977) 121 Sol Jo 224; *Buckenham* v. *Dickinson* [1997] CLY 661; *Hoff* v. *Atherton* [2004] EWCA Civ 1554; *Cattermole* v. *Prisk* [2006] 1 FLR 693; and *Scammell* v. *Farmer*

[2008] EWHC 1100 (Ch): and also in *Key* v. *Key* [2010] EWHC 408 (Ch), in which the solicitor was criticised for failing to follow the 'golden rule':

[6] [The solicitor's] failure to comply with what has come to be well known in the profession as the Golden Rule has greatly increased the difficulties to which this dispute has given rise and aggravated the depths of mistrust into which his client's children have subsequently fallen.

…

[8] Compliance with the Golden Rule does not, of course, operate as a touchstone of the validity of a will, nor does non-compliance demonstrate its invalidity. Its purpose, as has repeatedly been emphasised, is to assist in the avoidance of disputes, or at least in the minimisation of their scope. As the expert evidence in the present case confirms, persons with failing or impaired mental faculties may, for perfectly understandable reasons, seek to conceal what they regard as their embarrassing shortcomings from persons with whom they deal, so that a friend or professional person such as a solicitor may fail to detect defects in mental capacity which would be or become apparent to a trained and experienced medical examiner, to whom a proper description of the legal test for testamentary capacity had first been provided.

It is, however, important to note that the golden rule is in fact guidance and not a rule of law. The aim of the rule is to minimise or avoid post-death disputes regarding the capacity of the testator. It does not replace the test for testamentary capacity, and following the rule does not ensure the validity of the will. Following the golden rule, especially where time is of the essence, is not always straightforward.

In *Wharton* v. *Bancroft* [2011] EWHC 3250 (Ch), the solicitor's failure to follow the golden rule was raised in proceedings but dismissed as an issue by Norris J:

[110] … I consider the criticism of Mr Bancroft for a failure to follow 'the golden rule' to be misplaced. His job was to take the will of a dying man. A solicitor so placed cannot simply conjure up a medical attendant. He must obtain his client's consent to the attendance of and examination by a doctor. He must procure the attendance of a doctor (preferably the testator's own) who is willing to accept the instruction. He must make arrangement for any relevant payment (securing his client's agreement). I do not think Mr Bancroft is to be criticised for deciding to make his own assessment (accepted as correct) and to get on with the job of drawing a will in contemplation of marriage so that Mr Wharton could marry.

When instructed by a client in the preparation of a will, the solicitor's primary duty is to prepare the will with due skill and care, and within a reasonable time. In *Feltham* v. *Bouskell* [2013] EWHC 1952 (Ch), the solicitor was found to be liable to the testatrix's intended beneficiary when, as a consequence of delay in the preparation of the will, the testatrix proceeded with a home-made will that was later subject to a challenge.

Balancing the golden rule with a solicitor's duty to prepare the will with due skill and care, and within a reasonable time is not always straightforward.

Practical guidance for solicitors in addressing capacity issues, while avoiding unnecessary delay is given in Simon Taube's article, 'All that glitters' (*PS Magazine*, November 2014, **http://communities.lawsociety.org.uk/private-client**).

Dealings with the client's doctor are considered in more detail at **2.5.1**.

1.4.4   Techniques for assessment of capacity

When trying to determine whether a client has capacity to make a particular decision, it is essential to see the client personally. How and when you see the client may be important. It is suggested that, to put the client at ease, you first chat about matters other than the business that you intend to carry out. It is helpful to know from other sources something of the family background and client's career or history so that you can verify the client's recollection. Also ask a few questions about current affairs and past events.

See the client again if there remain doubts as to capacity because first impressions can be misleading (either way) and you may have called at a time when the client could not concentrate for some reason.

At any subsequent interview seek to discuss some of the same matters and see if there is consistency in what the client says. Also, seek detailed instructions again – if they are materially different there is a good chance that the client may lack capacity in respect of that particular transaction.

Do not rely upon the views of other persons without question. However well qualified they may seem they may have applied the wrong legal criteria or they may be influenced by a personal interest in the outcome. In some circumstances, it may be appropriate to involve the client's GP, hospital staff or carers (but always be mindful of your duty of confidentiality, see **2.5.2**).

Try to see the client at such time of the day as is best for the client and in the most favourable circumstances. Remember that you are testing the client's understanding of the decision to be made, not whether you agree with this or whether the client could make other decisions.

Meal times at carehomes

Optimising the conditions for assessing capacity

The MCA 2005 Code of Practice (para.4.46) states that, wherever possible, it is important to assess people when they are in the best state to make the decision in question. Chapter 3 of the Code suggests practical steps to support people to make decisions for themselves which also be helpful in creating the best environment for assessing capacity. These include the following suggestions to optimise the conditions for assessing a client's capacity at its highest level of functioning:

- Try to minimise anxiety or stress by making the person feel at ease. Choose the best location where the client feels most comfortable and the time of day when the client is most alert.

- If the person's capacity is likely to improve, wait until it has improved (unless the assessment is urgent). If the cause of the incapacity can be treated, a doctor should treat it before the assessment of capacity is made.
- If there are communication or language problems, consider using a speech and language therapist (often referred to within the NHS as SALT) or interpreter, or consult family members on the best methods of communication.
- Be aware of any cultural, ethnic or religious factors which may have a bearing on the person's way of thinking, behaviour or communication.
- If more than one test of capacity has to be applied, try to do each assessment on a different day, if possible, or allow time for a break and relaxation between each test.
- Consider whether or not a friend or family member should be present to help reduce anxiety. But in some cases the presence of others may be intrusive.

Previous solicitor and assessment of capacity

When introduced to a new client who is elderly, ascertain if another solicitor has previously acted and seek the client's permission to enquire of that solicitor whether there is anything that you ought to know. Be cautious if such permission is not forthcoming without an adequate explanation, especially if a member of the family or a carer discourages such contact. The former solicitor may have more infor-mation than you or may have declined, on grounds of the client's lack of capacity, to take the step that you are now being asked to take and, while you are not bound by his or her view, it is likely to be influential in your own assessment.

Another solicitor may have known and acted for the client for many years and the family may now be diverting the client to you in order to bypass advice which is inconvenient to them but in the best interests of the client.

1.5   LEGAL TESTS OF CAPACITY

Different legal tests of capacity apply to different types of decisions or transactions. The core principles and statutory test of capacity in MCA 2005 will apply in all situations covered by the Act, that is: financial, healthcare and welfare decisions which may need to be made for an individual by someone else.

There has been considerable judicial debate regarding the extent to which the MCA 2005 test of capacity replaces common law tests in contexts outside the scope of MCA 2005. Even where MCA 2005 does not strictly apply to the assessment of capacity, it will be prudent to consider its requirements and to have regard to the MCA 2005 Code of Practice, since they provide a thorough and comprehensive approach to lack of capacity derived from the common law.

The legal tests of capacity which are most relevant to elderly clients are described in the following sections. More detailed guidance is given in *Assessment of Mental Capacity: A Practical Guide for Doctors and Lawyers* (BMA and Law Society, 4th edn, 2015).

1.5.1   The test of capacity under MCA 2005

MCA 2005 sets out a comprehensive integrated jurisdiction for the making of personal welfare decisions, healthcare decisions and financial decisions on behalf of people who may lack capacity to make specific decisions for themselves. MCA 2005 starts with five guiding principles (s.1) setting out the values that underpin the legal requirements in MCA 2005 and govern all decisions made and actions taken under its provisions:

(1)   The following principles apply for the purposes of this Act.
(2)   A person must be assumed to have capacity unless it is established that he lacks capacity.
(3)   A person is not to be treated as unable to make a decision unless all practicable steps to help him to do so have been taken without success.
(4)   A person is not to be treated as unable to make a decision merely because he makes an unwise decision.
(5)   An act done, or decision made, under this Act for or on behalf of a person who lacks capacity must be done, or made, in his best interests.
(6)   Before the act is done, or the decision is made, regard must be had to whether the purpose for which it is needed can be as effectively achieved in a way that is less restrictive of the person's rights and freedom of action.

These principles confirm that MCA 2005 is intended to be enabling and supportive of people lacking capacity, not restrictive or controlling of their lives (see MCA 2005 Code of Practice, p.19). The aim is to protect people who may lack capacity to make particular decisions, but also to maximise their decision-making abilities, or their ability to participate in decision-making, as far as they are able to do so. Anyone using the powers or provisions of MCA 2005 must act in accordance with the statutory principles.

In assessing capacity under MCA 2005, the first three of these principles are particularly relevant. The starting point, at MCA 2005, s.1(2), is to enshrine in statute the presumption that an adult has full legal capacity unless it is established that they lack capacity, even when they make an unwise choice (s.1(4)). All practicable steps must first be taken to help the person make the decision in question (s.1(3)).

Defining lack of capacity

MCA 2005 adopts the common law notion that capacity is a functional concept, relating to a specific decision and not the person's ability to make decisions generally. This means that individuals should not be labelled incapable simply on the basis that they have been diagnosed with a particular condition, or because of any preconceived ideas or assumptions about their abilities due, for example, to their age, appearance or behaviour (MCA 2005, s.2(3)). Rather it must be shown that they lack capacity for each specific decision at the time that decision needs to be made. Individuals retain the legal right to make those decisions for which they continue to have capacity.

MCA 2005, s.2(1) sets out the definition of a person who lacks capacity:

> For the purposes of this Act, a person lacks capacity in relation to a matter if at the material time he is unable to make a decision for himself in relation to the matter because of an impairment of, or a disturbance in the functioning of, the mind or brain.

Capacity is therefore both decision specific and time specific and the inability to make the decision in question must be *because of* 'an impairment of, or a disturbance in the functioning of, the mind or brain'. The impairment or disturbance may be permanent or temporary (MCA 2005, s.2(2)) and the matter is decided on the balance of probabilities (MCA 2005, s.2(4)). Loss of capacity can be partial or temporary and capacity may fluctuate.

Test of capacity

The definition imposes a two-stage test in order to decide whether a person lacks capacity to make a decision. The MCA 2005 Code of Practice (paras.4.11–4.13) gives guidance on applying the test to establish that:

1. there is an impairment of, or a disturbance in the functioning of, the person's mind or brain, and if so
2. the impairment or disturbance is sufficient to cause the person to be unable to make that particular decision at the relevant time.

MCA 2005, s.3 sets out the test for assessing whether a person is unable to make a decision for himself or herself. A person is unable to make a decision if they are unable (s.3(1)):

(a) to understand the information relevant to the decision,
(b) to retain that information,
(c) to use or weigh that information as part of the process of making the decision, or
(d) to communicate his decision (whether by talking, using sign language or any other means).

Information relevant to the decision will include the particular nature of the decision in question, the purpose for which it is needed, the effect(s) of the decision and the likely consequences of deciding one way or another or of making no decision at all (MCA 2005, s.3(4)). In *CC* v. *KK and STCC* [2012] EWHC 2136 (COP), Baker J criticised the local authority for failing to provide sufficiently detailed information to enable the person being assessed to make an informed decision. Every effort must be made to provide the information in a way the individual can understand, using the means of communication that is most appropriate for the person's circumstances (MCA 2005, s.3(2)). The ability to retain information for a short period only should not automatically disqualify the person from making the decision (MCA 2005, s.3(3)) – it will depend on what is necessary for the decision in question. The ability to use or weigh the relevant information as part of the process of making the decision has already been considered extensively by the courts (see, for example, *Re MB (Adult: Medical Treatment)* [1997] 2 FLR 426 and *R* v. *Collins and Ashworth Hospital Authority, ex p Brady* (2001) 58 BMLR 173). In using the information, the person may be assisted by professional advice or support from family and friends (*Masterman-Lister* v. *Brutton & Co* [2002] EWCA Civ 1889). In *PCT* v. *P, AH and A Local Authority* [2009] EW Misc 10 (COP), Hedley J considered this limb of the test and described it as 'the capacity actually to engage in the decision-making process itself and to be able to see the various parts of the argument and to relate the one to another'. In considering P's capacity to make decisions regarding where he should live and his care and treatment, Hedley J identified that P's complex relationship with his adoptive mother combined with his other disabilities to hinder his ability to 'use or weigh' the relevant information.

The final criterion – that the person is unable to communicate the decision by any possible means – is likely to affect a minority of people (such as those with so-called 'locked-in syndrome') where it is impossible to tell whether the person is capable of making a decision or not. Strenuous efforts must first be made to assist and facilitate communication before any finding of incapacity is made. The MCA 2005 Code of Practice (para.4.24) suggests that in cases of this sort, professionals with specialist skills in verbal and non-verbal communication will be required to assist in the assessment.

MCA 2005 requires that any assessment that a person lacks capacity must be based on a reasonable belief backed by objective reasons. This requires taking reasonable steps to establish that the person lacks capacity to make the decision in question (MCA 2005, s.5(1)). The MCA 2005 Code of Practice (paras.4.44–4.45) provides guidance on 'reasonable belief' and on possible steps to take to establish a lack of capacity. Practitioners should keep careful records of the steps they have taken and of their reasons for believing that the person lacks capacity to make the decision in question.

Where the question of capacity is to be decided in proceedings before the Court of Protection, it has been held that the threshold for engagement of the court's powers (under MCA 2005, s.48) is lower than that of evidence sufficient in itself to rebut the presumption of capacity (see *Re F (Mental Capacity: Interim Jurisdiction)* [2009] EWHC B30 (Fam) at 44). The proper test in such circumstances is whether there is evidence giving good cause for concern that the person may lack capacity in some relevant regard.

1.5.2 Capacity to marry or enter into a civil partnership

The marriage ceremony and the civil partnership ceremony require both parties to enter into a contract. Capacity to enter into a marriage contract was considered by the courts in a number of cases in the 1880s. In *Hunter* v. *Edney* (1885) 10 PD 93 at 95, a distinction was made between marriage and the wedding ceremony itself:

> The question ... is not whether she was aware that she was going through the ceremony of marriage, but whether she was capable of understanding the nature of the contract she was entering into.

In order to understand the marriage contract, the person must be free from the influence of any 'morbid delusions'.

The degree of understanding required in order to have capacity to enter into the marriage contract was considered in *Durham* v. *Durham* (1885) 10 PD 80 at 81, in which it was held that:

> the contract of marriage is a very simple one, which does not require a high degree of intelligence to comprehend. It is an engagement between a man and a woman to live together, and love one another as husband and wife, to the exclusion of all others.

These considerations were upheld by the Court of Appeal in *Re Estate of Park (Deceased)* [1954] P 89, where the level of understanding was expressed as a broad understanding of 'the duties and responsibilities normally entailing to a marriage'.

In *Sheffield City Council* v. *E and S* [2004] EWHC 2808 (Fam), Munby J confirmed that the question of capacity to marry was quite distinct from whether someone was wise to marry (either wise to marry at all or wise to marry a particular person). The court also has no jurisdiction to consider whether marriage is in the person's best interests. He summarised the key questions as follows (at para.[141]):

(ix) There are thus, in essence, two aspects to the inquiry whether someone has capacity to marry. (1) Does he or she understand the nature of the marriage contract? (2) Does he or she understand the duties and responsibilities that normally attach to marriage?

(x) The duties and responsibilities that normally attach to marriage can be summarised as follows: Marriage, whether civil or religious, is a contract, formally entered into. It confers on the parties the status of husband and wife, the essence of the contract being an agreement between a man and a woman to live together, and to love one another as husband and wife, to the exclusion of all others. It creates a relationship of mutual and reciprocal obligations, typically involving the sharing of a common home and a common domestic life and the right to enjoy each other's society, comfort and assistance.

Munby J's approach was endorsed by Hedley J in *A, B and C* v. *X and Z* [2012] EWHC 2400 (COP) at para.[30]:

> In particular, am I in agreement with the words that appear at 144 as follows:
> 'There are many people in our society who may be of limited or borderline capacity but whose lives are immensely enriched by marriage. We must be careful not to set the test of

17

capacity to marry too high, lest it operate as an unfair, unnecessary and indeed discriminatory bar against the mentally disabled.'

Nevertheless, the subsequent case of *A Local Authority* v. *AK* [2012] EWHC B29 (COP), in which an individual was deemed to lack capacity to marry (after the marriage had taken place), confirms that the ability to use and weigh information remains a relevant part of the test for capacity to enter into a marriage.

Similar considerations would apply in assessing capacity to enter into a civil partnership.

Implications of marriage or civil partnership

The level of understanding required for marriage (and now, civil partnership) is less than that required for some other decisions or transactions. Since the status of marriage or civil partnership affects other matters, such as financial affairs and rights to property, subsequent arrangements may need to be made for a person who lacks capacity to manage these affairs. In particular, a valid marriage or civil partnership revokes any existing will made by either of the parties, including a statutory will. If one person lacks testamentary capacity (see **1.5.3**), an application may need to be made to the Court of Protection for a statutory will to be made on the person's behalf (see **4.7**).

Capacity to separate, divorce or dissolve a civil partnership

There have been a number of reported decisions concerning the capacity required to separate or divorce in the Canadian courts – such decisions being regarded as persuasive but not binding on UK courts. In the Ontario Court in *Calvert (Litigation Guardian)* v. *Calvert* (1997) 32 OR (3d) 281, a distinction was drawn between the varying levels of capacity required to make different decisions and separate consideration was given to the three levels of capacity which were relevant: capacity to separate, capacity to divorce and capacity to instruct counsel in connection with the divorce. It was held that:

> Separation is the simplest act requiring the lowest level of understanding. A person has to know with whom he or she does or does not want to live. Divorce, while still simple, requires a bit more understanding. It requires the desire to remain separate and to be no longer married to one's spouse. It is the undoing of the contract of marriage ... If marriage is simple, divorce must be equally simple ... the mental capacity required for divorce is the same as required for entering into a marriage ... The capacity to instruct counsel involves the ability to understand financial and legal issues. This puts it significantly higher on the competence hierarchy.

Subsequently, in the British Columbia Court of Appeal, *Wolfman-Stotland* v. *Stotland* 2011 BCCA 175 confirmed that the test of capacity 'to separate' involves 'an ability to appreciate the nature and consequences of abandoning the marital relationship'.

Similar considerations are likely to apply when assessing capacity to dissolve a civil partnership.

1.5.3   Capacity to make a will

A person making a will should have testamentary capacity at two important stages:

- first, when giving instructions for the preparation of a will, or if it is prepared or typed by the will-maker personally, at the time of writing or typing it;
- secondly, when the will is executed.

If the person making the will becomes ill or deteriorates between giving instructions and executing the will, the will may still be valid if it has been prepared in strict accordance with the instructions and the will-maker recalls giving instructions to a solicitor and believes that the will complies with those instructions (*Parker* v. *Felgate and Tilley* (1883) LR 8 PD 171). The rule in *Parker* v. *Felgate* was upheld in *Perrins* v. *Holland* [2009] EWHC 1945 (Ch) at para.[52], where it was clarified that:

> in a case in which the principle in *Parker v Felgate* is applied it is not necessary to prove knowledge and approval of the will, provided that (a) the testator believes that it gives effect to his instructions and (b) it does in fact do so.

Testamentary capacity – the common law

The most important case on testamentary capacity is *Banks* v. *Goodfellow* (1870) LR 5 QB 549, in which the Lord Chief Justice set out the following criteria for testamentary capacity:

> It is essential … that a testator shall understand the nature of the act and its effects; shall understand the extent of the property of which he is disposing; shall be able to comprehend and appreciate the claims to which he ought to give effect; and, with a view to the latter object, that no disorder of the mind shall poison his affections, pervert his sense of right, or prevent the exercise of his natural faculties – that no insane delusion shall influence his will in disposing of his property and bring about a disposal of it which, if the mind had been sound, would not have been made.

The first three elements (understanding the nature of the act and its effects, and the extent of the property being disposed of) involve the will-maker's understanding, that is, the ability to receive and evaluate information which may possibly be communicated or explained by others. The final test (being able to comprehend the claims to which he or she ought to give effect) goes beyond understanding and requires the person making the will to be able to distinguish and compare potential beneficiaries and make a choice. This requires other qualities, such as: judgment, the ability to reason, moral responsibility, memory, sentiment and affection. A person making a will can, if mentally capable, ignore the claims of relatives and other potential beneficiaries.

It is important to remember that, when someone's capacity is being assessed, it is the ability to make a decision (not necessarily a sensible or wise decision) that is under consideration. In *Bird* v. *Luckie* (1850) 8 Hare 301, the judge specifically remarked that, although the law requires a person to be capable of understanding the nature and effect of an action, it does not insist that the person behave 'in such a manner as to deserve approbation from the prudent, the wise, or the good'. Similarly, in *Sheffield City Council* v. *E and S* [2004] EWHC 2808 (Fam), the court was concerned with the client's capacity, not his or her wisdom. This principle is confirmed in MCA 2005 (s.1(4)): 'A person is not to be treated as unable to make a decision merely because he makes an unwise decision.'

Testamentary capacity – impact of the Mental Capacity Act 2005

The courts confirmed that, in respect of wills made before MCA 2005 came into effect on 1 October 2007, the question of testamentary capacity should be based on the common law test set out above, without reference to MCA 2005 (*Scammell* v. *Farmer* [2008] EWHC 1100 (Ch) at paras.[25]–[29]). The main difference then identified between the two tests was that the onus of proof under MCA 2005 is on the person alleging lack of testamentary capacity, while at common law, the position was different. This point was reaffirmed in *Perrins* v. *Holland* [2009] EWHC 1945 (Ch) where the will in question was made before MCA 2005 came into effect, when Lewison J commented (at para.[40]):

> However, there are six points that I should make. First, since the test is a common law test it is capable of being influenced by contemporary attitudes. Second, our general understanding of impaired mental capacity of adults has increased enormously since 1870. Third, we now recognise that an adult with impaired mental capacity is capable of making some decisions for himself, given help. Thus fourth, we recognise that the test of mental capacity is not monolithic, but is tailored to the task in hand: *Hoff* v. *Atherton* [2005] WTLR 99, 109. Fifth, contemporary attitudes toward adults with impaired capacity are more respectful of adult autonomy. Sixth, even the traditional test must be applied in the context of the particular testator and the particular estate. A testator with a complex estate and many potential beneficiaries may need a greater degree of cognitive capability than one with a simple estate and few Claimants.

In most other respects, the court then held that the test of capacity in MCA 2005, s.3 is a 'modern restatement' of the test in *Banks* v. *Goodfellow* (see *Scammell* v. *Farmer* [2008] EWHC 1100 (Ch) at para.[24]), and directed that assessment of testamentary capacity subsequent to implementation of MCA 2005 should therefore have regard to the provisions set out in MCA 2005, ss.1–3 as described above (**1.5.1**), and in particular, whether the testator is able to understand the likely effects of making, or not making, a will at this time, or deciding to make a different will (MCA 2005, s.3(4)).

However, the recent case of *Walker* v. *Badmin* [2014] All ER (D) 258 (Nov) reviewed the various conflicting decisions on whether the correct test of testamentary capacity is the MCA 2005 test or that established in *Banks* v. *Goodfellow*. It was concluded that the *Banks* v. *Goodfellow* test is the correct test (although it is possible that an appellate court might reach a different conclusion).

Capacity to revoke a will

The capacity required to revoke a will was considered in *Re Sabatini* (1970) 114 SJ 35, which established that a person who intends to revoke his or her will must have the same degree of understanding as when he or she made the will. The person must therefore be capable of:

- understanding the nature of the act of revoking a will;
- understanding the effect of revoking the will (this might even involve a greater understanding of the operation of the intestacy rules than is necessary for the purpose of making a will, although there is no direct authority on the point and it would be extremely difficult to prove retrospectively);
- understanding the extent of his or her property; and
- comprehending and appreciating the claims to which he or she ought to give effect.

1.5.4   Capacity to make a gift

People who are, or are becoming, incapable of looking after their own affairs are at particular risk of financial abuse and one of the easiest forms of abuse is the improper gifting of their money or other assets. The careful assessment of capacity to make a gift is therefore an important safeguard against financial abuse.

The common law

The most important case on capacity to make a gift is *Re Beaney (Deceased)* [1978] 1 WLR 770. The judge in the case set out the following criteria for capacity to make a lifetime gift (at 774):

> The degree or extent of understanding required in respect of any instrument is relative to the particular transaction which it is to effect ... Thus, at one extreme, if the subject matter and value of a gift are trivial in relation to the donor's other assets a low degree of understanding will suffice. But, at the other extreme, if its effect is to dispose of the donor's only asset of value and thus, for practical purposes, to pre-empt the devolution of his estate under [the donor's] will or ... intestacy, then the degree of understanding required is as high as that required for a will, and the donor must understand the claims of all potential donees and the extent of the property to be disposed of.

The judge added that, even where the degree of understanding in making a gift of lesser value is not as high as that required for a will, the donor must be capable of understanding that they are making an outright gift and not, for example, merely transferring property to someone else so that it can be sold.

21

It was later held that where a person makes a substantial gift, he should be capable of understanding the consequences for himself (in terms of tax liability, paying for care, etc.) during the remainder of his lifetime (*Hammond* v. *Osborn* [2002] EWCA Civ 885).

Impact of the Mental Capacity Act 2005

As in the case of testamentary capacity, there has been uncertainty as to whether the common law test for capacity to make a gift has been superseded by the MCA 2005 test. *Kicks* v. *Leigh* [2014] EWHC 3926 (Ch) reviewed the conflicting case law and concluded that the common law test remains the correct test. (It is, however, possible that an appellate court might reach a different conclusion.)

Further details on the law relating to gifts and dispositions of property are given in **Chapter 4**. See also the Law Society Practice Note: Making Gifts of Assets (6 October 2011).

1.5.5 Capacity to make an enduring power of attorney

Since MCA 2005 came into effect on 1 October 2007, it has no longer been possible to create an enduring power of attorney (EPA). However, EPAs made prior to that date remain valid and questions may still arise as to the capacity of a donor at the time of making the EPA. The law and practice relating to EPAs are described at **4.5**.

The Enduring Powers of Attorney Act 1985 (now repealed and replaced by MCA 2005, Sched.4) gave no indication of the mental capacity required of the donor at the time of creating an EPA. The problem was resolved in the test cases *Re K, Re F* [1988] Ch 310.

Having stated that the test of capacity to create an enduring power of attorney was that the donor understood the nature and effect of the document, the judge in the case set out four pieces of information which any person creating an EPA should understand:

- First (if such be the terms of the power), that the attorney will be able to assume complete authority over the donor's affairs.
- Secondly (if such be the terms of the power), that the attorney will in general be able to do anything with the donor's property which he himself could have done.
- Thirdly, that the authority will continue if the donor should be or should become mentally incapable.
- Fourthly, that if he or she should be or should become mentally incapable, the power will be irrevocable without confirmation by the court.

It is worth noting that the donor was not required to have the capacity to do all the things which the attorney would be able to do under the power. The donor needed only to have capacity to create the EPA.

The decision in *Re K, Re F* has been criticised for imposing too simple a test of capacity to create an EPA. But the rigour of the test depends largely on the way in which questions were asked by the person assessing the donor's capacity. It was confirmed by the Court of Appeal in *Re W (Enduring Power of Attorney)* [2001] 1 Ch 609 at paras.[23] and [25], that questions susceptible to the answers 'Yes' or 'No' may be inadequate for the purpose of assessing capacity.

1.5.6 Capacity to make a lasting power of attorney

MCA 2005 introduced a new type of power of attorney, called a lasting power of attorney (LPA). The LPA scheme replaces that provided under the Enduring Powers of Attorney Act 1985 and extends the areas in which donors can authorise others to make decisions on their behalf. In addition to making property and financial affairs LPAs, donors are now able to appoint attorneys (called 'donees' in the Act) to make decisions concerning their personal welfare, including healthcare and consent to medical treatment, when they lack capacity to do so for themselves. The law and practice relating to LPAs are described at **4.6** (for property and affairs LPAs) and **11.3** (for health and welfare LPAs).

The test of capacity to make an LPA is that set out in MCA 2005, ss.2–3, having regard to the principles of MCA 2005, s.1 (as described at **1.5.1** above). While MCA 2005 sets out the framework for assessing capacity in relation to the matter in question (making an LPA) at the material time, case law in relation to EPAs (as described above) is of some assistance in determining questions concerning capacity to make an LPA. In *Re Boar* (unreported, Court of Protection 11663606, 19 February 2010), Senior Judge Lush confirmed this but noted the significant differences between EPAs and LPAs, and as such the criteria in the test of capacity to make an EPA set out in *Re K, Re F* cannot be directly applicable to LPAs as the criteria would need to be adapted, to show that the donor understands:

- that the LPA cannot be used until it is registered by the Public Guardian;
- that (unlike a property and affairs LPA) the attorney under an LPA for health and welfare can only make decisions that the donor is contemporaneously incapable of making for him or herself;
- that under a property and affairs LPA, the attorney will, in general, be able to do anything with the donor's property which he or she could have done personally, unless any restrictions have been specified in the LPA;
- that the donor can revoke the LPA at any time when he or she has capacity to do so, without the court having to confirm the revocation;
- that if the donor lacks capacity to make a decision covered by the registered LPA, he or she could not revoke the power without confirmation by the court;
- that the authority conferred is subject to the provisions of MCA 2005, in particular the principles (s.1) and best interests (ss.4 and 9(4));
- the reasonably foreseeable consequences of making and not making the LPA or of deciding one way or another.

Solicitors accepting instructions to prepare an LPA for a client must be satisfied that the client has the required mental capacity to make the LPA. See the Law Society Practice Note: Lasting Powers of Attorney (8 December 2011), para.4.1.

In addition, MCA 2005 requires that in order to be valid, an LPA must include a certificate completed by an independent third party, confirming that in the certificate provider's opinion at the time the donor signs the LPA (MCA 2005, Sched.1, para.2(1)(e)):

(i)   the donor understands the purpose of the instrument and the scope of the authority conferred under it,

(ii)   no fraud or undue pressure is being used to induce the donor to create a lasting power of attorney, and

(iii)   there is nothing else that would prevent a lasting power of attorney from being created by the instrument.

The 2015 prescribed forms 'translate' this opinion into a statement of the certificate provider that 'as far as he is aware' the donor has the requisite understanding.

Former *Guidance for People Who Want to Make a Lasting Power of Attorney for Property and Financial Affairs* (Office of the Public Guardian, 2014) suggests that the certificate provider should discuss with the donor the following topics to establish the donor's capacity and understanding:

- What is your understanding of what an LPA is?
- What are your reasons for making an LPA?
- Why have you chosen me to be your certificate provider?
- Who have you chosen to be your attorneys?
- Why them?
- What powers are you giving them?
- In what circumstances should the power be used by your attorneys?
- What types of decision would you like them to make, and what (if any) should they not take?
- If there are any restrictions in the LPA, what do you believe they achieve?
- What is the difference between any restrictions and any guidance made in the LPA?
- Have the chosen attorneys provided you with answers to any of these questions?
- Do you have any reason to think they could be untrustworthy?
- Do you know when you could cancel the LPA?
- Are there any other reasons why the LPA should not be created?

Certificate providers should also have in mind the functional and diagnostic tests of capacity set down in MCA 2005 (ss.2–3). But the questions the certificate provider is asked to confirm are limited to the donor's understanding of the purpose and scope of the LPA (while other tests of capacity to perform a legal act refer to the nature and effect of the act in question, which arguably require a greater degree of understanding).

Greater responsibility is placed on professional certificate providers, as reflected in the fee they may charge. In cases of borderline capacity where the certificate provider is not a professional, it may be advisable to seek an opinion from a medical practitioner or other expert, to support the certificate provider's opinion (*Kenward v. Adams* (1975) *The Times*, 29 November – see also 'the golden rule' at **1.4.3**).

In *A, B and C* v. *X and Z* [2012] EWHC 2400 (COP), Hedley J emphasised that as a consequence of the fluctuating (and deteriorating) nature of X's condition, the making of an LPA 'unless accompanied by contemporaneous medical evidence of capacity, would give rise to a serious risk of challenge or refusal to register'.

The importance of any medical evidence being 'contemporaneous' had already been considered in the earlier case of *Re Collis* (unreported, 27 October 2010, COP), when the court preferred the evidence of the solicitor acting as professional certificate provider to that of the Court of Protection Visitor, who was also a medical practitioner, because the medical evidence 'had the major disadvantage of being retrospective'.

Capacity to revoke an enduring or lasting power of attorney

The Senior Judge of the Court of Protection summarised the evidence which the Court of Protection would require to see in order to be satisfied that the donor has the necessary capacity to revoke the power (*Re S*, unreported, 13 March 1997). The donor should know:

- who the attorney(s) are;
- what authority the attorney(s) have;
- why it is necessary or expedient to revoke the EPA or LPA; and
- what are the foreseeable consequences of revoking the power.

In practice, where the donor of a registered EPA or LPA wishes to revoke it, the attorney often disclaims (that is, gives notice to the Public Guardian). The court must then decide whether the donor has capacity to resume management of his or her own affairs or, in health or welfare cases, capacity to make the decision in question, or whether a deputyship order or some other order should be made in respect of the donor.

The Court of Protection has authority under s.22(4)(b) of the Act to revoke an LPA if the donor lacks capacity to do so.

In *Re DT* [2015] EWCOP 10, Senior Judge Lush highlighted the different criteria for the court to revoke an EPA. Whereas MCA 2005, s.22(3) and (4) provide that the court may revoke an LPA if (a) the donor lacks the capacity to revoke the LPA, and (b) the attorney has behaved or is behaving in a way that contravenes his authority or is not in the donor's best interest, or proposes to behave in such a way, in the case of an EPA, the court does not need to be satisfied that the donor lacks the capacity to revoke it himself. It merely needs to be satisfied that, having regard to all the circumstances, and in particular the attorney's relationship to or connection with the donor, the attorney is unsuitable to be the donor's attorney.

In *Re Harcourt* (2012) MHLO 74 (LPA) Senior Judge Lush made clear that the Court of Protection can only exercise its powers under MCA 2005, s.22(4) to revoke an LPA if the donor lacks the requisite capacity to revoke the LPA themselves. Evidence will therefore be required of the lack of capacity before the court's jurisdiction is engaged.

In *Re DP, Public Guardian* v. *JM* [2014] EWCOP B4, a Visitor's report was commissioned by the Office of the Public Guardian (OPG), pursuant to MCA 2005, s.58(1)(d), which considered the test of capacity to revoke the LPA, by reference to MCA 2005, ss.2–3 as follows:

[34] ... the Visitor replied ... 'I am able to confirm that DP has a specified mental condition that conforms to the requirements of the Mental Capacity Act 2005 so as to meet the first stage of the Mental Capacity Assessment. The Diagnostic Test is met in that a diagnosis of dementia exists.'

[35] The Visitor then stated:

'Moving on to the second stage Functional Test:

Understand

DP was able to understand the meaning of the LPA but did not understand the implications of the LPA in any meaningful sense.

Retain

She did not have the ability to retain information. I demonstrate this in that I reminded her who she had nominated and when I returned to this information she was unable to recall this 15 minutes later.

Use and weigh

When I presented her with information such as to who JM was, why she had chosen him or who else could act as her attorney she was unable to acknowledge or process this information and use it in any meaningful way.

Communicate

Although the donor has speech, she was unable to assimilate the information that I had given her in order to communicate an opinion of the LPA.

I am, therefore, able to conclude that it is my professional opinion that DP does not have mental capacity in relation to a decision about revoking or suspending the LPA.'

1.5.7 Capacity to manage property and affairs

The law prior to implementation of the Mental Capacity Act 2005

The only context in which the previous law relating to capacity to manage property and affairs remains directly applicable concerns the registration of EPAs made before MCA 2005 came into effect. An attorney acting under an EPA has a duty to register the power with the Public Guardian if he 'has reason to believe that the donor is or is becoming mentally incapable' (MCA 2005, Sched.4, para.4(1)–(2)). In this context, 'mentally incapable' means 'in relation to any person, that he is incapable by reason of mental disorder of managing and administering his property and affairs' (MCA 2005, Sched.4, para.23(1)).

The definition of 'mentally incapable' in this context contains three prerequisites:

- first, that the person is suffering from mental disorder; and
- secondly, that the person has property and affairs that need to be managed; and
- thirdly, that, because of the mental disorder, the person is incapable or becoming incapable of managing and administering his or her property and affairs.

'Mental disorder' is as previously defined in the Mental Health Act (MHA) 1983, s.1(2) for these purposes before it was amended by the Mental Health Act 2007 (MCA 2005, Sched.4, para.23(1A)). It means mental illness, arrested or incomplete development of mind (in other words, a learning disability), psychopathic disorder (sometimes referred to as personality disorder) or any other disorder or disability of mind. People are not to be regarded as suffering from mental disorder if their only problem is promiscuity, immoral conduct, sexual deviancy, or dependence on alcohol or drugs.

Property and affairs means 'business matters, legal transactions, and other dealings of a similar kind' (*F* v. *West Berkshire Health Authority* [1989] 2 All ER 545 at 554). It does not include personal matters such as where to live or medical treatment decisions.

Assessing someone's capacity to manage and administer property and affairs is extremely subjective to the person and his or her particular circumstances. Such capacity involves not just the carrying out of a single act such as making a gift or a will, but the carrying out of a series of actions which may or may not be connected to each other. It will depend on the value and complexity of the property and affairs as well as the extent to which the person may be vulnerable to exploitation.

Until 2002, there had been no reported decisions on the meaning of the term 'capacity to manage property and affairs'. It was generally accepted that the extent, importance and complexity of the individual's property and affairs must be taken into account (*Re CAF*, unreported, 1962). Another consideration is the extent to which the person may rely upon the advice or support of others (*White* v. *Fell*, unreported, 1987).

In *Masterman-Lister* v. *Jewell* [2002] EWHC 417 (QB), the judge at first instance, Wright J, reviewed all of the existing authorities and guidance relating to capacity to manage property and affairs. He set out the following principles, summarised below:

- Legal capacity depends on understanding rather than wisdom – the quality of the decision is irrelevant so long as the person understands what he was deciding.
- Capacity to manage property and affairs is a question of functional capacity and essentially a subjective matter; the nature and extent of the individual's property and affairs are therefore relevant.
- Personal information must also be considered, including the condition in which the person lives, family background, family and social responsibilities and the degree of back-up and support available.

This decision was upheld by the Court of Appeal (*Masterman-Lister* v. *Brutton & Co* [2002] EWCA Civ 1889), which confirmed the 'issue-specific nature' of the test of capacity, which must be considered in relation to the particular transaction (its nature and complexity) under consideration. A distinction was drawn between capacity to manage day-to-day affairs, capacity to deal with the complexities of personal injury litigation; and capacity to manage a large award of damages.

Capacity to manage property and affairs under MCA 2005

MCA 2005 confirms that a person's capacity must be assessed in relation to each particular decision about property and financial affairs at the time that decision needs to be made, rather than capacity to 'manage' those affairs generally. The test of capacity to make a decision about property or affairs is that set out in MCA 2005, ss.2–3, having regard to the principles of MCA 2005 in s.1 (as described at **1.5.1** above). The MCA 2005 test requires the presence of an impairment of, or a disturbance in the functioning of, the person's mind or brain that causes the person to be unable to understand information relevant to the decision, retain it and use or weigh the information as part of the process of making the decision in question. If the impairment or disturbance is ongoing or long term, this may be relevant to an assessment of the person's capacity to manage his or her property and affairs generally (MCA 2005 Code of Practice, paras.4.28–4.30).

The common law tests of capacity to manage and administer property and affairs are also likely to be of assistance if relevant to the circumstances under consideration (*Masterman-Lister* v. *Brutton & Co* [2002] EWCA Civ 1889). In particular, the term 'understanding' may need further consideration in the context of capacity to manage property and affairs. Thus in *Mitchell* v. *Alasia* [2005] EWHC 11 (QB), Cox J relied on qualities such as impulsiveness and volatility when deciding that the claimant was, by reason of his mental disorder, incapable of managing and administering his own affairs. Also, in *Lindsay* v. *Wood* [2006] EWHC 2895 (QB), Stanley Burnton J observed (at para.[18]):

When considering the question of capacity, psychiatrists and psychologists will normally wish to take into account all aspects of the personality and behaviour of the person in question, including vulnerability to exploitation.

In *A, B and C* v. *X and Z* [2012] EWHC 2400 (COP), Hedley J considered the common law tests when coming to the conclusion that X lacked the necessary mental capacity to manage his own property and affairs:

> [41] ... the general concept of managing affairs is an ongoing act and, therefore, quite unlike the specific act of making a will or making an enduring power of attorney. The management of affairs related to a continuous state of affairs whose demands may be unpredictable and may occasionally be urgent.

In line with the above judgments, *Assessment of Mental Capacity: A Practical Guide for Doctors and Lawyers* (BMA and Law Society, 4th edn, 2015) includes a checklist of factors to be taken into account when assessing capacity to administer property and affairs.

In addition, Empowerment Matters has published free guidance focused primarily on how to assess an individual's capacity in relation to financial decision-making and gives practical suggestions about how to support someone to manage his or her money and financial decisions. It suggests what could be done to support an individual who is finding it difficult to make decisions about money in a way that maintains his or her independence for as long as possible (**www.empowermentmatters.co.uk/**).

1.5.8 Capacity to claim and manage social security benefits

If a person is entitled to social security benefits, but is considered to be incapable of claiming and managing them, another person (known as an appointee) can be appointed to act on the claimant's behalf. Appointeeship is governed by Social Security (Claims and Payments) Regulations 1987, SI 1987/1968, reg.33 which provides that an appointee may be appointed by the Secretary of State where (reg.33(1)):

(a)   a person is, or is alleged to be, entitled to benefit, whether or not a claim for benefit has been made by him or on his behalf; and

(b)   that person is unable for the time being to act; and ...

(c)   no deputy has been appointed by the Court of Protection ... with power to claim or, as the case may be, receive benefit on his behalf ...

The test of capacity is therefore that the person is 'unable for the time being to act'. The regulation does not define this phrase, but internal guidance published by the Department for Work and Pensions (DWP) suggests that people may be unable to act 'for example, because of senility or mental illness' (*Decision Makers Guide*, para.02440). There are no formal legal criteria which specify the capacity required. The DWP agency will usually arrange for a visiting officer to visit the person to make an independent assessment of their ability to manage their financial affairs and, more specifically, their ability to understand how to make and manage a claim to benefit.

Further guidance states that 'the visiting officer must assess whether the customer shows comprehension of the rights and responsibilities of making the claim' (DWP, *Agents, Appointees, Attorneys and Deputies Guide*, para.5171). The guide also makes the following suggestions for its visiting officers when assessing a customer's capabilities (at para.5180):

- assume they are capable until they demonstrate otherwise
- focus on the customer's abilities to understand and function in making particular decisions, e.g.
  - can they pay bills?
  - do they know what income they have?
- do they have a general understanding of their benefits and what is involved in managing them – claiming, reporting changes, methods of payment?
- do they have a general understanding of the consequences of not claiming, reporting a change, not having a bank account?
- do they have an ability to understand and weigh up the information relevant to their decision?
- it may be helpful to have an independent person who is familiar with the customer present at the interview, e.g. a family member or social worker
- if the customer lives in a [care home or nursing home], do not assume they are incapable – they may be quite capable of managing their affairs
- if the customer has lost the ability to communicate, e.g. because of a stroke, do not assume they are incapable. Make every effort to find out their views and wishes by all possible means
- record the details of the visit and the assessment of the customer's ability to act in their own right.

1.5.9 Capacity and direct payments

Direct payments allow local authorities to make cash payments to service users who have been assessed as having an eligible need, so that they can buy their own services directly in order to meet that need. Direct payments can be paid in respect of people who lack capacity to consent to receiving direct payments, as well as to those who lack capacity to make decisions about managing direct payments. The appropriate test is one of capacity to request a direct payment (rather than capacity to consent to a direct payment) and allow for direct payments to continue to be made in cases of fluctuating capacity.

In cases where the person in need of care and support has been assessed as lacking capacity to request the direct payment, an authorised person can request the direct payment on the person's behalf (see **14.1** for further detail).

1.5.10 Capacity to litigate

People who lack capacity to conduct legal proceedings (known as lacking 'capacity to litigate' or 'litigation capacity') may also become parties to proceedings in the High Court, the County Court, the Family Proceedings Court, as well as in the Court of Protection. When an adult who lacks litigation capacity, or a child, is involved in legal proceedings, a procedure is then needed to enable the proceedings to continue by appointing someone else (generally known as a litigation friend) to give instructions to lawyers and otherwise conduct the proceedings on their behalf. These procedures are to be found in the relevant rules of court for the type of proceedings, which are:

- Civil Procedure Rules 1998, SI 1998/3132 (CPR), Part 21.
- Family Procedure Rules 2010, SI 2010/2955 (FPR), Part 15 (adults) and Part 16 (children).
- Family Procedure (Adoption) Rules 2005, SI 2005/2795 (FP(A)R), Part 7.
- Insolvency Rules 1986, SI 1986/1925 (IR), Part 7, Chapter 7.
- Court of Protection Rules 2007, SI 2007/1744 (COPR) Part 17.

The adult litigant who lacks litigation capacity is referred to in civil, family and adoption proceedings as a 'protected party, and in insolvency proceedings as an 'incapacitated person'. The litigant may also be a 'protected beneficiary' if they will lack capacity to manage any money recovered in the proceedings. Any proceedings involving a child or protected person conducted without a representative will be invalid and any settlement set aside, unless the court retrospectively gives its approval: *Dunhill* v. *Burgin* [2014] UKSC 18. Further details on the conduct of legal proceedings concerning people lacking litigation capacity, and on when the Official Solicitor to the Senior Courts should be involved, are set out in **Chapter 5**.

The common law

Although it is not specifically stated in the wording of the various rules, the Court of Appeal held in *Masterman-Lister* that the test of capacity is 'issue specific' and in the context of litigation, relates to capacity to manage the particular legal proceedings rather than the whole of the person's affairs (*Masterman-Lister* v. *Brutton & Co* [2002] EWCA Civ 1889 at para.[18]). This case (at para.[75]) established the test of capacity for legal proceedings to be:

> whether the party to legal proceedings is capable of understanding, with the assistance of such proper explanation from legal advisers and experts in other disciplines as the case may require, the issues on which his consent or decision is likely to be necessary in the course of those proceedings.

The Court of Appeal confirmed the approach adopted in *White* v. *Fell*, unreported, 1987, that capacity to litigate requires the person:

- to have 'insight and understanding of the fact that [she] has a problem in respect of which [she] needs advice';
- to be able to instruct an appropriate adviser 'with sufficient clarity to enable [the adviser] to understand the problem and advise [her] appropriately';
- 'to understand and make decisions based upon, or otherwise give effect to, such advice as [she] may receive'.

However, the Court of Appeal in *Masterman-Lister* also stressed that the test of capacity includes the ability to weigh information (and advice) in the balance as part of the process of understanding and acting on that advice (at 172) but that it does not require a detailed understanding of how that advice is to be carried out (at 190).

Impact of the Mental Capacity Act 2005

It is suggested in the MCA 2005 Code of Practice (paras.4.32–4.33) that the old common law tests of capacity to litigate (as set out above) may still apply, although the Code acknowledges that judges (sitting elsewhere than in the Court of Protection) may decide to adopt the MCA 2005 statutory test of capacity in relation to decisions outside the scope of MCA 2005 if that is appropriate, including for example where the issue is capacity to litigate. However, after the Code was published and at the same time as MCA 2005 came into effect on 1 October 2007, amendments were introduced into the CPR, the FPR and the FP(A)R so as to incorporate the same definition of capacity as applies under MCA 2005. The test to be applied is therefore the statutory test under MCA 2005. This was confirmed by the High Court in *Saulle* v. *Nouvet* [2007] EWHC 2902 (QB).

However, in *Dunhill* v. *Burgin* [2014] UKSC 18 at para.[13], the Supreme Court, in applying the test contained in the CPR, endorsed the approach adopted to determining capacity to conduct proceedings by the Court of Appeal in *Masterman-Lister* (above). It is therefore clear that the principles that evolved under the common law will continue to be of assistance in applying the statutory test in the context of capacity to conduct legal proceedings.

In *Re S; D* v. *R (Deputy of S) and S* [2010] EWHC 2405 (COP), S had made some significant gifts to D, who had befriended him. Proceedings were initiated by S's daughter and property and affairs deputy to have the gifts set aside for undue influence. S did not want the Chancery claim pursued and the court had to decide whether S had capacity to continue the litigation. Henderson J found:

> [43] At a superficial level, the nature of the decision may be simply stated … whether to discontinue or to continue … But that decision cannot be taken … without at least a basic understanding of the nature of the claim, of the legal issues involved, and of the circumstances which have given rise to the claim.

The Supreme Court also made clear in *Dunhill* v. *Burgin* [2014] UKSC 18 that the test must be applied to the claim that the party in fact has, not to the claim as formulated by their lawyers. Lady Hale (para.[18]) said:

the test of capacity to conduct proceedings for the purpose of CPR Part 21 is the capacity to conduct the claim or cause of action which the claimant in fact has, rather than to conduct the claim as formulated by her lawyers.

The Court of Appeal in the case ([2012] EWCA Civ 397 para.[25]) had already confirmed that: 'Capacity to litigate involves the capacity to understand a large variety of issues that arise between deciding to issue the claim up to the point of judgment.'

Careful assessment of a client's capacity to conduct the particular proceedings with which they are involved is therefore essential.

Insolvency proceedings

Following implementation of MCA 2005, special rules apply (IR, rule 7.43):

(1) … where … it appears to the court that a person affected by the proceedings is one who lacks capacity within the meaning of the Mental Capacity Act 2005 to manage and administer his property and affairs either –

   (a) by reason of lacking capacity within the meaning of the Mental Capacity Act 2005, or

   (b) due to physical affliction or disability.

Although a wider definition and different causes of incapacity are accepted in insolvency proceedings compared with other types of litigation, it would appear that the initial qualification of 'lacks capacity within the meaning of the Mental Capacity Act 2005' restricts this to the statutory definition. However, the approach to assessing the person's mental incapacity (as opposed to physical disability) is assumed to be the same as under the other court rules.

In *De Louville De Toucy* v. *Bonhams 1793 Ltd* [2011] EWHC 3809 (Ch), Vos J held that the IR supplement the provisions of the CPR for purposes of insolvency proceedings. Consideration should therefore be given to the appointment of a person to represent somebody who lacks capacity under the IR, in addition to consideration of the appointment of a litigation friend under Part 21 of the CPR. Although this would be wasteful and unnecessary in any normal case, the court must consider all the powers available to it in any particular case.

1.5.11 Contractual capacity

The law relating to contractual capacity is a complex combination of common law and statutory rules from which four general rules have emerged which apply when trying to assess an individual's capacity to enter into a contract:

• *Specificity*: contractual capacity relates to a specific contract, rather than to contracts in general. For example, this means that a person could have capacity to buy a bus ticket but not the capacity required to enter into a credit agreement.

- *Understanding*: the person must be capable of understanding the nature and effects of the specific contract and of agreeing to it (*Boughton* v. *Knight* (1872–75) LR 3 P&D 64). Obviously, the degree of understanding varies according to the kind of agreement involved.
- *Timing*: contractual capacity must be assessed at the time that the contract was to be entered into (i.e. not the day before or even the hour before). The capacity of an individual can fluctuate over a period of time – a lucid interval is sufficient. Evidence of capacity or lack of capacity at a different time is irrelevant, and would be inadmissible in any court proceedings about the validity of the contract, although evidence of a general lack of capacity may be significant.
- *Intention to create legal relations*: the parties must have intended to enter into a contract that is legally binding. In the case of social and domestic arrangements (e.g. financial arrangements within the family) there is a presumption that there is no such intention although this presumption may be rebutted by evidence to the contrary.

In dealing with contracts made by people whose mental capacity is in doubt, the courts have had to counterbalance two important policy considerations. One is a duty to protect those who are incapable of looking after themselves, and the other is to ensure that other people are not prejudiced by the actions of persons who appear to have full capacity. So, people without capacity will be bound by the terms of a contract they have entered into, unless it can be shown that the other party to the contract was aware of their mental incapacity or should have been aware of this (*Imperial Loan Co. Ltd* v. *Stone* [1892] 1 QB 599). The fact that the contract is unfair will not by itself be sufficient for the contract to be set aside: see *Hart* v. *O'Connor* [1985] 2 All ER 880.

Sale of Goods Act 1979

The Sale of Goods Act 1979 imposes a special rule to apply to contracts for 'necessaries'. A person without mental capacity who agrees to pay for goods or services which are necessaries is legally obliged to pay a reasonable price for them. Although the 1979 Act applies to goods, the rule regarding necessaries would also govern the provision of essential services (*Re Rhodes*; *Rhodes* v. *Rhodes* (1890) LR 44 ChD 94).

These rules are now brought together and given statutory force by MCA 2005 (s.7). This clarifies that the obligation to pay a reasonable price applies to both the supply of necessary goods and the provision of necessary services to a person lacking capacity to contract for them. Necessaries are defined in MCA 2005 as goods or services which are suitable to the person's condition in life (that is, to his or her place in society, rather than any mental or physical condition) and his or her actual requirements at the time of sale and delivery (for example, ordinary drink, food and clothing) (MCA 2005, s.7(2), based on the definition in Sale of Goods Act

1979, s.3(3)). The MCA 2005 Code of Practice (para.6.58) states that the aim of this provision is to make sure that people can enjoy a standard of living and way of life similar to those they had before lacking capacity. For example, the MCA 2005 Code of Practice suggests that if a person who now lacks capacity previously chose to buy expensive designer clothes, these are still necessary goods, as long as they can still afford them. But they would not be necessary for a person who always wore cheap clothes, no matter how wealthy they were.

Whether something is necessary or not is established in two stages by asking the following questions:

1. Are the goods or services capable of being necessaries as a matter of law?
2. If so, were the goods or services necessaries, given the particular circumstances of the incapacitated person who ordered them?

Case law has established that goods are not necessaries if the person's existing supply is sufficient. So, for instance, a person who buys a pair of shoes would probably be bound to pay for them, but if the same person purchased a dozen pairs, the contract might be voidable at the person's option. A contract for necessaries cannot be enforced against a person who lacks mental capacity if it contains harsh or onerous terms. The requirement that only a reasonable price is to be paid is an extension of this principle because a reasonable price need not be the same as the agreed or sale price (MCA 2005, s.7(1), based on Sale of Goods Act 1979, s.8(3)).

In relation to contracts for necessary goods and services as provided for under MCA 2005, the test for capacity to enter into a contract is the standard statutory test as set out in MCA 2005, ss.2–3 (see **1.5.1**) since the statutory test applies 'for the purposes of this Act'. This suggests that the MCA 2005 statutory test would also apply in relation to capacity to enter into other types of contracts, unrelated to necessaries. The MCA 2005 Code of Practice (paras.4.32 and 4.33) suggests that judges may choose to adopt the statutory test if they consider it to be appropriate, but the issue in relation to contractual capacity has not yet been considered by the courts. Elements of the previous common law approach are in any event present in the new statutory definition, particularly that capacity must be assessed in relation to the specific contract at issue at the time it is entered into.

In *Wychavon District Council* v. *EM* [2012] UKUT 12 (AAC), the Upper Tribunal Judge, Judge Mark, reviewed his earlier decision concerning entitlement to housing benefit because he had overlooked MCA 2005, s.7, which provides that: 'If necessary goods or services are supplied to a person who lacks capacity to contract for the supply, he must pay a reasonable price for them.' Although a purported tenancy agreement between P and her father was void because the father knew of her lack of capacity, under s.7, P was still 'liable to make payments in respect of the dwelling which she occupies as her home'. Consequently, she was entitled to housing benefit. Alternatively, even if s.7 was not wide enough to include the provision of accommodation, the common law rules as to necessaries would still apply, with the provision of accommodation being 'an obvious necessary'.

Subsequently, the *Court of Protection Guidance on tenancy agreements* (February 2012) confirmed:

> If the person has a registered attorney under an EPA or LPA, or has a deputy appointed to make decisions on their behalf, then the deputy or attorney can terminate or enter into a tenancy agreement without further authorisation from the court. Please note, however that deputies acting under an old style short order or receivership order made before the Mental Capacity Act came into force, may not have sufficient authority to sign the agreement, and it may be necessary to apply for 'reappointment' with the full powers of a deputy.

Deputies and attorneys

A person whose financial affairs are managed by an attorney acting under a registered EPA or LPA or by a deputy appointed by the Court of Protection (see **Chapter 4**), cannot generally enter into any contract which is inconsistent with the attorney's powers under the EPA or LPA, or the deputy's powers as determined by the court. Any such contracts are void, unless the person had contractual capacity at the time when entering into it. (Before MCA 2005 came into effect, any such contracts were automatically voidable, regardless of whether the person had contractual capacity and regardless of whether the other party was aware of the Court of Protection's involvement: *Re Walker* [1905] 1 Ch 160 and *Re Marshall* [1920] 1 Ch 284. However, since MCA 2005 became law, it is unlikely that this line of case law is still applicable.)

The Court of Protection has the power to make orders or give directions or authorities for the carrying out of any contract entered into by a person subject to its jurisdiction.

1.5.12 Capacity to consent to medical treatment

The starting point is the presumption that each adult has the necessary capacity to make his or her own healthcare and treatment decisions, unless there is evidence to rebut that presumption. The assessment of an adult patient's capacity to consent or to make a decision about his or her own medical treatment falls to be determined by the healthcare professional or doctor proposing the particular treatment, by the application of the statutory test for capacity set out in MCA 2005, ss.2–3 with regard to the principles within s.1 of the Act. All practicable steps must be taken to help the individual to make his or her own decision (s.1(4)). Information should be shared with the person in a way that facilitates his or her understanding of the nature and effects of the treatment, why it is necessary, the risks and benefits, the prospects of success, any alternatives, and the consequences of either receiving or not receiving the treatment. The person then needs to retain the information for long enough to use it and weigh it in the balance in order to arrive at a decision.

The test in MCA 2005 enshrines, with some modifications, the common law tests established in the judgments of *Re C (Adult: Refusal of Medical Treatment)* [1994] 1

All ER 819 and *Re MB (Medical Treatment)* [1997] 2 FLR 426, which continue to provide assistance in applying the MCA 2005 test of capacity in relation to decisions about medical treatments. Detailed guidance for healthcare professionals is given in *Assessment of Mental Capacity: A Practical Guide for Doctors and Lawyers* (BMA and Law Society, 4th edn, 2015).

The courts have also held, particularly in medical treatment cases, that a person's capacity must be commensurate with the gravity of the decision: the more serious the condition or complex the treatment proposed, the greater the capacity required (*Re T (An Adult) (Refusal of Treatment)* [1993] Fam 95). This case also affirmed the principle that a person has the right to refuse treatment, provided they can make a free and informed choice. It is irrelevant whether refusal is contrary to the views of most other people if it is broadly consistent with the individual's own value system.

In relation to the third limb of the capacity test – the need to be able to 'use and weigh the information relevant to the decision' – Macur J in *LBL* v. *RYJ* [2010] EWHC 2665 (COP) at para.[24] recognised that 'different individuals may give different weight to different factors' when using and weighing information relevant to a particular decision.

1.5.13 Capacity to make an advance decision to refuse medical treatment

Adults who are capable of making decisions about their healthcare and medical treatment can, if properly informed of the implications and consequences, also make anticipatory decisions about their preferences for medical treatment, intending them to apply at a later stage when they lose capacity to make such decisions for themselves. The legal enforceability of one type of anticipatory decision, known as 'an advance decision to refuse medical treatment' has been established by the common law and given statutory authority by MCA 2005 (ss.24–26). Section 24(1) defines an advance decision as:

> … a decision made by a person ('P'), after he has reached 18 and when he has capacity to do so, that if –
>
> (a) at a later time and in such circumstances as he may specify, a specified treatment is proposed to be carried out or continued by a person providing health care for him, and
>
> (b) at that time he lacks capacity to consent to the carrying out or continuation of the treatment,
>
> the specified treatment is not to be carried out or continued.

An advance decision to refuse treatment, which is both valid and applicable to the treatment in question, is as effective as a contemporaneous refusal of a person with capacity to make that decision, with the effect that the treatment cannot be carried out. The meanings of 'valid' and 'applicable' are set out at **11.8.5**.

It is important to note that an advance decision cannot be used to give effect to an unlawful act, such as euthanasia or assisted suicide or any intervention with the express aim of ending life (MCA 2005, s.62).

There have been no reported cases where the courts have closely examined the various components of MCA 2005, ss.2–3 in relation to capacity to make an advance decision. In his December 2012 paper, *Advance Decisions: Getting It Right?* (**www.39essex.com/advance-decisions-getting-it-right/**), Alex Ruck Keene considered the extent of the information a person must be able to understand to have capacity to refuse treatment:

> **17.1** The *'salient details'* relevant to such a decision are, it seems to me, few in number, and can be reduced to the following:
>
> 17.1.1 the nature of the treatment(s) that is/are to be covered by the advance decision, including, if various forms of intervention are necessary to support a particular purpose, that there is more than one intervention, and the core elements of those forms of intervention which are to be covered;
>
> 17.1.2 the circumstances (if such are specified) under which the treatment(s) are not to be started or continued;
>
> 17.1.3 the consequences of refusing the start or the continuation of that treatment (and, in the case of life-sustaining treatment, that such may result in death);
>
> 17.1.4 that the decision can be withdrawn or changed at any time whilst the person still has capacity to do so; but that
>
> 17.1.5 if the decision is not withdrawn or changed, and the person loses capacity to consent to the carrying out or continuation of treatment, that decision will bind the medical professionals and may do so even if – at the time – the individual is indicating that they do not wish it to.

In *A Local Authority* v. *E* [2012] EWHC 1639 (COP), Peter Jackson J considered whether E, a woman with severe anorexia, had capacity to make an advance decision to refuse force-feeding or other life support. E had made an advance decision, which satisfied all of the formalities required by MCA 2005, s.25 on the day she was detained under MHA 1983. E had the benefit of advice from her independent mental health advocate and from a solicitor but no formal capacity assessment was undertaken.

Peter Jackson J concluded (para.[65]):

> … on the balance of probabilities … E did not have capacity at the time she signed the advance decision in October 2011. Against such an alerting background, a full, reasoned and contemporaneous assessment evidencing mental capacity to make such a momentous decision would in my view be necessary. No such assessment occurred in E's case and I think it at best doubtful that a thorough investigation at the time would have reached the conclusion that she had capacity.

The court also considered whether the question of capacity in this instance had to extend to each of the various components of any intervention involved in force-feeding, and concluded (at para.[67]) that it was:

> … artificial to treat the various forms of intervention involved in forcible feeding individually. They are all central to or supportive of a single purpose. I therefore find that E lacks capacity to accept or refuse treatment in relation to any interventions that are necessary in conjunction with forcible feeding.

In the earlier case of *X Primary Care Trust* v. *XB and YB* [2012] EWHC 1390 (Fam), an advance decision to refuse life-sustaining treatment by a person with motor neurone disease was held to be effective by Theis J. Although at the time of the hearing XB could no longer communicate at all and therefore lacked capacity to make treatment decisions, he had made the advance decision just a few months previously when he was still able to communicate by eye movement, supported by his wife, his general practitioner and his local authority mental capacity coordinator, all of whom were able to give evidence that the necessary formalities had been complied with.

Further details about the creation and effect of advance decisions are given at **11.8**.

Advance statements

Other advance statements expressing wishes and preferences, as opposed to advance refusals of treatment, have a different status in common law: see *R (on the application of Burke)* v. *General Medical Council* [2005] EWCA Civ 1003. Such advance statements are also reflected in MCA 2005. Doctors cannot be compelled to carry out treatments which are contrary to their clinical judgment or to guidance given by the National Institute for Health and Clinical Excellence. However, under MCA 2005, s.4(6)(a) such wishes and preferences set out in an advance statement are treated as indicative of the person's past wishes and feelings, and in written form as relevant written statements, which must be considered when determining whether any proposed treatment is in the incapacitated person's best interests (see **1.6** and *RGB* v. *Cwm Taf Health Board* [2013] EWHC B23 (COP)).

1.5.14 Capacity to consent to sexual relations

Unlike capacity to consent to sexual relations to be considered under the criminal law, such capacity under the civil law is act specific, not person or situation specific. The focus of the criminal law will always be upon a particular specific past event with any issue relating to consent being evaluated in retrospect with respect to that singular event. In contrast, the context in which civil proceedings are usually brought is to protect an adult at risk of sexual exploitation or vulnerability in the future. Any other approach would be impractical or inappropriate: *D Borough Council* v. *AB* [2011] EWHC 101 (COP); *X City Council* v. *MB, NB and MAB* [2006] EWHC 168 (Fam); *Local Authority X* v. *MM and KM* [2007] EWHC 2003 (Fam); *A Local Authority* v. *H* [2012] EWHC 49 (COP); *IM* v. *LM* [2014] EWCA Civ 37.

The courts have in a number of cases over recent years considered the issue of whether a person had capacity to consent to sexual relations under MCA 2005 and have identified the following relevant information pertinent to the decision:

- an understanding of the basic mechanics of the act;

- an understanding of the reasonably foreseeable consequences to his or her health; and
- an understanding that he or she has a choice and can refuse (see *Tower Hamlets LBC* v. *TB* [2014] EWCOP 53).

Any 'moral' component has no specific role in any capacity assessment, but emotions are part and parcel of the question of whether the individual knows they have a choice and can refuse consent (*A Local Authority* v. *H* [2012] EWHC 49 (COP)). However, the process of using and weighing the relevant information should not involve a refined analysis of the sort which does not typically inform the decision to consent to sexual relations made by a person of full capacity, as such an approach would be discriminatory against a person with an impairment (see *A Local Authority* v. *TZ* [2013] EWHC 2322 (COP) and *IM* v. *LM* [2014] EWCA Civ 37).

There is an obvious overlap between capacity to consent to sexual relations and capacity to decide contact. However, decisions about contact with another person may be person specific, since without taking into account information about the other person and any particular risks they pose, the assessment of capacity will have nothing to bite on (*PC* v. *City of York Council* [2013] EWCA Civ 478). The consequence is that a person may be found to have capacity to consent to sexual relations, but not possess capacity to decide to have contact (*Derbyshire CC* v. *AC* [2014] EWCOP 38).

1.6 BEST INTERESTS DECISION-MAKING FOR PEOPLE WHO LACK CAPACITY

1.6.1 The best interests checklist

Where someone lacks capacity to make a particular decision, MCA 2005, s.1(5) establishes 'best interests' as the criterion for any action taken or decision made on that person's behalf:

> An act done, or decision made, under this Act for or on behalf of a person who lacks capacity must be done, or made, in his best interests.

In view of the wide range of decisions and actions covered by the Act and the varied circumstances of the people affected by its provisions, the concept of best interests is not defined in MCA 2005. Instead, MCA 2005, s.4 sets out a checklist of common factors which must be considered when determining what is in a person's best interests. The checklist can be summarised as follows:

1. **Equal consideration and non-discrimination** (MCA 2005, s.4(1)). The person determining best interests must not make unjustified assumptions about someone's best interests merely on the basis of his or her age or appearance, condition or an aspect of his or her behaviour.
2. **All relevant circumstances** (MCA 2005, s.4(2)). Try to identify all the issues

and circumstances relating to the decision in question which are most relevant to the person who lacks capacity to make that decision.

3. **Regaining capacity** (MCA 2005, s.4(3)). Consider whether the person is likely to regain capacity (e.g. after receiving medical treatment). If so, can the decision wait until then?

4. **Permitting and encouraging participation** (MCA 2005, s.4(4)). Do whatever is reasonably practicable to permit and encourage the person to participate, or to improve his or her ability to participate, as fully as possible in any act done or any decision affecting them.

5. **The person's wishes, feelings, beliefs and values** (MCA 2005, s.4(6)). Try to find out the views of the person lacking capacity, including:

   - the person's past and present wishes and feelings – both current views and whether any relevant views have been expressed in the past, either verbally, in writing or through behaviour or habits;
   - any beliefs and values (e.g. religious, cultural, moral or political) that would be likely to influence the decision in question;
   - any other factors the person would be likely to consider if able to do so (this could include the impact of the decision on others).

6. **The views of other people** (MCA 2005, s.4(7)). Consult other people, if it is practicable and appropriate to do so, for their views about the person's best interests and to see if they have any information about the person's wishes, feelings, beliefs or values. In particular, the following people must be consulted:

   - anyone previously named by the person as someone to be consulted on the decision in question or matters of a similar kind;
   - anyone engaged in caring for the person, or close relatives, friends or others who take an interest in the person's welfare;
   - any attorney of a lasting or enduring power of attorney made by the person;
   - any deputy appointed by the Court of Protection to make decisions for the person.

In *Re M; ITW* v. *Z* [2009] EWHC 2525 (Fam) Munby J held that it may be appropriate to consult with former carers and to take into account oral statements made by the person who lacks mental capacity in determining best interests. But be aware of the person's right to confidentiality – not everyone needs to know everything. The Senior Judge of the Court of Protection has held that where consultation is likely to be unduly onerous, contentious, futile or serve no useful purpose, it is not 'practicable or appropriate' (*Re Allen*, unreported, 2009, Court of Protection 11661992).

For decisions about serious medical treatment or a change of residence and where there is no one who fits into any of the above categories, the NHS body or the local authority involved has a duty to appoint an independent mental capacity advocate (IMCA), who must be consulted before any decision is made. MCA 2005, ss.35–41 established the IMCA service to provide a statutory right to advocacy services for particularly vulnerable people who lack capacity to make certain serious decisions.

7. **Life-sustaining treatment** (MCA 2005, s.4(5)). Where the decision concerns the provision or withdrawal of life-sustaining treatment (defined in MCA 2005, s.4(10) as being treatment which a person providing healthcare regards as necessary to sustain life), the person determining whether the treatment is in the best interests of someone who lacks capacity to consent must not be motivated by a desire to bring about the individual's death (MCA 2005, s.4(5)).

1.6.2 Applying the best interests checklist

Detailed guidance on determining best interests is given in Chapter 5 of the MCA 2005 Code of Practice.

Not all the factors in the best interests checklist will be relevant to all types of decisions or actions, but they must still be considered if only to be disregarded as irrelevant to that particular situation. Any option which is less restrictive of the person's rights or freedom of action must also be considered, so long as it is in the person's best interests (MCA 2005, s.1(6)).

The Court of Protection has confirmed that there is no hierarchy in the checklist – the weight to be attached to the various factors will depend on the specific circumstances, although in any particular case, one or more factors may be of 'magnetic importance' in influencing or even determining the outcome (*Re M*; *ITW* v. *Z* [2009] EWHC 2525 (Fam) at para.[32]).

Neither the person's own views (past or present) nor the views of those consulted (including family or close friends) will be determinative, but must be weighed up alongside other factors. In *Re S and S (Protected Persons)*; *C* v. *V* [2009] EWHC B16 (Fam), the Court of Protection considered the weight to be given to the wishes and feelings of the person lacking capacity and held that there is a presumption in favour of implementing the person's wishes unless they are irrational, impractical, or irresponsible (with reference to resources), or there is a sufficiently countervailing consideration. The need to give great weight to the person's wishes was confirmed in *Re P* [2009] EWHC 163 (Ch) at para.[41], although in this case Lewison J considered that it was overstating the importance of the person's wishes to speak in terms of presumptions. Further guidance is given in *Re M*; *ITW* v. *Z* [2009] EWHC 2525 (Fam) and in *Re GC* [2008] EWHC 3402 (Fam).

It is, however, clear from the decision in *Aintree University Hospitals NHS Trust* v. *James* [2013] UKSC 67, the first case on MCA 2005 to come before the Supreme Court, that the purpose of undertaking the best interests determination is to enable the decision to be taken that is right for the individual concerned, looking at the decision from his or her point of view. (See also *Re M (Best Interests: Deprivation of Liberty)* [2013] EWHC 3456 (COP).)

In *Re MN (Adult)* [2015] EWCA Civ 411, the President considered the nature of the Court of Protection's jurisdiction and the approach it should take when a local authority or care provider is unwilling to provide or pay for the specific care or services requested by an individual or their family. He concluded that the Court of Protection has no more power, when acting on behalf of an adult who lacks capacity, to obtain resources or facilities from a third party, whether a private or public entity, than the adult, if he had capacity, would be able to secure himself.

In cases where the court is not involved, carers (both professionals and family members) and others who are acting informally can only be expected to have reasonable grounds for believing that what they are doing or deciding is in the best interests of the person concerned (MCA 2005, s.4(9)), but they must still, so far as possible, apply the best interests checklist and therefore be able to point to objective reasons to justify why they hold that belief. This also applies to donees and deputies appointed to make welfare or financial decisions, as well as to those carrying out acts in connection with the care and treatment of a person lacking capacity. In deciding what is 'reasonable' in any particular case, higher expectations are likely to be placed on those appointed to act under formal powers and those acting in a professional capacity than on family members and friends who are caring for a person lacking capacity without any formal authority.

CHAPTER 2

Acting for the elderly client

Sheree Green

2.1 INTRODUCTION

According to the Office for National Statistics, current trends indicate that by 2035, 23 per cent of the population in the UK will be over 65 years of age (Statistical Bulletin: Older People's Day 2011 (ONS, 29 September 2011)). This represents a growing cohort of clients who deserve quality and comprehensive advice and representation.

For the elderly client, any one or more of the following factors may increase the level of risk involved in a particular transaction, in turn highlighting the need for bespoke advice from an experienced and independent professional:

- The nature of the transaction – a will providing for the devolution of his or her entire estate, a gift of a significant asset, a lasting power of attorney placing considerable decision-making powers and control in the hands of third parties.
- The potential lack of future opportunities to grow his or her income or capital, resulting in a greater focus on the need to preserve the available capital.
- The prospect that a proposed transaction may impact disproportionately on his or her current and future standard of living.
- Frailties that may impact on decision-making capacity or introduce an element of dependence on others, rendering the person vulnerable to the undue influence of others.
- The increased likelihood that they may lose capacity subsequent to the transaction, preventing any future revocation.

All clients are to be treated fairly and with respect. Assumptions about a person's decision-making capacity are not to be made on the basis of his or her age or appearance, nor is there a duty upon solicitors in general to obtain medical evidence on every occasion upon which they are instructed by an elderly client, just in case they lack capacity, as this would be both wholly inappropriate and potentially patronising (*Thorpe* v. *Fellowes Solicitors LLP* [2011] EWHC 61 (QB)).

However, it is nevertheless important to recognise that there are significant issues to factor into our delivery of legal services for the older client. Our approach will need to reflect our duties as set out in Chapter 1 of the Solicitors Regulation Authority (SRA) Code of Conduct 2011, and emphasised specifically in indicative behaviour 1.6:

> in taking instructions and during the course of the retainer, [have] proper regard to your client's mental capacity or other vulnerability, such as incapacity or duress.

In addition, our obligations under the Mental Capacity Act 2005 and the Equality Act 2010, which provides protection for people with defined 'protected characteristics', may require us to make 'reasonable adjustments'.

2.2 THE CLIENT

Before any work is carried out, it is of crucial importance to:

- identify who the client is (this may not be the person who first approaches the firm, as, for example, a relative or carer may make the first contact on the client's behalf);
- take instructions from and advise that client; if information or instructions come from an intermediary then it is all the more important to see the client and obtain confirmation;
- ensure that the client can give instructions freely and is not under the influence of another person (and always ensure that the solicitor sees the client alone on at least one occasion);
- ascertain that the client has the required capacity for the proposed course of action (see **1.5**);
- identify potential conflicts of interest at an early stage, and if appropriate recommend independent legal advice either for the would-be elderly client or for the other party or parties;
- continue to act in the best interests of the client, even if instructions are communicated by the client's attorney or deputy.

2.2.1 Communication

A client should not be prevented from giving his own instructions just because of communication difficulties. Best practice and good client care are given a statutory basis by MCA 2005, s.1(3) which makes it clear that a person cannot be assumed to lack capacity to make a decision 'unless all practicable steps to help him to do so have been taken without success'. It is the responsibility of the solicitor – in the same way as any other person seeking to establish whether he can act on another person's instructions – to make every effort to overcome any communication difficulties, for instance by:

- using an interpreter when necessary;

- using physical aids where these may assist – for example, some elderly clients may need to rely on hearing aids or glasses;
- allowing a friend or carer to be present initially to reassure the client and explain the best methods of communication;
- arranging to see the client at a convenient time for the client;
- seeing the client in familiar surroundings (a visit to a solicitor's office may be tiring or even slightly intimidating);
- accepting a simple 'yes' or 'no' response to questions if the client has severe communication problems, or even particular signs such as the movement of a finger, the blinking of an eye or a raised eyebrow.

Interview techniques

A different technique is required when interviewing clients who are mentally frail or otherwise vulnerable. In general:

- Speak clearly, at an appropriate pace, and use short sentences, avoiding jargon but taking care not to patronise the client.
- Take great care to avoid leading or closed questions, and do not rely on simple 'yes' or 'no' answers without exploring the issues further.
- Do not keep repeating questions as this may suggest that the solicitor does not believe the answers and encourages a change; but the same question may be asked at a later stage to check that consistent answers are being given.
- Do not move to new topics without explanation.
- Try to avoid abstract questions.
- Allow the client to tell his or her story and do not simply ignore information which does not fit in with your assumptions.
- Be patient, allow time for pleasantries and put the client at ease. Questions about family ('how many children do you have? … tell me about them') or personal history ('when did you retire … when did you get married … where did you live?) all provide a way of establishing a rapport with the client as well as securing information that may be relevant to assessing capacity.
- If the client is required to read a document, try to avoid unnecessarily long or complicated precedents.
- Be prepared to provide information to the client in a number of different formats, e.g. large print, braille, audio, DVD or easy read format. Do not go on too long without a break.
- Be prepared to arrange a further meeting or an independent assessment and be tactful in explaining why this is required.

Avoiding pitfalls

When interviewing the client, keep an open mind but be prepared to check the validity or accuracy of the information the client is sharing. Solicitors may have to justify their conduct in court and while there is a legal presumption of capacity, you need to be alert to any matters that raise a doubt over capacity, and mindful of the risk of a potential future challenge. The solicitor needs to be confident of the client's capacity and therefore it is the client who needs to demonstrate that he or she has capacity. Remember to:

- Take great care with simple 'yes' and 'no' responses; the client must have received, retained, understood and weighed sufficient information to make an informed decision.
- Make detailed and contemporaneous attendance notes.
- Always see the client alone or with an independent witness, even if additional time needs to be spent initially with an intermediary.
- Take care where seeing a couple together: one may be more informative than the other, either out of many years' custom or to compensate for the lack of capacity of the other.
- Do not make assumptions about the client. A couple seen together may have an inherent conflict of interest, for instance if they have children from other relationships; a client may also present well and give information that appears correct but which turns out to be wrong (this problem is dealt with in more detail at **2.6**).
- If in doubt, obtain medical evidence and follow the 'golden rule' emphasised by Templeman J in *Kenward* v. *Adams* (1975) *The Times*, 29 November, and restated subsequently by Briggs J in the case *Key* v. *Key* [2010] EWHC 408 (Ch) (see **1.4.3**).

Assessing capacity is dealt with in more detail at **1.4**, but it is not the only issue that is relevant when taking instructions from the elderly client. The client may, for instance, be subject to undue influence or pressure to do something that he is not inclined to do. Conversely, the client may want to do something which you believe is not in his or her best interests. MCA 2005, s.1(4) sets out the principle that a person should not be assumed to lack capacity simply by virtue of making an unwise decision. The client may have strong views, and in the words of Chadwick LJ in *Masterman-Lister* v. *Brutton & Co and Jewell and Home Counties Dairies* [2002] EWCA Civ 1889 at para.[78]:

> It is unnecessary to deny [clients of borderline capacity] the opportunity to take their own decisions if they are not being exploited. It is not the task of the courts to prevent those who have mental capacity to make rational decisions from making decisions which others may regard as rash or irresponsible.

See also *Thompson* v. *Foy* [2009] EWHC 1076 (Ch), where the clearly documented advice of the solicitor was crucial in showing that the client understood the risks inherent in her decision.

2.3 THE SOLICITOR

2.3.1 Importance of the solicitor's role

There is clear benefit to an elderly client, contemplating an important legal decision, in having an experienced solicitor providing independent advice and guidance on the proposed transaction. The solicitor not only provides the mechanism for the client to see through his or her instructions, but can also ensure that appropriate safeguards are in place to avoid any potential risk to the client of financial abuse. If the solicitor decides that the client is capable and goes ahead and completes the will or lasting power of attorney (LPA) or transfer deed, that document will be presumed to be valid and will be all the more difficult to overturn at a later date. It is also in the interests of any potential beneficiary to a transaction for the elderly client to receive the best possible advice and guidance. A helpful child who assists and supports his elderly parent to prepare a will or LPA benefits from knowing that the outcome is both legally effective and a true reflection of the parent's wishes, while being protected himself from subsequent allegations of inappropriate behaviour in supporting the procurement of the document for the parent.

2.3.2 Who is the client?

Instructions often come in the first instance from an intermediary, who may be a spouse, a son or daughter, carer or concerned neighbour, social worker, accountant or financial adviser. In the majority of cases the intermediary is well intentioned and they are communicating on behalf of the client, at the request of the client. But conflict of interest situations do arise and the fundamental rule in all such cases is to ask at the outset: 'Who is my client?'

A solicitor must act on the instructions of the client or, when these are given on behalf of a client who lacks capacity, in the best interests of that client. The SRA Handbook, Principle 4, provides a duty to act in the best interests of each client.

If the client lacks capacity for the proposed transaction, and instructions are received from his or her properly authorised agent, then a balancing exercise will always be necessary to determine what course of action is in the client's best interests. As part of that balancing exercise, the elderly client's past and present views and wishes must nevertheless be listened to and respected, even if they cannot always be followed.

This overriding duty to the client applies even if the solicitor is taking instructions from an agent such as a deputy or an attorney. The principal is still the client (*Re EG* [1914] 1 Ch 927 and MCA 2005, s.19(6)) and if it becomes necessary, the solicitor must inform the agent that the planned course of action may not be in the best interests of his or her principal and if necessary the solicitor should decline to act on those instructions. The solicitor should not abandon the client at this stage, although it may be that he will have to decide whether he can act for either the agent or the principal on the basis that the principal will need to be separately represented.

In certain situations, however, the solicitor is deemed to be acting for the agent rather than the principal:

- Where the attorney instructs the solicitor to apply to the Office of the Public Guardian for registration of the enduring power of attorney (EPA) or LPA.
- Where a prospective deputy instructs the solicitor to apply to the Court of Protection for the appointment of a deputy (the Court of Protection Practice Direction, Authority to Solicitors to Act for Patients or Donors (9 August 1995) is still good practice in such cases).
- Where the solicitor represents the deputy, attorney or other party to Court of Protection proceedings when there is a potential or actual conflict of interest: in such a situation, the solicitor may act for the party to the proceedings and the Court of Protection will appoint the Official Solicitor or another independent solicitor to act as litigation friend or alternatively appoint an accredited legal representative to represent the interests of the principal (Court of Protection Rules 2007, SI 2007/1744, rule 73(4), and Court of Protection (Amendment) Rules 2015, SI 2015/548, rule 40 and see generally **Chapter 4**).
- Where the solicitor believes that there is a conflict of interest and that he must act for the agent rather than the principal (who should then be separately represented).

2.3.3 Termination of retainer

The SRA Code of Conduct 2011 provides for the possibility that a client may subsequently lose capacity to instruct his or her solicitor in relation to a particular matter. Indicative behaviour 1.6 of the Code (mentioned at **2.1**) indicates that the solicitor should always remain alert to the risk of loss of mental capacity or other vulnerability, such as duress.

A solicitor must not terminate a retainer with an existing client except for good reason and upon reasonable notice.

Generally, a retainer terminates by operation of law when a client loses the capacity to give or confirm instructions. However, there are exceptions to this rule (in particular where the retainer has provided for the potential loss of such capacity, as in *Blankley* v. *Central Manchester and Manchester Children's University Hospitals NHS Trust* [2014] EWHC 168 (QB)). In this case, which concerned a person known to have fluctuating capacity, who had entered into a conditional fee arrangement, Phillips J held; 'There is no reason, as a matter of authority or legal principle, why an inability to instruct solicitors in the intervening period (which may be quite short) should be taken to have the effect of immediately ending a solicitor's retainer.'

In relation to instructions for a will, if the client has testamentary capacity when they give instructions, but then his or her capacity deteriorates before they sign the will, then the will may still be valid, if it has been prepared strictly in accordance with those instructions and the client remembers giving those instructions and believes the will accords with his or her previous instructions (*Parker* v. *Felgate and Tilley* (1883) LR 8 PD 171).

Arguably, the point at which the client loses capacity is the time when they may be most in need of good professional advice. Where an existing client loses capacity to instruct the solicitor, the solicitor should as far as practicable take action to protect the client's interests. It may be possible to identify an authorised agent who is able to give instructions, to enable the solicitor to continue to act.

Otherwise, the solicitor should consult those closely involved in the client's care and welfare – whether relatives, close friends, carers, a social worker or doctor – and, if appropriate, take steps to ensure that the client's affairs will continue to be dealt with in a proper manner.

If the client has appointed attorneys who refuse to apply to the Office of the Public Guardian to register the EPA or LPA, or close relatives or friends refuse to apply to the Court of Protection for the appointment of a deputy, the solicitor needs to record the advice provided to the relatives clearly and give them notice that any person may apply to the court for the appointment of a deputy. If there is no response to this or if there is a danger of financial abuse or neglect, it would be appropriate for the solicitor to apply in his or her own name either for the appointment of the solicitor or a panel deputy as deputy for the client, or for a specific court order. The Court of Protection would accept representations from other parties and may well appoint someone else as deputy. The court has the final say over who should be appointed and this is considered in more detail at **4.8.4**. The court is reluctant on the grounds of fairness and public policy to refuse a solicitor the costs of the application. A solicitor may, however, be at risk over costs if:

- the client has capacity and the Court of Protection has no jurisdiction;
- the solicitor acts in an aggressive or contentious manner, or becomes a protagonist in his own right, when all that is required is for the client's circumstances to be brought to the court's attention (see *EG* v. *RS* (unreported, 2010, Court of Protection 10237109) which is described by the judge as 'a cautionary tale for all those who put themselves forward as professional deputies when too closely associated with one party in a dispute before the Court of Protection';
- there is a valid LPA or EPA in existence; or
- there are insufficient assets in the estate to cover the cost of the solicitor's work.

2.4 CARERS

2.4.1 Definition

The Care Act (CA) 2014 in England defines a carer in s.10(3) as 'an adult who provides or intends to provide care for another adult (an "adult needing care")'. This definition is qualified in CA 2014, s.10(9) and (10), as follows:

(9) An adult is not to be regarded as a carer if the adult provides or intends to provide care –

(a)   under or by virtue of a contract, or

(b)   as voluntary work.

(10)   But in a case where the local authority considers that the relationship between the adult needing care and the adult providing or intending to provide care is such that it would be appropriate for the latter to be regarded as a carer, that adult is to be regarded as such (and subsection (9) is therefore to be ignored in that case). [This might be, for example, where a family member receives some payment through a direct payment for providing care for their relative.]

In Wales, the equivalent but not identical provision is found in Social Services and Well-being (Wales) Act 2014, s.3(4), (7) and (8) and s.187(1), as its legislation covers child carers.

2.4.2   Status

Relatives and friends who fulfil the role of carer tend to find informal ways of dealing with circumstances as they arise, but situations may occur where they need to be aware of their rights to make decisions on behalf of the person they provide care for (if the person does not have the requisite capacity to make a specific decision for themselves).

Family relationship by itself does not confer any legal rights. In practice blood relatives may be consulted although this may (wrongly) be in preference to a person who has (or had, prior to the lack of capacity) a far closer relationship with the individual, such as a cohabitee or partner. MCA 2005 brings both clarity and confusion to the status of the carer. MCA 2005, s.4(7) requires a person making a decision in the best interests of another person who lacks capacity to take into account the view of and if practicable, consult 'anyone engaged in caring for the person or interested in his welfare'. The Act therefore allows for a carer to have standing as a person 'to be consulted'. Carers' interests and views may well have been overlooked in the past, but now the decision-maker must take account of their views. However, a carer's formal rights are limited. They can make decisions in the best interests of the person they care for within their caring role, if the person cannot make that decision for themselves. But they cannot make wider decisions, outside their caring role or, for example, insist on access to the person or access to their medical records. An attorney under a property and affairs LPA is someone who must also be consulted under MCA 2005, s.4(7). (Interestingly, an attorney acting under an EPA is not specifically someone who should be consulted, unless he or she also falls into one of the other categories, for example as a carer.)

When more than one person has to be consulted by the decision-maker, and different viewpoints are expressed, then the decision-maker is left to balance and weigh the competing views, in the best interests of the person. The property and affairs attorney has particular standing, as he or she is the person with authority to pay for the donor's care or treatment and so is often deferred to as a result.

It is easy, when these situations arise, to see the wisdom in the appointment of an attorney, while a person still has capacity. An attorney under a health and welfare lasting power of attorney has authority to make decisions on behalf of the donor when the donor no longer has capacity to make the decision for himself.

2.4.3 Consulting carers

Where a client lacks (or is beginning to lack) capacity, the adviser or decision-maker may need to develop a dialogue with those responsible for the day-to-day care or supervision of the client. It may also be necessary to establish a link with the family or next of kin – or to use the terminology of MCA 2005, 'those who are engaged in caring for the person or interested in his welfare'. At the same time, the adviser or decision-maker also needs to be sensitive to the needs of those who are there day-to-day caring for the client, sometimes at great personal cost to themselves. Information must be sought and assimilated. The views of carers will help to provide a picture of the client's needs and highlight problems, especially where there is a dispute or the potential for a dispute.

The adviser or decision-maker must, however, also be careful not to be unduly influenced by one person's views and retain a necessary degree of professional discretion. Carers may not appreciate how much help is needed or make assumptions about the client's capacity or lack of capacity. The adviser or decision-maker must still form his own view, taking into account all the available evidence. Carers in particular may be influenced by other factors and cannot be assumed always to be acting in the best interests of the client. They may have their own concerns or issues or only have an incomplete picture of a person's interests. The final decision rests with the person or body making the decision and the views of the carers – whether family, friends or interested persons – are simply factors that must be taken into account. Any one of those factors may be persuasive but it cannot be determinative.

2.4.4 Caring for carers

It is important not to assume that informal carers have chosen this role. They are often involuntary carers needing encouragement and support because they:

- have a severely restricted lifestyle;
- face substantial costs of caring and loss of personal income;
- feel a mixture of emotions including inadequacy, frustration, resentment, embarrassment and guilt that they are not doing enough;
- need recognition, reassurance and information;
- need practical help in the form of services, financial support and respite care;
- may not always wish to take responsibility for the types of decisions that are often referred to them.

CA 2014 and the equivalent Welsh legislation put carers on 'an equal legal footing to those they care for', with carers' needs also 'at the centre of the legislation'. Local authorities have similar duties towards carers, as they have towards those needing care. For more information on a person's right to care and support see **Chapters 7** and **8**. It is also a crucial duty for any person acting as attorney or deputy, especially in a professional role, to make sure that the client can fulfil his practical as well as moral duties to persons who are caring for the client. The carer may be financially dependent, whether by way of remuneration for help given or because they are unable to work and are supported by the client while also acting as carer. Even if there is no history of financial support for such persons, an attorney or deputy can exercise these responsibilities on behalf of the client. An attorney under an EPA may 'so act in relation to himself or in relation to any other person if the donor might be expected to provide for his or that person's needs respectively, and … may do whatever the donor might be expected to do to meet those needs' (MCA 2005, Sched.4, para.3(2)). A deputy will usually have similar authority conferred on them. There is, however, no equivalent power for attorneys acting under a registered LPA and in such cases an attorney may be advised to obtain the consent of the court before providing any degree of financial support for a carer beyond incidental expenses or clearly measurable consideration.

2.5 OTHER PROFESSIONALS

When acting for elderly clients a solicitor must be prepared to develop relationships with other professionals in the interests of the client. Often these professionals will already be involved with the client, but on occasions the solicitor will take the initiative by seeking their involvement, with the consent and authority of the client.

2.5.1 Medical practitioners

Assessing capacity

Capacity is a legal test (see **1.5**) and it is for the solicitor (and ultimately for the courts) to decide whether a person is capable of performing a specific juristic act. Therefore, the solicitor needs to decide whether they can accept and act on the client's instructions. Obviously, medical advice may be crucial in informing the solicitor and any solicitor who acted against clear medical advice to the contrary would be foolish at the very least.

Doctors may be reluctant to make decisions concerning capacity and may be wary of becoming a party to what may become a contentious act, especially if there is a dispute in the family. Paradoxically, doctors make decisions about capacity on a regular basis where they are deciding whether patients can give consent to treatment. When obtaining medical evidence, remember to:

- Provide the client's written consent if this can be given or confirm that the client has agreed to be assessed.
- Explain clearly the purpose of the assessment and appropriate test of capacity (see **1.5**).

- Supply sufficient background information to enable the doctor to make an informed assessment. There is no point asking simply whether the client can make a gift – the doctor needs to know in general terms the size of the proposed gift relative to the size of the estate, whether the gift affects the will, whether there is a history of making gifts or whether the gift is unusual in some way. The information the doctor receives may well affect his assessment, which places a burden on the solicitor to provide the right information.
- Set out any concerns about the client, especially about the appropriateness of the proposed action and whether the doctor is in fact being asked to reinforce the solicitor's opinion.
- Provide a timescale for any response, especially if the matter is urgent, and monitor and chase as necessary. (A solicitor was found to be negligent in *Feltham* v. *Bouskell* [2013] EWHC 1952 (Ch) when a medical report was not obtained quickly enough, and the testator, impatient at the delay, executed a home-made will that was later subject to a challenge.)
- Ask the doctor if he requires payment for the assessment. Some doctors are more prepared to go out of their way to assist if they know they will be paid. (You will first need to discuss this with your client, if the client has the requisite capacity, and secure the client's agreement to the doctor's fee.)

Importance of consulting a doctor generally

A doctor's opinion is not only required to provide an assessment of capacity. A medical opinion may be extremely useful because the doctor may:

- have a pre-existing professional relationship with the client;
- hold clear views about the client's capacity or lack of capacity;
- have records of past treatment or symptoms which support a particular view;
- provide a diagnosis of a condition which either produces odd behaviour without there being impairment of reason or which affects reason without this being apparent;
- provide a prognosis as to whether any such condition is likely to be temporary or permanent, worsening or improving, changing rapidly or slowly.

Choosing the right doctor

Not all doctors will have a sufficient level of knowledge or expertise to determine issues of capacity. Many people can be assessed by their general practitioner (GP). A close and long-term acquaintance with the person being assessed may be helpful, particularly if the client feels more at ease with a familiar doctor. However, such familiarity, and knowledge of the client's family may make an objective assessment more difficult. In such cases, or where the client's medical condition is complex, it may then be more appropriate to request an assessment from a specialist practitioner, such as a psychiatrist or a geriatrician, who has expertise in the client's particular medical condition. Where the GP is the first point of reference, it is worth finding out as soon as possible whether the GP is able and willing to complete an assessment. There may already be involvement with a specialist or the GP may refer the assessment to a consultant or other specialist.

See *Assessment of Mental Capacity: A Practical Guide for Doctors and Lawyers* (BMA and Law Society, 4th edn, 2015).

2.5.2 Confidentiality

Carrying out an assessment of capacity requires the sharing of information about the personal circumstances of the person being assessed. Yet doctors, lawyers and other professionals are bound by a duty of confidentiality towards their clients, imposed through their professional ethical codes and reinforced by law. As a general principle, personal information may only be disclosed with the client's consent, even to close relatives or 'next of kin'. However, there are circumstances when disclosure is necessary in the absence of consent, such as where it is in the interests of the patient, required by statute, ordered by the court or where the patient has a notifiable disease.

In relation to people who lack capacity to consent to (or refuse) disclosure, a balance must be struck between the public and private interests in maintaining confidentiality and the public and private interests in permitting, and occasionally requiring, disclosure for certain purposes. Some guidance has been offered in *R (on the application of S)* v. *Plymouth City Council* [2002] EWCA Civ 388, which established 'a clear distinction between disclosure to the media with a view to publication to all and sundry and disclosure in confidence to those with a proper interest in having the information in question' (at para.[49]).

A similar balancing act must be carried out by professionals seeking or undertaking assessments of capacity. It is essential that information concerning the person being assessed which is directly relevant to the decision in question is made available to ensure that an accurate and focused assessment can take place. Every effort must first be made to obtain the person's consent to disclosure by providing a full explanation as to why this is necessary and the risks and consequences involved. If the person is unable to consent, relevant disclosure – that is the minimum necessary to achieve the objective of assessing capacity – may be permitted where this is in the person's interests. However, this does not mean that everyone has to know everything. Any medical evidence used in legal proceedings, including an assessment for the Court of Protection, will also be subject to legal privilege.

2.5.3 Nurses and professional carers

Do not overlook the fact that professional carers are the people who may be in closest day-to-day contact with your client and they may have considerable experience. They can provide valuable information and their views may be relevant although they may not be able to give expert evidence.

2.5.4 Social workers

Social workers are employed by local authority adult social care departments. They have clients whose welfare and interests they look after by providing support, guidance and advice, and an introduction to services. They also have a statutory role and may need to use their powers to protect the client. Some social workers have special knowledge, training and responsibilities and are approved mental health professionals under MHA 1983 (as amended) with certain statutory powers (see **12.6**).

Local authorities have extensive care and support duties and responsibilities under CA 2014 or the Social Services and Well-being (Wales) Act 2014. If a client becomes unable to cope and does not have the necessary support within the family, the solicitor should take the initiative by contacting the duty social work team for the area where the client lives and asking for an assessment of their care and support needs (see **Chapter 8**). Consent of the client should be obtained if the solicitor is not the attorney or deputy (or acting on instructions from such person). Alternatively, the solicitor may signpost a concerned friend or relative to the relevant local authority department.

2.5.5 Accountants, stockbrokers, etc.

A client may have used the services of various other professionals before becoming incapable of instructing them personally and the solicitor may now have taken on the role of coordinating the management of the client's affairs.

It would be inappropriate to disregard these professionals unless there were good reasons to do so (in the client's best interests, not the solicitor's). It would not be sufficient that the solicitor could more conveniently deal with a firm that they usually employ. The client's own professional advisers may have considerable knowledge of the client's affairs and preferences, and this represents part of the resources that the solicitor can draw upon.

The reality may be that the client has never taken the professional advice that his circumstances require. Whether or not the client has capacity, it may be appropriate for the solicitor to be involved in the choice of suitable firms to provide services, or provide them directly if they have the resources and expertise to do so.

The solicitor may work with other professionals, as part of a team acting in the mutual client's best interests and should not see themselves as being in competition with these other firms, but should ensure that advice is obtained when appropriate.

Remember that any action taken may at a later date be challenged by some interested person or by a disappointed beneficiary or former beneficiary after the client's death. Solicitors should therefore keep adequate records and notes of interviews, telephone attendances and deliberations. Where advice is given by other professionals that is to be acted upon, ensure that it is also confirmed by them in writing. Above all, ensure that any adviser is suitably qualified to give advice appropriate to the needs of the older client and receives all information necessary to do so. (The SRA allows solicitors to refer clients to non-independent financial advisers following on from the Retail Distribution Review within the financial services industry in December 2012. Solicitors need to ensure, however, that they have undertaken necessary due diligence before making any specific referral to a financial adviser.)

Advise your client wherever possible and appropriate of the need to notify members of the family of your involvement and the involvement of other professional advisers. This may be done by a suitable letter retained with the client's copy of the will, EPA or LPA. The solicitor's role may be made known at the earliest possible stage, when the documents are prepared. Where a client makes a will, executors or beneficiaries need to know where the will is stored. Where a client makes an LPA it is appropriate for the solicitor to write to the attorneys to execute their part of the document to let them know whom they should contact if the power of attorney needs to be acted upon (if immediate use is not required).

2.6   OBTAINING INFORMATION ABOUT THE CLIENT

2.6.1   The client

Clearly the first source of information is the client from whom instructions are obtained, but be prepared to verify any such information if the client is mentally frail or there is doubt about mental capacity. Significant documents should be inspected, rather than relying on the client's interpretation. Where circumstances justify this, a visit to the client's home greatly assists in forming a view about memory and understanding. It is often the case that a client is vague about how much money they have or the solicitor is not sure the client can have as much or as little as he claims. A visit to the client and a quick look at bank statements, passbooks or portfolio valuations will soon clear up any such confusion.

If the client has a property, the solicitor should have some idea of what the property is worth. The client's own valuation may be several years out of date and it may be worth checking Land Registry data, or one of the many websites that hold specific property valuation data, or asking relatives, neighbours or a local estate agent to obtain an approximate idea of the value. It is also advisable to check the title to the property and obtain office copy entries (assuming the property is registered). The client's wishes may well be inconsistent with the manner in which the property is held, as in *Re Ernest Chittock (Deceased)* [2001] EWCA Civ 915, in which the matrimonial home was assumed to be in joint names and to have passed by survivorship to the widow. In fact, it was in the late husband's sole name and subject to a partial intestacy.

Where the client lacks capacity

Obtaining information from a client who lacks capacity is much harder. Banks and other financial institutions should not divulge confidential information without formal authority. As such the solicitor must go through the client's papers and look at recent bank statements, passbooks, valuations, share certificates and correspondence. If an EPA or registered LPA is in place, then certified copies can be sent out and up-to-date statements and valuations will be supplied to the attorney.

If there is no EPA or registered LPA in place, then an application to the Court of Protection may be necessary. The solicitor will need to provide the Court of Protection with as much information as is available. If the assessment of the client's estate is incomplete do not delay the application. Once a deputy has been appointed, information will be released to a deputy on production of a sealed copy of the court order. If even the minimum information to prepare a full application cannot be supplied, then the application should still be made and the court will supply an interim authority to make enquiries on behalf of the client.

2.6.2　Couples

When acting for a couple, it is essential to see them both at an early stage. All clients need to be identified to satisfy anti-money laundering requirements (see **3.1.3**) and it is important to assess as early as possible whether there are problems with capacity or conflicts of interest. As with most couples, one may take more interest in the matter than the other. Telephone calls, letters or emails may come from one party to the relationship. One of them may call in to collect documents to be signed. In most cases, this is simply a practical and private arrangement between two clients who have a shared interest. A solicitor must, however, always take care and ensure that at the very least both clients are seen when executing important documents, especially a will or power of attorney. A solicitor must also be alert to conflicts of interest or potential conflicts of interest, as well as the capacity of the clients. Particular issues may arise if there have been earlier relationships and children from those other relationships, or if there are no children and different views as to how the estates should be dealt with on the survivor's death. There may also be different levels of capacity, where one party dominates the discussions and deliberately or even subconsciously conceals the lack of capacity of the other. If there is any doubt whatsoever about different interests or different levels of capacity, the couple should be seen separately or one party must obtain independent advice.

2.6.3　Carers and family

When the client is no longer living a fully independent life it can be helpful to talk to care workers, nurses, etc., as well as other members of the family, sometimes in the presence of the client. Where the client has capacity, these discussions should only take place with the client's express agreement.

If the client lacks the requisite capacity, then the solicitor will need to consider whether the best interests of the client require the solicitor to make these enquiries, which will involve proper consideration of the client's wishes and views in relation to any discussion of his or her personal affairs. It is desirable to explain the nature of the professional involvement to such persons and give them the solicitor's contact details. Do not omit to check whether anyone else in the practice has acted for the client and whether they have any insights that might help.

2.6.4   Financial bodies

With the authority of the client when capable, or otherwise with an EPA, registered LPA or order of the Court of Protection, useful information or confirmation about the client's financial position can often be obtained from:

- the client's bank, as to balances and documents or valuables held in safe custody;
- HM Revenue and Customs (HMRC) by requesting a copy of the last tax return or statement of account;
- the Department for Work and Pensions to ascertain what benefits are paid to the client, and details of the arrangements for payment;
- the client's accountant or tax adviser (if there is one);
- the client's stockbroker or insurance broker (if there is one);
- company registrars to obtain confirmation of shareholdings;
- any trustees making regular payments to the client from a trust;
- a care home to check who is paying, the level of fees payable, whether there are any arrears and the costs of additional extras which may be required for the client.

2.6.5   Care authorities

Good contacts at a personal level with those involved in the NHS, the relevant clinical commissioning group (CCG) (in England) or local Health Board (in Wales), local authority adult social care and housing departments for the area where you practise are invaluable:

- In ascertaining any involvement they have previously had with the client.
- If the solicitor needs to assist in arranging services for the client.
- In avoiding or resolving disputes about service provision or charges.
- In building up the firm's elderly client practice. (In CA 2014, s.4 there is a requirement that local authorities 'establish and maintain a service for providing people in its area with information and advice relating to care and support for adults and support for carers', which includes information on 'how to access independent financial advice on matters relevant to the meeting of needs for care and support'. It is therefore useful to ensure that key individuals within your local authority area, such as social work leads, are aware of your

firm's expertise in these matters. Section 17(1) of the Social Services and Well-being (Wales) Act 2014 is the equivalent but not identical provision in Wales, as it does not require the provision of information to access independent financial advice.)

Although solicitors may not routinely deal with these matters, if they are acting for the client in respect of the client's general financial affairs, their remit extends to seeing if they can improve the personal financial circumstances of the client or reduce the cost to the client. Advice should be informed by knowledge of the range of services and care provision available in the private and public sectors and the criteria for obtaining those services. Solicitors should also be aware of the authority and department responsible for identifying, arranging or providing these services and the officials who actually make the decisions. It may be necessary to make a formal complaint on behalf of a client who is in receipt of inadequate or reduced services, and so the solicitor should be familiar with complaints procedures and the mechanism for referring any unresolved complaint to the relevant Ombudsman.

2.7 FREEDOM OF INFORMATION

2.7.1 Legislation

The Freedom of Information Act 2000 created rights of access to information. The Act amended the Data Protection Act 1998 and the Public Records Act 1958.

Freedom of Information Act 2000

The Act created a statutory right of access, which provides for an extensive scheme for making information publicly available and covers a wide range of public authorities including: local government, NHS bodies, schools and colleges, the police and other public bodies and offices. The provisions in the Act are regulated by the Information Commissioner (the same person who acts as Commissioner under the Data Protection Act 1998) to whom the public has direct access. The Act permits people to apply for access to documents, or copies of documents, as well as to the information itself. The Public Records Act 1958 reorganised the arrangements for the preservation of public records. It places a duty on the Keeper of the Public Record Office to provide reasonable facilities for inspecting and obtaining copies of such records. The statutory rights under the Act and the Information Commissioner's regulatory powers extend to information contained in these records.
    The Act:

- provides a right of access to recorded information held by public authorities and specifies the conditions which need to be fulfilled before an authority is obliged to comply with a request;
- creates exemptions from the duty to disclose information;

- establishes the arrangements for enforcement and appeal;
- allows public authorities to charge fees in accordance with regulations made by the Secretary of State;
- provides time limits for complying with a request;
- requires public authorities to provide advice and assistance to applicants;
- requires public authorities to state the basis for refusal of a request;
- requires public authorities to adopt and maintain a publication scheme and to publish information in accordance with it.

Data Protection Act 1998

Individuals have the right to see most information stored about themselves on any relevant filing system. This includes information stored on a computer as well as manual data. There is a right to have incorrect or misleading information corrected or erased and provision for compensation, but certain types of data are exempt. The Information Commissioner keeps a register of data controllers who hold personal information, and fees for subject access are set by regulations.

Further provision must be made to comply with the EU Data Protection Directive (95/46/EC) which came into effect in the United Kingdom on 24 October 1998. The Commissioner publishes from time to time codes of practice.

See information on the Data Protection Act 1998 and the Freedom of Information Act 2000 available from the Information Commissioner (at **www.ico.org.uk**) or request by email (casework@ico.org.uk) or by post to the Information Commissioner, Wycliffe House, Water Lane, Wilmslow, Cheshire SK9 5AF, Tel: 0303 123 1113 (local rate).

Access to Medical Reports Act 1988

People have a right, in respect of a medical report about them prepared after January 1989 for an employer or insurance company, to see the report before it is sent and for six months afterwards and to ask for corrections to be made. Before applying for a report the employer or insurer must obtain the individual's written consent and inform him of these rights. A doctor can withhold information about any third party or which is likely to cause serious harm to the individual.

Access to Health Records Act 1990 (as amended)

Personal representatives are allowed to see and copy information which has been manually recorded on the deceased's health records (as defined) since November 1991. This includes health records in the private sector (e.g. private nursing homes) as well as the NHS.

If the solicitor needs access to a client's health records, they need to submit their request in writing or by email (with a copy of the client's written permission if possible) to (as appropriate):

- the person's GP surgery;
- the person's optician;
- the person's dentist;
- the health records manager at the hospital trust where the person was treated;
- any other body that holds personal information.

If the solicitor is applying for records on behalf of another individual (the client) in exercise of their rights, this is known as a 'subject access request' (SAR).

The health records manager, GP or other healthcare professional will decide whether the request can be approved. They can refuse to supply part of the request if, for example:

- it is likely to cause serious physical or mental harm to the patient or another person, or
- the information you have asked for contains information that relates to another person.

Under the Data Protection Act 1998, requests for access to records should be met within 40 days. However, government guidance for healthcare organisations says they should aim to respond within 21 days.

2.7.2   Local government

A member of the public has the right to attend any meeting of the council or a committee (or sub-committee) unless the council has exercised its power to exclude the public from all or part of the meeting, which it may only do for certain reasons.

Local Government (Access to Information) Act 1985

This Act extends the right of members of the public to information from and about local government. See Local Government Act 1972, Part VA, ss.100A–100K, as inserted by the Local Government (Access to Information) Act 1985. However, certain categories of information are exempt from disclosure: see the 1985 Act and Part I of Sched.12A to the 1972 Act.

You can inspect the registers of councillors, committees and delegated decision-making powers, and should be able to obtain copies of agendas, minutes, reports discussed at meetings, background papers, etc.

2.7.3   Persons who lack capacity

The right to apply for information is given to the individual about whom the information is held, and there is no provision for another person to apply on the individual's behalf. This causes problems when the individual lacks capacity, yet it is precisely in that situation that information is likely to exist and be needed by those seeking to make arrangements for care or support. The difficulty lies in identifying those who have a legitimate interest in obtaining the information – the right to confidentiality does not lapse by reason of lack of competence and family or carers might have an ulterior motive for seeking information.

If the client is unconscious or unable to give permission or communicate a decision about release of records, then health professionals must decide what information to disclose and to whom.

This decision must be made on the basis of what is in the person's best interests, taking account of any previous decisions or wishes they may have expressed and the views of others as to his or her likely wishes or feelings on the matter. Information should only be released in the person's best interests, and then only as much information as is required to support his or her care and treatment needs.

A deputy or attorney may have authority to access relevant confidential information, depending on the scope of their deputyship order or, EPA or LPA. This will remain a problem for the person applying to be appointed as deputy, who has no right of access to the information he may need to provide to the court (see **2.6.4**).

For those who need to make a decision but have no formal authority to access confidential information, such as someone wishing to rely on MCA 2005, s.5 in making a care and/or treatment decision, it is probably better to approach this on the basis of when confidential information should be disclosed (rather than to whom). Carers or next of kin can always ask for information from the NHS body or local authority and, although there may be no statutory obligation to provide this, the authority may recognise that it is in the best interests of the individual to do so (see **2.5.2**). Policies on disclosure of information should cover this. A climate of mutual co-operation is usually preferable to undue reliance upon legal rights. But there remain situations where information is withheld with no effective remedy aside from an application to the Court of Protection for an order for disclosure.

CHAPTER 3

The elderly client practice

Susan Lowe

3.1 RULES AND GUIDANCE

3.1.1 Rules for all practitioners

Solicitors are subject to the general law applicable to solicitors' practice such as the Solicitors Act 1974, Administration of Justice Act 1985, Courts and Legal Services Act 1990, and Legal Services Act 2007. There is also an increasing burden on solicitors of compliance with regulations in areas such as: money laundering, the proceeds of crime, and financial services.

The regulation of solicitors by the Solicitors Regulation Authority (SRA) is based on 'outcomes-focused' regulation and underpinned by a Handbook which includes the Code of Conduct, the Accounts Rules, the Authorisation and Practising Requirements, Client Protection and Discipline and Costs Recovery. The Handbook is a 'living document' which is amended regularly (most recently in November 2015). It sets out the standards and requirements expected from the profession.

The Handbook is underpinned by 10 fundamental and mandatory Principles which affect every aspect of legal practice. The Principles are:

1. uphold the rule of law and the proper administration of justice;
2. act with integrity;
3. not allow your independence to be compromised;
4. act in the best interests of each client;
5. provide a proper standard of service to your clients;
6. behave in a way that maintains the trust the public places in you and in the provision of legal services;
7. comply with your legal and regulatory obligations and deal with your regulators and ombudsmen in an open, timely and co-operative manner;
8. run your business or carry out your role in the business effectively and in accordance with proper governance and sound financial and risk management principles;
9. run your business or carry out your role in the business in a way that encourages equality of opportunity and respect for diversity; and
10. protect client money and assets.

Solicitors can keep up to date with regulatory developments by visiting the SRA's website at **www.sra.org.uk** and by receiving the SRA update email.

Firms must ensure that all employees – even non-qualified and non-fee earners – receive training in relation to the Handbook, albeit to a level appropriate for their role in the firm.

All firms must also have a Compliance Officer for Legal Practice (COLP) and a Compliance Officer for Finance and Administration (COFA). The role of compliance officers is all about risk management and ensuring proper governance. The compliance officers are responsible for ensuring processes are in place to enable the firm to comply with the Handbook. They must record and report all 'material breaches' and it is up to them whether a breach is 'material'.

Solicitors appointed by the Court of Protection as deputies for property and financial affairs – and support staff assisting solicitors who are appointed as deputies – need to be aware of the Office of the Public Guardian's professional deputy standards. The standards clearly set out what is expected of professional and public authority deputies and provide an important checklist of actions and behaviours every deputy should follow. Professional deputies are going to be assessed against these standards, either in face-to-face interviews or through assurance visits.

3.1.2 Good practice information from the Law Society

The Law Society publishes Advice and Practice Notes containing the Society's advice and view of good practice on a variety of topics. The following Practice Notes are relevant generally to the management and regulatory compliance of solicitors' firms (see also **Appendix B**):

- Anti-Money Laundering
- Client Care Information
- Compliance Officers
- Conflict of Interests
- Consumer Contracts Regulations 2013
- Equality Act 2010
- In-House Practice: Regulatory Requirements
- Initial Interviews
- Meeting the Needs of Vulnerable Clients
- Outcomes-Focused Regulation: Overview
- Provision of Services Regulations 2009
- Publicising Solicitors' Charges
- Redundancy
- Setting Up a Practice: Regulatory Requirements
- Supervision

The Practice Notes likely to be of most interest to elderly client practice are:

- Appointment of a Professional Executor
- Conflict of Interests

- Disputed Wills
- Equality Act 2010
- Estate Administration: Banking Protocols
- File Closure Management
- File Retention: Wills and Probate
- Holding Client Funds
- Lasting Powers of Attorney
- Making Gifts of Assets
- Meeting the Needs of Vulnerable Clients
- Powers of Attorney for Banking
- Preparing a Will When Your Client is Leaving a Gift for You, Your Family or Colleagues

With the growing emphasis on making customer service a priority for vulnerable people, one of the most relevant Practice Notes for elderly client practices is Meeting the Needs of Vulnerable Clients, which defines vulnerable clients; discusses how to enable vulnerable clients to access your services and emphasises the importance of tailored and appropriate communication. It gives guidance on assessing capacity in different circumstances and on taking instructions on behalf of a client who lacks capacity. It considers the role of carers, highlights the need for awareness of undue influence and gives case studies for practitioners. Finally, it explains how, if you fail to meet the needs of a vulnerable client, you could be at risk of a claim under the Equality Act 2010.

The SRA has also called on solicitors and firms generally to raise the bar in customer service, to help and protect vulnerable people. According to the SRA, 'vulnerable people have a greater need to be protected from poor service and they need more support when it comes to getting redress if things go wrong' (Risk Outlook 2015/16).

Solicitors can keep up to date with Practice Notes published by the Law Society by checking the Society's website and subscribing to the Law Society's Professional Update email circular (see **www.lawsociety.org.uk/news/newsletters**).

The Law Society's Practice Advice Service provides a helpline for solicitors on all areas of legal practice and publishes a range of FAQs. You can contact them on 0207 320 5675 or by email to practiceadvice@lawsociety.org.uk.

The Law Society also has a specific helpline for advice on client care and complaints handling including how to engage effectively with the Ombudsman. *Lawyerline* can be contacted on 0207 320 5720 or by email to lawyerline@lawsociety.org.uk.

There is also a PII helpline to advise on all aspects of professional indemnity insurance (0207 320 9545).

Finally, the SRA administers the Professional Ethics helpline for solicitors which can be contacted on 0370 606 2577.

3.1.3 Anti-money laundering

The Law Society has produced comprehensive guidance in its Practice Note: Anti-Money Laundering (22 October 2013), which is intended to:

- outline the legal and regulatory framework;
- outline good practice on implementing the legal requirements;
- outline good practice in developing systems and controls to prevent solicitors being used to facilitate money laundering and terrorist financing; and
- provide direction on applying the risk-based approach to compliance effectively.

Compliance with the Law Society Practice Note is not mandatory, but a solicitor may be asked by the SRA to justify a decision to deviate from it.

Complying with the risk-based approach to customer due diligence permitted by the Money Laundering Regulations 2007, SI 2007/2157 may at times create difficulties for solicitors with an elderly client practice. For instance, some elderly clients may have problems producing passports, driving licences or other documents that have a photograph and/or address to satisfy the recommended procedures. It is sufficient to accept a bus pass, a letter from the Department for Work and Pensions and/or a letter from a nursing home to confirm that the older person is resident at a particular home. Introductions from social workers or other professionals would also be acceptable but this should be recorded in the anti-money laundering record book to demonstrate that anti-money laundering procedures have been thought about in each case and followed as far as is practicable.

In all cases, it is essential to assess the individual risk, i.e. whether your client is in a higher risk category. For example, what is the matter you are being asked to deal with? Are you being asked to handle funds without an underlying transaction and are there any particular aspects of the retainer which would make the transaction a higher or lower risk? Will writing, for example, is not covered by the Money Laundering Regulations.

3.1.4 Equality and diversity

The Equality Act (EA) 2010 provides a legislative framework to protect the rights of individuals and advance equality of opportunity for all. The Act consolidates and simplifies discrimination laws dating back to 1970 and imposes duties on, among others, employers and service providers (including solicitors) not to discriminate against anyone on the grounds of age, disability, gender, race, religion or belief or sexual orientation.

EA 2010 identifies four different types of discrimination: direct, combined, discrimination arising from disability and indirect discrimination. Discrimination in relation to the provision of services is contained in s.29 of the Act and in summary, a service provider (even if the service is provided pro bono) must not discriminate or victimise: by not providing the service; in relation to the terms of the service; by terminating the service provision; and must not subject the person to any detriment, including harassment.

This discrimination may manifest itself in a variety of ways, including a refusal of service, providing a service on different terms, or providing a service of a different standard or manner.

Solicitors also need to take into account the Codes and guidance made under the Act and have regard to Chapter 2 of the SRA Code of Conduct 2011, which deals with equality and diversity. The required outcomes are:

(O)2.1   you do not discriminate unlawfully, or victimise or harass anyone in the course of your professional dealings;

(O)2.2   you provide services to clients in a way that respects diversity;

(O)2.3   you make reasonable adjustments to ensure that disabled clients, employees or managers are not placed at a substantial disadvantage compared to those who are not disabled, and you do not pass on the costs of these adjustments to these disabled clients, employees or managers;

(O)2.4   your approach to recruitment and employment encourages equality of opportunity and respect for diversity;

(O)2.5   complaints of discrimination are dealt with promptly, fairly, openly, and effectively.

Solicitors' practices may want to sign up to and promote their allegiance to the Law Society's Diversity and Inclusion Charter.

3.1.5   Safeguarding vulnerable adults

The Disclosure and Barring Service (DBS), which replaced the Criminal Records Bureau (CRB) and Independent Safeguarding Authority, was formed under the Protection of Freedoms Act 2012, to help employers make safer recruitment decisions and prevent unsuitable people from working with vulnerable groups.

It is a legal requirement in the UK for 'regulated activity' employers (such as care agencies and care homes) to refer safeguarding concerns to the DBS. It is illegal for anyone barred by the DBS to work, or apply to work with the sector (children or adults) from which they are barred. It is also illegal for an employer knowingly to employ a barred person in the sector from which they are barred.

Employees carrying out certain 'regulated activities' for older clients may require an enhanced DBS check of the barred lists, which identify individuals who are unsuitable for working with vulnerable adults and children.

The DBS has a useful guide to eligibility for DBS checks and the Department of Health has produced relevant booklets available at **www.gov.uk**.

3.1.6   Practice management guidance

The Law Society's accreditation scheme, called 'Lexcel', is open to all solicitors' practices to join, providing they meet the practice management standards specified by the scheme and successfully pass assessment by an independent assessor.

Solicitors can also opt to join the Law Society's Law Management Section which provides members with advice, information and support on all issues relating to the management of law firms (see **http://communities.lawsociety.org.uk/law-management**). Membership is open to solicitors, management staff of legal practices/departments, trainee solicitors and suppliers of financial or management services to legal practices. A membership fee is payable.

Good practice guidance and advice on practice management issues is provided by the Law Society in Advice and Practice Notes on a variety of topics (see **3.1.2**). The Law Society also publishes a wide range of books on practice management topics that will be useful to solicitors managing an elderly client practice or in the process of setting up a new practice. Anyone wishing to set up a practice will need to be familiar with the Authorisation and Practising Requirements including forms, the Practice Framework Rules and the Authorisation Rules, which can be found on the SRA website.

3.2 OFFICE MANAGEMENT

Running an efficient office combines management skills, interpersonal skills and common sense. The aim of this chapter is to highlight those skills generally relevant to the elderly client practice, as well as those which are essential. You should not assume that simply because some of your clients are old, you have the makings of a professional, profitable elderly client practice.

The practice must have the relevant knowledge and expertise to handle the many problems that arise. It should also have efficient, robust office systems to cope with the level of administration. Clients or those assisting with their affairs will soon become dissatisfied if there is delay and uncertainty or they are not kept advised. Elderly clients and their families come to a solicitor because they have a problem, often in distressing circumstances. The elderly client or their family may be asked to confront their own or their family member's failing health and mental faculties or other disability or even violence of a partner. In all circumstances, they need non-judgmental reassurance followed by clear, courteous and practical advice.

A solicitor has a very valuable role in such situations, especially in providing personal contact. In an increasingly impersonal society, elderly clients, more than most, appreciate knowing where to turn for advice. Many institutions – banks, government departments, hospitals and insurance companies – are prone to treat their customers as numbers, statistics or targets: customers can never get hold of a person or have to negotiate a telephone obstacle course to speak to a person. The aim of an elderly client solicitor must be to use the benefits of modern technology and good management practice to provide clients with a personal and professional service.

3.2.1　Staff

Staff must receive training in relation to the Handbook, to a level appropriate for their role in the firm. As a minimum, staff should be aware of the Principles. Solicitors should be aware of the outcomes required in Chapters 1–9 of the SRA Code of Conduct 2011.

Staff must be aware of the basic standards of good practice which they are expected to follow. It is important to value their contribution and recognise the particular stresses working with the elderly client can cause. A firm should ensure that all staff:

- Receive proper training and are continually updated on changes in the law, regulations and procedures (and see outcome 7.6).
- Can recognise particular problems which may arise in working with older clients, e.g. questions of capacity, inter-generational conflicts, long-term care issues. They should also be aware of the possibilities of undue influence and elder abuse. There is guidance in para.7.70 of the MCA 2005 Code of Practice; in addition, Action on Elder Abuse and Solicitors for the Elderly have useful guides.
- Are aware of the principles set out in Mental Capacity Act (MCA) 2005, s.1, its Code of Practice and the need to communicate effectively with those with a disability. The Alzheimer's Society has a range of useful factsheets including 'Communicating', which gives tips and advice for communicating with some-one with dementia.

Staff may obtain specialist qualifications (e.g. Society of Trust and Estate Practitioners (STEP)) or join specialist groups (e.g. STEP Special Interest Group Mental Capacity, Solicitors for the Elderly and the Law Society's Private Client Section). The Alzheimer's Society runs a Dementia Friend initiative, through which people can learn a little bit more about what it is like to live with dementia.

3.2.2　Delegation and supervision of staff

An efficient and profitable office aims to delegate case-work to staff, leaving the supervising partner or senior solicitor to cope with problems and develop a relationship with the client. However, this can cause its own problems with the client not knowing whom to contact and the solicitor and his or her staff working at cross-purposes.

Moreover, it is far more personal, especially in long-running cases, to explain to clients how the office works and introduce the staff who will be the other points of contact. Many clients can end up feeling more comfortable dealing with a junior fee earner or a secretary.

For any delegation to be effective, the client needs to be informed from the outset who will be dealing with the case, not only as a professional requirement, but as a reflection of common sense and professional courtesy. However, delegation cannot be an excuse for avoiding responsibility. Staff must not be allowed to do work beyond their capabilities or to overlook matters through neglect, embarrassment or because the solicitor is too busy (see outcomes 1.1, 1.4, 1.5 and 1.16). Neither should the possibility of financial mismanagement and even fraud be ignored (see outcomes 1.6, 1.13, 1.15 and 1.16).

Finally, if you are considering outsourcing any of your work, e.g. dictation, you should be aware of the Law Society Practice Note: Outsourcing (29 April 2015).

3.2.3 Departments

As should be clear from the areas of law covered by this work, the needs of the elderly client do not sit neatly with the conventional departmental structure used by most firms. Often work falls between two or more departments or involves more than one department. A seemingly simple case of appointing a deputy may, for example, involve conveyancing on the sale of the property, litigation on an Inheritance (Provision for Family and Dependants) Act 1975 claim or civil debt, contract law in respect of the nursing home, community care law and welfare benefit law to make sure (a) the client is receiving all the benefits they are entitled to and (b) no benefits are being overclaimed, investment advice which should recognise and make provision for payment of care fees, employment law as regards carers, company law in respect of the family business and issues of capacity concerning residence and treatment. Finally, according to Age UK, in 2013 there were over 1.1 million older people with problem debt issues, so knowledge of debt issues and possibly insolvency may also be required.

It is, perhaps, a clichéd saying but 'people do business with, and refer business to, people they know, like and trust'. Some firms have set up specialist departments or found a single fee earner who has become the firm's expert and main point of reference, usually within an existing private client or probate client department. It is often the case that what the client values most in his or her solicitor is a single point of contact and a relationship with the client coupled with access to specific expertise is generally more valuable than expertise in a particular field of law but no knowledge of the client.

Links between departments

Where work is done by more than one department for the same client, departments must inform each other, and the principal client contact, of all major developments. Modern technology facilitates this so that correspondence and emails can be copied very easily from one file to another across two or more departments within a firm.

The role of the practice is as much in giving support to the client as providing legal advice and this should be conveyed to colleagues who may be unfamiliar with the character and history of the client.

3.2.4 Ongoing monitoring

Clients will not always know when they need further legal assistance especially as their circumstances and needs can change quite radically in a relatively short period of time. A couple with a young family may not change their wills for 20 years, while an older client may unexpectedly find that he is intestate or that a carefully planned gift in a will has adeemed owing to a disposal of the asset. You may be dealing with a client whose mental capacity to make a specific decision deteriorates or improves over time. You need to take a proactive role with elderly clients who will often be unaware of the problems inherent in their situations. It is better to be hands-on and risk your client ignoring your advice than not to have proffered the advice at all.

As the client's circumstances change:

- Do not overlook the need for a will to be updated or a statutory will to be considered.
- Check whether an enduring power of attorney (EPA) is still operable or whether it should be registered. Was it properly executed?
- Check whether an LPA which is not registered, should be and that it is properly executed.
- Check that all current state benefits are being claimed in the light of benefit changes or the qualifying conditions of the client.
- Should the client be advised on community care services and how to obtain best delivery of services?
- Consider advising those with old EPAs to change to LPAs, if appropriate.
- Remind those clients with EPAs that an EPA does not cover any aspect of health and welfare – a separate LPA is required for those matters.
- Is assistance needed in negotiating any care contract?
- Do the client's present housing arrangements still meet the client's needs?

The client's financial affairs require particular attention to ensure they are still being handled properly and have been reviewed in the light of changes in circumstances:

- Is it time for a change of investment policy?
- Is the client living on capital and if so how long will this last? Can/should changes be made?
- Can the client afford the level of care to which he or she is committed?
- Should the client consider tax planning measures?
- Should assistance be offered to cope with self-assessment?
- Is there any reason to suspect that the client is vulnerable to financial exploitation or any other form of abuse? Be aware of guidance in the MCA 2005 Code of Practice and take sufficient action if abuse is discovered.

You can provide a useful service by offering advice and support to appointed deputies and attorneys so they are aware of the law regarding their role and responsibilities, including their strict fiduciary duties. These are set out in para.9 of the Law Society Practice Note: Lasting Powers of Attorney (8 December 2011) and

Chapters 7 and 8 of the MCA 2005 Code of Practice (see *Re Buckley; Public Guardian* v. *C* [2013] EWHC 2965 (COP)). This could include:

- ensuring that an EPA attorney knows when they need to register the power so they contact you when the need arises;
- offering assistance to a deputy with the preparation and submission of annual accounts;
- providing advice about their ability to maintain others or make gifts – even if for tax planning purposes; and
- giving assistance and advice on keeping accounts of transactions, not mixing their own funds with the person for whom they are appointed to act or using those funds for their own needs.

Make sure that your retainer and terms of business are up to date. Do they cover the additional work being carried out? Have you undertaken to do more than your client has asked you to do?

It is a matter of judgment and practice as to how best to monitor clients' needs. Some firms have systems for regular contacts and reminders. While you cannot monitor your clients all the time and there is always a danger of creating hostages to fortune in offering to do more than is practicable, doing nothing is no longer an option. Outcomes 1.2 and 1.5 require that 'you provide services to your clients in a manner which protects their interests' and which 'takes account of your clients' needs and circumstances'. SRA Principle 5 says 'you must provide a proper standard of service to your clients'. Note 2.9 to Principle 5 says: 'You should, e.g., provide a proper standard of client care and of work. This would include exercising competence, skill and diligence, and taking into account the individual needs and circumstances of each client.' Potentially, failure to keep the client updated could result in a complaint or a threat of litigation.

The aim of the elderly client solicitor should be to think proactively, anticipating the future needs of the client, putting out markers for further action being required. If you cannot monitor the client yourself, make sure those who are in regular contact will monitor the client and know when to contact you.

The solicitor who can achieve this is not only acting in the client's best interests but also marketing his or her business and securing future work for the firm and complying to the fullest extent with their professional obligations (see also **3.7**).

3.2.5 Systems

Systems introduced in the office make monitoring clients' affairs and safe custody of papers and documents more effective. Systems can be manual but the use of computerised systems will assist with:

- access to current files;
- archiving of old files;

- storage of documents, including deeds, wills, ordinary powers of attorney, EPAs and LPAs, securities, completed funeral plans and birth, death or marriage certificates;
- maintenance of accounting records;
- upkeep of diaries;
- reminders of significant dates (not just deadlines but also to review the client's needs or simply to send a birthday card);
- effective use of client databases to target or review for new work;
- reviewing files and work in progress.

3.2.6 Computers

Computers are ubiquitous in every office but they are not always used to their full potential. Often they are used simply for accessing the internet, emails, word processing and checking ledgers. However, there are many ways in which computers can help to provide a more effective and efficient service. For example, they can be used for:

- standard form letters;
- precedents of regularly used documents;
- storage of clients' previous wills for easy amendment;
- amending documents to make them more accessible, e.g. using larger fonts or heavier type;
- databases of:
  - clients with whom regular contact should be maintained, or those falling into specific work areas or age groups;
  - deeds and documents held in safe custody – in compliance with the requirements of the Information Commissioner;
  - current and old files;
  - key dates in respect of archiving and file destruction;
- spreadsheets of schedules of investments, tax returns and interest schedules for reproducing annually;
- keeping deputies' and attorneys' accounts up to date;
- accounting software for clients' accounts and trust accounts with facilities to calculate interest;
- time recording to ensure that work is properly costed and the client is kept informed of costs arising;
- diaries to manage appointments and reminders of action to take;
- internet access for up-to-date information from the SRA, the Law Society and **www.gov.uk** which hosts a 'front-desk service' for the government departments, as well as charities, publishers and lobby groups.

In addition, there are innumerable specialist software packages to assist with everything from practice management, compliance, dictation and form filling to will writing.

Client database

You may have a database containing information about individual clients from which all other storage records are derived. All relevant information can then be seen in respect of a client at a glance, while lists of deeds, wills, securities, etc. can still be produced (according to categories of client, date, name or otherwise as desired).

Data protection issues

If you send, receive, process or store material containing personal data, you should be registered with the Information Commissioner and you must ensure that you comply with the provisions of the Data Protection Act 1998 and guidance. The Information Commissioner's Office (ICO) produces a guide relating to the principles of the data protection legislation.

Clients should be advised how confidential information is being stored electronically. The Privacy and Electronic Communications (EC Directive) Regulations 2003, SI 2003/2426 govern the electronic storage of information about clients used for electronic marketing purposes.

Further information can be obtained from:

- Information Commissioner's Office (**www.ico.org.uk**).
- Law Society Practice Note: Data Protection (6 October 2011).
- Law Society Practice Note: Information Security (11 October 2011).
- The Law Society Library's 'Forms and Precedents', a 'template policy' for data protection, confidentiality and information security.

3.3   DUTIES TO THE CLIENT

It is vital to remember that professional duties are owed to the client, so it is important to correctly identify who is your client (see **2.3.2**). Do not be too easily persuaded by third parties as to the client's intentions or instructions, because however well-intentioned they may seem, they may have a personal interest and you should always be aware of duress or undue influence, particularly if there is a 'relationship of trust and confidence' between them. Be especially alert to the potential for financial abuse with EPAs and LPAs.

Solicitors should be aware of a person's mental capacity and whether they have the capacity to give informed instructions or whether they are being unduly influenced by another. Although note 6(c) of the guidance to rule 2 of the Solicitors'

Code of Conduct 2007 is no longer applicable, it does still provide good guidance about best practice for dealing with duress, specifically in relation to elderly clients:

> It is important to be satisfied that clients give their instructions freely. Some clients, such as the elderly, those with language or learning difficulties and those with disabilities are particularly vulnerable to pressure from others. If you suspect that a client's instructions are the result of undue influence, you need to exercise your judgement as to whether you can proceed on the client's behalf. For example, if you suspect that a friend or relative who accompanies the client is exerting undue influence, you should arrange to see the client alone or if appropriate with an independent third party or interpreter. Where there is no actual evidence of undue influence but the client appears to want to act against their best interests, it may be sufficient simply to explain the consequences of the instructions the client has given and confirm that the client wishes to proceed. For evidential purposes, it would be sensible to get this confirmation in writing.

Indicative behaviours 1.25–1.28, set out in Chapter 1 of the SRA Code of Conduct 2011, tend to show when you have not achieved the outcomes and therefore have not complied with the Principles.

3.3.1 Client care

Chapter 1 of the SRA Code of Conduct 2011 is all about client care which includes providing clients with the information they need to make informed decisions, about the services they need, how those services will be delivered and how much they will cost. This will enable you and your client to understand each other's expectations and responsibilities. If clients are not happy with the service they have received, they should know how to make a complaint and that all complaints are dealt with promptly and fairly.

The Law Society has an Advice Note: Saving Costs, Time and Improving Communication (15 May 2013) and a Practice Note: Client Care Information (26 March 2013), which makes clear that there are relatively few outcomes that require a solicitor to provide information in writing to a client and certainly, it is no longer mandatory to provide a client care letter. Nevertheless, it is still best practice to provide an initial letter to the client along with any terms of business. It can be helpful to refer to it at a later date and it may be used as positive evidence against complaints of insufficient information or inadequate professional service. It is imperative that the information is clear and that important details are highlighted, otherwise its value will be limited.

While much of the information given in the initial interview will help clients come to an informed decision, the written information given at the start of a retainer, whether in a client care letter or some other format, will also be important in meeting this outcome.

It is best practice that at the end of the matter you:

- confirm to the client, in writing, how the matter has been concluded;
- explain any continuing consequences and risks from his or her action or inaction;

- render your bill as promptly as possible and account to the client for all money due;
- consider with the client whether any papers and property are to be handed over or retained by your firm.

It is also useful to send out a simple questionnaire on the service rendered. This allows the client to evaluate the solicitor's work which will either provide welcome reassurance or identify improvements which may be necessary. A questionnaire can also be a useful marketing tool in reminding the client of his or her importance to the firm and also introducing the client to other areas of work.

3.3.2   Costs

Outcomes 1.13 and 1.14 stipulate that clients must receive the best possible information, both at the time of engagement and when appropriate as their matter progresses about the likely overall cost of their matter. They should also be informed of their right to challenge or complain about your bill and the circumstances in which they may be liable to pay interest on an unpaid bill. Indicative behaviours 1.13–1.21 list ways by which you may show that these outcomes have been achieved and you have complied with the Principles.

Further guidance on solicitors' charges is available from the Law Society's Practice Advice Service.

Any publicity provided by your firm must not be misleading or inaccurate (outcome 8.1) and publicity relating to your firm's charges must be clearly expressed, and state whether disbursements and VAT are included in the quoted sum (outcome 8. 2).

To comply with these outcomes, you should avoid:

- estimating charges pitched at an unrealistically low level (indicative behaviour 8.7);
- advertising additional 'sundries' or 'catch all' amounts for such without providing details about the purpose of the charges;
- providing estimated or fixed charges plus disbursements, if expenses which are in the nature of overheads are then charged as disbursements; and
- providing estimated or fixed charges for conveyancing services which may require additional charges for work on a related mortgage loan or repayment, including work done for a lender, unless the publicity makes it clear that additional charges may be payable (e.g. by including a clear statement such as 'excluding VAT, disbursements, mortgage related charges and charges for work done for a lender').

Costs for clients lacking capacity

It is arguable that a solicitor owes a higher duty of care to a client for whom he or she is acting in a fiduciary role and who may not be able to comprehend the legal issues being dealt with, let alone the contract between himself and his solicitor.

Where the solicitor is an attorney, the instrument may well provide authority to charge in the same way as a charging clause in a will. However, although the solicitor has a legal right to charge, in reality there may be little de facto oversight of the charges. There have regrettably been cases of solicitors abusing their roles as attorneys and charging excessively for their work to the point of committing a fraud against the client.

If a solicitor is appointed by the Court of Protection as deputy for property and financial affairs, Practice Direction 19B of the Court of Protection Rules 2007 will apply. There is now much greater oversight of a solicitor's charges and the Office of the Public Guardian is beginning to require annual cost estimates. It is therefore essential that solicitors acting in any kind of fiduciary role keep careful accounts which can be audited by the Supreme Court Costs Office or a beneficiary on the death of the client. Time ledgers and detailed fee accounts should also be retained with the file.

3.4 FINANCIAL SERVICES

3.4.1 Financial Services and Markets Act 2000

The Financial Services and Markets Act (FSMA) 2000 regulates the financial services industry. It is a criminal offence to carry on 'regulated activities', as defined in the Financial Services and Markets Act 2000 (Regulated Activities) Order (RAO) 2001, SI 2001/544, without authorisation, which must be obtained from the Financial Conduct Authority (FCA). Financial institutions undertaking regulated activities are regulated and supervised by the Prudential Regulation Authority (PRA).

Part XX of FSMA 2000 enables firms authorised and regulated by the SRA (because the Law Society is a designated professional body) to be treated as exempt professional firms and to carry on activities known as 'exempt regulated activities' provided that these firms are able to meet the conditions specified in FSMA 2000, s.327 and comply with the SRA Financial Services (Scope) Rules 2001 (as amended), which set out the scope of the activities which may be undertaken (see **3.4.4**).

These rules set out restrictions, and the basic conditions which those firms must satisfy when carrying on any regulated activities. Firms which are not regulated by the FCA are prohibited from carrying on certain regulated activities.

The following activities may involve a solicitor who is acting for the elderly in regulated activities:

- advice on or arrangements made for the purchase or sale of investment bonds or other specified investments;
- advice on or arrangements made for the purchase of a funeral plan contract;
- advice on or arrangements made for the purchase of an annuity;
- advice on or arrangements made for the acquisition of an insurance policy (e.g. term policy, contents or buildings policy);
- acting for a policyholder in respect of claims made under an insurance policy;
- advice on or arrangements made in respect of certain equity release schemes (including home reversion plans and sale and rent back agreements);
- acting as trustee or executor or acting on the administration of a trust fund or estate on behalf of an outside trustee or executor.

3.4.2 Regulated activities

'Regulated activities' are defined in RAO 2001 and are potentially undertaken when a solicitor is involved in any one of the activities referred to in arts.5–61 and relating to any one of the specified investments listed in arts.74–89. The most common activities will be:

- advice on the merits of buying or selling a specified investment;
- arranging on behalf of a client the sale or purchase of a specified investment;
- discretionary management of specified investments (this will arise where the trustees or executors are all partners or employees in the firm, or where a solicitor is a donee under a power of attorney which allows discretion in relation to the purchase/sale of specified investments);
- assisting in the administration and performance of a contract of insurance. This activity includes claims handling on behalf of the insured;
- safeguarding and administration of specified investments.

Shares, bonds, unit trusts, annuities, funeral plan contracts, home reversion plans, sale and rent back agreements and ISAs constitute common specified investments. Furthermore, all insurance contracts (investment, life and indemnity insurance policies) are specified investments.

Advising the client on or arranging the purchase or sale of the following investments does not constitute a regulated activity since these activities in relation to the investments are not caught by the definition of regulated activities:

- a normal bank or building society current or deposit account;
- National Savings and Investments products.

Similarly, generic investment advice is not within the definition of regulated activities in RAO 2001. Generic advice is advice about general categories of investment, as opposed to particular investments. Recommendations to the client that 'it would be wise to invest capital in equity shares/unit trusts' or 'you should take out an annuity' or 'you should purchase a funeral plan' are examples of generic advice.

3.4.3 Exclusions

Solicitors can avoid the need for authorisation by showing that certain exclusions contained in RAO 2001 apply. The most important exclusions are:

- Arrangements made with or through an authorised person (i.e. an independent financial adviser (IFA)) are excluded where the transaction is entered into on advice given to the client by an authorised person.
    This exclusion does not apply if the solicitor receives from any person other than the client any pecuniary award or advantage, for which he does not account to the client, arising out of his entering into the transaction (see **3.4.6**).
- Introductions are excluded where a solicitor introduces a client to an authorised person and the introduction is made with a view to the provision of independent advice (i.e. an introduction to an IFA).
- Arranging deals, discretionary management, safeguarding and administration and investment advice are all excluded if undertaken by a solicitor who is a trustee or executor (but not if a solicitor is merely acting for outside trustees or executors).

Note that for this exclusion to apply, the solicitor must not be remunerated for these activities in addition to any remuneration received for acting as a trustee or executor. Furthermore, for the exclusion to apply to discretionary management or safeguarding and administration activities, the solicitor must not hold himself out as providing such services.
    None of these exclusions apply where the specified investment is an insurance policy.

3.4.4 Exempt regulated activities

Where an exclusion is not available for any reason or where the regulated activity involves an insurance policy, the need for authorisation can be avoided by using FSMA 2000, Part XX, which contains provisions relating to 'exempt regulated activities' (see **3.4.1**).
    FSMA 2000, s.327 provides that the prohibition against carrying on regulated activities contained in the Act does not apply to the carrying on of a regulated activity by a member of a profession if certain conditions apply:

(a) the person must be a member of a profession or controlled or managed by one or more such members;
(b) the person must not receive from anyone other than his client any pecuniary reward or other advantage, for which he does not account to his client, arising out of his carrying on of any of the activities;
(c) the manner of the provision of any service in the course of carrying on the activities must be incidental to the provision by him of professional services;
(d) only regulated activities permitted by the designated professional body's rules may be carried out.

The SRA Financial Services (Scope) Rules 2001 cover the requirements of (d) above. These rules limit the scope of solicitors benefiting from Part XX. The prohibited activities include:

- market making;
- buying, selling, subscribing or underwriting as principal where the firm holds itself out as engaging in the business of buying investments with a view to selling them;
- acting as a trustee or operator of a regulated collective investment scheme (CIS);
- acting as a stakeholder pension scheme manager;
- entering as provider into a funeral plan contract;
- entering into regulated home reversion plans or sale and rent back agreements as plan or agreement providers.

Further restrictions in the use of Part XX are contained in the Scope Rules.

Retail investment products

These are defined as long-term insurance contracts (including annuities but excluding 'pure protection policies' such as term assurance), units or shares in a regulated CIS (e.g. unit trusts or shares in open ended investment companies) or an investment trust savings scheme, in each case whether or not held within an ISA, a CTF or a group or personal stakeholder pension scheme. Where such investments are involved, firms cannot use the 'incidental' exception in Part XX in relation to recommendations or arrangements to purchase a retail investment product but should instead use an authorised person (i.e. an IFA). Firms may, within Part XX:

- pass on and endorse the advice of an authorised person;
- recommend or arrange the disposal of a retail investment product;
- recommend or arrange the acquisition of a retail investment product by means of an assignment;
- recommend that a client should not buy a retail investment product (i.e. give negative advice).

Other investments

Recommending that an individual buy an investment is not permitted if the transaction is with a person whose business it is to deal in those investments (e.g. a stockbroker), or the transaction is on an investment exchange or in response to an invitation to subscribe for an investment admitted or to be admitted on an investment exchange. However, firms may, within Part XX:

- pass on and endorse the advice of an authorised person;
- recommend or arrange the disposal of such investments;
- arrange the acquisition of such investments;

- recommend that a client should not buy such investments (i.e. give negative advice).

Managing investments

Discretionary management of investments can only fall within Part XX if the management is undertaken by a solicitor who is a trustee, personal representative, donee under a power of attorney, or a deputy appointed by the Court of Protection. Further, to benefit from Part XX, it must be shown that all routine or day-to-day decisions are taken by an authorised person, or that any decision taken to buy or subscribe for an investment is taken in accordance with the advice of an authorised person.

Regulated home reversion plans and regulated sale and rent back agreements

A regulated home reversion plan is a form of equity release arrangement under which a person buys all or part of an interest in land in the UK from an individual who is entitled under the arrangement to occupy at least 40 per cent of the land in question as or in connection with a dwelling. The arrangement specifies one or more qualifying termination events, on the occurrence of which that entitlement will end (typically death or permanent residence in a nursing home).

A regulated sale and rent back agreement is one under which a person buys all or part of an interest in land in the United Kingdom from an individual seller and the seller (or a related person) is entitled to occupy at least 40 per cent of the land in question as or in connection with a dwelling, and intends to do so. Such an arrangement is not a regulated sale and rent back agreement if it is a regulated home reversion plan.

Activities such as arranging and advising on such plans or arrangements are regulated. Entering into and administering such arrangements will also be regulated activities.

The SRA Financial Services (Scope) Rules 2001 have been amended to prevent solicitors from using FSMA 2000, Part XX in relation to recommending particular plans and arrangements but solicitors can endorse the advice of an authorised person where such endorsement is incidental to other work.

3.4.5 Conduct of Business Rules

The SRA Financial Services (Conduct of Business) Rules 2001 are applicable to solicitors seeking exemption under Part XX. These include rules relating to:

- status disclosure – requiring firms to indicate in writing that they are not authorised by the FCA but are regulated by the SRA;

- execution of transactions – requiring firms to carry out transactions as soon as possible;
- records of transactions – requiring firms to keep records of instructions received and instructions given;
- record of commissions – where a firm receives commission which is attributable to regulated activities carried on by a firm, it shall keep a record of the amount of the commission and how the firm has accounted to the client;
- execution only – requiring firms to give written confirmation of execution-only transactions involving retail investment products;
- insurance activities – requiring firms to inform clients whether or not any recommendation is given on the basis of a fair market analysis of the type of product and requiring firms to give clients a demands and needs statement setting out the client's demands and needs and an explanation of why a particular insurance contract was recommended.

3.4.6 Commissions

Life assurance companies and the providers of some other types of investment product have paid commissions to intermediaries on the sale of their products but the FCA is now working towards a fee-based system and it is likely that commission-based earnings will be phased out. A solicitor who introduced a client to an authorised person would usually receive a commission for the introduction; whether this will be authorised by the rules on referral fees is not known at the date of publication.

Any commission received by the solicitor is subject to the SRA Code of Conduct 2011. Outcome 1.15 says you must properly account to clients for any financial benefit you receive as a result of your instructions. Acting in accordance with indicative behaviour 1.20 may help demonstrate you have achieved this.

3.4.7 The marketplace for financial services

Research and the experience of many practitioners indicate that elderly people are very receptive to the idea of seeking financial advice through their solicitor. Having encountered the constant marketing of financial services and products through advertisements and mailshots, a client may believe that he will not be sold something or indeed rushed into anything against his interests by his solicitor. It is far safer to introduce your elderly client to an independent financial adviser whom you know and trust. If you ignore the client's financial requirements, all your good work in other areas could be rendered ineffective by someone selling the client an inappropriate or unwise investment.

In addition, it may be easier to manage a client's tax and other affairs if you are fully aware of the financial products being sold to them. You should be aware of the need to 'know your client' and therefore to have some knowledge of his or her investments and assets the ownership of which may otherwise be inconsistent with other advice you have given in connection with tax or welfare benefits. Few solicitors are, themselves, authorised to provide financial advice. Yet whether advice is provided by your firm in-house or with an authorised party (AP), you will need to understand in broad terms the advice being given to the client. You may act as an intermediary and be responsible for providing the AP with sufficient details about your client to enable sound advice to be given. You may otherwise be asked to interpret, comment upon, endorse or provide 'negative advice' on the AP's recommendations.

3.4.8 General advice

You should not be deterred from providing any financial advice to your client simply by reason of FSMA 2000, because much of the advice that a typical elderly client needs will not come within the scope of that legislation. Such advice may be general or strategic and often the client's affairs may be neglected and simply need to be tidied up and simplified.

You should therefore consider whether:

- Money is safely invested and, at the very least, providing a good rate of interest. The client may have large sums of cash in the house which should be banked or a large balance on current account which could be put on deposit or invested to make full use of the annual ISA limits. The client may have a number of small building society accounts which could be amalgamated or on which a better rate of interest could be obtained in a different class of account. Matured savings certificates should be encashed and you should check with NS&I whether the client has any (usually long forgotten) premium bonds or unclaimed prizes.
- Income is being paid net of tax if the client would benefit from gross income, and recoverable tax deducted is actually being recovered.
- Any increase or decrease in income would affect welfare benefits.
- The client is claiming all benefits to which they might be entitled including housing benefit, council tax benefit and discounts in respect of council tax, e.g. the single person reduction. According to Age UK, billions of pounds-worth of benefits are going unclaimed despite rising poverty. Age UK has a useful online benefits calculator.
- The client might be better advised to reduce the value of his taxable estate through capital expenditure or lifetime gifts rather than necessarily generate a larger income.
- Capital could be preserved by purchasing an annuity or long-term care plan to fund residential or nursing care, so enabling the client to be self-funding with the consequent beneficial effects on state benefits and in preserving assets.
- Capital could be raised by using appropriate equity release schemes.

It used to be advisable to recommend to clients to pay for their funeral plan, as this was considered 'permitted expenditure' and could be useful for bringing a client under the capital threshold for pension credit. Although there is no mention in the DWP's 2014 publication, *A Detailed Guide to Pension Credit*, of the phrase 'permitted expenditure', it is still a useful thing to recommend to a client, because it will undoubtedly make things easier for the family and it will save money but if the client is near the qualifying threshold for pension credit, such a purchase might be questioned by the DWP.

Solicitors must be able to recognise the need to obtain expert and regulated financial advice when it is needed and, if possible, know where to obtain it.

3.5 THE MARKET FOR THE ELDERLY CLIENT ADVISER

It should be clear from the very nature of this work just how extensive is the need for specialist advice for the elderly client, and as the number of elderly clients grows, so does the market for their business. For more information on the elderly population see Age UK's research papers and statistical publications, including *Older People in the United Kingdom: Key Facts and Statistics* (see **www.ageuk.org.uk**).

Marketing is often seen as promoting your practice or particular specialist services which you can offer to potential clients. Advertising is one aspect and may not appeal to you; other possibilities can and should be considered. The best and simplest marketing involves making existing clients and people you deal with aware of the services you provide. You can easily spend a small fortune on clever brochures and adverts and overlook the large number of elderly clients and potential referrers of elderly clients you already have.

Although marketing is often seen as a complex and separate area, involving large resources and the recruitment of specialist staff or consultants, practitioners can at least seek to identify matters of particular significance to elderly clients which should be considered in developing a practice.

The Law Society publishes several books designed to help practice managers understand more about marketing legal services and developing marketing strategies.

3.5.1 Trends

Solicitors do not have a monopoly in providing for the legal needs of elderly people and it is regrettable that, in 2013, the then Justice Secretary, despite a robust recommendation from the Legal Services Board, decided not to regulate will writing. However, the Law Society has responded by launching the Wills and Inheritance Quality Scheme, which aims to be a best practice quality mark for wills and estate administration advice that consumers can trust. Solicitors for the Elderly, an organisation for lawyers specialising in this increasingly complex area of law, has also responded with the Older Client in Care Practice Award for existing members and STEP has introduced an Advanced Certificate in Advising Vulnerable Clients.

The solicitor in general practice is uniquely qualified to respond to the legal needs of older members of the local community, and the consequence of doing so may be a wide range of new work and an introduction to new clients (not only elderly ones, as many satisfied clients will have families, friends or other professional connections).

Financial and legal problems of older people are increasing because they are living longer and demographics and lifestyle mean that families do not live so close and cannot always provide support. Older people tend (and wish) to be cared for in the community rather than in hospitals or institutions and have more money (from home ownership, pensions and state benefits).

The need for delegation arises more often in the case of women because men generally die younger and are more reluctant to give up management of their affairs.

3.5.2   Areas of work

The law relating to the elderly client is unlike other areas of law which are subject-based. Instead of identifying an area of law such as divorce or crime and then finding the clients to service, elderly client law is entirely client focused and the solicitor needs to apply different areas of law to properly meet the needs of the client. To develop an elderly client practice, a solicitor or a firm of solicitors needs to provide expertise in many different areas of work.

Financial

See:

- Social security benefits, **Chapter 13**.
- Local authority benefits, **Chapters 13** and **14**.
- Financial planning, **Chapter 16**.
- Tax and tax planning, **Chapter 16**.
- Providing for infirm or disabled relatives, **Chapter 19**.
- Wills and gifts, **Chapters 18** and **19**.
- Loans to relatives and guarantees for their liabilities, **Chapter 17**.
- Long-term care planning, **Chapters 8**, **9** and **10**.

Management

See:

- Coping with mental and/or physical frailty, **Chapters 1** and **4**.
- Issues as to capacity, **Chapter 1**.
- Handling financial affairs and dealing with problems, **Chapters 1**, **4** and **16**.
- EPAs and LPAs, **Chapter 4**.
- Court of Protection applications and deputyship, **Chapter 4**.
- Negotiating service delivery for domiciliary, residential or nursing care, **Chapters 7–9**.

Personal

See:

- Involvement with the police, **Chapter 6**.
- Issues of civil status, **Chapter 6**.
- Planning for the future (e.g. residential care, home adaptations, funeral), **Chapters 8**, **9** and **20**.
- Community care provision and funding and advocacy services for service delivery, **Chapters 7** and **8**.
- Accidents (e.g. tripping on pavement), **Chapter 5**.
- Consumer problems, **Chapter 6**.

Relationships

See:

- Supporting carers and dealing with professionals, **Chapters 2** and **8**.
- Marriage, civil partnership and cohabitation difficulties, **Chapter 6**.
- Problems with family, **Chapter 6**.
- Abuse and domestic violence, **Chapter 6**.
- Disputes with others, **Chapters 5** and **6**.

Housing

See:

- Moving house, **Chapter 17**.
- Sharing the home or moving in with relatives, **Chapter 17**.
- Exercising the 'right to buy' council accommodation, **Chapter 17**.
- Disabled facilities and grants, **Chapter 15**.
- Home income plans, **Chapters 16** and **17**.
- Sheltered housing schemes, **Chapter 17**.
- Moving into a care home, **Chapter 9**.

Health

See:

- Coping with the NHS, **Chapters 10** and **15**.
- Private medical schemes, **Chapter 10**.
- Medical negligence and personal injury claims, **Chapter 5**.
- Implications of mental incapacity, **Chapter 1**.
- Implications of mental illness, **Chapter 12**.
- Advance decisions to refuse medical treatment, **Chapter 11**.

- Deprivation of liberty, **Chapter 11**.
- Arrangements immediately following death, **Chapter 20**.

The areas of law covered by this work as outlined above encompass almost all areas of legal practice. However, this is far more than a summary of the general law applicable to private clients. Making a will or a personal injury claim may involve similar legal issues whether the client is 30 years old or 80 years old. However, for the elderly client the issues may be very different and the elderly client practitioner needs to be aware of this. In these two examples, the will of a parent with a young family will be different from that of, for example, an elderly spinster with no dependants or an elderly widow or widower with warring children and step-children. Similarly, a personal injury claim will involve very different conse-quences in terms of life expectancy, lost prospects, dependants and long-term care. Moreover, these general areas of law very often do interact with legal principles applicable to the elderly client especially in areas of capacity and financial manage-ment. Taking these two examples again, an elderly client's will may involve issues of capacity or substituted decision-making through the Court of Protection, issues which would not apply to the youthful parent; while the elderly litigant may need to be represented by a litigation friend.

3.6 DEVELOPING AN ELDERLY CLIENT PRACTICE

Developing a successful elderly client practice requires more than giving high quality advice to elderly clients and having expert knowledge of the law relevant to their needs. It may also require a different approach to marketing, physical altera-tions to premises, awareness of communication difficulties associated with old age and with disability, and a more sensitive attitude to all communications with the client.

Before it is thought that no one can acquire all these qualities, it should be borne in mind that while change cannot take place instantly, firms can plan to update and improve what can be offered over a period of time.

In addition to making changes to their practice that better suit their clients, solicitors must also comply with their statutory obligations as a service provider under the Equality Act 2010 to facilitate access to services for all and, where a client lacks capacity, have regard in particular to Chapter 3 of the MCA 2005 Code of Practice.

3.6.1 A user-friendly office: checklist

Examine the facilities your firm has, and the services that are offered from the point of view of the elderly client.

Access

- Is the location of your office easily accessible by road (one way systems are not user friendly for anybody, least of all the elderly)?
- Is there provision for parking close by?
- Is there convenient access to public transport?
- Is the street near your office easy to cross?
- Can you provide a map or written travel instructions?
- Does your office have aids to improve physical accessibility (signs, steps, staircases, stair rails, ramps, door widths, etc.)? Are these enough to comply with the provisions of the Equality Act 2010?
- Is your office free of obstructions?
- Are there clear signs to the reception area?
- Is the lighting in and outside your office sufficient?
- Do you offer home visits when the client wishes this? The client may ask for this even if able to visit your office (remember that the client is paying the fee and if they would feel more comfortable at home then it is for the adviser to accommodate this). Do you charge extra for home visits or treat them as part of the service you provide? If you do charge, make sure you advise the client of the extra cost.

Waiting area

- Is your waiting area secure? Is there room to leave bags, shopping trolleys, umbrellas, etc.?
- Is your waiting area warm and draught free (and cool in summer)?
- Is there a choice of seating in your waiting area (e.g. higher/upright chairs with arms)?
- Do you have accessible toilet facilities (a disabled toilet may not always be feasible, but a toilet should be available on the same level as the waiting room)?

Interview room

- Is your interview room situated on the ground floor?
- Does your interview room offer a choice of seating (e.g. higher/upright chairs with arms)?
- Is it private (especially if having to speak loudly)?
- Is the lighting sufficient (also consider that a window behind the solicitor will create a silhouette effect making it difficult for the client to see)?
- Do you offer any adaptations to assist those with disabilities? Consider a hearing loop, for example. Action on Hearing Loss (now the trading name for the Royal National Institute for Deaf People (RNID)) and the Royal National Institute of Blind People (RNIB) will be able to assist you with information.

Impressions

- Do you have ground floor premises?
- Do your premises appear well cared for?
- Are your office furniture, carpets, and decorations in good condition?
- Can the impression your office creates be improved with pictures and flowers?
- Are your staff cheerful, polite and presentable?
- Are your staff well trained and able to be helpful and efficient?
- Have your support staff had any special training for working with elderly clients?

Communication

- Does your receptionist project a positive image of your firm to elderly clients?
- Does your receptionist communicate clearly with elderly clients, both in person and on the telephone?
- Do you provide elderly clients with information on the legal services you have available, e.g. the people in your office; costs; common legal issues (such as wills, long-term care, and LPAs)?
- Are clients kept informed about the progress of their case and the reasons for any delays?
- Have you considered suitable methods of communication such as large print in letters and documents; plain English in letters, documents and speech; installing an induction loop or minicom (for more information contact Action on Hearing Loss (the RNID))?

Convenience

- Do you offer appointments that suit the client including, if necessary, on a Saturday morning?
- Do you always make appointments and never keep clients waiting?
- Do your staff offer assistance to clients with their travel arrangements (e.g. offering to ring for a taxi or escorting clients across the road, etc.)?
- Are there clinics or surgeries close by?
- Do you always offer clients the opportunity of home appointments?
- Have you considered the problems caused by limited mobility, use of wheelchairs, visual and hearing impairments and communication difficulties?
- Have you complied with the Equality Act 2010?
- If sending documents to the client which need to be signed and returned, do you either have a Freepost address or provide a stamped, self-addressed return envelope?

3.6.2   Relationship with elderly clients

Dealing with older people is often based upon a one-to-one relationship, working at the client's pace and level of understanding:

- Do not see working with elderly clients to be as competitive as when dealing with other solicitors or commercial clients. Investing the time to establish a good relationship with your client will, in most cases, reap its own rewards.
- Ensure that the client knows who you are and that you are dealing personally with his or her matter.
- Explain how you may be contacted when the need arises.
- Introduce an alternative contact for occasions when you are not available.
- Make sure the client has the option of private discussion with you and thus is alerted to any potential problems or conflicts which may arise.
- If the client wishes to bring a friend to interviews, see the client on their own at first, to assess mental capacity and special needs. Do not discourage the client from bringing a friend, however, because that friend will discuss the matter with the client when you are not there and may be able to provide valuable assistance as advocate for the client.
- Always be aware of undue influence but do not see this as a spectre in every situation.
- Avoid being impatient or patronising and do not assume that older people are less legally competent merely because they are mentally or physically infirm.
- Be gentle when raising painful subjects such as mental incapacity or death.
- Treat the client professionally at all times – as you would wish your elderly parent (or grandparent) to be treated in this situation or indeed how you will want to be treated when you become an elderly client yourself.

3.6.3   Addressing the client

Establish a policy throughout the firm as to the manner in which clients are addressed, particularly in letters. Do not assume that a first name approach should be encouraged as many elderly clients prefer a more formal approach.

Although partners and senior staff may wish to be on first name terms with clients, would you wish employees to follow suit and to address them in that manner in letters?

Make sure that clients are addressed correctly. A long-standing client may be on first name terms with the senior partner, but may not expect to be addressed in the same way by a trainee. Be polite, find out how the client wishes to be addressed and let the client dictate the style of the relationship. Check that you and your staff are consistent in their dealings and use the right form of address:

- 'Dear Madam'.
- 'Dear Mrs Smith'.

- 'Dear Ms Smith'.
- 'Dear Ethel'.

Take care with titles, decorations, religious offices and military ranks. If such designations are used, then they should be used correctly.

How does the client view you?

Do you:

- Dress outrageously (nose rings, short skirts, loud ties)? The older client probably expects professionals to look professional.
- Appear too busy to discuss the client's problem or not easily available?
- Talk down to the client?
- Explain matters clearly to the client and appear to enjoy doing so?
- Offer the client alternatives or impose your own viewpoint?
- Give the client time to decide and consider matters with a follow-up letter?
- Greet the client in reception or expect him or her to find your room and enter while you are working?
- Take care how you address the client and invite the client to address you?

How can the client help you (and indirectly himself)?

Ensure the client can (if able):

- Prepare for the meeting by drawing up a statement of facts and questions.
- Give you clear instructions.
- Explain if there are any important time constraints.
- Be sure that you have understood each other.
- Seek reassurance if they are either unsure or worried about anything.
- Keep in regular touch with you.
- Deal promptly with any important or urgent questions that arise.
- Ask for a progress report if the client has not heard from you when expecting to do so.
- Talk about his or her family and history so that the client feels you are interested in what he or she has to say – this will help the client to feel at ease and you can gather valuable background information to assist with your advice or in assessing capacity.
- Write rather than telephone unless it is urgent.
- Make an appointment if wanting to see you.
- Avoid unnecessary calls (which may increase the cost).
- Speak to someone else whose time may be less expensive to the client, especially if the call is not urgent.

How can you help older clients?

Consider the following as a matter of routine:

- Have information packs to send in advance of an appointment to help prepare for any meeting relating to wills, tax planning, EPAs, LPAs, advanced decisions to refuse medical treatment and long-term care.
- Visit elderly clients at their homes if it is difficult for them to get out or if your office premises are not suitable for visits by them and cannot be adapted.
- Visit just for a chat when they have not asked to see you and you have no specific business but feel concerned about their welfare.
- Consider paying a social call if you are passing or visiting another client in the same nursing home.
- Remember to send birthday or Christmas cards especially when the client has few other relatives or friends.
- Tell clients in advance that you are willing to visit them (without adding substantially to the bill).
- Make appointments at a time that suits them or, if the client is in a care home or hospital at a convenient time (check with the home manager or nurse in charge); keep these appointments and conduct them in a cheerful manner.

3.6.4 Office brochures

Each firm will have its own style and the use of a 'logo' may create continuity between documents and give the firm an identity. Different brochures may be produced for different purposes, and it may be relevant to ask clients what their needs are. The following general brochures may be helpful to the older client.

An introduction to the firm

A marketing brochure or leaflet can inform potential clients about your firm and create the appropriate image. However, the brochure or leaflet needs to be appropriate to the client for whom it is designed. A glossy brochure promoting the firm's corporate business with bright pictures of glamorous lawyers in designer offices may deter some elderly clients.

A brochure or leaflet should at the very least provide reassurance that your firm is reputable and can provide expertise in different areas of law as well as basic information (with photographs) about the firm's:

- name, address and telephone numbers;
- history (formation, growth, previous partners, names and locations);
- premises (history, location, access and facilities);
- partners (qualifications, expertise, interests and backgrounds);
- staff (number, nature and any special experience);
- availability during and outside normal office hours;

- areas of work, particular expertise;
- philosophy;
- other relevant information used in marketing.

A guide for clients

You may provide separate client brochures to provide a range of information to persons who are or become clients of the firm. These may include:

- Basic information relating to the firm (name, full contact details, list of partners, list of department managers or fee earners, office hours, emergency telephone numbers).
- Specific details, added to the printed brochure, of persons with whom the client may become involved (the person dealing with the client's matter, another person in the event that this person is unavailable, the supervising partner).
- Guidance to the client on dealing effectively with the firm (e.g. standards that the firm seeks to maintain, the basis of charging, and complaints procedures).
- An overview of legal services provided by the firm (e.g. details of the general range of work undertaken, specialist services which are unique to the firm, a list of any newsletters promoting different services and issues).

3.7 PROMOTING LEGAL SERVICES

3.7.1 Establishing a reputation

Some firms will already have a sound reputation for specialising in elderly client work built up over several generations, but positive steps can be taken either to ensure that the firm is known locally as being willing and able to undertake this area of work, or to maintain the reputation. Remember that existing clients will bring your firm the most work.

Some suggestions for positive steps to improve your firm's reputation in the area:

- Join specialist legal groups, e.g. Society of Trust and Estate Practitioners, Solicitors for the Elderly, the Law Society's Private Client Section (see **3.8.2**).
- Offer a free initial interview for retired people.
- Join a hobby group in which you are interested.
- Give public talks to the Women's Institute, Rotary or other groups (if you are a trained and confident speaker and can provide talks at the right level for the group).
- Provide support for suitable organisations (e.g. staff associations, pensioners' groups, charities working with the elderly).
- Use the media to provide guidance about legal matters concerning the elderly (e.g. articles in local newspapers, writing letters on relevant subjects to local and national newspapers, making appearances on local radio and television).

- Sponsor suitable local events, or activities provided by voluntary services and organisations.
- Place advertisements targeted at older people and their needs (in magazines for older people, nursing home guides, local papers, etc.).
- Distribute information leaflets of interest to elderly clients (through Citizens Advice Bureaux, health centres, day centres or by inserts into local magazines, newspapers, etc.).
- Use mailshots to existing clients (to advise on the extent of your services) or potential new clients about particular services.

But beware the scattergun approach. This is actually less effective than specially targeted campaigns to become known. It is also worth assessing, prior to launching a campaign, whether the firm has the relevant expertise and can actually service the work. Marketing without the necessary back-up is a waste of skills and energies. Bringing in work and not being able to service it is a pointless exercise. In fact, it may do more harm than good.

3.7.2 Contacts

Developing personal contacts in the community reaps its own rewards, and willingness to offer your services without charge on occasions can be valuable:

- Give talks to local groups or societies, e.g. Rotary, Age UK (if possible, keep material for talks in stock on subjects such as LPAs, wills, state benefits, community care and the role of a solicitor, and tie these in with information packs).
- Contact your local sheltered housing associations; find out if they offer information events to residents and offer to participate.
- Attend national conferences and seminars on issues relevant to older people (these may involve other professionals working with the elderly, e.g. specialist financial advisers, local and health authorities, accountants and charities).
- Attend business meetings (Rotary, Institute of Directors) and talk to other attendees.
- Work with other professionals to inform them of the services you can provide (e.g. accountants may know all about your tax planning expertise but they also have older clients who may benefit from your expertise).
- Attend local charity-run fetes and open days at nursing homes and other places relevant to the elderly (try not to refuse an invitation to a residential home's Christmas party).
- Volunteer for work for local societies and join any relevant committees providing services to elderly people (e.g. Age UK, the Alzheimer's Society).
- Cultivate contacts with retirement and nursing homes and sheltered housing complexes (make it known that you are prepared to visit residents, preferably at no extra cost).

- Cultivate contacts with officers of the NHS and local authority (they need to know who specialises so ask if they keep a register of solicitors for their clients – not all will be without assets).
- Organise a firm's seminar on matters of concern to older people. Consider whether to advertise or to make it invitation only. Also consider whether or not to make a charge to attend.
- Consider joining a networking organisation where many professions are represented. Build links with, for example, local accountants and bank managers, hairdressers and florists. Your fellow members may have services you could recommend to your clients. If you recommend people you know and trust through your networking, hopefully they will recommend you.

3.7.3   Suitable topics for seminars

These include:

- providing for long-term care;
- financial management for those who become incapable;
- employment issues for residential care and nursing homes;
- LPAs and how they work (and how they do not work);
- asset protection for the family;
- inheritance tax planning;
- provision for disabled dependants;
- wills;
- housing options for older people.

3.7.4   Image

The current use of advertising and publicity by solicitors is something which many older clients do not associate with the professions. However, it is part of modern practice and is significant in this particular marketplace when so many people are competing for other clients' business. Thus, although the more formal approach may be appropriate, in today's competitive marketplace this needs to be linked with the use of information technology and systems as well as well-trained, informed staff.

A conservative approach

Consider the term you use: is it 'old', 'older', 'elder', 'elderly', or 'senior'? Fashions change and some consider 'old' to be a derogatory term. It is advisable to ask your clients. Think about it very carefully before ordering expensive brochures.
   Your brochure should also reflect this approach:

- Avoid garish colours, fussy designs and youth-orientated pictures.

- Avoid negative pictures of elderly persons, i.e. lolling in an orthopaedic chair in a crowded nursing home sitting room.
- Use a clear font for text (preferably a sans serif variety such as Arial).
- Ensure the size of the text is as high as is practical (at least font size 12, but preferably 14).
- Use background colour and text colour sensibly (black text on a white background or black on bright yellow).
- Ensure that the words 'authorised and regulated by the Solicitors Regulation Authority and recognised as [insert firm's name] under SRA Number . . .' are on all marketing material.
- Ensure you comply with the outcomes in the SRA Code of Conduct 2011, Chapter 8 – in particular, that publicity must not be misleading or inaccurate.

A professional image

It is important to become known not only as having expertise in working with and for older clients but also for:

- being able to understand and communicate with them;
- being flexible and allowing them to develop their own wishes;
- not promoting a level of expertise which your firm does not have!

It may also be helpful to market your image and professionalism as a member of the solicitors' profession and the benefits that membership gives to your clients:

- independence;
- all-round advice;
- adherence to strict standards of professional conduct;
- professional indemnity insurance.

Elderly clients will in general be resistant to an over-aggressive commercial approach to marketing and promotion, but beware of taking a patronising tone as well. Remember that elderly clients also have the sophistication and experience to be discerning.

3.7.5 Websites

Your website is a valuable, yet frequently overlooked, tool for marketing. Many older people – particularly the 'active retired' – are increasingly 'internet-savvy' so make sure your website is clear and user-friendly. It should contain enough information to be useful but not so much that it becomes boring to read. Ideally, it should be a welcoming, open invitation for a client to contact you and your contact details should be obvious on every single page (see Law Society Practice Note: Information on Letterheads, Emails and Websites (24 August 2015)). Make sure your website is 'mobile device' friendly too – so it will adapt to being accessed on a tablet or a mobile phone.

Another useful tool is to have a 'news' section on your website, which is updated regularly. Also include links to other useful organisations, such as the Alzheimer's Society, When They Get Older and Age UK. Finally, consider whether you need a social media presence. Many firms have a Facebook page.

The importance to an elderly client practice of having a website is illustrated by statistics gathered by the Office for National Statistics bulletin *Internet Access: Households and Individuals 2014*. According to the bulletin, of the adults aged 55–64, daily internet use has doubled from 36 to 74 per cent. Of the adults aged 65 and over, daily internet use has increased more than fourfold, from 9 to 42 per cent. The proportion of adults aged 65 and over who have never used the internet has reduced from 65 to just 28 per cent – more than a two-thirds reduction (see **www.statistics.gov.uk**). For many busy modern families, life with the internet has become vital for staying in touch with older relatives. This is demonstrated by the popularity of tools such as Skype.

Remember too that it is not just the elderly who would access a website, but their children and relatives who may live in other countries or in other parts of the United Kingdom. They will be looking for solicitors who may be able to help them to sort out problems arising when they discover their relatives are becoming frail or forgetful and they cannot reach their elderly relatives quickly.

Unless you wish to go down the full route of an interactive site with clients accessing their own files, etc., use your website as a window box to tell visitors about your services. Use it to inform older people of services useful for them and have links to local organisations if those organisations agree for you to link up with them; they may agree to include your website on their own useful links.

For more information about the use of the internet by older people see:

- *Web Accessibility for Older Users: A Literature Review* (World Wide Web Consortium (**www.w3.org**).
- *Web accessibility implementation in private sector organizations: Motivations and business impact* published by Springer Berlin Heidelberg.

British Standard 8878: *2010 Web accessibility – Code of Practice* provides a framework for web accessibility when designing or commissioning web products. It provides guidance on meeting the requirements of the Equality Act 2010, which states that web products must be accessible to all. The standard is recognised by the UK government's e-Accessibility Action Plan as a key tool for developing accessible online services. See **www.equalityhumanrights.com** for this Code of Practice.

The World Wide Web Consortium (W3C) also produces the *Web Content Accessibility Guidelines* to help owners of websites design sites more accessible to people with a disability, which will be of interest to an elderly client practice considering the design and accessibility of its website.

3.7.6 Quality of service

However much trouble you take to develop your reputation and to cultivate the right image, it will be wasted if your firm does not have the knowledge and expertise to do the work and the staff and facilities to do it efficiently, as has been reiterated previously.

3.7.7 Providing information

Clients need information as well as advice. It can be time-consuming to provide this information so consider the following:

- Keep a supply of leaflets on relevant topics for handing to clients (HM Revenue and Customs leaflets, Department for Work and Pensions leaflets, Office of the Public Guardian booklets, Age UK leaflets and the Law Society leaflets, etc.).
- Create your own in-house information packs and make them available to your clients.
- Print and distribute your own elderly client newsletter.
- Create and print your own booklets on particular topics and make them available to your clients (including an introduction to the services you offer). Members of Solicitors for the Elderly have free access to material to help provide information, ranging from factsheets, leaflets and DVD recordings as part of their subscription. This can be adapted to the firm's requirements.
- Buy in inexpensive booklets and leaflets and provide them to your clients.

3.7.8 Packages of services

A fixed fee regime could be implemented for wills, LPAs and related matters such as advance decisions, severance of joint tenancy, financial planning.

Simple packages may be appropriate in providing your services to older clients:

- Offer an LPA when you make a will, but advise as to the dangers as well as the potential advantages (see **4.6**).
- Discuss an advance decision to refuse medical treatment when making a will, but be tactful as many people have no wish to address this issue (see **11.8**).
- Provide a stockbroker's valuation with recommendations when completing annual tax returns or repayment claims.

You may wish to market special packages in conjunction with other professionals for older clients, such as:

- an annual 'wealth check' (e.g. an investment review, tax planning assessment, and state benefit survey);
- a 'plan ahead' programme (e.g. consideration of appropriate options for housing and care based upon the client's wealth and needs);

- a 're-housing' package (e.g. support and legal services on finding and moving to a more suitable home);
- a 'balance the family' package (e.g. advice and preparation of wills and LPAs for cohabitees or second marriages);
- a 'family support' programme (e.g. support for children looking after parents);
- a 'care' package (e.g. legal assistance in respect of a move into a care home and disposal of the home);
- a 'financial management' package (e.g. legal services in respect of the registration of an LPA or application for deputyship followed by first year support for the attorney or deputy).

3.8 SUPPORT GROUPS

3.8.1 Solicitors for the Elderly

Solicitors for the Elderly is a national organisation that provides appropriate training and assistance to solicitors wishing to specialise in elderly client practice. Applicants must have some detailed knowledge in the field to be a full member but those who do not have sufficient experience but are working towards it can become associate members. Solicitors for the Elderly was set up specifically to enable solicitors, barristers and legal executives to exchange ideas, information on practice development and legal issues affecting older people as well as being part of an organisation that charities and voluntary bodies would feel confident referring clients to. It organises an annual conference but also provides specialist training at local level. It provides a monthly newsletter, resource and marketing information on its website, an email forum and discounts on some books and journals. It is organised by way of local county branches (see **www.sfe.legal**).

3.8.2 Law Society's Private Client Section

The Law Society's Private Client Section is dedicated to the interests of the solicitors' profession, and offers a number of benefits, including:

- practice development (news and data on the competition and client needs; research on market trends);
- opportunities for contact, communication, and information sharing with other members;
- media and PR campaigns to focus attention on the value of using a solicitor;
- discounts on conferences and publications;
- regular newsletters providing succinct authoritative legal updates;
- free regional seminars;
- specialist software buyers' guides;

- a website (**http://communities.lawsociety.org.uk/private-client**) for updates and sharing information;
- a guide to marketing to your existing clients.

All enquiries to: Section Co-ordinator, Private Client Section, The Law Society, 113 Chancery Lane, London WC2A 1PL, DX 56 London/Chancery Lane.

3.8.3 Society of Trust and Estate Practitioners

The Society of Trust and Estate Practitioners (STEP) is a worldwide organisation that deals with trust issues including the taxation and law relating to trusts. It has a large membership of lawyers and accountants throughout the world. Contact STEP, Artillery House (South), 11–19 Artillery Row, London SW1P 1RT; tel. 020 7340 0500.

CHAPTER 4

Managing the financial affairs of the elderly

Martin Terrell

4.1 INTRODUCTION

We all hope to go on managing our own affairs for as long as possible and no elderly person should be prevented from so doing where possible. If the elderly client's needs increase, so will the extent to which someone else needs to intervene to manage a part, or the whole, of the client's estate. The manner in which this is done then depends on a wide range of factors according to the nature of the client's estate and whether the client has planned for these eventualities. Not every client will lose capacity at a specific time and date – this may be part of a gradual process. Often the client can be supported with practical help and reassurance from family, friends and professional advisers. A relative may help with bank statements and setting up direct debits; a stockbroker or financial adviser may keep an eye on the investments and meet once or twice a year to check on valuations, income and expenditure levels; an accountant can deal with the annual tax return. There are many ways of providing advice and support which are available to clients of all abilities and these may often work very effectively.

Where a more formal level of involvement is needed, some assets can be dealt with individually with minimal formality. In other cases, a person is able to give an authority to deal with the full extent of his or her assets and if this is inadequate or no such authority is in place, the involvement of the Court of Protection may be required. However, an application to the Court of Protection is likely to involve a degree of effort and expense as well as intrusiveness, and should only be justified if there is no other alternative.

4.2 STATE BENEFITS

State benefits may be paid directly to another person when the claimant is unable to claim personally, without requiring an attorney or deputy to be in place (see the Social Security (Claims and Payments) Regulations 1987, SI 1987/1968).

4.2.1 Appointee

If the claimant is 'unable for the time being to act' and a deputy has not been appointed, an adjudication officer can appoint someone (known as an appointee) to claim any state benefits on his behalf (SI 1987/1968, reg.33). The appointee can collect and spend the money for the benefit of the claimant but the appointee's powers do not extend beyond receiving and dealing with the benefit in question.

Application is in writing (using form BF56) to the Department for Work and Pensions (DWP) which must be satisfied as to the claimant's inability to manage his affairs and the suitability of the appointee. A close relative who lives with or someone else who cares for the claimant is usually the most suitable person to be the appointee. The manager of a care home can also act as an appointee. The appointee is under a duty to disclose relevant information to the DWP when claiming benefits (and may be personally liable in the event of non-disclosure) and if the appointee is not acting properly or in the best interests of the claimant, the appointment may be revoked. Where a deputy has been appointed then benefits cannot be paid to an appointee (see also **4.8.1**).

4.2.2 Other powers

An adjudication officer may also direct that benefits be paid to another person acting on behalf of the claimant if this appears necessary for protecting the interests of the claimant or a dependant (SI 1987/1968, reg.34).

The costs of housing, accommodation and fuel and water services may be deducted from certain benefits and paid direct to third parties on behalf of the claimant in accordance with detailed procedures (SI 1987/1968, reg.35 and Sched.9).

4.3 OTHER ASSETS

4.3.1 Bank or building society accounts

An elderly client may have legal capacity but require assistance with the management of day-to-day finances. There are a number of ways in which practical help can be given to an elderly individual using conventional banking arrangements:

- A third party mandate can be completed allowing another person to manage the account. This arrangement may be convenient in cases of physical disability.
- Online banking may be used to allow access to a person's account.
- The account can for convenience be held in the joint names of the individual and another person on the basis that either may sign. Such authority may be revoked if either account holder loses mental capacity. It needs to be understood that in the absence of any contrary direction, the account will pass to the survivor on the death of either account holder. Depending on the intentions of

the parties, it may need to be recorded that this is not intended to be a joint account that passes to the survivor on death but that the money belongs to the elderly individual.

- The account can be in the name of another as express nominee for the elderly individual.
- The account can simply be in the name of another although it belongs to the elderly individual.

These arrangements can cause their own problems. They work where the account holder is able to understand what the third party is doing, and the account holder's affairs are relatively straightforward. If the account holder lacks capacity, any mandate is ineffective and there is a danger of the third party exceeding his or her authority. Problems often occur where authority is given to access accounts while the account holder has capacity and this is still being acted on after the account holder has lost capacity.

A joint account should also be severed where one account holder loses capacity, and this can give rise to problems if one account holder dies or there is uncertainty as to the beneficial ownership of any money in the account. Nominee or trust arrangements can also cause problems. There may be confusion over whom the money belongs to, especially if the named account holder becomes incapable, is made bankrupt or dies.

4.3.2 Income tax

Tax returns must be signed by the taxpayer in person under Taxes Management Act 1970, s.8. However, HMRC will permit a return to be signed by a deputy appointed by the Court of Protection (or the equivalent for Scotland and Northern Ireland) or an attorney under a registered enduring power of attorney (EPA) or lasting power of attorney (LPA).

HMRC will also disclose information to a tax adviser (the taxpayer must complete form 64-8), who may be authorised directly by the taxpayer to submit a return online. HMRC will also allow a taxpayer to register a friend or family member to manage the taxpayer's tax online who can be designated a 'trusted helper'.

4.3.3 Trusts

Where it is desired to make provision for a person who lacks or may lack capacity, problems may be avoided by appointing trustees and transferring property to them on suitably worded trusts. This is often done where a parent wishes to provide for an adult child with mental disabilities. A trust may also be appropriate where a person receives an award for a personal injury and this is excluded from assessment to means-tested benefits (Income Support (General) Regulations 1987, SI 1987/1967, reg.51(1)(a) and Sched.10, para.12; the Care and Support (Charging and Assessment of Resources) Regulations 2014, SI 2014/2672 (applicable in England); and until April 2016, National Assistance (Assessment of Resources) Regulations 1992, SI 1992/2977 (as amended) (applicable in Wales), after which new regulations will be passed).

Where a trust is in existence, the trustees may hold and manage the trust property with power to apply it for the benefit of the beneficiary. For example, care home fees can be paid directly to the home for the beneficiary's benefit without involving the beneficiary.

Informal trusts

Money may be held in the name of another person who acknowledges (formally or informally) the true ownership. In some family situations a trust is not even created, but money or assets are simply given to children or other relatives in the expectation that it will be made available in case of need. This arrangement is, however, only suitable for relatively small sums that can be dealt with on an informal basis. Tax and other complications can arise especially if the understanding goes wrong. Without clear evidence of the separate status of the trust, there is no simple way of protecting the fund if ownership is called into question on the death, bankruptcy, mental incapacity or divorce of the asset holder.

4.3.4 Hospitals and care homes

A hospital or care home does not provide for all of a person's personal needs and some spending money in the hands of the patient or resident may be desirable. If relatives are dealing with the person's financial affairs they may hand over regular sums in cash when they visit, but if these visits are not regular or it is not possible to deal with cash then other arrangements need to be made.

Snack trolley expenditure

Where a person is a long-term patient in a hospital then a hospital welfare officer may be able to assist with holding cash in a hospital account. Care homes will generally have a procedure for holding residents' funds, usually for small amounts, which can be drawn down on for personal expenditure.

4.4 POWERS OF ATTORNEY

A power of attorney is a document whereby a person (the donor) gives another person (an attorney) power to act on his behalf in his name in regard to his property and financial affairs. Note that the power:

- must be executed as a deed (see the Law of Property (Miscellaneous Provisions) Act 1989 as to execution);

- may be in general terms or limited to specific acts or circumstances, for instance a general power under the Powers of Attorney Act 1971;
- can only be granted by a competent adult person;
- subject to any express limitation in the power, subsists until revoked by an act of the donor, the death of the donor or the attorney, or the bankruptcy of the attorney.

A power of attorney is also revoked by operation of law on the donor becoming mentally incapable of managing his or her property and affairs. Enduring powers of attorney and lasting powers of attorney are an exception to this principle (see **4.4.3**, **4.5** and **4.6**).

This chapter is limited to the property and affairs of persons who lack capacity. A health and welfare LPA is similar in form to a property and financial affairs power but deals solely with decisions relating to personal welfare. However, such a power can only be exercised where the donor lacks capacity; as it relates to the donor's welfare the financial status of the attorney is not relevant and therefore it is not revoked in the event of the attorney's bankruptcy. Health and welfare LPAs are dealt with in more detail at **11.3**.

4.4.1 Evidence of power

A photocopy which bears a certificate signed by a solicitor at the end of each page that it is a true and complete copy of the original must be accepted as proof of the contents of the original. A certified copy must be accepted if satisfying these requirements (this also applies to EPAs and LPAs) (Powers of Attorney Act 1971, s.3). An office copy of an LPA or EPA is evidence of the contents and that it has been registered with the Public Guardian (MCA 2005, Sched.1, para.16 and Sched.4, para.15(3)).

4.4.2 Nature of a power of attorney

Any power of attorney by which one person (the donor) grants authority to another (the attorney) creates a fiduciary relationship between the two parties. Thus an attorney is expected to manage the donor's property and affairs in accordance with the authority given to him under the power and his other legal powers and responsibilities. A body of common law principles applies to the relationship between donor and attorney regardless of the mental capacity of the donor. Note that an attorney:

- has a fiduciary duty towards the donor and must use such skill as he or she possesses and show such care as the attorney would in conducting his or her own affairs;
- must avoid any conflict of interest which may benefit the attorney at the expense of the donor;

- cannot seek any profit or commission, although the attorney is entitled to reimbursement of out-of-pocket expenses and an attorney acting in a professional role may be remunerated;
- if being paid, must exercise the care, skill and diligence of a reasonable person, and if acting in the course of a profession must exercise proper professional competence;
- may not appoint a substitute or otherwise delegate the attorney's general authority, but may employ persons to do specific tasks;
- has no power over the donor so cannot dictate where he or she shall live (although the attorney may have considerable influence over such matters);
- must retain any money or other assets of the donor in the name of the donor, so that there is a clear separation between the donor's property and the attorney's property.

4.4.3 Nature of power where donor lacks capacity

An ordinary power of attorney is revoked on the donor becoming incapable of managing his or her property and affairs. The donor no longer has capacity to understand what the attorney is doing on behalf of the donor and cannot therefore be assumed by any third party to have approved of such acts. A power of attorney can only continue to operate in these circumstances if it is in a form permitted by statute, namely:

- an enduring power of attorney (EPA) created prior to 1 October 2007 in accordance with the Enduring Powers of Attorney Act 1985 and registered by the Public Guardian;
- a lasting power of attorney (LPA) created after 1 October 2007 in accordance with MCA 2005 and registered by the Public Guardian.

An attorney acting under an EPA or LPA is still bound by the same fiduciary relationship as exists under a power of attorney (see in particular the helpful summary of these duties at paras.7.58–7.68 of the MCA 2005 Code of Practice). However, MCA 2005 imposes an additional level of responsibility where the donor lacks capacity. In that situation, the attorney is also making decisions on behalf of the donor and must make those decisions in the donor's best interests (therefore having regard to the principles set out in MCA 2005, ss.1 and 4 and its Code of Practice). For instance, an attorney must take account of a record of the donor's wishes even if it is not legally binding. As capacity is function specific, a donor may still have capacity to make decisions even though the attorney is acting under a registered power of attorney. An attorney may, when acting for the same donor, need to distinguish between situations where the donor is making his or her own decisions or is otherwise capable of making decisions, and situations where the attorney is making decisions which the donor lacks capacity to make for him- or herself.

The following considerations apply to any attorney acting under MCA 2005:

- An attorney has authority to make limited gifts on behalf of the donor; an attorney acting under an EPA also has authority to maintain a person the donor might be expected to provide for.
- The Public Guardian is responsible for maintaining a register of registered instruments which is open to inspection.
- Where the attorney disclaims the power he must notify the Public Guardian.
- An LPA in favour of a spouse or civil partner is revoked on a dissolution of the marriage or civil partnership to that person unless the instrument provides otherwise.
- Any competent adult may act as an attorney under an EPA or LPA, although a trust corporation can only act as attorney in relation to property and affairs under an LPA.
- The bankruptcy of an attorney terminates the appointment of that attorney where the power of an attorney is an EPA or a property and affairs LPA.
- A donor of an LPA who has capacity may at any time revoke the power but must notify the attorney and the Public Guardian.
- The Public Guardian must be notified on the death of the donor.
- The Court of Protection has authority to intervene where the donor lacks capacity or is alleged to lack capacity.

4.4.4 Enduring powers of attorney under the Mental Capacity Act 2005

MCA 2005 came into force on 1 October 2007, setting out a single statutory framework for decision-making on behalf of persons who lack capacity. The same statute covers decisions made by court-appointed deputies as well as by attorneys, in relation to both welfare and financial decisions. The Act introduced LPAs which operate within this framework, addressing a person's property and affairs as well as welfare decisions. As a result, the Enduring Powers of Attorney Act 1985 was repealed and no new EPA could be created (MCA 2005, s.66(2)). However, MCA 2005 provides for EPAs validly created before this date to remain effective. Schedule 4 to MCA 2005 governs the operation of EPAs so that EPAs operate within the same statutory framework of MCA 2005, although subject to the same principles which governed their creation under the Enduring Powers of Attorney Act 1985. They are therefore an anomaly, in that different principles and definitions apply to when and how an attorney may act under an EPA compared to an LPA; at the same time, an attorney acting under an EPA must also act in the donor's best interests and is bound by MCA 2005 in the same way as any other person who makes a decision under that Act. Attorneys acting under an EPA are not under an express duty to have regard to the MCA 2005 Code of Practice, but it can be used as guidance. Furthermore, an attorney who fails to act in the donor's best interests may be regarded as unsuitable.

4.4.5 Powers of attorney and solicitors

Often a solicitor is first contacted by a relative or an attorney, whether to make a power of attorney or for advice in connection with registering or using the power. In all such cases the solicitor must have a clear understanding of who the client is. Where the power is being created, the solicitor is acting for the donor so must see the donor personally and alone so that independent advice may be given and where appropriate, a certificate of understanding may be completed (see **4.6.3**). Where the attorney is involved (and it is often good practice to involve the attorney), information can be given with the consent of the client. There may also be matters that the donor wishes to address in private, such as whether the will should be disclosed or whether there are any family problems that might arise.

When a solicitor receives instructions from an attorney, the attorney will usually be the client in respect of the registration process or any application to the Court of Protection; in other respects, the donor remains the client and the attorney will simply provide instructions on behalf of the donor. However, the solicitor still owes a duty to the donor. Where the donor retains capacity, then the donor's instructions can be confirmed and must be acted upon. Regardless of the donor's capacity, if there is a dispute or conflict of interest between the attorney and the client, it may be necessary for the parties to be separately represented.

Issues of conflict of interest are considered below in connection with deputies acting in a fiduciary role (see **4.8.2**), for example in cases where applications are made to the Court of Protection by a deputy (or attorney) and the Official Solicitor is appointed to act as litigation friend for the person who lacks capacity. See also **2.3.2**.

These issues are comprehensively addressed in the Law Society Practice Note: Lasting Powers of Attorney (8 December 2011).

4.5 ENDURING POWERS OF ATTORNEY

4.5.1 Relevant legislation

- Powers of Attorney Act 1971.
- Enduring Powers of Attorney Act 1985.
- Mental Capacity Act 2005, Sched.4.
- Enduring Powers of Attorney (Prescribed Form) Regulations 1990, SI 1990/ 1376.
- Enduring Powers of Attorney (Welsh Language Prescribed Form) Regulations 2000, SI 2000/289.
- Lasting Powers of Attorney, Enduring Powers of Attorney and Public Guardian Regulations 2007, SI 2007/1253 (as amended).

4.5.2 Formal requirements

For an EPA to be valid, it must have been executed in the manner and form prescribed. Most EPAs in existence used the form prescribed by the 1990 Regulations. A Welsh language version of the same form was introduced by the 2000 Regulations. Forms prescribed by the previous 1986 (SI 1986/126) and 1987 (SI 1987/1612) Regulations could only be used for EPAs executed prior to June 1988 and July 1991 respectively.

For a power of attorney to take effect as a valid EPA, it must be executed by the donor as well as by the attorney(s). Execution is required from the attorney to signify acceptance and to acknowledge the duty to register in certain circumstances. Therefore, an EPA must have been executed by the donor and all the attorneys before 1 October 2007 if it is to remain valid under Sched.4 to MCA 2005. Where attorneys have been appointed jointly and severally and an attorney has failed to execute his part of the form, the EPA will remain valid in favour of the other attorneys.

4.5.3 Validity

Completion of a valid EPA presupposes that the donor had sufficient capacity to grant the power. Although the Enduring Powers of Attorney Act 1985 did not define the degree of capacity required to grant a power, the distinction between creation of the EPA and the criteria for its use helped clarify an important legal principle, since embodied in MCA 2005. Capacity is specific to the function for which it is required. Therefore, the creation of the power by a person is a function separate from the managing and administering of the same person's property and affairs. Thus the same person may have been capable of creating an EPA while being mentally incapable of managing and administering his property and affairs. The degree of understanding specific to an EPA was considered by Hoffmann J in *Re K, Re F* [1988] 1 All ER 358 where an EPA had been made very shortly before being registered (on the grounds that the donor was mentally incapable). The judge upheld the validity of the EPA so long as the donor understood (at 363):

key >

> first, if such be the terms of the power, that the attorney will be able to assume complete authority over the donor's affairs; second, if such be the terms of the power, that the attorney will in general be able to do anything with the donor's property which the donor could have done; third, that the authority will continue if the donor should be or become mentally incapable; fourth, that if he should be or become mentally incapable, the power will be irrevocable without confirmation by the court.

An EPA which has been properly executed is presumed to be valid. In *Re W* [2001] Ch 609, it was held that the burden of proof when challenging the validity of an EPA rested on the objectors. Unless the objectors could satisfy the court that the instrument was invalid, the court had to register the EPA.

The moaners have to prove it is invalid

4.5.4 Restrictions

An EPA may be general in its terms or for specific purposes only, and the donor may have placed restrictions or conditions on the power. For example, a donor may have limited the scope of the EPA to certain property or have excluded certain property from its scope. It was also common for a donor to restrict the power to operate when he became mentally incapable (so that the power did not operate as a general power immediately). This could, however, lead to difficulties if the donor remains mentally capable but is physically incapable and needs the attorney to operate the power (a similar restriction is contained as an option in the 2015 property and affairs LPA prescribed form (see **4.6.3**)).

There are also statutory restrictions (MCA 2005, Sched.4, para.3) on what an attorney under an EPA can do, so that the attorney cannot:

- benefit himself or persons other than the donor except to the extent that the donor might have been expected to provide for his or their needs;
- make gifts (except for presents of reasonable value at Christmas, birthdays, weddings and such like to persons related to or connected with the donor or charitable gifts which the donor might have been expected to make).

The donor can, if he wishes, further restrict these powers.

4.5.5 Registration

In the event that the donor is or is becoming mentally incapable, the EPA must be registered with the Public Guardian. If it is not so registered, the power is voided by the supervening incapacity of the donor. Registration also provides some safeguards against misuse, as the donor and certain relatives must be given notice and can object to registration. The registration process is then suspended and the objectors have an opportunity of bringing their concerns to the attention of the Court of Protection. Note that:

- An attorney is under a duty to apply to the Public Guardian for registration of the EPA as soon as practicable once the attorney has reason to believe that the donor is or is becoming mentally incapable (MCA 2005, Sched.4, para.4).
- 'Mentally incapable' means in relation to any person that he is 'incapable by reason of mental disorder of managing and administering his property and affairs'.
- The definition of 'mental disorder' is provided by MHA 1983, s.1(2) as 'any disorder or disability of the mind'.
- Once an application for registration has been made, then until the EPA is registered, the attorney has limited but potentially very useful powers to maintain the donor and prevent loss to the donor's estate (MCA 2005, Sched.4, para.1(2)).

Notices

Notice must first be given to the donor and to the donor's closest relatives in the prescribed form (EP1PG), which states that the attorney proposes to apply for registration of the EPA and that the recipient may object to this within five weeks of receiving the notice on any of the grounds specified. Notice must be handed to the donor personally but other relatives may be served by first class post.

Notice need not, in any event, be given to anyone who has not attained 18 years, is mentally incapable or cannot be traced. Application can be made to dispense with giving notice to any other person for special reasons, although such an application must be made separately to the Court of Protection (MCA 2005, Sched.4, para.7(2)). The court is generally unwilling to remove the donor's statutory safeguards. Application must be made in form COP1 and must be supported by medical evidence to show that it would be undesirable or impracticable for the attorney to give notice or some other clear evidence to show that no useful purpose is served by the giving of notice.

Subject to these exceptions, the relatives who must be notified must be taken in order of priority from the statutory list, class by class:

(a) the donor's husband or wife;

(b) the donor's children (no distinction is made between legitimate or illegitimate children);

(c) the donor's parents;

(d) the donor's brothers and sisters, whether of the whole or half blood;

(e) the widow or widower of a child of the donor;

(f) the donor's grandchildren;

(g) the children of the donor's brothers and sisters of the whole blood;

(h) the children of the donor's brothers and sisters of the half blood;

(i) the donor's uncles and aunts of the whole blood; and

(j) the children of the donor's uncles and aunts of the whole blood.

At least three relatives must be served but if anyone from a class has to be served then all members of that class must be served, even if more three persons are notified. For example, if the donor has two children and six grandchildren, then all eight relatives must be notified. If the attorney is a relative, then the attorney counts as one of the persons who must be notified and if there are fewer than three relatives, then only those relatives need to be notified. If there are no persons who are capable of being notified, then the Public Guardian cannot register the EPA without undertaking 'such inquiries as he thinks appropriate in all the circumstances' (MCA 2005, Sched.4, para.13(7)).

Application for registration

The attorney or attorneys applying for registration must send the application in form EP2PG together with the original EPA and registration fee of £110 to the Public

Guardian once all the relevant notices have been served. If no objections are received within five weeks of the last notice being served, the Public Guardian must register the power. The original EPA is returned to the attorney or the attorney's solicitor, duly marked. The Public Guardian also retains a copy and maintains a record of registered EPAs.

Objections

Although the Public Guardian has responsibility for registration, he only has limited authority to refuse a properly made application on the grounds that:

- a deputy has been appointed and the deputy's powers conflict with those of the attorney if the EPA were registered (MCA 2005, Sched.4, para.13(2)); or
- an objection has been made by a person entitled to receive the EP1PG notice within the five-week period (MCA 2005, Sched.4, para.13(4)). In such a case the EPA can only be registered on the direction of the court.

A person to whom notice is given may object to registration on one or more of the grounds contained in MCA 2005, Sched.4, para.13(9):

(a)   the power was not validly created;
(b)   the power no longer subsists;
(c)   the application is premature because the donor is not yet becoming mentally incapable;
(d)   fraud or undue pressure was used to induce the donor to create the power;
(e)   having regard to all the circumstances and in particular the attorney's relation-ship to or connection with the donor he is unsuitable to be the donor's attorney.

An objection to registration must be made to the court in form COP8 and the Public Guardian must also be notified in form EP3PG. The former ensures the matter is determined by the court, and the latter ensures the registration process is suspended, pending the court's decision. There is therefore a procedural threshold for the objector to cross if he wishes to make an objection. A simple letter expressing a general concern is not enough; the objector must instigate a formal court process with evidence and take the risks that go with it. A person who does not receive notice of registration or a person who subsequently wishes to object to the validity or operation of the EPA must make an application in form COP1.

Implications of registration

Once an EPA is registered the attorney(s) have authority to act within the scope of the power, and the EPA cannot be revoked by the donor without the confirmation of the court. The court has jurisdiction to supervise, restrict, revoke or supplement the powers of the attorney contained within the EPA, and in the event that the EPA is revoked, direct that a deputy be appointed. The attorney may also apply to the court for a substantial gift to be made (MCA 2005, Sched.4, para.16(2)(e)) and has

Don't have to die intestate if you lack capacity and have never made a will

standing to apply to the court to exercise any other powers available to it under MCA 2005, s.18, such as the making of a statutory will.

The register is open to the public. An application to inspect is made on form OPG100. There is no fee charged for this service.

4.6 LASTING POWERS OF ATTORNEY

£82

4.6.1 Introduction

LPAs were introduced by MCA 2005 from 1 October 2007 and replaced EPAs as the method by which one person can appoint another to make decisions in advance of losing capacity. Although LPAs appear to fulfil a similar function and operate within the same legal and statutory framework (see **4.4**), there are some considerable differences. These can be summarised as follows:

- A separate LPA can be made to authorise the making of personal welfare decisions.
- An LPA is not effective or valid as a power of attorney until it is registered with the Public Guardian, so that registration can be effected at an early stage regardless of the donor's capacity.
- While the LPA is being registered, there are no temporary or limited powers that can be used by the attorney during the registration process.
- The instrument that creates an LPA contains a certificate of understanding to provide a contemporary record of the donor's capacity at the time the instrument is made.
- The donor (who has capacity) may apply for registration.
- Instead of relying on a prescribed class of relatives who must be notified, the donor may select persons (up to a maximum of five) who are notified on registration.
- On an application for registration by an attorney, the Public Guardian is responsible for notifying the donor and any other attorney (where there is more than one attorney and the attorneys are appointed jointly and severally).
- A property and affairs LPA can be used at any time once it has been registered, unless the donor has specified to the contrary.
- A health and welfare LPA can only be used to make decisions which the donor lacks capacity to make.

slight differences

4.6.2 Relevant legislation

- Powers of Attorney Act 1971.
- Mental Capacity Act 2005.
- Lasting Powers of Attorney, Enduring Powers of Attorney and Public Guardian Regulations 2007, SI 2007/1253 (the 2007 Regulations).

Must be registered

- Lasting Powers of Attorney, Enduring Powers of Attorney and Public Guardian (Amendment) Regulations 2009, SI 2009/1884 (the 2009 Regulations).
- Lasting Powers of Attorney, Enduring Powers of Attorney and Public Guardian (Amendment) Regulations 2013, SI 2013/506.
- Lasting Powers of Attorney, Enduring Powers of Attorney and Public Guardian (Amendment) Regulations 2015, SI 2015/899 (the 2015 Regulations).

4.6.3   Prescribed forms

For an LPA to be valid, it must be executed in the manner and form prescribed and then registered. Unless and until the instrument is registered by the Public Guardian, it has no validity as a power of attorney (MCA 2005, s.9(2)). The current prescribed forms came into force on 1 July 2015 (SI 2015/899). Forms made under the 2007 Regulations could be signed by the donor until 31 March 2011 and forms made under the 2009 Regulations could be signed by the donor until 31 December 2015. As long as the donor executes the form before the prescribed date, the LPA can be registered at any time.

There are separate forms for a lasting power of attorney for property and financial affairs (LP1F) and a lasting power of attorney for health and welfare (LP1H) on the sensible grounds that where two powers are given, they may involve different attorneys operating at different times in very different circumstances.

The prescribed forms are set out in a series of logical sequences that reflect the order in which they are made and registered (sections 1 to 15) as explained below.

Section 1 – the donor

The prescribed form provides space for the donor to write or print his or her name and address and date of birth. Thus the donor's details are shown on the very first page of the form, making it easier to use in practice (there is also space for details of the registration to be entered on the same page).

Sections 2 and 3 – the attorneys

These sections set out the details of the appointment of the attorney or attorneys and the scope of their authority. The donor must specify whether one or more attorneys are appointed and if more than one, whether they are to act jointly, jointly and severally or jointly in respect of some matters and jointly and severally in respect of others. MCA 2005, s.10(4) allows the donor to appoint more than one attorney provided that the attorneys are appointed to act 'jointly' or 'jointly and severally' or 'jointly in respect of some matters and jointly and severally in respect of others'. This may appear to be an unnecessary complication. However, a donor may wish to appoint attorneys to act jointly and severally in respect of his investments but require them to act jointly where a major decision was required, for instance to sell his home or in a welfare power, to withhold consent to life-sustaining treatment. If it

115

is unclear whether attorneys are appointed jointly or jointly and severally, the appointment is construed in favour of their being appointed jointly.

There is space for four attorneys in the prescribed form and space for four further attorneys on Continuation Sheet 1.

Section 4 – replacement attorneys

The appointment of a replacement attorney is often desirable. Attorneys cannot appoint their own successors in the same way that trustees can and an LPA may need to be used for many years after it has been made. Under MCA 2005, s.10(8)(b) the donor may appoint a person to replace the attorney (or one of the attorneys) on the occurrence of a specified event (disclaimer, death or bankruptcy, dissolution of a marriage, or incapacity) which has the effect of terminating the attorney's appointment (MCA 2005, s.13(6)).

Generally, replacement attorneys will act as soon as an original appointment fails, thus the donor may appoint A as his attorney and B as his replacement attorney. However, care needs to be taken when appointing replacement attorneys where there are more than two attorneys involved. For example:

- The donor appoints A and B to act jointly and severally and then C as a replacement attorney; C will be appointed to act automatically on the failure of either of the first appointments.
- The donor appoints A and B to act jointly and severally and then C and D as replacement attorneys; if the appointment of A fails, then C and D will step in automatically and act jointly and severally with B.
- The donor appoints A and B jointly and then C as a replacement attorney; if the appointment of A fails, then the appointment of B also fails and C is appointed (if in this scenario the donor wants B to go on acting, then the donor should make a second LPA which comes into play when the first LPA fails).
- The donor appoints A and then B and C as replacement attorneys; the donor needs to specify in Continuation Sheet 2 how B and C are to act; if the donor does not specify, they are presumed to act jointly.

A further problem with replacement attorneys is that if the instrument is registered in favour of the original attorneys, any notified persons have no knowledge of the identity of the replacement attorneys who may find themselves acting at a later date without the notified persons fulfilling their role of being able to object to the suitability of the new attorneys.

There is space for two replacement attorneys in the prescribed form and space for four further replacement attorneys on Continuation Sheet 1.

Section 5 – when the LPA comes into effect (property and affairs)

In most respects the two types of LPA are similar. However, section 5 is different for each form (see **11.3**). On a property and affairs LPA the donor is asked: 'When do you want your attorneys to make decisions?' and is then provided with a choice of two options, each with its own tick-box. The first allows the LPA to be used as soon as it has been registered, i.e. while the donor still has capacity; the second allows the LPA only to be used when the donor lacks capacity. This choice reflects the status of an EPA (see **4.5.4**), which must be registered when the donor lacks capacity (it was not uncommon to restrict EPAs so that they could not be used if the donor still had capacity). However, it is difficult to use in practice, as any third party dealing with the attorney will require proof of the donor's lack of capacity to make the decision which the attorney is purporting to take, and set out how that is to be established when incapacity is not a continuing state. Furthermore, an LPA is not only useful if the donor lacks capacity; it may also be useful if the donor is physically disabled and requires assistance from the attorney. This option also presupposes that the attorney cannot be trusted to intervene at the right time.

Section 6 – persons to be notified

This section contains space for the donor to select up to four persons who are to be notified of an application to register the power. The maximum number of persons who can be notified is five, so if five persons are to be notified, this part of the LPA has to be extended by using Continuation Sheet 2. The use of named persons to be notified on registration can be an important safeguard for the donor, and such persons should be chosen carefully. The named person cannot be an attorney or replacement attorney.

In forms made under the 2007 Regulations or 2009 Regulations the donor may dispense with notice being given, in which case, the donor must obtain two certificates of understanding. However, the 2015 forms allow the donor to dispense with naming any persons to be notified without any additional safeguard. It may therefore be assumed that a requirement to give notice of registration does not provide any greater level of protection for the donor. Nevertheless, it remains important for a donor to ensure that relatives, close friends or professional advisers are at least aware of the existence of the LPA. This can be done just as easily with a short letter, without the need to go through a notification process.

Section 7

There is space for preferences and instructions, which distinguish between guidance for the attorney (which the attorney must take into account when acting in the donor's best interests) and formal instructions, which are binding on the attorney. Specific instructions which are often used in practice may provide for:

- a charging clause for professional attorneys;
- power to delegate investment management to a discretionary fund manager;

- a requirement to keep accounts or submit accounts to audit by an accountant or a solicitor;
- a requirement to take advice when making specific decisions.

Preferences may include an expression of general wishes, for example as to where the donor wishes to live. A donor may wish to live in a particular area or particular style of care home or to avoid a care home for as long as possible. They set out expectations that the attorneys will consult with or take account of the views of others, for example where the donor appoints only one or two of his or her children as attorneys and does not appoint other children.

Generally, such additional clauses should be drafted carefully. Prescriptive instructions sit uneasily with the principle that donors should be able to trust their attorneys and respect their judgment as to when and how they should act. They can be awkward to draft and can cause their own problems for the attorneys. The Public Guardian frequently delays registration and refers LPAs to the Court of Protection so that clauses are severed. Where possible, the concerns of the donor should be addressed as guidance which does not complicate the drafting or challenge the validity of the LPA but which the attorneys are obliged to take into account when making decisions in the donor's best interests. This can be contained in the LPA itself or in a separate letter of wishes.

Section 8 – prescribed information

The prescribed information is headed 'Your legal rights and responsibilities' and set out at section 8, so before the LPA is executed by the donor, and must be read prior to execution. However, this section must also be read by the certificate provider and each attorney. It contains the following essential information:

Everyone signing the LPA must read this information
In sections 9 to 11, you, the certificate provider, all your attorneys and your replacement attorneys must sign this lasting power of attorney to form a legal agreement between you (a deed).
By signing this lasting power of attorney, you (the donor) are appointing people (attorneys) to make decisions for you.
LPAs are governed by the Mental Capacity Act 2005 (MCA), regulations made under it and the MCA Code of Practice. Attorneys must have regard to these documents. The Code of Practice is available from www.gov.uk/opg/mca-code or from The Stationery Office.
Your attorneys must follow the principles of the Mental Capacity Act:
1. Your attorneys must assume that you can make your own decisions unless it is established that you cannot do so.
2. Your attorneys must help you to make as many of your own decisions as you can. They must take all practical steps to help you to make a decision. They can only treat you as unable to make a decision if they have not succeeded in helping you make a decision through those steps.
3. Your attorneys must not treat you as unable to make a decision simply because you make an unwise decision.

Be enablers

4.   Your attorneys must act and make decisions in your best interests when you are unable to make a decision.

5.   Before your attorneys make a decision or act for you, they must consider whether they can make the decision or act in a way that is less restrictive of your rights and freedom but still achieves the purpose.

Your attorneys must always act in your best interests. This is explained in the Application guide, part A8, and defined in the MCA Code of Practice.

Before this LPA can be used:

- it must be registered by the Office of the Public Guardian (OPG)
- it may be limited to when you don't have mental capacity, according to your choice in section 5

Cancelling your LPA: You can cancel this LPA at any time, as long as you have mental capacity to do so. It doesn't matter if the LPA has been registered or not. For more information, see the Guide, part D.

Your will and your LPA: Your attorneys cannot use this LPA to change your will. This LPA will expire when you die. Your attorneys must then send the registered LPA, any certified copies and a copy of your death certificate to the Office of the Public Guardian.

Section 9 – execution by donor

This section contains a brief summary of what the donor has read and understood and sets out the act of appointment of the attorneys. The wording is then followed by space for the donor to sign and date the form and for the witness to sign beneath the donor's signature and set out his or her name and address.

Section 10 – certificate of understanding

Before the LPA can be completed, there is a further safeguard to protect the interests of the donor, providing a contemporary record of the donor's understanding at the time the LPA is made. MCA 2005 requires a certificate by a person of a prescribed description, given at the time of execution or as soon as reasonably practicable thereafter, that in his or her opinion (Sched.1, para.2(1)(e)):

(e)   ... at the time when the donor executes the instrument –

(i)   the donor understands the purpose of the instrument and the scope of the authority conferred under it,

(ii)   no fraud or undue pressure is being used to induce the donor to create a lasting power of attorney, and

(iii)   there is nothing else which would prevent a lasting power of attorney from being created ...

The certificate provider must be chosen by the donor from one of two categories of persons (SI 2007/1253, reg.8). Regulation 8(1)(a) defines a certificate provider as someone who has known the donor personally for at least two years; reg.8(1)(b) defines a certificate provider as a person who 'on account of his professional skills and expertise, reasonably considers that he is competent to make the judgments necessary' to certify the matters described above.

Regulation 8(2) provides examples of persons who can act as certificate provider in a professional capacity:

(a)   a registered health care professional;
(b)   a barrister, solicitor or advocate called or admitted in any part of the United Kingdom;
(c)   a registered social worker; or
(d)   an independent mental capacity advocate.

LPAs made under the 2007 Regulations and 2009 Regulations included spaces for the certificate provider to show the capacity in which he or she has known the donor (when acting in a personal capacity) or his or her particular skill or expertise (when acting in a professional capacity). The current forms provide no room for any such details; it is therefore important for a solicitor preparing an LPA to keep a record of the certificate provider's details and any professional qualifications in case the certificate provider needs to provide evidence of the donor's capacity or freedom from undue pressure.

Certain persons cannot act as a certificate provider, namely:

- a family member of the donor;
- an attorney of the power;
- an attorney of any other LPA or EPA which has been executed by the donor (whether or not it has been revoked);
- a family member of an attorney of the power;
- a director or employee of a trust corporation acting as an attorney of the power;
- a business partner or employee of the donor, or an attorney of the power (so that where the attorney is a partner in a firm of solicitors, no other partner or employee of the firm can give a certificate of capacity);
- an owner, director, manager or employee of any care home in which the donor is living when the instrument is executed or a family member of such a person.

The responsibilities of the certificate provider are considered in more detail in the context of the donor's capacity to create a valid LPA at **1.5.6**. See also Law Society Practice Note: Lasting Powers of Attorney (8 December 2011), para.7.1.

Section 11 – attorney's certificate

As with an EPA, there is a separate page for completion by each attorney. This must be dealt with carefully and should not be signed as a formality. The attorney's certificate provides the attorney with a useful reminder of his obligations under the power and MCA 2005 and the Code of Practice as well as a point of reference if the attorney fails to meet those obligations. The attorney is required to declare as follows:

- I am aged 18 or over

- I have read this lasting power of attorney (LPA) including section 8 'Your legal rights and responsibilities', or I have had it read to me
- I have a duty to act based on the principles of the Mental Capacity Act 2005 and to have regard to the Mental Capacity Act Code of Practice
- I must make decisions and act in the best interests of the donor
- I must take into account any instructions or preferences set out in this LPA
- I can make decisions and act only when this LPA has been registered and at the time indicated in section 5 of this LPA

Further statement by a replacement attorney:

> I understand that I have the authority to act under this LPA only after an original attorney's appointment is terminated. I must notify the Public Guardian if this happens.

There is no reference to the attorney's limited authority to make gifts or to the requirement to keep accounts and financial records and produce these to the Public Guardian or Court of Protection (although, curiously, these points are addressed in the equivalent page for completion by an attorney which is a trust corporation). It is therefore all the more important for professional advisers to ensure that donors and attorneys are aware of what attorneys can or cannot do and that they may be called to account for their actions.

Sections 12 to 15

The application to register the LPA is contained in these sections of the form itself, which reflects a policy to encourage early registration. The advantages and disadvantages of early registration and the registration process are dealt with at **4.6.5**.

4.6.4 Continuation pages

Great care needs to be taken when drafting LPAs. Although they appear to be user friendly, the forms contain several pitfalls for the unwary. It is perhaps simple enough if the donor appoints one or two attorneys without any instructions or replacement attorneys. If any more attorneys are appointed, or additional information included, there are several different supplementary pages that need to be added to the end of the form. However, these need to be cross-referenced to the parts of the form which they supplement and must be signed and dated by the donor at the same time as execution. A separate continuation sheet should be used for each section which it relates to. For example, if the donor requires space for both preferences and instructions (at section 7) then a separate sheet must be added for each of them. The 2015 Regulations provide for the following continuation pages:

- Continuation sheet 1 – Additional people – to be used in conjunction with sections 2, 4 or 6.
- Continuation sheet 2 – Additional information – further information for sections 3, 4 or 7 of the LPA form.

- Continuation sheet 3 – If the donor cannot sign or make a mark – to be used if the donor cannot sign or make a mark (someone else can sign on behalf of the donor and two people must witness the donor's signature).
- Continuation sheet 4 – Trust corporation appointed as an attorney.

4.6.5 Registration

Advantages and disadvantages of early registration

Because an LPA is ineffective unless it is registered, MCA 2005 has the effect of encouraging early registration. The aim of the legislation is to allow a property and affairs LPA to be used both as an ordinary power while the donor has capacity and as a lasting power when the donor lacks capacity. The instrument is neutral on the subject of capacity and does not therefore discriminate against a donor who has limited or fluctuating capacity.

The donor may also be uncomfortable leaving an unregistered instrument in safe custody, for it to be registered only when it is needed. There is then a danger that it will be needed quickly, for instance where the donor has gone into hospital and decisions need to be taken quickly to sell a property and find a care home. There is then a risk that the LPA will not be available when it is needed and unlike with an EPA (see **4.5.5**) the attorney has no authority to act under the power while it is being registered. If there are no problems with the form and no objections, registration will take several weeks. If the form contains a provision which the Public Guardian considers is ineffective, would prevent the power from operating or if there are objections, the application must be referred to the Court of Protection before registration can take place, causing yet further delay in bringing the donor's affairs under proper control.

There is also a risk that if registration is delayed for a lengthy period, the persons who are to be notified on an application for registration may have lost contact, died or become incapable so rendering them ineffective as a practical safeguard.

Although early registration is advisable in most cases, it also has a number of disadvantages:

- Donors may be deterred from making LPAs because of the additional cost and complexity of the registration process (see below).
- Donors may not want to confer authority on attorneys at an early stage before it is acted on (although suitable restrictions can be included to cover this).
- Circumstances may change before the power needs to be used so that a new LPA needs to be prepared.
- Once the LPA is registered, if it is to be replaced then the donor needs to contact the Public Guardian with evidence of revocation.

Application for registration

The registration process is a straightforward one and designed to give formal recognition to the power as well as provide a measure of protection to the donor. Unlike the EPA registration process, an application to register an LPA can be made by the donor as well as by the attorney. The applicant must complete sections 12–15 of the LPA form and then submit the complete document to the Public Guardian, enclosing a cheque for £110. The same fee is payable in respect of each LPA even if two applications for registration are made at the same time.

Where the LPA has been made in accordance with the 2007 Regulations or the 2009 Regulations prior to 1 July 2015, the completed instrument must be submitted with an application in form LP2.

The person making the application must give notice in form LP3 to any persons named by the donor in the LPA for that purpose (see **4.6.3**) (the application form does not specify when the notices were served; the applicant merely states that he or she has notified the persons named in the form). No other notices need to be served and it is the Public Guardian who must give notice in form LPA003B to the donor if, as will usually be the case, the application is made by the attorney. The Public Guardian is also responsible for giving notice in form LPA003A to the attorney where the application is made by the donor or to an attorney where another attorney makes the application.

Unless the Public Guardian receives a valid notice of objection within four weeks of the date of the notice given by the Public Guardian or there is a defect in the instrument preventing registration the Public Guardian must register the instrument as an LPA (MCA 2005, Sched.1, para.5). Once registered, the original instrument is stamped and returned to the applicant. The Public Guardian also gives notice in form LPA004 to the donor and attorney that the LPA has been registered.

Objections to registration and cancellation by Public Guardian

Although the Public Guardian is responsible for registration, he has a limited right or ability to assess the validity of the power. His power is only to refuse registration on certain technical or factual grounds unless directed otherwise by the court. He can also cancel the registration directly if satisfied that one of the specified grounds exists, whether due to a defect in the power or on receipt of a valid notice of objection which has been made to the court. An objection on a substantive ground that might involve a determination of fact must be dealt with by the court.

Refusal of Public Guardian to register

The Public Guardian is obliged to refuse registration if:

- it appears to the Public Guardian that the instrument is not made in accordance with MCA 2005, Sched.1 (e.g. where the incorrect form was used or there was a technical defect in the form which prevented it from operating as a valid LPA).

Reasons

This provision has been relied on by the Public Guardian to refuse registration where boxes or fields in the 2007 prescribed form were omitted;

- the court has already appointed a deputy and it appears to the Public Guardian that the powers conferred on the deputy would conflict with the powers conferred on the attorney in which case the power cannot be registered unless directed by the court;

- it appears to the Public Guardian that there is a provision in the instrument which would be ineffective as part of an LPA or which would prevent the power from operating as an LPA, in which case the power must be referred to the court for determination. If the instrument contains a restriction or condition or other provision which would prevent the power from operating, then the court has power to sever the offending provision;

- the Public Guardian receives a notice of objection from the attorney or named person on one of the specified grounds (see below) and it appears to the Public Guardian that the ground for making the objection is satisfied, in which case the Public Guardian must not register the power unless directed by the court;

- the court receives a notice of objection from the attorney or named person on one of the prescribed grounds (and notice is given to the Public Guardian), in which case the Public Guardian must not register the power unless directed by the court.

Objections to Public Guardian on factual grounds

An objection to registration on one of the factual grounds can only be made to the Public Guardian by a donor using form LPA006 or by an attorney or named person using form LPA007. The objector must file his notice before the end of the period of only three weeks beginning with the date on which the notice is given. The 'factual' grounds on which a person can 'object' in this way are specified by MCA 2005, s.13(3) and (6):

(3)
- in so far as the LPA relates to the property and affairs of the donor, the bankruptcy of the donor or the attorney or where the attorney is a trust corporation, its winding up or dissolution;

(6)
- the LPA has been disclaimed by the attorney;
- the death of the attorney;
- the dissolution or annulment of a marriage or civil partnership between the donor and the attorney (unless the power excludes revocation in these circumstances);
- the attorney lacks capacity.

On receipt of an objection on the factual grounds, the Public Guardian will simply stop the registration process. It is then for the person applying for registration to accept the situation or apply to the court to consider the matter and direct the Public Guardian to register the power.

Cancellation of registration by Public Guardian

The Public Guardian may also at any time cancel the registration of the power in the following circumstances:

- he is satisfied that one of the above grounds specified in MCA 2005, s.13(3) and (6) has been established;
- he is satisfied that the power has been revoked by the death of the donor;
- he receives a notice that the donor has revoked the LPA and is satisfied that the donor has taken such steps as are necessary in law to revoke the power; or
- the court directs the Public Guardian to cancel the registration if it revokes the power on one of the 'prescribed grounds', determines the power has been revoked by the donor or otherwise come to an end or it determines that a requirement for creating the power was not met.

Revocation by Court of Protection

Where an attorney or a named person receives a notice of registration and objects on one of the 'prescribed grounds' the Public Guardian cannot register the LPA until directed to do so by the Court of Protection. An objection on one of these grounds must be made by way of application to the court in form COP7 and notice must also be given to the Public Guardian in form LPA008. The person making the objection must make an application to the court before the end of the period of only three weeks beginning with the date on which the notice is given.

If an objection to registration on these grounds is made by any other person or any person (including a donor, attorney or named person) wishes to apply for revocation of the LPA after it has been registered, then a formal application needs to be made to the court in form COP1.

The court may direct that a power is not to be registered or if the donor lacks capacity, revoke the power on the following grounds if it is satisfied that:

- the power has been revoked (by the donor) or otherwise come to an end;
- one of the requirements for the creation of a LPA has not been met;
- fraud or undue pressure was used to induce or create the LPA; or
- the attorney has behaved, is behaving, or proposes to behave in a way that contravenes his authority or is not in the donor's best interests.

4.6.6 After registration

Powers of the Court of Protection

The court has wide powers to intervene in the operation of the LPA. MCA 2005, s.23 provides the court with the following powers:

(1) The court may determine any question as to the meaning or effect of a lasting power of attorney or an instrument purporting to create one.

(2)   The court may –

    (a)   give directions with respect to decisions –

        (i)   which the donee of a lasting power of attorney has authority to make, and

        (ii)   which P lacks capacity to make;

    (b)   give any consent or authorisation to act which the donee would have to obtain from P if P had capacity to give it.

(3)   The court may, if P lacks capacity to do so –

    (a)   give directions to the donee with respect to the rendering by him of reports or accounts and the production of records kept by him for that purpose;

    (b)   require the donee to supply information or produce documents or things in his possession as donee;

    (c)   give directions with respect to the remuneration or expenses of the donee;

    (d)   relieve the donee wholly or partly from any liability which he has or may have incurred on account of a breach of his duties as donee.

(4)   The court may authorise the making of gifts which are not within section 12(2) (permitted gifts).

Powers of Public Guardian after registration

The Public Guardian has no formal or continuing role in connection with attorneys of LPAs in the same way as deputies (see **4.8.9**). His only statutory duty is to maintain a register of LPAs. However, the Public Guardian is also obliged, under MCA 2005, s.58(1)(h), to deal with representations (including complaints) about the way in which an attorney is exercising his powers. The Public Guardian therefore has investigatory powers and if such investigations disclose a concern about the operation of the power, he must apply to the Court of Protection for the power to be revoked. Under the 2007 Regulations (reg.46) the Public Guardian may where it appears to him that the attorney has contravened or might contravene his authority, not act in the donor's best interests or fail to comply with an order or direction, require the attorney to:

- provide specified information or information of a specified description;
- produce specified documents or documents of a specified description;
- direct a Court of Protection Visitor to visit the donor.

4.6.7   Solicitors and LPAs

Greater understanding and practice, with revisions to the forms at the end of 2009 and again in 2015 have at least made the forms manageable, even if they remain far from perfect. There are only two ways of responding to these problems: give up in despair or tackle them head on and do what needs to be done to make them work. It is vital to remember that LPAs are not simple and straightforward documents that can be sold on the back of a set of wills. They raise countless issues, creating a legal relationship that may last for several years and during a period during which the donor's voice will not be audible. A donor needs to be aware of the risks involved as well as the obvious benefits of the LPA to ensure that an informed decision can be made. Considerations that need to be addressed may include:

- whether there are issues of capacity and whether further evidence or advice needs to be obtained;
- whether there is a potential conflict of interest between husband and wife or civil partners purporting to act together;
- who should be the attorney and in what circumstances they should act;
- whether there should be replacement attorneys;
- whether the donor clearly understands what the attorney can or cannot do;
- what restrictions and conditions will protect the client and the attorney;
- whether there are any family or background issues that need to be considered, especially family conflicts;
- whether there are any other relatives who need to be aware of what is being done or who should receive information from the attorneys;
- who the named persons should be and whether the solicitor should offer this as a service;
- who will complete the certificate of capacity, and whether the solicitor can give this;
- whether the LPA should be registered immediately or whether registration can be left for a future date;
- where the original LPA should be stored;
- whether certified copies should be provided and on what basis these might be disclosed in the future;
- ensuring that the attorneys have enough information to know what they can and cannot do, when they can act and whom to contact if they need advice.

4.7 THE COURT OF PROTECTION

4.7.1 Introduction

The Court of Protection is a distinct court – a superior court of record created by MCA 2005 – but which exercises its statutory powers through designated judges within the mainstream judicial framework. The judges of the Court of Protection are the judges of the High Court (one of whom is President and another Vice President) and a number of circuit judges and district judges nominated by the President. Currently all judges of the Chancery and Family Divisions of the High Court have been nominated, together with around 100 circuit judges and district judges. At the time of writing five district judges together with the Senior Judge, Denzil Lush (who is a circuit judge), are permanently based at the court's central registry at First Avenue House in London. The other judges sit at their own courts in England and Wales. Only the permanent judges at First Avenue House deal solely with Court of

Protection proceedings; other judges combine this with other mainstream practice in civil and family law.

The aim of the jurisdiction is to allow cases to be dealt with at an appropriate level and in a location that best serves the interests of the parties. In practice, serious welfare cases are dealt with by High Court judges and most other cases are dealt with by district judges, with appeals referred upwards to the circuit judges or directly to the High Court, depending on the seriousness and urgency of the case. However, all applications are dealt with through the central registry at PO Box 70185, First Avenue House, 42–49 High Holborn, London WC1A 9JA (DX 160013 Kingsway 7), but where a hearing it to take place, the case may be referred to a regional court. Approximately half of all hearings are held outside London.

4.7.2 Relevant legislation

- Mental Capacity Act 2005.
- Lasting Powers of Attorney, Enduring Powers of Attorney and Public Guardian Regulations 2007, SI 2007/1253 (as amended).
- Court of Protection Rules 2007, SI 2007/1744 (COPR) (as amended by Court of Protection (Amendment) Rules 2015, SI 2015/548).
- Court of Protection Fees Order 2007, SI 2007/1745 (as amended by Court of Protection Fees (Amendment) Order 2009, SI 2009/513).

4.7.3 The jurisdiction

MCA 2005 came into force on 1 October 2007 and provides a comprehensive jurisdiction for the Court of Protection to make single decisions or declarations or appoint a deputy for people who lack mental capacity to make decisions relating to their property and financial affairs and/or their personal welfare. The court's administration is managed by Her Majesty's Courts and Tribunals Service.

4.7.4 Powers of the Court of Protection

The court may only make decisions on behalf of a person who lacks capacity or in relation to such a person. However, a person may be the subject of proceedings where his capacity is in dispute, or to determine that he does in fact have capacity or indeed has recovered capacity. The legislation therefore refers somewhat brusquely to the person who lacks capacity or who is alleged to lack capacity as 'P'.

The Court of Protection can exercise its jurisdiction in a number of ways, depending on the requirements of the case and the best interests of P. Under MCA 2005, ss.15 and 16, the court may:

- make a declaration as to a person's capacity to make a decision (therefore confirming that the person concerned can make a valid decision or that he lacks capacity and a decision can be made on behalf of that person);

- make a declaration that a particular act done in relation to a person who lacks capacity is lawful;
- make a decision on behalf of a person who lacks capacity; or
- appoint a deputy to make decisions on behalf of a person who lacks capacity to make those decisions.

Thus the Court of Protection can declare that a doctor may lawfully carry out an operation or withdraw life-sustaining treatment from a person who lacks capacity. Where a person's property and affairs are concerned, the court can confirm that a person has capacity to make a will or a substantial lifetime gift. In these cases, the court prefers to allow (where possible) a person to make his own decision. This sensitive and flexible approach is required by several important principles enshrined in MCA 2005:

- The court can only make decisions on behalf of P where P lacks capacity (s.16(1)).
- 'Before the act is done, or the decision is made, regard must be had to whether the purpose for which it is needed can be as effectively achieved in a way that is less restrictive of the person's rights and freedom of action' (s.1(6)).
- When the court is considering the exercise of its powers to appoint a deputy, the court must have regard (in addition to the matters mentioned in s.4) to the principles that '(a) a decision by the court is to be preferred to the appointment of a deputy to make a decision, and (b) the powers conferred on a deputy should be as limited in scope and duration as is reasonably practicable in the circumstances' (s.16(4)).

The court must therefore allow a person to make his own decisions where possible and formal intervention should be as brief and limited as possible. However, where a person lacks capacity to make a decision that needs to be made, then the court can make that decision on the person's behalf or delegate that power to another person, known as a deputy. The court's principal powers in respect of P's property and affairs are contained in MCA 2005, s.18, which extend in particular to:

(a) the control and management of P's property;
(b) the sale, exchange, charging, gift or other disposition of P's property;
(c) the acquisition of property in P's name or on P's behalf;
(d) the carrying on, on P's behalf, of any profession, trade or business;
(e) the taking of a decision which will have the effect of dissolving a partnership of which P is a member;
(f) the carrying out of any contract entered into by P;
(g) the discharge of P's debts and of any of P's obligations, whether legally enforceable or not;
(h) the settlement of any of P's property, whether for P's benefit or for the benefit of others;
(i) the execution for P of a will;
(j) the exercise of any power (including a power to consent) vested in P whether beneficially or as trustee or otherwise;
(k) the conduct of legal proceedings in P's name or on P's behalf.

There are further administrative powers relating to property and affairs contained in MCA 2005, Sched.2:

- vesting orders in respect of any settlement made by P or power exercised on behalf of P to appoint trustees or retire as a trustee (para.5);
- varying a settlement made by virtue of s.18 (para.6);
- vesting stock in a curator appointed outside England and Wales (para.7);
- preserving an interest in P's property to take effect as the same interest under a will or intestacy (para.8);
- appointing a properly qualified person to exercise P's powers as patron of a benefice (para.10).

While the court is in principle expected to exercise limited powers on a case-by-case basis, in practice it has to be able to delegate powers to a deputy, especially where ongoing financial decisions need to be taken. Therefore, all the powers set out in s.18 can be delegated to a deputy apart from the following powers which are expressly reserved to the court (s.20(3)):

(a) the settlement of any of P's property, whether for P's benefit or for the benefit of others;
(b) the execution for P of a will; or
(c) the exercise of any power (including a power to consent) vested in P whether beneficially or as a trustee or otherwise.

The role of a deputy and the criteria for selecting a deputy are dealt with at **4.8.3–4.8.4**.

4.7.5 The Public Guardian

The Public Guardian, whose role is derived from MCA 2005, is principally responsible for registering EPAs and LPAs and dealing with the supervision of deputies appointed by the Court of Protection. This reflects the principle enshrined in the legislation that there is a clear separation of powers and functions between the Court of Protection (comprised of judges) and the Public Guardian (comprised of civil servants). The problem in practice (where deputies are concerned) is that only the court has power to make decisions on behalf of P and access to the court is limited by its procedures. The Public Guardian can inspect accounts and query or even investigate the work of a deputy, but he cannot advise a deputy as to what he can or cannot do and he cannot take direct action to remove or control a deputy, as these powers can only be exercised by the court.

The role of the Public Guardian in the supervision of deputies is considered in more detail at **4.8.9**.

The Public Guardian's functions are administered by the Office of the Public Guardian (OPG) and carried out at offices in London, Birmingham and Nottingham. There is a central address at PO Box 16185, Birmingham B2 2WH (DX 744240 Birmingham 79).

4.7.6 Official Solicitor

The Official Solicitor is part of the judicial system of England and Wales, appointed by the Lord Chancellor and administered as part of the Ministry of Justice. The principal function of the Official Solicitor and his staff is to ensure, by intervention in proceedings or otherwise, that the legal rights and duties of persons under a disability are recognised and enforced (Senior Courts Act 1981, s.90). In Court of Protection proceedings, the Official Solicitor is usually directed to act as litigation friend for P, in the same way as a litigation friend may represent a person under disability in civil proceedings. In practice, in a case where the interests of P are affected, such as an application for a statutory will or lifetime gift, P will be joined as a party and the Official Solicitor will be appointed to act as litigation friend. The role of the Official Solicitor is to give priority to the interests of P in the proceedings. The Official Solicitor serves a vital function in terms of protecting P's interests but is often very helpful to the other parties to proceedings, for example by establishing any common ground between the parties and putting forward a consensus for consideration by the court, thereby avoiding the expense and delay of an attended hearing.

The Official Solicitor can be contacted at Victory House, 30–34 Kingsway, London, WC2B 6EX (and see **Appendix A**).

4.7.7 Court of Protection Visitors

MCA 2005, s.61 gives the Lord Chancellor power to appoint Visitors who can, on the direction of the court or the Public Guardian, visit a person who lacks capacity or is alleged to lack capacity and prepare a report. The court's powers to direct a report are contained in MCA 2005, s.49. Section 58(1)(d) defines one of the functions of the Public Guardian as directing a Visitor to visit a deputy or a donor or an attorney of an LPA. SI 2007/1253, reg.48 has extended this function to EPA attorneys. Visitors may be either General Visitors or Special Visitors, the latter having a medical qualification and being experienced in assessing capacity. Most persons under the jurisdiction of the court will be seen at least once by one of the General Visitors who report to the Public Guardian. These are reports carried out as part of a person's routine supervision. In more difficult cases, usually where there is a dispute about a person's capacity or best interests, a report is specially commissioned by the court or Public Guardian.

4.8 THE DEPUTY

4.8.1 When is it necessary to appoint a deputy?

The appointment of a deputy presupposes that P lacks capacity to make a decision for himself in relation to the matter because of an impairment of, or a disturbance in the functioning of, the mind or brain and there is no other way of dealing with P's assets which cannot be dealt with by:

- an appointee responsible for receiving state benefits (see **4.2**);
- an attorney acting under a registered EPA (see **4.5**);
- an attorney acting under a registered LPA (see **4.6**).

Where there is no power of attorney available and day-to-day decisions need to be taken to manage or supervise the property and affairs of a person who lacks capacity, the Court of Protection will delegate authority to a deputy. This may sit uneasily with the principles of MCA 2005 outlined above (see **4.7.4**), as a long-term appointment of a deputy should be seen as a last resort. If, however, there are assets that need to be administered, it is simply impractical to assume that a person who cannot manage his property and affairs should rely on one-off decisions being made by an application to the Court of Protection.

A person may lack capacity to manage all his property and affairs but may also have capacity to make certain decisions. The threshold of capacity to manage property and affairs is dealt with at **1.5.7**. The difficulties faced by a deputy in this type of situation are dealt with at **4.8.3**.

4.8.2   Status of a financial deputy

A deputy appointed under MCA 2005 has a difficult and unusual task to perform, combining a number of different roles in different situations, depending on the nature of the assets that need to be dealt with and the capacity of their owner. Despite the aims of MCA 2005 that a deputy's authority should be as limited as possible in scope and duration, most deputies receive an order that appears unlimited. The order will in most cases extend to the whole of the person's estate and be without limit. Where P is completely incapable of managing his property and affairs, for instance where there is a case of advanced dementia, this does not present any difficulties for the deputy. It is, however, more complicated where P has a degree of capacity, or capacity which fluctuates perhaps due to a psychiatric illness or a brain injury. The order will have no validity in respect of any decisions that P has capacity to make. In an ideal scenario, P makes his own decisions where he can, perhaps running his own bank account and paying for his day-to-day needs. The deputy deals with investments and purchases, keeping an eye on budgets and care costs and making sure the tax returns are completed. However, not all situations are so straightforward and it is possible for a deputy to find himself in conflict with P or making a decision which is possibly invalid.

A deputy needs to be aware of the following considerations:

- A deputy is the statutory agent of P – but only in relation to anything done within the scope of his authority (MCA 2005, s.19(6)).
- A deputy is not liable for the proper debts and expenses of P, and legal fees and expenses incurred by the deputy are payable by P's estate.

- Property in the name of P does not vest in the deputy but remains in P's legal ownership and the deputy acts 'as deputy for' P and not on his own account.
- A deputy is a fiduciary and has a duty of care to P, similar to the relationship between an attorney and the donor of an EPA or LPA (see **4.4.2–4.4.3**).
- The client is P who gives instructions through the deputy and where there is a conflict of interest which might prejudice the interests of P, the parties should be separately represented.
- A third party dealing with the agent is entitled to act on the authority of the deputy unless he or she has notice that P has capacity in relation to the matter.
- Where the deputy deals with a matter that P has or may have capacity to deal with, then the deputy should obtain P's consent to any action he takes.
- A deputy must act in P's best interests and, even where P lacks full capacity to make a decision, must nevertheless attempt to ascertain P's likely wishes.

A deputy still has a great deal of discretion as to how he carries out his duties. Not only will the deputy be responsible for the management of P's assets and ensuring those assets are utilised for P's benefit, the deputy must also act in P's best interests, having regard to P's wishes – whether ascertainable, previously recorded or the factors that P would have considered if he had capacity. The authority conferred on a deputy will also extend to maintaining a person whom P might be expected to provide for as well as to the making of small gifts. A deputy may have to contend with conflicting demands, balancing the wishes of P, the extent of P's assets and the demands and interests of family members. It is often a difficult task, made all the more difficult because the only person or body the deputy can turn to if he has any doubt over what he can or cannot do is the Court of Protection. Each time the court needs to be approached, a formal application needs to be made, with the payment of a fee, the submission of evidence and inevitably, a degree of expense. However, if the deputy is in doubt as to whether or not a particular decision is lawful or might be open to challenge, an application to the court should be made.

4.8.3 Duties of the deputy

A prospective deputy should consider carefully whether or not to take on the role. It should not be considered a right or a privilege. To ensure that a prospective deputy understands the nature and extent of his duties, the Deputy's Declaration (form COP4) which accompanies an application for the appointment of a deputy (see **4.8.5**) sets out 17 personal undertakings which the prospective deputy is required to give. These emphasise the core fiduciary duties of the deputy as well as the deputy's wider duties under MCA 2005:

1. I will have regard to the Mental Capacity Act 2005 Code of Practice and I will apply the principles of the Act when making a decision. In particular I will act in the best interests of the person to whom the application relates and I will only make those decisions that the person cannot make themselves.

2.   I will act within the scope of the powers conferred on me by the court as set out in the order of appointment and will apply to the court if I feel additional powers are needed.

3.   I will act with due care, skill and diligence, as I would do in making my own decisions and conducting my own affairs. Where I undertake my duties as a deputy in the course of my professional work (if relevant), I will abide by professional rules and standards.

4.   I will make decisions on behalf of the person to whom the application relates as required under the court order appointing me. I will not delegate any of my powers as a deputy unless this is expressly permitted in the court order appointing me.

5.   I will ensure that my personal interests do not conflict with my duties as a deputy, and I will not use my position for any personal benefit.

6.   I will act with honesty and integrity, and will take any decisions made by the person to whom the application relates while they still had capacity, into account when determining their best interests.

7.   I will keep the person's financial and personal information confidential (unless there is a good reason that requires me to disclose it).

8.   I will comply with any directions of the court or reasonable requests made by the Public Guardian, including requests for reports to be submitted.

9.   I will visit the person to whom the application relates as regularly as is appropriate and take an interest in their welfare.

10.   I will work with the person to whom the application relates and any carer(s) to achieve the best quality of life for him or her within the funds available.

11.   I will co-operate with any representative of the court or the Public Guardian who might wish to meet me or the person to whom the application relates to check that the deputyship arrangements are working.

12.   I will immediately inform the court and the Public Guardian if I have any reason to believe that the person to whom the application relates no longer lacks capacity and may be able to manage his or her own affairs.

13.   I understand that I may be required to provide security for my actions as deputy. If I am required to purchase insurance, such as a guarantee bond, I undertake to pay premiums promptly from the funds of the person to whom the application relates.

14.   I will keep accounts of dealings and transactions taken on behalf of the person to whom the application relates.

15.   I will keep the money and property of the person to whom the application relates separate from my own.

16.   I will ensure so far as is reasonable that the person to whom the application relates receives all benefits and other income to which they are entitled, that their bills are paid and that a tax return for them is completed annually.

17.   I will take reasonable steps to maintain the property of the person to whom the application relates (if applicable), for example arranging for insurance, repairs or improvements. If necessary I will arrange and oversee a sale or letting of property with appropriate legal advice.

The practical responsibilities a deputy may face when managing a person's property and affairs are further considered at **4.12**.

4.8.4   Choice of deputy

Any person can make an application for the appointment of himself, another or a trust corporation as a deputy. However, no person can be appointed as a deputy unless he is over the age of 18 and has consented to his appointment. A trust corporation can only act as a financial deputy.

No one individual has the right to assume the role of a deputy. Who should be appointed as deputy for P is ultimately a matter for the Court of Protection, which must make the appointment in P's best interests. Often a close relative (usually the spouse or an adult child) makes an application and is therefore proposed as deputy, but if the spouse is of advanced age it may be preferable to appoint a younger member of the family, such as one of P's adult children. If no relatives are willing or able to act, a friend or neighbour, a solicitor or other professional adviser, or an officer of the local social services authority may be appointed. The court is, however, generally reluctant to appoint as deputy anyone who:

- is resident outside England and Wales – although this is not automatically a bar to appointment;
- is an accounting party (e.g. the trustee of a trust in which P has an interest); or
- has interests that conflict with those of P, unless the court is satisfied that P's interests will not be prejudiced.

These are, however, only grounds for caution rather than obstacles. Most family members will have an inherent conflict of interest where they are beneficiaries under P's will. The question is whether the conflict might lead to P's best interests being compromised.

As for residence, the Court of Protection is more willing to appoint deputies in other countries as families are more widespread and modern communication methods make distance less of an obstacle. Each case needs to be dealt with on its own merits, but the onus rests with the applicant to address any unusual circumstances and demonstrate that these will not prejudice the safe management of P's property and affairs. If the estate is substantial or there is property in England and Wales, then the court will prefer to have at least one deputy who is resident in the jurisdiction.

Joint and successive appointments

Occasionally, applications are made for the appointment of joint deputies, especially where there are two or more opposing factions within P's family. Although such appointments are possible (see MCA 2005, s.19(4)), they have historically been discouraged by the court as they are often proposed in contentious applications. Where there is a history of family conflict, each decision will become a bone of contention, and the joint appointment can therefore give rise to unnecessary delays and additional costs. However, the appointment of joint deputies is becoming more common in non-contentious cases, especially in view of the effort and expense involved in changing deputies if this is a likely possibility. Where an elderly spouse is appointed deputy, it is sensible for an adult child or a professional deputy to be appointed as well so that the deputyship can continue uninterrupted if the spouse becomes unable to act as deputy or dies. In such a case deputies can be appointed jointly and severally. Joint deputies are also appointed where there is a large estate and the appointment of a relative with a solicitor provides both P and the relative with a further degree of protection.

Although MCA 2005, s.19(5) allows the court to appoint one deputy to succeed another, this is extremely rare in practice. The court prefers to appoint a person whose suitability to act can be assessed at the time of the appointment. However, in *Re H, F and M* [2015] EWCOP 52, the court agreed to appoint successor deputies to make welfare decisions. P was a disabled young adult whose parents acted as her deputies. They did not require joint deputies to act with them, but would have peace of mind if they had certainty that close family members would act as deputies if they died or became unable to act as deputies.

4.8.5 Procedure on first application

The application forms can be obtained free of charge from the Customer Service Unit of the Court of Protection or the government website at **www.gov.uk/become-deputy**.

An application for the appointment of a deputy is commenced in the same way as any other first application, which must be made in accordance with COPR Part 9. The procedure described below for the appointment of a deputy is therefore the same for any first application to the court.

Any person can make an application if he has reason to believe that P lacks capacity and it is in his best interests that a deputy is appointed. Where the application is for the appointment of a welfare deputy then permission to apply must be obtained. An application for permission can be made as part of form COP1.

On a first application, the following documents must be lodged with the Court of Protection:

- application form (COP1) in duplicate;
- a supporting information form, COP1A (form COP1B is the equivalent form in welfare applications). This is a detailed questionnaire which is designed for all types of estate and no distinction is made between the small estate where a simple order is required and a large and complex estate involving investments, trusts, properties and business interests. The applicant should attach any further information that is relevant, such as copies of a will or power of attorney and details of properties, investments, business assets or trusts and estates in which P has an interest;
- assessment of capacity form (the medical certificate) (COP3) which must be provided by a registered medical practitioner, psychologist, psychiatrist or experienced social worker who has examined and assessed P in connection with the matter to which the application relates. It is crucial that the court has clear medical evidence addressing P's lack of capacity before it will accept jurisdiction;

- the Deputy's Declaration (COP4), which provides the consent of the proposed deputy to act as well as a list of undertakings and obligations that he is prepared to accept (see **4.8.3**);
- cheque for £400 in respect of the application fee.

Proceedings are not formally started until the court issues the application form and official time limits are by reference to the date of issue of the application. Once the court has examined the papers, it will issue the application form and return an endorsed copy to the applicant.

4.8.6 The application form and the parties to the application

The application form which starts the judicial procedure is form COP1. This sets out the essential details of the application and has two principal functions. First, it serves to clarify what it is that the court is being asked to do for P and why the application is in P's best interests; second, it defines the status or role of the parties or persons connected with the application. Most applications to appoint a deputy are not contentious so there are no defendants or respondents to the application. The only person involved formally in the proceedings is the applicant. P and close relatives are simply persons who are notified. They are aware of the application being made and the onus is on them to take positive steps to apply to be joined as a party if they oppose the application or propose a different order. The persons notified on an application to appoint a deputy are dealt with at **4.8.7**.

A person notified who, for instance, opposes the application to appoint a deputy must file an acknowledgement of service form (COP5) in which he or she applies to be joined as a party to the proceedings. This must be filed with evidence within 14 days of service or notification (COPR rule 72(2)). This imposes a tight deadline on anyone who wishes to challenge an application. If there is insufficient time to file evidence or the deadline is missed, the person concerned must apply for an extension of time to serve his evidence. A person who wishes to respond out of time or who has not been notified or served must apply separately, using form COP9. No fee is payable.

4.8.7 Application procedure and notices

Notification to P

Where P is concerned, the general principle is that P must be notified in person that an application form has been issued. It is irrelevant whether or not P has capacity to understand the information being given to him. P must be notified 'as soon as practicable and in any event within 14 days of the date on which … the application … was issued' (COPR rule 46). P may be notified by the applicant, his agent or 'such person as the court may direct'. The person effecting notification of P must do so in person and provide P in a way that is appropriate to his circumstances with an explanation as to:

- who the applicant is;
- the fact that the application raises the question of whether P lacks capacity in relation to a matter or matters, and what that means;
- what will happen if the court makes the order or direction that has been applied for; and
- where the application contains a proposal for the appointment of a person to make decisions on P's behalf in relation to the matter to which the application relates, details of who that person is.

Although the Rules refer to P being given an explanation of the application, P must also be provided with a prescribed notification form (COP14). Form COP14 is not very helpful as it is largely left blank for the applicant to complete. The form provides spaces for P's name and address, the case number and date of issue, the name of the applicant and then a large blank space headed 'this notice is to tell you that ...'. The guidance notes (form COP14A) describe the form as one 'which explains the matter for which notification is being provided'. COP14 should simply serve as a record of the information that must be given to P.

The difficulty for the applicant is that in most cases P will lack any meaningful insight into the procedure or P will have limited insight, in which case it will prove awkward for both P and the person notifying. Nevertheless, it is considered an essential safeguard of P's rights and dignity that this information is given. Those involved in the process cannot assume that P will lack some insight into the decision or while lacking capacity to make the decision in issue cannot also make other decisions.

P must also be provided with a form for acknowledging notification (form COP5).

The person giving notice to P must then, within seven days of giving notice, file a certificate of notification (COP20A) with the court. This must include a description of the steps taken to 'enable P to understand, and the extent to which P appears to have understood, the information' (COPR rule 48(2)). The form goes on to ask the person giving notice to describe (at section 3.8) 'what if anything the person to whom the application relates said or did in response to that notification'. If notification cannot be provided, this needs to be explained in section 4, and the form should be returned to the court with an application notice (form COP9) requesting that notification of P is dispensed with (COPR rule 49).

Notification of other named persons

As well as notifying P, the applicant must also notify the persons named in form COP1. This must be done as soon as practicable – and no more than 14 days after an application has been issued. In deciding whom to notify, the applicant must refer to

Practice Direction 9B – *Notification of Other Persons that an Application Form Has Been Issued* which states as follows:

4. The applicant must seek to identify at least three persons who are likely to have an interest in being notified that an application form has been issued ...

5. Members of P's close family are, by virtue of their relationship to P, likely to have an interest in being notified that an application has been made to the court concerning P. It should be presumed, for example that a spouse or civil partner, any other partner, parents and children, are likely to have an interest in the application.

6. This presumption may be displaced where the applicant is aware of circumstances which reasonably indicate that P's family should not be notified, but that others should be notified instead. For example, where the applicant knows that the relative in question has had little or no involvement in P's life and has shown no inclination to do so, he may reasonably conclude that that relative need not be notified. In some cases, P may be closer to persons who are not relatives and if so, it will be appropriate to notify them instead of family members.

Although Practice Direction 9B allows close friends to be notified in place of blood relatives, it also sets out a list of classes of relationship. At least three people should be notified in the following descending order:

(a) spouse or civil partner;
(b) person who is not a spouse or a civil partner but who has been living with P as if they were;
(c) parent or guardian;
(d) child;
(e) brother or sister;
(f) grandparent or grandchild;
(g) aunt or uncle;
(h) child of a person falling within subparagraph (e);
(i) step-parent; and
(j) half-brother or half-sister.

If a class of relatives needs to be used to reach a figure of three notified persons, then the entire class must be notified. If, however, it is not appropriate to notify a relative who has had little or no involvement in P's life, the applicant should show in form COP1A why that person was not notified.

In addition to the list of relatives, the following persons should also be notified where appropriate:

- where P is under 18, any person with parental responsibility for P within the meaning of the Children Act 1989;
- where there is a deputy or an attorney appointed under either an EPA or an LPA to make decisions on behalf of P in regard to a matter to which the application relates, the deputy or attorney; and
- any other person not already mentioned whom the applicant reasonably considers has an interest in being notified about matters relating to P's best interests.

The notified person must be provided with notice in form COP15. As with form COP14, this provides room for some very basic details and then requires the applicant to explain both the matter the court has been asked to decide and the order the court has been asked to make. However, unlike form COP14 which must be given in person, form COP15 can be delivered personally, delivered at a person's home or last known address or sent by first class post to that address. A notified person must also be provided with a form for acknowledgement (form COP5). This provides a period of 14 days in which the person notified can apply to the court to object to the application and be joined as a party. The procedure is clear but may appear overly formal or even hostile, when this is not the case. The way in which a person responds to a notice may well depend on the information contained in form COP15 and the manner in which it is presented. In a close family these matters might be discussed beforehand; even in a more formal situation the form should be accompanied by a letter explaining the need for the application and briefly what a deputy may or may not do and how he is supervised.

The applicant must within seven days of giving or sending the notice form, file a certificate of notification (COP20B) with the court in respect of each person notified.

4.8.8 Order appointing deputy

Unless the application and notification procedure give rise to any objections, and if at least 14 days have elapsed since the last notice was given, the court will proceed to issue the order appointing the deputy. This will also set out the scope of the deputy's authority to act, provide for payment of any costs and set the security that must be provided. On receipt of the order the deputy must comply with the requirement to provide security and in most cases the order will not be effective until security is in place.

The deputy must also arrange for P to be notified (for a second time), to confirm that a final order of the court has been made, provide an explanation of the effect of the order and provide P with a copy of the order (COPR rule 44(1)). This must be done within 14 days of the order being made, or (to allow time for the order to be drawn up by the court and sent out) 14 days of the order being served on the person effecting notice (COPR rule 46(3)). The person notifying P must also inform P that he or she may seek advice and assistance in relation to the matter of which P is notified. However, the court does not usually require confirmation that notification has been effected.

The order confirming the appointment of the deputy will generally be set in wide terms. As mentioned at **4.8.2**, a deputy has a great deal of discretion as to how he or she carries out the duties of a deputy. Although MCA 2005 only allows the court to make such decisions that P lacks capacity to make, the order itself does not generally specify what P can or cannot do. It is for the deputy to act in P's best interests in accordance with the terms of the order, MCA 2005 and the Code of Practice. Thus the order, typically, confirms the appointment of a named individual or individuals (or in property and affairs matters, a trust corporation) as deputy 'to make decisions on behalf of [P] that he is unable to make for himself in relation to his property and affairs subject to any conditions or restrictions set out in this order'. To remind the deputy that his authority is not just limited by the order, the order will also usually confirm that the deputy 'must apply the principles set out in MCA 2005, s.1 and have regard to the guidance in the Code of Practice to the Act'.

In defining the scope of a deputy's authority, the following provisions are typically used:

1. The court confers general authority on the deputy to take possession or control of the property and affairs of [P] and to exercise the same powers of management and investment as he has as beneficial owner, subject to the terms and conditions set out in this order.

2. The deputy may make provision for the needs of anyone who is related to or connected with [P], if he provided for or might be expected to provide for that person's needs, by doing whatever he did or might reasonably be expected to do to meet those needs.

3. The deputy may (without obtaining any further authority from the court) dispose of [P]'s money or property by way of gift to any charity to which he made or might have been expected to make gifts and on customary occasions to persons who are related to or connected with him, provided that the value of each such gift is not unreasonable having regard to all the circumstances and, in particular, the size of his estate.

4. For the purpose of giving effect to any decision the deputy may execute or sign any necessary deeds or documents.

The deputy's authority to take 'possession or control' extends to calling in and receiving any property or income that P owns or is entitled to. The authority to buy and sell property is contained within the power of management and is confirmed by the power to execute or sign deeds and documents.

Restrictions and conditions in order

Although in most cases the order appointing the deputy is generally very widely drawn, it will typically contain various 'tailored' restrictions that limit what the deputy can do in practice. Restrictions might be imposed if the deputy has been appointed to administer a large estate or damages award or there are concerns that the deputy may be unable to manage the award. Thus orders may contain one or more of the following limitations:

*   requiring the deputy to provide security (under MCA 2005, s.19(9) the court will require a deputy to provide security for a specified amount by entering in an insurance bond);
*   a 'sunset' clause, limiting the operation of the order to a particular period, so that it comes to an end on the expiry of a fixed period of time;

- a cap or limit on the amount the deputy can spend in any one year or withdraw from the Court Funds Office;
- excluding from the order the power to buy, sell or charge property (so that a new application would need to be made to deal with property transactions);
- excluding an investment portfolio from the scope of the deputy's authority (so that the deputy cannot release capital from an account without the express permission of the court);
- requiring a deputy to have accounts professionally audited;
- where P is in receipt of a compensation award that covers all care costs, preventing a deputy from applying for specified state financial support without further application to the court; or
- requiring the deputy to make a new application to deal with a further matter that cannot be dealt with immediately (for instance where a deputy is appointed to conduct proceedings and manage an interim award, a further application needs to be made to deal with the substantive award).

In practice most orders are not limited beyond the requirement to provide security and to act in accordance with MCA 2005 and the Code of Practice. Limitations often cause more inconvenience for the deputy than intended, for instance preventing the deputy from releasing funds to invest. Every time the deputy needs to go back to the court, a new application needs to be made with the effort, expense and delay that attends such a process. Where possible a deputy should be trusted to manage the estate and get on with the job. If the deputy acts dishonestly or carelessly, then that is a problem to be dealt with after the event, following investigation by the Public Guardian. Therefore, unless there is a problem, the Court of Protection should have no further involvement in the case. For the future, it is the role of the Public Guardian to supervise (see **4.8.9**) and monitor accounts and deal with any complaints about the role of the deputy.

4.8.9 Supervision of deputy

One of the principal functions of the Public Guardian is to supervise deputies appointed by the court (MCA 2005, s.58(1)(c)). The Public Guardian has a limited but very important role to ensure that deputies are carrying out their functions properly. He cannot make decisions for deputies or advise them as to what they can or cannot do. He can, however, receive complaints or concerns from concerned friends or relatives or statutory bodies about the conduct of a deputy. In the great majority of cases supervision is by way of a routine reporting exercise. Most deputies must submit an annual return showing that they have accounted for P's money and property and that they have acted in P's best interests. In general, reports are often inadequate in their detail and not closely monitored in practice. The financial details required are by way of a summary so that detailed accounts or bank statements do not need to be supplied. They do, however, provide a measure by which deputies are expected to act and any failure in their duty can be judged. Also, where a deputy fails to submit a report, he is likely to be investigated. Any conscientious deputy will therefore take his reporting duties seriously. A modest amount of supervision provides a greater degree of protection and public confidence than might first be expected.

The amount of formal supervision required in a particular case is set by the Public Guardian. When the Public Guardian first began assessing levels of supervision in 2008, four basic levels were set which would be allocated to each case according to various factors such as risk, complexity, complaints or abuse. Since early 2015, the OPG has implemented a revised supervision model, so supervision is determined by deputy type, namely lay, professional and public authority, managed by teams within the OPG, with each case being treated as unique, assessing risk and supporting as required rather than following set procedures governed by case type. The team take an end-to-end approach to supervising each case.

The OPG has also introduced deputy standards to support and supervise professional and public authority deputies. The standards set out what is expected of professional deputies and provide a checklist of actions and behaviours every deputy should follow. Deputies will be assessed against the standards through either face-to-face assurance visits, assurance reviews conducted by telephone or during a case review.

In addition to these changes, a new digital reporting system for deputies is in the final stages of development and will be introduced during the 2015–16 financial year.

4.9 OTHER APPLICATIONS

4.9.1 Contested or formal applications involving respondents

Procedure

Any application begins in the same way, using the same application form COP1 (see **4.8.5**) and requiring an application fee of £400. The procedure is, however, more complicated if there are other parties involved and evidence is to be relied upon to persuade the court to exercise its powers.

Defining the parties

Most applications for the appointment of a deputy are not contentious, and no one is prejudiced by the application or expected to take part in the proceedings. However, in a contentious application, for instance where a current deputy is being replaced, or in an application for a gift, will or settlement (see **4.10**) the applicant must treat anyone with a material interest in the application as a respondent. This will include not just someone who may receive less by virtue of the application being successful but also someone who may receive more. The applicant therefore has the responsibility of specifying the names of the respondents in form COP1 and as soon as the application has been issued, must serve the application on any respondent, together with the evidence relied on to support the application and a form for acknowledging service (form COP5) (COPR rule 66(1)).

A respondent is not, however, a party to proceedings unless and until he has filed an acknowledgement of service form. This must be filed with evidence within 14 days of service or notification (COPR rule 72(2)). As with notifying a person on an application to appoint a deputy (see **4.8.7**), this imposes a tight deadline on anyone who wishes to challenge an application. If there is insufficient time to file evidence or the deadline is missed, the person concerned must apply for an extension of time to serve his evidence. A person who wishes to respond out of time or who has not been notified or served must apply separately, using form COP9.

P as a party

In most such cases where P is deemed to have an interest in the outcome or an interest in the matter, then he will need to be a party. In such cases it will be for the court to decide whether P should be a party to the application (COPR rules 73(4) and 85(2)(c)). If the court decides that P is to be a party then it will also appoint a litigation friend to represent P, who will generally be the Official Solicitor. It is then the responsibility of the litigation friend to involve P as far as possible and in most cases where the Official Solicitor acts in that role, a personal visit to P is made.

Subsequent procedure

Once the court has issued the application, the court will usually make a number of directions, exercising its wide discretion under rule 85 and also using its case management powers in COPR rule 25. The first direction will usually be to join P as a party and appoint a litigation friend. The next direction will be to confirm the other parties and provide directions and time limits for the service and exchange of evidence. The court or the parties may require further evidence, such as medical reports. The case may also be allocated to a regional court outside London or if the matter is particularly complex or contentious, to a High Court judge. A complex case may require a telephone directions hearing at which detailed directions can be agreed with the parties. The court will then set the case down for a hearing.

4.9.2 Application within the proceedings

Part 10 of the COPR sets out a procedure for applications within the proceedings, which is a simplified procedure for use where a case is already before the court and a party or other person requires the court to make a direction or order. The procedure may be used in the following instances:

- to join a party;
- to remove a party;

- to terminate the proceedings (for instance where P recovers capacity or dies);
- to move the hearing or management of the case to a different court;
- to appoint a litigation friend for P or another party who is a protected party;
- to dispense with notice being given to P or another party;
- to allow further evidence to be admitted in proceedings;
- to extend the time limit allowed in an existing direction;
- to require a party or witness to produce evidence, for example where a doctor or solicitor holds confidential records that will be required as evidence;
- to obtain an interim order to access property of P (for example where funds are urgently required before a deputy has been appointed);
- to obtain a copy of a final order where a person notified or served has not responded in form COP5;
- to ask for a decision made without an attended hearing to be reconsidered.

Procedure

The person making an application under Part 10 must file with the court an application notice (form COP9) with any evidence in support. No fee is payable. Once the form has been issued, the applicant must, within 21 days of issue, serve a copy of the application and any evidence filed in support on anyone named as a respondent in the application notice, every other party to the proceedings and such other person as may be directed by the court (COPR rule 80). The applicant must also file a certificate of service (COP20B) within seven days of service.

4.9.3 Routine and subsequent procedures – by deputies and attorneys

Not every application requires the formality of an application and the involvement of other parties. It would be clearly inappropriate for a deputy wanting authority for a small gift or authority to buy or sell a property to go through a formal application process with notification or service on other people every time an order is required. Practice Direction (PD) 9D – *Applications by Currently Appointed Deputies, Attorneys and Donees in Relation to P's Property and Affairs* – therefore provides a simplified procedure for applications by existing deputies and attorneys. This still requires an application form (COP1), a supplementary form (COP1E), a witness statement and an application fee of £400, but there is no requirement to give notice to P or any other person unless specifically directed to do so by the court.

PD 9D provides the following list of cases where the short procedure would be appropriate:

(a) applications for regular payments from P's assets to the deputy in respect of remuneration;
(b) applications seeking minor variations only as to the expenses that can be paid from P's estate;
(c) applications to change an accounting period;

(d)   applications to set or change the time by which an annual account may be submitted;

(e)   applications in relation to the sale of property owned by P, where the sale is non-contentious;

(f)   applications for authority to disclose information as to P's assets, state of health or other circumstances;

(g)   applications to make a gift or loan from P's assets, provided that the sum in question is not disproportionately large when compared to the size of P's estate as a whole;

(h)   applications to sell or otherwise deal with P's investments, provided that the sum in question is not disproportionately large when compared to the size of P's estate as a whole;

(i)   applications for the receipt or discharge of a sum due to or by P;

(j)   applications for authority to apply for a grant of probate or representation, where P would be the person entitled to the grant but for his lack of capacity;

(k)   applications relating to the lease or grant of a tenancy in relation to property owned by P;

(l)   applications for release of funds to repair or improve P's property;

(m)   applications to sell P's furniture or effects;

(n)   applications for release of capital to meet expenses required for the care of P;

(o)   applications to arrange an overdraft or bank loan on P's behalf;

(p)   applications to open a bank account on behalf of P or for the purpose of the deputyship at a private bank, a bank that is not located in England and Wales, or at a bank which has unusual conditions attached to the operation of the account; and

(q)   applications for the variation of an order for security made pursuant to rule 200.

There are two further important conditions that an applicant must be able to demonstrate before this procedure can be used: first, that the order sought is not likely to be significant to the estate; and second, that there are unlikely to be any objections. The applicant must be able to show that he reasonably believes these conditions to be fulfilled. If the applicant cannot satisfy these conditions or the court is not so satisfied, the applicant must make a formal application, serving the evidence on the other parties affected by the application.

4.9.4   Reconsideration and appeal

Where the applicant is dissatisfied with the order made, where it was made without a hearing, he can request that the court reconsiders the matter by submitting a COP9 within 21 days of the order being served under COPR rule 89. The reconsideration can occur with or without a hearing.

Part 20 of the COPR contains the provisions relating to an appeal, and is supported by PD 20A. Permission is generally required before an appeal can be made and applications made by submitting COP35 in duplicate (appellant's notice) with the court fee of £400. The permission request is contained within COP35. It should be supported by a skeleton argument (COP37), which sets out the grounds for appeal, a sealed copy of the order being appealed, and any witness statements.

Where an appeal is to the Court of Appeal, the Civil Procedure Rules 1998 apply.

The appeal can be made at the hearing or within 21 days of the decision being made, or such other time as the judge specifies at the hearing (COPR rule 175).

Once the court has issued the appellant's notice, it will need to be served on each respondent within 21 days of issue. The appellant must confirm service by completing and filing with the court a certificate of service (COP20B) within seven days. A respondent who wishes to challenge the matter must file a respondent's notice (COP36) in duplicate, within 21 days of receiving service of the appellant's notice or such other time as set by the judge. This should be accompanied by a skeleton argument (COP37) and any witness statement in support. The court will then decide whether to list the matter for a hearing and notify the parties.

4.10 GIFTS AND DISPOSITIONS OF PROPERTY

4.10.1 Gifts not requiring the approval of the court

A deputy or attorney is by definition someone who acts in a fiduciary role and should not benefit from his role. Neither can a fiduciary act to benefit someone other than his principal. However, exceptions need to be provided for, to reflect the practical reality of most situations as well as to prevent the Court of Protection being inundated with applications. Thus an exception is made as a matter of practice where a deputy or attorney is acting in a professional role and should be remunerated. Thus the power of attorney will provide authority for an attorney to be remunerated while an order appointing a professional deputy will provide authority for his costs to be assessed.

While any transfer of property from one person to another is a gift, the role of an attorney or deputy makes an important distinction between a gift which is purely bounty and a gift which represents the performance of an obligation. A birthday or wedding present is a gift pure and simple; the payment of a spouse's care costs, a child's mortgage payments or a grandchild's school fees is a carrying out of a moral obligation. With the former the powers of an attorney or deputy are very limited; with the latter they can be more generously interpreted. However, where the attorney is acting under a registered LPA, MCA 2005 only refers to the attorney's limited authority to make gifts.

Power to make gifts

An order appointing a deputy will typically contain an express authority to make gifts (see **4.8.8**) to a charity 'to which he made or might have been expected to make gifts' or 'on customary occasions' to a person 'related to or connected with him'. There is an important proviso that 'the value of each such gift is not unreasonable having regard to all the circumstances and, in particular, the size of the estate'. Thus a deputy may make gifts on P's behalf to members of the family at Christmas or on the occasion of a birthday, wedding or other celebration. An attorney acting under an LPA or EPA has a similar authority conferred by statute unless it is expressly limited by the power of attorney (respectively MCA 2005, s.12 and Sched.4, para.3(3)).

There is no formal limit or even guidance as to the value of any such gift. It is a matter for the deputy or attorney to decide in each case. In a small estate, a gift of £250 or even £100 may represent a large sum of money; in a larger estate, gifts of up to £3,000 might be more appropriate especially if the estate may be liable to inheritance tax. For guidance on the limited gifts that might be made without court approval see the decision of Senior Judge Lush in *Re GM* [2013] EWHC 2966 (COP). If there is any doubt as to what is reasonable, the attorney or deputy should either err on the side of caution or apply to the Court of Protection for authority. Depending on the sums involved, the procedure may be quite straightforward (see **4.9.3**).

Maintenance

As well as providing authority to make gifts, an order appointing a deputy may confer on the deputy authority to 'make provision for the needs of anyone who is related to or connected with [P], if he provided for or might be expected to provide for that person's needs, by doing whatever he did or might reasonably be expected to do to meet those needs'. An attorney acting under an EPA (but not under an LPA) has a similar authority conferred by statute unless it is expressly limited by the power of attorney (MCA 2005, Sched.4, para.3(2)).

As with gifts, the amount that can be spent by way of 'maintenance' is not defined even though in practice this may greatly exceed the amount of any gift. This can confer a very wide discretion. For instance, in *Re Cameron (Deceased)* [1999] Ch 386) an attorney under a registered EPA created a settlement for the education of the donor's grandchild. In *Bouette* v. *Rose* [2000] Ch 662 the Court of Appeal held that a mother who had given up her job to look after her severely disabled child should be provided for on the grounds that providing for the child's needs extended to the needs of the mother caring for the child. In the more recent case of *Re A* [2015] EWCOP 46, the court endorsed the deputy's decision to pay the school fees of P's sibling. Maintenance may extend to the considerable expense of paying for a spouse's nursing care or the provision of a family budget for parents of a severely disabled child. The sums involved when maintaining another person especially over an extended period of time can be considerable and if the attorney or deputy is any doubt as to the extent of the authority conferred or whether the payments are in the best interests of P, an application should be made to the Court of Protection.

4.10.2 Gifts, settlements and wills – decisions requiring the approval of the court

Where larger gifts are involved or the gift involves the creation of a settlement or the execution of a will then a formal application is required. The express authority of the court is required for an order under MCA 2005, s.18. A gift which might be significant in relation to the size of the estate is not appropriate for a short procedure application (see **4.9.3**); a decision to make a settlement or a will cannot be made by a deputy and is reserved to the court (MCA 2005, s.20(3)). In any such case there must be a proper consideration of P's best interests, taking account of the interests of any other person affected by the proposed disposition.

Who may make an application

MCA 2005, s.50 sets out the general rule that no application can be made without permission unless one of the exceptions applies, principally that the application is made by P, a deputy or an attorney or where it relates to the property and affairs of P.

Application

An application for a gift, settlement or will must be made by way of a formal application as described at **4.9.1**. Thus the applicant must submit an application form COP1 in duplicate together with a supplementary form COP1C, a fee of £400 and medical evidence in form COP3 addressing specifically the decision which P lacks capacity to make and which the court is being asked to make on P's behalf. It is also helpful to include a copy of form COP1A as a summary of P's financial and personal details.

The applicant must also provide evidence to support his view that the decision should be made. The detailed evidence required is summarised in Practice Direction 9F – *Applications Relating to Statutory Wills, Codicils, Settlements and Other Dealings with Property* – which should always be referred to before such an application is made. Paragraph 6 provides as follows:

> In addition to the application form COP1 (and its annexes) and any information or documents required to be provided by the Rules or another practice direction, the following information must be provided (in the form of a witness statement [using form COP24], attaching documents as exhibits where necessary) for any application to which this practice direction applies:
>
> (a) where the application is for the execution of a statutory will or codicil, a copy of the draft will or codicil, plus one copy;
> (b) a copy of any existing will or codicil;
> (c) any consents to act by proposed executors;
> (d) details of P's family, preferably in the form of a family tree, including details of the full name and date of birth of each person included in the family tree;
> (e) a schedule showing details of P's current assets, with up to date valuations;
> (f) a schedule showing the estimated net yearly income and spending of P;
> (g) a statement showing P's needs, both current and future estimates, and his general circumstances;
> (h) if P is living in National Health Service accommodation, information on whether he may be discharged to local authority accommodation, to other fee-paying accommodation or to his own home;

(i) if the applicant considers it relevant, full details of the resources of any proposed beneficiary, and details of any likely changes if the application is successful;

(j) details of any capital gains tax, inheritance tax or income tax which may be chargeable in respect of the subject matter of the application;

(k) an explanation of the effect, if any, that the proposed changes will have on P's circumstances, preferably in the form of a 'before and after' schedule of assets and income;

(l) if appropriate, a statement of whether any land would be affected by the proposed will or settlement and if so, details of its location and title number, if applicable;

(m) where the application is for a settlement of property or for the variation of an existing settlement or trust, a draft of the proposed deed, plus one copy;

(n) a copy of any registered enduring power of attorney or lasting power of attorney;

(o) confirmation that P is a resident of England or Wales; and

(p) an up to date report of P's present medical condition, life expectancy, likelihood of requiring increased expenditure in the foreseeable future, and testamentary capacity.

Subsequent procedure

The application proceeds in the same way as any other formal application (see **4.9.1**). The court will issue the application form and return this to the applicant. It is then for the applicant to serve the application and supporting evidence on any respondent. The court will also issue a direction joining P as a party and appointing a litigation friend, whereupon the application will be served on the litigation friend. P must be notified in person that a litigation friend has been appointed on his behalf (COPR rule 41A), and must be provided with form COP14 (see **4.8.7**). Any person served with the application must be provided with form COP5; only if this is returned by the person served indicating that he or she opposes the application or seeks a different order will that person be joined as a party. A person who simply wishes to reserve a position pending further evidence being disclosed will have to indicate a wish to oppose the application. As form COP5 also assumes that the respondent (or where P is served, a litigation friend) must attach evidence, it is usual to apply within the form for an extension of time to submit further evidence.

Once evidence has been filed and served, the court will either make an order without a hearing or proceed to an attended hearing. The final order will be effective as soon as it is pronounced, although a statutory will is not effective as a will until it has been executed in accordance with MCA 2005.

Form and execution of statutory will

An order authorising the making of a will on behalf of P will also authorise a named person to execute the will approved by the court. Once a statutory will has been approved by the court, the applicant or other person authorised by the court must execute the will in accordance with MCA 2005, Sched.2, para.3 which provides as follows:

(1)   Sub-paragraph (2) applies if under section 16 the court makes an order or gives directions requiring or authorising a person ('the authorised person') to execute a will on behalf of P.

(2)   Any will executed in pursuance of the order or direction –

       (a)   must state that it is signed by P acting by the authorised person,

       (b)   must be signed by the authorised person with the name of P and his own name, in the presence of two or more witnesses present at the same time,

       (c)   must be attested and subscribed by those witnesses in the presence of the authorised person, and

       (d)   must be sealed with the official seal of the court.

To comply with the statutory requirements, Practice Direction 9F provides a draft or model testimonium and attestation clause for a will:

This is the last will of me AB [the person who lacks capacity] of _____ acting by CD the person authorised in that behalf by an order dated the _____ day of _____ 20____ made under the Mental Capacity Act 2005.

I revoke all my former wills and codicils and declare this to be my last will.

1. I appoint EF and GH to be executors and trustees of this my will.

2. I give _____

In witness of which this will is signed by me AB acting by CD under the order mentioned above on (date).

SIGNED by the said AB [the person who lacks capacity] by the said CD [authorised person] and by the said CD with his (or her) own name pursuant to the said order in our presence and attested by us in the presence of the said CD.

AB [person who lacks capacity]

CD [authorised person]

[Names and addresses of witnesses]

Sealed with the official seal of the Court of Protection the _____ day of _____ 20____

The statutory will therefore needs to be signed twice by the person authorised, first with P's own name and then with his or her own name. Any will executed in this way has the same effect for all purposes as if P had been capable of making a valid will and the will had been executed by him in accordance with the Wills Act 1837. The will is executed by the authorised person on behalf of P who, not being a witness, may be a beneficiary under the will. However, no other beneficiary or spouse of a beneficiary can act as a witness to the will as they would be barred from benefiting from the will under the Wills Act 1837, s.15. As soon as the statutory will has been signed and witnessed in this way, it is valid and effective as the testator's last will.

In all other respects, the statutory will is no different from a will made by a competent testator who is properly advised. It is therefore the responsibility of the solicitor drafting the statutory will to ensure that it is correctly drafted. The will should cover matters such as ademption where the testator's estate might fall in value and substitutional provisions where beneficiaries and executors might predecease the testator. It should have up-to-date and flexible administrative clauses which are appropriate to the size and complexity of P's estate.

Once the will has been executed, the original is sent to the Court of Protection with two certified copies and the draft will be approved by the court, together with any outstanding fee (there is a further fee of £500 payable on an attended hearing). The court checks that the will has been correctly executed and then seals the will with the seal of the Court of Protection. The applicant's solicitors are usually authorised to retain the will in their safe custody and shall hold the will to the order of the court during the lifetime of P and for so long as P lacks capacity.

Considerations on making a will or other dispositions on behalf of P

It is to some extent a considerable intrusion into the autonomy of a person to make a decision of such significance as disposing of that person's property or deciding how it should be disposed of on that person's death. Most people make a will assuming that it will be their last word, or live with the consequences of not making a will. That reflects their wishes so long as they have capacity. The court is exercising an awesome responsibility in taking that person's autonomy and making a decision which it decides is better than the one made by P when P had capacity.

How then should the court, or anyone involved in the process of applying to the court or involved in these proceedings, approach such a difficult dilemma? For many years the court's approach under the MHA 1983 jurisdiction was determined by the guidelines set out by Sir Robert Megarry in *Re D(J)* [1982] Ch 237. The court should proceed on the assumption that it was making the decision which the testator (and by implication the donor of a gift or settlor of a settlement) would make if at the precise moment the decision was made, he or she had perfect capacity. In this hypothetical lucid moment, the testator has a clear and complete understanding of the circumstances surrounding the decision such as the state of any earlier wills, the size of his estate and the claims on his bounty. The court must take account of the actual person making the decision, with all his likes and dislikes rather than an objectively reasonable person ('it is the actual patient who has to be considered and not a hypothetical patient on the Clapham omnibus'). However, there was an important caveat to the effect that the court should not be obliged to 'give effect to antipathies or affections of the patient which are beyond reason'. The court would also allow for the fact that the will was being professionally prepared and that the hypothetical testator had access to proper legal advice and would make a will that also took a 'broad brush' approach to claims on his bounty.

When MCA 2005 came into force on 1 October 2007 it was assumed that this approach would be reflected in the new jurisdiction. A decision made on behalf of a person who lacked capacity had to be in that person's best interests. It must therefore take account of past and present wishes and feelings, the beliefs and values that would be likely to influence the person's decision if that person had capacity, and the other factors that he or she would be likely to consider if able to do so. However, the former approach of the court in the light of the new legislation was considered by Lewison J in *Re P* [2009] EWHC 163 (Ch). In his carefully considered decision the judge held that an attempt to replicate or substitute the court's judgment for that of the person who lacked capacity was no longer appropriate. This was not the same as making a decision in a person's best interests. The earlier approach could no longer apply to decisions made under the new Act for a number of reasons (at para.[38]):

(i)   The 2005 Act does not require the counter-factual assumption that P is not mentally disordered. The facts must be taken as they are. It is not therefore necessary to go through the mental gymnastics of imagining that P has a brief lucid interval and then relapses into his former state.

(ii)   The goal of the enquiry is not what P 'might be expected' to have done; but what is in P's best interests. This is more akin to the 'balance sheet' approach than to the 'substituted judgment' approach. The code of practice makes this clear in that it points out that the test of best interests was one that was worked out by the courts mainly in decisions relating to the provision of medical care (para.5.1).

(iii)   The previous guidance was concerned with deciding what P would have wanted if he were not mentally disordered. But the 2005 Act requires the decision maker to consider P's present wishes and feelings, which *ex hypothesi* are wishes and feelings entertained by a person who lacks mental capacity in relation to the decision being made on his behalf.

(iv)   The same structured decision-making process applies to all decisions to be made on P's behalf, whether great or small, whereas the previous guidance was specific to the making of a will, gift or settlement. Moreover, it is a decision-making process which must be followed, not only by the court, but by anyone who takes decisions on P's behalf.

(v)   In making his decision the decision maker must consider 'all relevant circumstances'.

(vi)   The Act expressly directs the decision maker to take a number of steps before reaching a decision. These include encouraging P to participate in the decision. He must also 'consider' P's past and present wishes, and his beliefs and values and must 'take into account' the views of third parties as to what would be in P's best interests.

The court is therefore making a decision in P's best interests, which may, but might not necessarily, be the one that P would have made if he had capacity. This approach has caused some consternation and it has been seen as a green light to a speculative approach to making decisions on P's behalf. However, the case has to be seen in the light of its own facts, where the testator's known wishes were inherently irrational. The correct approach therefore is that where P's wishes cannot be ascertained reliably or are irrational or unjust then the court can take a wider or objective view of P's best interests. Thus where P has no known testamentary history and it cannot be said with any certainty what P may or may not have done, a decision can be made in his best interests. The judge addressed this point carefully (at para.[44]):

There is one other aspect of the 'best interests' test that I must consider. In deciding what provision should be made in a will to be executed on P's behalf and which, *ex hypothesi*, will only have effect after he is dead, what are P's best interests? Mr Boyle stressed the principle of adult autonomy; and said that P's best interests would be served simply by giving effect to his wishes. That is, I think, part of the overall picture, and an important one at that. But what will live on after P's death is his memory; and for many people it is in their best interests that they be remembered with affection by their family and as having done 'the right thing' by their will. In my judgment the decision maker is entitled to take into account, in assessing what is in P's best interests, how he will be remembered after his death.

It should, however, remain the case that where P's wishes or likely wishes can be ascertained by evidence from earlier wills, relationships, charitable bequests or past conduct, the court must try to give effect to those wishes. Subsequent cases have emphasised the importance of giving effect to P's wishes or likely wishes when making decisions in P's best interests. See, for example, *Re JC; D* v. *JC, JG, A, B, C* [2012] COPLR 540.

4.11   FEES AND CHARGES

4.11.1   Court of Protection fees

The fees payable to the Court of Protection are set out in the Schedule to the Court of Protection Fees Order 2007, SI 2007/1745 (amended by the Court of Protection Fees (Amendment) Order 2009, SI 2009/513). In summary, the main fees are:

- Application fee. An application fee of £400 is payable on the making of any first application under Part 9 of the COPR. Thus all applications are treated in the same way, whether made by deputies, attorneys or other persons or bodies. An application fee is also payable on an application for permission, although if permission is given, it is not payable again on the making of the application.
- Appeal fee. An appeal fee of £400 is payable on an appeal against a decision of the court under Part 20 of the COPR.
- Hearing fee. A further fee of £500 is payable on an attended hearing. Thus the cost to P's estate will be £900 if the application is dealt with at a hearing – whether this is a short informal appointment or a lengthy trial.

Remission of fees

The Court of Protection operates a single but extremely complex remissions system. In general, the calculations are assessed on household means, including jointly held capital. However, applicants will be assessed as single where:

- the fee payer is 'P' (applicable in property and financial affairs cases); or
- the partner of a third party applicant is 'P'.

Stage 1 is determined by the level of the applicant's capital. If the applicant is aged 60 or under and has over £3,000 of disposable capital, they have to pay the full court fee, even if they are in receipt of means-tested state benefits. There are complex rules as to what is 'disposable capital'. If they have under £3,000, the applicant moves on to stage 2 – the income test.

If the applicant is aged 61 or over (the current state retirement age for women) and they have disposable capital of under £16,000, they will move on to stage 2 – the income test.

Stage 2 applies a single tapered income assessment test. Applicants who have under the disposable capital limit, and a gross monthly income (including those in receipt of prescribed (i.e. not all) means-tested benefits) below a certain threshold are automatically entitled to a full remission.

Gross monthly income thresholds

Gross monthly income with	Single	Couple
No children	£1,085	£1,245
1 child	£1,330	£1,490
2 children	£1,575	£1,735
Add £245 for each additional child		

Applicants with a gross monthly income over the relevant threshold set out above will be required to make a contribution towards their fee of £5 for each additional £10 income above the threshold, up to the value of the fee. Further details and the remission application form EX160 can be obtained from **www.justice.gov.uk/ courts/fees**.

4.11.2 Public Guardian fees

Separate fees are charged by the Public Guardian for the carrying out of his duties to register powers of attorney and supervise deputies. These are set out in the Schedule to the Public Guardian (Fees, etc.) Regulations 2007, SI 2007/2051 (as amended by the Public Guardian (Fees, etc.) (Amendment) Regulations 2013, SI 2013/1748). The fees set out in the table to the Regulations are as follows:

- enduring power of attorney registration – £110;
- enduring power of attorney office copy – £25;
- lasting power of attorney registration – £110;
- lasting power of attorney office copy – £25;
- appointment of deputy – £100;
- supervision (paid annually): £325 for most cases.

Remission

A donor is exempt from paying any fee if he or she is in receipt of any of the following means-tested benefits when an application to register is made:

- income support;
- income-based employment and support allowance;
- income-based jobseeker's allowance;
- guarantee credit element of state pension credit;
- housing benefit;
- council tax reduction/support – also known by other names (not the 25 per cent single person discount or the class U exemption);
- local housing allowance;
- a combination of working tax credit and at least one of – child tax credit, disability element of working tax credit or severe disability element of working tax credit.

If the donor has been awarded personal injury damages of more than £16,000, the exemption does not apply.

If the donor's gross annual income is less than £12,000, they may be eligible for a 50 per cent reduction of the fee. The applicant must complete form LPA120A with evidence in support to qualify.

4.11.3 Solicitors' costs – when payable

All costs incurred in relation to Court of Protection proceedings are in the discretion of the court, which may order them to be paid by P or charged on or paid out of P's estate, or to be paid by any other person attending or taking part in the proceedings.

The question of costs was considered in detail in *Re Cathcart* [1892] 1 Ch 549, which established a number of principles that still apply over a century later:

- Unlike proceedings in other civil courts, costs in the Court of Protection do not necessarily follow the event.
- Where an application is made in good faith, supported by medical evidence, is in the best interests of the person concerned, and without any personal motive, the applicant is generally entitled to his costs from the estate, even if he is unsuccessful.
- The court has an unlimited discretion to make whatever order for costs it considers that the justice of the case requires.
- In exercising its discretion, the court must have regard to all the circumstances of the case, including, though not limited to: the relationship between the parties, their conduct, their respective means, and the amount of costs involved.
- Where a person places himself in a hostile position to the person concerned, or where his conduct results in the costs of the proceedings being more expensive than they might otherwise have been, the court may consider it appropriate to penalise him as to costs.

Although these principles must now be considered in the light of MCA 2005 and the overriding requirement that any decision of the court, including a decision on costs, must be in P's best interests, they are also reflected in the COPR which now govern the issue of costs. Rule 156 sets out the following general rule:

> Where the proceedings concern P's property and affairs the general rule is that the costs of the proceedings or of that part of the proceedings that concerns P's property and affairs, shall be paid by P or charged to his estate.

Rule 156 of the COPR applies to proceedings concerning property and affairs. Where the proceedings concern P's welfare, then rule 157 adopts a general rule that there should be no order for costs. Thus each party is expected to pay its own costs. However, both rules also allow the court to depart from the general principles they embody 'if the circumstances so justify'. Rule 159 provides that, in deciding whether to depart from the general principles:

(1) ... the court will have regard to all the circumstances, including –

    (a) the conduct of the parties;
    (b) whether a party has succeeded on part of his case, even if he has not been wholly successful; and
    (c) the role of any public body involved in the proceedings.

(2) The conduct of the parties includes –

    (a) conduct before, as well as during, the proceedings;
    (b) whether it was reasonable for a party to raise, pursue or contest a particular issue;
    (c) the manner in which a party has made or responded to an application or a particular issue;
    (d) whether a party who has succeeded in his application or response to an application, in whole or in part, exaggerated any matter contained in his application or response; and
    (e) any failure by a party to comply with a rule, practice direction or court order.

The order most commonly made in property and affairs cases is that the costs of the parties be subject to detailed assessment and paid from P's estate. However, while it is important that the parties should not make assumptions about this, the court wishes to discourage parties from defending their interests in a matter or bringing their concerns before the court. A finding against a party over costs will usually arise in a contentious matter where there has been an attended hearing and a party's conduct has been examined carefully and a determination made. The court will generally allow costs unless there is a strong argument that costs should not be paid.

4.11.4 Solicitors' costs – basis for payment

A solicitor can only charge costs to the extent that an order of the Court of Protection permits. There are only four bases on which costs can be charged.

(1) Detailed assessment

The detailed assessment of costs under orders or directions of the Court of Protection is dealt with in accordance with the Civil Procedure Rules 1998. Solicitors should lodge a request for a detailed assessment at the Senior Courts Costs Office, Thomas More Building, Royal Courts of Justice, Strand, London, WC2A 2LL. Form N258B should be used if the costs are payable out of a fund, or form N258 if payable by one party to another, together with the authority for assessment, the bill of costs, all supporting papers and the fee of £220 payable in respect of a detailed assessment.

The request for assessment must include a detailed narrative bill in the form shown in the Schedules to the Civil Procedure Rules 1998, setting out the title of the matter, the names of the parties, the details of the authority for assessment, the period covered by any general management work, a brief narrative of the work covered by the bill, the charging rates of the fee earners involved and each chargeable item of work in chronological order and any disbursements incurred.

The Senior Courts Costs Office will deal with most assessments on a provisional basis by post. If the solicitor is not satisfied with the assessment, he must inform the Costs Office within 14 days of receipt of the provisionally assessed bill and provide an explanation of any points not agreed. The Costs Office will usually review the bill in the light of any submissions made, only fixing a date for a hearing if the costs are not agreed by the solicitor. Where other parties are involved in proceedings, the solicitor must serve a copy of the provisionally assessed bill on the other parties, who then have 14 days in which to file any points of dispute with the Costs Office. If these cannot be dealt with through correspondence, the costs will be dealt with at a hearing.

On receipt of the provisionally assessed bill, the solicitor must complete the summary on the bill certifying the castings as correct, and return the original bill to the Costs Office for the issue of the costs certificate. There is no further fee payable on sealing the certificate.

The rates at which work can be charged for are also prescribed for all work involving civil proceedings. Guideline rates apply to work carried out in four different grades or bands of fee earner as follows:

A.   Solicitors with over eight years' post-qualification experience including at least eight years' litigation experience.
B.   Solicitors and legal executives with over four years' post-qualification experience including at least four years' litigation experience.
C.   Other solicitors and legal executives and fee earners of equivalent experience.
D.   Trainee solicitors, paralegals and other fee earners.

For work carried out after 1 April 2010, the rates, which are unchanged at the time or writing, are as follows:

	Band A	Band B	Band C	Band D
London 1	£409	£296	£226	£138
London 2	£317	£242	£193	£126
London 3	£229–£267	£172–229	£165	£121
National 1	£217	£192	£161	£118
National 2/3	£201	£177	£146	£111

www.gov.uk

(2) Short form assessment

Where the amount of the bill does not exceed £3,000 (excluding VAT and disbursements) the solicitor may request the Senior Courts Costs Office to assess the costs using the short form assessment procedure. The procedure for applying for assessment is the same as that for an application for detailed assessment above, except that solicitors may use a simplified form of bill and a reduced fee of £110 is payable.

(3) Fixed costs

Fixed costs were first introduced to reduce the volume of excessive cases in which the amount of costs at issue was relatively small. Practice Direction 19B provides for six categories, and in each case the costs should not exceed the amount stated. The rates for bills submitted on or after 1 February 2011 are as follows:

Category I	Work up to and including the date upon which the court makes an order appointing a deputy for property and affairs.	£850 (plus VAT)
Category II	Applications under ss.36(9) or 54 of the Trustee Act 1925 or s.20 of the Trusts of Land and Appointment of Trustees Act 1996 for the appointment of a new trustee in the place of 'P' and applications under s.18(1)(j) of MCA 2005 for authority to exercise any power vested in P, whether beneficially, or as trustee, or otherwise.	£385 (plus VAT)
Category III	(Where a solicitor acts as a deputy) Annual management fee where the court appoints a professional deputy for property and affairs, payable on the anniversary of the court order:	
	(a) for the first year: amount £1,500 (plus VAT)	£1,500 (plus VAT)

	(b) for the second and subsequent years: amount £1,185 (plus VAT)	£1,185 (plus VAT)
	provided that, where the net assets of P are below £16,000, the professional deputy for property and affairs may take an annual management fee not exceeding 4.5 per cent of P's net assets on the anniversary of the court order appointing the professional as deputy.	
Category IV	Where the court appoints a professional deputy for health and welfare. The deputy may take an annual management fee not exceeding 2.5 per cent of P's net assets on the anniversary of the court order appointing the professional as deputy for health and welfare up to a maximum of £500.	
Category V	Preparation and lodgement of the annual report or annual account to the Public Guardian.	£235 (plus VAT)
Category VI	Preparation of an HMRC income tax return on behalf of P.	£235 (plus VAT)

www.judiciary.gov.uk

In addition to the fixed costs in each category, VAT and disbursements are allowed.

Solicitors are under no obligation to accept fixed costs, and retain the option of having a bill of costs drawn up and a detailed assessment, if they prefer.

(4) Agreed costs

A deputy who is not a solicitor will generally have authority within the scope of the order appointing the deputy to agree the costs of a solicitor instructed by him on an application or in connection with the general management of P's estate.

4.11.5 Costs in general management

A solicitor must have authority to charge for general management work which is distinct from an application to appoint a deputy or a formal application which is covered by an order for assessment. General management relates only to P's financial affairs and property although for a professional deputy it is often difficult to separate this role from the wider personal duties of a deputy to act in P's best interests. For example, personal visits or attendance at case conferences should be delegated where possible to relatives or friends and if this cannot be done for whatever reason, the deputy must explain the reason why the costs of such attendance should be recovered.

General management costs can be high, especially where a solicitor is appointed deputy in complex cases where there are no relatives to take on this role. Costs should also be assessed annually, to coincide with a deputy's accounting period. Because the deputy would otherwise have to carry out a year's work before the deputy can even begin the assessment process, let alone receive payment, Practice Direction 19B permits the deputy to take payments on account for the first three quarters of the year. Interim quarterly bills must not exceed 20 per cent of the estimated annual management charges – that is up to 60 per cent for the whole year. Thus at the year end, the last quarter's work remains unbilled and provides a cushion or float in the event of any reduction in the solicitor's costs on assessment. Once the year's costs have been assessed, a final bill can be entered showing the deduction of payments on account and the balance due. In the unlikely event that costs on account exceed the amount allowed on assessment the excess must be repaid immediately to P with interest.

4.12   ADMINISTRATION OF P'S PROPERTY AND AFFAIRS

4.12.1   General considerations

Managing a personal estate can be time consuming and involve a series of many small transactions that can be overlooked, especially in a busy legal practice. It is important therefore to use standard procedures and checklists to ensure that essential obligations are not overlooked. At the same time, sound legal experience, knowledge of MCA 2005 and its principles and common sense should be assumed prerequisites in every case. Nevertheless, mistakes and oversights are easy to make.

The following points are not exhaustive but are intended to assist the deputy who should:

- Check the wording of any new order and make sure that the details are set out correctly and that the deputy has the authority needed to deal with P's estate.
- Retain all original orders but obtain office copies and produce these to third parties as required.
- Notify persons dealing with P (e.g. the staff at a care home) of the deputy's appointment so that they do not inadvertently seek to enter into transactions with P directly.
- Notify all asset holders and other organisations dealing with P including banks, building societies, stockbrokers, company registrars, NS&I for National Savings, local authority, insurance companies, pension and annuity providers, HMRC and the DWP.
- Where P has moved out of a property, consider a postal redirection so that details of assets and liabilities are not overlooked.

- Where P owns a property, ensure it is adequately insured and that any conditions in the insurance policy are observed.
- Where P lives at home, ensure that P and any other occupiers of the property have contact details for emergencies (service contracts for supplies to the property may be an effective way of providing cover and peace of mind).
- Record and if necessary prepare an inventory and/or valuation of P's personal effects (a frequent complaint against former deputies is that allegedly valuable items have been sold or cleared).
- Arrange to visit P. Giving P notice of a final order (see **4.8.8**) provides an opportunity to visit P and ensure that P's care needs are being met. A deputy should in any event visit P in person or arrange for P to be visited at least once a year.
- Open a bank account in the deputy's name as deputy for P for the purpose of receiving all income due to P, discharging liabilities and providing such funding as P requires; all financial dealings entered into by P should be conducted through this account so that there is a clear audit trail and to assist in preparing the deputy's report.
- Sign any authorised document in the deputy's own name adding: 'as deputy for [P]'.
- Where the deputy is authorised to execute a deed, sign this twice, once with P's name and then with the deputy's own name (however, for execution of a statutory will see **4.10.2**).
- Remember that P's money is there to be used for P's benefit rather than preserved for those who would inherit on P's death; financial arrangements should reflect the needs of P and be structured so as to be as supportive and provide as much freedom to P as circumstances and P's capacity permit.
- Check the location and contents of P's will and who the executors are; also identify any specific items referred to and consider any funeral arrangements in the will: if these are not recorded in the will, should a funeral plan be considered? Can P be consulted on this?
- Take into account the terms of P's will and any disposals of property and changes in the value of the estate in the light of that will; if P has capacity to make a new will then the deputy should obtain medical evidence and may take instructions directly from P; if there is doubt over P's capacity the court can make a declaration of capacity under MCA 2005, s.15; if P lacks capacity, a statutory will should be considered.
- In cases where guidance is needed on P's capacity, consult P's doctor or other suitably qualified expert.
- Where there is doubt over whether the deputy is acting within the scope of his or her authority, apply to the Court of Protection. An application may well be dealt with quickly and simply under the short procedure (see **4.9.3**).
- Whenever issues arise concerning P's welfare and residence, act in P's best interests: consult with family members, P's doctor and the social services department for the area in which P lives and seek a consensus as to what is in P's

best interests; a deputy appointed to deal with property and affairs cannot determine these for himself, although he may have an opinion and influence the outcome in terms of P's available resources; however, the deputy's main role is to apply P's resources for P's needs, while also acting in P's best interests.

- Remember that if there is no consensus over how or where P should be looked after, the Court of Protection has authority to make decisions on P's behalf including deciding where P is to live, and who should have contact with P and on what terms.

- Be aware of conflicts of interest and the need to remain objective; to whom is the deputy's duty of care owed? A deputy may rely on a close relative for information about P's wishes and feelings, but that relative is not the client and may require separate representation.

- Take account of P's longer term needs, bearing in mind that continuity of care is desirable so P should not be moved to a private nursing home where the costs would be likely to exhaust resources (while also bearing in mind that it is not necessarily in P's best interests to preserve assets for their own sake and that a better quality of life in the short term may be more important than long-term security, especially where life expectancy is limited).

- Disclose assets to the DWP and social services department where means assessment applies and ensure that all benefits to which P is entitled are claimed.

- Obtain specialist investment advice from a regulated financial adviser where any money or investments are to be invested, especially in a climate of historically low interest rates.

- Notify the Public Guardian if there are any concerns about P, if for example there are suspicions of financial abuse and also if there any major changes in P's circumstances that have a bearing on the nature of the estate and the assets under the deputy's control (such as the sale of a property) or the amount of work being carried out (such as a family dispute or investigation of financial abuse).

A deputy may sometimes feel obliged to do everything that P would have done, without being able to do this in practice, given the constraints of other work and the costs involved. But a deputy does not have to do everything, and should not be expected to. Thus specialist advice should always be sought where necessary, especially when dealing with investments or properties. Specialist advice can also be brought in to assist with care arrangements and welfare reports.

4.12.2 Conclusion

A professional deputy should never treat deputyship work as being of low priority or importance. If the estate is administered effectively, there may be other work to be done, in terms of further applications to the court as well as dealing with property and investments. Regardless of size or complexity, the deputy's role is of vital importance to the elderly client and if the work is dealt with efficiently, it can also be

properly remunerated, therefore achieving the rare combination in most professional lives of doing a worthwhile job and being properly paid for it.

CHAPTER 5

Legal proceedings

Hugh Cumber

5.1 INTRODUCTION

It would be impossible to categorise all of the circumstances in which an older person may become involved in proceedings before civil courts or tribunals. This chapter sets out a general introduction to proceedings before the civil courts and then looks in greater detail at some of the causes of action and remedies that may be of particular significance to the affairs of older people.

5.2 CIVIL PROCEEDINGS

An older person may have difficulty coping as a party to proceedings, or as a witness at a hearing, because of some physical or mental impairment. While the court staff should be helpful and judges are being trained so as to become 'disability aware', a litigant is only treated in a different manner by the rules in the case of serious mental disability. Advisers should, whenever necessary, draw to the attention of the court any situation where disabled facilities or special directions are needed. Many courts will require notice in advance where, for example, a British Sign Language (BSL) translator is required.

5.2.1 Discrimination

The 'judicial function' is exempted from the provisions of the Equality Act 2010, but this is likely to be limited to the adjudicative and listing functions. The civil courts themselves are not exempted from the provisions of the Equality Act 2010, and could find themselves in breach of this legislation if they do not take into account the needs of disabled people. To the disabled individual it does not matter whether the problem is physical access to the court, hearing and understanding the proceedings or being heard and understood by the judge – each could be seen as discrimination. In practice the courts take 'making reasonable adjustments' for disabled people extremely seriously.

For more detailed information on the Equality Act 2010 see **6.14**.

5.2.2 Court rules

There are several sets of rules that apply to different types of proceedings:

- Civil Procedure Rules 1998, SI 1998/3132 (as amended) (CPR) for all civil proceedings in the High Court or County Court. The CPR are supplemented by Practice Directions (PDs) that indicate how the rules should be applied. These are made by the Lord Chief Justice and should always be referred to when considering a rule.
- Family Procedure Rules 2010, SI 2010/2955 (as amended) (FPR) for all family proceedings, whether in the High Court or the new Family Court: certain provisions of the CPR also apply (in particular in relation to costs).
- Insolvency Rules 1986, SI 1986/1925 (as amended), for insolvency proceedings: the CPR will fill any gaps.
- Non-Contentious Probate Rules 1987, SI 1987/2024 (as amended), for non-contentious probate proceedings: the Rules of the Supreme Court in their final form fill any gaps. These rules have been subject to a review and a draft bill, simply called the 'Probate Rules' was published in 2013. Since then, the Ministry of Justice has remained silent on the issue of updating the rules.
- Court of Protection Rules 2007, SI 2007/1744 (as amended) (COPR) and Lasting Powers of Attorney, Enduring Powers of Attorney and Public Guardian Regulations 2007, SI 2007/1253 (as amended) for matters dealt with by the Court of Protection.

5.2.3 Civil Procedure Rules 1998

Since 26 April 1999, civil proceedings in England and Wales have been governed by the Civil Procedure Rules 1998 (CPR). The introduction of the CPR was intended to represent a change of culture in the civil justice system; they offered a complete replacement of the old rules. In April 2013, the system was reformed again following the Costs Review carried out by Sir Rupert Jackson, placing a renewed emphasis on carrying out litigation at proportionate cost, and ensuring rule compliance. This has led to a much stricter approach to sanctions for non-compliance with rules, with potentially very serious consequences for litigants.

Proceedings under the CPR are governed by the overriding objective of enabling the court to deal with cases justly and at proportionate cost, which means:

- ensuring that the parties are on an equal footing;
- saving expense;
- dealing with cases in ways which are proportionate to the money involved, importance of the case, complexity of the issues and financial position of each party;
- ensuring that cases are dealt with expeditiously and fairly;
- allotting to cases an appropriate share of the court's resources;
- enforcing compliance with rules, Practice Directions and orders.

The court must seek to give effect to the overriding objective and the parties are required to help. The court is under a duty of active case management; this includes encouraging the parties to co-operate, identifying the issues at an early stage and deciding how they can best be resolved, and fixing timetables. A cost-benefit approach is adopted and hearings will be dealt with without the need for the parties to attend at court if possible. Alternative dispute resolution (ADR) is encouraged and attempts should be made to settle proceedings at an early stage. For example, a well-planned mediation is an effective way of solving many disputes.

Cases are allocated to one of three 'tracks' (with different timetables and procedures) according to the amount in issue, complexity and other factors. The tracks are:

- The small claims track for most cases up to £10,000 (although different rules apply for personal injury claims, claims by tenants for repairs, claims for damages for harassment or unlawful eviction against landlords, and claims involving a disputed allegation of dishonesty).
- The fast track for most claims between £10,000 and £25,000 which can be disposed of within a day (though the fact that a trial will last longer than a day is not necessarily a conclusive reason for allocation of a case to the multi-track).
- The multi-track for claims over £25,000 and trials likely to exceed a day.

Although the primary rules for track allocation are based on the value of the claim, a claim may be allocated to a different track if the judge decides it can be dealt with more justly on another track.

5.2.4 Pre-action protocols

Various pre-action protocols exist relating to certain types of proceedings such as professional negligence cases, personal injury claims and judicial review. In addition to these specific protocols, the Practice Direction on Pre-Action Conduct contains provisions which apply to all cases. Underlying these protocols is a hope that they may assist the parties to resolve their dispute without having to resort to litigation. Even where proceedings need to be issued, the protocol may have assisted with case management of the claim by identifying the issues at an early stage.

The court will expect the parties to have complied with the protocol relevant to the claim, though the court is not likely to be concerned with minor and technical non-compliance. It is important to consider using a form of ADR. The court has power under the CPR to take into account compliance with a protocol when giving directions and when making orders for costs, and has a general power to impose sanctions; this may include imposing a stay of the proceedings until steps which ought to have been taken are taken.

5.2.5 Bringing a claim

Proceedings to which the CPR apply are brought by the issue of a claim form. Several types of claim form exist for different types of claim, but the principal forms are the Part 7 claim form (form N1) which should be used where there is a factual dispute between the parties and the Part 8 claim form (form N208) which is generally used where the claim is unlikely to involve a substantial dispute of fact. Some types of claim are required by the rules to be brought by a specific procedure (e.g. claims under the Inheritance (Provision for Family and Dependants) Act 1975 must be brought under CPR Part 8).

With effect from April 2015, the cost of issuing civil claims for money has increased. For claims valued between £10,000 and £200,000 the court fee will be 5 per cent of the value of the claim. Above that, the fee is capped at £10,000. For non-money claims, a fixed fee of £480 applies for the High Court (£280 for the County Court). A remission system is available to those who would have difficulty paying a fee and meet certain criteria (see **www.justice.gov.uk/courts/fees**).

5.2.6 Choice of court

Regional County Courts in England and Wales have been replaced by a single County Court. In practice the County Court will continue to sit in different locations around the country. For most types of proceedings, the County Court and the High Court have concurrent jurisdiction. However, some types of claim can only be issued in certain courts.

- Claims for damages may only be issued in the High Court where the value of the claim is more than £100,000 (£50,000 in the case of damages for personal injury) (CPR PD 7A, para.2.1).
- Claims of discrimination under the Equality Act 2010 relating to premises and the provision of services must be brought in the County Court.
- The County Court's jurisdiction for claims in equity (e.g. claims relating to trusts) is limited to claims worth less than £350,000, although the parties can agree to confer jurisdiction on the court to hear the claim (see County Court Jurisdiction Order, SI 2014/503 and County Courts Act 1984).

Both the High Court and County Court have wide powers to transfer proceedings from one court to another (CPR Part 30).

5.2.7 Part 7 claims

Where a claim is brought on a Part 7 claim form, the claimant has four months to serve the claim form (see **5.2.5**). The claimant must serve particulars of claim either with the claim form or within 14 days of its service on the defendant (but in any event within four months of the issue of the claim form). The defendant must acknowledge service no later than 14 days after the particulars of claim were served upon him. A defence must then be served within 28 days of the service of the particulars of claim.

5.2.8 Part 8 claims

Where the claim is brought by way of Part 8, the claimant must serve the evidence on which he wishes to rely with the claim form. The defendant must acknowledge service within 14 days of the service upon him of the claim form and is required by the rules to file his evidence at the same time. In practice the time for the service of the defendant's evidence is frequently extended by agreement. The claimant has a further 14 days from the date of service of the defendant's evidence to file any evidence he wishes to adduce in reply. Part 8 claims are treated as allocated to the multi-track and the parties do not need to complete a directions questionnaire.

The court will then list the matter for a hearing. The nature of the hearing will depend upon the case. Some cases will be suitable to be listed for disposal at the initial hearing. In other cases, the court may give directions for the future conduct of the case, and this may include a direction that it should continue as if it had been commenced under Part 7.

An important difference between Part 7 and Part 8 proceedings is that costs management provisions of the CPR do not apply to Part 8 proceedings unless the court orders that they should.

5.2.9 Costs management

For all multi-track Part 7 proceedings commenced after 22 April 2014 (with the exception of claims valued over £10 million), the costs management regime implemented by the Jackson reforms applies. Under these provisions, parties are required to file and exchange costs budgets. The court will then make a costs management order. Non-compliance with these rules can have very serious implications for the defaulting party (as illustrated by the approach to relief from sanctions taken by the Court of Appeal in *Mitchell* v. *Alasia* [2005] EWHC 11 (QB) and *Denton* v. *TH White Ltd* [2014] EWCA Civ 906). However, the court has discretion to order parties to, for example, file costs budgets in other types of proceedings, including in Part 8 proceedings.

5.2.10 Allocation

If a defendant files a defence, a court officer will then decide the track which appears to be the most suitable track, and serve on each party a notice of proposed allocation. The parties will be invited to fill in a directions questionnaire; there are different forms of directions questionnaire for small claims track claims and fast and multi-track claims. The court may hold an allocation hearing, if necessary before making an allocation decision. After a claim has been allocated to a track, the court may make a subsequent order reallocating it to a different track.

5.2.11 Applications

The general rules for applications for court orders are set out in CPR Part 23. Where a party wishes to make an application he should file form N244 together with any evidence he wishes to rely upon in support with the court and serve copies on the other parties. In general, the minimum time for the service of an application is three clear days before the hearing. The court may deal with certain applications without a hearing.

Where injunctions are being sought it may be necessary to make an application without notice being given to the other party. This may be because the application is urgent, or because to give notice would destroy the purpose of the application (for example where the court is being asked to make a freezing order). Where the court makes an order on a 'without notice' basis, it will direct that a further hearing should take place with the other party being put on notice.

5.2.12 Appeals

Appeals are governed by CPR Part 52, Part IV of the Access to Justice Act 1999 and the Access to Justice Act 1999 (Destination of Appeals) Order 2000, SI 2000/1071. In general, permission is required to appeal from any decision of any judge or Master in the High Court or County Court (the most important exception to the requirement for permission being appeals against committal orders). Permission may be given either by the judge who made the decision under appeal or by the court that will hear the appeal. However, where the decision under appeal was itself made on an appeal, permission can only be given by the Court of Appeal.

Appeals lie as follows:

- from a County Court district judge to a County Court circuit judge;
- from a County Court circuit judge, where the decision under appeal is a final decision made in multi-track or specialist proceedings, to the Court of Appeal;
- from a County Court circuit judge, where the decision under appeal was itself made on appeal, to the Court of Appeal;
- in all other cases from a County Court circuit judge to a High Court judge;
- from a district judge or Master of the High Court to a High Court judge;
- from a High Court Judge to the Court of Appeal;
- from the Court of Appeal, to the Supreme Court of the United Kingdom.

Where a party wishes to appeal a decision he must file an appellant's notice (form N161 for all appeals apart from on the small claims track in which case an N164) within 21 days of the decision. This must then be served on other parties within seven days of being filed with the court. Where the party requires permission to appeal, this is sought on the same form. The court has power in an appropriate case to extend the time for filing form N161.

5.3 LITIGANTS WITH PHYSICAL DISABILITIES

5.3.1 Implications and solutions

Many forms of physical disability (or mental impairment falling short of incapacity) may affect the ability of an older person to participate in litigation, but when the problem is drawn to the attention of the court, steps may be taken to cope with the impairment:

- Impaired mobility may render it impossible to gain access to the court or cope in a particular courtroom – transfer the case to a court in the area where the disabled party resides or with disabled access.
- Impaired hearing or vision may make it difficult to follow what is going on – move the hearing to a courtroom or chambers with facilities for the hard of hearing or produce all documents in large print.
- Communication limitations may prevent others from understanding the individual, or vice versa – arrange for an interpreter to be present and allow a longer time estimate.
- Limited concentration spans or the need for regular medication may make it impossible to remain in court for more than a limited period – arrange regular adjournments or shorter hearings.
- Some ailment may make it impossible to attend court at all – arrange for the evidence of the disabled person to be taken away from the court prior to the hearing or for the hearing to take place other than in a courtroom.

5.3.2 Evidence

Need to attend court

The court now controls the issues on which it requires evidence and the way that evidence is given. It will only be necessary for a party or witness to attend a hearing (other than the trial) to give evidence if cross-examination is required. A statement or pleading verified by a 'statement of truth' may be treated as evidence of the facts stated if it has been duly served on the other parties.

At the trial itself oral evidence is generally required. Witness statements will have been served in advance and will generally stand as evidence in chief, being amplified only with the permission of the court. The court may take into account the age or infirmity of a potential witness when deciding whether evidence is required from that source.

For evidence see CPR Part 32 and the Practice Direction. For the need to attend court see CPR Part 34 and the Practice Direction.

Taking evidence away from court

When an elderly person is too infirm to attend the hearing, arrangements may be made for that person's evidence to be taken in advance in a manner that suits the circumstances (the procedure is known as taking depositions). This could be in a local court before the district judge, or in the individual's own home or a nursing home before an independent solicitor appointed for the purpose. The power is discretionary but an order will usually be made (and is often made by consent) where the witness:

- is too old and frail to attend the trial;
- is so ill or infirm that there is no prospect of being able to attend the trial;
- might die before the trial;
- intends to leave the country before the trial.

The procedure for taking depositions is to be found in CPR rules 34.8–34.12.

Hearings other than in a courtroom

Where the circumstances render it expedient in the interests of justice the court may arrange the trial at, or adjourn it to, the place where a party or witness is, so as to allow for the participation and oral examination of that person at the trial itself. This could be the individual's own home or a nursing home. See CPR rule 2.7 which provides that a court may sit anywhere.

Interpreters

The Equality Act 2010 places an obligation on the court, as a service provider, to make reasonable adjustments for disabled persons. For example, in the Royal Courts of Justice, defendants or claimants who are hearing impaired may request a BSL interpreter; the court requires at least three days' notice of such a requirement. For more information on the Equality Act 2010, see **6.14**.

5.3.3   Representation

Rights of audience in court are strictly controlled. A party to proceedings has a right of audience in his capacity as such but exercising a right of audience is a reserved legal activity and only an individual authorised by a regulator (such as a barrister, solicitor or Fellow of the Institute of Legal Executives) may carry out such activities (see Legal Services Act 2007). The judge may refuse to hear a person who would otherwise have a right of audience in a specific instance, but reasons must be given.

An attorney under an EPA does not have a right of audience on behalf of the donor (*Gregory* v. *Turner* [2003] EWCA Civ 183). By analogy an attorney under an LPA would not have a right of audience on behalf of the donor. This does not prevent the attorney from applying to the court to become the litigation friend on behalf of the person for whom they act (see **5.4**). In exceptional circumstances the court may grant a lay person a right of audience for particular proceedings (*Clarkson* v. *Gilbert* [2000] 3 FCR 10).

McKenzie friend

During a hearing in open court (and generally also in private) a litigant in person has the right to be accompanied by a 'friend' to take notes, quietly make suggestions and give advice. The judge has discretion to refuse this if the friend is not acting in the best interests of the litigant (e.g. pursuing a personal agenda). This is not the same as allowing such person to act as a representative although where a litigant in person is elderly, disabled or inarticulate the judge may seek assistance from any such person present in court who clearly has the confidence of the litigant. There has been a worrying trend of 'professional' McKenzie friends who charge for their services. Such individuals are unlikely to possess professional indemnity insurance and are not subject to regulation.

Lay representatives

At a small claims hearing any person (known as a lay representative) may speak on behalf of a party. This is a right of audience only and does not extend to the conduct of the litigation generally. The permission of the court is required if the party is not present (CPR PD 27, para.3.2(3)) and permission is unlikely to be refused in the case of a responsible representative where the party is unable to attend due to infirmity or disability. The judge may refuse to hear an unsuitable lay representative but the reasons should be stated and the court is entitled to expect the representative to behave honestly, reasonably and responsibly.

5.4 LITIGANTS WITH MENTAL DISABILITIES

Special procedures apply in respect of proceedings by and against a mentally incapacitated litigant. These ensure that a representative is appointed, the court approves compromises and settlements of claims, and there is supervision of any money recovered.

5.4.1 Rules

The procedures are to be found in the following rules (see **5.2.2**):

- CPR Part 21 'Children and Protected Parties', and PD 21.
- FPR, Part 15 'Representation of Protected Parties'.

- Insolvency Rules 1986, Part 7, Chapter 7 'Persons incapable of managing their affairs'.
- COPR Part 17, rules 140–149 'Litigation Friend'.

Definitions

In proceedings by and against a person under a disability, the rules refer to a child where the person is under 18, or to a protected party. 'Protected party' is defined as: 'a party, or an intended party, who lacks capacity to conduct the proceedings' (CPR rule 21.1). 'Lacks capacity' has the same meaning as within the Mental Capacity Act (MCA) 2005. The old terminology of referring to protected parties as 'patients' should be avoided.

The same definition is also used to establish the jurisdiction of the Court of Protection to administer the property and affairs of adults lacking capacity (see generally **4.6**). The test of capacity to conduct proceedings was considered by the Supreme Court in *Dunhill* v. *Burgin* [2014] UKSC 18 (see also *Masterman-Lister* v. *Jewell* [2002] EWCA Civ 1889). The Supreme Court considered that the test of capacity to conduct proceedings should be applied to the claim the claimant in fact has, rather than the claim formulated by her lawyers. Although in general capacity is issue specific, the approach to capacity to conduct proceedings would appear to be holistic (i.e. addressed to proceedings as a whole rather than individual decisions during proceedings), provided of course that the protected person's capacity does not fluctuate. As the Supreme Court in *Dunhill* said (at para.[15]):

> ... a party whose capacity does not fluctuate either should or should not require a litigation friend throughout the proceedings. It would make no sense to apply a capacity test to each individual decision required in the course of the proceedings.

5.4.2 Assessing capacity

In accordance with MCA 2005 there is no longer a presumption that a person who lacks capacity to manage his property and affairs also lacks capacity to conduct legal proceedings. The rules assume that you know whether a party lacks mental capacity. In case of doubt the proceedings should be stayed while the court deals with this as a preliminary issue. This may raise particular issues in the context of settling proceedings with a party who may lack capacity.

Unlike the Court of Protection, other courts do not have specific facilities to investigate (e.g. to obtain medical evidence):

- The Official Solicitor may be referred to where assistance is required.
- Under the CPR the court can give permission for steps to be taken before the finding has been made and a representative appointed (CPR rule 21.3(2) and see FPR rule 15.3(1) (in very similar terms)).
- A medical report is likely to be necessary (see *Masterman-Lister* v. *Brutton & Co* [2002] EWCA Civ 1889).

If the Court of Protection has already assumed jurisdiction over the property and affairs of the person who lacks mental capacity and specifically authorised a person to conduct proceedings, then that person will be entitled to conduct proceedings.

The judge may be prepared to find that the party is incapable of conducting the relevant litigation by reason of conduct in or giving rise to the proceedings, and the question is then whether this is by reason of an impairment of, or a disturbance in the functioning of, the mind or brain. There is no difficulty in the case of a claimant because the proceedings may be stayed until that party submits to a medical examination. A defendant who will not submit to a medical examination does, however, present a problem.

5.4.3 Procedure

Need for a representative

A protected party must have a representative to conduct proceedings, whether bringing or defending them. In civil proceedings and family proceedings this representative is a 'litigation friend'. Any step which might normally have been taken in the proceedings may be taken by the representative, but steps otherwise taken on behalf of a protected party may not be effective. The protected party's solicitor may be personally liable for the costs wasted even though ignorant of the incapacity: see *Yonge* v. *Toynbee* [1910] 1 KB 215.

In the absence of a person being authorised to conduct proceedings by the Court of Protection, a representative may nominate himself and provided he gives the required notice to the other party and to the court, he may act as such without a court order. In default, the court may appoint a representative. If a party becomes a protected party during the course of proceedings an application must be made for such an appointment to be made.

The procedure for appointing, removing or changing the representative is to be found in the relevant court rules.

Who is appointed

A person within the jurisdiction not being under an incapacity and not having an interest adverse to the protected party or being connected to an opposing party may be a litigation friend. For instance, a person authorised by the Court of Protection to conduct proceedings on behalf of a person who lacks mental capacity (usually the deputy, unless there is a clear conflict of interest) is entitled to become the representative. Otherwise it should be a substantial person and a relation of or person connected with the protected party, or friend of the family, and not a mere volunteer. If no suitable person can be found the Official Solicitor may be appointed but should first be consulted and give his consent.

A person may become the litigation friend of a protected party if he (CPR rule 21.4(3)):

(a)   can fairly and competently conduct proceedings on behalf of the ... protected party; and

(b)   has no interest adverse to that of the ... protected party.

If the protected party is a claimant and the litigation friend wishes to be appointed without a court order he must also undertake to pay any costs which the protected party is ordered to pay in the proceedings.

Unless he or she is also a deputy appointed by the Court of Protection or an attorney under a registered EPA or LPA, the representative will have no status in regard to the affairs of the person who lacks mental capacity outside the proceedings.

Service of proceedings

If a party is a protected party, proceedings must be served upon, initially, the person authorised by the Court of Protection (if any, including an attorney under a registered EPA, the donee of an LPA or a deputy) or (if there is no such person) an adult with whom the protected party resides or in whose care he is and thereafter the duly authorised representative of the person who lacks mental capacity (or solicitor on the record) (see CPR rules 6.13, 6.25).

The court may make an order for deemed service or dispensing with service in appropriate circumstances and can order that proceedings be served on the protected party himself or some other person.

Compromises and settlements

No compromise or settlement of a claim for a protected party is valid without the approval of the court, but an action may be brought solely for that purpose:

- this extends to costs and applies even if the representative is the deputy or attorney;
- the overriding consideration is the interest of the protected party, having regard to all the circumstances of the case;
- the approval of the Court of Protection is not required.

Following the decision of the Supreme Court in *Dunhill* v. *Burgin* [2014] UKSC 18 (see **5.4.1**), extreme care must be taken in settling proceedings with parties who may lack capacity to carry out litigation. In that case, a compromise agreement was set aside more than a decade later on the basis that a party to the compromise had lacked capacity at the relevant time and therefore that the approval of the court was required by the relevant rules.

See CPR rule 21.10 and PD 21, para.5.

5.4.4   General matters

Evidence

In civil and family proceedings evidence may only be given by an individual who is considered by the judge to be competent to give evidence. Evidence may be admitted as to the capacity of the witness in general terms but not as to the likelihood of being able to give a truthful account.

A different technique is required when examining vulnerable witnesses and the judge should control this where necessary. The aim is to elicit true and accurate information and not to break the already vulnerable witness. You should take account of the general considerations relevant to communicating with any elderly or potentially incapable client which are set out at **2.2.1**.

Limitation of actions

The limitation period will vary depending on the cause of action (e.g. six years for an action on a contract and three years for a personal injury claim). Special rules apply if the person was under a disability when the right of action accrued:

- the action may be brought within six years of the date when the disability ceased or the person died;
- where a disability arises after the cause of action has accrued, time will continue to run;
- the court has a discretion to extend the time for bringing personal injury claims;
- a person is treated as under a disability while he lacks capacity (within the meaning of MCA 2005) to conduct legal proceedings.

Whether a person lacks capacity is a question of fact to be decided in each individual case (see **Chapter 1** and **5.4.1**). There are no longer any presumptions that a person is under a disability for the purposes of limitation.

See the Limitation Act 1980, ss.28(1), 33(3)(d), 38(2) and (3) (as amended).

Stay of execution

If proceedings are taken to enforce a judgment against a protected party a court would stay execution to enable steps to be taken on the protected party's behalf, for example:

- an application to the Court of Protection for the appointment of a deputy;
- registration of an EPA; or
- presumably, the execution of an LPA if the protected party has capacity to do so.

Injunctions

Being a protected party is not itself a bar to the granting of an injunction and the question is whether the person understood the particular proceedings and the nature and requirements of the injunction. An injunction ought not to be granted against a person who is incapable of understanding what he is doing or that it is wrong since he would not be capable of complying with it, and:

- Any breach would not be subject to effective enforcement since he would have a defence to an application for committal for contempt (*Wookey* v. *Wookey*; *Re S (A Minor)* [1991] 3 All ER 365).
- The use of MHA 1983 powers of compulsory admission to hospital might be considered but if the protected party's mental state does not justify this no effective remedy is available.

The court could make a hospital order under Contempt of Court Act 1981, s.14(4) where the party was suffering from serious mental incapacity at the time of the contempt proceedings but if that incapacity had existed earlier it would have precluded any contempt (*Wookey* v. *Wookey*).

5.4.5 Costs

Solicitor and client

Unless the court otherwise directs, the costs payable in most proceedings by a protected party to his own solicitor must be assessed by the court and no costs are payable to that solicitor except the amount so allowed. Solicitors should be aware that the rule extends to costs payable to a protected party by another party. If those costs can be agreed and the protected party's solicitor waives any claim to further costs, the district judge may waive detailed assessment if satisfied with the amount notified (see CPR PD 46, para.2.1(b)).

Conditional fee agreements (CFAs)

Before 1 April 2013, conditional fee agreements were a popular means of funding civil litigation. The structure of the regime under the Access to Justice Act 1999 was that a party would enter into an arrangement with his legal advisers such that they would work on a 'no win no fee' basis, but would be entitled to a 'success fee' in the form of an uplift in the event they were successful. The party would take out 'after the event' (ATE) insurance to cover their potential costs liability if they were unsuccessful. Both the success fee and the ATE premium were recoverable from the unsuccessful parties. For conditional fee agreements entered into before 1 April 2013, ATE premiums and success fees remain recoverable. A challenge to these provisions on the basis that they were incompatible with the European Convention on Human Rights was unsuccessful in the Supreme Court (see *Coventry* v. *Lawrence* [2015] UKSC 50, but see also *MGN Ltd* v. *United Kingdom* (2011) 53 EHRR 195).

However, following changes introduced by the Legal Aid, Sentencing and Punishment of Offenders Act (LASPO) 2012, these are a much less attractive option for parties. The main change introduced by LASPO is that the success fee and ATE premium must be paid by the party and are not recoverable by the defendant. A litigation friend is able to apply to recover the amount payable in respect of ATE insurance or a success fee, provided that it has been reasonably incurred and is reasonable in amount (CPR rule 21.12).

Costs of another party

The representative may be ordered to pay the costs of the proceedings (and will on commencing them have had to give an undertaking to pay any costs which the protected party may be ordered to pay). In the absence of misconduct on his part, the representative will be entitled to recover any costs awarded against him from the property of the protected party (if any) (CPR rule 21.4).

Liability of solicitor

A solicitor may be ordered to pay the wasted costs incurred where he or she brings or continues an action for a claimant, or defends an action for a defendant, who is or has become a protected party, without a litigation friend acting for him (*Yonge* v. *Toynbee* [1910] 1 KB 215, CA).

Public funding

The availability of funding from the Legal Aid Agency does not depend upon age or mental capacity. It may be sought on behalf of a protected party based upon the merits of the case and his financial circumstances. The application will be submitted by the person acting (or proposing to act) for the protected party but the financial circumstances of this representative will not be taken into account. Unfortunately, public funding has been the subject of wide-ranging cuts, and is available in increasingly fewer circumstances.

5.4.6 Disposal of damages

The court must decide how damages awarded to a protected party are to be handled. The award itself should allow for the additional cost of administering the damages.

Procedure

A protected beneficiary is a protected party who lacks capacity to manage and control money recovered by him or for his benefit in proceedings (CPR rule 21.1(2)). If a protected party has capacity to manage and control his damages they can be paid directly to him.

Money awarded or otherwise paid to a protected beneficiary must be dealt with in accordance with the court's directions under CPR rule 21.11. CPR PD 21, para.8.1 provides that the court may:

1. direct the money to be paid into court for investment in which case directions should be given as to the general aims for the fund and also of the type of investment;
2. direct that sums be paid directly to the protected beneficiary or his litigation friend or his legal representative either to defray expenses or otherwise for the benefit of the protected party;
3. direct that the application in respect of investment be transferred to a local district registry.

However, CPR PD 21, para.10.2 limits the court's powers. It provides that where the amount awarded exceeds £50,000 the directions must specify that the litigation friend must apply to the Court of Protection for the appointment of a deputy, unless a person has been appointed to manage the protected beneficiary's property and affairs as:

- an attorney under a registered EPA;
- the donee of an LPA;
- a deputy appointed by the Court of Protection.

Where the amount is less than £50,000 the funds may be retained in court and invested in accordance with the court's directions in the same manner as the court would deal with funds held on behalf of a child (i.e. possibly by directing that the funds be paid directly to the litigation friend to invest in a bank or building society). The Court of Protection may also authorise a sum of £50,000 or more to be retained in court and dealt with in this way.

There is therefore a tension between the wide scope of para.8.1 and the narrower focus of para.10.2. The editors of *Heywood & Massey: Court of Protection Practice* suggest that CPR PD 21, para.8.1 permits the court to use funds for the immediate needs of the protected beneficiary but that their long-term investment and use is a matter for the Court of Protection. An order transferring a fund to the Court of Protection should follow the wording of form N292.

See generally: CPR rules 21.1 and 21.11 and PD 21, paras.8 and 10.

5.5 CHALLENGING DECISIONS

5.5.1 General

There are many situations in which you may need to help an older client challenge a decision made by the authorities, or even a failure to make a decision. The emphasis in this chapter is upon the provision of services by the local authority, but the following are examples of other situations in which older clients may seek your assistance:

- appeals against decisions on claims for state benefits (see **Chapter 13**);
- appeals against decisions of local authorities on claims for housing benefit or council tax rebate (see **Chapter 13**);
- appeals against decisions of valuation officers on council tax banding (see **Chapter 13**);
- refusals of planning permission (see generally the appeal procedures under the Town and Country Planning Acts);
- compulsory purchase and compensation relating to highway development;
- decisions relating to registration of residential care homes or private nursing homes (see **Chapter 9**);
- decisions on healthcare or medical treatment (see **Chapters 10, 11** and **12**; for the provision of community care services see **Chapter 8**).

When acting for a client in dealings with the authorities, do not be too quick to use your letter heading as this can be counter-productive. It may result in a premature reference to the legal department! Assist the client to write a well-reasoned letter and then monitor progress. Advising the client in the background is not a sign of weakness and may be effective in clarifying the approach of the authority before seeking to challenge this when necessary.

5.5.2 Entitlement to services

Assessments and case conferences are part of the procedure for the provision of services. Delay and indecision by the authority may be used to avoid provision when shortage of funds or lack of facilities make it difficult to fulfil a request.

Before embarking on a course of action against an authority, consider using the following checklist.

5.5.3 Checklist when dissatisfied with local authority

- Has a decision been made by the relevant authority?
- Is it a request which the authority is obliged to consider? The statutory duties of the authority may be general in nature and not enforceable in respect of an individual.

181

- Identify the authority, department and officer responsible for providing the services required and complain to this officer.
- Ask for a review of a decision and be prepared to compromise.
- Follow any complaints or appeal procedure.
- Check the time limits for taking any other available legal action.
- Should the Minister be asked to use his default powers?
- Is it a case for judicial review?
- Is it maladministration which can be referred to an Ombudsman?

5.5.4 Structure of local authorities

Most parts of England have two tiers of local government:

- county councils, generally responsible for provision of services to elderly persons through their adult social services departments;
- district (or borough or city) councils, responsible for housing and environmental health.

In some areas, e.g. metropolitan districts, Greater London boroughs and unitary authorities, the responsibilities of the county level and the district level are combined in a single local authority.

Parish (or community or town) councils operate at a level below district and borough councils and in some cases, unitary authorities. They address local issues such as providing community centres.

The powers of councils are generally delegated: elected councillors are collectively responsible for policy decisions, officers are appointed to carry out policy decisions but have delegated powers and administration is divided into departments each headed by a senior officer:

- housing: deals with provision of housing (including homeless persons);
- environmental health: covers public health and the environment;
- social services: responsibilities include welfare of the elderly.

5.5.5 Complaints procedures

In many instances internal complaints procedures are available and you should be given information about these on enquiry. Any complaint must be in the appropriate form to the right person, but whether or not there is a formal procedure you may make representations to elected councillors, the chief executive or head of department. Most local authorities now have service charters advising of their standards and complaints procedures.

Local authorities must establish and publicise the existence of a procedure for considering any representations or complaints with respect to the discharge of their social services functions or the failure to discharge those functions. This must provide:

- a definition of a complaint and identify who can bring a complaint;
- for the role of the independent person;
- support for persons who need assistance in bringing a complaint.

See **Chapter 8** for further details of social services complaints procedures and **Chapter 10** for the complaints procedures available in respect of healthcare.

5.5.6 Appeal procedures

If not satisfied with a decision always enquire whether there is a formal appeal procedure and if so the time limits for invoking this. The decision-making authority will be under an obligation to tell you if there is a procedure. There is no 'appeal' against a financial assessment for community care, although it is possible to evoke the complaints procedure if guidance has not been followed, complain to the Ombudsman or seek judicial review.

5.6 OMBUDSMEN

Ombudsmen are independent people who investigate and report on complaints by UK residents about treatment by particular public bodies. At the time of writing, the government has indicated that the draft Public Services Ombudsman Bill will be published in the 2015–16 parliamentary session. This follows proposals to reform public services ombudsmen and a consultation. The proposed measure includes absorbing the functions of the Parliamentary and Health Service Ombudsman, the Local Government Ombudsman and potentially the Housing Ombudsman.

Complaints about Welsh bodies are made to the Public Service Ombudsman for Wales (see **www.ombudsman-wales.org.uk**).

5.6.1 Key points

There is generally a 12-month time limit for bringing a complaint to an ombudsman. All existing means of seeking redress must first be exhausted and matters before the courts cannot be investigated.

The complaint is normally made by a person who has been personally affected. Where he or she is for any reason unable to act for him or herself the complaint may usually be made by a member of his or her family or some body or individual suitable to represent him or her. Legal representation is not usually necessary but a solicitor may be able to assist in presenting the complaint.

The procedure is usually private but the resulting report may be published. Findings are not legally enforceable but the report may result in redress where there is no legal remedy, e.g. compensation or an apology and an attempt to discourage similar administrative action in the future.

5.6.2   Parliamentary and Health Service Ombudsman

The Parliamentary and Health Service Ombudsman is someone completely independent of the government who can investigate complaints by members of the public about the way they have been treated by government departments and agencies.

These departments and agencies include the Department for Business, Innovation and Skills, Department for Work and Pensions, Department for Transport, the Department for Culture, Media and Sport and the Department of Energy and Climate Change. Also included are certain non-departmental public bodies such as HMRC, the Legal Aid Agency, the Law Commission, the Land Registry, the Information Commissioner and the Commission for Equality and Human Rights – the list is frequently updated.

Complaints about government policy or the content of legislation are not included but are matters for Parliament. Complaints must be channelled through an MP who will usually seek to sort the matter out with the department concerned first. A complaint must normally be made within a year of when a problem first becomes apparent. The Ombudsman decides whether to carry out a full investigation and he may inspect government files and papers and can summon anyone to give evidence in an investigation (see **www.ombudsman.org.uk**).

5.6.3   The Local Government Ombudsmen

The three Local Government Ombudsmen deal with complaints by anyone who considers that he has suffered injustice because of maladministration by a local authority. The LGO is the Social Care Ombudsman and investigates all complaints about adult care services.

Their remit does not include parish councils or certain other authorities (e.g. police authorities). If the complaint passes initial screening it will be taken up in correspondence but there is power to examine the authority's internal papers and to take written and oral evidence from anyone who can provide relevant information (see **www.lgo.org.uk**).

5.7   LEGAL CHALLENGES

When negotiation and persuasion, and the use of complaints procedures when available, do not result in the needs of the client being met it becomes necessary to consider the legal remedies that are available. There may be a choice of remedies but equally none may offer the certainty of positive results within an acceptable timescale. Nevertheless, the threat to use one of these remedies or the taking of the initial steps may be sufficient to draw a response and create a further climate for negotiation.

5.7.1 Complaint to the Minister

Many statutes vest supervisory powers in government ministers and codes of guidance are issued by government departments. Some statutes giving powers to or imposing duties on local authorities authorise the Minister to make regulations prescribing how they shall exercise or perform these. A complaint may be made direct to a Minister if the authority does not comply with his directions and he may exercise default powers, although these are appropriate to deal with a general breakdown in some service provision rather than individual cases.

The Minister may call the authority to account for failure to exercise its functions, direct the authority to comply and take over the authority's functions (e.g. National Health Service Act 2006, s.66).

There is a power for the Secretary of State to declare local authorities in default if they fail to comply with their social services duties, to direct compliance within time limits and to enforce this by judicial review (mandatory order): Local Authority Social Services Act 1970, s.7D (as amended).

5.7.2 Small claims procedure

Do not overlook the possibility of assisting the client with a claim in the County Court where operational failings by a service provider (including a local authority) have resulted in financial loss to an elderly client or carer. An example is repeated failure to provide agreed transport to a day care centre resulting in expenditure on taxis so that the carer can meet other commitments. Under the above principles there remains some prospect of success, and the threat of a claim or the issue of proceedings may in itself be sufficient to persuade the service provider to be more careful in the future. Repeat claims could be brought if there was a continuing failure.

If the claim is under £10,000 (£1,000 for a personal injury or housing disrepair claim) it is likely to be allocated to the small claims track which may provide advantages to the claimant (see **5.2.3**).

Also, while you may assist with the preparation of the case your client should be able to cope at the hearing itself if funds are limited as:

- the hearing is relatively informal and before a district judge;
- the district judge without 'entering the arena' must seek to make good the deficiencies of an unrepresented party;
- a lay representative (e.g. a relative or friend) will be permitted to address the court.

If funding from the Legal Aid Agency is not available, resist any application that the case should not be allocated to the small claims track by arguing that:

- there is no difficult issue of law or exceptional complexity in the facts;
- the client cannot afford legal representation whereas the local authority has the resources of its legal department;

- the client could not pursue the claim if faced with an open court trial and the risk of costs.

See CPR Part 27 and PD 27.

5.7.3 Judicial review

Judicial review enables people to challenge the lawfulness of decisions made by public bodies and others exercising public functions through the process of litigation. The High Court may review the legality of a course of action by a public body and provide one or more of the following remedies in a final order:

- a mandatory order: requiring the performance of a specific public law duty;
- a quashing order: quashing a decision which is invalid;
- a prohibiting order: prohibiting the body from acting in an unlawful manner;
- a declaration: declaring what the law is.

A typical order might include a quashing order to quash an unlawful decision and a mandatory order to require a new decision according to the law. As an interim measure the court may grant an injunction (which may be of a mandatory nature).

Claims for judicial review are heard by the Administrative Court. Relief is available where the decisions of public bodies (and also inferior courts and tribunals) are unlawful, which includes exercises of powers and decisions that are:

- illegal (in the sense that they are done without the legal power to do so). This includes:

    - going beyond the scope of the power;
    - using a power for an improper purpose;
    - ignoring a relevant consideration or taking into account an irrelevant consideration;
    - unlawfully delegating a power or decision;

- unreasonable/irrational;
- procedurally improper or unfair (this includes decisions affected by actual or apparent bias);
- contrary to a legitimate expectation; or
- contrary to the Human Rights Act 1998 (see below).

These categories of grounds of review are neither exhaustive nor mutually exclusive. In addition to these traditionally recognised grounds, English courts are increasingly recognising 'proportionality' as a distinct ground of judicial review (see e.g. the discussion in *Pham* v. *Secretary of State for the Home Department* [2015] UKSC 19, per Lord Mance, Lord Reed and Lord Sumption).

The claim must be made promptly and in any event within three months of the grounds arising unless time is extended by the court (e.g. because of the need to get public funding) (a different time limit applies to a claim under the Human Rights Act 1998, see below).

The applicant should normally first comply with the pre-action protocol for judicial review. This requires the applicant to send a letter before action to the potential defendant identifying the decision or act that is being challenged and explaining the reasons for the challenge. A standard letter form is annexed to the protocol.

Before he can pursue the claim the applicant must obtain permission to proceed from a High Court judge. The claim is commenced by issuing the Part 8 claim procedure, as modified by CPR Part 54. This should be filed with the court accompanied by:

- a detailed statement of the grounds for bringing the claim;
- a statement of the facts relied upon;
- any applications for extending time for bringing the claim or directions;
- any written evidence in support of the claim;
- a copy of any order that the applicant wishes to have quashed;
- an approved copy of the decision of any court or tribunal that is being challenged;
- copies of any documents upon which the applicant relies;
- copies of any relevant statutory material;
- a reading list (see CPR PD 54A, para.5.6).

The claim form must be served on the defendant and any interested party within seven days of issue.

The statutory framework for applications for judicial review under Senior Courts Act 1981, s.31 was modified by the Criminal Justice and Courts Act 2015, with effect from 13 April 2015. The amendments require the court to refuse permission on an application for judicial review if it considers it highly likely that the defendant's conduct in the matter in question would not have affected the outcome for the applicant.

In the first instance the court will usually determine whether permission to proceed should be granted on the papers alone. If permission is refused at this stage, the applicant can request the matter to be reconsidered at an oral hearing. If permission is refused after an oral hearing an appeal lies to the Court of Appeal.

Where permission is given the court may give directions. The defendant and any other person served with the claim form has 35 days from the date of the grant of permission to serve a response and any written evidence. Disclosure is not usually required. Hearings normally take place before a single judge in open court and are often short (an expedited hearing may be sought) usually consisting of oral argument on legal matters based on the written evidence. The court may hear oral evidence, although it is rare for this to occur.

The claimant must have a sufficient interest in the matter to bring a claim in judicial review. Judicial review is a last resort, and generally other available remedies should be pursued first. Moreover, the remedies in judicial review are discretionary and detailed rules have developed to define the circumstances in which the court will intervene.

5.7.4 Breach of statutory duty

In certain limited situations a private action may be brought against public authorities for breach of statutory duty. Claimants must generally be able to establish a specific duty owed to them personally, rather than a duty owed to society at large.

In *X (Minors)* v. *Bedfordshire CC* [1995] 2 AC 633, the House of Lords considered that a private law cause of action will arise only if it can be shown as a matter of construction of the statute, that the duty was imposed for the protection of a limited class of the public, and that Parliament intended to confer on members of that class a private right of action for breach of that duty. Where there is already an adequate remedy under the law of tort or under the statute, it is unlikely that a cause of action for breach of statutory duty will arise. Generally, the courts are reluctant to impose liability, particularly where the authority is performing a welfare role or a regulatory role.

5.7.5 Negligence

In the absence of express statutory authority, a local authority is liable for torts in the same way as an individual. Although ordinary principles of negligence apply, the application of these principles to public authorities gives rise to considerable complexity in practice.

In common with all actions in negligence, the claimant must establish that the authority owed her a duty of care. In contrast with claims for breach of statutory duty, the first question the court will consider is whether the statute excludes a cause of action in negligence. If the policy of a statute is not to create a statutory liability to pay compensation, the same policy will usually exclude the existence of a common law duty of care. Another preliminary question is whether the conduct complained of is an act or an omission. As a very general rule, an omission to act is very unlikely to give rise to a cause of action in negligence: *Stovin* v. *Wise* [1996] AC 923 (failure by highway authority to modify a dangerous junction where the claimant had an accident).

Even if there is no duty to provide a service (e.g. where there is merely a general duty or a power) there may be a common law duty of care in the manner in which it is carried out. This may possibly extend to administrative or operational failure to provide or in the provision of an agreed service: see *Barrett* v. *Enfield LBC* [2001] 2 AC 550 and *Phelps* v. *Hillingdon LBC* [2001] 2 AC 619. The negligent manner in which a public authority carried out its statutory duty could give rise to liability where it created the danger which caused the injury: *Capital and Counties plc* v. *Hampshire CC* [1997] QB 1004 (negligence by fire brigade which owed a duty of care when it turned off a sprinkler system).

The fact that the acts which are claimed to be negligent are carried out within the ambit of a statutory discretion is not of itself a reason to prevent a claim in negligence arising (*Barrett* v. *Enfield*). However, where what has been done has involved the weighing of competing public interests or has been dictated by considerations on which Parliament could not have intended that the courts would substitute their views for the views of Ministers or officials, the court should decide that the issue is non-justiciable on the basis that the decision was made in the exercise of a statutory discretion (*Phelps* v. *Hillingdon* and also *D* v. *East Berkshire Community Health NHS Trust* [2005] UKHL 23).

In practice where a claim is brought in negligence, a claim for breach of a statutory duty in the strict sense is often pleaded in the alternative (see above).

An authority may also be vicariously liable for the torts of its employees. There is no public policy reason why an authority may not be vicariously liable for the acts of a social worker who fails to provide significant information to foster parents: *W* v. *Essex CC* [2001] 2 AC 592 (they were not told that the foster child was an active sexual abuser and their own children were abused); *DN* v. *Greenwich LBC* [2004] EWCA Civ 1659 (the local authority was liable for the negligence of its education psychologist in failing to identify the claimant's complex social and communication needs). An authority will not be vicariously liable for an independent act by an employee outside the course of employment. However, a range of acts may be connected with the employment: *Lister* v. *Hesley Hall Ltd* [2001] UKHL 22 (employer vicariously liable for sexual abuse of children by warden of school boarding house).

5.7.6 Breach of contract

If a promise has been made it may be enforceable as such against the authority. This may possibly extend to the provision of agreed services for which a payment is made by the recipient (see the Supply of Goods and Services Act 1982).

5.7.7 Human Rights Act 1998

European Convention on Human Rights

The following substantive rights guaranteed by the European Convention on Human Rights may be of direct relevance to the older citizen, although these are subject to qualifications not mentioned here.

- Article 2: 'Everyone's right to life shall be protected by law.' This creates a positive obligation to safeguard life and can be relevant to the provision of medical treatment.
- Article 3: 'No one shall be subjected to ... inhuman or degrading treatment ...' This may be relevant to standards of care provision.

- Article 5: 'Everyone has the right to liberty and security of person.' The 'lawful detention of ... persons of unsound mind' is allowed for but everyone who is deprived of his or her liberty by detention is entitled to have the lawfulness tested by a court and to compensation if it was unlawful. This will be relevant in the fields of mental health and other care provision (see **11.6**).
- Article 6: 'In the determination of his civil rights and obligations ... everyone is entitled to a fair and public hearing within a reasonable time by an independent and impartial tribunal established by law.' This is relevant to access to justice for people with disabilities.
- Article 8: 'Everyone has the right to respect for his private and family life, his home and his correspondence.' This may prove relevant to standards in residential care and nursing homes as well as sheltered housing, but has far wider potential reach.
- Article 9: 'Everyone has the right to freedom of thought, conscience and religion ...' This right has to date received little scrutiny but may be infringed by procedures to protect an elderly person who is perceived to be vulnerable.
- Article 12: the right to marry and found a family. Only the first part of this right is likely to be relevant to the older person but procedures for assessing capacity for marriage could be questioned.
- Article 14: 'The enjoyment of the rights and freedoms set forth in this Convention shall be secured without discrimination on any ground such as sex, race ... religion ... property, birth or other status.'
- Article 1 First Protocol: 'Every ... person is entitled to the peaceful enjoyment of his possessions.' It may be that the absence of accessible legal procedures for decision-making on behalf of those who lack capacity could lead to a breach of this right.

Human Rights Act 1998

The Convention is incorporated into UK domestic law by the Human Rights Act 1998, though with some limitations. The Act came into effect on 1 October 2000. It is unlawful for a public authority to act in a way which is incompatible with a Convention right:

- Individuals are able to rely upon the provisions of the Convention in any legal proceedings although claims brought expressly under it will only be permitted in certain courts.
- A party who wishes to rely on the provisions of the 1998 Act must give full details of his contentions in his statement of case (CPR PD 16, para.16).
- All legislation must be read so far as is possible to give effect to the Convention in a way that is compatible with the rights that it lays down.
- When a court seeks to determine a question arising in connection with a Convention right it must take into account the case law of the European Court of Human Rights.

- Only a victim of an action by a public authority which is incompatible with a Convention right may complain under the Act and the law cannot be challenged in the abstract.
- There is a one-year time limit for bringing proceedings under the Act with discretion to extend this.

If primary legislation proves to be incompatible with the Convention, despite the duty not to so interpret it if possible, all the higher courts can do is make a 'declaration of incompatibility' which may result in the legislation being amended. Courts may, however, within the limit of their general powers, give relief against subordinate legislation. If relief is not granted in our courts, it may still be sought in the European Court of Human Rights.

The 1998 Act may be of assistance in various types of claim. However, it must first be established that the body whose decision is being challenged is a public authority. A housing association may be a public authority in relation to certain actions (*Poplar Housing Association and Regeneration Community Association Ltd* v. *Donoghue* [2001] EWCA Civ 595) but a charity with whom a local authority had arrangements for the provision of accommodation was considered not to be a public authority (*R (on the application of Heather)* v. *Leonard Cheshire Foundation* [2002] EWCA Civ 366; [2002] 2 All ER 936).

Courts which have the power to award damages or order the payment of compensation in civil proceedings have limited powers to award damages in respect of a breach of a person's human rights (see Human Rights Act 1998, s.8).

Authorising deprivations of liberty

In the context of the regime under MCA 2005 (as amended by the Mental Health Act 2007), deprivations of liberty must be authorised using 'deprivation of liberty safeguards' (DOLS). This change was intended to address the so-called 'Bournewood gap', whereby adults who were informally detained, for example in residential care homes, were being deprived of their liberty without adequate safeguards, contrary to art.5 of the European Convention on Human Rights.

In *P* v. *Cheshire West and Chester Council; P and Q* v. *Surrey CC* [2014] UKSC 19, the Supreme Court gave an expansive definition to the concept of a deprivation of liberty. The majority of the Supreme Court applied an 'acid test', asking whether the individual in question was (1) subject to continuous supervision and control; and (2) not free to leave.

Although the decision applies to deprivations of liberty made by the state (e.g. by a local authority or by the NHS), this will apply, for example, where the care is taking place in a care home, in supported living, or in the home of the person. It may also apply when the deprivation of liberty occurs privately, as the UK's positive obligations under art.5 of the Convention may still arise. This is a developing area of law. A number of important practical questions have arisen out of the decision. For example, it would appear that the adult without capacity needs to be a party to the proceedings (see *Re X (Court of Protection Practice)* [2015] EWCA Civ 599). Specialist legal advice should be sought if it appears likely that an older person will be deprived of his or her liberty.

5.8 THE EUROPEAN DIMENSION

5.8.1 The Court of Justice of the European Union

The Court of Justice of the European Union (CJEU), formerly known as the European Court of Justice, is based in Luxembourg and is the ultimate appeal court on matters relating to EU law. Its decisions are binding upon our courts. The CJEU consists of three courts: the Court of Justice, the General Court and the Civil Service Tribunal. The Court of Justice has one judge for each member state and nine Advocates-General. The judges and the Advocates-General are each appointed for a renewable term of six years. They are chosen by member states 'by common accord'. The role of the Advocate-General is to provide a written opinion with a recommendation at the end of the oral procedure; this is not binding but assists the judges who hand down a single judgment. It is notable that there is no provision for dissenting judgments.

Where an issue of EU law arises before a national court, questions of interpretation or validity can be referred to the CJEU for a preliminary ruling:

- The procedure is available to the national court rather than to the parties.
- It is the court which decides the question to be referred although a party may make the initial request for a reference.
- The CJEU may grant legal aid in certain circumstances.

The General Court (European Union), formerly known as the Court of First Instance, is also part of the CJEU, and has 28 judges. The General Court has jurisdiction to determine actions brought by natural or legal persons against acts of the institutions of the European Union and against regulatory acts of those institutions. It also considers actions brought by the member states against the Commission and against the Council. The decisions of the General Court may be subject to an appeal before the Court of Justice on points of law.

5.8.2 European Court of Human Rights

An aggrieved person is able to make a direct complaint to Strasbourg whereupon it will be considered either by a single judge, or by a committee of three or of seven judges. Meritorious complaints are then considered by a Chamber unless they are of particular importance in which case they may be considered by the Grand Chamber.

Complaints can be made only by a victim who has suffered by reason of a violation of one or more of the articles of the European Convention on Human Rights or the First Protocol. Complaints should be made only after all remedies within a domestic legal system have been exhausted and within six months of the exhaustion of those remedies. There is limited legal aid (subject to a means test) which may be available from the Council of Europe.

The Committee of Ministers of the Council of Europe supervises the execution of judgments made by the court, although it cannot force a state to comply and the ultimate sanction is expulsion from the Council of Europe.

It should be noted that the procedure is slow as the court has a large backlog of cases. Changes introduced by the 14th Protocol were intended to streamline applications and reduce the backlog. The 15th Protocol to the Convention will introduce a number of reforms, most notably reducing the time limit to apply to the Strasbourg court from six months to four. On 10 April 2015, the United Kingdom ratified the 15th Protocol; however, it will not enter into force until it has been ratified by all state parties to the Convention. In 2014 the Conservative/Liberal Democrat Coalition government announced that it would not be signing or ratifying Protocol 16 to the Convention (which permits a national court to seek an advisory opinion from Strasbourg in certain circumstances).

CHAPTER 6

The elderly client, society and the law

Hugh Cumber with Julia Krish

6.1 INTRODUCTION

This chapter looks at the civil rights of the elderly client and the way in which these may be affected by increasing age and disability. While **Chapter 4** considered the legal framework for the management of the client's property and affairs, not every aspect of the client's life can at every stage be dealt with in this way. Autonomy, self-determination and dignity are important rights protected by art.8 of the European Convention on Human Rights. For any client, we should begin with a presumption of capacity and provide practical assistance to the client to preserve his or her independence and autonomy as long as possible. Capacity and in particular the issue-specific test of capacity contained in the Mental Capacity Act (MCA) 2005, ss.1–3 are considered in more detail in **Chapter 1**. And there are also personal decisions and circumstances which affect the elderly client and the way he or she conducts life in society. In July 2015, the Law Society published guidance on 'Meeting the needs of vulnerable clients', which sets out the Law Society's view of good practice in this area.

6.2 THE IMPACT OF CAPACITY ON SPECIFIC CONTRACTS

6.2.1 General contracts

A contract may be set aside at the option of a party if it can be shown that he did not understand its nature due to mental incapacity and that the other party knew (or should have been aware) of this. The fact that the contract is unfair will not by itself be sufficient. However, the court may interfere with so-called 'unconscionable bargains' in certain limited circumstances, namely where the terms of the contract are oppressive, one party is at a serious disadvantage in relation to the other, and there is unconscionable conduct on the part of the other party (see *Hart* v. *O'Connor* [1985] 2 All ER 880).

For the contract to be valid, the individual must understand the nature and effect of what he is doing and be capable of agreeing to it. The extent of that understanding depends upon the implications of the contract (in the case of an elderly person it may need to extend to the effect upon state benefits and local authority support). Capacity is judged in respect of each transaction at that moment. Therefore, if a person has capacity to enter into the contract during a lucid interval, then that is sufficient. The appointment of a deputy for a person by the Court of Protection will not prevent him from contracting if he has sufficient capacity to enter into the specific contract which he proposes to enter.

Necessary goods and services

A person who lacks capacity to contract may be required to pay a reasonable price for goods and services that are deemed to be 'necessary'. MCA 2005 defines 'necessary' as 'suitable to a person's condition in life and to his actual requirements at the time when the goods or services are supplied' (s.7(1)); the statutory definition of 'necessary' precisely mirrors the common law rule (see *Aster Healthcare Ltd* v. *Estate of Shafi* [2014] EWCA Civ 1350). This legislation protects both the shop-keeper who may obtain payment for goods and services as well as the incapable person, who is obliged to pay only a 'reasonable price'. Clearly a care home or care agency must be able to expect payment for essential services provided before a deputy has been appointed.

6.2.2 Specific contracts

Bank accounts

In regard to bank and building society accounts (as well as credit or charge cards):

- The duty and authority to pay a customer's cheque is determined by notice of incapacity of a sufficient degree to prevent an understanding of the transaction. The size and nature of the cheque or payment is relevant (see *Drew* v. *Nunn* (1878–79) LR 4 QBD 661).
- By custom a bank is entitled to charge simple interest at a reasonable rate upon overdrafts but a loan is a matter for specific agreement.
- A guarantor may not be liable if the fact of mental incapacity on the part of the debtor was known to all parties but a separate contract of indemnity could be enforced.
- National Savings Bank accounts may be opened on behalf and in the name of persons who lack capacity by that person's deputy (National Savings Bank Act 1971, s.8(1)(f); National Savings Regulations 2015, SI 2015/623, reg.10).
- Accounts may be opened by a deputy or the donee of an LPA or the attorney under a registered EPA for a person without capacity.

Until such time as a bank receives actual notice of a person's incapacity, it tends to look for the ability to provide a consistent signature rather than applying more sophisticated tests. However, once a bank has notice of incapacity, especially formal notice of the appointment of a deputy or of a registered EPA it will generally prevent any use of the account by the customer, even if technically the customer has capacity to manage such an account. Such a practice is likely to be inconsistent with the principles of MCA 2005.

Insurance policies

Any relevant disability must be disclosed on the proposal form and also on renewal, and a policy may be void for non-disclosure. Attorneys and deputies need to take great care when taking out policies or renewing policies where the disability might be relevant, such as health policies or travel insurance. An express declaration as to medical condition or disability may be required.

If the policyholder is incapable when money is payable the insurers will only make payment to a donee of an LPA or an attorney under a registered EPA or pursuant to an order of the Court of Protection. Where money is payable under a life insurance policy, this requirement can be avoided (with sufficient foresight) if the policy is written in trust so that the proceeds are payable to trustees rather than to the incapable proposer.

Agency

The traditional view of agency in the context of the incapacity of the principal is that the authority of an agent depends on the mental capacity of the principal at the time of appointment and throughout the period of the agency, so that it terminates once there is a loss of capacity. However, the current edition of *Bowstead & Reynolds on Agency* casts doubt on the correctness of this view, and in the Supreme Court case of *Dunhill* v. *Burgin* [2014] UKSC 18 the issue was expressly left open by Baroness Hale in her judgment at [31] (see *Bowstead & Reynolds on Agency* (20th edn, 2014) at 2-009 and 10-020).

A power of attorney involves the appointment of an agent, and this agency may be terminated by incapacity unless the power is an EPA that was created under the Enduring Powers of Attorney Act 1985 and duly registered with the Office of the Public Guardian (or the Court of Protection before 1 October 2007) or the agent is the donee of an LPA created under MCA 2005.

6.2.3 Trustees

There is no upper age limit for a trustee but a trustee who is incapable is thereby unable to act in that capacity and should be replaced at the earliest opportunity. Problems most commonly arise where spouses own a property together and therefore hold the legal title as trustees of land. A trustee of land who also has a beneficial interest in the land can delegate his trusteeship under the Trustee Delegation Act 1999 using an EPA or LPA and this delegation can continue even if he loses capacity.

Where the trust involves assets other than land in which the trustee has a beneficial interest, the situation is more complicated. It is obviously desirable to replace the trustee as soon as practicable. There are various means of doing so (for example, under s.36 or s.41 of the Trustee Act 1925), and the method used will depend on whether the trustee is also a beneficiary under the trust (see **17.3.3**).

6.3 CIVIL STATUS

6.3.1 Driving licences

It is an offence to drive a motor vehicle on a road unless the driver holds a licence authorising him or her to drive a vehicle of the class being driven. An applicant for a licence must state whether he is suffering from a 'relevant disability':

- This means either a disability prescribed by the Secretary of State or any other disability which is or may become likely to cause the driving of a vehicle by the applicant to be a source of danger to the public (being under a guardianship order under the Mental Health Act (MHA) 1983 is a prescribed disability).
- The holder of a licence must also report any subsequent 'notifiable' medical condition or disability, which includes Alzheimer's disease and visual impairments, and fines may apply if the holder fails to notify the Driver and Vehicle Licensing Agency (DVLA) which may revoke the person's licence.
- A doctor is required to inform the DVLA if he or she believes a patient is unfit to drive. If the patient does not agree to disclosure, the doctor must notify the patient that the DVLA will be advised, and then write to the DVLA in confidence. The patient must also be informed.
- A deputy needs to notify the DVLA of a patient's incapacity (this can be done by sending the DVLA the licence together with a copy of form COP3, with the doctor's consent or the Court of Protection's approval as of course the medical certificate is for court purposes only); an attorney acting under a registered EPA or donee of an LPA, if the donor has become incapacitated should likewise inform the DVLA of the donor's incapacity.
- DVLA medical officers tend to adhere to rigid guidelines so it is difficult to persuade the DVLA to reverse a decision.
- A right of appeal against a refusal to grant or revocation of a driving licence lies to the magistrates' court for the local justice area in which the aggrieved person resides and few applications are successful. The DVLA usually instructs lawyers and calls medical evidence and costs may be awarded against the appellant (Road Traffic Act 1988, ss.87–94 and 100).

6.3.2 Passports

Where a person is unable to sign a passport application form through mental disability a declaration signed by a person responsible for the applicant's welfare may be accepted. This could be a son or daughter, doctor, social worker or officer in charge of a care home, or a deputy or attorney. The signatory should explain in the 'Other Information' section of the form, or in a separate letter if preferred, that the applicant is incapacitated and that the signatory (in whatever relevant capacity) has signed on his or her behalf.

6.3.3 Privileges

Certain privileges or concessions may be available to older people:

- parking schemes (the 'blue badge scheme' allows parking concessions to be made to assist people with mobility problems);
- older and disabled persons may travel free in London under the Freedom Pass scheme;
- older people may be eligible for free travel on local buses in England, but the age at which you can apply varies by location;
- disabled persons' rail travel may apply to older people and enables an escort to travel with them at a discounted rate;
- those over 60 can also obtain a Senior Railcard which provides reduced fares for the holder;
- for concessionary payments see **Chapter 15**.

6.3.4 Voting

There is no upper age bar to voting. Section 73 of the Electoral Administration Act 2006 abolished any common law rule which provides that a person is subject to a legal incapacity to vote by reason of his mental state. Moreover, the Electoral Commission's own guidance provides that 'persons who meet the other registration qualifications are eligible for registration regardless of their mental capacity or lack thereof'. As MCA 2005 expressly excludes voting rights from the scope of decision-making under the Act, a donee of an LPA may not exercise such rights as a proxy; a person must therefore have capacity to appoint a proxy.

6.3.5 Jury service

An individual is eligible for jury service up to the age of 70 years. When it is brought into force, s.68 of the Criminal Justice and Courts Act 2015 will increase the upper age limit to 75. This is with the aim that 'juries better reflect the current demographic make-up of the adult population' allowing juries to 'benefit from the experience and knowledge of those aged 70 to 75' (Lord Faulks, *Hansard*, 28 July 2014). The individual must also be registered as a parliamentary or local government elector and have been ordinarily resident in the United Kingdom (or the Isle of Man or the Channel Islands) for at least five years since the age of 13 years.

Various categories of person are ineligible or disqualified including:

- anyone liable to be detained under MHA 1983;
- anyone in a hospital on account of mental disorder;
- a person in guardianship under MHA 1983, s.7 or subject to community treatment under MHA 1983, s.17A;
- a person lacking capacity within the meaning of MCA 2005 to make the decisions required of a juror.

See the Juries Act 1974, Sched.1 (as amended).

A judge may discharge a juror who is considered unable to understand the nature of the oath or the evidence. If a person called for jury service is not thought fit to sit the jury officer or court clerk should be informed and the summons may be withdrawn. When a person with a disability is called for jury service it is for the judge to determine whether or not that person should act as a juror:

- The presumption is that they should unless the judge is of the opinion that the person will not, on account of disability, be capable of acting effectively.
- There have been many cases in which blind persons have served on juries.
- No evidence has ever been presented that a deaf juror is less able to assess the demeanour of a witness but the need for a communicator in the jury room would be a fundamental obstacle.

See the Juries Act 1974, ss.1, 9B (as amended).

6.4 CIVIL RESPONSIBILITY

6.4.1 Council tax

Council tax is a property tax with a personal element charged on an adult resident in a dwelling which is his or her sole or main residence. Joint and several liability can arise but not every individual will be liable. See **13.7** for detail on council tax reductions.

6.4.2 National insurance contributions

National insurance contributions are not payable by those over state pension age but an adequate contributions record of the individual (or spouse) is required if the normal state retirement pension is to be paid; this is true for both the old state pension, and the new state pension (which will be provided to those who reach retirement age on or after 6 April 2016). A pensions forecast can be obtained by contacting the 'Future Pension Centre' (**www.gov.uk/future-pension-centre**) or by using the online service at **www.gov.uk/state-pension-statement**. A copy of a national insurance account can be obtained from HMRC.

Gaps in the national insurance record may also be made up by credits, e.g. while unemployed and claiming jobseeker's allowance or employment and support allowance. It is also possible to make voluntary contributions in order to protect a pension record. For pensions generally see **16.2**.

6.4.3   Income and capital taxes

For income and capital taxes see **16.3**.

6.5   DISCRIMINATION

The Equality Act (EA) 2010 consolidated the voluminous discrimination legislation dating back to the 1970s.

The following types of conduct are prohibited by the EA 2010 regime:

- Direct discrimination (i.e. less favourable treatment of A because A has a protected characteristic, or because A is wrongly believed to have a protected characteristic).
- Associative discrimination (i.e. less favourable treatment of A because of B's protected characteristic).
- Direct discrimination on the basis of dual characteristics (but only certain characteristics may be the grounds of dual characteristics claims).
- Indirect discrimination (i.e. applying to A, a 'provision, criterion or practice' which is discriminatory in relation to a relevant protected characteristic).
- Harassment.
- Victimisation.

For EA 2010 more generally, see **6.14**.

6.5.1   Age discrimination

Age is a protected characteristic under EA 2010. Age groups are self-defined and would include, for example 'over fifties' or 'twenty-one year olds' (see Explanatory Notes to the Equality Act, paras.36–37). A number of specific exceptions to the regime have been issued under the Equality Act 2010 (Age Exceptions) Order 2012, SI 2012/2466, including, for example, the provision of financial services. Age is unique among the protected characteristics under EA 2010 in that employers may justify *direct* discrimination on the basis of age. However, the operation of the justification test in the context of direct age discrimination is narrower, despite being worded identically, and will only apply to legitimate aims of a 'public interest nature' (see *Seldon* v. *Clarkson Wright and Jakes (a partnership)* [2012] UKSC 16).

In order for a person to show that he or she has been directly discriminated against, the claimant must prove that he has been treated less favourably and that the ground for that less favourable treatment was the person's age. Indirect discrimination occurs where a criterion, provision or practice puts one or more persons of a particular age or age group at a specific disadvantage when compared with other people. Any requirement in a job advert for a particular length of service would be likely to be indirectly discriminatory.

Although legitimate aims which justify direct discrimination are limited to those of a public interest nature, no such limitation applies to legitimate aims to justify indirect discrimination. There is no statutory definition of what amounts to a legitimate aim. These aims could include:

- health and safety;
- the particular training requirements of the job;
- promoting loyalty;
- economic factors such as business needs and efficiency; however, there must be a real need shown on the part of the employer for such a factor to be justified.

6.5.2 Disability discrimination

EA 2010 provides the legislative scheme governing disability discrimination law. The Equality Act 2010 (Disability) Regulations 2010, SI 2010/2128 have been issued under the power to create secondary legislation under that Act.

Code of Practice and guidance

The Statutory Code of Practice on Employment has been published by the Equality and Human Rights Commission. Government guidance on various aspects of the Equality Act regime can be found at **www.gov.uk/government/publications/equality-act-guidance**.

Definitions

The Equality and Human Rights Commission has published 'Guidance on matters to be taken into account in determining questions relating to the definition of disability' which can be found at **www.equalityhumanrights.com**.

EA 2010 defines a disabled person as a person with a disability. A person has a disability for the purposes of the Act if he or she has a physical or mental impairment and the impairment has a substantial and long-term adverse effect on his or her ability to carry out normal day-to-day activities (EA 2010, s.6)). Certain conditions (notably alcohol or substance dependency) are expressly excluded from this definition by the regulations. Certain conditions (including HIV and cancer) automatically qualify as disabilities. The definition in s.6 is supplemented by Sched.1 to EA 2010.

Service providers

A service provider (defined as a person concerned with the provision of a service to the public or a section of the public whether for payment or not) is prohibited from discriminating against disabled persons. Provision of a service includes providing goods or facilities.

Prohibited conduct

The duty to make reasonable adjustments applies to service providers. Furthermore, alongside the prohibition on direct and indirect discrimination, harassment and victimisation, the following forms of discrimination are specifically prohibited by EA 2010 in respect of the provision of services (see EA 2010, s.29 and guidance published by the Equality and Human Rights Commission):

- refusing to provide services to a person because of his or her protected characteristic;
- terminating the provision of services to an individual having a protected characteristic;
- when providing services, discriminating as to the terms on which they are provided;
- when providing services, providing someone a service of worse quality than would usually be provided.

Enforcement, remedies and procedure

Proceedings for discrimination must be brought in the County Court and brought within six months (although the court may extend time if it considers that it is just and equitable to do so).

The court may award damages as compensation for injury to feelings. Furthermore, the court may grant any remedy which is available in the High Court for a claim in tort or in a claim for judicial review, so the court could, for example, grant a declaration that there has been discrimination (see EA 2010, ss.114, 118, 119).

The Equality and Human Rights Commission

The Equality and Human Rights Commission is an executive non-departmental public body. In addition to promoting equal opportunities and encouraging good practice the Commission will provide information and advice and may provide legal help to people including elderly and disabled people. The goal of the Equality and Human Rights Commission is to promote equality and human rights and to create a fairer Britain.

6.6 MARRIAGE AND CIVIL PARTNERSHIP

The Marriage (Same Sex Couples) Act 2013 is now in force, and permits marriage between same sex couples. It also permits existing civil partners to convert their civil partnership into a marriage. Private legal instruments (notably wills and trusts) made before the coming into force of s.11 of the Act will not be taken to include the spouse in a same sex marriage, though references to marriage or spouses in such instruments after 13 March 2014 will include same sex marriages.

6.6.1 Competence

'The marriage contract is a very simple one, which does not require a high degree of intelligence to comprehend' (*Durham* v. *Durham* (1885) LR 10 PD 80). The same is true of entering into a civil partnership. For capacity to contract a valid marriage or civil partnership see **1.5.2**. Civil partnerships are governed by the Civil Partnership Act 2004.

6.6.2 Formalities

A caveat can be entered at the relevant register office, church or place registered for the celebration of marriage if it is believed that a party to a proposed marriage does not have the necessary capacity. This puts the registrar or clergyman on notice and creates a requirement to investigate the matter: see Marriage Act 1949, s.29. The reading of banns in church may give an opportunity to concerned persons to record an objection to a proposed marriage, in which event an enquiry is made as to the capacity of the parties to enter into the ceremony.

It is now possible for a marriage ceremony to take place in a mental hospital for a detained patient: see Marriage Act 1983, s.1. This is also possible in the case of a civil partnership.

The various formalities for entering into a civil partnership are contained in the Civil Partnership Act 2004, ss.5–27.

6.6.3 Implications

Despite the relative ease with which a person can marry, there is a change of status with long-term financial implications and no warning is given to the parties of this:

- assets/chattels owned and used jointly need to be clearly defined and proper transfer on death ensured (this avoids potential litigation and post-death claims);
- assets may be redistributed in the event of a divorce or the dissolution of a civil partnership;
- entitlement to state benefits and community care services may be affected (a widow's pension may be lost and a joint means test may apply);

- remarriage or the formation of a subsequent civil partnership may lead to loss of a surviving spouse pension under an occupational pension scheme;
- marriage or civil partnership revokes an existing will unless made in contemplation of the marriage or civil partnership; this can cause problems because of the low capacity threshold for marriage and the high threshold for testamentary capacity; a statutory will may be considered, see **4.10**;
- claims can arise under the Inheritance (Provision for Family and Dependants) Act 1975, see **Chapter 19**.

Cohabitation (or sharing a home) may be an alternative to marriage or civil partnership and does not have all the above implications (see **6.9**). Proper legal and financial advice is still needed.

6.6.4 Ante-nuptial agreements

Ante-nuptial agreements are particularly appropriate for second, or subsequent, marriages usually between an older couple, when either or both have children and wish to keep their own property separate in order to protect the children's inheritance. Although ante-nuptial agreements are not currently strictly binding, they are strongly persuasive and generally the courts will uphold a nuptial agreement that is freely entered into by each party with a full appreciation of its implications unless, in the circumstances, it would not be fair to hold the parties to the agreement (see *Radmacher* v. *Granatino* [2010] UKSC 42).

In February 2014, the Law Commission published its report *Matrimonial Property, Needs and Agreements*, recommending the introduction of 'qualifying nuptial agreements', subject to certain requirements, including a draft Bill. It remains to be seen whether the government will take forward the Law Commission's proposals in the next Parliament.

6.7 BREAKDOWN OF MARRIAGE OR CIVIL PARTNERSHIP

Family law was substantially reformed in changes brought about in April 2014. On 22 April 2014, a single Family Court came into existence, bringing together the work of the High Court, County Court and Family Proceedings Court. It is intended to create a much simpler system. Moreover, the Children and Families Act (CaFA) 2014 brought about extensive changes in this area, covering both public and private children proceedings. The Family Procedure Rules 2010 were amended to accommodate these changes. CaFA 2014 also finally repealed the unimplemented provisions contained in Parts II and III of the Family Law Act 1996. The changes introduced compulsory 'mediation, information and assessment meetings' (MIAMs) before applying for certain types of court order.

For the law relating to the breakdown of marriage, see the Matrimonial Causes Act (MatCA) 1973 (as amended). For the procedures adopted by the court, see the Family Procedure Rules 2010, SI 2010/2955 (as amended).

6.7.1 Nullity

Marriages may be void or voidable (MatCA 1973, ss.11–13). Check whether the marriage was before or after 31 July 1971 because the Nullity of Marriage Act 1971 changed the common law from that date (previously the grounds were restricted but may have made the marriage void).

A marriage after 31 July 1971 will be void if, inter alia, the parties are within the prohibited degrees of relationship. A marriage which results from the purported conversion of a void civil partnership is also void.

A marriage is now voidable at the instance of one party (inter alia) on proof:

- of incapacity by either party to consummate the marriage;
- of wilful refusal by the respondent to consummate the marriage;
- that either party did not validly consent to the marriage (this may be due to duress, mistake, unsoundness of mind or otherwise);
- that at the time of the marriage either party, though capable of consenting, was suffering from mental disorder within the meaning of MHA 1983, of such a kind or to such an extent as to be unfitted for marriage;
- that at the time of the marriage the respondent was suffering from a venereal disease or pregnant by another.

It must be noted that the grounds relating to consummation do not apply to same sex marriages. Bars to the granting of a decree in respect of a voidable marriage now include:

- for lack of consent, disease or pregnancy by another, proceedings were not commenced within three years;
- the petitioner, knowing that the marriage could be avoided, so conducted him- or herself in relation to the respondent as to lead him or her reasonably to believe that he or she would not seek to do so, and it would be unjust to grant a decree (this may be relevant to a marriage for companionship only).

Part 2, Chapter 2 of the Civil Partnership Act 2004 deals with the dissolution and nullity of a civil partnership and other related proceedings.

6.7.2 Divorce

Divorce is based on irretrievable breakdown of the marriage but no petition may be presented before the expiration of one year from the marriage, and one of five facts must also be established (MatCA 1973, ss.1–3):

1.   The respondent has committed adultery and the petitioner finds it intolerable to live with the respondent.
2.   The respondent has behaved in such a way that the petitioner cannot reasonably be expected to live with the respondent.
3.   The respondent has deserted the petitioner for a continuous period of at least two years immediately preceding the presentation of the petition.
4.   The parties to the marriage have lived apart for a continuous period of at least two years immediately preceding the presentation of the petition and the respondent consents to a decree being granted.
5.   The parties to the marriage have lived apart for a continuous period of at least five years immediately preceding the presentation of the petition.

The respondent may oppose dissolution on grounds of hardship when the petition is based upon 'living apart' (MatCA 1973, ss.5 and 10). This will usually mean financial hardship though loss of pension rights may be relevant.
    Orders may be made in the divorce proceedings dealing with:

- arrangements for any relevant children;
- molestation and occupation of the home;
- temporary maintenance;
- a final financial settlement.

Judicial separation

A decree of judicial separation is obtained on the same basis as a divorce and orders relating to financial matters and children may be made but:

- a petition may be presented in the first year;
- the parties are not free to remarry;
- pension rights should not be affected;
- intestacy rights (but not the right to inherit under a will) are affected.

6.7.3   Financial provision

Orders made

The court can make all or any of the following ancillary relief orders for the benefit of a spouse:

- on or after filing of the petition: maintenance pending suit;
- on or after granting a decree (but with effect in the case of divorce or nullity from decree absolute):
    - periodical payments (including secured periodical payments);
    - order for the payment of a lump sum;

- property adjustment (transfer/settlement of property, variation of settlement);
- pension adjustment;
- avoidance of dispositions intended to reduce financial relief;
- release of future inheritance claims against the estate of the other spouse (see Inheritance (Provision for Family and Dependants) Act 1975, s.15);
- variation of periodical payments orders following a change of circumstances.

Most cases are resolved by consent orders but these must be approved by the judge after full disclosure of the financial position of each party. For orders that may be made see MatCA 1973, ss.21–24G.

Matters taken into account

When making financial orders the court must 'have regard to all the circumstances of the case', first consideration being given to the welfare of any relevant minor child. The court will in particular have regard to the following matters:

- the income, earning capacity, property and other financial resources which each of the parties to the marriage has or is likely to have in the foreseeable future, including in the case of earning capacity any increase in that capacity which it would in the opinion of the court be reasonable to expect a party to the marriage to take steps to acquire;
- the financial needs, obligations and responsibilities which each of the parties to the marriage has or is likely to have in the foreseeable future;
- the standard of living enjoyed by the family before the breakdown of the marriage;
- the age of each party to the marriage and the duration of the marriage;
- any physical or mental disability of either of the parties to the marriage;
- contributions made by each of the parties to the welfare of the family, including any contribution made by looking after the home or caring for family;
- the conduct of each of the parties, if that conduct is such that it would in the opinion of the court be inequitable to disregard it.

For the basis of financial provision see MatCA 1973, s.25.

Outcome

The court seeks to achieve a clean break wherever possible, i.e. no continuing financial provision between the parties (see MatCA 1973, s.25A). This may not be possible following a long marriage where pension rights are involved and there is little further employment potential unless there is adequate capital to provide for the security of both parties or both parties are likely to depend on state benefits. The court also now has powers to make provision involving pension schemes (see

MatCA 1973, ss.25B, 25C and 25D). It is currently unclear how liberalisation of pension rights for defined contribution pension schemes introduced in April 2015 will affect claims for financial provision, but the fact that money in pension schemes is much more accessible for divorcing spouses is likely to be a relevant consideration in some cases.

Ownership and continued occupation of the former matrimonial home is usually of paramount importance and this may be:

- ordered to be sold and the net proceeds divided in specified proportions with a view to each party making his or her own provision;
- transferred to one party outright or with a deferred charge to the other for a fixed sum or share of the value;
- settled on one spouse for their life or until their remarriage.

6.8   GRANDCHILDREN

Grandparents may become involved in disputes relating to their grandchildren following the breakdown of the marriage of the parents. They may find themselves looking after these grandchildren on a full-time basis or wish to seek regular contact with them when this is denied. The law in this area was substantially reformed by CaFA 2014, which amended the Children Act 1989.

6.8.1   Children Act 1989

The Children Act 1989 (as amended) governs:

- private law disputes (involving the family) about the upbringing of children;
- public law applications (involving local authorities) relating to their welfare.

Key principles

The emphasis is on parental responsibility and agreement being reached as to the future upbringing of children. The court will not make an order unless it considers that doing so is better for the child than making no order at all (s.1(5)). CaFA 2014 introduced a presumption that involvement by the parent in the life of the child will further the child's welfare (s.1(2A)). The purpose of this amendment is to reinforce the importance of children having an ongoing relationship with both parents after family separation, where that is safe, and in the child's best interests. The welfare of the child is the paramount consideration and when considering whether to make most orders, the court must have particular regard to the matters stated in s.1(3):

- the ascertainable wishes and feelings of the child;
- the physical, emotional and educational needs of the child;
- the likely effect on the child of a change of circumstances;

- the age, sex, background and any characteristics of the child which the court considers relevant;
- any harm which the child has suffered or is at risk of suffering;
- how capable each of the child's parents (and any other person) is of meeting the child's needs;
- the range of powers available to the court.

Although the wishes and feelings of the child, if of sufficient age and maturity, are ascertained and taken into account, a child should not be expected to choose. For key principles in regard to the welfare of a child, see Children Act 1989, s.1.

Parental responsibility

Parental responsibility means all the rights, duties, powers, responsibilities and authority which by law a parent of a child has in relation to the child and the child's property, and is concerned with bringing the child up, caring for the child, and making decisions about the child (s.3(1)). Married parents automatically each have parental responsibility, as do single mothers. Unmarried fathers who are named on the birth certificates automatically have parental responsibility (Adoption and Children Act 2002, s.111). Unmarried fathers may also acquire parental responsibility by means of a 'parental responsibility agreement' or by court order. A 'child arrangements order' relating to residence also confers parental responsibility in the case of the father of the child.

For parental responsibility in respect of a child, see Children Act 1989, ss.2–4ZA, including in relation to a second female parent and a step-parent.

6.8.2 Private law applications

CaFA 2014 introduced new terminology into the Children Act 1989 in relation to the orders a court may make. Certain existing types of order were replaced by a 'child arrangements order' (CAO). This is defined as an order regulating arrangements relating to with whom a child is to live, spend time or otherwise have contact, and when a child is to live, spend time or otherwise have contact with any person. This replicates the previous concepts of 'residence' and 'contact'. The court can also make:

- a prohibited steps order: an order that no step which could be taken by a parent in meeting his parental responsibility for a child, and which is of a kind specified in the order, shall be taken by any person without the consent of the court;
- a specific issue order: gives directions for the purpose of determining a specific question which has arisen, or which may arise, in connection with any aspect of parental responsibility for a child.

Collectively these orders are referred to as 'section 8 orders'. The court has power to make a desired order even if no application has been made. Where a court has power to make a section 8 order, it may do so at any time during the course of the proceedings in question even though it is not in a position to dispose finally of those proceedings, i.e. an interim order. No order is ever final although the court may be reluctant to disturb the status quo unless there are compelling reasons to do so.

One reason behind the change from 'residence' and 'contact' orders to 'child arrangements orders' was to move away from terminology that implies that there is a winner or loser in disputes concerning children (the perception often being that the parent with residence is the winner, while the parent with contact is the loser).

Role of grandparents

Grandparents may initiate or become involved in applications to the court for orders governing their relationship with grandchildren. In *Re B (A Child) (Care Proceedings: Joinder)* [2012] EWCA Civ 737, Black LJ stated that 'the prospects of a grandparent taking over the child's care must, of course, always be looked into carefully because it can be greatly to a child's benefit to be kept within the family by such a placement'. The courts have long recognised that grandparents potentially have an important role to play in the upbringing of children.

When appropriate in the best interests of the child, a grandparent may be joined as a party in proceedings between the parents. In these cases, it should be shown that there is a need for such intervention, as usually the grandparent will co-operate with and support the case of a parent. This may be appropriate when the grandparent is at odds with both parents.

A grandparent is entitled to apply for a CAO if the child has lived with the grandparent for a period of three years (s.10(5)(b)). This period need not be continuous but must not have begun more than five years before, or ended more than three months before, the making of the application (s.10(10)). Moreover, as a 'relative', a grandparent is entitled to apply for a CAO relating to where the child concerned is to live, provided that the child has lived with the grandparent for at least one year immediately preceding the application (s.10(5B)). In other circumstances they can make such an application with leave of the court (s.10(9)).

An order may be made requiring the person with whom a child lives, or is to live, to allow the child to visit or stay with a grandparent, or for that grandparent and the child otherwise to have contact with each other. Although it is generally in the best interests of a child to remain with the parents or one of them, a grandmother supported by a grandfather may be able to make out a stronger case especially if the parents are not stable. Where a child is living with grandparents with the agreement of parents, it may be necessary to apply for a CAO to achieve stability.

If grandparents are able to see both sides of the problem and avoid taking sides, they can be particularly helpful in facilitating contact in the best interests of the child or children when the relationship between the parents is hostile (see e.g. *Re B (A Child) (Residence: Biological Parent)* [2009] UKSC 5).

6.8.3 Public law applications

When a child is suffering, or likely to suffer, significant harm and this is attributable to inadequate care by the parent(s) the local authority in whose area the child is ordinarily resident may apply for a care order or a supervision order. In this instance the grandparents may apply for leave to be made parties and to be heard and an order for reasonable contact may be made in favour of grandparents.

One of the major changes introduced by CaFA 2014 was a 26-week outside time limit for care proceedings although extensions are possible under the rules. Proceedings follow the Public Law Outline (PLO). The accompanying flow chart is likely to be of assistance to practitioners.

Where a care order is made in favour of the local authority, the child may be accommodated with grandparents. The court cannot order this but failure by the authority to carry out its care plan might justify subsequent revocation of the care order on an application by the grandparents for a CAO. The grandparents may be paid an allowance if the child is placed with them by the authority but may not receive financial support under a CAO unless the parents are able to provide this or the authority makes payments under its discretionary powers.

For local authority applications see the Children Act 1989, Part IV, ss.31–42.

6.8.4 Adoption

Grandparents are unlikely to be permitted to adopt a grandchild because of their age and the confusion of roles that would result. An adoption order will only be made if it is in the best interests of the child but if a grandchild is placed for adoption all legal ties with the grandparents are severed so:

- the grandparents may apply for leave to intervene and oppose this step;
- there can be post-adoption contact with parents or grandparents but this is unusual and likely to be restricted in its nature;
- adoption is a last resort so grandparents may wish to consider an application for a CAO.

See the Adoption and Children Act 2002.

6.9 COHABITATION

An elderly couple may contemplate living together and it may be convenient, economical and mutually supportive for them to do so. In that event a formal agreement may be prepared. Note that cohabitation can also give rise to an inheritance claim under the Inheritance (Provision for Families and Dependants) Act 1975.

6.9.1 Checklist of legal and practical implications to be discussed in advance of cohabitation

- Where are they to live?
- Who is to own the home or hold the tenancy?
- Is the non-owning party to make a capital contribution and on what basis?
- If the home is to be owned jointly, on what basis will it be held beneficially?
- In what shares and what manner are they to meet household expenses?
- Will there be a pooling of expenses?
- Is a joint bank account appropriate?
- Is one party to be merely a lodger at home and if so on what terms?
- On what basis will they live together?
- Is an intimate relationship intended or merely companionship?
- Will they take holidays together and share leisure activities?
- What will be the attitude of their respective families?
- What will be the effect on any benefit claims or services provided?
- Will they be 'living together as man and wife' for benefits purposes?
- Will any services be withdrawn or restricted?
- Will increased charges be made for services?
- Is the relationship intended to be mutually supportive for life?
- Does this mean financially or on a caring basis, or both?
- What will be the effect upon any pension entitlement of the parties?
- Should any home and furnishings be owned jointly?
- Should an LPA be completed?
- If financially supportive, is this until the first death or the second death?
- If until death of survivor, what steps are to be taken to secure the intention?
- Should the home be held as joint tenants or on a tenancy in common?
- Are new wills required to ensure that the needs of the survivor are protected and dependency claims avoided?

6.9.2 Marriage or civil partnership

Advice may be sought as to whether it is in the parties' best interests to marry or enter into a civil partnership, but if there is a possible conflict of interest each party should be separately advised. The parties must carefully consider:

- the effect on any benefits claims or liabilities, e.g. funding for community care services (what happens if one of them goes into a residential care home?);
- the implications for income tax and capital taxes;
- the consequences of any existing will being revoked by marriage or civil partnership so that they are effectively intestate.

6.10   ABUSE AND DOMESTIC VIOLENCE

6.10.1   Nature of abuse

Abuse of older people is more prevalent than previously recognised and may:

- take place in a family or domestic environment, in the community, or in a care home;
- be by a relative, a friend or neighbour (or even a stranger), or be by an informal carer or a professional carer or trustee;
- take the form of physical assault or threatening behaviour; sexual abuse; verbal or emotional pressure; neglect, abandonment or isolation; misuse of money or property;
- amount to a criminal offence; the tort of trespass to the person (assault, battery or false imprisonment); the tort of negligence; or theft.

The abused individual may not be in a position to complain or to seek a remedy so lawyers must be vigilant. Failure to recognise the personal and civil rights of an elderly person is a form of abuse, and this includes:

- undue influence and denial of access to independent legal advice;
- medical paternalism whereby the doctor administers treatment on the basis that he knows best without troubling to obtain the informed consent of the patient or ascertain what the patient would have wished.

Lawyers should not make the same mistake by advising relatives or carers without seeking to communicate with their elderly client. For more information, see **www.elderabuse.org.uk** and 'A Safeguarding Strategy for Recognising, Preventing and Dealing with the Abuse of Older and Vulnerable People', available from **www.sfe.legal**.

6.10.2   The right to intervene

Unless the abuse amounts to a serious criminal offence the victim is expected to initiate his or her own remedies or at least complain. We can counsel and advise, but cannot initiate action without the consent of the individual involved, if he or she is competent. Older people are entitled to put themselves at risk and no one can legally interfere in their lives simply because it is considered that they are vulnerable to abuse. Any form of intervention against their wishes can only be justified when they lack the mental capacity to take the particular decision involved. It will then be lawful if it is in the best interests of the incapacitated person, but any intervention should be the least restrictive possible.

There will be occasions, however, where the person is mentally competent but vulnerable to abuse and not in a position to take steps to protect themselves, such as those under duress, coercion or undue influence or substantially handicapped by illness, injury or congenital deformity. In such cases, a referral should be made to

213

social services, adult protection team, who may then take action on behalf of the person at risk. The High Court retains inherent jurisdiction to make appropriate orders, to protect such persons (see *DL* v. *A Local Authority* [2012] EWCA Civ 253).

6.10.3 Remedies

Recourse to the law, whether civil or criminal, may not be the only way of achieving a remedy. Unless the abuse is particularly serious the victim will not be seeking compensation or retribution but merely wish to ensure that the abuse does not continue or is not repeated. Remedies that may be available include:

- Civil court proceedings (the standard of proof is the balance of probabilities). A claim may be made for damages or an injunction (see below). For the ability to initiate proceedings when the individual is mentally incapacitated (see **Chapter 5**).
- Criminal proceedings (the standard of proof is beyond reasonable doubt). The police may prosecute on information given by a third party. A compensation order may be made (if the offender can pay). A claim may be made to the Criminal Injuries Compensation Authority under the statutory scheme.
- Non-legal remedies: the victim may be moved away from the abusive situation; the abuser may be a carer who simply cannot cope without additional help; a professional carer may be dismissed.
- Use of complaints procedures. If the abuse is by a care professional this may be appropriate and sufficient. For the regulation of care homes see **Chapter 9**.
- Report the situation to the appropriate authority. The social services department of the local authority should investigate all alleged incidents of abuse where a vulnerable older person is involved.
- Put financial affairs on a proper footing (see **Chapter 4**).

Failure to intervene may allow abuse to continue, but too much intervention may be a greater abuse than that which it is intended to prevent.

6.10.4 Injunctions

Enhanced protection for people who suffer from violence or harassment is now available through the courts. The victim may be given protection under one of the three statutes mentioned below in addition (or as an alternative) to bringing an action in tort.

Local courts provide effective remedies in a wide range of abusive situations.

Effect of mental disorder

An elderly person may become an abuser. Where persistent inappropriate behaviour is due to mental disorder an injunction may not be available to control this.

An injunction ought not to be granted against a person who is incapable of understanding what he is doing and that it is wrong, because a breach could not then be the subject of effective enforcement proceedings: *Wookey* v. *Wookey* [1991] 3 All ER 365. However, it is possible for an injunction to be granted against a person who lacks or may lack capacity to manage his or her property and affairs or alternatively to conduct legal proceedings because the tests of capacity are different. See *Re de Court* (1997) *The Times*, 27 November, clarified in *P* v. *P (Contempt of Court: Mental Capacity)* [1999] 2 FLR 897.

There may be a 'gap' with an elderly mentally disordered individual causing disruption to the lives of others which is not restrained by the health or social services authorities yet cannot be controlled by the courts.

Family Law Act 1996, Part IV

Proceedings may be brought against an abuser in the Family Court or High Court by an associated person which includes:

* existing and former spouses and cohabitants;
* those who live or have lived in the same household, other than merely by reason of one of them being the other's employee, tenant, lodger or boarder;
* 'relatives' as widely defined;
* persons who have agreed to marry one another.

Various orders may be made or provisions included in the order. Urgent relief can even be obtained without giving notice to the other party (known as an ex parte or 'without notice' order) although notice is then given of a later hearing when the need for continuing orders will be considered.

Non-molestation order

Under a non-molestation order, the respondent is forbidden to use or threaten violence against the applicant or to intimidate, harass or pester the applicant. The respondent may also be ordered not to instruct, encourage or in any way suggest that any other person should do these things. The court must have regard to all the circumstances including the need to secure the health, safety and well-being of the applicant. What behaviour amounts to molestation will depend on the facts of the particular case, but implies some quite deliberate conduct which is aimed at a high degree of harassment of the other party, so as to justify the intervention of the court (see *C* v. *C (Non-molestation Order: Jurisdiction)* [1998] Fam 70).

Occupation order

An occupation order controls occupation of the home (see **6.10.5**).

Undertaking

Instead of an injunction the respondent may undertake (i.e. promise the court) not to behave in a particular way in future. The alleged behaviour is not admitted and the court makes no findings but a contested hearing is avoided and there is usually no costs order. Breach is contempt of court so committal proceedings can be brought, but a power of arrest cannot be attached to the undertaking so the court should not accept it if this protection is needed.

Power of arrest

A power of arrest is attached to the order if violence has been used or threatened against the applicant unless the applicant will be adequately protected without it. A constable may then arrest without warrant a person whom he has reasonable cause for suspecting to be in breach. An arrested person must be brought before a court within 24 hours but the court can remand the arrested person in custody or on bail pending a hearing. The court has power to remand to enable a medical report to be obtained.

Warrant for arrest

Where breach of an injunction is alleged (and there is no power of arrest) an application may be made for the issue of a warrant.

Committal proceedings

An application can still be made on notice for a committal order under the 'show cause' procedure.

A power to make rules providing for a representative to act on behalf of another person in applying for or enforcing an occupation order or a non-molestation order has not yet been implemented. Such power could be used to assist a vulnerable elderly person.

Protection from Harassment Act 1997

The wording of the Protection from Harassment Act 1997 is broad enough to encompass a wide range of activities which may include 'elder abuse'. A person must not pursue a course of conduct (i.e. conduct on at least two occasions) which amounts to harassment of another and which he knows or ought to know amounts to harassment of the other. Harassment of a person includes alarming the person or causing the person distress, and under s.1(2) 'conduct' includes speech where 'if a reasonable person … would think that the course of conduct amounted to or involved harassment' then 'the person whose conduct is in question ought to know' (there is an exception if in the circumstances the course of conduct was 'reasonable'). The Act has been amended to introduce the offence of stalking.

Harassment is made a criminal offence as well as a tort, and breach of a civil injunction is a specific offence in addition to civil enforcement procedures:

- civil proceedings are brought in a County Court (or the High Court);
- criminal proceedings are dealt with in the magistrates' court or (for the more serious offences) the Crown Court.

An actual or apprehended breach of the prohibition on harassment may be the subject of a claim in civil proceedings by the victim of the course of conduct:

- The court may grant an injunction to restrain such conduct and damages may be awarded for any anxiety caused or financial loss resulting from the harassment.
- If the claimant thereafter considers that the defendant has done anything which is prohibited by the injunction he may apply to the court without notice to the other party for a warrant of arrest against the defendant.
- If after considering all the evidence the defendant is found to have been in breach of the injunction he may be fined or committed to prison for contempt, or be tried for a separate statutory offence.

This legislation was hastily enacted to control 'stalking' but is not restricted to this and may assist in a wide range of other situations.

Injunctions against anti-social behaviour: Anti-Social Behaviour, Crime and Policing Act 2014

An injunction under this Act may be made against a person aged 10 or over if the court is satisfied, on the balance of probabilities (the civil standard of proof), that the person has engaged in, or is threatening to engage in, anti-social behaviour and that it is just and convenient to grant the injunction. 'Anti-social behaviour' means:

- conduct that has caused, or is likely to cause, harassment, alarm or distress to any person;
- conduct capable of causing nuisance or annoyance to a person in relation to that person's occupation of residential premises; or
- conduct capable of causing housing-related nuisance or annoyance to any person.

Various entities are entitled to apply for such injunctions, including a local authority, a housing provider, Transport for London, and the chief officer of police for a police area (s.5). These provisions replace the much-maligned 'ASBO' regime.

6.10.5 Occupation of the home

Under the Family Law Act 1996, Part IV (see **6.10.4**) a wide range of orders can also be made to regulate the occupation of a dwelling-house as between spouses, civil partners and cohabitants. The terms and duration of the order depend upon whether or not the applicant has an estate or interest in the home:

- this could include matrimonial home rights, i.e. the right by virtue of a subsisting marriage to live in the home of the spouse;
- where the parties are not existing or former spouses or cohabitants but are within some other category of 'associated person' (see above), the applicant must have some pre-existing right to occupy before an order can be made.

Where a party is to be excluded from the home a 'balance of harm' test is applied. 'Harm' means ill-treatment or impairment of health, and 'ill-treatment' includes non-physical forms. The court must have regard to all relevant circumstances including:

- the housing needs and resources of the parties;
- the financial resources of the parties;
- the nature and length of the parties' relationship;
- the parties' conduct in relation to each other;
- the effect of an order upon the health, safety or well-being of the parties or a child.

These orders relate to 'dwelling-houses' but this includes a part of a building occupied as a dwelling-house, a caravan, houseboat or structure occupied as a dwelling-house, and any yard, garden, garage or outhouse occupied with the dwelling-house. Mortgagees or landlords are given a chance to make representations, but an order may include provision that in respect of the home or a part of the home:

- the applicant is entitled to occupy it and the respondent shall allow this;
- the respondent shall not obstruct, harass or interfere with peaceful occupation;
- the respondent shall not occupy it at all or between specified times or dates;
- the respondent shall leave it by a specified time and not return to, enter or attempt to enter it or go within a specified distance of it;
- a party maintains and repairs the home or furnishings and contents, and pays the rent or mortgage.

Where, for example, a drunken grandson or drug-using granddaughter is abusing an infirm grandmother in her own home while posing as a carer, it may be more effective to exclude this person from the home and arrange alternative support (if required) rather than to move the grandmother to a care home.

It is unfortunate that in many cases, the victim suffers twice, once from the abuse and then again from the remedy. Often the victim is incapable of providing clear evidence of abuse or does not want to exclude a close relative. Such painful cases are all too common notwithstanding a wide range of legal remedies which are technically available.

6.11 VICTIMS OF CRIME

6.11.1 Reporting and investigation

When it is alleged that an offence has been committed there must be an early decision about involving the police.

Where the victim has been subjected to a serious offence, such as violence or sexual abuse, immediate police involvement is important to ensure a medical examination takes place promptly, and to secure corroborative forensic evidence.

The victim will be asked to make a statement about the offence, which will contain a statutory declaration as to its truth; in some cases, statements will be taken by means of video interview, which is then used as evidence in chief at trial.

The victim should also be given the opportunity to provide a 'victim personal statement', covering the following matters:

- How the crime has affected them him/her physically, emotionally or financially.
- Whether they feel vulnerable or intimidated.
- If they are worried about the defendant being given bail.
- Whether they are considering claiming compensation.
- Anything they think may be helpful or relevant.

Where the identity of the perpetrator of a crime is unclear or unknown, the victim may also be asked to take part in the identification of suspects, either informally or by means of a video identification or an identification parade, and/or to identify photographs.

The victim may go to the police direct or with help from a third party, but should be consulted and where possible consent to a referral to the police. Many police forces have specially trained officers who are experienced in interviewing mentally vulnerable victims and investigating reports of crimes involving them, and also in investigating and interviewing in particular types of crime, e.g. sexual offending.

6.11.2 Prosecution

The decision as to whether or not to prosecute is, in almost all cases now, taken by the Crown Prosecution Service (CPS) rather than the police. The 'CPS Code for Crown Prosecutors' (January 2013: **www.cps.gov.uk/publications/code_for_crown_prosecutors/**) provides guidance to prosecutors on the general principles to be applied when making decisions about prosecutions. In deciding whether a prosecution is required in the public interest, prosecutors should take into account any views expressed by the victim regarding the impact that the offence has had on him or her. Under the Code, prosecutors must consider the circumstances of and harm caused to the victim (see **6.12.4**). A victim may even not wish to 'press charges'; this is a matter which should be taken into account by the CPS, but is not determinative.

There may be no prosecution in the case of a victim who would make a poor witness because of lack of reliable evidence or corroboration.

Victims can seek a review of decisions not to charge, to discontinue or otherwise terminate all proceedings.

6.11.3 Information

The 'CPS Code of Practice for Victims of Crime' provides that victims of crime must be provided with timely, accurate information about their case, at all stages of the criminal justice process. This includes where a prosecution is discontinued, or the charges are substantially altered.

Where a defendant offers a 'plea bargain', that is, a guilty plea or pleas to fewer or less serious charges than he originally faced, the views of the victim where possible should be taken into account, although the decision as to whether or not these should be accepted rests with the prosecutor.

The care of victims and witnesses is managed by the victim's local Witness Care Unit, with a dedicated officer who will act as a single point of contact and will keep the victim informed of the case's progress from the point of charging the suspect, to sentencing or acquitting of the defendant. Practical and emotional support is also available to a victim by volunteers from Victim Support.

Legal Aid Agency funding is not available for a vulnerable witness in connection with a prosecution because that person is not a party to the proceedings.

Reports of the offence in the press can cause distress and the victim may suffer media attention during or after the trial. Victims of sexual offending must not be identified (Sexual Offences (Amendment) Act 1976). Victims of other offences and witnesses may, in certain circumstances, be eligible for a reporting direction (prohibiting the reporting of the witness's identity (Youth Justice and Criminal Evidence Act (YJCEA) 1999, s.46). The age of the victim/witness is one of the factors the court is required to take into account when determining whether to make a reporting direction (s.46(4)(b)).

6.11.4 Giving evidence in court

The presumption is that at every stage of criminal proceedings, all persons (whatever their age) are competent to give evidence, unless it appears to the court that he is not a person who is able to understand questions put to him as a witness, and give answers to them which can be understood (YJCEA 1999, s.53). Competence is determined by the judge, on the balance of probabilities and expert evidence may be called on the point (YJCEA 1999, s.54). Once the decision has been made to admit the evidence it is for the jury to decide what weight to attach to it. The prosecution cannot call medical evidence to support the reliability of one of its witnesses unless this is to rebut a challenge by the defence.

There have been significant recent developments aimed at enabling all those who appear before the courts to participate effectively in the proceedings and give their best evidence. The Criminal Procedure Rules 2015, SI 2015/1490 require the court to take 'every reasonable step' to encourage this. Under Part 3 of the Rules the court must identify the needs of a witness at an early stage. Those needs may include the use of special measures (see below).

Judges are directed to intervene and stop repetitive or over-vigorous cross-examination in the case of a vulnerable witness; ground rules hearings are required where an intermediary is used; and the Advocacy Training Council has prepared a series of 'toolkits' to assist advocates preparing to question vulnerable people at court. The Court of Appeal has endorsed this approach.

Part II of the Youth Justice and Criminal Evidence Act 1999 (as amended by the Coroners and Justice Act 2009) provides that the court may make a 'special measures direction' in respect of the evidence of certain vulnerable and intimidated witnesses, in the following circumstances, if the court considers that the quality of evidence given by the witness is likely to be diminished by reason of any of the following circumstances (YJCEA 1999, s.16):

- the witness suffers from a mental disorder within the meaning of MHA 1983; or
- the witness otherwise has a significant impairment of intelligence and social functioning; or
- the witness has a physical disability or is suffering from a physical disorder.

YJCEA 1999, s.17 empowers the court to make a 'special measures direction' in respect of witnesses, the quality of whose evidence is likely to be diminished by reason of fear or distress in connection with testifying in the proceedings.

The age of the witness is one of the factors to be taken into account by the court (s.17(2)(b)).

The special measures which the court may direct in YJCEA, ss.16 and 17 cases are set out in YJCEA 1999, ss.23–30 and are as follows:

- screening the witness from the accused;
- allowing the witness to give evidence by a live TV link;
- excluding persons (other than the accused and the legal representatives) from court while the witness is giving evidence;
- judge and counsel removing wigs and gowns;
- the use of video recorded evidence in chief;
- the use of video recorded cross-examination or re-examination;
- the examination of a witness through an intermediary;
- aids to communication.

In certain circumstances only the court may make a 'witness anonymity order' (Coroners and Justice Act 2009, ss.86–90).

A written statement by a victim may be admissible in evidence if the victim is unfit to give evidence because of his bodily or mental condition, provided it is in the interests of justice to allow this (Criminal Justice Act 2003, ss.114 and 116).

The CPS website (**www.cps.gov.uk**) contains a thorough and very helpful summary for victims and witnesses of crime, with sections on reporting a crime, going to court, vulnerable victims and witnesses, the CPS commitment to support victims and witnesses, and the victim's right of review. The 'Resources' link gives access to all current CPS policies and practice in relation to the treatment of victims and witnesses, and to the relevant Codes of Practice.

6.12   CRIMINAL RESPONSIBILITY

Particular considerations arise in the case of those individuals suffering from a mental disorder who become caught up in the criminal justice system as suspects and/or as defendants.

It is important to identify any mental disorder at an early stage so that:

- the safeguards of the Police and Criminal Evidence Act 1984 (PACE) Codes of Practice are observed by the police in the detention, treatment and questioning of such an individual;
- alternatives to prosecution are investigated with a view to the avoidance of prosecution altogether;
- issues such as fitness to plead and potential defences such as insanity are explored;
- adaptations to the trial process in accordance with the Practice Direction relating to vulnerable defendants (see below) can be considered;
- MHA 1983 disposals and other sentencing options are considered;
- where appropriate, treatment is given rather than punishment.

Mental disorder is defined as 'any disorder or disability of the mind' (MHA 1983 (as amended), s.1(2)). The term is used throughout PACE and its Codes of Practice, as well as MHA 1983.

6.12.1   Police investigation

Stop and search, seizure, and the detention, treatment and questioning of persons by police at the police station are governed by the Codes of Practice, issued pursuant to PACE. Code C governs the detention, treatment and questioning of detained suspects.

6.12.2   At the police station – general rights

A detained person has the general rights:

- to be given information about and a notice of rights under PACE;
- to have someone informed of arrest;
- to be told that free and independent legal advice is available;
- to consult privately with a solicitor;
- to consult the Codes of Practice.

6.12.3   Additional safeguards

Clinical treatment and attention

The custody officer must make sure a detainee receives appropriate clinical attention as soon as reasonably practicable if the person:

- appears to be suffering from physical illness;
- is injured;
- appears to be suffering from a mental disorder; or
- appears to need medical clinical attention.

This applies even if the detainee makes no request for clinical attention and whether or not he or she has already received clinical attention elsewhere. If the need for attention appears urgent, e.g. when indicated in Annex H, the nearest available healthcare professional or an ambulance must be called immediately (C.9.5/9.5A).

Whenever an 'appropriate healthcare professional' (formerly known as police surgeon) is called to examine or treat a detainee, the custody officer is required to ask his/her opinion about:

- any risks or problems which the police need to take into account when making decisions about a detainee's continued detention;
- when to carry out an interview if applicable; and
- the need for safeguards (C9.13).

Any medication that a detainee requires (whether or not previously prescribed) must be authorised by an appropriate healthcare professional (AHP) and will be administered by that AHP or by the custody officer with permission from the AHP (C9.9/9.10).

Mental illness, vulnerability

If an officer has any suspicion, or is told in good faith, that a person of any age may be mentally disordered or otherwise mentally vulnerable, in the absence of clear evidence to dispel that suspicion, the person shall be treated as such for the purposes of this code (C1.4/Annex E.1).

The term 'mentally vulnerable' applies to any detainee who, because of his or her mental state or capacity may not understand the significance of what is said, of questions or of their replies. Where the custody officer has any doubt about the mental state or capacity of a person detained, the detainee should be treated as mentally vulnerable and as a vital protection have the right to have an appropriate adult (C.1.G).

A detainee's solicitor cannot be that detainee's appropriate adult.

The appropriate adult will be:

- a relative, guardian or other person responsible for his or her care or custody;

- someone experienced in dealing with mentally disordered or mentally vulnerable people but who is not a police officer or employed by the police;
- failing these, some other responsible adult aged 18 or over who is not a police officer or employed by the police.

The role of the appropriate adult is to safeguard the welfare of the detainee. The appropriate adult's duties include exercising the right on behalf of the detainee to legal advice where the appropriate adult considers it should be taken up, facilitating communication, being present at the interview, observing whether it is being conducted fairly (and intervening if not), and making representations about the need for detention.

A solicitor should not take instructions from the detainee in the presence of the appropriate adult. It is important to note that, unlike conversations between a solicitor and the detainee, those between the appropriate adult and the detainee (whether or not in the presence of the solicitor) are not covered by legal privilege.

Failure by the police to observe these Codes could lead to the exclusion of evidence at a subsequent trial if the breach is significant and substantial.

6.12.4 The decision to prosecute

The decision as to whether or not to prosecute is, in almost all cases, taken by the CPS rather than the police. The CPS Code for Crown Prosecutors (see **6.11.2**) sets out the two stages which need to be satisfied before a prosecution should take place or should continue:

1. The 'evidential stage': prosecutors must be satisfied that there is sufficient evidence to provide a realistic prospect of conviction. They must ask themselves:

    - Can the evidence be used in court?
    - Is the evidence reliable?
    - Is the evidence credible?

2. The 'public interest stage': prosecutors must ask themselves:

    - How serious is the offence committed?
    - What is the level of culpability of the suspect?
    - What are the circumstances of and the harm caused to the victim?
    - Was the suspect under the age of 18 at the time of the offence?
    - What is the impact on the community?
    - Is prosecution a proportionate response?

Paragraph 4.12(b) of the Code sets out some common public interests factors against prosecution (i.e. the circumstances in which a prosecution is less likely to be required); these include where the suspect is, or was at the time of the offence, suffering from significant mental or physical ill health, unless the offence is serious or there is a real possibility that it may be repeated.

Consideration should be given to alternatives such as cautioning and diversion to the health and social services systems (see **6.12.5**). The individual may, however, wish to be given the opportunity to answer any charges in court.

Solicitors can make written representations, supported by medical evidence where appropriate, as to whether prosecution properly meets the public interest test.

6.12.5   Alternatives to prosecution

Out-of-court disposals allow the police to deal quickly and proportionately with low-level, often first-time offending which does not merit prosecution at court, allowing the police to spend more time on frontline duties and tackling serious crime.

The CPS has developed specific guidelines on 'Diverting offenders with mental health problems and/or learning disabilities within the National Cautioning Framework' (**www.cps.gov.uk/legal/**).

Current out-of-court disposals are as follows:

*   caution/conditional caution (adults and youths);
*   fixed penalty notice/penalty notice for disorder;
*   sectioning under MHA 1983 (where applicable).

A caution or conditional caution will not be appropriate if there is any doubt about the reliability of any admissions made or if the defendant's level of understanding prevents him or her from understanding the significance of the caution or conditional caution and giving informed consent.

6.12.6   Prosecution

Representation

Everyone arrested and taken to a police station is entitled to free legal advice, whatever his or her means. After being charged or served with a summons, a person's eligibility for further legal assistance becomes means tested. This will cover the work that a solicitor will need to do to prepare the case and representation at the magistrates' court and the Crown Court.

It must also be established that it is in the interests of justice for a person to be granted legal aid. If a person is found guilty, they may be required to repay his or her legal costs. The rules are constantly changing and it is important to take specialist advice from a solicitor who specialises in the criminal law.

The duty solicitor is available to represent defendants at their first appearance at the magistrates' court.

Remand status

All cases start in the magistrates' court. The majority of offences are dealt with in these courts. Some offences are 'summary only' (i.e. they can only be tried in the magistrates' courts, e.g. driving with excess alcohol). Some offences are 'either way', that is, a defendant can choose whether to have his or her case tried either in the magistrates' court or in the Crown Court (e.g. theft). The most serious offences are 'triable only on indictment', that is, in the Crown Court (e.g. rape, murder).

If a case is not concluded at the first appearance in the magistrates' court, a defendant may be remanded in custody or on bail. The age, physical and mental health of the defendant are all matters that the court can take into account when considering bail.

Conditions of bail can be imposed where necessary. If the defendant requires medical treatment, a condition to reside at a hospital could be imposed. A defendant who left would be in breach of his terms of bail and liable to arrest and remand in custody.

If the defendant appears to be mentally disordered but bail is not appropriate the court has powers under MHA 1983 to remand to hospital rather than prison:

- to remand for psychiatric reports (MHA 1983, s.35), for periods of 28 days at a time to a maximum of 12 weeks;
- (Crown Court only) to remand for treatment (MHA 1983, s.36), again for periods of 28 days at a time to a maximum of 12 weeks.

Both sections require medical evidence and confirmation that arrangements have been made for the defendant's admission to hospital, within seven days.

The Home Secretary has the power to transfer a mentally disordered remand prisoner from prison to hospital when there is an urgent need for treatment (MHA 1983, s.48).

6.12.7 Pleas and defences

Once criminal proceedings have started, where issues arise as to a defendant's ability to participate in those proceedings, expert evidence needs to be sought. The following list sets out in broad terms the points and stages at which expert assessment may be important:

- mental state at time of the offence (*mens rea* issues);
- mental state at time of police interview (reliability of interview);
- current mental state/level of functioning (fitness to plead);
- remand period issues/transfer from prison to hospital (where co-morbid mental disorder);
- fitness to stand trial/ability to participate effectively in trial process;
- sentence/risk assessment.

Fitness to plead

Every year a small number of defendants facing prosecution in a criminal trial are found 'unfit to plead and stand trial'. The law, dating back to 1836, has developed in a piecemeal way and independently of developments under the European Convention on Human Rights on 'effective participation' as part of the right to a fair trial. The law and procedures differ according to whether a defendant is tried in summary proceedings or on indictment, as do the disposals available to the court.

The Law Commission has been working on reform of the law in this area for some time. In 2010 a consultation paper was published. More recently this has been followed by an 'Issues Paper' (**www.lawcom.gov.uk/project/unfitness-to-plead/**).

At present, the common law test for fitness to plead remains that set down in *R* v. *Pritchard* (1837) 7 C&P 303: 'Has D sufficient intellect to comprehend the course of proceedings in the trial so as to make a proper defence, to challenge a juror to whom he might wish to object, and to understand the details of the evidence?'

The most widely favoured modern reformulation comes from *R* v. *M* [2003] EWCA Crim 3452, in which the Court of Appeal approved the trial judge's direction that the defendant should be found unfit to plead if any one or more of the following was beyond his capability:

- understanding the charges;
- deciding whether to plead guilty or not;
- instructing solicitors and counsel;
- exercising his right to challenge a juror (indictable offences);
- following the course of proceedings;
- giving evidence in his own defence.

The written or oral evidence of two doctors (at least one of whom must be approved under MHA 1983, s.12) is required before the court can make a finding of unfitness. The courts will look closely at the availability of special measures (see **6.11.4**) and particularly as to whether the use of an intermediary may enable a defendant to participate effectively in the normal criminal process.

If a defendant is found to be unfit to plead, a jury will be sworn to consider whether the defendant 'did the act or omission charged against him as the offence'. If satisfied that he did, they must find accordingly; if not they must acquit. If the former, the court's powers of disposal are limited to:

- hospital order (with or without a restriction order);
- supervision order;
- absolute discharge.

This procedure and these disposals apply only in the Crown Court. There is a (broadly) equivalent summary procedure available to the magistrates' court (MHA 1983, s.37(3)).

The vulnerable defendant and effective participation

The 'central thesis' of the Law Commission's paper on fitness to plead is that 'the normal criminal process is the optimum outcome where the defendant faces an allegation in our criminal justice system. We consider that this is the best outcome not just for the accused but also for victims, witnesses and society more generally. The full criminal trial process engages fair trial guarantees for all those involved, under art.6 of the ECHR, and allows robust and transparent analysis of all the elements of the offence, and any defence advanced, whilst offering the broadest range of disposals'.

Provisions introduced in 2000 in response to the decision of the European Court of Human Rights in *T* v. *United Kingdom*; *V* v. *United Kingdom* (1999) 30 EHRR 121 (the Jamie Bulger/Thompson and Venables case) in respect of young defendants have been substantially expanded to cover adults suffering from mental disorder or some other significant impairment of intelligence or social functioning.

The previous version of the Practice Direction (Vulnerable Defendants) addressed, in quite general terms, the steps needed to be taken to enable the defendant to give his/her best evidence, comprehend the proceedings and engage fully with his/her defence, with the following adaptations to the 'normal' trial process to be considered in cases where a defendant is vulnerable by virtue of age or otherwise:

- frequent breaks;
- assistance in understanding the meaning of language used;
- special seating arrangements;
- a supporting adult present;
- to give his evidence by live link;
- use of an intermediary.

The most recent Practice Direction ([2013] EWCA Crim 1631) takes matters a stage further and contains more detailed provisions as to the use of intermediaries, who it appears are likely to play an increasingly important role in the trial of vulnerable defendants. See also 'toolkits' to assist advocates as they prepare to question vulnerable people at court at **www.theadvocatesgateway.org**.

Other trial issues

A defendant who does not give evidence is at risk of having an inference drawn against him, unless he or she can show that his physical or mental condition makes it undesirable for him/her to testify (Criminal Justice and Public Order Act 1994, s.35).

The reliability of a police interview can be challenged by means of expert evidence as to reliability; given the defendant's level of functioning, can the answers be relied upon? Did he or she understand the caution? Is he or she suggestible and if so have answers been obtained as a result of leading questions? Is he or she prone to confabulation?

For a very small number of defendants (generally speaking, those with psychotic illness who are unwell at the time of the commission of the offence) there is the question of whether the defence of legal insanity is available. The current rules date back to 1843 (*M'Naughton's Case* (1843) 10 CL&F 200): the test is whether (on the balance of probabilities) at the time of committing the act:

- the defendant was acting under such a defect of reason, from disease of the mind;
- that he or she did he not know the nature and quality of the act he or she was doing; or
- if he or she did know it, that he or she did not know that it was wrong.

If a defendant is found not guilty by reason of insanity, and to have 'done the act' the disposals open to the Crown Court are identical to those where a defendant has been found unfit to plead and to have 'done the act' (see above). In the magistrates' court, a finding of not guilty by reason of insanity will result in an outright acquittal.

The Law Commission has produced a 'Discussion Paper' directed to the question of 'when should a person not be criminally liable because of their mental condition at the time they committed an alleged offence?'. Provisional proposals for reform are set out, based on lack of capacity.

Sentencing

With the aim of achieving consistency, a series of definitive sentencing guidelines (covering an increasing range of offences) have been introduced (by the Sentencing Guidelines Council, and its successor the Sentencing Council). A sentencing court must identify and follow the appropriate guideline unless it would be 'contrary to the interests of justice to do so', and, if contrary to the interests of justice, must state why.

Very generally, a sentencing court has to make an assessment of a defendant's culpability, of harm caused and/or intended, and of future risk. The principal tool is the Sentencing Guidelines Council Guideline on 'Seriousness'. Aggravating and mitigating factors to be identified are listed; of the latter, the most relevant (in the context of this chapter) are 'mental illness or disability', and 'youth or age, where it affects the responsibility of the individual defendant'.

Before imposing either a custodial sentence or a community sentence the court is generally required to obtain a pre-sentence report, which will be prepared by the probation service (Criminal Justice Act (CJA) 2003, s.156).

There is an additional requirement in the case of a mentally disordered defendant: before passing a custodial sentence upon such a defendant: the court must consider any information it has on the defendant's mental condition, and the likely effect such a sentence will have on that condition of the defendant and on any treatment which may be available for it (CJA 2003, s.157).

Possible disposals other than immediate custody include the following:

- absolute discharge;
- conditional discharge;
- financial penalties, such as a fine, costs, compensation, and victim surcharge;
- community order, which must include one of the CJA 2003 requirements (e.g. supervision by the probation service, mental health treatment requirement, alcohol or drug rehabilitation if appropriate);
- suspended prison sentence with or without a CJA 2003 requirement as above;
- hospital order (MHA 1983, s.37);
- hospital order with restriction order (MHA 1983, ss.37/41) (only where necessary to protect the public from future serious harm);
- guardianship order (MHA 1983, s.37).

6.13   UN CONVENTION ON THE RIGHTS OF PERSONS WITH DISABILITIES

The UK ratified the Convention on 8 June 2009. The Optional Protocol was ratified on 7 August 2009. At the time of writing 144 countries have signed the Convention and 84 have ratified it. The Convention provides for states to have legally binding obligations under international law to protect the human rights of persons with disabilities. However, the Convention does not create new rights. By art.1 of the Convention its purpose is to:

> ... promote, protect and ensure the full and equal enjoyment of all human rights and fundamental freedoms by all persons with disabilities, and to promote respect for their inherent dignity.

The UN suggests that the Convention represents a paradigm shift whereby persons with disabilities are not treated as 'objects' of charity or medical treatment but 'subjects' with their own rights who can make their own decisions and be active members of society.

Although the Convention is not directly incorporated into our domestic law, the CRPD is recognised by the Strasbourg court as part of the international law context within which the guarantees of the European Convention are to be interpreted, as the Supreme Court noted in *P* v. *Cheshire West and Chester Council* [2014] UKSC 19.

Article 3 deals with general principles including the respect for inherent dignity, individual autonomy, non-discrimination (both direct and indirect with the need for reasonable accommodation of the disability), inclusion in society, respect for difference and diversity, equality of opportunity and accessibility among others.

Article 4 provides states with general obligations to legislate and amend legislation to comply with the Convention, to respect the rights of persons with disabilities, to protect persons with disabilities from having their rights infringed by third parties (i.e. private individuals) and also to fulfil the rights of persons with disabilities by taking measures which lead to the improvement of the enjoyment of human rights by such disabled persons.

The following articles deal more specifically with individual aspects of the rights of disabled persons:

- Article 5: equality and non-discrimination.
- Article 6: women with disabilities.
- Article 7: children with disabilities.
- Article 8: awareness-raising.
- Article 9: accessibility.
- Article 10: right to life.
- Article 11: situations of risk and humanitarian emergencies.
- Article 12: equal treatment before the law.
- Article 13: access to justice.
- Article 14: liberty and the security of person.
- Article 15: freedom from torture or cruel, inhuman or degrading treatment or punishment.
- Article 16: freedom from exploitation, violence and abuse.
- Article 17: protecting the integrity of the person.
- Article 18: liberty of movement and nationality.
- Article 19: living independently and being included in the community.
- Article 20: personal mobility.
- Article 21: freedom of expression and opinion, and access to information.
- Article 22: respect for privacy.
- Article 23: respect for home and the family.
- Article 24: education.
- Article 25: health.
- Article 26: habilitation and rehabilitation.
- Article 27: work and employment.
- Article 28: adequate standard of living and social protection.
- Article 29: participation in political and public life.
- Article 30: participation in cultural life, recreation, leisure and sport.

The Optional Protocol establishes the right of the Committee on the Rights of Persons with Disabilities to consider complaints by individuals or groups who claim to be victims of the violation of the Convention by the state. The Committee can enquire into the alleged violation by the state and require the state to provide a written explanation and report on the outcome of its enquiry. Therefore, advisers may consider a complaint to the Committee.

For more information on the Convention see the UN Enable website (**www.un.org/disabilities**).

6.14 EQUALITY ACT 2010

The Equality Act (EA) 2010 grew out of a paper by the Government Equalities Office: *Framework for a Fairer Future* (2008, Cm 7431). The aims of the Act are to rationalise the law on equality and discrimination into one statute as the previous legislation in its various statutes and statutory instruments was overly complex and also to strengthen the law to increase progress towards the government's equality objectives, including eliminating the gender pay gap, for people from ethnic minorities to have the same job prospects as white people and for disabled people to have the same job prospects as their able-bodied counterparts and for the Senior Civil Service and the House of Commons to be representative of society as a whole.

The broad and ambitious aims of the Act are as follows:

- To introduce a new duty on public authorities to reduce socioeconomic inequalities (s.1 and also Part 11 in particular Chapter 1).
- To introduce a new 'equality duty'. This will overtake the piecemeal duties relating to gender, race and disability, etc. which already exist.

There are various 'protected characteristics' which are listed in Part 2 Chapter 1 on the basis of which it is not permitted to discriminate (s.4). These are:

- s.5 – age;
- s.6 – disability; see also s.15:

    - the duty to make reasonable adjustments is found at s.20 *et seq* and also s.189;
    - transport is dealt with in Part 12. There are specific sections dealing with taxis (Chapter 1); public service vehicles (Chapter 2); rail vehicles (Chapter 3);

- s.7 – gender reassignment (see also s.16);
- s.8 – marriage and civil partnership;
- s.9 – race;
- s.10 – religion or belief;
- s.11 – sex (i.e. gender) – see for pregnancy and maternity discrimination s.17 (for non-work cases) and s.18 (for work cases) and further ss.72–76;
- s.12 – sexual orientation.

Both direct discrimination (s.13) and indirect discrimination (s.19) are considered, as is combined discrimination as a result of dual characteristics (s.14). Comparison is to be made by reference to circumstances (s.23). Harassment and victimisation are also prohibited (ss.26 and 27) (see also **6.5**).

- Part 3 deals with the provision of services.
- Part 4 deals with premises.
- Part 5 deals with discrimination at work and in situations analogous to work, e.g. barristers offering pupillage or tenancy and also qualification bodies.

- Part 6 deals with education.
- Part 7 deals with private associations.
- Part 9 deals with enforcement.
- Part 14 permits general exceptions.

The aims of the Act are:

- to end age discrimination, e.g. extending the prohibition on age discrimination outside the workplace (s.5);
- to require transparency, e.g. in relation to gender, pay and ethnic minority and disability employment and to outlaw secrecy clauses which prevent discussion of pay (ss.77 and 78 on disclosure of information);
- to extend the scope of positive action – so that employers can take into account under-representation of a disadvantaged group when selecting between two equally qualified candidates (Part 11 in particular Chapter 2);
- to protect carers so that it is illegal to discriminate against them because of their link to a protected person (s.13) and also indirect discrimination (s.19);
- to ban discrimination in private members' clubs although discriminatory associations such as male-only clubs will still be permitted (Part 7);
- to improve protection of disabled people in relation to commonly owned properties by imposing a new duty on landlords and managers of residential properties to make reasonable adjustments for disabled people (Part 3 and in particular s.36 and also Part 13, s.190 on improvements to let dwelling houses);
- to strengthen enforcement of the law (Part 9).

PART B

Welfare and medical treatment

CHAPTER 7

Community care policies

Serdar Celebi, Caroline Bielanska and David Foster

7.1 SOURCES

7.1.1 Reports

The Law Commission undertook a series of reports to reform adult social care in England and Wales culminating in May 2011 in its final report, *Adult Social Care* (Law Com No.326), which contained its recommendations. This was followed soon after, in July 2011 by the Commission on Funding Care and Support's report (chaired by Andrew Dilnot) on *Fairer Care Funding* (available at **www.ageuk.org.uk/home-and-care/dilnot-commission-on-funding-of-care-and-support/**). The government published its White Paper, *Caring for Our Future: Reforming Care and Support* (Cm 8378, July 2012), which set out its reform priorities, and described its approach to legislation. The Welsh Assembly published its White Paper, *Sustainable Social Services for Wales: A Framework for Action* (WAG10-11086) and decided to introduce its own legislation, amalgamating social care provision for children. This chapter will only cover how legislation affects adults.

7.1.2 Legislation

In April 2015, in England, most of the Care Act 2014 came into force, consolidating the complex legislation in the area (including the National Health Service and Community Care Act 1990 and the National Assistance Act 1948) and imposing new duties on local authorities. The introduction of the so-called 'funding cap', which is the maximum sum an adult should pay for their social care during their lifetime, has been postponed until April 2020.

For Wales, the Social Services and Well-being (Wales) Act (SSWB(W)A) 2014 is due to come into force in April 2016.

7.1.3 Regulations

The following regulations have been issued in England:

• Care and Support (Assessment) Regulations 2014, SI 2014/2827.

- Care and Support (Eligibility Criteria) Regulations 2015, SI 2015/313.
- Care and Support (Independent Advocacy Support) Regulations 2014, SI 2014/2824.
- Care and Support (Independent Advocacy Support) (No.2) Regulations 2014, SI 2014/2889.
- Care and Support (Charging and Assessment of Resources) Regulations 2014, SI 2014/2672.
- Care and Support (Preventing Needs for Care and Support) Regulations 2014, SI 2014/2673.
- Care and Support (Choice of Accommodation) Regulations 2014, SI 2014/2670.
- Care and Support (Deferred Payment) Regulations 2014, SI 2014/2671.
- Care and Support (Personal Budget: Exclusion of Costs) Regulations 2014, SI 2014/2840.
- Care and Support (Provision of Health Services) Regulations 2014, SI 2014/2821.
- Care and Support (Discharge of Hospital Patients) Regulations 2014, SI 2014/2823.
- Care and Support (Children's Carers) Regulations 2015, SI 2015/305.
- Care and Support (Ordinary Residence) (Specified Accommodation) Regulations 2014, SI 2014/2828.
- Care and Support (Disputes Between Local Authorities) Regulations 2014, SI 2014/2829.
- Care and Support (Continuity of Care) Regulations 2014, SI 2014/2825.
- Care and Support (Cross-border Placements and Business Failure: Temporary Duty) (Dispute Resolution) Regulations 2014, SI 2014/2843.
- Care and Support (Market Oversight Criteria) Regulations 2015, SI 2015/314.
- Care and Support (Market Oversight Information) Regulations 2014, SI 2014/2822.
- Care and Support (Sight-impaired and Severely Sight-impaired Adults) Regulations 2014, SI 2014/2854.
- Care and Support (Business Failure) Regulations 2015, SI 2015/301.

At the time of writing, the following regulations have been issued in Wales, to come into force on 1 April 2016:

- Care and Support (Assessment) (Wales) Regulations 2015, SI 2015/1305 (W 111).
- Care and Support (Care Planning) (Wales) Regulations 2015, SI 2015/1335 (W 126).
- Care and Support (Disputes about Ordinary Residence, etc.) (Wales) Regulations 2015, SI 2015/1494 (W 166).
- Care and Support (Ordinary Residence) (Specified Accommodation) (Wales) Regulations 2015, SI 2015/1499 (W 171).

- Care and Support (Eligibility) (Wales) Regulations 2015, SI 2015/1578 (W 187).
- Care and Support (Direct Payments) (Wales) Regulations 2015, SI 2015/1815 (W 260).
- Care and Support (Choice of Accommodation) (Wales) Regulations 2015 (SI 2015/1840 (W 268).
- Care and Support (Deferred Payment) (Wales) Regulations 2015, SI 2015/ 1841 (W 269).
- Care and Support (Review of Charging Decisions and Determinations) (Wales) Regulations 2015, SI 2015/1842 (W 270).
- Care and Support (Charging) (Wales) Regulations 2015, SI 2015/1843 (W 271).
- Care and Support (Financial Assessment) (Wales) Regulations 2015, SI 2015/ 1844 (W 272).
- Care and Support (Provision of Health Services) (Wales) Regulations 2015, SI 2015/1919 (W 285).
- Care and Support (Business Failure) (Wales) Regulations 2015, SI 2015/1920 (W 286).

7.1.4 Guidance

The guidance to the Care Act 2014 is contained in the Care and Support Statutory Guidance (CSSG) published in October 2014.

A local authority is under a positive duty to comply with the guidance, and can only depart from it if there is very good reason (see *R* v. *Islington LBC, ex p Rixon* [1997] ELR 66).

The Social Services and Well-being (Wales) Act 2014 requires the Welsh government to publish a Code of Practice, which provides both guidance and imposes requirements on local authorities when exercising their social services functions (s.145). Local authorities do not have to follow the Code, where there is good reason, provided the authority has published an alternative policy for the exercise of its functions (s.147).

7.2 ROLE OF LOCAL AUTHORITIES

7.2.1 Responsibilities

The local authority's duty to assess for care and support services and determination of eligibility is set out in **Chapter 8**. This chapter looks at the overarching responsibilities of local authorities.

The well-being principle

There is a duty on the local authority to promote the individual's well-being (Care Act 2014, s.1(1); SSWB(W)A, ss.1(3) and 5). What is meant by 'well-being' is slightly different in Wales. In England, it includes personal dignity, physical and mental health and emotional well-being, protection from abuse and neglect, control by the individual over his or her everyday life, participation in work, education, training or recreation and suitability of accommodation. In Wales, there is no mention of the need to ensure the personal dignity of the individual but the definition extends to securing the person's rights and entitlements (s.2). Under the CSSG, in England the local authority must have regard to factors including the importance of beginning with the assumption that the individual is best-placed to judge the individual's well-being and the individual's views, wishes, feelings and beliefs (para.6.30). *One knows oneself*

Abuse and neglect enquiries

There may be safeguarding issues with older clients, for example where there is abuse or neglect (or risk of the same). Where a local authority has reasonable cause to suspect that an adult in its area:

- has needs for care and support (whether or not the authority is meeting any of those needs);
- is experiencing, or is at risk of, abuse or neglect; and
- as a result of those needs is unable to protect himself or herself against the abuse or neglect or the risk of it,

then the local authority must make (or cause to be made) whatever enquiries it thinks necessary to enable it to decide whether any action should be taken in the adult's case and, if so, what and by whom (Care Act 2014, s.42; SSWB(W)A, s.126).

Prevention of needs

Preventing needs for care and support is now provided for in the legislation (Care Act 2014, s.2; SSWB(W)A, s.15).

A local authority must provide or arrange for the provision of services, facilities or resources, or take other steps, which it considers will:

- contribute towards preventing or delaying the development by adults in its area of needs for care and support;
- contribute towards preventing or delaying the development by carers in its area of needs for support;
- reduce the needs for care and support of adults in its area;
- reduce the needs for support of carers in its area.

The Welsh legislation also requires local authorities to contribute towards preventing people from suffering abuse or neglect and to minimise the effect on disabled people of their disabilities (s.15(8)).

In England, there is a power to charge for prevention services, subject to the exceptions of community equipment and reablement care (Care and Support (Preventing Needs for Care and Support) Regulations 2014, reg.3).

A local authority must establish and maintain a service for providing people in its area with information and advice relating to care and support for adults and support for carers (Care Act 2014, s.4(1); SSWB(W)A, s.17(1)).

The service must provide information and advice on matters such as how to access the care and support that is available, how to access financial advice on matters relevant to the meeting of needs for care and support and how to raise concerns about the safety or well-being of an adult who has needs for care and support. In England, there is a specific requirement to provide information on how to access independent financial advice (Care Act 2014, s.4(2)(d)).

Provision of advocates

An English local authority must arrange for an 'independent advocate' to represent and support the individual for the purpose of facilitating the individual's involvement in carrying out an adult's or carer's needs assessment, and preparing or revising plans for care, where the individual would experience substantial difficulty in understanding, retaining, using information given or communicating his or her views, wishes or feelings, and where there is nobody else appropriate to involve (Care Act 2014, s.67). The Welsh legislation only creates a power for local authorities to provide advocates, which will in due course be underpinned by regulations (SSWB(W)A, s.181(1)).

7.2.2 Social services department

Social services is the relevant department within the local authority responsible for implementing the above responsibilities, unless their functions have been delegated (see **7.3**).

7.2.3 Co-operation and integration with other partners

Local authorities and their relevant partners or departments, such as health, health-related services and housing must co-operate generally in performing their functions related to care and support and, in specific individual cases they must co-operate in performing their respective functions, wherever they can. This responsibility includes integrating with partners for developing strategic plans, commissioning services, to prevent, reduce or delay needs for care and support, assessments and care planning and delivery (Care Act 2014, ss.2(3), 3, 6, 7, 22, 23, 74; SSWB(W)A, ss.162–169(1)). For example, local authorities in England are expected to draw on existing analyses such as the Joint Strategic Needs Assessment (JSNA) and joint health and well-being strategies and work with the NHS to develop a broader, shared understanding of current and future needs, and support integrated approaches to prevention and delivery.

7.2.4 Powers and duties

A distinction must be drawn between a power to provide a service and a duty to do so; and between a general duty to provide services and a duty to a particular individual.

Where an authority is not under a duty to a specific individual action may only be taken if there is discrimination on grounds of sex, race or disability, the authority blindly follows a particular policy without considering the individual circumstances, or the authority makes an unreasonable decision (the *Wednesbury* principle).

There is a duty on the local authority to meet eligible needs of carers and adults, where the person needing care is ordinary resident in their area, and there is no charge; or they are of limited means; or the adult lacks mental capacity and has no one to arrange his or her care (see **8.3.1**). There is a discretionary power to meet non-eligible needs (Care Act 2014 ss.18–20; SSWB(W)A, ss.36, 45). Local authorities also have wide discretion as to how to meet eligible needs (see **8.3.5**). The following are examples of what may be provided to meet needs:

- accommodation in a care home or in premises of some other type;
- care and support at home or in the community;
- counselling and other types of social work;
- goods and facilities;
- information, advice and advocacy (Care Act 2014, s.8) but could also extend to social work;
- payments (including direct payments);
- aids and adaptations; and
- occupational therapy (SSWB(W)A, s.34(2)).

Power to charge

Local authorities have the power to charge for meeting needs but if they do charge, they must first carry out a financial assessment (Care Act 2014, s.14; SSWB(W)A, s.59). The individual's income must not fall below a minimum amount specified in the regulations – in England, where the person is living in his or her own home, it is equivalent to the applicable amount under benefits regulations plus 25 per cent. In Wales, home care costs are capped. This sum increases annually, and for 2015/16 it is £60 per week.

From April 2020, it is proposed the maximum a person should pay for his or her care will be capped at £72,000. For those living in a care home, the calculation will exclude daily living costs (capped at £12,000 per year). The Welsh government has no pending plans to introduce a cap on care.

If a service user has capital that exceeds £23,250 in England, or £24,000 in Wales (2015/16) the local authority is not permitted to pay towards the cost of care. In England, capital between £14,250 and £23,250 is treated as creating a weekly income of £1 for each complete £250 in excess of £14,250. Capital under £14,250 in England or £24,000 in Wales is ignored in the financial assessment. **Chapter 14** provides more detail.

From April 2020, it is proposed that the upper capital limit in England will rise to £118,000 for those living in a care home, where their former home forms part of the financial assessment.

7.2.5 Ordinarily resident   *Have to be resident*

The duty of a local authority to provide and fund care generally applies in respect of an individual who is ordinary resident in its area. In contrast, in England, an individual who may be in need (or about to be in need: see *R (on the application of B)* v. *Camden LBC* [2005] EWHC 1366 (Admin)) of care services does not need to be ordinarily resident to be assessed for services.

The concept becomes particularly complex when people move area as it determines which local authority funds the cost of residential care, domiciliary care, deprivation of liberty processes, delayed discharge processes and responsibility for Mental Health Act 1983, s.117 aftercare. It is also relevant to NHS bodies when exercising partnership arrangements with local authorities.

In England, the Care and Support (Ordinary Residence) (Specified Accommodation) Regulations 2014 and the Care and Support (Disputes Between Local Authorities) Regulations 2014 apply, as well as chapter 19 of CSSG. The Department of Health ordinary residence guidance (LAC (93) 7) has application in Wales until 2016. The Care Act 2014, ss.37–38 and the Care and Support (Continuity of Care) Regulations 2014 apply in England in respect of moves between local authorities and continuity of care.

Guidance for the NHS is set out in *Who Pays? Determining Responsibility for Payments to Providers* (August 2013).

Meaning of ordinarily resident

The term 'ordinarily resident' is not defined in legislation and so the term should be given its ordinary and natural meaning, subject to any interpretation in the courts. It involves consideration of the length of time a person has been in the area, his intention and degree of continuity. For a person with mental capacity, this will be identified by where the person has chosen to be settled as part of the regular order of his life (*R* v. *Barnet LBC, ex p Shah* [1983] 2 AC 309).

If the person lacks mental capacity to make the choice of where they live, the *Shah* test is adapted. Instead, ordinary residence is determined by where the person's usual home is based or considering the person's physical presence, and the nature and purpose of that presence. The Supreme Court has held in *R (on the application of Cornwall Council)* v. *Secretary of State for Health* [2015] UKSC 46 that the key point is whether the person's residence was sufficiently settled to constitute ordinary residence.

If the person has more than one place of residence, ordinary residence is determined by where the person has the strongest links.

People of no settled residence or in urgent need should be treated as being ordinarily resident in the local authority area where they are present (*R* v. *Redbridge LBC, ex p East Sussex CC* (1993) *The Times*, 3 January; see also Care Act 2014, ss.18(1), 19(1) and 20(1); SSWB(W)A, ss.35, 40 and 194).

Non-residential care services

In respect of non-residential services, where a person moves from one local authority area to another, the receiving local authority will be responsible for assessing and arranging care. This may result in a change in services, as there is no obligation to provide the same services as the outgoing local authority. There is an expectation in such cases that both local authorities should work together to enable portability of care, which is embedded in the new care legislation (Care Act 2014, ss.37, 38; SSWB(W)A, ss.56–57).

'Deeming provisions' for specified accommodation

Where an out-of-area placement is arranged in specified accommodation, 'deeming provisions' are triggered. Under the English regulations 'the specified accommodation' is a care home, shared lives scheme accommodation (i.e. adult fostering) or supported living accommodation. Until the 2015 Welsh regulations are in force, the deeming provisions only apply to care home accommodation; after April 2016, they are the same as the English regulations.

The effect of this is that the placing local authority remains responsible for provision and funding of care in another local authority area. This applies when the person has been assessed and the local authority has accepted responsibility to provide.

If the person has independently moved into another area, such as those who self-fund and subsequently seek local authority assistance, the person will be ordinarily resident in the new local authority area. This applies even if the former local authority provides advice and information about the move.

Where there is a break in local authority provision, for example a person who qualified for the 12-week property disregard, then becomes self-funding, but later seeks local authority support, the placing local authority is responsible during the initial 12-week period but the receiving local authority is responsible following the break in provision, but if the person funds his or her care through a deferred payment agreement, the placing local authority remains responsible, as it is that local authority which has agreed to fund the care shortfall, but taken a charge on the person's former home as security.

Funded nursing care

Residents in nursing homes are entitled to a contribution for their nursing care provided by a registered nurse. The authority responsible is the clinical commissioning group in England/Health Board (HB) in Wales where the resident is registered with a GP. It means that local authorities have to liaise with their local NHS body, where they previously had no partnership arrangements.

NHS continuing healthcare

If the full cost of care is being met as the person qualifies for NHS continuing healthcare, the authority responsible is the NHS body that originally clinically assessed the person.

Aftercare services under Mental Health Act 1983, s.117

Section 75(3) of the Care Act 2014 amends s.117 of the Mental Health Act 1983, applicable in England and Wales, so that the relevant responsible local authority in respect of aftercare is:

(a)   if, immediately before being detained, the person concerned was ordinarily resident in England, the area in England in which he was ordinarily resident;

(b)   if, immediately before being detained the person concerned was ordinarily resident in Wales, the area in Wales in which he was ordinarily resident; or

(c)   in any other case, for the area in which the person concerned is resident or to which he is sent on discharge by the hospital in which he was detained.

See **8.2.3** on aftercare services.

Dispute resolution

Disputes between local authorities regarding ordinary residence in England should be resolved locally, but if this is not achieved, they are determined by the Secretary of State. The local authority which is meeting the needs of the adult or carer on the date on which the dispute arises must continue to meet those needs until the dispute is resolved.

If no local authority is meeting the needs on the date on which the dispute arises the duty is on:

(a)   the local authority in whose area the adult needing care is living; or

(b)   if the adult needing care is not living in the area of any local authority, the local authority in whose area that adult is present (Care Act 2014, s.40).

In Wales, disputes are resolved by the Welsh Ministers or someone appointed by them (SSWB(W)A, s.195). The 2015 regulations in Wales are similar to the English regulations.

7.3 ROLE OF THE PRIVATE SECTOR

Care watch

Since the early 1990s, there has been a big shift towards service provision being made by the independent sector. Few local authorities run their own care homes or have their own agencies, yet the independent sector is often reliant on the state which funds their clients. This has produced difficulties for service users, who may find their provider goes out of business or the care provided is basic or limited as state commissioners pay as little as possible for the service. In England, the Care Act 2014 has attempted to recognise this problem, by giving local authorities responsibility to create a regime to oversee the market and take action to avoid or mitigate care provider failure (ss.53–57). In Wales, local authorities have a more limited role, to step in and arrange care and support where a care provider's business fails (SSWB(W)A, ss.189–191).

In England, local authorities also have wide powers to delegate most of their functions under the Care Act 2014 with the exceptions being those relating to charging, safeguarding and integration and co-operation. Assessments, eligibility decisions and care planning can all be delegated. The Welsh legislation does not contain the same power of delegation. However, the role of the private sector is likely to expand further.

England authorities can delegate a lot to the private sector

246

CHAPTER 8

Care and support services

Caroline Bielanska

8.1 ASSESSMENT FOR SERVICES

Care and support services may be for the well-being of a disabled or ill person or to assist a carer to provide care. They can include domiciliary services provided in the home, comprising personal care (bathing, washing, dressing, eating, etc.) and domestic help (often limited to cooking and laundry); day services provided outside the home; and residential services (short- or long-term care). There can also be assistance for people with physical disabilities with aids and appliances (continence pads, walking aids, wheelchairs, etc.) and the home (adaptations or provision of a suitable home). These are not exhaustive examples of services, as care provision should be flexible to meet the person's needs.

Provision or arrangement of care and support services is dependent on an assessment of the individual's needs, but should be seen as a critical intervention in its own right, rather than merely a gateway to help, as it can assist people to understand their situation and the needs they have, enable them to take action to reduce or delay the onset of greater needs and know how to access support when they require it.

Although it is not necessary to ask for an assessment, the person will need to come to the local authority's attention, either by a direct approach to the local adult social services department or indirectly, such as through the housing department (*R (on the application of P)* v. *Newham LBC* (2000) 4 CCL Rep 48).

Chapter 7 explains how the social care legislation and policy has changed in England since April 2015 and will change in Wales from April 2016.

8.1.1 The well-being principle

There is a general duty on each local authority when exercising its functions, to promote the individual's well-being (Care Act 2014, s.1: Social Services and Well-being (Wales) Act (SSWB(W)A) 2014, s.5. It applies equally to adults with care and support needs and their carers. This is known as the 'well-being principle', which intends to put well-being at the heart of care and support, by actively seeking improvements to the person's life to achieve his or her desired outcomes. It is a broad concept, which includes the individual's well-being in relation to his or her personal dignity; physical and mental health and emotional well-being; protection from abuse and neglect; control over his or her day-to-day life; suitability of living accommodation; participation in work, education, training or recreation; domestic, family and personal relationships; social and economic well-being; and the individual's contribution to society. In Wales, there is no mention of the need to ensure the personal dignity of the individual but the definition extends to securing the person's rights and entitlements (SSWB(W)A, s.2). It is not intended to specify the activities which should take place.

During the assessment process, the local authority should explicitly consider the most relevant aspects of well-being to the individual concerned, and assess how his or her needs impact on them. Taking this approach will allow for the assessment to identify how care and support, or other services or resources in the local community, could help the person to achieve his or her outcomes. During care and support planning, when agreeing how needs are to be met, promoting the person's well-being may mean making decisions about particular types or locations of care (Care and Support Statutory Guidance (CSSG), para.1.12).

8.1.2 Duty to assess an adult with care and support needs

In England, the duty to assess an adult who may have needs for care and support arises under the Care Act 2014, s.9. Overarching Care and Support Statutory Guidance (CSSG) was published in October 2014, which includes guidance on assessments, eligibility, financial assessments and care planning. There is no need to request an assessment, but in practice a request must be made before an assessment will be undertaken. Wales has its own Statutory Code of Practice, which contains similar but not identical guidance.

A similar duty to assess arises in Wales, under SSWB(W)A, s.19, which comes into force on 6 April 2016. In the meantime, the National Health Service and Community Care Act 1990 (the 1990 Act), s.47 applies to create a statutory duty to assess needs on Welsh local authorities where it appears to them that a person for whom they may provide or arrange community care services appears to need such services. Transitional arrangements mean that people in Wales who have been assessed and their care arranged pre-April 2016 will continue to be subject to the old legislation until they are assessed.

The term 'community care services' is defined by reference to specific service provision under:

- Part III of the National Assistance Act 1948 (welfare services for disabled persons, including under the Chronically Sick and Disabled Persons Act 1970, s.2 and residential care principally for elderly, ill and disabled people).
- Section 45 of the Health Services and Public Health Act 1968 (including practical assistance in the home for old people).
- Section 192 of, and Schedule 15 to, the National Health Service (Wales) Act 2006 (home helps for a person who is 'aged', night sitting service, day centres,

meals and social work support to prevent illness and for the care and aftercare of persons suffering from illness).

- Section 117 of the Mental Health Act 1983 (aftercare services for people with a mental disorder).

The legislative focus of community care services is not on meeting a need but on providing a prescribed service. If the assessed person is disabled, the Welsh local authority must provide a written statement, which sets out the needs of the disabled person, which the local authority should provide, and its proposals as to how it will meet those needs (1990 Act, s.47(2) and Disabled Persons (Services, Consultation and Representation) Act 1986, s.4).

The Welsh government published guidance in December 2013 setting out the duties and responsibilities on social services departments when carrying out needs assessments and care planning, specifically in regard to people aged 65 and over. The guidance is called: *Integrated Assessment, Planning and Review Arrangements for Older People: Guidance for Professionals in Supporting the Health, Care and Well-being of Older People. The Unified and Fair System for Assessing and Managing Care* (UFSAMC) applies to people who are aged under 64 years (NAFWC 09/02, WHC (2002) 3). The Welsh Code of Practice contains guidance in Parts 3 and 4.

8.1.3 Duty to assess a carer with support needs

In England, any carer of an adult who may have a need for support (whether currently or in the foreseeable future) is entitled to have an assessment of their own needs for support (Care Act 2014, s.10). There is no need to request an assessment, but in practice it is usual to seek an assessment before one will be undertaken. The right to an assessment applies to any informal carer, regardless of the level or frequency of care. The aim of the assessment is to ensure the sustainability of care and prevent the care situation from breaking down. As such the assessment is focused on the carer being able and willing to care and the impact of providing care on the carer's day-to-day life, including whether they work or wish to work, participate or wish to participate in education, training or recreation. It is useful to note that family carers who are also employed have the right to request flexible working from their employers under the Work and Families Act 2006.

The local authority should not use the presence of a carer as an excuse for not looking at the needs of the cared for person and for failing to provide the services that are needed. The local authority must take into account the results of that assessment in making its decision. The carer may be charged for any service they receive, but this may be subject to a financial assessment of his or her own financial resources.

An identical duty applies in Wales from 6 April 2016 (SSWB(W)A, s.24). Until then, Welsh local authorities are under a duty to inform carers that they may be entitled to a carers' assessment (Carers (Equal Opportunities) Act 2004, s.1) and can consider the carer's needs:

1.   Under the Disabled Persons (Services, Consultation and Representation) Act 1986, s.8 when assessing the needs of the cared for person, the authority must have regard to the carer's ability to continue to provide care on a regular basis. It is not an assessment of the carer and will only apply where the carer is already providing a substantial amount of care on a regular basis and is not employed to do so by a statutory body or private agency.

2.   When undertaking an assessment of the cared for person under the 1990 Act, s.47, the local authority can carry out an assessment of the carer's ability to provide or to continue to provide a substantial amount of care on a regular basis. This should happen before the local authority makes its decision as to whether the needs of the cared for person call for the provision of any services (Carers (Recognition and Services) Act 1995, s.1).

3.   When the carer asks the local authority to carry out an assessment of his or her ability to provide and to continue to provide care on a regular basis for the cared for person. This is independent of any assessment of the cared for person and is particularly useful if the cared for person refuses either to be assessed or to receive services (Carers and Disabled Children Act 2000, s.2(2)). Unlike services provided under the Carers (Recognition and Services) Act 1995, the carer can be means tested for the services they receive under the Carers and Disabled Children Act 2000.

The Carers (Recognition and Services) Act 1995 and Carers and Disabled Children Act 2000 are silent on the definition of 'substantial and regular care'. It is for the assessor to identify the impact of the caring role on the carer, in light of the carer's age, health, employment status, interests and other commitments.

8.1.4   Threshold for an assessment

Low threshold

The threshold for appearing to need care and support is a low one, which means that the local authority cannot refuse an assessment even if there is no service need identified. The duty to assess is independent of provision, so exists regardless of the level of the person's needs or his or her financial resources. Any local authority which attempts to sift out assessments where there is no hope of meeting any need would be acting unlawfully (*R* v. *Bristol City Council, ex p Penfold* (1998) 1 CCL Rep 315). It should be noted that the duty to assess does not extend to creating a duty to provide.

Where services are required as a matter of urgency they may be temporarily provided prior to an assessment. Provision will be made subject to a full assessment being conducted at a later date, following which, depending on the outcome, the service may continue, be reduced, altered or withdrawn.

Literally every carer regardless of caring duties + wealth is eligible for an assessment

8.1.5 The involvement of other public bodies

There is a new expectation on each local authority to co-operate with 'relevant partners', in particular, NHS bodies, private registered providers of social housing, police, other local authorities, and other departments, including children's services and housing. If during the assessment it is apparent the assessed person has a need which could be addressed by a relevant partner, the assessor should request their input. There are reciprocal duties of co-operation given to the relevant partners (Care Act 2014, ss.6 and 7; SSWB(W)A, s.164).

The NHS body must be involved where a place in a nursing home is sought, as the NHS will be responsible for funding the nursing care provided by a registered nurse, known as 'funded nursing care'.

8.1.6 Form of assessment

A local authority must establish and maintain a service for providing people with information and advice relating to care and support. Information and advice should be provided at key touch points, throughout the care journey, so that people understand what to expect, what they are or are not to receive, with reasons, how to delay or reduce their care needs, how provision is financed, and how to challenge an adverse decision (Care Act 2014, s.4; SSWB(W)A, s.17).

A local authority must carry out an assessment in a manner which is appropriate and proportionate to the needs and circumstances of the individual to whom it relates. The nature of the assessment will not always be the same for all people, and depending on the circumstances, it could range from an initial contact which helps a person with lower needs to access support in their local community, to a more intensive, ongoing process which requires the input of a number of professionals over a longer period of time. Where an individual may lack capacity a face-to-face assessment must be arranged.

Assessments may be:

- Face-to-face and co-produced, where the person being assessed takes a collaborate role in the assessment.
- A supported self-assessment, which may be done online or over the telephone, and is carried out jointly by the adult with care and support needs or the carer and the local authority. It places individuals in control of the assessment process to a point where they complete their own assessment. People should be asked to complete the same assessment questionnaire that the local authority uses in its assessments.
- Integrated, to prevent one person from having multiple assessments with other agencies and partners, such as the NHS.
- Combined assessment with carers, if both are in agreement.
- Specialist assessment for people who are deafblind.

The local authority must involve the person, any carer and any person they ask to be involved, or where the person lacks mental capacity, anyone who appears to be interested in the person's welfare. Where a carer's assessment is being undertaken, the cared for person does not have to be involved.

Local authorities commonly use assessment tools to help collect information about potential service users, so the outcome of the assessment provides a full picture of the individual's needs, including where those needs fluctuate, before the local authority moves on to consider the person's eligibility and what provision could meet those needs. People who have been assessed should be provided with a copy of the assessment.

Local authorities must carry out an assessment within a reasonable period of time and they should publish realistic timescales (CSSG, para.6.29 and in Wales in accordance with UFSAMC, Annex 10, para.2.17). In Wales, the *Integrated Assessment, Planning and Review Arrangements Guidance* requires that assessments are timely and appropriate (para.6.10). Part 2 of the Welsh Code of Practice repeatedly reminds those involved with the assessment and planning process that responses should be proportionate and timely.

8.1.7   Advocacy support

In England, the local authority must provide independent advocacy to facilitate the person's involvement in the care and support assessment, planning and review processes, where an individual would experience substantial difficulty in understanding, retaining or using information given, or in communicating his or her views, wishes or feelings and there is no one appropriate and available to act on the person's behalf. In Wales see Part 10 of the Code of Practice.

8.2   ELIGIBILITY FOR SERVICES

8.2.1   Duty of local authority to consider impact of needs on well-being

If the local authority is satisfied that the person has care and support needs or support needs, it must then consider whether the person meets the eligibility criteria. In doing so it must consider how the need for care and support impacts on the assessed person's well-being, what that person wants to achieve from his or her day-to-day life and whether and to what extent the provision of a service could contribute to achieve those outcomes (see **8.1.1** and **7.2.1**) (Care Act 2014, ss.9(4), (6), 10(5), (8) and 13(1); SSWB(W)A, ss.19(4), 24(4) and 32(1)).

Until 6 April 2016, in Wales, the local authority should have regard to the results of the assessment, and then decide whether the person's needs call for the provision by the authority of specified services (1990 Act, s.47(1)). This is determined by comparing the person's assessed needs to eligible criteria.

8.2.2   Eligibility criteria

The Care Act 2014, s.13 and SSWB(W)A, s.32 set out the provision for eligibility criteria. In England, the Act is supported by the Care and Support (Eligibility Criteria) Regulations 2015, SI 2015/313 that contain a mandatory national minimum threshold for eligibility which establishes what level of needs must be met. The written outcome of the determination of eligibility should be given to the assessed person. Local authorities can decide to meet needs that are not deemed to be eligible if they choose to do so. Similar but not identical regulations will come into force in Wales on 6 April 2016 (Care and Support (Eligibility) (Wales) Regulations 2015, SI 2015/1578 (W 187)).

The threshold is based on identifying how an adult's needs which arise from or are related to a physical or mental impairment or illness, affect his or her ability to achieve at least two specified outcomes, namely:

- managing and maintaining nutrition;
- maintaining personal hygiene;
- managing toilet needs;
- being appropriately clothed;
- being able to make use of their home safely;
- maintaining a habitable home environment;
- developing and maintaining family or other personal relationships;
- accessing and engaging in work, training, education or volunteering;
- making use of necessary facilities or services in the local community including public transport, and recreational facilities or services; and
- carrying out any caring responsibilities the adult has for a child, and how this significantly impacts on their well-being.

The Welsh Assembly has a wider and lower eligibility threshold, which covers people whose needs arise because of physical or mental ill-health, age, disability, dependence on alcohol or drugs, or other similar circumstances and only one specified outcome needs to be met.

A carer's needs are only eligible where their needs arise as a consequence of providing necessary care for an adult, the effect of which is that the carer's physical or mental health is either deteriorating or is at risk of doing so, or the carer is unable to achieve any of the prescribed outcomes, such as being able to look after a child or others to whom the carer provides care, engaging in work, training, education, volunteering or recreational activities, which has a significant impact on the carer's well-being.

Being 'unable to achieve' an outcome means:

- unable to achieve it without assistance; or
- able to achieve it without assistance, but doing so causes the adult significant pain, distress or anxiety; or doing so endangers or is likely to endanger the health or safety of the adult, or of others; or able to achieve it without assistance but it takes significantly longer than would normally be expected.

Individuals with fluctuating needs may have needs which are not apparent at the time of the assessment, but may have arisen in the past and are likely to arise again in the future. As such local authorities must consider the individual's need over an appropriate period of time to ensure that all of his or her needs have been accounted for when eligibility is being determined.

The term 'significant' is not defined by the English regulations, but must be understood to have its everyday meaning.

Pending the introduction of the 2014 Welsh legislation, guidance has been issued in *Integrated Assessment, Planning and Review Arrangements for Older People* (**http://gov.wales/docs/dhss/publications/131217reporten.pdf**), which provides councils with a framework for determining eligibility for older people. It provides that councils should make similar decisions in their area. It does not go as far as to say that different councils should make identical decisions about eligibility or what services should be provided. In setting eligibility criteria, Welsh local authorities have to take account of the eligibility guidance, their own resources, local expectations and local costs, and also the Equality Act 2010 and the Human Rights Act 1998 (*R (on the application of Chavda)* v. *Harrow LBC* [2007] EWHC 3064 (Admin)).

The Welsh framework is graded into four bands, based on the seriousness of the risk to independence if problems and issues are not addressed. Local authorities do not need to adopt all bands as it depends on their own resources. Eligibility for an individual is determined by comparing the risks to his or her autonomy, health, safety, ability to manage daily routines and involvement in family and wider community life with the eligibility criteria.

8.2.3 Aftercare services under Mental Health Act 1983, s.117

A joint duty is imposed by Mental Health Act 1983, s.117 on local authorities and NHS bodies to arrange or provide aftercare services to those who leave hospital after ceasing to be detained under ss.3, 37, 47 or 48. These services must have the purposes of 'meeting a need arising from or related to the person's mental disorder' and 'reducing the risk of a deterioration of the person's mental condition and, accordingly, reducing the risk of the person requiring admission to a hospital again for treatment for mental disorder' (s.117(6)). Services provided under this section are broad (including residential and domiciliary care) and must not be charged for (*R* v. *Manchester City Council, ex p Stennett* [2002] UKHL 34). Aftercare services do not need to be provided indefinitely and will cease if the need for the service no longer exists. In the case of a person with dementia this may be unlikely (see judicial comments in *R* v. *Richmond LBC, ex p Watson* [1999] All ER (D) 899).

8.2.4 Local Government Act 2000 – overarching provision

Independent of the social care legislation the local authority has a wide general power under Local Government Act 2000, s.2 to do anything which it considers is likely to promote or improve the social well-being of its area, which may be for the benefit of all persons or an individual person, either resident or present in its area. This extends to providing accommodation to any person (s.2(4)(f) and *R (on the application of J)* v. *Enfield LBC* [2002] EWHC 432 (Admin)). There is a wide general power to charge for such services and guidance was issued by the Office of the Deputy Prime Minister, entitled *General Power for Best Value Authorities to Charge for Discretionary Services: Guidance on the Power in the Local Government Act 2003*.

8.3 PROVISION

8.3.1 Duty to arrange or provide

If the person's assessed needs meet the eligibility criteria, the local authority must then consider what could be done to meet those needs. In England, the local authority will also consider at this stage whether the adult is ordinarily resident in their area, whereas from 6 April 2016, in Wales this is considered at the assessment stage. For more details of the term 'ordinarily resident' see **7.2.5**. (Care Act 2014, s.13(3), (4); SSWB(W)A, s.32; and, before 1 April 2016, the 1990 Act, s.47(1) applies.)

A local authority must meet eligible needs if:

- the adult is ordinarily resident in the local authority's area; and
- there is no charge for meeting the needs; the adult (or the carer if it relates to a carer's needs) has limited financial resources (see **Chapter 14**); or the adult lacks mental capacity and there is no person who can arrange their care on their behalf (Care Act 2014, ss.18 and 20; SSWB(W)A, ss.35 and 40).

From April 2020 local authorities in England will meet the eligible needs, if the adult has exceeded the 'care cap', i.e. the financial limit on what an individual is expected to pay for their care during their lifetime on meeting their eligible needs (Care Act 2014, s.18(5)). See **Chapter 14** for more detail about the care cap.

8.3.2 Arrangements for self-funders

The new care legislation gives people with eligible needs who have sufficient financial assets to fund their own care and/or support, the right to ask their local authority to meet their needs. This is a right to ask, but not a right to have the arrangements made by the local authority, which means they may either directly contract on behalf of the person or broker care to meet their needs. In the event that the local authority arranges the care and/or support, an arrangement fee may be charged.

8.3.3 Delayed discharge from hospital

Local authorities should provide services promptly once they have agreed to do so. Where waiting is unavoidable, they should ensure alternative services are in place to meet the person's eligible needs.

Delays can occur at the point of discharge from hospital, as social services may not have assessed the patient or put arrangements in place for their move. In England, under the Care Act 2014, Sched.3 there is a financial incentive for local authorities to provide care and support services for adult patients who may need local authority support. The hospital serves formal notice on the local authority which then has a short period of time to assess the patient and arrange service provision so they can safely be transferred to a more appropriate setting. If the local authority fails to do this, it must pay a daily sum to the hospital until the patient is discharged. Prior to the notice being served, the patient and/or his carer should be consulted.

8.3.4 Care planning

A core feature in establishing good service provision is understanding what will be provided, when, by which service provider, and the objectives in providing that service. The local authority must prepare a 'care and support plan' for the adult or 'support plan' for the carer and the legislation sets out what should be contained in the plan (Care Act 2014, s.25; SSWB(W)A, s.54). A copy of the plan should be provided to those involved.

8.3.5 Provision and local authority resources

Once the local authority has determined it is under a duty to meet the person's eligible needs it must do so and cannot use lack of resources as an excuse for failing to act.

Although care planning has for many years attempted to be person centred, in practice because of the severity of needs which the individual has to have, to be eligible for services, the local authority is usually heavily involved in deciding the service to be provided. This gives the local authority wide discretion as to how best to meet the need within its budget. Any upper cost parameters should only ever be used as a guide, as the local authority must cater for exceptional circumstances to avoid fettering its discretion. Budgetary considerations should not be prioritised over the legal requirement to meet the assessed need, which would amount to maladministration and be unlawful. As such, local authorities have discretion as to how to meet the eligible need but no discretion as to whether to meet the need. The duty continues until the need has been fulfilled (*R* v. *Sefton MBC, ex p Help the Aged* [1997] 4 All ER 532 at 543; *R* v. *Wigan MBC, ex p Tammadge* [1998] 1 CCLR 581: *R (on the application of Batantu)* v. *Islington LBC* [2000] All ER (D) 1744).

Where the local authority can meet the assessed need by an alternative care package, the cheaper option can be selected (*R* v. *Gloucestershire CC, ex p Barry* [1996] 4 All ER 421 at 439). In effect, the local authority may decide to provide residential home care rather than 24-hour care in the home, provided that it is suitable to meet the assessed need (*R* v. *Lancashire CC, ex p Ingham and Whalley* (unreported, 5 July 1995); *R (on the application of Khana)* v. *London Borough of Southwark* [2001] EWCA Civ 999) or one type of residential accommodation over another (*R* v. *Kensington and Chelsea Royal London Borough, ex p Kujtim* [1999] 4 All ER 161). Continence pads have been found to meet the need for help with safe toileting at night, for a person who was not incontinent. Although this may interfere with the service user's right under art.8 of the European Convention on Human Rights, for respect to his or her family life and privacy, it was not breached, as it was proportionate and justified as 'necessary in a democratic society' (*McDonald* v. *United Kingdom* (2014) 60 EHRR 1).

8.3.6   Identifying default

The following matters should be addressed if problems are encountered in securing adequate care provision:

- Has an assessment of needs been requested (or the need for this arisen)?
- If so, what has been the response?
- If not, make the request (it cannot be refused).
- Has an assessment of needs been made?
- If so, what are the assessed needs (inspect the assessment)?
- If not, why not?
- Was the assessment properly made?
- Did those who made the assessment listen to the elderly person and carer (and any advocate)?
- Was it a fair assessment of needs?
- If not, use the complaints procedure.
- Has a decision been made as to whether those needs should be provided for?
- If so, what is that decision?
- If not, why not?
- Has a decision been made not to provide for assessed needs?
- If so, what are the reasons for that decision?
- Does this reflect the eligibility criteria for determining when services should be provided?
- Has a decision been made as to provision for assessed needs?
- If so, what is that decision and will the provision meet those needs?
- If not, why not?
- What provision is actually being made to meet the assessed needs?
- Does this fulfil the decision to provide for assessed needs?
- If not, why not and what provision is available to meet these needs?

- Is any restriction or condition being imposed?
- If so, is it necessary?
- What purpose is it intended to fulfil?
- Can this purpose be fulfilled in some other way?
- Has an existing service been withdrawn or restricted?
- If so, is this the result of a reassessment?
- If not, does it follow a decision or has it just happened?
- On what basis (if at all) can this be justified?
- Should the needs be reassessed?
- If so, start from the first question again!
- If not, the existing provision should continue.
- Does this assessment/reassessment suggest that the issues are primarily health-care so that the responsibility should lie with the NHS? (See *R* v. *North and East Devon Health Authority, ex p Coughlan* [2001] QB 213.)

8.3.7   Withdrawal of services

Services cannot be withdrawn once provided until the person has been reassessed, the results conclude that they no longer meet the eligibility criteria or his or her needs can be met in another way, and that withdrawal of the service will not put the person at serious physical risk. The person should also be advised of the complaints procedure to appeal the decision if they wish.

8.4   COMPLAINTS PROCEDURE

8.4.1   Statutory basis for complaints

In England, local authority social services departments must follow the Local Authority Social Services and National Health Service Complaints (England) Regulations 2009, SI 2009/309 in resolving complaints. In Wales, the Social Services Complaints Procedure (Wales) Regulations 2014, SI 2014/1794 (W 187) apply. These are to be read alongside *A Guide to Handling Complaints and Representations by Local Authority Social Services* (2014: **http://gov.wales/docs/ dhss/publications/140730complaintsen.pdf**).

Each local authority must appoint a complaints manager and make arrangements for dealing with complaints in relation to the discharge of, or failure to discharge, its social services functions in respect of persons for whom it has a power or duty to provide and whose needs (or possible needs) have come to its attention. The aim is that complaints are dealt with efficiently, are properly investigated, and appropriate action is taken in the light of the outcome.

8.4.2 Timescale

The complainant can be the service user or a representative and another person may make a complaint on behalf of a person who has died or on behalf of someone who cannot make the complaint due to his or her physical or mental incapacity. Complaints must be made within 12 months of the cause of the complaint arising or when it first came to their attention.

8.4.3 Procedure

A complaint can be made orally, electronically or in writing. In England, the local authority must acknowledge receipt within three working days, whereas in Wales it is within two working days. The complainant must be provided with a copy of the complaint, if made orally. The complainant must be offered the opportunity to discuss the complaint in an attempt to resolve the matter informally.

In England, there is no set timeframe, but a plan of action should be agreed, including timescales for when and how the complainant will hear back about his or her complaint. There is no prescribed independent investigation, but the complaints manager can arrange for an independent conciliator or mediator to be brought in to help resolve the complaint.

In Wales, the discussion should take place within 10 working days of the date upon which the local authority acknowledged receipt of the complaint. The complainant has a right to ask the local authority for a formal investigation of his or her complaint. At this stage, the complaint will be investigated by an 'independent investigator', i.e. someone who is not employed by the local authority which is the subject of the complaint. A report with findings, conclusions and recommendations must be produced. The local authority must respond to the complainant within 25 working days of the request for the independent investigation.

The complaint should be finalised within six months from the date when the complaint was received. If this timescale is not possible, the complainant must be given written reasons why. Once any investigation is completed a written response explaining the outcome and what action has been taken should be sent to the complainant. If the complainant is dissatisfied with the decision, it is possible to refer the matter to the Local Government Ombudsman for England or the Public Services Ombudsman for Wales.

8.4.4 Alternative remedies

The following alternative methods may be available of challenging the local authority and enforcing its duties:

- complaint to the Local Government Ombudsman;
- judicial review;
- request to the Secretary of State to exercise default powers;
- civil action in damages for breach of statutory duty or negligence.

See **5.6** and **5.7**.

8.5 RETIREES RETURNING TO THE UK

8.5.1 Health and social care

Much of the provision of health and community care services is determined by whether or not the individual is ordinarily resident in the clinical commissioning group/local Health Board or local authority area (see **7.2.5** for the meaning of 'ordinarily resident'). Local authorities are under a duty to arrange or provide services for those people who are eligible and ordinarily resident in their area. If they are not ordinarily resident the local authority only has discretion to provide services.

8.5.2 Immediately necessary or emergency treatment

Every GP practice or walk-in centre has an obligation to provide any immediately necessary or emergency treatment to any patient that presents, regardless of all other considerations. In the case of treatment given in an accident and emergency department the exemption from charges will cease to apply once the patient is formally admitted as an in-patient or registered at an outpatient clinic.

Drugs and dressings, which are necessary, are prescribed on an NHS prescription and supplied in the usual way, subject to NHS prescription charges.

8.5.3 Registering with a GP surgery

Any person living lawfully in the UK on a settled basis is regarded as ordinarily resident in the UK and entitled to free primary medical services.

8.5.4 Hospital treatment

Anyone who is deemed to be ordinarily resident in the UK is entitled to free NHS hospital treatment. If the person intends to live permanently in the UK they will qualify for free NHS care from the date of their arrival in the UK. However, they will need to prove their intention and their right to reside.

UK pensioners residing six months in UK and less than six months in an EEA country or Switzerland, but are not registered as resident there, are classed as ordinarily resident in the UK.

Anyone who is not ordinarily resident is subject to the National Health Service (Charges to Overseas Visitors) Regulations 2015, SI 2015/238 and the National Health Service (Charges to Overseas Visitors) Regulations 1989, SI 1989/306 which apply in Wales. Guidance on the English regulations was published in 2015. The regulations place a responsibility on NHS hospitals to establish whether a person is ordinarily resident; or exempt from charges under one of a number of exemption categories; or liable for charges. Compulsory psychiatric treatment is exempt.

8.5.5 British citizens living in another EEA country or Switzerland

British citizens living in another EEA country or Switzerland but who are in the UK on a temporary visit, and are insured by their resident state, should present a valid European Health Insurance Card (EHIC) from that member state to access any medical treatment and care. If they cannot show their EHIC, they may instead produce a Provisional Replacement Certificate (PRC) for that card to prove entitlement.

UK pensioners living in EEA countries and with an 'S1 document' (a certificate of entitlement to healthcare) registered in that country will be exempt from payment for elective healthcare. The person's spouse/civil partner is also exempt when lawfully visiting the UK with them, unless they are entitled to hold a non-UK EHIC. The UK will recover the cost of that healthcare from the other member state.

8.5.6 British citizens living in a non-EEA country

Where there is a reciprocal healthcare agreement between the UK and a country outside the EEA, the person will be entitled to free necessary medical treatment. This by its nature is very limited. If they are not covered under an exemption category under the regulations, they will be charged for services they receive at the point of accessing care.

CHAPTER 9

Commissioning care

Cate Searle

9.1 ENGLAND: CARE STANDARDS LEGISLATION AND REGULATION

9.1.1 Health and Social Care Act 2008 and underpinning regulations

The system for regulation and monitoring of care homes and care services has changed a number of times over the past 15 years. Since 2009, regulatory responsibility has rested with an independent body, the Care Quality Commission (CQC), which was established by the Health and Social Care Act 2008. The CQC replaced the Commission for Social Care Inspection (CSCI), which had itself replaced the National Care Standards Commission. Prior to that and until 2002, regulatory and inspection responsibility lay with individual local authorities and health authorities, which had resulted in unacceptable differences in standards of care across the country.

The CQC is responsible for the registration, review and inspection of certain health and adult social care services in England irrespective of whether these are provided by the NHS, local authorities, private companies, charities or voluntary organisations. The CQC has combined the work and functions previously performed by the Mental Health Act Commission, CSCI and the Healthcare Commission, with the aim of ensuring common standards of care across all services.

Notwithstanding the role and function of the CQC, local authority social services departments and NHS clinical commissioning groups (CCGs) also continue to exercise regulatory, inspection and monitoring roles in relation to services that they commission (fund) and also in relation to Safeguarding Adults at Risk. In a consultation and review process undertaken by the Department for Business, Innovation and Skills (*Review of the Adult Care Home Sector: Focus on Enforcement Regulatory Reviews* (October 2013) a large number of care providers commented upon the 'very extensive duplication' required of them by social services in addition to their CQC reporting obligations, and some conflict between those standards required by the CQC, CCGs and local authorities.

The main sources of legislation and regulation in England are found in:

- Health and Social Care Act 2008.
- Care Quality Commission (Registration) Regulations 2009, SI 2009/3112 (2009 Regulations).

- Care Quality Commission (Registration) and (Additional Functions) and Health and Social Care Act 2008 (Regulated Activities) (Amendment) Regulations 2012, SI 2012/921.
- Care Act 2014.
- Health and Social Care Act 2008 (Regulated Activities) Regulations 2014, SI 2014/2936 (2014 Regulations).
- Health and Social Care Act 2008 (Regulated Activities) (Amendment) Regulations 2015, SI 2015/64.

There are 14 regulated activities covered by the Health and Social Care Act 2008 (Regulated Activities) Regulations 2014 and monitored by the CQC. These apply equally to care at home services and care services and include the provision of:

- personal and/or nursing care for adults in care homes or their own homes;
- accommodation for people who require nursing and/or personal care;
- accommodation for people who require treatment for substance misuse;
- treatment, care and support provided by hospitals, GPs dentists, ambulances and mental health services; and
- services for people whose rights are restricted under the Mental Health Act 1983.

Providers pay a fee to the CQC to cover registration and compliance requirements, which is paid upon initial registration and thereafter annually. The amount of the fee is determined by a number of factors including the nature of the service provided; the turnover; the number of locations; and the number of service users.

9.1.2   The 12 fundamental standards

The 'fundamental standards' contained in the 2014 Regulations came into effect from 1 April 2015, which replaced the CQC's former 'Essential Standards of Quality and Safety'. All regulated providers must meet the fundamental standards – these are the standards below which care must never fall. A failure to meet them will result in the CQC taking action against the provider. Guidance and full details of the fundamental standards are available at **www.cqc.org.uk**, but in summary the standards are:

1. *Person-centred care*: care and treatment must be appropriate, and be based upon an assessment that reflects the person's individual needs and preferences (reg.9).
2. *Dignity and respect:* this includes ensuring that people have privacy when they need and want it, treating them as equals and providing any support they might need to be autonomous, independent and involved in their local community (reg.10).
3. *The need for consent*: the intention is to ensure that all people using the service, and those lawfully acting on their behalf, have given consent before any care or treatment is provided. The CQC recognises that this fundamental

standard may create tension with some of the other regulations and warns that providers must not provide unsafe or inappropriate care 'just because someone has consented to care or treatment that may be unsafe' (reg.11).

4.   *Safe care and treatment*: this includes obligations to undertake risk assessments in relation to a person's care and treatment and in relation to premises and equipment. It covers the safe administration of medication and the prevention and control of the spread of infection. In addition, providers must ensure that staff have the qualifications, competence, skills and experience to keep people safe (reg.12).

5.   *Safeguarding against abuse and improper treatment*: providers must have a zero tolerance approach to abuse, unlawful discrimination and restraint, covering neglect; subjecting people to degrading treatment; unnecessary or disproportionate restraint; and inappropriate deprivation of liberty (reg.13).

6.   *Meeting nutritional and hydration needs*: providers are required to assess a person's individual needs; to reduce the risk of malnutrition and dehydration; and to take into account the person's preferences, religious and cultural background (reg.14).

7.   *Premises and equipment*: must be clean, suitable, maintained, secure and used properly (reg.15).

8.   *Receiving and acting on complaints*: from people using the service, people acting on their behalf or other stakeholders. A requirement to undertake a thorough investigation to take necessary action where a failure is identified (reg.16).

9.   *Good governance*: providers must demonstrate that they have systems and processes in place to comply with the regulations; and to assess, monitor and drive improvement in the safety and quality of the services provided (reg.17).

10. *Staffing*: to provide sufficient numbers of suitably qualified, competent, skilled and experienced staff to meet the needs of the people using the service at all times and to meet the other regulatory requirements. This includes supporting, training and supervision of staff (reg.18).

11. *Fit and proper persons employed*: covering robust recruitment and monitoring procedures; appropriate checks and arrangements in place to deal with staff who are no longer fit and appropriate (reg.19).

12. *Duty of candour*: to ensure that providers are open and transparent with service users (and relevant others) about care and treatment, specifically when things go wrong; and a duty to provide truthful information (reg.20). It includes a requirement to display CQC performance assessments (reg.20A).

9.1.3   Requirement to be fit and appropriate to undertake the regulated activity

Regulations 4–7 of the 2014 Regulations cover the CQC's requirements and expectations of those who are registered providers, those who have director level responsibility, and of registered managers. Prosecutions cannot be brought in respect of a breach of these regulations, but the CQC can take regulatory/ enforcement action and must not register a person who cannot satisfy the requirements. In particular:

- Regulation 4 – applies where the registered provider is an individual or a partnership.
- Regulation 5 – covers those who have director level responsibility for the quality and safety of care, and for meeting the fundamental standards.
- Regulation 6 – applies where the registered provider is a body other than a partnership; and requires a nominated individual.
- Regulation 7 – registered managers – the regulated service must be managed by an appropriate person who must:
  - be of good character;
  - be able properly to perform tasks that are intrinsic to their role;
  - have the necessary qualifications, competence, skills and experience to carry on the regulated activity or supervise its management;
  - be able to supply CQC with documents that confirm their suitability.

A person will not be regarded as fit to undertake regulated activities if they are on the children's or adults' barred list; declared bankrupt; subject to a formal debt arrangement; or precluded from acting by any other statute. A person will not be regarded as being of good character if they have been removed from a professional register; convicted of any offence in the UK; or convicted of an offence overseas, if it would constitute an offence in the UK.

9.1.4 CQC inspections and monitoring

CQC inspectors assess services against five key questions giving a rating of 'outstanding', 'good', 'requires improvement' or 'inadequate'. If a service is rated as requiring improvement or inadequate, the CQC then determines whether a regulation has been breached or not. The five key questions are:

1. Are they safe?
2. Are they effective?
3. Are they caring?
4. Are they responsive to people's needs?
5. Are they well led?

It is a legal requirement for providers to display their CQC ratings within 21 days of the CQC inspection report. The CQC ratings must be displayed on each and every premises where a regulatory activity is delivered; in the main place of business; and also on the provider's website.

The CQC publishes its inspection reports on its website and also provides online press releases, a list of the most recently inspected services and an email alert subscription to track particular service providers.

9.1.5 CQC enforcement

The CQC has a wide set of powers that allow it to protect the public and hold registered providers and managers to account. Its new enforcement policy (1 April 2015) is used where it identifies poor care, or where registered providers and managers do not meet the standards required in the regulations. The aim of the policy is to:

- Protect people who use regulated services from harm and the risk of harm, and to ensure they receive health and social care services of an appropriate standard.
- Hold registered providers and managers to account for failures in how the service is provided.

The CQC's 'Enforcement Decision Tree' requires it to conduct a four-stage process of:

1. initial assessment;
2. legal and evidential review;
3. selection of the appropriate enforcement action; and
4. final review.

The CQC's enforcement powers for breach of the regulations include:

- Suspending registration (of a registered person due to serious concerns that may be capable of remedy within a fixed period).
- Cancelling registration (of a registered person due to serious concerns that may be capable of remedy within a fixed period).
- Imposing, varying or removing conditions of registration (to secure improvement).
- Requirement notices (no immediate risk of harm; no history of poor performance).
- Warning notices (past or continuing breach; can be made public).
- Urgent measures (immediate effect, e.g. to cancel registration; right of appeal).
- Special measures (administrative framework to manage providers in relation to inadequate care).
- Criminal law cautions (formal record of an offence admitted but not prosecuted; achieving improvements appears to be a realistic alternative).
- Criminal law penalty notices (as an alternative to prosecution).
- Criminal law prosecutions (for breaches of any of the prosecutable fundamental standards/for carrying on a service without registration/obstructing a CQC inspection/providing false or misleading statements in an application to register).

The regulations set out a process for providers/registered managers to make representations in respect of, or appeal against CQC enforcement decisions.

Whether the right is to make representations or to appeal will depend upon the nature of the enforcement action the CQC has decided upon. Rights include:

- Inspection reports: right to make factual accuracy comments.
- Warning notice: right to make written representations.
- Notices of proposal: right to make written representations.
- Notices of decisions: right to appeal to First-tier Care Standards Tribunal (Health, Education and Social Care Chamber).
- Urgent cancellation: right to appeal to First-tier Tribunal.
- Notices served under the urgent procedure: right to appeal to First-tier Tribunal.

9.1.6 Complaints about care homes and care providers

The registered person must bring the complaints system to the attention of service users or persons acting on their behalf. The complaints system has to be in an appropriate format. The registered person must then ensure that any complaint is fully investigated and resolved – as far as reasonably practicable – to the satisfaction of the complainant. The CQC may request a summary of complaints and responses from the registered person.

If the complainant is not satisfied with the response provided by the care home or care service, then they can ask the Local Government Ombudsman to investigate the complaint (see **5.6.3**).

The CQC does not have a complaints procedure for people to make complaints about care providers in England, although it uses complaints as a way of monitoring, investigating and taking regulatory action.

9.2 WALES: CARE STANDARDS, LEGISLATION AND REGULATION

9.2.1 The Care Standards Act 2000, underpinning regulations, and proposed changes

In Wales, regulatory responsibility lies with the Care and Social Services Inspectorate Wales (CSSIW) – formerly the Care Standards Inspectorate for Wales. The CSSIW regulates social care and social services, including children's services. For the purpose of this publication, regulation for children's services is omitted. The Care Standards Act 2000 was amended to bring CSSIW broadly in line with the functions of the CQC, and still has application in Wales.

The CSSWI carries out its functions on behalf of Welsh Ministers under the following legislation – the standards for measurement of care service providers being found in the first two Acts.

- Care Standards Act 2000 (as amended).
- Health and Social Care (Community Health and Standards) Act 2003.

- Care Homes (Wales) Regulations 2002, SI 2002/324.
- Care Homes (Amendment) (Wales) Regulations 2003, SI 2003/947.
- Care Homes (Wales) (Amendment No.2) Regulations 2003, SI 2003/1004.
- Care Homes (Wales) (Miscellaneous Amendments) Regulations 2011, SI 2011/1016.
- Domiciliary Care Agencies (Wales) Regulations 2004, SI 2004/219.
- Domiciliary Care Agencies (Wales) (Amendment) Regulations 2013, SI 2013/225.
- Adult Placement Schemes (Wales) Regulations 2004, SI 2004/1756.
- Adult Placement Schemes (Wales) (Miscellaneous Amendments) Regulations 2010, SI 2010/2585.

There is a raft of other regulations applying to nursing care services and associated regulations in Wales.

The Regulation and Inspection of Social Care (Wales) Bill was introduced in February 2015. The purpose of the Bill is to 'improve the quality of care and support in Wales and strengthen protection for citizens'. Its aims include to reform the care and support regulatory regime; reform the inspection regime for local authority social services functions; reconstitute the name the Care Council for Wales as Social Care Wales and broaden its remit; set out the regulation of the care workforce and establish requirements for Welsh Ministers and local authorities to undertake assessments of the sector's future sustainability.

9.2.2   Welsh national minimum standards

CSSIW has different sets of minimum standards dependent upon the type of service provided and to whom the service is provided. There are different sets of standards for example for care homes for younger people than for care homes for older people; adult placement schemes, care and nursing agencies each get their own set of national minimum standards. CSSIW expects care providers of all types not only to meet the standards but also to aim to exceed them.

All are available on the CSSIW website at **www.cssiw.org.uk** as PDF documents.

The standards set out in great detail what the Welsh care home resident should expect, including:

1.   *Choice of home* – Prospective residents must have the information they need to make an informed choice about where to live. Each home must produce:

   –   a 'statement of purpose' setting out its aims and objectives, the kinds of services it offers to residents, and the range of residents' needs which the service is intended to meet, location of care home, legal status and full name of the service provider and details of any registered manager;
   –   a 'service user's guide';
   –   a contract, with content as set out in the regulations.

These standards also cover needs assessments, the capacity of the provider to meet those needs and trial visits.

2. *Planning for individual needs and preferences* – which covers the service user plan and record keeping standards.

3. *Quality of life* – including:

   – valuing autonomy and choice;
   – social and community contact;
   – rights and confidentiality.

4. *Quality of care and treatment* – a wide range of standards which include:

   – privacy and dignity in personal care;
   – healthcare;
   – meals and mealtimes;
   – medication;
   – safe working practices; and
   – expectations around dying and death.

5. *Staffing* – staffing levels, qualifications, training, recruitment, supervision and volunteers.

6. *Conduct and management of the home* – which include:

   – the registered manager;
   – ethos;
   – quality assurance
   – financial procedures; and
   – service users' money.

7. *Concerns, complaints and protection.*

8. *The physical environment standards* – which include:

   – space requirements and furniture/fittings for individual accommodation;
   – adaptations and equipment; and
   – expectations around shared facilities, lavatories and washing facilities, etc.

The 27 minimum standards for domiciliary care ensure that services are user-focused, requiring the service provided to be matched to the needs of the service user, which take into account his or her wishes and preferences when planning and delivering the service. Specific terms and conditions should be provided to the service user before the service is provided. These extend to how they will personally be cared for and protected from harm.

9.2.3 The registered person

Section 11(1) of the 2000 Act applicable to Wales provides that any person/ organisation that carries on or manages a care home, adult placement scheme or care agency must be registered. Failure to register is a criminal offence. In Wales each establishment should have a registered owner or proprietor. If the proprietor/ service provider is not in day-to-day control of the care establishment or agency, a manager is required to be appointed who must also be registered by the registration authority (see 2000 Act, s.22 and 2008 Act, s.13(3)).

9.2.4 CSSIW inspections and monitoring

The CSSWI undertakes inspections to assess the quality of care provided by all care establishments and agencies. The registration authorities use the national minimum standards in Wales and regulations to assess to what extent service providers exceed, meet, or fail to meet care requirements. They aim to work with the registered person to identify problems and help them agree an action plan with a suitable timescale that will enable them to comply with expectations.

9.2.5 CSSIW enforcement

The CSSWI in Wales has less extensive enforcement powers than the CQC in England. If it finds that a service user's quality of life is affected by provider failings or the service user is put at risk, it will issue and publish a non-compliance notice. This identifies the regulations that have not been met; sets out the evidence to back that up; and a list of actions required within a specified timeframe. In non-urgent cases, providers are given time to improve before a further compliance inspection is undertaken.

If a Welsh service provider becomes a 'service of concern', the CSSIW will:

- formally meet with the provider;
- share the concerns with other agencies – for example the local authority;
- consider/take urgent enforcement action including suspension of the service; cancelling registration; or prosecution of the organisation/manager.

9.2.6 Complaints investigation Wales

Under the Care Homes (Wales) Regulations 2002, the Adult Placement Schemes (Wales) Regulations 2004 and the Domiciliary Care Agencies (Wales) Regulations 2004, the CSSWI has established a complaints procedure through which service users and family members can lodge complaints about the care establishment or agency, whether this is the local authority or a private, voluntary or charitable provider. It is expected that all complaints, if appropriate, are made to the care establishment or agency initially, through their internal complaints procedure. The procedure should be set out in the statement of purpose which should be provided to every service user or be made available upon request for inspection by the service user or their representative.

9.3 CARE HOME CONTRACTS, SERVICE USER GUIDES AND STATEMENT OF PURPOSE

9.3.1 Contracts

The Care Quality Commission (Registration) Regulations 2009 require the registered provider in England to supply the service user/their representative with a written statement of terms and conditions in respect of the services, to include the amount and method of payment, including a form of contract where applicable. As far as is practicable, this should be supplied prior to the commencement of the services; and should be supplied whether the service user pays for his or her care in full or in part.

In Wales, the statement of terms and conditions (Standard 5.2) must as a minimum include details of:

- rooms to be occupied;
- overall care and services (including food) covered by fee;
- fees payable and by whom (service user, local or health authority, relative or another);
- additional services (including food and equipment) to be paid for over and above those included in the fees;
- rights and obligations of the service user and who is liable if there is a breach of contract;
- terms and conditions of occupancy, including period of notice (e.g. short/long-term intermediate care/respite).

If the local authority has accepted responsibility to pay the individual's care fees, subject to his or her income contribution, then the contract will generally be between the local authority and the care provider, not the service user. This will usually take the form of a simple one or two-page 'individual placement agreement' or 'individual service agreement', which focuses primarily on the weekly fee. The service user/their representative should still be provided with a written statement of other terms and conditions. If the care provider has not accepted the local authority rate fees, then the service user/their representative or a third party will be asked to enter into a separate contract to cover the 'third party' or 'first party top up' payments. The contractual requirements of such agreements in England are set out in helpful detail in the Care and Support Statutory Guidance (DoH, 2014) Annex A (see also **14.2.6**).

If the CCG in England or Local Health Board in Wales has accepted responsibility to pay the individual's care fees through an award of NHS continuing healthcare, then the contract or commissioning documentation will be between the NHS body and the care provider, not the service user. If the care provider is unwilling to accept the NHS body's weekly fee rate, which is more common when NHS continuing healthcare is granted to someone who has historically paid private market rate fees, then the service user/their representative may be told that they need to enter into a separate contract such as a 'Lifestyle Payment Agreement' or 'Silver Service/Gold Tap Agreement'. This is an increasingly common response on the part of care providers who say that the NHS rate of payment – while typically higher than the local authority rate of payment – is not adequate to cover the actual costs of providing a service. The service user/their representative should take further advice to challenge this (see also **10.2.6**).

9.3.2   What should be in the care home contract?

The English standard requires that the terms and conditions include:

- details of the room to be occupied;
- information about overall care and services (including food) covered by the fee;
- fees payable and by whom (service user, local or health authority, relative or another);
- details of additional services (including food and equipment) to be paid for over and above those included in the fees;
- rights and obligations of the service user and registered provider (care home) and who is liable if there is a breach of contract;
- terms and conditions of occupancy, including period of notice, e.g. short/long-term intermediate care/respite.

9.3.3   Unfair contract terms

In October 2003, the Office of Fair Trading (OFT) conducted a market study on care homes for older people and found that a number of care home contracts for self-funding residents were unfair or unclear. The main areas of the study focused on:

- The lack of price transparency (the cost of care, what services the price includes, how often the price is reviewed).
- The need for better complaints procedures.
- Complex or unfair terms that make it difficult to assess true rights and obligations of the resident and of the care home under the contract.
- The procedure for termination of a contract.
- The administering of medication.

While some of these contractual issues have subsequently been addressed through the regulatory regimes (for example, a better complaints process), some others remain as issues of concern to residents and/or their representatives. The OFT research highlighted the importance of looking out for the following examples (not a definitive list) when considering whether or not to enter into the contract:

- Whether the care home is excluded from liability from causing death or injury.
- Whether the care home is permitted to make significant changes to what it supplies to the resident without consultation.
- Whether the room can be changed without consultation.
- Whether the terms are not clear about how long the fees are payable after death.

Advisers should also consider whether the resident or their representative should enter into a contract which:

- Charges a 'placement fee' or 'administration fee' for the work which the care home undertakes in accepting and registering the resident with them, including writing up a care plan and setting up accounting records, which is an operational overhead and likely to amount to an unfair term.
- Requires the resident or their representative to disclose to the care home when the resident's financial resources have reduced to the equivalent of one year's care fees.
- Requires a third party to act as guarantor, who will pay the care fees if the resident is unable to pay the fees.

9.3.4   Service user guides and statement of purpose

In England and Wales, the care home is required to produce an information pack or service user's guide for each resident or prospective resident. This may include a brochure (or 'statement of purpose'), and should be made available in advance. Any changes to these should be brought to the service user's attention before the agreement is entered into. The Office of Fair Trading has said that it is likely to challenge terms that provide for the agreement to supersede any statements in guides, information packs or the brochure. These could allow the care home to deny liability for material discrepancies, and effectively to mislead the consumer.

The Welsh standards are more prescriptive than the English standards. The CQC requires the care provider to supply residents with a statement of purpose, which appears to be somewhat like a business plan. The CSSIW requires the care provider to supply residents and potential residents with an up-to-date statement of purpose setting out its aims, objectives, philosophy of care, services and facilities, its terms and conditions (Standard 1.1).

The Welsh service user's guide must, as a minimum, contain (Standard 1.3):

- a brief description of the accommodation and services provided;
- relevant qualifications and experience of the registered provider, manager and staff;
- the number of places provided and any special needs and interests catered for;
- a statement on whether service users can expect choice in the gender of those who provide their personal care;

- the home's policy on pets;
- a copy, or summary, of the most recent inspection report;
- a copy of the complaints procedure; and
- a summary of the home's most recent care quality review report which shall indicate, wherever practicable, service users' views about the home.

9.4 TYPES OF CARE HOMES

'Care home' is the correct legal terminology (as set out in the Care Standards Act 2000, s.3(1)), but many service providers and service users still refer to residential, nursing, or elderly mentally ill (EMI) homes. Different types of care homes have different conditions attached to their registration:

1. Care home – accommodation and personal care.
2. Care home registered to provide nursing care – accommodation, nursing and personal care.
3. Dual registered care home.

Each of these may be generalist or may have certain specialisms such as dementia care, acquired brain injury care, learning disability care, etc.

9.4.1 Choice of care home

A care home may be run by:

- a company or an individual for profit;
- a charity or non-profit making organisation (voluntary homes);
- relatively rarely now, the social services department of a local authority.

The Office for National Statistics undertakes a census analysis of the main changes and trends in the care home population in England and Wales, each analysis spanning data for the previous decade. The most recent was published in 2014, covering the period 2001 to 2011. The key findings were:

- There were 291,000 people aged 65 or over living in care homes in 2011, representing 3.2 per cent of the total population at that age; 164,000 were aged 85 or over.
- The care home resident population for those aged 65 and over has remained almost stable since 2001 with an increase of 0.3 per cent, despite growth of 11.0 per cent in the overall population at this age.
- The gender gap in the older resident care home population has narrowed since 2001. In 2011 there were around 2.8 women for each man aged 65 and over compared to a ratio of 3.3 women for each man in 2001.

- The resident care home population is ageing: in 2011, people aged 85 and over represented 59.2 per cent of the older care home population compared to 56.5 per cent in 2001.

Many care home residents rely upon public funding in respect of the fees for accommodation at some point during their residence, if not for the duration of their residence.

Those people who need social services funding assistance to pay care home fees, whether from the outset or when assessable capital has been used up and they can no longer self-fund, should be provided with their own choice of accommodation, which is suitable for their assessed needs and does not cost the local authority more than usual for the type of accommodation preferred. The care home must also agree to enter into a contract with the local authority. In England the Choice of Accommodation Directions have been replaced by the Care Act 2014 and specifically Annex A of the Care and Support Statutory Guidance (DoH, 2014), which outlines the rules relevant to third party and first party top-ups for 'more expensive accommodation'. The Choice of Accommodation Directions currently apply in Wales, although they are similar to the English regulations and statutory guidance (see **14.2.6**). For assessment of need see **8.1** and for funding and means tests see **14.2.3**.

A number of organisations provide factsheets and guidance about the factors to consider when choosing a care home. There are also a growing number of private organisations and individuals with health and social care backgrounds who will work with individuals and their families to find and match suitable residential care or care at home packages for their needs.

See, for example, Age UK Information Booklet IG06: *Finding the Right Care Home* and Age UK Factsheet 29: *Finding Care Home Accommodation* (both from **www.ageuk.org.uk**).

9.5   CARE HOME CLOSURES

9.5.1   Reason for home closures

From time to time care homes will close. The reasons for home closures are complex but it is a fact that local authorities are the main commissioners of care beds and restrict the amount they will pay. There are a number of care home groups and individual care homes that will not take local authority funded residents at all, or who will do so only if a family member is prepared to sign a 'third party top-up' contract (see **14.2.6**). Other providers take local authority funded residents but charge a higher rate for self-funding clients and a lower rate for local authority funded residents, which cross-subsidises their business, enabling them to continue to operate and avoid the risk of closure. The overheads of running a care home are high, including the cost of regulation, training and payment of quality staff. Many struggle and close through their own choice, while others are forced to close as a result of being unable to comply with the regulatory requirements; and may close as a result of safeguarding investigations.

9.5.2 Moving older residents

There is concern that moving an older and frail person, particularly if they have been in a care home for many years, may bring about his or her premature death. There have been a number of well-publicised cases of this happening, although formal evidence of such is often inconclusive (see *R (on the application of Wilson)* v. *Coventry City Council* [2008] EWHC 2300 (Admin)). There is no guidance for social services on this type of situation but the NHS Executive issued Good Practice Guidance in April 1998 on the procedure for transferring frail older NHS patients to other long-stay settings under Health Service Circular 1998/048. This is available on the Department of Health website in the Archive section. The Personal Social Services Research Unit has also published *Guidelines for the Closure of Care Homes for Older People: Prevalence and Content of Local Government Protocols* (2003: **www.pssru.ac.uk/pdf/dp1861_2.pdf**). NHS England has published practical guidance, *Safe, Compassionate Care for Frail Older People Using an Integrated Care Pathway* (2014) (**www.england.nhs.uk**), which provides matters for commissioners to consider.

Local authorities do not have to follow the guidance but many refer to it as good practice. In summary before deciding to close the facility there should be full consultation with residents, a flexible project plan, an assessment and care plan for each person prior to any move. The move should be planned but postponed if the person is not well enough, until such time as they are.

Closure of a person's care home may trigger concerns about an infringement of their human rights, in particular their right to life (art.3) and not to suffer degrading treatment (art.2) under the European Convention on Human Rights, although there has been little reported success in seeking to enforce such rights (*R (on the application of Haggerty)* v. *St Helens Council* [2003] EWHC 803 (Admin); *R (on the application of Dudley)* v. *East Sussex CC* [2003] EWHC 1093 (Admin)).

Some care home residents are asked to move or may want to move for reasons other than closure or service provider failure. This may be a matter of choice when the resident wants to be in a care home closer to other relatives, or has a spouse or partner who also now needs care and they want to be in the same care home. Sometimes the care home may give notice because it can no longer meet the resident's needs; or because of disputes with the resident's family; or because of care fee arrears.

9.5.3 Home for life?

Following the introduction of the National Health Service and Community Care Act 1990, there was a big shift in care being provided by the independent sector. As a consequence, there was closure of a significant number of council-run homes.

Although councils are able to do this, there must be adequate consultation with residents (*R* v. *Wandsworth LBC, ex p Beckwith* [1996] 1 WLR 60).

In *R* v. *North and East Devon Health Authority, ex p Coughlan* [2001] QB 213 the Court of Appeal held that the health authority had made a promise to the resident that the home would be hers for life and this bound them. The decision to close the home constituted unfairness amounting to an abuse of power, which was in breach of art.8 (the right to family life) of the European Convention on Human Rights. This decision has been followed in *R (on the application of B)* v. *Camden LBC* [2001] EWHC Admin 271 and *R* v. *Merton, Sutton and Wandsworth Health Authority, ex p P* [2001] Lloyd's Rep Med 73. The tide turned, however, in *R (on the application of C)* v. *Brent, Kensington, Chelsea and Westminster Health NHS Trust* [2002] EWHC 181 (Admin), *Cowl* v. *Plymouth City Council* [2002] EWCA Civ 1935 and *R (on the application of Dudley)* v. *East Sussex CC* [2003] EWHC 1093 (Admin), where the homes did close, as the facts were distinguished from the *Coughlan* case.

There is usually very little that one can practically do to stop closure of an independent home, although Health and Social Care Act 2008, s.145, makes local authority assisted residents cared for in independent care homes entitled to the protection of the Human Rights Act 1998.

9.6 COMMISSIONING CARE AT HOME: BEING AN EMPLOYER

9.6.1 Introduction

The aim of this section of the chapter is to help those who advise the elderly client to understand how employment legislation affects the elderly client as an employer (perhaps in their own right or through their attorney or deputy, acting as their agent) and therefore how to stay on the right side of employment law.

Many people with long-term care needs now choose to arrange a package of care that allows them to remain living at home, rather than choosing to live in a care home. This may involve a rota of carers who attend for an agreed number of care visits each day, or having a live-in carer. Some people choose to use a care agency to make the arrangements and provide the care staff, so that they do not have to take on any employer responsibilities. Others find the agency approach unsatisfactory as it may not allow much choice or control about who the individual carers are, or even about what time they attend. As a result, there is an increasing move towards people or their family members/representatives employing their own personal carers or personal assistants.

While the option of commissioning care at home can be empowering and maintains independence, the responsibility of becoming an employer and comply-ing with the huge and fast changing employment law developments can be very onerous. The typical employment law issues relevant to those commissioning care in their own home include:

- Fair and efficient recruitment practices which avoid discrimination.

- Preparing employment contracts and staff handbooks.
- Preparing licences for live-in carers.
- If a care agency is used, ensuring that their terms are fair.
- Dealing with management issues such as poor performance or conduct, including grievances or disciplinary proceedings.
- Redundancy and termination of the employment contract.
- Defending employment tribunal claims.
- Avoiding discrimination in employment practices.
- Any Transfer of Undertakings Protection of Employment (TUPE) considerations when outsourcing or insourcing (which may be relevant when the cared for person has a significant care at home package/uses an agency).

9.6.2   Is the personal assistant employed or self-employed?

It is essential that the personal assistant's (PA's) employment status is clearly and correctly defined from the outset. While many people would prefer their PA to be self-employed – thus avoiding the huge range of employers' legal duties – simply saying that someone is self-employed does not mean that they are. The person providing care at home services may be an employee, an independent contractor, a worker, a part-time worker or an agency worker.

The courts and employment tribunals look at the individual underlying factors in order to determine whether the arrangements really are equivalent to self-employment under a service provider agreement or consultancy agreement; or whether the circumstances actually amount to an employment contract in all but name. The courts and employment appeal tribunals have devised a number of tests of employment; no single one is determinative, but factors to be considered are:

- *Mutuality of obligation* – whether there is an obligation on the part of the hirer to provide work for the service provider and whether he or she is obliged to take work when it is offered.
- *Control* – for example, what work is done, how, where and when it is done. The greater the degree of control exercised by the hirer, the more likely this is to be an employer/employee relationship.
- *Personal services* – whether someone has to deliver their services personally to the hirer or can they send along a substitute at their own cost (the right must exist even if it is not used in practice to establish a non-employment relationship).

The above so-called irreducible minimums of an employment relationship must exist for the relationship to start to look like one of employment. Then other key aspects are looked at, such as: who provides the tools and equipment; if it takes longer to do the job than the provider estimates or promises, is the price or fee the same or does it reduce; is there a disciplinary process or absence reporting process; what are the holiday arrangements (paid or unpaid?) and are the above the same for employees? Even if a tribunal is satisfied that the relationship is not one of employment the income tax authority, Her Majesty's Revenue and Customs (HMRC), may reach a different conclusion on the same facts.

It should be noted that even if it is established that someone is not an employee in the conventional meaning, the opportunity may exist for them to argue that they are workers (a 'worker' is someone who works under a contract by which they agree to do or perform, personally, any work or services for another whose status is not that of a client or customer of any profession or business undertaking: Employment Rights Act 1996, s.230). Certain employee rights such as entitlement to the National Minimum Wage, protection under the Working Time Regulations and the right to be protected from certain types of discrimination have been extended to workers who are not employees.

9.6.3 Avoiding discrimination as an employer

The Equality Act 2010 applies to protect employees with 'protected characteristics' from unfair treatment. Protected characteristics include gender, marital status, gender reassignment, pregnancy, maternity, race, disability, sexual orientation, religion or belief, and age.

The legislation is relevant to job applicants in addition to employees and workers, and is thus important to consider at the recruitment stage. Discrimination in recruitment extends to the arrangements for selection for determining who should be offered employment; the terms of the offer; or not offering or refusing to offer employment. Avoiding discrimination applies all of the way through the employment relationship, including when dealing with performance management issues and when terminating employment.

The Advisory, Conciliation and Arbitration Service (ACAS) website pages on equality are a useful resource: **www.acas.org.uk/equality**.

9.6.4 Working with vulnerable adults or adults at risk

The Criminal Records Bureau (CRB) and Independent Safeguarding Authority have merged and are now known as the Disclosure and Barring Service (DBS). What were commonly referred to as CRB checks are now known as DBS checks.

The individual who proposes to employ personal assistants to provide care at home services should undertake the appropriate checks as to the person's suitability to work in regulated activities in relation to working with adults. The definitions of the regulated activities and those who are afforded protection by the DBS regime are contained in the Safeguarding Vulnerable Groups Act 2006.

The employer should arrange a DBS check only in relation to the successful applicant(s) and can withdraw the offer if anything in the results would make the applicant unsuitable. The employer also needs to undertake an identity check as part of the DBS check.

Once the employer has submitted the application, the DBS certificate is sent to the job applicant, not to the prospective employer. The employer can choose to accept a previous DBS certificate and undertake a free status check, but this will only be effective if the job applicant has joined the DBS Update Service. The DBS warns employers that they accept 'out of date' certificates at their own risk.

The DBS operates Barred Lists for individuals unsuitable to work with adults or children. The employer has a legal duty to refer any individual if the employer:

- sacked them because they harmed someone;
- sacked them or removed them from working in a regulated activity because they might have harmed someone; or
- was planning to sack them for either of these reasons, but they resigned first.

9.6.5 Contracts and terms of employment

Once an employee is appointed, or an offer is accepted, a contract comes into existence. The terms may be express (oral or in writing) or implied but cannot override certain terms implied by statute. Those commissioning care within their own home may find that it is preferable to have a written contract setting out all the main terms and conditions of employment. Without a formal contract, disputes often occur due to different understandings and expectations about terms.

Statement of terms of employment and implied terms

Employees have the right to a written statement of employment particulars after a month's service. Under the Employment Rights Act 1996, s.1 the written statement setting out specified basic terms must be provided no later than two months after the beginning of the employee's employment; a penalty of two weeks' pay is payable by an employer for failure to provide written particulars of employment (Employment Act 2002). The particulars should confirm:

- The start date, hours of work, starting salary (and whether this is gross or net and intervals at which it is paid), holidays, sickness and sick pay.
- The period of notice and any terms relating to pensions.
- Any other benefits that the employee may be entitled to (for example, use of a car, motor expenses).
- Disciplinary and grievance procedures.

While not obligatory, it is good practice to make sure that the particulars and/or contract include a detailed description of the employee's duties.

The employer should keep in mind that the stated terms are not conclusive if the employer and employee have behaved in a manner inconsistent with them. That behaviour is likely to be the best evidence relating to the relevant term. The terms of the contract may be deduced from custom or implication in so far as not specified. Terms may be implied because of long-established custom and practice or simply because it is reasonable to do so.

National Minimum Wage and PAYE

Generally, everyone who 'provides a personal service' is entitled to be paid at least the National Minimum Wage. This includes employees, workers (including agency workers), and certain people who might regard themselves as self-employed. The current gross hourly rates can be checked at **www.gov.uk/national-minimum-wage/what-is-the-minimum-wage**. This site also includes a calculator to allow employers and employees to check whether current and past pay is compliant with the legislation.

Exceptions and special situations that may be relevant to commissioning care at home include:

1. Situations where accommodation is provided as part of a worker's remuneration package, in which case an employer is entitled to offset a specified maximum daily figure against the amount that should otherwise be paid.
2. Workers who sleep on the premises, who need not be paid the minimum wage for any period that they are not actually working, provided that the employment contract clearly sets out the period when the worker is permitted to sleep, and the employer provides suitable sleeping facilities.
3. Workers who receive a low salary while having to work a large number of hours in the same pay period, who may be paid less than the National Minimum Wage on an hourly basis during that period.
4. Where a worker is 'on call'. Generally, workers are entitled to be paid for all time when they are at or near work, and where they are required to be available to work – but this will often exclude time spent at home, and it always excludes time spent sleeping. Cases of this nature are often a 'grey area' and specialist advice should be sought.

An employee is entitled to a payslip, which must show earnings before and after any deductions, explain any deductions and show how the wage is paid. Apart from any legal deductions like tax or national insurance, employers cannot make any deductions from wages unless it is specified in the employment contract, or the employee has said in writing that they accept the deduction before it is made.

The employer commissioning care at home is legally obliged to keep adequate records of what is paid. These need not be in a specific format and the PAYE records may be sufficient. HMRC can demand records, interview employees, and take enforcement action for failure to keep adequate records, or for keeping false records. Where there is a breach of the minimum wage requirements, the employer will be ordered to pay the arrears within 14 days, plus a penalty equivalent to 100 per cent of the unpaid wages. They may also be subject to prosecution and a fine.

There are payroll companies who can assist with the PAYE and HMRC functions, including some that specialise for those commissioning care at home. Some of these also provide standard forms of contract that can be adapted by the person commissioning the care at home.

The person commissioning care at home may need specialist advice in certain circumstances such as how to manage the employee's rights when there is no work in a specified period – for example, when the cared for person is in hospital or in respite care; and relevant notice and pay requirements, including redundancy, on the death of the cared for person or on a permanent but unplanned admission to a care home.

Other statutory pay and leave requirements

As a result of fast changing employment legislation, including EC Directives, and the effects of case law, information on statutory pay obligations quickly goes out of date. Those commissioning care at home will find the ACAS website to be a very valuable resource for keeping abreast of employer responsibilities.

When commissioning care at home, it is vital to have an understanding of the employer's statutory duties in relation to:

- maternity leave and statutory maternity pay, including time off to attend antenatal appointments for example;
- paternity leave and statutory paternity pay;
- adoption leave and statutory adoption pay;
- shared parental leave and shared parental pay;
- statutory sick pay;
- statutory redundancy payments;
- considering requests for flexible working;
- auto-enrolment into a pension;
- statutory minimum provisions in regard to the notice period on termination of the employment contract.

In addition, employees are entitled to equal pay with those of the opposite sex (Equal Pay Act 1970; see now Equality Act 2010, Part 5, Chapter 3) for doing like work, work rated as equivalent or work of equal value.

Working Time Regulations, breaks and holidays

The Working Time Regulations 1998, SI 1998/1833 (as amended) govern the minimum standards in relation to employees' holidays, working hours and rest breaks. The aim of the regulations is to protect employees' health, safety and welfare in line with the EU Working Time Directive.

Employees are entitled to work a maximum of 48 hours a week, unless they choose to work longer hours and voluntarily opt out from this limit. The regulations include requirements for work breaks and for rest periods between working days. Employees have a statutory paid holiday entitlement of a minimum of 5.6 weeks' paid leave a year, which applies on a pro rata basis to part-time workers. The holiday entitlement can and usually does include public holidays such as bank holidays.

Special rules apply to young employees, night workers and Sunday working. If the employee regularly works at night, the employer may have to offer them a free health assessment to make sure that they are fit to work at night.

Individuals commissioning care at home from a live-in carer or carers will need to be particularly mindful about the relevant Working Time Regulations, particularly in relation to the requirements around sleeping hours, on-call hours and rest periods/breaks.

9.7 OTHER FACTORS TO CONSIDER WHEN COMMISSIONING CARE AT HOME

9.7.1 Insurance

The person commissioning care at home must ensure that they have appropriate employer's liability insurance (ELI) and public liability insurance in place. This is the case whether the PA is employed through social services direct payments or individual budgets, NHS continuing healthcare, personal health budgets, or personal funds (see **14.1.4**). The ELI protects the employer in the event that the PA becomes injured or ill while they are working and they seek compensation from the employer. People commissioning care at home can be fined by the Health and Safety Executive if they do not have the right insurance in place as an employer.

If care is commissioned from a self-employed carer, then the person receiving that care is not required to have ELI, as the paid carer must have his or her own insurance in place. However, it is advisable to err on the side of caution and obtain ELI; and to ask to see the insurance certificate of a self-employed carer.

9.7.2 Health and safety

The person commissioning care at home has duties to take care of the employee's health and safety, including the duty to protect them from reasonably foreseeable mental or physical harm associated with risks such as hazards like cables that they may trip over, polluted air such as cigarette smoke, injuries from lifting, bullying which can cause stress and acute anxiety, and may lead to depression and the possibility of a nervous breakdown.

9.7.3 Health or social services funding and commissioning care at home

The person at home who receives direct payments, a personal budget or personal health budget from either social services or the NHS needs to be aware that the statutory organisation may impose additional requirements in relation to how and by whom that care is commissioned and how it is managed (see **14.1.4**). There may also be issues and difficulty around 'topping-up' the funds made available by health or social services. In addition, there may be restrictions upon employing a family member as a carer or PA using health or social services funding.

9.7.4 Data protection

All employers owe statutory duties to hold, process and deal with personal data fairly and lawfully (not used other than for the purposes of managing or administering the employment relationship). Data should not be kept longer than is necessary after the relationship ends. Any data that is capable of identifying a person (by date of birth, name, address, or job) is personal data and as such needs to be handled very carefully to ensure that it does not fall into the wrong hands. The Data Protection Act 1998 and the Codes of Practice deal with everything from how medical information is dealt with by an employer to the giving of employers' references. All employees can find out what information (data) their employer holds about them by making a formal written data subject access request and sending £10 to the employer in order to have any data which identifies them as a data subject disclosed to them. This could include any memos, letters, emails and other media that mention their name or give sufficient details by which their identity can be discerned. If an employer fails to deal with the request properly or at all a complaint can be made to the Information Commissioner who has extensive powers to fine employers.

Other resources

See Skills for Care (**www.skillsforcare.org.uk**) and **www.beingtheboss.co.uk** – a website run by disabled people for disabled people who employ their own personal assistants/carers.

CHAPTER 10

Provision of healthcare

Caroline Coats with Caroline Bielanska

10.1 THE NATIONAL HEALTH SERVICE

10.1.1 Legislation

- Health Act 1999.
- Health and Social Care Act 2001.
- National Health Service Reform and Health Care Professions Act 2002.
- Health (Wales) Act 2003.
- Health and Social Care (Community Health and Standards) Act 2003.
- Mental Capacity Act 2005.
- National Health Service Act 2006.
- National Health Service Act (Wales) Act 2006.
- National Health Service (Consequential Provisions) Act 2006.
- Local Government and Public Involvement in Health Act 2007.
- Health and Social Care Act 2008.
- Health Act 2009.
- Health and Social Care Act 2012.
- Care Act 2014.
- Social Services and Well-being Act (Wales) 2014.
- Local Authority Social Services and National Health Service Complaints (England) Regulations 2009, SI 2009/309.
- Care and Support (Charging and Assessment of Resources) Regulations 2014, SI 2014/2672.
- Care and Support (Discharge of Hospital Patients) Regulations 2014, SI 2014/2823.
- Care and Support Statutory Guidance (CSSG) (October 2014).

10.1.2 Reform

The National Health Service (NHS) was established by the NHS Act 1946 to provide a health service, based on clinical need that is free for all at the point of delivery. It was not long before the NHS was taking steps to reform, with the introduction of prescription charges. The NHS has since undergone almost constant reorganisation in an effort to produce a more efficient service that puts the patient first, providing more choice and reinforcing the main aim of the NHS which is to help people live longer and enjoy a better quality of life.

More recently, in July 2010, the government published its White Paper, *Equity and Excellence: Liberating the NHS* (Cm 7881) containing proposals for:

- giving groups of GP practices 'real' budgets to buy care;
- abolishing all primary care trusts and strategic health authorities, and creating a new NHS Commissioning Board;
- scrapping performance targets, including waiting times; and
- transforming the health service regulator, 'Monitor', into an economic regulator.

In the same year, the government published *Healthy Lives, Healthy People: Our Strategy for Public Health in England* (Cm 7985) a public health strategy with plans to create a new organisation – Public Health England – whose sole responsibility would be to provide advice and influence public health issues and transferring public health responsibility from the NHS to local authorities. Eventually the Health and Social Care Act 2012 was passed, bringing major reform, on 1 April 2013.

The Health Act 2009 imposed a duty on English NHS bodies to have regard to the NHS Constitution, which was launched in January 2009 and last updated in July 2015. The aim is for the NHS to be fair and effective and so sets out the rights of patients and staff and the responsibilities they have towards each other.

Following the passing of the Government of Wales Act 1998 and the establishment of the National Assembly, Wales has its own policy and law governing the NHS. These are broadly similar to those in England, but not identical. For example, there is no equivalent NHS Constitution in Wales. All NHS Wales organisations work to their quality assurance system. See **www.wales.nhs.uk/governance-emanual/organisational-structure**.

10.1.3 Structure

The Secretary of State retains overall responsibility for the NHS in England with the Minister for Health and Social Services having this responsibility in Wales. In addition to setting the strategic direction he has a number of other specific functions (e.g. under MHA 1983) and may:

- provide any services which he considers appropriate for the purpose of discharging any of his statutory duties;
- do any other thing calculated to facilitate, or conducive or incidental to, the discharge of such duties.

Public Health England

Public Health England provides national leadership and expert services to support public health. It also works with the NHS and local government in response to emergency situations and:

- coordinates a national public health service;
- supports development of the public health workforce;
- supports the public to make healthier choices; and
- builds an evidence base to support local public health services.

In Wales these functions are provided by Public Health Wales.

NHS England

NHS England, although legally called the 'NHS Commissioning Board', is an independent body whose role is to improve health for people in England, by:

- providing national leadership for improvement and driving up the quality of care;
- overseeing the operation and allocation of resources to clinical commissioning groups;
- commissioning primary care and specialist services.

It operates through local area teams, which are responsible for operating the independent review panels for NHS continuing healthcare appeals from local clinical commissioning groups.

Clinical commissioning groups (CCGs)

Clinical commissioning groups (CCGs) comprise GPs, consultants, nurses and other clinicians and are responsible for 60 per cent of the NHS budget and commission secondary healthcare services for their local area, for example:

- community health services;
- mental health and learning disability services;
- rehabilitative care;
- planned hospital care;
- out-of-hours, urgent and emergency care.

They also have a duty to involve patients and carers in decisions they make about the services they commission, taking into account guidelines from the National Institute for Health and Care Excellence (NICE) and data about providers from the Care Quality Commission (CQC).

Special health authorities

These have particular functions and provide services for the whole population in England, such as NHS Blood and Transplant (NHSBT) and NICE.

NHS trusts and foundation trusts

Hospital trusts usually offer a range of services to meet general health needs. Some trusts act as a regional or national centre of expertise for more specialised care, while some are attached to universities and help to train health professionals. Trusts may also provide services in the community through health centres, clinics or in people's homes, for example ambulance services. Other than in an emergency, hospital treatment is arranged by a referral through the GP. Most trusts operate as foundation trusts, which are public benefit corporations, authorised and regulated by Monitor. They are locally governed and accountable to their local population, so they can be more responsive to their local communities.

Care trusts

The Health Act 1999 created flexibility for the NHS and social care to work together to provide better-integrated services. This is particularly important in regard to groups such as the elderly infirm, but is made difficult by the fact that health/local authority boundaries do not coincide.

A care trust is an NHS organisation to which local authorities can delegate health-related functions, in order to provide integrated health and social care to their local communities. They are established on a voluntary basis and in partnership, where there is a joint agreement at a local level that this will be the best way to deliver better health and social care services.

Structure in Wales

The Welsh Assembly Government is responsible for policy direction and for allocating funds to the NHS in Wales.

There are seven local Health Boards (HBs), each with a decision-making board, made up of local doctors, nurses, other health professionals, members of the local council and voluntary organisations, and others to represent the voice of patients. They also have a small executive team to put the decisions into action and provide services for the public. HBs plan and pay for most hospital and family health services with the exception of certain specialist services. These are the responsibility of the Health Commission Wales (Specialised Services).

Public Health Wales (**www.publichealthwales.wales.nhs.uk**) gives advice and guidance to HBs on a range of issues such as disease prevention and control.

Patient representation in England

PATIENT ADVICE AND LIAISON SERVICE

The Patient Advice and Liaison Service offers confidential advice, support and information on health-related matters. It helps to resolve concerns or problems involving the NHS and provides advice on how to get independent help to make a complaint.

PATIENT FORUMS

Patient forums are run by independent volunteers with wide-ranging experience by local people with a desire to improve services. They work to influence the commissioning of services.

INDEPENDENT COMPLAINTS ADVOCACY SERVICE

The Independent Complaints Advocacy Service is a free independent service to assist patients or their families make a complaint about NHS care or treatment. Trained advocates guide the complainant through the complaints procedure and provide support.

Patient representation in Wales

Community Health Councils represent the interests of patients and advise on complaints with regard to hospital and community health services in Wales.

Healthwatch

The Health and Social Care Act 2012 established local Healthwatch, operating at local level, and Healthwatch England, which operates nationally.

Healthwatch England is a national body that enables the collective views of the people who use NHS and social care services to influence national policy, advice and guidance. It provides leadership, guidance and support to local Healthwatch organisations.

Local Healthwatch aims to give communities a stronger voice in influencing and challenging how health and social care services are provided in their areas, as the views and feedback from people who use services are an integral part of local commissioning of health and social care.

10.1.4 Joint planning and funding

Health and wellbeing boards

The Health and Social Care Act 2012 establishes health and wellbeing boards (HWBs) in England as a forum for commissioners across the NHS, social care and public health services to improve the health and well-being of their local population and reduce health inequalities. A member of the local Healthwatch must sit on the HWB.

10.2 DELIVERY OF HEALTHCARE

10.2.1 NHS choice

The NHS Choice Framework explains the legal right to choice about treatment and care in the NHS. Everyone who is cared for by the NHS in England has legal rights that cover:

- rights about access to health services;
- rights about quality of care and environment, such as the provision of same sex hospital accommodation;
- rights about treatments and drugs;
- rights about consent and confidentiality;
- rights about patient choice;
- rights about your own involvement in your healthcare – for example, through schemes such as personal health budgets;
- rights to complaints and redress.

The legal right to choice does not apply to all healthcare services. Where there is not a legal right to choice, some choices may still be offered, depending upon what is available locally.

10.2.2 Types

There are three types of healthcare provided under the NHS, though healthcare may also be purchased or arranged by the NHS privately:

1. primary healthcare provided in the community by family doctors, dentists, opticians and others;
2. secondary healthcare provided through hospitals and the ambulance services;
3. tertiary healthcare provided through specialist hospitals, e.g. for cancer.

The NHS Constitution in England provides that all patients have the right to:

- start consultant-led treatment within a maximum of 18 weeks from a referral for non-urgent conditions; and

- be seen by a cancer specialist within a maximum of two weeks from GP referral for urgent referrals where cancer is suspected.

There is no longer a prescribed time limit on how quickly the patient should be able to see a GP.

Primary care services

In addition to seeing a GP other services include:

- Local pharmacists: give advice on minor ailments; can suggest non-prescription medicines to ease symptoms; answer questions about prescriptions.
- NHS 111 or NHS Direct Wales: national, confidential NHS non-emergency numbers, available 24 hours a day, 365 days a year, which provide telephone advice and health information service staffed by nurses and professional advisers. They also connect to the ambulance service. They hold details of GP practices and dentists offering NHS treatment, local pharmacies including late opening pharmacies, emergency dental services, NHS walk-in centres and minor injuries units. There is a confidential interpretation service, and 24-hour textphone service on 0845 606 46 47. NHS Direct Wales phone line is 0845 4647.
- NHS walk-in centres: open seven days a week from early morning until late evening. Run by experienced nurses and managed by CCGs, they provide a range of services to treat minor ailments.
- Minor injuries units: for patients with non-life-threatening injuries, such as broken bones, minor burns, head and eye injuries, insect and animal bites, that do not need the attention of accident and emergency (A&E) staff.
- NHS Choices website: **www.nhs.uk**.
- Accident and emergency: all patients are assessed on arrival and the most serious cases given priority. The aim is for a patient to be seen, diagnosed and treated within four hours of arrival at A&E with a suspected serious illness or injury.

10.2.3 In the community

The NHS is responsible for providing community health services to people in care homes on the same basis as to people in their own homes. The NHS provides relevant equipment in addition to the standard equipment that the home provides as part of its services. Each CCG or HB should have its own published criteria for the type of help it will provide, based on guidance issued by the government. NHS services that may be provided include assessment and support from community-based NHS staff such as district nurses and continence nurses, care provided in a nursing home by a registered nurse, palliative care services, and rehabilitation and recovery services such as speech therapy.

General practitioners

Family doctors (GPs) provide their services in medical practices to persons who register with them. Practices may offer a wider range of services with more emphasis on promotion of good health and prevention of disease. Practice nurses may undertake specialist training which allows them to prescribe certain medicines and other items, such as wound dressings. GP contracts allow GPs to take on responsibilities where they have clinical specialist interests, such as dermatology. They are able to carry out procedures in the practice rather than in hospital. Directories are produced of local GPs giving details of their practices which should produce an annual leaflet with details of the services provided.

Everyone has the right to be registered with a GP:

- the patient may approach a GP and ask to join his or her list of patients (but the GP is not obliged to accept a particular patient);
- the CCG/HB will allocate a patient to a GP if he or she is unable to find one but there is then a risk of periodic transfer so the patient should seek to find their own GP;
- patients may change GP without giving reasons or getting permission.

Patients have the right to see a GP (not necessarily their own) at the surgery during surgery hours which should be displayed on a notice outside. The surgery should provide a telephone number for messages at all times. An appointment system may prevail except in an emergency. Home visits cannot be insisted upon and are at the doctor's discretion, but should be available to patients who genuinely need them.

Patients aged 75 and over must be offered an annual assessment and home visit to see how they are managing, but not necessarily at a time of year of their choice.

Patients away from home for up to three months can ask to be treated as a temporary patient by another GP and even if the patient is not accepted, that GP must give any treatment that is immediately necessary.

Out-of-hours care may be managed by a deputising service or a co-operative. It may be that the GP's emergency telephone number will refer the caller to NHS 111 or NHS Direct Wales who will then determine if the patient should go to hospital or make an appointment with the GP, or it may give advice.

Dental care

Patients may be accepted on to a dentist's NHS 'continuing care' list. All necessary treatment must be offered to continuing care patients under the NHS but private treatment can be arranged in addition or as an alternative. Registration usually lasts for 15 months which is renewed each time a new course of NHS treatment begins. NHS 111 or NHS Direct Wales will be able to assist in finding a dentist.

Continence services

Contact details for the local NHS continence advisory service are available from the Bladder and Bowel Foundation, the CCG's Patient Advice and Liaison Service (PALS) or local Community Health Council in Wales. GP referral is not required, although that is the main way of accessing the service. A plan to treat or manage the condition will be discussed and agreed with the patient, along with a review date. If this plan is not successful, there may be referral to a hospital consultant for further investigation. Pads or other products necessary should be available from the NHS. What is available varies from region to region: in England each CCG has its own eligibility criteria and contract to supply continence products including pads. Eligibility to receive long-term continence supplies is reassessed at least annually.

Hearing difficulties

A referral can be made from the patient's GP for an investigation and diagnosis of hearing difficulties and treatment/dispensing of a hearing aid. NHS hearing aids are provided on loan; batteries are supplied free of charge.

Chiropody

The GP or PALS in England or Community Health Council in Wales will advise about local eligibility criteria for NHS chiropody. This usually means a medical foot problem or health condition leading to higher risk of foot-related problems. Routine care such as nail cutting is unlikely to be offered as NHS treatment.

End of life care

End of Life Care Strategy: Promoting High Quality Care for All Adults at the End of Life published by the Department of Health and by the Welsh Assembly in July 2008 aimed to:

- ensure that high quality care is available to people as they approach the end of their life, wherever they are cared for; and
- make it easier for people to die at home, if that is their preference.

Services must be able to meet the needs of patients with any terminal illness, not just cancer, and be available to people in their own home, a care home, or a hospice as well as in hospital. Local NHS bodies and their respective local authorities must identify what services and additional staff need to be in place to provide 24-hour support for patients. The Leadership Alliance for the Care of Dying People has published *One Chance to Get It Right* (June 2014, available from **www.gov.uk**), which replaces what unfairly became the controversial Liverpool Care Pathway. As end of life approaches, individuals and those close to them need to be able to access high quality care that is compassionate, competent and respectful. For this to happen health and social care staff need to make sure they deliver the right person-centred care 'the first time, every time'. Good end of life care means:

1. The possibility that a person may die within the next few days or hours is recognised and communicated clearly, decisions made and actions taken in accordance with the person's needs and wishes, and these are regularly reviewed and decisions revised accordingly.
2. Sensitive communication takes place between staff and the dying person, and those identified as important to them.
3. The dying person, and those identified as important to them, are involved in decisions about treatment and care to the extent that the dying person wants.
4. The needs of families and others identified as important to the dying person are actively explored, respected and met as far as possible.
5. An individual plan of care, which includes food and drink, symptom control and psychological, social and spiritual support, is agreed, coordinated and delivered with compassion.

Coordination of care can be made through Electronic Palliative Care Coordination Systems (EPaCCS) and/or other mechanisms. See **www.dyingmatters.org** for more information.

NICE has published quality standards in respect of end of life care for adults updated in October 2015 which should be followed when providing end of life care and guidelines for caring for dying adults published in December 2015 which require that:

- there is recognition when someone is dying and the patient and his or her relevant family are told of the situation honestly and to the degree they wish;
- those treating the patient include the patient and his or her family in discussions and care planning;
- the patient is helped to stay comfortable, so that any pain, breathlessness, nausea and vomiting, anxiety, delirium and agitation, noisy breathing, and hydration are properly and appropriately managed.

10.2.4 Hospital care

Patients generally need to be referred to a hospital by a GP, but in an emergency an A&E department will provide treatment:

- there is no absolute right to choose the hospital or consultant, but a preference may be expressed to the GP;
- there is no right to a second opinion but patients can request one if in doubt;
- for hospital discharge see **10.5**.

10.2.5 Private medical care

Medical care and treatment outside the NHS is provided under direct contracts between the provider and the patient. A private hospital may be set up as a commercial enterprise or a charity. There may be separate contracts with the private hospital, consultant, etc. Fees are charged which may be recovered as a civil debt and a matter of complaint may also be a breach of contract.

Health professionals involved are governed by the same professional bodies as govern those working in the NHS (some also work part-time for the NHS). The NHS can commission care in the private sector if the patient has been on a waiting list for an extended period of time.

The Care Quality Commission is responsible for registering private hospitals and clinics in England. The Health Care Inspectorate Wales carries out this function for private hospitals situated in Wales.

Private medical insurance

The potential fees for private medical care may be covered by tailor-made insurance policies or schemes, providing a level of cover for an annual premium or subscription. Refer to the conditions of the particular policy or the rules of the scheme:

- not all forms of medical treatment are eligible for a claim;
- any additional cost of the treatment must be paid by the patient but cash benefits may be available for those who receive treatment under the NHS;
- there may be age restrictions on taking out a policy or joining a scheme.

10.2.6 NHS continuing healthcare

- National Framework for NHS Continuing Healthcare and NHS-Funded Nursing Care in England (November 2012).
- Continuing NHS Health Care: The National Framework for Implementation in Wales (June 2014, WG 22091).
- National Health Service Commissioning Board and Clinical Commissioning Groups (Responsibilities and Standing Rules) Regulations 2012, SI 2012/2996.
- NHS Continuing Healthcare (Responsibilities of Social Services Authorities) Directions 2013.
- Care and Support (Discharge of Hospital Patients) Regulations 2014, SI 2014/2823.

NHS continuing healthcare is a package of care arranged and funded solely by the NHS to meet assessed health and personal care needs that may relate to physical and/or mental health. To qualify for fully funded NHS continuing healthcare the individual must fall within the eligibility criteria. The care needs must relate primarily to one of health. The criteria are based on the nature, intensity, instability, unpredictability or complexity of healthcare needs or need for the use of routine healthcare equipment or the requirement for palliative care. Approximately 10 per cent of care home places are fully funded by the NHS. However, care can be provided in any setting, including the person's own home. The person will be the responsibility of social services (and therefore means tested) if the nursing services provided are ancillary or incidental to the provision of a care and support service and of a nature one would expect social services to provide (see *R* v. *North and East Devon Health Authority, ex p Coughlan* [2001] QB 213; Care Act 2014, s.22; Social Services and Well-being (Wales) Act 2014, s.47(1)).

The CCG/HB that holds the contract with the GP practice at the time of assessment is responsible for arranging and funding a suitable care package. Each CCG/HB has a manager responsible for NHS continuing healthcare. The individual remains an NHS patient and no charge is made, but social security benefits may be withdrawn or reduced.

The National Framework in England

The National Framework for NHS Continuing Healthcare and NHS-Funded Nursing Care was developed and first introduced in England in October 2007. It aimed to reduce scope for local interpretation and improve the clarity, transparency and consistency of the decision-making process by providing:

- clear principles and processes to be followed throughout England for establishing eligibility for NHS continuing healthcare;
- guidance that must be followed by all CCGs in conjunction with their local authorities and by hospital staff involved in the assessment process;
- clarification of the interaction between the assessment for NHS continuing healthcare and NHS-funded nursing care;
- common paperwork to record evidence that will inform decision-making.

The National Framework guidance and tools (checklist tool, decision-support tool and fast-track tool) to support decision-making have been updated a number of times, most recently in November 2012.

Checklist and decision-support tools

Characteristics of the different levels of need that feature in the checklist tool and decision-support tool help to indicate whether the care need is primarily a health need. The features are:

- *Nature* – the type of needs, the overall effect of those needs, and the interventions required to manage them.
- *Intensity* – both the extent and severity of the needs and the need for regular interventions to manage them.

CCG: Clinical Commissioning Groups

- *Complexity* – how the different needs arise and interact to increase the skill needed to monitor and manage care.
- *Unpredictability* – unexpected changes that are difficult to manage and the degree of risk if adequate and timely care is not provided.

A review should be requested as health deteriorates. If hospital admission occurs due to failing health, then review should take place as part of hospital discharge procedures.

THE CHECKLIST

The checklist is based on the 12 domains or areas of need in the decision-support tool. For each domain, there are descriptions for 'no and low', 'moderate' and 'high' needs. A full assessment is required if there are:

- high levels of need in two or more domains; or
- moderate levels of need in five or more domains; or
- one high and four moderate levels; or
- one high level of need in one of the four domains that carries a priority level in the decision-support tool and any levels of need in other domains.

Once the checklist is completed, the decision may be made. A copy of the completed checklist should provide enough detail to explain the decision made. The CCG can be asked to reconsider the decision and it may take into account any further information. Subsequently, complaint is through the NHS complaints procedure.

THE DECISION-SUPPORT TOOL

If the person is referred for a full assessment, the CCG is responsible for coordinating the whole process until a decision about eligibility and funding has been reached and a care plan agreed. An appropriate range of health and social care professionals should contribute to the assessment (multidisciplinary team). Information collected during the assessment is used to complete the decision-support tool.

The tool features 12 domains or areas of need. Each domain is broken down between four and six levels of need: 'no need', 'low', 'moderate', 'high', 'severe' and 'priority'. The domains are: Behaviour; Cognition; Psychological and emotional needs; Communication; Mobility; Nutrition; Continence; Skin including tissue viability; Breathing; Drug therapies and medication, symptom control; Altered states of consciousness; and Other significant care needs to be taken into consideration.

When completing the tool:

- all care domains should be completed, ideally on the same day;
- the team should use the assessment evidence and their professional judgment to select the level that most closely describes needs;

297

- needs should not be placed between levels. If it proves difficult to choose between two levels, the higher level should be selected and the reasons for differences of opinion recorded;
- interactions between needs should be considered as appropriate;
- needs not covered by one of the 11 specific domains should be recorded in the 12th domain and taken into account when making an eligibility decision;
- needs should not be marginalised because they are successfully managed.

Well-managed needs are still needs and should be recorded appropriately.
   A clear recommendation of eligibility would be expected if:

- there is a priority level of need in any of the four domains with that level; or
- there are two or more instances of severe needs across all domains.

A primary health need may also be indicated if:

- there is one domain recorded as severe together with needs in a number of other domains; or
- there are a number of domains with high and/or moderate needs.

The completed decision-support tool, guidelines indicating the threshold needed to constitute a primary health need and the professional judgment (consideration of what the evidence indicates about the nature and/or complexity and/or intensity and/or unpredictability of needs) of the multidisciplinary team (MDT) who will make a recommendation to the CCG combine to make an informed decision. Only in exceptional circumstances should the MDT's recommendation not be followed.
   The CCG should provide its decision verbally and in writing, giving clear reasons and the basis on which the decision was made. A copy of the completed decision-support tool should also be made available. Ongoing reviews should be included.

Fast-track tool

Decisions to fast track should be made case by case and supported by a prognosis, where possible, and not be based on life expectancy. The CCG should follow the principles set out in the *End of Life Care Strategy* (see **10.2.3**) and take into account any stated preferences and wishes and any advance care plan.

NHS continuing healthcare in Wales

The Welsh Assembly introduced a similar national framework in August 2010, which was last updated in June 2014. Only the decision-support tool has been adopted, although locally agreed 'fast track' protocols have been developed. The use of a screening tool or checklist is not mandated, although it is acknowledged there may be circumstances where such a tool may be useful. For example, care home residents whose condition has changed requiring an earlier than planned review or to provide a structured rationale where the multidisciplinary team believes a complex care package is clearly not required. In those circumstances where a checklist is employed, the English checklist tool should be used in order to ensure that a consistent approach is adopted (paras.3.34–3.35 of the Welsh National Framework).

The guidance documents *Integrated Assessment, Planning and Review Arrangements for Older People: Guidance for Professionals in Supporting the Health, Care and Well-being of Older People* or *Creating a Unified and Fair System for Assessing and Managing Care* (National Assembly for Wales, 2002), which apply to people who are aged under 64 years (NAFWC 09/02, WHC (2002) 3), are used to assess the domains of care, although it is down to the assessor to form his or her own view as to the level of care that the person requires.

Challenging the decision in England

There are two stages in the review process:

- a local review process at CCG level;
- a request to NHS England (also known as the National Commissioning Board (NCB)), which may refer the matter to an independent review panel (IRP).

Each CCG should have a local review process, including timescales, publicly available which should be provided if a review is requested. The procedure may provide for the case to be referred to another CCG. Once local procedures are exhausted the case should be referred to the IRP. If using the local review process would cause undue delay, the NCB has discretion to put the case straight to the IRP, which considers:

- the procedure followed in reaching the eligibility decision; and
- application of the criteria of eligibility, i.e. the primary health need test.

If the NCB decides not to convene a panel a full written explanation should be provided.

The IRP has a scrutiny and reviewing role and is required to make a recommendation to the NCB in the light of its findings. Legal representation is not usually necessary. The NCB should communicate the outcome of the review, with its reasons, to the individual and the CCG. If the original decision is upheld and further challenge is deemed necessary, a complaint can be made to the Parliamentary and Health Service Ombudsman.

Parliamentary and Health Service Ombudsman

The Ombudsman's office does not have to investigate every complaint. It will usually expect the local resolution and independent review stages to have been completed by the CCG/NCB, unless it would be unreasonable to do so. Reports may be accessed at **www.ombudsman.org.uk**.

MDT: Multi-disciplinary teams

Reviews

If the NHS is providing or funding any part of the care package, a case review should take place no later than three months after the initial eligibility decision, and annually thereafter, unless a specific recommendation about the timing of the next review was made by the MDT making the original recommendation.

Challenging the decision in Wales

The HB operates a similar review process to the local review process run by CCGs in England. When informal review has been exhausted, the HB can refer the matter to the independent review panel, similar to such panel established by the NCB in England. Those who are still dissatisfied can make a complaint to the Public Services Ombudsman for Wales.

10.2.7 NHS registered nursing care contribution

In all cases, a decision about eligibility for NHS continuing healthcare must be made before considering the need for NHS-funded nursing care. Nursing care needs may then be decided in two different ways:

- by the MDT: nursing needs should be recorded on the decision-support tool; or
- by a registered nurse making a needs assessment when the patient leaves hospital.

If a person is staying in a care home providing nursing care the NHS pays for the cost of nursing care provided by a registered nurse. Payment is made direct to the home by the CCG or HB in which the patient's GP is based. It covers care carried out by the registered nurse employed by the home but not care carried out by other care staff even where delegated by the registered nurse. A payment for nursing care is not made on behalf of residents of care homes not registered to provide nursing care (often referred to as 'residential homes'). Any nursing care these residents require from a registered nurse is provided by a nurse who visits the home such as a district nurse, not a nurse employed by the home.

Services provided by a registered nurse may involve:

- identifying and addressing potential health problems;
- monitoring/reviewing medication needs;
- planning and reviewing a care plan;
- provision of nursing care;
- supervising/monitoring care provided by a non-registered nurse.

Normally the NHS would not expect to pay for healthcare twice but sometimes it may continue to pay the nursing care contribution as a retainer during stays in hospital.

The sum paid is based on the nursing needs of the resident and in England prior to October 2007 it was assessed as lower, middle, or higher rate. Since 1 October 2007 there has been a single band of nursing care. For 2015/16 the weekly rate, paid directly to the nursing home, is £112.00. Those previously on the low or middle bands transferred to the single band. Those on the high band continue at a higher rate (£154.14 for 2015/16) until:

- death;
- eligibility for NHS continuing healthcare arises;
- the person is no longer resident in a nursing home;
- a review decision that nursing care is no longer needed;
- a review decision that nursing needs no longer match high band criteria (so transfer to the single band rate).

Wales has always operated a flat rate for nursing care.

Free nursing care also brings entitlement to free incontinence supplies in addition to the assessed entitlement. Specific needs should be included in the person's care plan.

Reviews

A review should take place no later than three months after the decision of ineligibility for NHS continuing healthcare and at least annually as a minimum thereafter. Each review should reconsider eligibility for NHS continuing healthcare by using the checklist. The care home manager should be aware of the CCG's/HB's arrangements for nursing care reviews.

10.3 INFORMATION

There is a general duty of confidentiality imposed upon health professionals at common law, so medical information concerning an older person may only be disclosed to third parties in certain defined circumstances. Older people may themselves wish to be told what the diagnosis of an illness is or to know what is held in their medical records. The obligations of an NHS body or medical practitioner in relation to the disclosure of information are dealt with in **Chapter 2**. Relevant legislation includes:

- Access to Medical Reports Act 1988.
- Access to Health Records Act 1990.
- Data Protection Act 1998.
- Human Rights Act 1998.
- Health Service (Control of Patient Information) Regulations 2002, SI 2002/1438.

See also Confidentiality: NHS Code of Practice (July 2003).

10.3.1 Confidentiality

A doctor is under a general duty not to disclose information which he or she has gained in his or her professional capacity but there are the following potential exceptions to this general principle:

- disclosure with the patient's consent;
- disclosure in relation to the clinical management of a patient;
- disclosure to a close relative or another third party in the best interests of the patient;
- disclosure required by statute;
- disclosure in connection with judicial proceedings or in the public interest;
- disclosure for the purposes of medical audit, teaching and research.

A doctor who discloses confidential information about a patient must be prepared to justify this under one of the above heads.

Consent to disclosure

A doctor is free to disclose medical information with the consent of the patient but the consent should cover the extent of the information disclosed and the persons to whom it is disclosed:

- if the patient is incapable of giving consent the other exceptions must be considered, e.g. is the disclosure in the best interests of the patient;
- wherever possible questions of disclosure will be discussed with the patient in advance and express consent obtained or inferred.

Disclosure to other professionals

Medical information may only be disclosed to those directly involved in the care and treatment of the patient on a 'need-to-know' basis in relation to such care – other purposes will not suffice:

- all medically qualified staff share the duty of confidentiality;
- a doctor releasing information to non-medical professionals (e.g. social workers) must ensure that they too will treat it in confidence;
- information required for administrative purposes should be on a basis which does not identify the patient;
- if a patient is particularly vulnerable disclosure of concerns about abuse to an appropriate source may be indicated.

Disclosure to others

Doctors may need to discuss with relatives or carers the nature of an illness and any treatment, and consent may often be presumed (unless expressly refused):

- if consent cannot be given the doctor must act in the patient's best interests;
- when it is undesirable, for medical reasons, to seek a patient's express consent, disclosure is essentially a matter of clinical judgment.

Public interest

It may be in the public interest for a doctor to disclose information about his patient where failure to disclose will expose the patient, or someone else, to a risk of death or serious harm, for example:

- where a doctor considers that the patient is no longer fit to drive (though he or she should advise the patient first and invite surrender of the licence); or
- if it is apparent that a perpetrator of abuse to the patient is also abusing other vulnerable adults.

10.3.2 Withholding information

It is suggested that information may only be specifically withheld from the patient if disclosure would be likely to cause serious harm to the patient's physical or mental health.

NHS Code of Practice

In July 2003 the Department of Health published Confidentiality: NHS Code of Practice (similar Codes exist in Scotland and Wales). Confidentiality: NHS Code of Practice Supplementary Guidance: Public Interest Disclosures was published in November 2010.

It provides that:

- complaints about non-disclosure, delays in disclosure or charges for information should be made to the appropriate NHS manager;
- if complainants are dissatisfied with the response received they should write to the chief executive of the NHS body;
- those still dissatisfied may complain to the Parliamentary and Health Service Ombudsman (who has required a health body to establish the specific exemption relied upon in order to justify refusal to disclose information).

Caldicott guardians

The Caldicott review of personally identifiable information in 1997 recommended that 'guardians' of personal information be created to safeguard and govern the uses made of confidential information within NHS organisations. The Caldicott principles and processes provide a framework of standards for the management of confidentiality and access to personal information under the leadership of a Caldicott guardian. The Caldicott standard is extended into local authorities with social services responsibilities with the aim to provide a good foundation for joint working between health and social services.

The Caldicott principles are:

1. Justify the purpose(s).
2. Do not use patient-identifiable information unless it is absolutely necessary.
3. Use the minimum necessary patient-identifiable information.
4. Access to patient-identifiable information should be on a strict need-to-know basis.
5. Everyone with access to patient-identifiable information should be aware of their responsibilities.
6. Understand and comply with the law.

10.4   COMPLAINTS

A client may be dissatisfied about the delivery of healthcare and wish to complain. You should only pursue this on the request or with the consent of the actual patient and be careful about complaints made by other people (unless the patient lacks mental capacity and is dependent upon other people looking after his or her interests). Before pursuing a formal complaint, it may be appropriate for the patient or someone on their behalf to discuss the problem with the professional involved and if not satisfied that this has been done you may wish to take the step yourself (it may be more appropriate to have the discussion with that person's manager). Help and advice should be available from the local PALS in England or Community Health Councils in Wales.

It is important to distinguish cases where there is the possibility of legal redress (e.g. damages for negligent treatment) and consider:

- it may not be appropriate to delay matters by pursuing a complaint;
- if the complaint arises in the private sector it may amount to an actionable breach of contract;
- there is no legal justification for attempts to persuade complainants to waive legal rights before a complaint will be investigated;
- the purpose of a complaint is to resolve a problem, not to increase it.

10.4.1   Procedures

On 1 April 2009, a two-stage system for resolving complaints was introduced for the NHS and local authorities in England with adult social care responsibilities. Stage one involves seeking local resolution; stage two involves taking the complaint to the relevant Ombudsman. Complaints may be instigated with the commissioner (the local CCG) or the provider of any NHS service.

Complaints should be made within 12 months of the event occurring or awareness of the event occurring. A complaint made after this time may be investigated at the discretion of the complaints manager if it is still possible to do so fairly and effectively.

When the complaint is acknowledged there should be an offer to discuss the complaint and information on:

- how it will be handled;
- how long it may be before any investigation is complete;
- when a response is likely to be received.

If a discussion is declined, the complaints manager will advise in writing how the complaint will be dealt with.

NHS complaints procedures

Organisations offering NHS services should produce information explaining their arrangements for dealing with complaints. All staff should know who is responsible for complaints handling and be able to signpost patients and relatives appropriately. Staff should also know how to direct patients to the local Patient Advice and Liaison Service (PALS) or the Independent Complaints Advocacy Service (ICAS). PALS will often help resolve problems before they exacerbate and, if unable to do so, will explain the complaints procedure and contact the local ICAS. ICAS is an independent service which provides support to raise complaints, assists in preparation and attendance at meetings and discusses options at every stage of the process. NHS 111 also has their contact details.

Complaints do not have to be made by the person receiving services, but may be:

- because you are affected by the issue being complained about;
- for a friend or relative if they agree, preferably in writing;
- on behalf of someone who, within the meaning of the Mental Capacity Act 2005, 'lacks the capacity' to complain;
- on behalf of someone who has died.

A complaint cannot be raised again if it has already been investigated under the previous system.

STAGE 1 – LOCAL RESOLUTION

The Local Authority Social Services and National Health Service Complaints (England) Regulations 2009, SI 2009/309 and the NHS Constitution do not stipulate the form local resolution must take but do include the following:

- The complaint may be made in person, by phone, letter or email. If the complaint is made in person or by phone, the person hearing it must send a copy of their recorded interpretation of the complaint.

- The complaint should be acknowledged within three working days of receipt and an opportunity to discuss the complaint at a convenient time offered.
- If an investigation is required, it should be proportionate and is expected to be completed and a response provided no later than six months from the date of receipt.

At the end of the investigation a written response is provided and should include:

- an explanation of how the complaint has been considered;
- conclusions reached on the specifics of the complaint;
- any remedial action to be taken;
- details of the right to take the complaint to the Parliamentary and Health Service Ombudsman.

STAGE 2 – TAKING A COMPLAINT TO THE OMBUDSMAN

If a person is dissatisfied with the way the complaint has been dealt with locally, the Parliamentary and Health Service Ombudsman (HSO) may be asked to investigate. The HSO is independent of the NHS and the government. If the complaint involves services from both the NHS and a local authority the HSO and the Local Government Ombudsman will work together to resolve it. The HSO provides further advice at **www.ombudsman.org.uk**.

Complaints in Wales

The National Health Service (Concerns, Complaints and Redress Arrangements) (Wales) Regulations 2011, SI 2011/704 (W 108) set out the common arrangements and duties that apply to NHS organisations in Wales in respect of the investigation and handling of complaints. 'Putting Things Right' guidance on dealing with concerns about the NHS was issued in 2011 and last updated in 2013. The aim is for the NHS to 'investigate once, investigate well', ensuring that concerns are dealt with in the right way, the first time round.

The arrangements are similar but not identical to the English complaints process, with some notable differences:

1. An acknowledgement to a complaint should occur within two working days of the complaint being received.
2. An interim report should be provided within 30 days of the complaint being received, which may set out a plan of action to deal with the complaint.
3. An investigation report (if part of the complaint plan) should be provided within 12 months of the complaint being received, although it may take longer.
4. HBs are able to investigate primary care complaints, rather than merely to facilitate resolution of complaints.
5. There is a duty to consider when investigating a concern, whether there is a

qualifying liability in tort in respect of a service which has been provided, although it does not apply to concerns raised and investigated relating to primary care practitioners.

Professional misconduct

Professional misconduct complaints against GPs or hospital doctors are made to the General Medical Council and dealt with under established procedures. Sanctions range from a warning letter through suspension to removal from the Register. Complaints against nurses, dentists, pharmacists and other professional groups are made to the professional association concerned.

NHS discipline procedure

Discipline in respect of family health services practitioners is dealt with separately from complaints by special disciplinary committees of a different NHS body. They hear evidence, make findings of fact and recommend an appropriate penalty. Appeal lies to the First-tier Tribunal (Primary Health Lists).

Human Rights Act 1998

Relevant articles in the European Convention on Human Rights, as set out in Schedule 1 to the Human Rights Act 1998, are:

- Article 2: the right to life.
- Article 3: the right not to be subject to torture or degrading treatment or punishment.
- Article 5: the right to liberty and security of the person.
- Article 6: the right to a fair hearing by an independent and impartial tribunal.
- Article 8: the right to respect for family life, home and correspondence.
- Article 14: the right not to be discriminated against.

Remedy may be sought if any right is violated by a public body.

10.5 DISCHARGE FROM HOSPITAL

Formal discharge from hospital is not possible until the medical condition of the individual is stable. There is no right to stay in hospital indefinitely if hospital care is no longer required but discharge to a care home may be refused. Patients may discharge themselves and leave hospital at any time unless detained under MHA 1983 (see **Chapter 12**) or admitted under a Justice of the Peace's order for an infectious disease. An elderly patient whose mental capacity is impaired is likely to come under the care of a psycho-geriatrician so if a report is needed as to mental capacity, refer to the consultant.

Before patients are discharged from hospital, proper arrangements must be made for their return home and for any continuing care that may be necessary. All local authorities and hospitals are required to have in place discharge procedures. The discharge process should ensure:

- hospital stays are no longer than necessary;
- a comprehensive care package is offered in a setting that maximises independence;
- social services are alerted if care and support services are likely to be needed.

Schedule 3 to the Care Act 2014 sets out the process for the NHS to discharge a patient who is likely to have ongoing care and support needs. It is underpinned by the Care and Support (Discharge of Hospital Patients) Regulations 2014.

Problems arise when it is proposed to discharge from hospital a patient who needs continuing nursing care, as there is a funding implication. There is no charge for services provided under the NHS although the individual will be means tested for any local authority services. The Care and Support (Discharge of Hospital Patients) Regulations 2014 place a duty on the NHS to assess whether a person needs continuing NHS care before serving a notice to social services that the patient may require care and support services. If discharge is delayed because social services fail either to assess needs and/or provide a suitable care package within a prescribed timescale the local authority must reimburse the NHS for every day that a patient remains in an acute hospital bed.

The NHS body is required to consult with the patient before making a referral to social services. Good practice requires full involvement of patients and carers in assessment and care planning. However, if the patient refuses the involvement of social services or any services put in place for them the patient becomes responsible for themselves. The patient and their carer should be informed of the discharge date at the same time as, or before, social services.

The prescribed delayed discharge process does not apply in Wales, although discharge guidance (WHC (2004) 066/NAFW 46/2004) and supplementary guidance was issued in March 2011 setting out the procedures when discharging patients from hospital to a care setting.

Anyone requiring nursing care by a registered nurse should receive a multi-disciplinary assessment and be assessed for continuing healthcare before the nursing care assessment is undertaken. For details as to how assessments are conducted, see **Chapter 8** on care and support services and **Chapter 14** for funding.

The majority of patients leaving hospital will not have needs that suggest eligibility for NHS continuing healthcare or NHS-funded nursing care. If the need for hospital care is over there may be eligibility for a period of intermediate care, also known as 'reablement service'.

PALS may be contacted to obtain information about the discharge process. It should be able to provide this information or indicate whom to contact to receive it. NHS 111 has details for PALS.

10.5.1 The care and support plan

The discharge process should:

- provide information about the discharge process;
- include assessment of the patient's needs and those of the main carer (the right to a care assessment exists whether the individual or social services is to fund any support required).

If an occupational therapist is involved a home visit may be suggested. This allows consideration of the home environment and provision of aids or special equipment. A separate carer's assessment should also be requested to identify any services they may need to support them in their caring role. Their willingness or ability to provide care should not be assumed.

The care and support plan addresses how and where eligible needs may be provided. If a person needs financial support from the local authority, and long-term care needs may be met equally well through care at home or care in a care home, the local authority may legitimately offer the option which is cheapest for it to arrange or provide. If a person is awarded NHS continuing healthcare the appropriate care plan and care package will be provided by the CCG/HB or arranged using direct payments.

A copy of the care plan must be provided. Under the Care Act 2014 and Care and Support Statutory Guidance, such a plan must set out:

- identified needs;
- whether, and if so to what extent, the needs meet the eligibility criteria;
- the needs that the local authority is going to meet and how it is going to meet them;
- the impact of the needs on the person's well-being; the outcomes the person wishes to achieve in their day-to-day life, and whether and if so to what extent the provision of care and support could contribute to the achievements of those outcomes or in the case of a carer's assessment whether they are able and willing to provide care; the impact on the well-being of the cared for person; the outcome the carer wishes to achieve in their day-to-day life, including whether they work or wish to participate in training, education and recreation; and whether, and to what extent, support provision could contribute to the achievement of those outcomes;
- the personal budget for the adult concerned;
- advice and information about what can be done to meet or reduce the needs in question; and what can be done to prevent or delay the development of needs for care and support in the future;
- where some or all of the needs are to be met by making direct payments, the needs to which the payment relates, and the amount and frequency of the direct payments; and
- the contingency plan, for example, where employed personal assistants are unavailable.

10.5.2   Implementing and monitoring the care plan

Discharge home should not take place unless:

- the patient is medically fit;
- the care package has been agreed and services are ready to start on arrival home.

If minor adaptations are required, such as a hoist or grab rails, 'interim' or 'transitional' care arrangements may be necessary. There is no power to place people compulsorily in a care home against their wishes.

If refusal to accept a place in a care home is unreasonable, social services are entitled to consider that they have fulfilled their statutory duty to assess and offer services, leaving the individual to make his or her own care arrangements. In order to fulfil their statutory duty, social services must show that a patient refusing a care package has persistently and unequivocally refused services, not simply refused them on a single occasion.

It is the CCG/HB area where the GP practice the individual is registered with is located that dictates who is responsible for arranging and funding NHS services, including fully funded NHS care. Responsibility for arranging social care services lies with the local authority in which the patient is ordinarily resident (see **7.2.5**).

10.5.3   Intermediate care

Intermediate care, also known as 'reablement services', may be offered as a short period of 'active' rehabilitation after acute hospital treatment for a person to regain confidence and physical skills in order to return home or to maximise independence in a care home. It is limited to a maximum of six weeks and may be for as little as one to two weeks. It may be provided in a care home, community hospital, a day care facility or own home and may involve different healthcare professionals and social care staff. No charge should be made for health or social care services provided as part of an intermediate care package (Care and Support (Charging and Assessment of Resources) Regulations 2014, reg.3 and CSSG; *Intermediate Care Guidance* (WHC (2002) 128 NAFWC 43/02: **www.wales.nhs.uk**). It is anticipated that intermediate care will remain part of services under the Social Services and Well-being (Wales) Act 2014 when it comes into force in Wales in April 2016).

10.5.4   Rehabilitation and recovery services

Rehabilitation services are to promote recovery and maximise independence, maybe following a heart attack or a stroke. Services may begin before or after leaving hospital, may continue for weeks or months and may involve a range of health professionals and therapies.

10.5.5 Palliative care

Palliative care is holistic care offered when an advanced progressive illness is no longer responding to treatment. Palliative care services may be offered at home, in a care home or in a hospice. They should include managing pain and other physical symptoms, and providing emotional support for patients and their families during and following an illness. They are designed to keep the patient comfortable and ensure the best quality of life possible. Palliative care services might include support from Admiral Nurses, Macmillan nurses, Marie Curie nurses or hospice support teams.

10.6 OVERSEAS RETIREES RETURNING TO THE UK

To access NHS care and social care in the UK, an individual needs to be ordinarily resident. The meaning of 'ordinarily resident' is considered at **7.2.5**. If emergency care is required treatment will be free of charge regardless of whether the patient is ordinarily resident. If a person is seeking hospital care or registering for primary care at a GP's surgery, evidence of residence in the UK will be required. The sort of evidence that may be required is utility bills for up to six months; if the individual is not able to provide this evidence charges will be levied for NHS or social care (for further detail see **8.5**).

CHAPTER 11

Health and welfare decisions

Julia Abrey and Imogen Davies

11.1 CONSENT TO TREATMENT

No medical treatment may be given to an adult patient without consent, and treatment involving physical contact is a trespass to the person (a battery) in the absence of consent. Provision of basic nursing care may be excusable in the absence of consent (e.g. cleaning up a protesting patient) but intrusive medical treatment is not. Section 5 of the Mental Capacity Act (MCA) 2005 may protect someone from liability in respect of acts done in the best interests of someone who lacks capacity (see **11.2.2**). Doctors cannot compel competent patients to accept treatment, however convinced they may be that it is in the patient's best interests. Special provision is made for patients who lack competence to make a decision about medical treatment. The Human Rights Act 1998 is likely to affect this area of the law. The European Court of Human Rights has recently ruled in *Lambert* v. *France* (2015) 145 BMLR 28 that French doctors can switch off the life support system of an incapable French national against the objections of his parents that withdrawing nutrition and hydration would be in breach of arts.2 and 3 of the European Convention on Human Rights. The ruling will form a precedent across the continent in other similar cases of dispute between families and the medical teams.

11.1.1 The nature of consent

A person is presumed to be capable of taking healthcare decisions unless the opposite is proved and must be given all practicable help in making the decision themselves before it can be concluded that they lack the capacity to do so (MCA 2005, s.1). The onus is on the patient to prove that he did not consent (*Freeman* v. *Home Office (No. 2)* [1984] QB 524). Consent may be in writing (a signed form), verbal or implied by conduct (e.g. where a patient presents himself for treatment, but not where only a diagnosis is requested). The signature on a form is merely evidence which may be rebutted and the question is not whether the patient signed the consent form but whether he decided to have the treatment (see generally **Chapter 1**).

Consent must be specific and valid, which means that the patient consents to the treatment actually given and does so voluntarily, i.e. consent is given freely, and not under threat (e.g. to discharge or use compulsory powers).

The doctor is under a duty to take reasonable care to ensure that the patient is aware of any material risks involved in any recommended treatment, and of any reasonable alternative or variant treatments. The test of materiality is whether, in the circumstances of the particular case, a reasonable person in the patient's position would be likely to attach significance to the risk, or the doctor is or should reasonably be aware that the particular patient would be likely to attach significance to it. The doctor is, however, entitled to withhold from the patient information as to a risk if he reasonably considers that its disclosure would be seriously detrimental to the patient's health. The doctor is also excused from conferring with the patient in circumstances of necessity, for example, where the patient requires treatment urgently but is unconscious or otherwise unable to make a decision (*Montgomery* v. *Lanarkshire Health Board* [2015] UKSC 11). Failure to inform of significant risks which would affect the judgment of a reasonable patient may nullify consent (*Pearce* v. *United Bristol Healthcare NHS Trust* [1998] EWCA Civ 865) and wrong information may give rise to an action in negligence if injury directly results, on the basis that the patient would not have consented if properly informed and damage resulted from the subsequent treatment.

The patient must have capacity to consent (which should be continually reassessed on the basis that capacity under MCA 2005 is assessed on a decision-by-decision basis) and this is based on understanding in broad terms what he is consenting to, so the degree depends on the complexity of treatment. A patient's wishes in regard to treatment may be recorded in advance (e.g. in the form of an advance decision (see **11.8**)).

The right of choice regarding treatment is not limited to decisions which others might regard as sensible but exists notwithstanding that the reasons for making the choice are rational, irrational, unknown or even non-existent (*Re T (An Adult) (Refusal of Treatment)* [1993] Fam 95). So long as the patient has capacity to make that decision, it will take priority over the decision of a welfare attorney or deputy with authority to make that decision.

See Chapter 23 of the Code of Practice 2015 under Mental Health Act (MHA) 1983, s.118 and the Department of Health's *Reference Guide to Consent for Examination or Treatment* (2nd edn, 2009), available at **www.gov.uk/government/ publications/reference-guide-to-consent-for-examination-or-treatment-second-edition**.

11.1.2 Refusal of consent

A patient who remains competent to make a decision about continuing treatment may refuse it and then it cannot be given even if death will result. For such a refusal to be legally binding the patient must:

- have capacity to make the decision and not have had his will overborne by the influence of a third party;
- have understood in broad terms the nature and effect of the treatment;
- in refusing contemplated the actual situation in which the treatment is needed.

The leading cases in this area are:

- *Re T (An Adult) (Refusal of Treatment)* [1993] Fam 95.
- *Re MB (Adult: Medical Treatment)* [1997] 2 FLR 426.
- *Re B (Adult: Refusal of Treatment)* [2002] EWHC 429 (Fam): a seriously physically disabled patient with the mental capacity to make decisions about treatment, even when a consequence of such decision could be death, had the right to decide to refuse treatment.
- *R (on the application of N)* v. *M* [2002] EWCA Civ 1789 on what makes a treatment a medical necessity.

The treating doctor determines whether the criteria are fulfilled but his or her view of the reasonableness or rationality of the patient's decision may influence his or her approach.

11.2   PATIENTS WHO LACK CAPACITY

11.2.1   Capacity

Capacity is presumed unless the contrary is proved, and means that the patient is able to:

- understand the information relevant to the particular decision which needs to be made;
- retain that information long enough to be able to make the decision;
- use or weigh up that information as part of the decision-making process;
- communicate that decision (MCA 2005, ss.2 and 3).

Key points:

- The ability to communicate can be impaired by mental or physical causes but the latter may often be overcome by imaginative techniques (see **2.2.1**).
- A diagnosis of mental disorder does not by itself prevent a patient from consenting (see *Re C (Adult: Refusal of Medical Treatment)* [1994] 1 WLR 290) and *Heart of England NHS Foundation Trust* v. *JB* [2014] EWHC 342 (COP)).
- The fact that a person can retain information for only a short period does not prevent them being regarded as able to make a decision.
- A person's capacity to consent may be temporarily affected by such matters as confusion, panic, shock, tiredness, pain or medication but the existence of such

factors should not lead to an automatic assumption that a person lacks the capacity to consent.

- While the decision of an incapacitated person cannot validate treatment, clinically unjustified withholding of treatment from such a person may give rise to an action for breach of a duty of care.
- Coercive pressure from another person may prevent the patient from being able to weigh up the information relevant to making a decision, such that they lack the capacity to consent (*Re A (A Child); Re C (Vulnerable Adult) (Deprivation of Liberty)* [2010] EWHC 978 (Fam)).

The personal power to consent to or refuse medical treatment may be delegated to others by means of a lasting power of attorney for health and welfare (LPAHW) (see **11.3**) or the appointment of a personal welfare deputy by the Court of Protection (see **11.5**). Further, a person may indicate his or her wishes when they retain capacity with regard to treatment at a time they do not, by means of an advance decision to refuse medical treatment, also known as an 'advance directive' or as a 'living will' (see **11.8**).

11.2.2 Treatment without consent

Emergency treatment may be given to save the life of an unconscious patient, although there may be an exception where it is known that the patient would not wish to be treated because of religious or other beliefs, because of the existence of an advance decision which is valid and applicable to the situation or the instruction of an attorney under an LPAHW who has the power to refuse consent to life-sustaining treatment.

Treatment without consent is also lawful in the case of an adult who lacks capacity where it is considered by the doctor to be necessary and in the best interests of a patient. Best interests is not defined in MCA 2005 but s.4 provides a checklist of factors which must be taken into account. These include whether the person may regain capacity and if so when; a person's past and present wishes and feelings and in particular any relevant written statement made while having capacity; and his beliefs and values (see **Chapter 1**).

A doctor must act in accordance with practice accepted as proper by a responsible body of medical practitioners, skilled and experienced in the relevant specialty: see *Bolam* v. *Friern Barnet Hospital Management Committee* [1957] All ER 118 and *F* v. *West Berkshire Health Authority* [1989] 2 All ER 545.

MCA 2005, s.5 makes provision to allow carers (both informal and those who are paid) and health professionals to carry out certain acts in connection with the personal welfare and healthcare or treatment of a person lacking capacity in the form of protection from legal liability for such acts. To be protected by MCA 2005, s.5 the decision-maker must have a reasonable belief that the individual lacks capacity and that the act, decision or treatment is in the individual's best interests. No formal authority to act is required in these circumstances but anyone interested in the individual's welfare including any attorney under an LPAHW or a personal welfare deputy should be consulted. Any such treatment or decision must accord with the principles of MCA 2005, s.1 and must not be contrary to any valid and applicable advance decision (MCA 2005, s.11(7)(b)).

In cases of serious doubt or dispute about a person's ability to consent or their best interests, an application can be made to the Court of Protection for a decision. See also Chapter 8 of the MCA 2005 Code of Practice, particularly para.8.18.

NHS Trust v. *FG* [2014] EWCOP 30 provides useful guidance as to how applications should be made when treating patients who lack capacity to make decisions, and *Re A (A Child); Re C (Vulnerable Adult) (Deprivation of Liberty)* [2010] EWHC 978 (Fam) contains guidance to local authorities as to the exercise of their powers in respect of the welfare of adults lacking capacity to consent. Where 'serious medical treatment' is proposed by an NHS body for a person who lacks the capacity to consent to that treatment and who has no one who may be consulted as to that person's best interests the NHS body must ensure that advice is sought from an independent mental capacity advocate (see **11.4**).

Treatment for a mental disorder (subject to safeguards) may be given to a patient detained under the treatment provisions of MHA 1983 (see **Chapter 12**).

Next of kin

The next of kin (whether the actual next of kin or those stated as such by the patient) do not have any legal right to consent or refuse consent on behalf of an adult patient:

- carers, home managers and social workers also do not have any legal status in regard to treatment decisions;
- there is no role for the 'nearest relative' similar to that for treatment under MHA 1983.

However, if the treating doctor is to determine the patient's best interests he or she would need to consult with such persons and it may be prudent to have their approval.

11.2.3 Allowing the patient to die

Codes of medical ethics have never required a doctor to prolong life at any cost; caring for a patient as he dies in peace and dignity may be the last service a doctor can perform.

'Double effect'

Drugs given to relieve suffering may shorten the life of the patient – the principle of 'double effect' (the successful defence of Dr Bodkin Adams). A decision may need to be made to change from treatment for living to treatment for dying:

- Administering a drug which will merely kill without first relieving suffering is murder (or attempted murder if there is no proof that it actually caused death).
- It is no defence that the patient pleaded to be put out of his misery, though juries are reluctant to convict doctors in this situation and it is also effective mitigation (*R* v. *Cox* (1992) 12 BMLR 38).

Withholding or withdrawing treatment

Doctors may withhold or withdraw treatment which is not in the best interests of their patient without being in breach of duty or in breach of the criminal law, even if death is the inevitable consequence. There is no difference between withholding and withdrawing treatment: both are omissions rather than positive acts (*Airedale NHS Trust* v. *Bland* [1993] AC 789).

Recent cases have given guidance on a number of aspects of this area:

- *Aintree University Hospitals NHS Foundation Trust* v. *James* [2013] UKSC 67 is a landmark case concerning an application relating to the timing of applications for declarations as to the lawfulness of withholding invasive treatment and cardio-pulmonary resuscitation (CPR) from a terminally ill patient at the end of life. The case also gave guidance as to the timing of applications concerning the withdrawal of life-sustaining treatment, the Supreme Court noting that if clinicians bring an application too early, there is a risk that the court will be unable to say that the treatment will not be in the patient's best interests. The Supreme Court did not provide further guidance on timing but did stress the need to be precise in setting out the declarations sought from the court.
- *United Lincolnshire Hospitals NHS Trust* v. *N* [2014] EWCOP 16 held that it was in the best interests of a patient in a minimally conscious state for the treating NHS trust not to make further efforts to establish and maintain a method of providing her with artificial nutrition. The patient was physically resistant to all attempts by medical staff to re-insert a feeding tube or establish an alternative method of providing her with nutrition.
- *AVS* v. *A NHS Foundation Trust* [2011] EWCA Civ 7, in which permission to appeal the decision of the Court of Protection not to continue medical treatment for a patient in a near vegetative state was refused, on the basis that there was no clinician prepared to provide treatment.
- *Re M* [2011] EWHC 1197 (COP) re-emphasised the requirement that all decisions relating to the withdrawing or withholding of artificial nutrition and hydration in relation to an adult in a minimally conscious state must be referred to the court. The case also referred to Court of Protection Practice Direction 9E which lists the types of decision to be regarded as serious medical treatment for the purposes of the Court of Protection Rules 2007.

The useful Parliamentary Office of Science and Technology Paper No. 489 (March 2015) on the medical, legal and ethical challenges associated with the care of patients in vegetative and minimally conscious states is available at **http://researchbriefings.parliament.uk/ResearchBriefing/Summary/POST-PN-489**.

11.2.4 Good medical practice

Directions as to the withdrawal of life-sustaining treatment may be included in an LPAHW or in a valid and applicable advance decision. The British Medical Association acknowledges that any patient may express views, orally or in writing, to his GP who will then be aware of them. Open sharing of views between patient, doctors and nurses, and also relatives and other carers (with the patient's consent where this is possible) should be encouraged and any conclusions should be noted on the patient's records. See the Department of Health's *Reference Guide to Consent for Examination or Treatment* referred to at **11.1.1** and the BMA guidance, *Withholding and Withdrawing Life-Prolonging Medical Treatment* (3rd edn, 2007).

11.2.5 Assisted suicide

In February 2010, the Crown Prosecution Service published a Policy for Prosecutors in respect of cases of encouraging or assisting suicide. This followed several high profile court cases particularly *R (on the application of Purdy)* v. *Director of Public Prosecutions* [2009] UKHL 45 in which the House of Lords required the DPP 'to clarify what his position is as to the factors that he regards as relevant for and against prosecution'. While committing or attempting to commit suicide is not, itself, a criminal offence, encouraging or assisting suicide carries a maximum penalty of 14 years' imprisonment (Suicide Act 1961, s.2). Mrs Purdy suffered from multiple sclerosis and could foresee a time when she would wish to travel to a Swiss clinic to die but would need the help of her husband to do so. She wished to ensure that her husband would not be prosecuted for assisting in her suicide. While the House of Lords rejected her application it issued the above direction.

The Crown Prosecution Service *Policy for Prosecutors in Respect of Cases of Encouraging or Assisting Suicide* (**www.cps.gov.uk/publications/prosecution/assisted_suicide_policy.html**) emphasises that there has been no change in the law. The policy lists the public interest factors for and against prosecution. Those for (16 in total) include the fact that the 'victim' was under 18; that they did not have the capacity (as defined in MCA 2005) to reach an informed decision to commit suicide; that the 'suspect' was not wholly motivated by compassion or pressured the victim to commit suicide. Factors tending against prosecution (six in total) include that the victim had reached a voluntary, clear, settled and informed decision to commit suicide; that the suspect was wholly motivated by compassion; that his or her actions were of only minor encouragement or assistance and could be characterised as reluctant.

The policy came into effect on 25 February 2010 and was updated in October 2014 following *R (on the application of Nicklinson)* v. *Ministry of Justice; R (on the application of AM)* v. *DPP* [2014] UKSC 38, three connected cases concerning the wishes of three seriously ill individuals to end their lives but who were unable to do so due to acute physical incapacity. In dismissing the three appeals against the refusal at first instance to grant the applications requested, the Court of Appeal said that the 2010 guidelines did not provide 'sufficient clarity' on whether doctors can help patients end their lives.

The 2014 update amended factor 14 tending in favour of prosecution – where the suspect was a doctor, nurse or healthcare professional, professional carer or person in authority (for example a prison officer) but only where the victim was in that person's care. Permission has been given in 2015 for judicial review of the 2014 changes to the 2010 guidelines.

In *R (on the application of AM)* v. *Director of Public Prosecutions* [2012] EWHC 470 (Admin), the court granted a declaration that solicitors retained by a terminally ill person wishing to end his life would not be encouraging or assisting suicide within the meaning of Suicide Act 1961, s.2(1) by obtaining information from third parties and appropriate experts to advise the client and then place before the court in support of the client's case. To hold otherwise would conflict with clients' fundamental rights to have access to the court and to engage lawyers to advise and represent them. In particular, the court held that there was no objection to solicitors communicating with Dignitas for general information about their service.

11.3 LASTING POWER OF ATTORNEY FOR HEALTH AND WELFARE

Lasting powers of attorney (LPAs) replaced enduring powers of attorney (EPAs) under MCA 2005, which came fully into force in England and Wales on 1 October 2007. See **4.6** concerning LPAs generally: form, validity, registration and powers and duties of attorneys and **Chapter 1** in relation to the capacity to grant an LPA.

11.3.1 Scope of LPAHW – personal welfare matters

MCA 2005, s.9(1)(a) provides that the donor of an LPA can confer on the donee authority to make decisions about the donor's personal welfare or specified matters concerning the donor's personal welfare.

The term 'personal welfare' is not defined in MCA 2005 although s.11 makes it clear that authority to make decisions about the donor's personal welfare 'extends to giving or refusing consent to the carrying out or continuation of a treatment by a person providing health care'. An LPAHW can therefore cover both welfare and healthcare decisions. In certain circumstances, the attorney's authority may even extend to giving or refusing of consent to life-sustaining treatment (see **11.3.2**).

Chapter 7 of the MCA 2005 Code of Practice gives examples of decisions which might be made under an LPAHW:

- where the donor lives and whom they should live with;

- the donor's day-to-day care, including diet and dress;
- whom the donor should have contact with;
- consenting to or refusing medical examination and treatment on the donor's behalf;
- arrangements needed for the donor to be given medical, dental or optical treatment;
- assessments for and provision of community care services;
- whether the donor should take part in social activities, leisure activities, education or training;
- the donor's personal correspondence and papers;
- rights of access to personal information about the donor; or
- complaints about the donor's care or treatment.

11.3.2   Life-sustaining treatment

The donor of an LPAHW must choose whether or not to give his or her attorney authority to give or refuse consent to life-sustaining treatment. Life-sustaining treatment is defined in MCA 2005, s.4(10) as treatment that, in the view of the person providing healthcare, is necessary to sustain life. There has been no case law to date as to what will be covered by this definition. MCA 2005, s.62 makes it clear that an LPAHW does not authorise euthanasia. It also does not give the attorney authority to demand a particular medical treatment although treatment preferences expressed by the attorney on behalf of the donor should be taken into account in determining the donor's best interests.

As with all decisions an attorney must act in the donor's best interests when making decisions about life-sustaining treatment. This will involve applying the best interests checklist and consulting with carers, family members and others interested in the donor's welfare. The MCA 2005 Code of Practice (paras.5.29–5.32) gives further guidance on the assessment of best interests in making decisions about life-sustaining treatment.

11.3.3   Attorneys' powers: special issues in welfare and healthcare matters

An LPAHW made after an advance decision to refuse medical treatment under MCA 2005, ss.24–26 which confers authority on the donee in respect of treatment to which the advance decision relates will take precedence over any refusal of consent in that advance decision. Similarly, an LPAHW made on the same day as an advance decision has the same effect, as the LPA is not created until it has been registered with the Office of the Public Guardian (see *Re E* [2014] EWCOP 27).

Furthermore, any person performing an act in connection with care or treatment under MCA 2005, s.5 will not be protected by that section if it conflicts with the decision of an attorney under an LPAHW acting within the scope of his or her power.

11.3.4 Limits on attorneys' powers under an LPAHW

- An attorney has no power to make a decision under the LPA if the donor has the mental capacity to make the particular health and welfare decision themselves.
- An attorney cannot make decisions about the donor's property and affairs.
- If the donor has previously made an advance decision to refuse the proposed treatment which is both valid and applicable (and the LPAHW does not give the attorney authority to give or refuse life-sustaining treatment) then the attorney will be unable to act in relation to decisions concerning the proposed treatment.
- The attorney may not make decisions relating to life-sustaining treatment if they have not been given the authority to make such decisions in the LPAHW.
- An attorney cannot make decisions in relation to a donor who is detained under MHA 1983 (as amended).
- The attorney cannot make decisions in relation to matters not relating to health and personal welfare or which are excluded decisions – for example family matters such as consenting to marriage or divorce or other personal decisions such as voting in an election (MCA 2005, ss.27 and 29).
- An LPAHW does not authorise the attorney to restrain the donor except in certain circumstances.
- The attorney's powers may be restricted by the terms of the LPAHW itself.
- A trust corporation cannot be appointed as an attorney under an LPAHW.

11.3.5 The prescribed form

An instrument cannot be valid as an LPAHW unless it is in the form prescribed (see **4.6.3** for details of the regulations).

The LPAHW follows the same structure as the property and financial affairs LPA (see **4.6**) but contains an additional section concerning consent to life-sustaining treatment – section 5. The donor must select option A or option B in the section on page 6 of the form in which the attorney either is or is not authorised to give or refuse consent in relation to life-sustaining treatment on the donor's behalf.

11.3.6 Drafting and case law

In January 2013, Jill Martin, then legal adviser to the Public Guardian published guidance on 'Avoiding invalid provisions in your LPA' (**www.gov.uk/government/uploads/system/uploads/attachment_data/file/435932/Avoid_invalid_LPA.pdf**).

Examples given of provisions which cannot be included in a health and welfare LPA are:

- Making decisions about property and financial affairs.
- Taking illegal actions – e.g. taking the donor to a euthanasia clinic.
- Telling attorneys that they can act if the donor becomes physically incapable.

- Giving directions as to how attorneys should make decisions about life-sustaining treatment if the attorneys do not have the power in the LPAHW to make this kind of decision.

In May 2015 the Office of the Public Guardian published leaflet LPA10 – *Getting Started as an Attorney: Health and Welfare* (**www.gov.uk/government/publications/getting-started-as-an-attorney-health-and-welfare**) to give attorneys guidance as to how they should carry out their role.

In *Public Guardian* v. *CS and PL* [2015] EWCOP 30 the court, in making an order to revoke an LPA for property and affairs granted by the donor to her two children on the basis that the animosity between the children had such a corrosive effect that it had created an impasse in the management of their mother's affairs, did not revoke the LPAHW granted to the children at the same time.

11.4 INDEPENDENT MENTAL INCAPACITY ADVOCATES

MCA 2005, ss.35–41 provide a statutory scheme for the creation of independent mental capacity advocates (IMCAs) and impose a duty on the Secretary of State for Health in England and National Assembly in Wales to make such arrangements as they consider reasonable to enable IMCAs to be available to represent and support a person who has difficulties in understanding and making decisions and for whom there is no one appropriate to consult in relation to:

- provision of serious medical treatment by an NHS body;
- provision of long-term accommodation by an NHS body; or
- provision of long-term accommodation by a local authority.

The purpose of the IMCA service is to help and support unbefriended vulnerable people who lack capacity who are facing important decisions made by the NHS and local authorities about serious medical treatment and changes in residence, for example, moving to a hospital or care home.

11.4.1 Structure, role and functions

The IMCA service is provided locally and commissioned by the local authority which approves those who are IMCAs. IMCAs must have specific experience, IMCA training, integrity, a good character and must be able to act independently. They must also undergo a Disclosure and Barring Service check to obtain a certificate that they can work with vulnerable people. An IMCA must be independent of the person they are helping and therefore a person cannot act as an IMCA if they care for or treat in a paid or professional capacity the person they will be representing or have links to the person instructing them, a decision-maker or other individuals involved in the person's care and treatment.

The functions of an IMCA are set out in MCA 2005, s.36 and supplemented by the Mental Capacity Act 2005 (Independent Mental Capacity Advocates) (General) Regulations 2006, SI 2006/1832 in England and the Welsh equivalent, which includes expansion duties in SI 2007/852. The local authority may make regulations as to the functions of IMCAs and in particular make provision requiring an IMCA to take such steps as may be prescribed for the purposes of:

- providing support for the person whom an IMCA has been instructed to represent so that the person may participate as fully as possible in any relevant decision;
- obtaining and evaluating relevant information;
- ascertaining what the represented person's wishes and feelings are likely to be and the beliefs and values that would be likely to influence the person if he had capacity;
- ascertaining what alternative courses of action are available to the person;
- obtaining a further medical opinion where treatment is proposed and the IMCA thinks that one should be obtained.

Chapter 10 of the MCA 2005 Code of Practice gives further details about IMCAs and confirms their functions. An IMCA must, in addition to the list above:

- confirm that the person instructing them has the authority to do so;
- interview the person (in private if possible) to evaluate his or her wishes, feelings and beliefs and examine and take home copies of health, social services or care home records which the person holding the records considers may be relevant to the IMCA's investigation;
- obtain the views of professionals and paid workers providing care or treatment for the person who lacks capacity and the views of anyone else who can give information about wishes, feelings, beliefs or values and any other information which they think will be necessary;
- find out what support the incapacitated person has to help them make the decision;
- write a report on their findings for the local authority or the NHS; and must act in accordance with the principles of MCA 2005 and take account of the guidance in the Code.

11.4.2 Duty to instruct an IMCA

NHS bodies

An NHS body is under a duty to instruct an IMCA and take into account any information given and submissions made by that IMCA before providing 'serious medical treatment' where there is no one for the provider of the treatment to discuss it with, i.e. no person nominated by the person, an attorney under an LPA or pre-existing EPA or a deputy plus non-professional carers or friends whom it would be appropriate to consult. The duty to instruct also arises where it is proposed that an incapacitated person should be accommodated in long-term accommodation in hospital or a care home or should be transferred to another hospital or care home where this accommodation is provided or arranged by the NHS and the accommodation is to last more than 28 days in a hospital or eight weeks in a care home.

Local authority

A local authority must instruct an IMCA and take into account any information given or submissions made by that IMCA where long-term accommodation is being arranged in a care home, nursing home, ordinary or sheltered housing, housing association or other registered social housing or in private sector housing which is provided by a local authority or in hospital accommodation on behalf of a local authority.

11.4.3   Expansion of the IMCA role

Following the Mental Capacity Act 2005 (Independent Mental Capacity Advocates) (Expansion of Role) Regulations 2006, SI 2006/2883 applicable to England, and SI 2007/852 in Wales, the role of IMCAs has been expanded such that an NHS body or a local authority may instruct an IMCA when reviewing accommodation arrangements or proposing to take protective measures to minimise the risk of abuse or neglect.

11.4.4   Deprivation of liberty cases

The Mental Health Act 2007 amended MCA 2005 to introduce a further role for IMCAs where a person is, or is to be, deprived of his or her liberty (see **11.6**).

11.4.5   Development

In March 2015 the Department of Health published a detailed report entitled *The Seventh Year of the Independent Mental Capacity Advocacy Service*. The report confirmed a year-on-year increase in the number of referrals since the service commenced in 2007. The report noted only 6 per cent of total referrals were for serious medical treatment by doctors in a hospital setting. It continues to be the case that there are wide disparities in the rate of IMCA instructions across different local areas which cannot wholly be explained by population differences.

11.5 POWERS OF THE COURT OF PROTECTION, WELFARE DEPUTIES AND SINGLE ORDERS

See **4.7** in relation to the Court of Protection generally, its structure and the principles within which it can make decisions.

11.5.1   MCA 2005, ss.15, 16 and 17

The general powers of the court are to make declarations and decisions and to appoint deputies. The powers in relation to the making of decisions and the appointment of deputies are set out in MCA 2005, ss.15 and 16, and MCA 2005, s.17 confirms the application of the s.16 powers as regards the personal welfare of a person who lacks capacity (P).

In summary, the court's powers in relation to personal welfare and healthcare extend in particular to:

- deciding where P is to live;
- deciding what contact, if any, P is to have with any specified person;
- making an order prohibiting a named person from having contact with P;
- giving or refusing consent to the carrying out or continuation of a treatment by a person providing healthcare for P;
- giving a direction that a person responsible for P's healthcare allows a different person to take over that responsibility.

Although MCA 2005, s.17 identifies the typical decisions which may be made in relation to personal welfare, the powers of the court are not limited to this kind of decision.

Chapter 8 of the MCA 2005 Code of Practice gives more details of the powers of the court.

A declaration of the court must be made in relation to the lawfulness of certain types of decision relating to serious medical treatment.

11.5.2   Limits on the court's powers

Although MCA 2005, s.17 powers are widely drafted, there are limitations on what the court can do:

- It cannot act where the person to whom the decision relates has capacity.
- Its decision should be limited in scope and time and must be made in a person's best interests.
- It may order the giving or refusing of consent to treatment but has no power to order that treatment be carried out.
- MCA 2005, ss.27 and 29 set out a number of decisions which are beyond the scope of MCA 2005 and cannot be authorised by the court. These include consent to marriage or a civil partnership, sexual relations, divorce on the basis

of separation for two years, a dissolution order relating to a civil partnership, a child being placed for adoption, the making of an adoption order or discharging parental responsibilities in matters not relating to a child's property, consent under the Human Fertilisation and Embryology Act 1990 or authorising a decision on voting at an election for any public office or at a referendum (although the court is not restricted in its powers in relation to voting in the case of private elections or contractual rights). The court also cannot consent to treatment for mental disorder where the treatment is regulated under MHA 1983.

11.5.3 Welfare deputies and single orders

See **4.8** for general information about deputies.

The court can exercise its powers in respect of an incapacitated person's welfare either directly by making an order or by appointing a deputy with powers delegated by the court. A single order is preferred to the appointment of the deputy (MCA 2005, s.16(4)) and there may be situations in a welfare context in which single orders are more appropriate; for example, where an order is required for a single issue such as where a person should live or authorising a particular course of treatment and it is not anticipated that further orders will be needed in the future.

Welfare deputies are therefore not commonly appointed and at present 80 per cent of applications are rejected.

Chapter 8 of the MCA 2005 Code of Practice indicates that deputies for personal welfare decisions will be only be required in the most difficult cases where:

- important and necessary actions cannot be carried out without the court's authority; or
- there is no other way of settling the matter in the best interests of the person who lacks capacity to make particular welfare decisions.

The Code of Practice gives examples of when a welfare deputy might be appointed:

- A series of linked welfare decisions needs to be made over time and it would not be beneficial or appropriate to require all these decisions to be made by the court.
- The most appropriate way to act in the person's best interests is to have a deputy who will consult relevant people but have the final authority to make decisions.
- There is a history of serious family disputes that could have a detrimental effect on the person's future care unless a deputy is appointed to make the necessary decisions.
- The person who lacks capacity is felt to be at risk of serious harm if left in the care of family members. Welfare decisions may therefore need to be made by someone independent of the family.

In *Re JK* (2013, unreported, COP Case 1185523T), District Judge Ralton gave a useful summary of circumstances in which it would be appropriate to appoint a welfare deputy. A case summary is available at **www.mentalhealthlaw.co.uk/ media/39_Essex_Street_MC_Law_Newsletter_September_2013.pdf**.

11.5.4   Restrictions on a welfare deputy's powers

MCA 2005, s.20 sets out further restrictions appropriate to the powers of a deputy responsible for welfare and healthcare matters:

* A deputy does not have power to make a decision for an incapacitated person if he knows or has reasonable grounds for believing that that person has capacity to make the decision themselves.
* A deputy has no authority to prohibit a person from having contact with the person.
* A deputy cannot direct a person responsible for the person's healthcare to allow a different person to take over that responsibility.
* A deputy cannot act in relation to settlement of the person's property or the execution of a will.
* A deputy may not refuse consent to the carrying out or continuation of life-sustaining treatment in relation to the person; only the court can make this decision.
* A deputy may not restrain the person other than under certain specified conditions.

In *PB* v. *RB* [2013] EWCOP B41 the court examined the powers of a deputy in relation to decisions about contact in the context of the difference between the authority to decide what contact P should have with a specified person in MCA 2005, s.17 and the restriction on prohibiting a named person to have contact with P in MCA 2005, s.20.

11.6   DEPRIVATION OF LIBERTY SAFEGUARDS

11.6.1   Current position

The deprivation of liberty safeguards (DOLS) are intended to apply to the cases of those who are not detained under MHA 1983 or are being treated for a mental disorder informally. Special authorisation is required for the care and treatment of a person in an NHS hospital or in an independent hospital or care home which is registered under the Health and Social Care Act 2008 in England or the Care Standards Act 2000 in Wales, where the person concerned does not have the capacity to reach their own decisions about what is happening to them, where this involves depriving them of their liberty.

Until April 2009, such patients fell into what was known as the 'Bournewood gap' after the decision of the European Court of Human Rights in *HL* v. *UK* (2004) 40 EHRR 761.

The Mental Health Act 2007 inserted provisions into MCA 2005 which came into force on 1 April 2009 and made it unlawful to deprive such a person of their liberty unless it is as a consequence of giving effect to an order of the Court of Protection on a personal welfare matter, or if the deprivation of liberty is in a hospital or care home and a standard or urgent authorisation is in force. The provisions are accompanied by a DOLS Code of Practice: Deprivation of Liberty Safeguards (26 August 2008), available at **www.webarchive.nationalarchives.gov.uk**.

Deprivation of liberty is a question of the degree or intensity of restrictions on personal freedom rather than the particular decisions to be made. It not only relates to being prevented from leaving the hospital or care home when a person wishes but can include any decision which such a person wishes to make in relation to where they are housed, for example who may visit them.

In order to obtain authorisation under DOLS, the managers of the hospital or care home (known as the 'managing authority') must apply to the local authority or in the case of a hospital in Wales to the local Health Board (known as 'the supervisory body').

An urgent authorisation will be considered where there is an immediate need to deprive someone of his or her liberty. It can last for no more than seven calendar days, unless there are exceptional circumstances in which case it may be extended by up to a further seven days.

A standard authorisation must be applied for before someone is deprived of his or her liberty and only where it is clear that less restrictive measures will not meet a person's needs. It can last for a maximum period of 12 months but should be for as short a time as possible. If deprivation of liberty needs to continue for a period of more than 12 months a new application must be made.

When it receives an application for a standard authorisation the supervisory body must carry out an assessment within 21 calendar days. The assessment procedure involves six separate assessments of such matters as the age of the person concerned (to ascertain they are over 18); whether a valid decision concerning the treatment has already been made by an attorney or a deputy or is one to which a valid and applicable advance decision relates; that the person concerned lacks the capacity to make the decision themselves; that the person is suffering from a mental disorder within the meaning of MHA 1983; that the person is eligible to be deprived of their liberty under DOLS, for example that they are not being detained under MHA 1983; that the deprivation is in their best interests, is necessary to prevent them from coming to harm and is a proportionate response to the likelihood of them suffering harm and the seriousness of that harm.

If a person meets the criteria under all six assessments the supervisory body will issue a DOLS authorisation in writing which will include details such as the purpose of the deprivation and the period for which it is to last. A representative will be appointed for the relevant person who can seek a review or challenge the authorisation.

For urgent authorisations the managing authority must at the same time apply for a standard authorisation and the six assessments must be carried out within seven days of the urgent authorisation being given.

Either authorisation may be challenged through the Court of Protection although it will be better to attempt to resolve any concerns informally first. The managing authority must carry out a review of the authorisation if one is requested by the 'relevant person's representative' or if circumstances change, for example the person no longer meets one or more of the criteria of the six assessments or there has been some other relevant change in the person's situation.

If, following the review, a person no longer meets the DOLS requirements, the authorisation must be terminated. Such a termination must be notified to the relevant person's representative in writing and the person should cease to be deprived of his or her liberty immediately. This also applies if the authorisation is suspended, which may be for a maximum of 28 days.

11.6.2   Change on the way

The DOLS provisions have been much criticised since their introduction as being overly complex and excessively bureaucratic. There was a commonly held view that staff in hospitals and care homes did not understand them and that there was confusion over the differences between the powers under MHA 1983 and DOLS.

In March 2014, a House of Lords Select Committee conducting post-legislative scrutiny of MCA 2005 found that DOLS were not 'fit for purpose' and called for them to be replaced. The committee also recommended that the new system should extend to cover those in supported living arrangements as well as hospitals and care homes. In the same month the Supreme Court handed down judgment in two cases, *P* v. *Cheshire West and Chester Council* and *P and Q* v. *Surrey CC* [2014] UKSC 19, which held that the acid test for a finding of deprivation of liberty was that the person was under constant supervision and control and not free to leave – regardless of the normality of the setting, the purpose of residence, or compliance of the person. The judgment has led to a considerable increase in the numbers of people in England and Wales who are considered to be 'deprived' of their liberty for the purposes of receiving care and treatment.

The Department of Health has accepted that there are difficulties with DOLS and has announced various measures designed to improve the way in which the safeguards operate. *Deprivation of Liberty: A Practical Guide* was issued by the Law Society on 9 April 2015 (**www.lawsociety.org.uk/support-services/advice/articles/deprivation-of-liberty**) and, as part of its Twelfth Law Reform Programme, the Law Commission has embarked on a project on mental capacity and detention which includes DOLS. The Commission hopes to have recommendations for reform and a draft Bill in 2016.

In *Re AJ (Deprivation of Liberty Safeguards)* [2015] EWCOP 5, Baker J gave detailed guidance in this area with particular reference to the burden on local authorities in making sure that individuals deprived of their liberty are afforded effective access to the Court of Protection to secure their rights under art.5(4) of the European Convention on Human Rights. The judgment also considers the role of the IMCA in DOLS matters.

11.7 ABUSE OF OLDER PEOPLE

Elder abuse is defined by the World Health Organization as 'a single or repeated act or lack of appropriate action, occurring within any relationship where there is an expectation of trust, which causes harm or distress to an older person'.

11.7.1 Types of elder abuse

Elder abuse includes:

- physical abuse;
- psychological abuse;
- financial abuse;
- discriminatory abuse;
- sexual abuse;
- neglect.

11.7.2 Prevalence of elder abuse

Statistical data on the prevalence of elder abuse is difficult to collect. Abuse is frequently hidden by the abuser and there is a general lack of awareness of what constitutes abuse. A study by the Health and Social Care Information Centre entitled *Abuse of Vulnerable Adults in England 2012–13*, carried out by Action on Elder Abuse and published February 2014, although it looked at adults of all ages, collected information from local authority adult safeguarding teams alerts and referrals. During the year, 176,000 alerts were reported by 132 councils, an increase of 20 per cent from the previous year. The most common types of abuse were physical abuse (28 per cent) and neglect (29 per cent) and the alleged abuse was more likely to occur in the vulnerable adult's own home (39 per cent) or in a care home (36 per cent). The source of harm was commonly reported as a social care worker (32 per cent) or a family member (32 per cent). Those over the age of 75 suffered the highest percentage of abuse and the area recording the highest levels of abuse were the West Midlands, North West and London.

MCA 2005, s.44 introduced a criminal offence of ill-treatment or neglect of a person without capacity. See *R* v. *Nursing* [2012] EWCA Crim 2521 and *R* v. *Heaney* [2011] EWCA Crim 2682.

The Criminal Justice and Courts Bill 2015 provides that it will be an offence for an individual who has the care of another individual by virtue of being a care worker to ill-treat or wilfully to neglect that individual. It is anticipated that MCA 2005, s.44 will be used in parallel where the ill-treatment or neglect has been by a family member or other person outside the category of paid care workers.

11.8 ADVANCE DECISIONS

11.8.1 Definition

An advance decision relates to a medical treatment decision made at a time when the maker has capacity but intended to apply at a future time when capacity has been lost. It is commonly used to refuse life-sustaining treatment.

MCA 2005, ss.24–26 provide a statutory basis for an advance medical decision made by a person (P) after he has attained 18 and when he has capacity to do so. If:

(a) at a later date and in such circumstances as P may specify, a specified treatment is proposed to be carried out or continued by a person providing healthcare for him or her; and

(b) at that date he or she lacks capacity to consent to the carrying out or continuation of the treatment,

the specified treatment is not to be carried out or continued.

An advance decision may be written or (other than in relation to the refusal of life-sustaining treatment) verbal. There are, however, obviously particular issues of evidence, validity and applicability in relation to verbal advance decisions. See the MCA 2005 Code of Practice paras.9.22 and 9.23.

11.8.2 Case law

Prior to the coming into force of MCA 2005, there had been a number of court decisions which confirmed that a competent adult might validly refuse treatment at the time of the decision but also at a future time when they were incapable of expressing their refusal and that if a person was treated in contravention of a valid refusal, such treatment was tortious. Case law had, however, confirmed that such an advance decision would only be valid if certain criteria were complied with. Other types of decision, for example a request for specific care or treatment, are directives or proxy directives and were not valid under the common law.

11.8.3 Advance medical decisions – forms and formalities

MCA 2005 does not specify any particular form for an advance decision with the exception of decisions relating to life-sustaining treatment (see **11.8.6**). It is recommended in all cases that the decision should be in writing, signed by the maker (or by another person in the maker's presence and at their direction) and that the signature should be made or acknowledged by the maker in the presence of a witness, who should sign or acknowledge his signature in the presence of the maker.

11.8.4 Capacity to make a valid advance decision

An advance medical decision will not be valid unless the maker has capacity to make it (see **Chapter 1**). The capacity test relating to this kind of decision is the test set out in MCA 2005, ss.2 and 3 and the principles set out in MCA 2005, s.1 will also apply. The starting point is the assumption that the maker of the advance decision has the capacity to make it unless it is established that the maker does not have such capacity. Case law had also provided a number of tests of capacity in relation to making an advance decision before the coming into force of MCA 2005. The test of capacity to make an advance decision is set out in *Re T (An Adult: Consent to Medical Treatment)* [1993] Fam 95.

The maker must:

- have all the information relative to the decision;
- understand and believe it; and
- be able to weigh that information and make an informed choice.

Combining the *Re T* test with the principles of MCA 2005 adds another limb: the fact that the decision seems unwise, particularly, it is assumed, to a medical practitioner, does not mean that the person making the decision does not have capacity to make it.

The MCA 2005 Code of Practice, Chapter 9 advises that healthcare professionals should always start from the assumption that a person who has made an advance decision has the capacity to make it unless they are aware of reasonable grounds to doubt the person has that capacity. If a healthcare professional is not satisfied that the person had capacity at the time they made the advance decision, or if there are doubts about its existence, validity or applicability, they can treat a person without fear of liability.

11.8.5 Validity and applicability

Under MCA 2005, s.25, an advance decision will only be effective if it is valid and applicable to the treatment to be carried out.

Validity

An advance decision will not be valid if the person making it had:

- withdrawn the decision at a time when he had capacity to do so;
- under an LPAHW, created after the advance decision was made, conferred authority on an attorney to give or refuse consent to the treatment to which the advance decision relates; or
- done anything clearly inconsistent with the advance decision remaining his fixed decision.

Applicability

An advance decision must still be applicable to the treatment at the material time. It will not be applicable if:

- the proposed treatment is not the treatment specified in the advance decision;
- the circumstances in the advance decision are absent;
- there are reasonable grounds for believing that circumstances exist, which the maker did not anticipate at the time of the advance decision and would have affected his decision had he anticipated them;
- the maker has the capacity to give or refuse consent.

Healthcare professionals

Healthcare professionals must follow an advance medical decision if it is valid and applicable. If they do not, they could face criminal prosecution or civil liability.

11.8.6   Life-sustaining treatment

An advance decision relating to the refusal of life-sustaining treatment will not be valid, in addition to the requirements specified above, unless it complies with the formalities set out in MCA 2005, s.25(5) and (6). These formalities require the decision to be in writing and signed by the maker, who must sign it in the presence of a witness, who must then sign the document in the presence of the maker. The maker and witness can acknowledge their signatures. The advance decision must also make it clear by specific statements that it is to apply to the specific treatment even if life is at risk. Life-sustaining treatment is defined in MCA 2005, s.4(10) as 'treatment which in the view of a person providing healthcare for the person concerned is necessary to sustain life'. An advance decision which seeks to refuse life-sustaining treatment, but which does not comply with these formalities, may still operate as a valid advance decision refusing other types of treatment (see *X Primary Care Trust* v. *XB and YB* [2012] EWHC 1390 (Fam)).

See **11.3.2** regarding the interrelationship of advance decisions and an LPAHW concerning life-sustaining treatment.

11.8.7   Format of the advance decision

Although there is no specified format, except in relation to any refusal of life-sustaining treatment, the following drafting points should be considered:

- **Introductory matters.** The decision should state what the document is, its date, the full name and other details of the maker and to whom it is addressed.
- **Record of discussions.** If the maker has discussed the advance decision with his doctor or any other member of the healthcare team, the fact should be recorded and details of the doctor or any other relevant members of the

healthcare team, both their emails and telephone numbers should be inserted. It would also be useful to note whether the maker's GP has had a copy of the document.

- **Dating and edition.** Although the advance decision should be dated (see below) it might also be sensible to indicate whether this is one in a series of documents – in other words, which 'edition' it is – so that it is clear whether the wishes in this advance decision combine with previous documents or override them.

- **Capacity issues.** The document should contain a statement that is to be used only if the maker lacks capacity to make a treatment decision. Under MCA 2005 it would probably otherwise not be applicable.

- **Circumstances in which the decision should apply.** This is often called the 'triggering event'. It normally forms two parts: defining what time and in what circumstances the decision will come into operation.

- **Treatment covered by the decision.** Once the triggering event has occurred and the advance decision is in operation, the document must then express clearly the treatment which is being refused. This does not have to be in medical language, but should be as precise as possible. A general decision refusing all treatment may be valid, if the maker explains his or her reasons for that decision.

- **The reasons for the decision.** These should be stated as they will help doctors decide whether there has been any relevant change of circumstances, which would render the decision inapplicable under MCA 2005.

- **Other wishes and statements.** These could include issues and matters which are important to the patient in the context of his healthcare. Not all of them may direct the medical team to take any particular action or refuse any particular medical treatment, but they can set out preferences or important facts about the patient.

- **Life-sustaining treatment.** See **11.8.6**.

- **Persons to be consulted.** The maker may want the healthcare team to consult with specific relatives and friends who are aware of his or her wishes. See **11.3** in relation to an LPAHW.

- **Signature and attestation.** Although the document being signed and witnessed is only a formal requirement under MCA 2005 in the case of refusal of life-sustaining treatment, it is recommended by Chapter 9 of the MCA 2005 Code of Practice that the document should be in writing and witnessed.

11.8.8 Letting people know

It is a good idea for the existence of an advance decision to be recorded in a patient's medical record or copies kept with either the family or the legal adviser, if the legal adviser is going to be involved in the future, for example, as attorney. It is very important that the LPAHW and the advance decision do not contradict each other (see **11.8.5**).

11.8.9 Precedents

A number of textbooks in relation to advice for the older client provide precedents for advance decisions to refuse medical treatment. Precedents are also available from charities interested in this area, including the Alzheimer's Society (see **www.alzheimers.org.uk**). A number of other charities produce factsheets. See Age UK's Factsheet 72: *Advance Decisions, Advance Statements and Living Wills* (**www.ageuk.org.uk**)

11.8.10 Review and cancellation

Advance decisions should be regularly reviewed as circumstances change: new or improved medical treatments may become available, or the personal circumstances of the maker may alter. The new document should make it clear whether it overtakes the previous version or adds to it. An advance decision can be cancelled at any time while the maker still has capacity to do so. The cancellation does not have to be in writing; a verbal statement cancelling the decision should be respected but evidential questions about the time and/or effect of cancellation may arise. Care should be taken not to have a review date included in the advance decision, unless it is an express decision, as it may otherwise prevent it from being operative if the maker forgets to update or reaffirm the advance decision.

11.8.11 What an advance decision cannot be used for

- Any actions which are illegal – for example euthanasia or help to commit suicide.
- Demanding any particular type of care which the healthcare team considers inappropriate.
- Refusal of the offer of food and drink by mouth.
- Refusal of the use of measures solely designed to maintain the patient's comfort (examples include providing warmth, shelter, pain relief and the control of distressing symptoms) and refusal of basic nursing care essential to keep the patient comfortable such as washing and bathing.
- Refusal of treatment for a mental disorder for a person detained under MHA 1983.

11.8.12 Powers of the court

The Court of Protection has power to make an order or declaration in relation to the existence, validity and applicability of an advance decision but cannot overturn a valid and applicable advance decision. The court can use its powers under MCA 2005, ss.16 and 17 to resolve disputes about personal welfare which involve advance decisions, for example whether a person has capacity to accept or refuse treatment at the time it is proposed. While the court decides, life-sustaining treatment or treatment to prevent a serious deterioration in a person's condition can be provided.

CHAPTER 12

Mental health legislation

Joanna Sulek

12.1 LEGISLATION

- MHA 1983 (as amended by Mental Health Act 2007 and other legislation).
- Human Rights Act 1998.
- Mental Capacity Act 2005.
- Mental Health (Discrimination) Act 2013.
- Mental Health (Hospital, Guardianship and Treatment) (England) Regulations 2008, SI 2008/1184.
- Mental Health (Approved Mental Health Professionals) (Approval) (England) Regulations 2008, SI 2008/1206.
- Mental Health (Approval of Persons to be Approved Mental Health Professionals) (Wales) Regulations 2008, SI 2008/2436 (W 209).
- Mental Health (Hospital, Guardianship, Community Treatment and Consent to Treatment) (Wales) Regulations 2008, SI 2008/2439 (W 212).
- Mental Health Act 1983 (Independent Mental Health Advocates) (England) Regulations 2008, SI 2008/3166.
- Mental Health (Wales) Measure 2010 (2010 nawm 7).
- Mental Health (Independent Mental Health Advocates) (Wales) Regulations 2011, SI 2011/2501 (W 273).
- Code of Practice to Parts 2 and 3 of the Mental Health (Wales) Measure 2010 (GEN-LD8880) (2012).

12.1.1 Rules

The following rules govern the procedure to be adopted by the courts and tribunals that deal with proceedings under the mental health legislation:

- Civil Procedure Rules 1998, SI 1998/3132 (as amended) (see County Court Rules 1981, SI 1981/1687, Ord.49, rule 12, which is reproduced in Sched.2).
- Tribunal Procedure (First-tier Tribunal) (Health, Education and Social Care Chamber) Rules 2008, SI 2008/2699.
- Mental Health Review Tribunal for Wales Rules 2008, SI 2008/2705.
- Court of Protection Rules 2007, SI 2007/1744 (as amended).

12.1.2 Scope

MHA 1983 applies to persons suffering from a mental disorder (called 'patients') and provides for:

- Part II: compulsory admission to and detention in hospital, etc.
- Part IV: medical treatment in hospital without consent and consent to medical treatment.
- Part 4A: treatment of community patients under community treatment orders (CTOs) not recalled to hospital.
- Part V: review by a tribunal of detention, including applications to the tribunal and its powers of discharge.
- Part II: guardianship in the community.
- Part III: special treatment in criminal proceedings (see **Chapter 5** and **6.12**).

Older people may suffer from mental disorder, bringing them within the scope of the legislation and allowing assessment for compulsory admission and treatment in hospital. These disorders include depression, Alzheimer's disease and other forms of dementia.

12.2 GUIDANCE, CIRCULARS AND GUIDANCE NOTES

Numerous documents provide guidance on the application of the legislation including:

- Code of Practice: Mental Health Act 1983 (Department of Health, 2015) and Mental Health Act 1983: Code of Practice for Wales (Welsh Assembly Government, 2008).
- *Reference Guide to the Mental Health Act 1983* (Department of Health, 2015 **https://www.gov.uk/government/publications/reference-guide-to-the-mental-health-act-1983**).
- *The Reference Guide to Consent to Treatment for Examination or Treatment* (Department of Health, August 2009).
- *The Care Programme Approach* (HC (90) 23/LASSL (90) 11).
- *Refocusing the Care Programme Approach: Policy and Positive Practice Guidance* (Department of Health, 2008 **http://webarchive. nationalarchives.gov.uk/20130107105354/http:/www.dh.gov.uk/en/ Publicationsandstatistics/Publications/PublicationsPolicyAndGuidance/ DH_083647**).
- *Guidance on the Discharge of Mentally Disordered People and Their Continuing Care in the Community* (HSG (94) 27/LASSL (94) 4) (paras.33–36 of this guidance are replaced by 'Independent investigation of adverse events in mental health services', 15 June 2005, concerning the conduct of independent inquiries into mental health services).
- *After-care under the Mental Health Act 1983* (LAC (2000) 3).

- Care Quality Commission publications (see the Biennial Reports). The Commission monitors the use of MHA 1983 and the Mental Capacity Act 2005 in England and its reports can be downloaded from the website **www.cqc.org.uk**. This also contains useful information on the rights of patients detained under MHA 1983 and those under community treatment orders, for example, electroconvulsive therapy (ECT), medication and independent mental health advocates. The Healthcare Inspectorate Wales performs an equivalent function in Wales.
- Law Society Practice Note: Representation before Mental Health Tribunals (22 January 2015).

12.3 DEFINITIONS

Several key definitions appear in MHA 1983, Part I, s.1:

- *Mental disorder* – defined as 'any disorder or disability of the mind' ('mentally disordered' is construed accordingly).
- *Learning disability* – defined as 'a state of arrested or incomplete development of the mind which includes significant impairment of intelligence and social functioning'. For most purposes under the Act, including treatment in hospital for mental disorder, a person with learning disability shall not be considered to be suffering from mental disorder by reason of that learning disability unless the disability is 'associated with abnormally aggressive or seriously irresponsible conduct on his part'.
- *Medical treatment* – defined as including nursing, psychological intervention and specialist mental health habilitation, rehabilitation and care (s.145(1)). Any reference in the Act to medical treatment in relation to mental disorder shall be construed 'as a reference to medical treatment the purpose of which is to alleviate, or prevent a worsening of, the disorder or one or more of its symptoms or manifestations' (s.145(4)).

12.4 NEAREST RELATIVE

12.4.1 Powers and functions

The rules for identifying a person's nearest relative are set out in MHA 1983, s.26 and he or she has the following powers and functions in respect of the 'patient', the person subject to a section of MHA 1983, namely to:

- Request an assessment with a view to admission to hospital, or be informed about an application for admission for treatment (under s.3) or assessment (which may be followed by treatment) (under s.2).

- Apply for admission to hospital for treatment or for assessment, or for admission to MHA 1983 guardianship (under s.7).
- Be consulted about, and object to, an application for admission to hospital for treatment, or for admission to MHA 1983 guardianship.
- Be informed about discharge from section and be consulted about a CTO application.
- Request discharge to hospital managers and apply to a mental health tribunal.

12.5 WHO IS THE NEAREST RELATIVE?

In relation to a patient the nearest relative will normally be the husband or wife, son or daughter, father or mother, brother or sister, grandparent, grandchild, uncle or aunt, nephew or niece. The elder of relatives in a class takes precedence and whole blood equates to half-blood but the former take precedence.

Living together as husband and wife, or civil partners, for six months is sufficient (MHA 1983 has been explicitly amended to include same sex partners: see s.26(1)(a) and *R* v. *Liverpool City Council and the Secretary of State, ex p SSG* (2002) 5 CCLR 639). A relative who ordinarily resides with or cares for the patient will take precedence, and this may apply to a non-relative after five years.

Certain persons are excluded, namely a separated spouse or civil partner, a person under 18 (unless a spouse or civil partner) and a person not ordinarily resident in the United Kingdom.

The nearest relative will not always be the next of kin and may be replaced. This may take place under a process known as 'displacement' in MHA 1983, s.29.

A nearest relative may be displaced on application to the County Court if he cannot be found, is incapable of acting, has used or is likely to use his power to discharge the patient without due regard for the patient's welfare or the interests of the public, objects unreasonably to an application for admission for treatment or for guardianship, or is otherwise not a suitable person to act as nearest relative. An application may also be made for the appointment of a nearest relative if the patient has no nearest relative within the meaning of MHA 1983, or it is not reasonably practicable to ascertain whether the patient has such a relative, or who that relative is. The application may be made by the patient, any relative of the patient, any other person with whom the patient is residing (or was last residing before being admitted to hospital), or an approved mental health professional.

There is a procedure which allows the nearest relative to delegate his or her functions to another person, if he or she is unable to act.

12.6 APPROVED MENTAL HEALTH PROFESSIONALS

Approved mental health professionals (AMHPs) are appointed by social services authorities pursuant to MHA 1983, s.114 and are approved as having appropriate competence to deal with persons suffering from mental disorder. A wide group of professionals may be appointed as AMHPs: in addition to social workers, these may be first level nurses practising in mental health or learning disability nursing, chartered psychologists, and occupational therapists, but not doctors ('registered medical practitioners'). They have various statutory duties and powers over persons believed to be suffering from a mental disorder. In their capacity as AMHPs, these professionals act on behalf of the local social services authority that appointed them. There are separate regulations for the approval of AMHPs in England and in Wales. It can be an offence to obstruct them in the performance of their duties: see s.114, s.129 and *Mental Health Act 2007 New Roles: Guidance for Approving Authorities and Employers on Approved Mental Health Professionals and Approved Clinicians* (National Institute for Mental Health in England, October 2008).

12.7   CODE OF PRACTICE

Under MHA 1983, s.118(4), a Code of Practice has been prepared by the Department of Health (for England) and the Welsh Assembly (for Wales). The Codes are broadly parallel in content and offer guidance on how the Act should be implemented. A reference to 'the Code' will often encompass both versions, as they are not always mentioned separately. The Code is updated periodically, and this took place most recently in 2015 in England and in 2008 in Wales.

The Code is primarily aimed at the needs, rights and entitlements of mentally disordered persons who are detained, but it may also be referred to as a good practice document for the care and management of informal patients (patients not subject to a section of the Act). It deals with matters such as assessment prior to admission, admission to hospital or guardianship, treatment and care in hospital, leaving hospital, community treatment orders and aftercare.

The Code lays down certain guiding principles. For example, the Code for England states that:

- Where it is possible to treat a patient safely and lawfully without detaining them under the Act, the patient should not be detained; if the Act is used, detention should be used for the shortest time necessary and in the least restrictive hospital setting available.
- Any restrictions should be the minimum necessary to safely provide the care or treatment required having regard to whether the purpose for the restriction can be achieved in a way that is less restrictive of the person's rights and freedom of action.
- Those taking decisions under MHA 1983 must recognise and respect the diverse needs, values and circumstances of each patient, including his or her age, disability, gender reassignment, marriage and civil partnership, pregnancy and maternity, race, religion or belief, sex and sexual orientation, and culture.

- Patients should be given the opportunity to be involved in planning, developing and reviewing their own care and treatment to help ensure that it is delivered in a way that is as appropriate and effective for them as possible.
- Commissioners and providers should give equal priority to mental health as they do to physical health conditions.
- Health and social care agencies should work together to deliver a programme of care that minimises the duration of detention, facilitates safe discharge from hospital and takes into account the patient's wishes.
- All decisions must be lawful and comply with the Human Rights Act 1998.

The Code of Practice for Wales also includes the following principles:

- alternatives to the use of compulsory powers should be explored before making an application for admission, and the least restrictive option should be considered;
- decision-making should be open and transparent, except where disclosure of information could harm the patient or others;
- care plans should focus on early discharge and providing aftercare at the earliest opportunity.

The Code does not have the same force as statute, but the House of Lords ruled in 2005 that the Code should be given great weight and departed from only if there are cogent reasons for doing so. A departure from the Code will not automatically be unlawful, provided that it does not amount to a breach of the European Convention on Human Rights (see *R (on the application of Munjaz)* v. *Mersey Care NHS Trust* [2005] UKHL 58). Departures from the Code may still, however, give rise to legal challenge, and a court will determine whether the reasons for any such departure are sufficient to justify it.

12.8 ADMISSION TO HOSPITAL

12.8.1 General

Admissions may be on a formal (compulsory) basis or an informal basis (where the patient is not subject to any sections of the Act). Admissions should be voluntary and take place with the consent of the patient wherever possible, but it is possible for an informal admission to take place where the patient is compliant but incapable of consenting. The admission must be in the patient's best interests (see MHA 1983, s.131(1) and **Chapter 1**). However, a patient who lacks the capacity to consent to admission cannot be admitted on an informal basis under MHA 1983, s.131 if the admission constitutes a deprivation of his or her liberty. The criteria for determining if a deprivation of liberty is occurring have been set out in *P* v. *Cheshire West and Chester Council; P and Q* v. *Surrey CC* [2014] UKSC 19 (see **11.6.2**). In such cases, formal procedures will be required. If the patient does not satisfy the criteria for formal detention under MHA 1983, then the MCA 2005 deprivation of liberty safeguards (DOLS) should be used (see **11.6**).

A compulsory admission under MHA 1983 is pursuant to a statutory power, often referred to as being 'under section'. There are several statutory powers and various safeguards (see below).

12.8.2 Statutory powers

The different statutory powers are used in the following circumstances.

Section 2 for assessment

The patient is suffering from mental disorder of a nature or degree which warrants detention in hospital for assessment (or for assessment followed by medical treatment) for at least a limited period and it is in the interests of the patient's health or safety or for the protection of others:

- two medical recommendations are necessary;
- application is made by an AMHP or nearest relative (although the AMHP is usually the more appropriate applicant);
- detention can be for up to 28 days but cannot be renewed;
- there is a right to apply to a mental health tribunal.

Section 3 for treatment

The patient is suffering from mental disorder of a nature or degree which makes it appropriate to receive medical treatment in hospital and necessary for the health or safety of the patient or protection of others:

- two medical recommendations are required;
- application is made by an AMHP or nearest relative (although the AMHP is usually the more appropriate applicant);
- detention can be for up to six months in the first instance, renewable for another six months and then one year at a time;
- there is a right to apply to a mental health tribunal.

Section 4 for assessment in emergency

The patient is admitted on the grounds set out in s.2 but on the recommendation of one doctor in case of urgent necessity on a diagnosis of mental disorder:

- application is made by an AMHP or nearest relative (although the AMHP is usually the more appropriate applicant);

- detention can be for up to 72 hours and although the s.4 detention cannot be renewed it is convertible to a s.2 detention on a second medical recommendation.

Section 5 for short-term detention for those already in hospital

A hospital in-patient may be detained by the treating doctor or by a nurse for short periods in certain circumstances. Powers of compulsion tend to be used less frequently in the treatment and care of older people; however, legal representatives and carers, and local authorities and hospitals need to be aware that a patient's circumstances may amount to a deprivation of liberty and that if the deprivation of liberty is not stopped, an application for a MCA DOLS authorisation is likely to be required to safeguard the patient's rights under the European Convention on Human Rights (see **11.6**).

12.8.3   Medical treatment

MHA 1983 contains powers for medical treatment to be given to a detained patient without his consent in certain closely defined circumstances, mainly treatment for his or her mental disorder or for symptoms closely linked or ancillary to the mental disorder, but apart from this, normal common law principles and the best interests principles in MCA 2005 apply (see **Chapter 1**):

- treatment for 'general medical or surgical' conditions cannot be given under the provisions of MHA 1983 but can be given under the common law, if the patient consents, and in certain emergency situations;
- if the patient lacks the capacity to consent to treatment, such treatment may not be given under MHA 1983 but can be given if it is in the patient's best interests, as defined in MCA 2005.

Detention under MHA 1983 does not mean that a patient lacks capacity to consent to general medical treatment or that consent should not be sought.

Treatment for mental disorder

A patient who is detained under the treatment sections of MHA 1983 (i.e. ss.2, 3, 36, 37, 38, 46, 47 and 48) can be given 'medical treatment for a mental disorder' without his consent. An exception to this general rule is where a detained patient with mental capacity to refuse ECT refuses it. The same applies where a patient has previously made a valid and applicable advance decision refusing ECT, or where a MCA health and welfare deputy or attorney have refused ECT, in which case, ECT cannot be given without consent except in an emergency (MHA 1983, ss.58A and 62; see **Chapter 11**). A patient detained under the 'short-term' sections, or subject to MHA 1983 provisions while in the community, such as CTOs or guardianship, cannot be given medical treatment for a mental disorder without his consent under the treatment regime of MHA 1983. Certain patients in the community, such as CTO patients, may, however, if recalled to hospital, be subject to compulsory treatment under the consent to treatment provisions of MHA 1983.

There are 'safeguards' whereby particular treatments require the consent of the patient and/or a second medical opinion, with regular reviews of such treatment (see MHA 1983, Part IV). There are special provisions for urgent treatment (see s.62). Section 57, for example, which governs treatment with neurosurgery (sometimes known as psychosurgery) and other specified forms of treatment, applies to all patients, whether detained under MHA 1983 or informal, as the consent of the patient, in addition to other safeguards, is required in order for such treatment to proceed. Where such treatment is being considered, patients are entitled to receive assistance and support from independent mental health advocates (IMHAs). Patients detained under certain sections are also eligible to receive IMHA support in respect of other matters connected with their detention. In Wales, all detained patients except those subject to ss.135 and 136 are eligible to receive IMHA support in respect of a wide range of matters, and this also includes all informal patients receiving in-patient care and treatment for mental disorder.

Section 58 additionally provides that a second opinion from a 'second opinion appointed doctor' (SOAD) appointed by the Care Quality Commission or Health-care Inspectorate Wales must be obtained where medicine for the treatment of mental disorder has been administered to a detained patient for three months. The treatment cannot continue unless the SOAD certifies that it is appropriate for the treatment to be given, or the patient consents and is capable of doing so.

12.8.4 Implications of detention – deprivation of liberty

Part 2 of the Mental Health Act 2007 made amendments to the Mental Capacity Act 2005 by the introduction of provisions for the deprivation of liberty safeguards. These came into force on 1 April 2009. The need for the introduction of these provisions was highlighted by the identification of the 'Bournewood gap', a situation sometimes arising in relation to patients such as the patient in *HL* v. *UK* (2004) 40 EHRR 761. In this case the European Court of Human Rights ruled that a man diagnosed with autism, receiving in-patient care but not formally detained under MHA 1983, was deprived of his liberty in breach of his rights under art.5 of the European Convention on Human Rights. The amendments set out to address the breach of an individual's rights to liberty which may occur when he or she is deprived of liberty without the use of procedures prescribed by law, such as sectioning under MHA 1983. They introduced a procedure in England and Wales for depriving a person of his or her liberty in NHS hospitals and nursing homes, where the person does not have capacity to consent to admission or treatment but is not formally detained. For further details of the deprivation of liberty safeguards, see **11.6**.

12.9 COMMUNITY POWERS

12.9.1 Power to inspect

An AMHP may enter and inspect premises in the area of the local social services authority in which a mentally disordered person is living if he has reasonable cause to believe that the patient is not under proper care (MHA 1983, s.115). There is no power to force entry, to restrain or remove the patient.

12.9.2 Removal to a place of safety

A constable has power to remove to a place of safety with a view to early examination, assessment and treatment of a person believed to be suffering from a mental disorder who is:

- ill-treated, neglected or not kept under proper control or unable to care for himself and living alone (MHA 1983, s.135); this must be under a warrant issued by a magistrate and the constable must be accompanied by an AMHP and a registered medical practitioner;
- in a public place in immediate need of care or control and this is necessary in the interests of the person or the protection of others (MHA 1983, s.136).

12.9.3 Statutory guardianship

A limited form of adult guardianship is available under MHA 1983, ss.7 and 8. This is used far less frequently than detention in hospital, and its use has decreased in recent years, possibly owing to the introduction of MCA DOLS. It enables the establishment of an authoritative framework for working with a patient with a minimum of constraint to achieve as independent a life as possible within the community, but must be part of the patient's overall care and treatment plan (Code of Practice for England, para.30.4; Code of Practice for Wales, para.6.2).

A patient may be received into guardianship provided he suffers from mental disorder and that both the following apply:

- the disorder is of a nature or degree which warrants guardianship;
- guardianship is necessary for the welfare of the patient or the protection of others.

Appointment

Guardianship initially lasts for six months but may be renewed for a further six months and thereafter annually. Application is made to the social services department by an AMHP or the patient's nearest relative, in each case supported by two doctors. The nearest relative can object or subsequently discharge the patient. There is a right of appeal to a mental health tribunal.

Who is appointed?

The guardian may be either the social services department or a private individual with the approval of the local authority, but a private guardian has duties which relate to notification of the local authority and appointment of a medical practitioner.

Powers

The guardian has very limited powers in respect of the patient but may require:

- that the patient resides at a specific place (but not with a specific person);
- that the patient attends at places and times specified for the purpose of medical treatment, occupation, education or training;
- access to the patient to be given at the patient's residence to any medical practitioner, AMHP or other person specified.

The guardian has no power to detain the patient and cannot restrict his movements but can only insist that the patient ordinarily resides at the place specified and return the patient to that place if appropriate. He cannot authorise or require physical removal of an unwilling patient, or authorise medical treatment (the treatment provisions of MHA 1983 do not apply). He has no power over the money and property of the patient and cannot authorise deprivation of liberty procedures (see **11.6**). However, the ability to use even limited powers when everyone else is powerless can be valuable and the guardian may adopt a dominant role, where, for example, it is useful for certain decisions in relation to a patient's living arrangements to be taken by a single individual or authority.

It is an offence to ill-treat or wilfully neglect a person subject to guardianship.

12.9.4 Aftercare

There is a specific duty on the health and social services authorities in co-operation with voluntary organisations to arrange or provide 'aftercare services' for persons who have been detained under the longer-term treatment sections of MHA 1983 (s.117). This therefore excludes patients who are being or have been discharged from s.2 detention, in contrast to patients discharged from s.3 detention. It arises prior to the discharge if that can only take place when the arrangements are in hand and continues until the aftercare authorities are satisfied that the person is no longer in need of such services.

The patient has a right to a care and support assessment (see **8.1**) and services provided under s.117 (including residential care) may not be charged for (*R* v. *Manchester City Council, ex p Stennett* [2002] UKHL 34). See also the Local Government Ombudsmen's Special Report, *Advice and Guidance on the Funding of Aftercare under Section 117 of the Mental Health Act 1983* (2003).

Consideration may be given to the use of guardianship if there is concern about risk of harm to the person or to others. A 'care plan' should be established in accordance with the Code of Practice and other guidance. This is often referred to as 'the Care Programme Approach'.

12.9.5 Community treatment orders

There may be discharge from hospital into supervised community treatment where a patient is placed under a CTO (MHA 1983, ss.17A–17G). The use of CTOs allows patients to receive care and treatment in the community instead of remaining in hospital under detention, and aims to prevent patients from relapsing by providing a stable framework for monitoring progress and treatment outside hospital. This is done by attaching certain conditions, with which a patient must comply, to the CTO, and giving the responsible clinician the power to recall a patient to hospital for breach of certain conditions of the CTO, or if recall is considered otherwise necessary for the management of the patient's care and treatment.

Application

The CTO is made in writing by the responsible clinician (RC) in charge of the patient's care in hospital. There are procedures that must be complied with and strict criteria as to the patients to whom this treatment may apply. Only patients detained in hospital for treatment under s.3, or unrestricted patients sent to hospital through the criminal justice system and detained for treatment, can be considered for CTOs. Patients detained in hospital for assessment (or for assessment followed by treatment) under s.2 are not eligible. The CTO lasts for six months and is renewable by the RC for a period of six months and for periods of one year thereafter.

Implications

Supervision of aftercare and monitoring of the care plan will be by a named supervisor, the 'care coordinator' (a community nurse, a social worker or other appropriate community mental health professional), working with the RC and the team responsible for the patient's care. There is no power to treat the patient in the community without his consent, but the RC may recall the patient to hospital, without the patient's consent, if the patient is no longer complying with CTO conditions or it is unsafe or inappropriate for the patient to remain in the community. There may be a change in the patient's circumstances leading to an increase in risk, or his or her condition may have deteriorated. As not all conditions in a CTO are mandatory, not every breach will automatically lead to recall. The important question is whether the breach results in increased risk to the patient or others. The RC may also vary or suspend any conditions in the CTO instead of recalling the patient.

On recall to hospital, the patient will be assessed and may be treated for mental disorder. The patient may then be detained for 72 hours. After this time, he or she must either be discharged back into the community still subject to the CTO, or continue to be detained in hospital following revocation of the CTO. If the patient requires treatment as an in-patient for longer than 72 hours, the RC must revoke the CTO in order to continue treatment, and the patient will then be detained under the original detention section, which was suspended during the CTO, and is now 'revived'.

The CTO will contain conditions such as the following:

- A requirement for the patient to make himself available for medical examination when this is necessary to consider extending the CTO, and to allow a SOAD to provide a certificate authorising certain forms of treatment (these conditions must be included).
- Other conditions necessary or appropriate to ensure that the patient receives medical treatment for mental disorder, to prevent a risk of harm to the patient's health or safety, and to protect others.

The AMHP must also agree to the proposed conditions before the CTO is made.

The patient has the right to apply to a mental health tribunal to be discharged from a CTO, although at present the tribunal has no power to vary CTO conditions. Only the RC can do this. The patient may also be discharged by the hospital managers, the RC, and, if a patient is a 'civil' patient, i.e. originally detained otherwise than through the criminal courts, by the nearest relative. The RC must discharge the patient if he or she no longer meets the criteria for a CTO, but may do so at any time.

See Chapter 29 of the Mental Health Act Code of Practice for England (Chapter 30 of the Code for Wales).

12.10 REVIEW AND APPEAL

12.10.1 Discharge

Detention or guardianship ceases if a written order for discharge is made (s.23). The order in respect of a hospital patient detained under s.2 or s.3 may be made by the RC, the hospital managers or nearest relative of the patient (and in respect of guardianship also by the responsible social services authority).

A nearest relative wishing to take the initiative must give at least 72 hours' notice in writing to the hospital managers. The RC may within that time report to the managers that in his opinion the patient, if discharged, would be likely to act in a manner dangerous to himself or to some other person. If such a report is made the discharge by the nearest relative will be of no effect but a similar order cannot be made within the next six months. However, in respect of certain detention sections (notably s.3) and CTOs, the production of such a report by the RC creates a right for the nearest relative to apply on behalf of the patient to the mental health tribunal, which is additional to the patient's own right to apply.

12.10.2   Mental health tribunal

A mental health tribunal is an independent tribunal comprising a legal member (the tribunal president (in Wales) or judge (in England)), a medical member (a psychiatrist) and another member (previously known as the 'lay member', usually a professional from a relevant field). The tribunals in both England and Wales come within the statutory oversight of the Administrative Justice and Tribunals Council and are administered by the Tribunal Service – Mental Health in England, and from the Welsh Assembly in Wales. Specific provisions and time limits are found in MHA 1983, s.66. The tribunal, previously known universally as the mental health review tribunal, has since November 2008 been divided into two separate jurisdictions, known by the official names of the First-tier Tribunal (Mental Health) in England, and the Mental Health Review Tribunal for Wales in Wales. There is a right of appeal to the Upper Tribunal from both the English and Welsh tribunals, but only on a point of law.

Applications and references to the tribunal

Under ss.25, 29, 66, 67, 68 and 69, cases relating to patients detained or subject to CTOs under MHA 1983, Part II, are referred to the tribunal by:

- applications from patients detained under s.2 or s.3, received into guardianship or subject to CTOs;
- references by hospital managers where a detained patient or community patient has not applied for a tribunal hearing within six months, and then after three years (one year for a patient under 18);
- references by the Secretary of State for Health for a patient liable to be detained or subject to guardianship;
- applications from a patient's nearest relative where the nearest relative has made a written request for discharge and the responsible clinician has barred the discharge (or an acting nearest relative if a County Court order has directed that the functions of the nearest relative be carried out by an acting nearest relative).

The tribunal may discharge the patient, decline to do so, or may make certain other orders (s.72).

Representation by lawyers is encouraged but is available free of charge (in the form of non-means tested legal aid) only from Law Society mental health accredited lawyers who will be experienced in these cases and have a public funded (legal aid) contract with the Legal Aid Agency. For details of suitable lawyers, visit the Find a Solicitor section of the Law Society website (**http://**

solicitors.lawsociety.org.uk/) and search under 'Social welfare, health and benefits' and 'Mental health'.

12.10.3 Care Quality Commission

The Care Quality Commission safeguards the rights of detained patients, including monitoring the welfare of community treatment order patients (known as CTO or 'community' patients) and review of complaints.

The Care Quality Commission protects the interests of detained (i.e. compulsorily admitted) patients and community patients by:

- regularly visiting those hospitals and nursing homes with detained patients, and community services with community patients;
- reviewing their care and treatment, and investigating complaints made by them or on their behalf;
- appointing doctors to review treatment under MHA 1983, Parts IV and 4A;
- in the case of detained patients, reviewing decisions to withhold postal packets.

Informal patients wishing to complain about matters relating to their treatment and care will need to follow the same complaints procedures as other non-detained patients, which currently consist of a local resolution process followed possibly by a referral to the Parliamentary and Health Service Ombudsman in England or the Public Services Ombudsman for Wales.

12.11 OVERLAP BETWEEN MENTAL HEALTH ACT AND MENTAL CAPACITY ACT

12.11.1 General

There are many situations where professionals involved in the care of patients subject to MHA 1983 will need to know whether MCA 2005 applies.

Approved mental health professionals will need to understand the principles of MCA 2005 in order to determine when alternative procedures to MHA 1983 detention, guardianship or CTOs would be appropriate, including DOLS procedures.

12.11.2 Treatment

Responsible clinicians and other mental health professionals, such as second opinion appointed doctors, will need to apply the capacity test in MCA 2005 (see **Chapter 1**) when offering medical treatment or authorising certain types of treatment under MHA 1983 safeguards (MHA 1983, ss.57, 58 and 58A). An assessment of capacity may be needed in order to provide the correct authorisation or determine whether treatment should take place. Capacity to consent to a particular form of treatment may be required before the treatment can take place, except in emergencies (s.62). Under s.58A, for example, ECT cannot be given without consent to an adult patient with the capacity to refuse it, under the compulsory treatment provisions (Parts IV and 4A) of MHA 1983. Also it may not be given if a valid and applicable advance decision refusing ECT has been made in accordance with the requirements of MCA 2005, or a court-appointed personal welfare deputy or attorney under a health and welfare lasting power of attorney (LPAHW) with such authority has refused the ECT on the patient's behalf (see **Chapter 11**). This is in contrast to the situation with most other types of treatment for mental disorder, which can be given in the absence of consent under the compulsory treatment provisions, even if it has been refused in advance by a valid and applicable advance decision, or by a relevant deputy or attorney on the patient's behalf. Other treatments regulated by s.57, such as neurosurgery for mental disorder (psychosurgery) can only be given to patients capable of consenting, with statutory certification that the patient has given consent and that the treatment should be given.

Treatment may be given in a detained patient's best interests (see **Chapters 1** and **11**) under MCA 2005 where a patient lacks the capacity to consent to or refuse it and it is not treatment for mental disorder given under the treatment provisions of MHA 1983 (Parts IV and 4A). MCA 2005 may not generally be used to give a CTO patient any medical treatment for mental disorder, but relevant attorneys, deputies and the Court of Protection may consent to such treatment on a patient's behalf, as long as he or she has not been recalled to hospital. They may also refuse treatment on a patient's behalf, except in emergencies. Treatment may not be given to a CTO patient contrary to a valid advance decision, if he or she has not been recalled to hospital.

12.11.3   Attorneys, deputies and guardianship

Patients subject to MHA 1983 in hospital or in the community may make lasting powers of attorney, if they have the mental capacity to do so, appointing attorneys to make healthcare and welfare decisions on their behalf. Personal welfare deputies may also be appointed by the court to make decisions on behalf of such patients. In particular, mental health professionals need to be aware that an LPAHW may authorise an attorney to apply on behalf of a patient to a mental health tribunal or to hospital managers for discharge, and personal welfare deputies may exercise the same rights. Attorneys authorised by patients to make decisions concerning property and affairs (see **Chapter 4**) on their behalf should be able to continue exercising the powers delegated to them, during the patients' detention, guardianship or CTO under MHA 1983.

Where a MHA 1983 guardianship patient has an attorney or a deputy authorised to make personal welfare decisions, when they are acting within the scope of their powers, they will continue to make these decisions, but a guardian will make decisions in relation to guardianship conditions. If the guardian is authorised to decide where the patient should reside, he or she will decide this question. It may not be necessary to use MHA 1983 guardianship if a patient lacks the capacity to make certain decisions, such as whether to move to residential care. It may be possible to take any action necessary on the basis of MCA 2005, s.5 (see **Chapter 11**), a decision of a relevant attorney or deputy, or MCA 2005 DOLS provisions. In cases of conflicting arguments, such as appropriate residence and whether DOLS should be used, it may be helpful to apply to the Court of Protection for a best interests decision (see **Chapters 1** and **11**).

12.11.4   The Mental Health Act and deprivation of liberty

As a general rule, the DOLS procedures cannot be used for anyone detained under MHA 1983, and this may include a person who is liable to be detained or who could potentially be detained, where certain conditions are met.

In *GJ* v. *Foundation Trust* [2009] EWHC 2972 (Fam) an informal patient, who had previously been detained, was assessed as falling within the potential scope of MHA 1983, because he met the criteria for detention under s.2 or s.3. He needed treatment and care relevant to mental and physical conditions. He lacked the capacity to make treatment decisions but had refused insulin and tried to leave hospital on previous occasions. His actions indicated that he objected to treatment in hospital. The package of care for which a deprivation of liberty was considered necessary was treatment for diabetes. The court found that he was not being deprived of liberty for treatment of his mental disorder and that he was eligible for DOLS procedures. The treatment for mental disorder and treatment for diabetes were different and separate, although both were promoted by the provision of nursing care and monitoring in a safe environment. It was concluded that he was not within the scope of MHA 1983 (see MCA 2005, Sched.1A). It is important to establish whether the patient would need detention in hospital but for the need for physical treatment, and whether the only effective reason for detention is the need for physical treatment.

The case also suggests that a person subject to MHA 1983 in the community, such as a CTO or guardianship patient, or a patient on s.17 leave, can be deprived of liberty under DOLS if he or she is not subject under MHA 1983 to any conditions conflicting with DOLS, such as a condition specifying where the person is to reside. It is likely therefore that DOLS could be used where, for example, the treatment is for a physical disorder, even where the patient also has care and treatment needs relevant to mental disorder, or where the patient needs treatment for mental disorder but this would take place somewhere other than in a hospital.

A MCA DOLS authorisation and MHA detention may in principle be both available where a person:

- is suffering from a mental disorder within the meaning of MHA 1983, s.1;

- needs to be assessed and treated or treated in hospital for mental disorder or for physical conditions related to that disorder (and meets the criteria for admission under MHA 1983, s.2 or s.3);
- has a care treatment package that may or will amount to a deprivation of liberty;
- lacks capacity to consent to being accommodated in the relevant hospital for treatment; and
- does not object to being admitted to hospital, or to some or all of the treatment they will receive for mental disorder.

MCA 2005, Sched.1A, however, specifies in greater detail those who are ineligible for MCA DOLS:

- Those currently detained in hospital under MHA 1983, ss.2, 3, 4, 35–38, 44, 45A, 47, 48 or 51.
- Those still liable to be detained because they are on leave from a detention section and a condition of leave is incompatible with DOLS because for example the deprivation of liberty would require residence elsewhere than stipulated by the leave condition, or the relevant care and treatment consists in whole or in part of treatment for mental disorder in a hospital.
- Those on a CTO in the community with a CTO condition incompatible with DOLS, or the relevant care and treatment consists in whole or in part of treatment for mental disorder in a hospital.
- Those under MHA 1983 guardianship with an incompatible condition, or it is proposed the patient should be detained in a hospital for treatment for mental disorder and they object, or are likely to object (and their healthcare attorney or deputy has not given a valid consent).
- Those within the scope of MHA 1983 (i.e. an application could be made under s.2 or s.3 and they could be detained in a hospital in pursuance of such an application if it were made) and objecting to being in hospital for treatment, or to being given some or all of that treatment (and their healthcare attorney or deputy has not given a valid consent).
- If a person needs treatment for *mental disorder* in a *hospital*, they are objecting to the treatment, the proposed deprivation of liberty is for the purpose of allowing the treatment to take place, and they meet the criteria for detention under MHA 1983, then MHA 1983 detention should be used instead of deprivation of liberty.

There are additional indications that MHA 1983 should be used instead of DOLS provided that the patient meets the criteria for detention, for example, if the patient is under 18, has made a valid and applicable advance decision refusing a necessary part of the treatment for which admission to hospital is taking place, or the use of DOLS would conflict with a decision of a relevant attorney, a deputy or the Court of Protection (see MHA 1983 Code of Practice for England, para.13.56). A further relevant consideration is that capacity is fluctuating and the patient is likely not to consent to treatment upon regaining capacity: MHA 1983 procedures are more appropriate in this situation.

The decision should always be made on the individual facts of the case, and one regime may prove to be less restrictive and of greater benefit than the other in respect of a particular patient.

Decision-makers are advised to exercise their professional judgment in respect of which regime should be applied (MHA 1983 Code of Practice England, para.13.68). There may be cases where both regimes are available but in most cases, only one will be. The eligibility for MHA 1983 detention, the availability of MCA DOLS authorisation, or an order from the Court of Protection authorising a deprivation of liberty should be considered. A court order may be sought to authorise a deprivation of liberty where DOLS are not available, for example where the patient is living at home (see **11.6**). The choice should never be based on a preference of one regime over the other, or an assumption that one has greater safeguards or is less restrictive than the other (*AM* v. *South London & Maudsley NHS Foundation and Secretary of State for Health* [2013] UKUT 365 (AAC); MHA 1983 Code of Practice for England, paras.13.58, 59).

For further information, see MHA 1983 Code of Practice for England chapter 13, and **Chapters 1** and **11**.

PART C

Finance and benefits

Social security benefits

Gary Vaux

13.1 SOCIAL SECURITY SYSTEM

13.1.1 Sources of law

The relevant enabling statutory provisions are:

- Social Security Administration Act 1992.
- Social Security Contributions and Benefits Act 1992.
- Social Security (Incapacity for Work) Act 1994.
- Jobseekers Act 1995.
- Social Security Act 1998.
- Child Support, Pensions and Social Security Act 2000.
- State Pension Credit Act 2002.
- Pensions Acts 2007 and 2014.
- Tribunals, Courts and Enforcement Act 2007.
- Welfare Reform Acts 2007, 2009 and 2012.

Regulations

Regulations are made under powers granted by the legislation and:

- Provide detailed law as to entitlement to particular benefits, for example:

    - Social Security (Widow's Benefit and Retirement Pensions) Regulations 1979, SI 1979/642.
    - Income Support (General) Regulations 1987, SI 1987/1967.
    - State Pension Credit Regulations 2002, SI 2002/1792.

- Specify procedure, in particular:

    - Social Security (Claims and Payments) Regulations 1979, SI 1979/628 and 1987, SI 1987/1968.
    - Social Security (Payments on Account, Overpayments and Recovery) Regulations 1988, SI 1988/664.
    - Social Security and Child Support (Decisions and Appeals) Regulations 1999, SI 1999/991.

– Social Security, Child Support, Vaccine Damage and Other Payments (Decisions and Appeals) (Amendment) Regulations 2013, SI 2013/2380.

Commissioners' decisions and judgments of the Upper Tribunal

Until November 2008, decisions on appeal from tribunals were made by the Social Security and Child Support Commissioners and some Commissioners' decisions remain sources of law:

- significant decisions were published;
- the reference indicates the type of benefit, number of decision and year:

    – R(IS)1/98 is the first reported income support decision of 1998;
    – an unreported income support decision might be referred to as CIS 13/98.

Since the establishment of the Upper Tribunal by the Tribunals, Courts and Enforcement Act 2007, the Social Security and Child Support Commissioners have become part of the Administrative Appeals Chamber of the Upper Tribunal, and most former Commissioners were appointed as judges in the Upper Tribunal.

Judgments are reported on the Upper Tribunal website at **www.administrativeappeals.tribunals.gov.uk/Decisions/decisions.htm.**

13.1.2 Administration

The Department for Work and Pensions (DWP) took over from the Benefits Agency in 2001 and the Pensions Disability and Carers Service in 2011, while national insurance contributions are dealt with by HM Revenue and Customs. Services for jobseekers are delivered by Job Centre Plus.

Some benefits are dealt with at local offices but others in a single location (e.g. carer's allowance in Preston). Income support and employment and support allowance claims are handled by local or district offices but attendance allowance and pension credit are administered by a national centre.

The assessment of war pensions and the welfare service for war pensioners and civilian personnel is provided by Veterans UK which is based at Norcross, Thornton-Cleveleys, Lancashire, FY5 3WP. For more information, see **www.gov.uk/government/organisations/veterans-uk** or contact the Veterans UK helpline on 0808 1914 218 or veterans-uk@mod.uk.

The Pension Service helps with state pension eligibility, claims and payments. See **www.gov.uk/find-pension-centre**.

A Customer Charter sets out the standards of service which all customers can reasonably expect from the DWP, how customers can help the DWP to help them and what they can do if things go wrong.

Decisions on benefit claims are made by the Secretary of State acting through authorised officers. Changes were made in 2014, with the introduction of a 'mandatory reconsideration' stage into the appeal process for most benefits and tax credits (Social Security, Child Support, Vaccine Damage and Other Payments (Decisions and Appeals) (Amendment) Regulations 2013, SI 2013/2380). The reconsideration by the DWP/HMRC must take place before a case can proceed to an independent First-tier Tribunal (see **13.4**).

13.1.3   Different countries

The same social security system covers Great Britain with some variations. A claimant living elsewhere in the European Economic Area (EEA) may qualify for benefits under the basic rules about going abroad or under EEA coordination rules but note that some benefits such as employment and support allowance are not payable if a person in receipt of the benefit moves permanently abroad. Since April 2013, people in receipt of attendance allowance or disability living allowance care component have been able to retain those benefits (or make a new claim) indefinitely in specific circumstances – see **www.gov.uk/find-pension-centre** or call the DWP Exportability Team on 01253 331 044.

13.1.4   Information

Practical information about benefits and claims is readily available, with free leaflets which can be collected from local DWP offices and most post offices.

You can get an order form from **www.gov.uk/government/publications/dwp-leaflets-order-form** and return it to:

iON
2nd Floor
One City West
Gelderd Road
Leeds
LS12 6NJ
Email: ion-pass@xerox.com.

The DWP publishes a quarterly benefits information guide called *Touchbase* which provides background information on changes to benefits.

For general benefit advice enquire of the local DWP office, by looking in local telephone directory (Business Section) under DWP. There are a number of informative websites with links to other sites, for example **www.turn2us.org.uk/Find-Benefits-Grants**.

Rights membership of Child Poverty Action Group brings an annual selection of invaluable books and material.

Reference may be made to the following literature:

* *Disability Rights Handbook: A Guide to Benefits and Services* published annually by Disability Rights UK.

- *Your Rights: A Guide to Money Benefits for Older People* published annually by Age UK. This is inexpensive and could be handed to clients.
- Age UK Factsheets deal with particular benefits.

See **www.ageuk.org.uk/money-matters/claiming-benefits/benefits-calculator**.

In the event of an appeal the relevant statutes, regulations and Commissioners' decisions should be referred to as the leaflets may have misled the client or matters of interpretation may arise. Up-to-date annotated statutory material is available at a moderate price.

When a dispute arises the leaflets issued by the DWP should not be treated as authoritative and reference should be made to the original statutory material and court or Upper Tribunal/Commissioners' decisions.

13.2   TYPES OF BENEFITS

13.2.1   Weekly benefits

Weekly cash benefits are paid to meet different needs, but rates change yearly and the qualifying criteria are constantly amended. A claimant may not receive two 'overlapping' benefits and it is important to claim the one that pays the highest rate.

Useful information can be found on **www.gov.uk** or from the Age UK Factsheets at **www.ageuk.org.uk**.

Contributory benefits

These depend upon national insurance contributions paid during normal working life, generally without reference to income or savings, or personal circumstances, e.g. the presence, income or savings of any partner that the claimant lives with. However, employment and support allowance can be reduced if a person has a private or occupational pension of more than £85 a week. Most contributory benefits are taxable and all are taken into account when claiming means-tested benefits. Those claimable by an older person are:

- retirement pension, over 80s pension and bereaved person's benefits (see **16.2**);
- incapacity benefit used to be paid beyond pension age. However, employment and support allowance (which began replacing incapacity benefit in 2008) stops at pension age.

See:

- Age UK Factsheet 19: *State Pension*.
- **www.ageuk.org.uk/money-matters/pensions/state-pension**.
- **www.ageuk.org.uk/money-matters/claiming-benefits/bereavement-benefits/what-are-bereavement-benefits**.

New state pension scheme

A new single-tier, flat-rate state pension of £155.65 (maximum award) (compared to current £119.30) is being introduced which will affect people reaching state pension age from 6 April 2016 onwards. In May 2014, Parliament agreed the Pensions Act 2014. As a result, the state pension age increases from 66 to 67 between April 2026 and April 2028 (it is already due to rise to 65 for women by 2018 and to 66 for men and women by 2020).

You can find out more about the state pension changes on **www.gov.uk** or on **www.ageuk.org.uk/money-matters/pensions/what-the-new-state-pension-reforms-mean-for-you/new-state-pension**.

Non-contributory benefits

There is no need to have paid national insurance contributions to qualify for non-contributory benefits and people resident in Great Britain are entitled regardless of personal means. There may be additions for dependants, but some benefits cannot overlap. Some are non-taxable and/or not taken into account for means-tested benefits. Many benefits awarded on disability are passports to other benefits and concessions.

Possible claims by an older person are listed below.

ATTENDANCE ALLOWANCE

Attendance allowance (AA) is available where disability begins at or after 65 and the person can show they have a need for personal care or supervision to prevent danger to self or others. It can be paid to those who live alone, is not means tested and has no negative impact on any other benefit that the person receives. It can be spent in any way that the claimant chooses. Special rules and rates apply for those terminally ill, and those who are in publicly funded or NHS care homes. There are two rates (higher rate for those needing supervision day and night) and it is tax free and non-contributory. Claim forms can be obtained by calling the attendance allowance helpline on 0345 605 6055 or downloaded or claims made online at **www.gov.uk/attendance-allowance**.

DISABILITY LIVING ALLOWANCE

Disability living allowance (DLA) is available where disability began before 65. If paid before 65, it could carry on beyond that age, as an alternative to attendance allowance. Special rules applied for those terminally ill. It is split into a care component at three levels and mobility component at two levels. No new claims for DLA are now possible, and all existing claimants (except those who turned 65 after 5 April 2013) are being assessed for the replacement benefit, the personal independence payment (PIP).

PERSONAL INDEPENDENCE PAYMENT (PIP)

PIP is similar to DLA, and also has two elements for daily living and mobility. But the assessment is different, and there are only two rates for daily living, so those who previously got DLA, or who were turned down, may get a different decision under PIP rules. Like DLA, it can continue to be paid beyond 65 if claimed before then. See **www.ageuk.org.uk/money-matters/claiming-benefits/ personal-independence-payment** and **www.ageuk.org.uk/money-matters/ claiming-benefits/disability-living-allowance** for information on both benefits.

CARER'S ALLOWANCE

Carer's allowance is paid to a carer of someone in receipt of AA or DLA care component (middle or higher rate) or PIP (either rate for daily living). Although there is no means test, the claimant has to be earning less than a specified sum (currently £110 a week), and must state that they are providing a minimum of 35 hours' care per week. It also overlaps with other state benefits, for example retirement pension, and is generally worth less so is not actually paid. However, pensioners should still claim it if getting any means-tested benefit as they can show 'underlying entitlement' which increases the value of those other benefits. It is taxable but provides national insurance contributions credits. See **www.ageuk.org.uk/money-matters/claiming-benefits/carers-allowance** for more information.

INDUSTRIAL DISABLEMENT BENEFIT

Industrial disablement benefit is paid to those who became ill or disabled as a result of work for an employer. See **www.gov.uk/industrial-injuries-disablement- benefit**.

Means-tested benefits

These are weekly income supplements to which residents in Great Britain may be entitled whether or not they have paid national insurance contributions. They are assessed on the needs of a family living in the same household which includes the claimant and any partner with whom he or she is living as a couple (in a civil partnership, marriage or cohabitation). Either partner may claim and the benefit may be non-taxable:

- Pension credit brings the income up to a minimum level (see **13.2.2**).
- Child tax credit is claimable by an older person if there is a dependent child. See **www.gov.uk/tax-credits-calculator**.
- Working tax credit can be paid to pensioners who are doing full- or part-time work although any pension income will be taken into account as 'earnings'. See **www.gov.uk/working-tax-credit**.

- Universal credit is being introduced for working-age claimants in the 2014–18 period. It replaces income support, income-related employment and support allowance and job seeker's allowance, housing benefit and tax credits. It does not replace pension credit (see **13.2.2**) but that benefit will ultimately have to change to include elements for children and rent as child tax credit and housing benefit will no longer exist.

Winter fuel payment and Christmas bonus

A non-taxable payment is paid to those receiving one or more qualifying benefits but each claimant is only entitled to one such payment. To qualify the claimant has to be over women's pension age (which is rising from 60 to 66 in stages every two months) in the qualifying week (it is usually the third week in September).

13.2.2   Pension credit

Pension credit is designed to provide pensioners with a minimum level of income but it also rewards those who have managed to save a little during their working life, up to a certain limit. There are two main parts:

- the guarantee credit; and
- the savings credit.

It is designed to bring the claimant's income from all sources up to a certain figure, which changes each year (guarantee credit). Those aged 65 or over may be credited with a small extra weekly sum if they have modest savings or private or occupational pensions (savings credit). The calculation involves a complicated formula based on income and notional income from capital. For couples, pension credit eligibility is based on the age of the oldest partner, but when universal credit is fully introduced (2018 perhaps), it will be based on the age of the younger partner for new claims. This will mean that, in couples where one is below 66, the younger partner may, at some point in the future, have to look for work as a condition of getting benefit.

To claim pension credit, call 0800 99 1234. Application forms will be completed by DWP officers and sent out to the applicant for checking and signing. A claim for housing benefit and council tax support can be made during the same call.

For further information, see:

- **www.gov.uk/pension-credit/overview**.
- **www.ageuk.org.uk/money-matters/claiming-benefits/pension-credit/ what-is-pension-credit**.

If pension credit is received, further 'passported' benefits become payable, e.g. cold weather payments or full council tax support.

13.2.3 The Social Fund

The discretionary element of the DWP Social Fund, to deal with emergency or vulnerability cases, has now largely disappeared. The budget for crisis loans and community care grants has been transferred to local authorities (and the devolved administrations in Wales and Scotland), for them to spend on 'local welfare assistance'. This means each local authority has its own scheme to deal with situations, such as buying furniture for people leaving residential or hospital care, or providing emergency financial help. See **www.cpag.org.uk/lwas** for details of each local scheme.

Loans

Budgeting loans, at 0 per cent interest, are still available from the DWP to assist in meeting important intermittent expenses for which it is difficult for those receiving pension credit to budget. There are maximum and minimum amounts:

- the maximum takes into account any outstanding balance of previous loans;
- any capital over £1,000 will reduce the amount;
- the amount may not exceed £1,500 or the amount which the applicant can afford to repay.

There are also short-term benefit advances available from the DWP where a benefit has been claimed, but delays in payment are causing hardship.

Cold weather payments

Payments are sent automatically to those on pension credit during periods of cold weather (as defined below). These are not discretionary. Payments are currently £25 a week (2015/16) when the average temperature has been, or is expected to be, 0°C or below for seven days in a row (between 1 November and 31 March).

Funeral grants

The DWP Social Fund can provide grants to people responsible for arranging a funeral. This only applies to the closest relative of the deceased, unless there is a good reason for someone else being responsible. The organiser has to be receiving certain means-tested benefits, such as pension credit or housing benefit or council tax support.

A claim should be made on Form SF200 Funeral Payment from the Social Fund available from the local DWP office or download it from **www.gov.uk**. You can also call the DWP Bereavement Service on 0345 606 0265 to make a claim. The amount of the payment varies, but should be sufficient to pay for a basic funeral. However, the DWP can recover the payment from the deceased's estate, and it is a first charge.

13.3 PROCEDURES

13.3.1 Claims

A properly completed form (obtained from the local DWP office or in some cases from the internet) must reach the appropriate DWP office in order for a claim to be validly made. Online claims are also possible for some benefits, but the claimant or their agent may need to register with the Government Gateway service first (**www.gateway.gov.uk**).

The claim may be amended or withdrawn before a decision is made but further information may be required in support of the claim. The claim may be treated as having been made on the date of receipt of a letter asking about the benefit if the form sent out in response is returned within a month. If the form is sent back because it is not properly completed but returned duly completed within a month, the claim is treated as made when first submitted.

Professional persons who claim benefits on behalf of elderly persons should make it clear to the DWP the capacity in which they act.

Backdating

Most benefits are paid from the date of claim and there are strict time limits on backdating which vary from benefit to benefit, so this needs to be checked on an individual basis:

- The maximum period for which almost all benefits can be backdated is three months. However:
  - Retirement pensions can be backdated for up to 12 months without the claimant having to show why they claimed late.
  - Pension credit can be backdated for up to three months in the same way.
  - Some benefits (e.g. carer's allowance) can be backdated for three months but this can be extended if the outcome of the claim depends on the result of a claim for another benefit (e.g. waiting for an attendance allowance claim to be decided).
  - Some benefits can be backdated (usually for up to three months) if there is a good reason for a late claim. This includes being given wrong or incomplete advice in writing by a solicitor or an advice agency, or the claimant was misinformed by the DWP.

For agents and appointees generally, see **4.2**.

13.3.2 Decisions

The claim is now decided by the Secretary of State for Work and Pensions delegated to authorised representatives ('decision-makers'). Payments of benefit are also controlled in certain ways:

- A claimant may not receive two overlapping benefits but receives the higher:

    - Social Security (Overlapping Benefits) Regulations 1979, SI 1979/597;
    - benefits providing for different purposes can be claimed simultaneously.

- Changes in circumstances that may affect entitlement must be reported, ideally to the office that administers the benefit (although it is arguable that this requirement can be discharged if the claimant or agent reasonably believes that they have made a valid disclosure to another part of the benefit system).
- A claimant may have non-means tested benefits such as attendance allowance, disability living allowance or personal independence payment withdrawn after a certain length of time (which does not have to be continuous) while in hospital or a care home, unless self-funding.
- Since April 2003 a person's retirement pension is not withdrawn after a period in hospital.

For more information, see the DWP guide, 'Financial help if you're disabled', at **www.gov.uk/financial-help-disabled**.

Revision and supersession

The Secretary of State for Work and Pensions may revise a decision of his own initiative or on an application within one month of notification. A decision (whether or not on appeal) may be superseded by the Secretary of State on his own initiative or on an application outside the one-month period. In some circumstances this may be backdated to the original decision if this is advantageous to the claimant.

Suspension

Payment of benefit may be suspended in certain circumstances (e.g. for failure to provide information or if an appeal is pending against a decision in a 'lead case').

13.3.3   Payment

Benefits can generally only now be obtained via a bank, building society, credit union or Post Office card account. If the client refuses to have an account that can be used for BACS, there is a system called 'simple payment'. This means that benefits can be accessed via Paypoint outlets on production of a payment card, a memorable date and suitable ID. Where practitioners are acting on behalf of a client the benefits should be paid direct into the client's bank account on a monthly basis, especially if the client is going into a care home.

Payment may be made direct into the account of the spouse or other person acting on behalf of the claimant, and this may be helpful to older people.

Delegation

There are procedures for authorising others to collect benefit:

- an agent may be nominated by the claimant organising this with their bank, etc.;
- an appointee may be appointed when the claimant is unable to act through mental or physical disability – the agent collects and spends the benefit for the claimant.

Those acting as appointees should be advised of the personal liability that can attach to this role (see generally **Chapter 4**).

Overpayments

An overpayment of benefit may be recovered where any person whether fraudulently or otherwise misrepresents, or fails to disclose, any material fact and this results in the overpayment:

- The original decision (either to pay benefit or determining the amount of benefit) must first be revised.
- A misrepresentation can be wholly innocent and a failure to disclose may be the result of forgetfulness but knowledge of the material fact by the person who fails to disclose it must be established.
- Disclosure need not be in writing but must be made in such a manner that it is likely to be brought to the attention of the office handling the claim and if it appears that it has not been further disclosure may be required.
- The claimant is expected to have read the information in any leaflets forwarded with payment, and these may indicate the changes of circumstances which affect the benefit and should be disclosed.
- Overpayment calculations tend to be complicated because of the need to take into account the claimant's position as it would have been if the overpayment had not been made – the diminishing income or capital rule.
- Overpayments may be recovered from the claimant (or the appointee) or the estate of a deceased claimant in cases of misrepresentation or failure to disclose.

Underpayments

Claimants are entitled to compensation if they are underpaid benefit of £50 or more resulting from clear and unambiguous error by the DWP and the delay in payment was more than 12 months:

- There is no leaflet or claim form, but the DWP Administrative Code instructs local offices to consider ex gratia payments in such cases (the onus is on the claimant to raise the issue with the office dealing with the claim).
- The benefit itself may also be backdated.

- See the guide that DWP produces for its own staff, *Financial Redress for Injustice Resulting from Maladministration*: **www.gov.uk/government/ publications/financial-redress-for-injustice-resulting-from-maladministration**.

DWP Compensation Recovery Unit

The Compensation Recovery Unit (CRU) works with insurance companies, solicitors and DWP customers, to recover:

- amounts of social security benefits paid as a result of an accident, injury or disease, if a compensation payment has been made (the Compensation Recovery Scheme);
- costs incurred by NHS hospitals and ambulance trusts for treatment from injuries from road traffic accidents and personal injury claims (recovery of NHS charges).

See **www.gov.uk/government/collections/cru** for more details.

13.4   RECONSIDERATIONS AND APPEALS

If your client is unhappy with the outcome of a decision about benefits or tax credits, they can usually challenge the decision. This section looks at the usual process for:

- most benefits administered by the DWP;
- local councils – housing benefit and council tax reduction schemes.

It is sometimes possible to get decisions looked at again outside the main process, for example, if there has been official error.

13.4.1   DWP benefit decisions

If your client is unhappy with a decision, they must usually challenge it within one month from the date on the decision letter. They can only put in a late challenge in exceptional circumstances and usually no later than 13 months after the original decision.

They can also ask for written reasons within the first month if the decision letter does not include these; this extends the time limit by 14 days of the original date, if the reasons are provided within that month, or 14 days of the statement date, if provided after that.

The client should be made aware that asking for a decision to be looked at again can sometimes result in the benefit going down instead of up, as the whole decision is looked at again.

Mandatory reconsideration

If the client wants to challenge a decision formally, they must first ask for a mandatory reconsideration where it will be looked at again by the DWP. It is best to do this in writing. Identify the decision being challenged, and explain why the client disagrees with the decision. If possible, supply extra information or evidence to support their case at this stage. The client should sign any reconsideration letter, unless incapable of doing so.

If the new decision-maker is likely to reach an adverse decision, it will phone the client and the client should use this opportunity to provide any further evidence that might help their case. Whether or not the DWP changes the decision, it will give the outcome in writing, and send two copies of the 'mandatory reconsideration notice' (MRN).

Appeals

There is then a further month to appeal to the independent Social Security and Child Support (SSCS) tribunal. The time limit can be extended in special circumstances but it cannot be extended to more than 13 months from the date of the decision being appealed against.

Tribunals are administered by HM Courts and Tribunals Service (HMCTS) and the appeal must be sent directly to HMCTS at SSCS Appeals Centre, PO Box 1203, Bradford, BD1 9WP or by fax to 0870 739 4108 – not the DWP. Use Form SSCS1, which is available from **www.gov.uk** and enclose the mandatory reconsideration notice, otherwise the appeal will be rejected.

There are no fees or risks of costs involved as the Tribunals Service is a free service. It cannot award costs either against or in favour of an appellant, nor can it award compensation or damages.

The rules relating to making an appeal can be found in the Tribunal Procedure (First-tier Tribunal) (Social Entitlement Chamber) Rules 2008, SI 2008/2685.

The DWP may look at the papers again and a new decision could be made at this stage. If this decision is favourable in whole or part, the appeal process will stop, so if the client wants to proceed, they have to start the reconsideration process again. If the DWP does not change its decision, it must return its appeal response to HMCTS within 28 days.

The SSCS tribunal will then look at the decision afresh. This can be done using the papers alone (paper hearing) or at an oral hearing. If the appeal is successful, any change is normally backdated to the time of the original decision.

The tribunal

This is drawn from a judicial panel appointed by the Lord Chancellor. Members of the panel have to be qualified in law, medicine or accountancy, or be an expert in the field of disability. The tribunal will consist of:

- (for disability living allowance or attendance allowance appeals) a tribunal judge, a medical practitioner and a disability expert;
- (for industrial injuries benefits, assessments for incapacity benefit or employment and support allowance) a lawyer and a medical practitioner;
- (for all other types of case) a tribunal judge alone.

The tribunal is less formal than a court in so far as there are no wigs or gowns worn and the evidence can be given by someone who is seated.

The decision

Although the hearing is in theory in public, the tribunal will consider the evidence and statements in private. In most cases, a decision will be made at the tribunal. If this is not possible, an adjournment may be called and another date will be set for the next hearing.

After the hearing

Application can be made to set aside the decision of the tribunal for the following reasons:

- a document relating to the proceedings was not sent or received in time; or
- a hearing had been arranged but the claimant did not attend; or
- there has been some other procedural irregularity.

An application to set aside must be made in writing within one month of the date of issue of the decision notice or statement of reasons.

Further appeal

Application can be made for permission to appeal against the decision of the tribunal to the Upper Tribunal, but the appeal is only on the ground of 'error of law'.

This decision will be considered by a senior tribunal judge. He may grant permission, or refuse permission or decide to set aside the decision of the tribunal.

The Upper Tribunal has the power to set aside the tribunal's decision and refer the case to a fresh tribunal or to substitute its own decision.

13.4.2 Upper Tribunal

The Upper Tribunal (Administrative Appeals Chamber) hears appeals from the First-tier Tribunal on points of law only, but this includes cases where the decision was based on a mistaken interpretation of the law, inadequate reasons and/or findings of fact were recorded so that it is unclear how or why the decision was arrived at, the decision is not supported by any or any sufficient evidence and is therefore perverse, or there was a breach of the rules of natural justice.

The procedures of the Upper Tribunal are set out in the Tribunal Procedure (Upper Tribunal) Rules 2008, SI 2008/2698. Appeals to the Upper Tribunal may take many months and most appeals are dealt with on written representations. The appellant can ask for an oral hearing. This is not always granted but a written decision is ultimately sent to the parties. The Upper Tribunal may make the final decision (if the tribunal determined all the material facts) or send the case back to the First-tier Tribunal with directions as to how it should be dealt with.

13.4.3   Courts

There is a further right of appeal to the Court of Appeal and this will be on a question of law. Leave to appeal must be obtained from the Upper Tribunal within three months or, if refused, from the Court of Appeal. After the Supreme Court the ultimate right of appeal is to the European Court of Human Rights and issues may be referred there at an earlier stage.

Legal aid is available for the first time at this stage, subject to means.

Judicial review

An application may be made to the High Court for judicial review but this will be refused if another remedy is available (e.g. the normal appeal process). Excessive delay by the DWP in carrying out its statutory duties may justify application. Some benefit decisions are taken by the Secretary of State without a right of appeal so there is scope for judicial review if he exercises his powers improperly.

European Court of Justice

Any issue of EU law arising before a national court concerning questions of interpretation or validity can be referred to this court for a preliminary ruling (art.177 of the Treaty of Rome). In social security matters, a reference can be made by the Appeals Service, a Commissioner or the courts.

13.4.4   Local council benefits

This section looks at challenging housing benefit and council tax reduction decisions. These benefits are administered by unitary, district or borough councils.

Housing benefit revision

If there is disagreement with a housing benefit decision, the client can ask the local authority to look at it again. They should do this in writing, normally within one month of the date the decision was made. This time limit can be extended in special circumstances but must be within 13 months of the date of the original decision.

Appeals

If the client is unhappy with the new decision, they can appeal to an independent tribunal. Use the form approved by the local council available by phone or from its website.

Appeals should be requested within one month of the decision being appealed against, although again, this can be extended to 13 months in special circumstances.

The client does not have to ask for a revision first but can go straight to the appeal stage, if preferred.

Discretionary housing payments

The local authority has to follow the law when making decisions about housing benefit. If the decision it has made is legally correct but the client is still struggling to pay their housing costs, the client may want to consider applying for a discretionary housing payment to top up their benefit. The client needs to be receiving some amount of housing benefit in order to get a payment and it is more likely to be granted if they have difficult personal circumstances, such as a disability or personal problems which would make it difficult for them to move to cheaper accommodation.

Discretionary housing payments cannot be made to cover shortfalls for recovery of overpaid housing benefit and, if refused, the client can only ask the council to review its decision – there is no formal right of appeal.

Council tax reduction schemes

Local authorities set their own rules for council tax reductions. If the client does not agree with a decision, they can ask the local authority to review it. If they are still not satisfied they can appeal to the Valuation Tribunal.

13.5 NATIONAL INSURANCE CONTRIBUTIONS

National insurance contributions are intended to be paid during a normal working life so are not payable by those over pensionable age.

13.5.1 Types

There are different classes of contribution depending on the status of the individual and a series of leaflets dealing with contributions is available from the DWP:

- Class 1 earnings-related contributions are paid by both employers and employees in respect of anyone in employment.
- Flat-rate Class 3 contributions can be paid voluntarily by those wishing to improve an incomplete record (within time limits).

- Self-employed people pay flat-rate Class 2 contributions together with profit-related Class 4 contributions if their profits exceed a certain sum up to a defined maximum.

National insurance contributions are not paid beyond the pension age, currently 65 for a man and rising to 65 by 2018 for a woman.

13.5.2 Contributions record

Entitlement to certain benefits (including retirement pension) depends upon an adequate contributions record. This can be made up by credits rather than by actual payment of contributions. Either the claimant or the spouse must have an adequate record. Those with an inadequate record should consider paying additional contributions before retirement.

Credits and protection

Credits are earned while a person is unemployed and registering for employment, off work sick or entitled to certain benefits paid during a working life, e.g. employment and support allowance.

Carer's credit (formerly known as home responsibilities protection) also provide some assistance with contribution conditions for periods when a person is unable to work because he or she is caring for someone. This might be a child or an elderly or disabled person. See **www.gov.uk/carers-credit**.

13.5.3 Pension forecasts

A comprehensive retirement pension forecast is available for those who have not yet drawn their pension and this indicates the effect of postponing the pension. Voluntary or late contributions can in some circumstances be paid in order to top up a pension contributions record. See **www.gov.uk/state-pension-statement** – which may be important for those approaching pension age, as the rules change from April 2016.

13.6 HOUSING BENEFIT

13.6.1 Relevant sources of law

- Social Security Act 1986.
- Social Security Contributions and Benefits Act 1992.
- Housing Benefit Regulations 2006, SI 2006/213.
- Housing Benefit (Persons Who Have Attained the Qualifying Age for State Pension Credit) Regulations 2006, SI 2006/214.
- Housing Benefit (Amendment) Regulations 2007, SI 2007/1356.

- Housing Benefit and Council Tax Benefit (War Pension Disregards) Regulations 2007, SI 2007/1619.
- Housing Benefit and Council Tax Benefit (Amendment) Regulations 2008, SI 2008/2299.
- Housing Benefit (Amendment) Regulations 2009, SI 2009/614.

13.6.2   Sources of information

- **www.gov.uk/housing-benefit/overview**.
- Age UK Factsheet 17: *Housing Benefit* (**www.ageuk.org.uk/publications/age-uk-information-guides-and-factsheets/**) and **www.ageuk.org.uk/money-matters/claiming-benefits/housing-benefit/what-is-housing-benefit**.

13.6.3   Purpose

Housing benefit helps people on low incomes to pay rent in respect of a dwelling they normally occupy. A dwelling includes a hotel, hostel or lodgings and other residential accommodation in the United Kingdom, whether furnished or unfurnished, in the public or private sector but does not include a care home.

Housing benefit provides help with the cost of providing (but not owning) a home for those on low incomes.

13.6.4   Entitlement

Benefit may be claimed by people who are in full-time work or self-employed as well as those who are unemployed, sick or retired. The claimant must be the person who is legally liable to pay the rent (or treated as such). In order to prevent abuse certain claimants are treated as not liable, for example someone living with the person to whom the rent is paid where that person is a close relative or the agreement is not on a commercial basis. Individuals are excluded from claiming if they move into a registered care home or hospital, although they may remain entitled for their 'normal' accommodation for up to a year if in a care home or hospital temporarily, or for 13 weeks if in a care home on a trial basis.

Amount

The amount depends upon the rent paid, how much of that rent is 'eligible' for benefit, the claimant's income and savings (including that of a spouse or partner), the size of the family and the age or disability of the claimant, partner or child. It is tax free, not dependent on national insurance contributions and paid in addition to other benefits:

- Up to 100 per cent of the eligible rent can be allowed.

- Claimants on income support, the income-related element of employment and support allowance or the guarantee credit part of pension credit receive maximum benefit and others a proportion according to their income.

Assessment

Assessment is complicated. Income is compared with the statutory sum needed to live on (the applicable amount), calculated as for income support or pension credit for those over pension age. The maximum benefit is then reduced by a percentage of any excess income. A deduction may also be made for non-dependants living with the claimant:

- Non-dependants are people who are not tenants and are over the age of 18 years.
- A person employed by a charitable or voluntary organisation as resident carer is not classed as a non-dependant.
- If a claimant is registered blind or receives attendance allowance or the highest or middle rate care component of disability living allowance or either rate of personal independence payment (daily living) then no non-dependant deductions will be made.

If a claimant receives attendance allowance, personal independence payment or disability living allowance these are disregarded when assessing income. A claimant may have up to £16,000 in capital:

- Capital is defined as for income support, and certain income and capital is disregarded.
- If a person has the guarantee credit element of pension credit, there is no capital limit, as the capital will already have been taken into account in the pension credit assessment.
- If the person has the savings element of pension credit, the first £10,000 of their savings are ignored (£6,000 if under pension age). Any amount above that figure is deemed to generate £1 per week for every £500 or part thereof (£1 per £250 if under pension age). At £16,000, housing benefit would no longer be payable.
- Notional income and capital rules apply as for income support.

Eligible rent

There are restrictions upon the amount and nature of the rent that can be claimed. Rent may include a non-eligible element. Non-eligible services must be identified and the cost deducted from the charges made so as to identify the true rent:

- Eligible charges include wardens and caretakers, removal of refuse, lifts, gardening and general management charges.

- Non-eligible charges include water and sewerage charges, meals, fuel, laundry, leisure items, cleaning of personal rooms, transport, medical expenses, nursing or personal care, and other services not connected with the provision of accommodation.

The local authority may reduce the rent in certain other circumstances too.

The penalty for under-occupation (sometimes known as the bedroom tax) does not apply to tenants of social sector housing who are over pension age. But if anyone rents in the private sector, they may be caught by the 'local housing allowance' rules, which set limits for maximum private sector rents in each council area. See your local council's website for details or **https://lha-direct.voa.gov.uk/ search.aspx**.

Prospective private tenants can request a pre-tenancy determination from their local council to get an indication of whether the rent will be acceptable for housing benefit purposes. Certain claimants are protected, for example claimants already receiving benefit prior to 1996 may not be affected unless they move home.

There is some discretion to allow an increase in the maximum eligible rent when exceptional hardship can be established (discretionary housing payments – see above).

Rules for entitlement change at intervals and are being made progressively more stringent so up-to-date material should be relied upon.

Some of the service charges paid by housing benefit have been transferred to local authorities, who fund providers of some types of supported accommodation for providing care and support to their residents.

13.6.5 Procedure

A claim form is submitted to the Housing and Council Tax Office of the local authority. Couples make a single claim but either partner may claim. There are time limits:

- The claim may be made up to 13 weeks in advance but claims by pensioners may only be backdated for a maximum of 13 weeks (but without having to give a reason for the late claim). A person below pension age can have up to 26 weeks' backdating but has to show a good reason for claiming late.
- Those away from home for a long period can still claim if they are intending to (and do) return within 52 weeks (shorter in some circumstances, e.g. prisoners, people in residential care for a trial period).
- Claimants should be supplied with a written statement of their claim calculation within six weeks of a request.

Claims should be dealt with within 14 days. Those in receipt of income support or entitled to the guarantee credit part of pension credit have a 'passported' claim.

Payment

Private tenants receive benefit by cheque or credit to a bank or building society account, but for council or housing association tenants the benefit simply reduces the rent. Benefit may be paid to the landlord where there are arrears. Overpayments may be recovered from the claimant (or the landlord) in certain circumstances.

Payment is made for a maximum period up to 60 weeks and will then have to be reclaimed.

Review and appeal

There may on request within one month be an administrative review of the decision followed by an appeal within one month thereafter to an independent tribunal.

13.7   COUNCIL TAX REDUCTIONS

13.7.1   Relevant sources of law

- Council Tax (Exempt Dwellings) Order 1992, SI 1992/558.
- Council Tax (Reductions for Disabilities) (Amendment) Regulations 1999, SI 1999/1004.
- Council Tax Reduction Schemes (Default Scheme) (England) Regulations 2012, SI 2012/2886.

13.7.2   Sources of information

- **www.citizensadvice.org.uk/benefits/help-if-on-a-low-income/help-with-your-council-tax-council-tax-reduction**.
- Age UK Factsheet 21: *Council Tax.*
- **www.ageuk.org.uk/money-matters/claiming-benefits/council-tax-benefit**.

13.7.3   Nature

There are a number of ways in which council tax bills can be reduced. The help varies according to the local authority but is also different in Wales, Scotland and Northern Ireland compared to England.

There are:

- Discounts (e.g. properties occupied by a single adult get a 25 per cent discount).
- Disability reduction (e.g. a property has been made more suitable for the needs of a disabled person).
- Exempt properties (e.g. an unoccupied dwelling).

- Exempt people (e.g. people who are severely mentally impaired are exempt, which may mean a property becomes 'exempt' by being treated as 'empty' or a property with two occupants gets the 25 per cent single person discount if one is severely mentally impaired).

None of the above are means tested.

Council tax support

Council tax benefit was abolished as a national scheme in 2013. It is now at each council's discretion as to how to operate a local council tax support scheme. A few councils have maintained the old national scheme but most others have set limits on how much help people can get (between 65 per cent and 95 per cent of the amount of council tax due) and/or introduced new rules on the treatment of earnings and savings, etc. People over pension age, however, are still assessed under the old national scheme.

Entitlement to council tax support does not depend on national insurance contributions and benefit is tax free and allowed in addition to other benefits. It is paid by the council tax section of the local authority to which claims must be made and can be claimed on the same form as housing benefit. A review can be requested within one month, and if necessary appealed to an independent tribunal within one month thereafter.

Council tax is payable on most residential dwellings and liability remains during temporary absences. Owners of care homes are usually liable rather than the residents. There are some exemptions:

- self-contained units occupied by a dependent relative, where the dependent relative is aged over 65; substantially and permanently disabled; severely mentally impaired;
- dwellings occupied by people who are severely mentally impaired;
- dwellings that are unoccupied as a result of the resident's hospital admission or entry into a care home, and where the former resident is receiving or providing personal care relating to old age, disablement or mental disorder.

Amount

Financial eligibility is broadly similar to that for housing benefit. A householder on the guarantee credit part of pension credit automatically has a 100 per cent rebate unless there are non-dependant deductions. If the property is in band F or higher, council tax benefit will be reduced. Payment is made in the form of a reduction in the bill.

Second adult rebate is available in some local authorities where another adult on a low income also lives in the home which can provide a rebate of up to 25 per cent for claimants even if they do not qualify for help based on their own income and savings.

The disability reduction scheme applies if there are additional facilities or adaptations for the use of a substantially and permanently disabled person. Council tax is reduced to that for the valuation band below. If the property is in band A then the bill is reduced by one-sixth.

A reduction of 25 per cent is given where there is only one adult resident and 50 per cent where there are none. A person is not a resident if they are:

- in a care home;
- resident in hospital;
- severely mentally impaired;
- a carer (in certain cases).

13.8 RETURNING TO THE UK

13.8.1 The habitual residence test

The habitual residence test was introduced into income-related benefit regulations by the Income-Related Benefits Schemes (Miscellaneous Amendments) (No. 3) Regulations 1994, SI 1994/1807 (now repealed). There have been a number of modifications to the test over time. Its purpose is to ensure that income-related benefits are paid to people who have reasonably close ties to the UK with an intention to settle here.

The habitual residence test acts as a gateway to state help and is additional to other required criteria to be satisfied by all British citizens residing in the UK to qualify for services/benefits.

Habitual residence is not defined in any of the regulations and so case law has evolved to clarify the position. It refers to the State in which the person concerned habitually resides and where the habitual centre of their interests is to be found. In that context, account should be taken in particular of the person's family situation; the reasons which have led them to move; the length and continuity of their residence; the fact (where this is the case) of proof of stable employment; and their intention to settle in the UK as it appears from all the circumstances. In some cases, habitual residence may be established immediately on returning to the UK (*Swaddling* v. *Adjudication Officer* (Case C-90/97) [1999] ECR I-1075), while in other cases it would be necessary to be in the UK for a period of time to satisfy the requirement (*Nessa* v. *Chief Adjudication Officer* [1999] 1 WLR 1937).

13.8.2 The right to reside

There is also a right to reside test for benefits, which is not an immigration test. A person may have a right to reside for immigration purposes but not have one for benefit purposes and vice versa. There are also separate rules for EEA nationals, returning British citizens and family members of British citizens, for example elderly parents from abroad who are sponsored to enter the UK. For more information, see **www.citizensadvice.org.uk/benefits/coming-from-abroad-and-claiming-benefits-the-habitual-residence-test**.

13.8.3 Benefits not caught by the habitual residence and right to reside tests

The habitual residence test or the right to reside test are not relevant for contributory benefits, such as employment and support allowance or a retirement pension, but the national insurance test for those benefits may make eligibility very difficult anyway.

13.8.4 State pension

If the person has paid full national insurance contributions they will continue to receive their full entitlement to the state pension if they move abroad within the EEA, updated annually. This also applies to certain other countries (e.g. Turkey, Jamaica or the USA) but the annual increase is denied in other countries (e.g. Australia, Canada and Trinidad).

13.9 USEFUL DWP CONTACTS

Disability Benefits Centre

Contact the Disability Benefits Centre (**www.gov.uk/disability-benefits-helpline**) for advice or information about a claim already made for:

- disability living allowance;
- attendance allowance; or
- personal independence payment.

See **Appendix A** for phone numbers and other contact details.

CHAPTER 14

Local authority support

Gary Vaux

14.1 NON-RESIDENTIAL CARE FUNDING

14.1.1 Sources of law and guidance

- Health and Social Services and Social Security Adjudications Act (HASSASSA) 1983, s.17.
- MHA 1983, s.117.
- Care Act 2014.
- Social Services and Well-being (Wales) Act 2014.
- Carers Strategies (Wales) Measure 2010.
- Community Care, Services for Carers and Children's Services (Direct Payments) (Wales) Regulations 2011, SI 2011/831 (W 125).
- Social Care Charges (Means Assessment and Determination of Charges) (Wales) Regulations 2011, SI 2011/962 (W 136).
- Social Care Charges (Direct Payments) (Means Assessment and Determination of Reimbursement or Contribution) (Wales) Regulations 2011, SI 2011/963 (W 137).
- Care and Support (Charging and Assessment of Resources) Regulations 2014, SI 2014/2672.
- Care and Support (Direct Payments) Regulations 2014, SI 2014/2871.
- Care and Support (Assessment) (Wales) Regulations 2015, SI 2015/1305 (W 111).
- Care and Support (Eligibility) (Wales) Regulations 2015, SI 2015/1578 (W 187).
- Care and Support (Direct Payments) (Wales) Regulations 2015, SI 2015/1815 (W 260).
- Care and Support (Choice of Accommodation) (Wales) Regulations 2015, SI 2015/1840 (W 268).
- Care and Support (Deferred Payment) (Wales) Regulations 2015, SI 2015/1841 (W 269).
- Care and Support (Review of Charging Decisions and Determinations) (Wales) Regulations 2015, SI 2015/1842 (W 270).

- Care and Support (Charging) (Wales) Regulations 2015, SI 2015/1843 (W 271).

- Care and Support (Financial Assessment) (Wales) Regulations 2015, SI 2015/ 1844 (W 272).

Sources of guidance

- *The Unified and Fair System for Assessing and Managing Care* (UFSAMC) applies to people who are aged under 64 years (NAFWC 09/02, WHC (2002) 3).

- Direct Payments Guidance: Community Care, Services for Carers and Children's Services (Direct Payments) (Wales) Guidance 2011 (April 2011).

- *Direct Payments 'Suitable Person' Guidance* (Wales) (April 2011).

- *Introducing More Consistency in Local Authorities' Charging for Non-Residential Social Services* (April 2011, WAG10-12408).

- *Sustainable Social Services: A Framework for Action* (2011, WAG 10-11086).

- *Carers Strategies (Wales) Measure 2010: Guidance* (December 2011).

- *Integrated Assessment, Planning and Review Arrangements for Older People* (December 2013, WG-19920).

- Care and Support Statutory Guidance (CSSG) (October 2014).

- Guide to the Care Act 2014 and the implications for providers at **www.local.gov.uk/documents/10180/6869714/L14-759+Guide+to+the+Care+Act.pdf**

- *Guidance for Welsh Local Authorities on Cross-border Placements for Adults* (February 2015, WG-23591).

- Social Services and Well-being (Wales) Act 2014 Statutory Code of Practice (June 2015).

For a comprehensive list of Care Act resources (legislation, guidance, Department of Health factsheets, parliamentary and local authority briefings and information) see **www.disabilityrightsuk.org/how-we-can-help/independent-living/care-act-resource-page**.

14.1.2 Services

Local authorities are responsible for funding non-residential community care services but may make whatever charges they think reasonable. Elderly people will have their needs assessed by the local authority for services such as: home help, meals on wheels, and day care (see **Chapter 8**).

The assessment by the local authority of a person's service needs is a separate process from the assessment of that person's means to pay for it. Failure to pay does not mean that the service will be withdrawn as the remedy for the local authority is an action in court to recover the debt (see **14.1.5** and **14.2.4**).

Local authorities in England must follow the national eligibility criteria set out in the Care and Support (Eligibility Criteria) Regulations 2015, SI 2015/313 (see **8.2** for more detail on eligibility). Until April 2016, Welsh local authorities must follow the guidance contained in *Integrated Assessment, Planning and Review Arrangements for Older People* which provides councils with a framework for determining eligibility for older people. After April, 2016 new regulations will be introduced which are similar but not identical to the eligibility criteria which operate in England.

The local authority may take into account the resources available to it when considering the eligibility criteria (see **Chapter 8**).

Supporting People services

Supporting People began on 1 April 2003 and was a scheme designed to provide people with housing-related support such as visiting support, provision of a warden, and community care services. From April 2010, the grants for this scheme were no longer ring-fenced, so local authorities now contract with service providers as they see fit by drawing on money from grants from the Department for Communities and Local Government or their own resources.

Those eligible for services being arranged or provided by the local authority are financially assessed in accordance with the charging regulations and guidance (see **14.1.1**).

14.1.3   Charges

On 17 July 2015, the English government announced that it was postponing until April 2020 the introduction of a cap on social care funding, so no one would pay more than £72,000 for the cost of their care and the accompanying more generous means test, which proposed to increase the capital disregard thresholds.

In England, the Care and Support (Charging and Assessment of Resources) Regulations 2014 and the Care and Support Statutory Guidance (CSSG) provide a charging framework for all local authorities to follow. However, local authorities have considerable discretion when charging for non-residential care so charges vary between local authorities. In Wales, no service user can be charged more than £60 per week (2015/16) towards the cost of their domiciliary care (*Introducing More Consistency in Local Authorities' Charging for Non-Residential Social Services*). As such most of this section applies to England, unless otherwise stated. Disregarded assets and notional capital are considered at **14.2.3**.

In most circumstances, it is the person receiving services who is charged. The local authority has no power to assess couples or civil partners according to their joint resources. Each person must be treated individually.

The local authority should not put an arbitrary ceiling on what it will fund for care at home. It depends entirely on the service user's assessed eligible needs. However, in practice there is often a ceiling on the amount of home care the local authority will provide, often set at the level where care in a care home is the cheaper option. Local authorities must not fetter their discretion so must allow some flexibility for exceptional circumstances.

Where the local authority decides to charge, the client will be financially assessed on what they can afford to pay and must follow the mandatory guidance in working out the client's contribution. If the recipient is unable to meet the charges the local authority must consider this and reduce or waive the charges as appropriate. If the service user does not provide information as to their personal means, the full charge will be imposed.

In England, charges for domiciliary care should not reduce the service user's income to below a minimum income guarantee set out in reg.7 of the Care and Support (Charging and Assessment of Resources) Regulations 2014 (aligned to the basic level of income support or pension credit, plus a buffer of 25 per cent). In addition to this buffer, local authorities disregard national insurance, income tax, housing costs and council tax. Benefits advice should be provided when the financial assessment takes place (see **Chapter 13**). State benefits available (from the Department for Work and Pensions) may include:

- **State retirement pension**: based on national insurance contributions, with additional elements based on previous schemes, e.g. State-Earnings Related Pension or State Second Pension. Major reform is planned for new claims for people who reach pension age after April 2016 – with a higher basic benefit but a stiffer test of national insurance contributions.
- **Attendance allowance** (AA): for those aged 65 or over who need help with personal care because of illness or disability. There are two rates dependent upon the level of assistance required.
- **Disability living allowance** (DLA): for people with disabilities from birth to 65, although paid beyond that age if awarded before 65. There are two parts, a care component and a mobility component.
- **Personal independence payment** (PIP): replacing DLA for people aged 16 or over. It can be paid beyond 65 if claimed beforehand. There are two parts – daily living and mobility.
- **Pension credit**: This is a top-up to the basic state pension, even for people who get a full pension but have limited other income. It is also in two parts. The guarantee credit is for people over women's pension age. The savings credit is for people aged 65 or over, who have savings or other pensions. The latter will be phased out for some new claimants from April 2016.
- **Constant attendance allowance**: there are four levels paid with industrial injuries benefit and war pensions.
- **Exceptionally severe disablement allowance**: if in receipt of higher levels of constant attendance allowance.

Most authorities take state benefits into account when considering ability to pay, although the mobility elements of DLA or PIP must be ignored. Authorities may take AA into account as well as the care element of DLA and the daily living element of PIP, but if they do, then disability-related expenditure should also be taken into account and offset against that income (see below). In addition, the local authority should also ignore the difference between the highest two rates of AA or the DLA care element if paid because the person needs night-time care, unless night-time care is actually being provided.

When calculating disability-related expenditure (often referred to as 'DRE'), some councils deduct a set amount rather than assess each individual. The amount set by each authority varies. An assessment may always be requested and this is recommended where actual expenditure is considerably higher than the set amount. Assessment of disability expenditure may take into account for example:

- extra heating costs;
- extra washing;
- special washing powder;
- special diet;
- special clothing/footwear, or extra wear and tear;
- additional bedding;
- gardening;
- cleaning;
- transport;
- equipment.

In the main, the same capital disregards apply for domiciliary care as they do for residential care (see **14.2**). The value of the service user's own or main home is not included in the financial assessment.

The local authority will provide the service user with a written statement of the amount to be paid and how to pay it. These payments should not be made directly to the service provider. Information on notice periods, so that arrangements may be made to cover holiday periods, will also be provided. If charges for services subsequently increase significantly, a phased implementation may be requested.

Charging carers

If services are provided directly to a carer the local authority may charge the carer for services. Local authorities are discouraged from charging carers but there may be circumstances where it is appropriate, in which case the same charging rules apply as they do to a service user (see **8.1.3** and CSSG, paras.8.49–8.54).

A carer may be eligible for carer's allowance if they are aged 16 or over and if, for 35 hours a week or more, they provide care for a person who receives one of the following benefits:

- attendance allowance; or
- disability living allowance with a care component paid at the middle or higher rate; or
- personal independence payment for daily living (either rate);

- constant attendance allowance at or above the normal maximum rate with an industrial injuries disablement benefit, or basic (full day) rate with a war disablement pension.

See **www.gov.uk** for further details.

Reviews

If the charge is considered unreasonable it is possible to request a review. Many local authorities have appeals panels for this purpose and the local authority complaints procedure may also be used (see **Chapter 8**).

Services with no charge

It is not lawful to charge for social work support, occupational therapy, advice and assessments of need.

Services provided under Mental Health Act 1983, s.117 where care is required as a result of a mental disorder, following discharge from detention under one of the longer treatment sections of MHA 1983 (usually s.3 or s.37) cannot be charged for. There is a joint duty on the NHS and local authority to provide the services required, unless it is decided by both that the person is no longer in need of these by virtue of his or her mental disorder (see **8.2.3**).

Social services and the NHS provide an integrated community equipment service at no charge.

Intermediate care services up to six weeks are provided by the NHS and social services working together at no charge to prevent readmission to hospital or to assist a person to regain the ability to live at home following discharge from hospital.

There is no power to charge where need is primarily a healthcare need (see *R* v. *North and East Devon Health Authority, ex p Coughlan* [2001] QB 213). The full cost of such care should be paid for by the NHS. This is often known as NHS continuing care (see **Chapter 10**).

A fund administered by the National CJD Surveillance Unit provides money so that no charge is made for any services provided to meet the needs of a person diagnosed with Creutzfeldt Jakob Disease.

14.1.4   Personalisation

The concordat between government departments and organisations involved in the delivery of social care, *Putting People First: A Shared Vision and Commitment to the Transformation of Adult Social Care* (Department of Health, December 2007) announced a policy initiative proposing to change the framework of social care provision so that people '... have maximum choice, control and power over the support services they receive'. This concordat has been incorporated into the

CSSG, throughout the care journey from undertaking an assessment to care planning and delivery. The Welsh Assembly Government has not adopted the term 'personalisation', although maintaining autonomy, health, safety, daily routines and involvement is core to its social care policy (*Sustainable Social Services for Wales: A Framework for Action* (WAG10-11086, 2011); UFSAMC); and SCIE Report 20: *Personalisation: A Rough Guide* (Social Care Institute for Excellence, October 2008, updated April 2010) describes personalisation as:

- tailoring support to people's individual needs;
- ensuring that people have access to information, advocacy and advice to make informed decisions about their care and support;
- finding new collaborative ways of working (sometimes known as co-production) that support people to actively engage in the design, delivery and evaluation of services;
- developing local partnerships to co-produce a range of services for people to choose from and opportunities for social inclusion and community development;
- developing the right leadership and organisational systems to enable staff to work in creative, person-centred ways;
- embedding early intervention, reablement and prevention so that people are supported early on and in a way that's right for them;
- recognising and supporting carers in their role, while enabling them to maintain a life beyond their caring responsibilities;
- ensuring all citizens have access to universal community services and resources – a total system response.

Personal budgets

Personal budgets are intended to increase choice and control over the services received.

In England, the Care Act 2014 provides the statutory basis for personal budgets, and makes them compulsory (CSSG, para.11.6). In Wales, the term 'personal budget' is not used; rather the focus continues to be on the provision of direct payments. Personal budgets are more flexible than direct payments alone and may be used to purchase assistance or services from a commercial provider (e.g. gym membership rather than day centre) or to pay friends and, in some circumstances, relatives.

A personal budget is a sum of money allocated to a person assessed as needing care and support services. The eligible person can choose to:

- Take the allocated fund as direct payments.
- Agree to the fund being used by the local authority to pay for care directly.

- Agree to the fund being paid into a user-controlled trust. Under this arrangement, the local authority contracts with the third party, while day-to-day arrangements are made by the eligible person and the third party provider.
- Allocate the fund to a combination of these options.

The funds in the personal budget may be taken as a lump sum or as a budget managed over the year.

The personal budget forms part of the care plan which is generally reviewed no later than every 12 months, although a light-touch review should be considered six to eight weeks after the plan and personal budget have been signed off. The local authority shall, following an assessment of need and an indicative calculation of how much the budget is likely to be, undertake an assessment of the eligible person's financial circumstances and calculate what the person's maximum contribution will be. This will be carried out in accordance with the CSSG (see p.207 onwards).

Service users are financially assessed on their personal budget and may have to contribute towards their care costs (see the Care and Support (Charging and Assessment of Resources) Regulations 2014 and Annex B (capital) and C (income) of the CSSG).

NHS personal budget

Personal health budgets are being introduced by the NHS to help people manage their care in a way that suits them (see **15.2**).

Direct payments

Direct payments is a scheme whereby the local authority makes a means-tested cash payment in place of social service provision to a person assessed as needing care and support. It is mandatory for local authorities to offer direct payments to those who are eligible. Direct payments allow people to manage their own care services rather than rely on those provided by social services.

The amount of the payment will not be more than it would cost social services to provide the service required. Payments are made to cover the cost of care for assessed needs. If there are no assessed needs then there is no payment. The local authority will monitor that the payments are used for the care needed and are able to request repayment if not satisfied.

The SCIE Report 20: *Personalisation: A Rough Guide* (2008 updated 2010) indicates that once a support plan has been devised, support can be purchased from:

- statutory social services;
- the private sector;
- the voluntary or third sector;
- user-led organisations;

- community groups;
- neighbours, family and friends.

Direct payments are not usually used to pay:

- a spouse, civil partner or someone living in the same house as though a spouse or civil partner;
- a close relative or their spouse living in the same house (although exceptions may be made);
- for services provided by the NHS;
- for residential accommodation for any period of more than four weeks in a 12-month period (although the English government is planning to introduce this from April 2016);
- for costs incurred in meeting needs by the provision to the person of intermediate care and reablement support services, where the local authority is not permitted to make a charge for meeting needs or has chosen not to do so (Care and Support (Personal Budget: Exclusion of Costs) Regulations 2014, SI 2014/2840).

If direct payments are made for equipment it is important to ascertain whether the individual or the local authority will own it and who is responsible for maintenance and repairs.

The means test for direct payments is applied in the usual way. Any contribution to be paid may be deducted from the payment, or the full amount paid and the contribution amount returned (advisable if there is any dispute as to the amount of the contribution). The service user must also be able to manage the payments.

Direct payments are also available to an eligible person even if that person lacks the mental capacity to consent to managing direct payments. In these circumstances a 'suitable person' (as they are known in Wales) or 'nominated person' (as they are known in England) is appointed to receive and manage the payments on behalf of the eligible person who lacks capacity. The local authority appoints the 'suitable or nominated person' in accordance with the direct payments regulations, CSSG (chapter 12) or *Direct Payments Guidance: Community Care, Services for Carers and Children's Services (Direct Payments) (Wales) Guidance 2011* (**www.gov.wales/topics/health/socialcare/directpayments**).

Direct payments can also be made to an attorney acting under a lasting power of attorney or a deputy or other suitable person. Direct payments can also be made to a suitable third party for those subject to guardianship or supervised discharge under MHA 1983.

Direct payments should be offered at the time needs are assessed and included in the care plan. They may be requested when the care plan comes up for review or at any time the individual no longer wishes to have services arranged by the local authority.

A person will not automatically qualify for direct payments if they are subject to restrictions under mental health or criminal justice legislation or receiving any form of aftercare under a compulsory court order. People subject to drugs and alcohol restrictions under criminal justice legislation also do not qualify.

A person receiving direct payments and paying directly for services may become an employer in some circumstances. If so, they need to be aware of such matters as the European Working Time Directive, sickness and holiday pay, and auto-enrolment into pension schemes. From 6 April 2015, employers of care and support workers have been able to claim the employment allowance. This is not a grant or benefit: it works by reducing the amount of employer national insurance contributions the cared for person has to pay, by up to £2,000 a year (see **www.gov.uk/ government/uploads/system/uploads/attachment_data/file/421000/carers-guidance.pdf**). There is guidance on an employer's responsibilities and on contracting with self-employed suppliers in *A Guide to Getting Direct Payments from Your Council: A Route to Independent Living* (DoH, September 2009). A service user can also use local care agencies, employment agencies and support groups to avoid the responsibilities of becoming a direct employer. Local authorities in England should provide access to independent advocacy and brokerage services as part of their duty to provide information and advice under the Care Act. No such specific duty exists in Wales.

Direct payments do not count as the service user's income when assessing any means-tested benefits, as they are to be used to meet needs not met by those benefits. They do not disqualify the person from attendance allowance, disability living allowance or personal independence payment either. However, if passed on to a carer, they may affect that person's benefits, such as carer's allowance, income support, housing benefit and council tax support, as they will be treated as earnings. The original recipient of the direct payment should also be aware that if they accumulate direct payments in their bank account, this may be counted as capital when benefits are assessed.

For more information, see **www.skillsforcare.org.uk/Employing-your-own-care-and-support/Information-hub.aspx**.

Independent Living Fund (ILF)

This method of funding personal care and support in the home was introduced in 1988 as a government-funded but independently administered (by trustees) scheme to help disabled people to remain at home as an alternative to going into a care home. It went through numerous changes but finally closed in June 2015. Those still in receipt of ILF funding, which could be quite generous, were transferred to their local authority for continued funding under the direct payments scheme instead.

See **www.gov.uk/government/publications/independent-living-fund-your-transfer-guide** for more information.

14.1.5 Enforcement

The Care Act 2014 and the Social Services and Well-being (Wales) Act 2014 introduce a new legal framework for the recovery of any debts that may have accrued as a result of a local authority meeting a person's eligible care and support needs. This is considered at **14.2.4**.

14.2 RESIDENTIAL CARE FUNDING

14.2.1 Sources of law and guidance

- National Assistance Act 1948, s.22.
- National Health Service and Community Care Act 1990.
- Health and Social Care Act 2001.
- Care Act 2014.
- Social Services and Well-being (Wales) Act 2014.
- Social Care Charges (Means Assessment and Determination of Charges) (Wales) Regulations 2011, SI 2011/962.
- Care and Support (Deferred Payment) Regulations 2014, SI 2014/2671.
- Care and Support (Charging and Assessment of Resources) Regulations 2014, SI 2014/2672.
- National Assistance (Sums for Personal Requirements) and Social Care Charges (Wales) (Miscellaneous Amendments) Regulations 2015, SI 2015/720 (W 58).
- Care and Support (Choice of Accommodation) (Wales) Regulations 2015, SI 2015/1840 (W 268).
- Care and Support (Deferred Payment) (Wales) Regulations 2015, SI 2015/1841 (W 269).
- Care and Support (Charging) (Wales) Regulations 2015, SI 2015/1843 (W 271).
- Care and Support (Financial Assessment) (Wales) Regulations 2015, SI 2015/1844 (W 272).
- Social Services and Well-being (Wales) Act 2014 Statutory Code of Practice (June 2015).
- Care and Support Statutory Guidance (CSSG).
- Charging for Residential Accommodation Guide (CRAG) (Welsh Assembly, April 2015).

See Age UK Factsheet 10: *Paying for Permanent Residential Care*; Factsheet 58: *Paying for Temporary Care in a Care Home* and Factsheet 39: *Paying for Care in a Care Home if You Have a Partner*: **www.ageuk.org.uk/home-and-care/care-homes**. Age Cymru have equivalent factsheets explaining the slightly different financial rules that apply in Wales: **www.ageuk.org.uk/cymru**.

From April 2015, CRAG was replaced in England by the Care and Support Statutory Guidance (CSSG). CRAG applies in Wales until April 2016, when it will be replaced by a new Code of Practice. There will be new underpinning regulations.

Local authorities are required to publish long-term plans covering social services, health and housing services for adults with difficulties associated with old age, long-term illness or disability and carers for these adults. These were originally incorporated in England into 'Better Care, Higher Standards' charters. However, the Care Act 2014 amended the National Health Service Act 2006 to provide the legislative basis for the establishment of a Better Care Fund, where funding would be shared between NHS clinical commissioning groups (CCGs) and local authority social care departments to provide integrated care and support services.

See **Chapter 8** for assessment of need for residential care.

14.2.2 Charges

Individuals who can afford to pay for a place in a care home may arrange this independently. Nevertheless, it is still advisable for all people with care needs to seek a care needs assessment prior to entering a care home in order to achieve continuity if local authority funding should be needed in future. The local authority may also have negotiated a better weekly rate than a person would be able to negotiate on their own. So even if the person has to pay the full cost to the local authority, it may be less than the person would have to pay the home, if they commissioned their care independently. If a request to assess in advance is met with a refusal from the local authority, the local authority should be reminded that the assessment of need for care provision does not depend upon the need for funding. However, local authorities are not obliged to arrange care home provision, where the person has sufficient resources, has mental capacity or lacks mental capacity but has people who are able and willing to arrange the placement. It may also be wise to ensure that the particular home is willing to accommodate residents on local authority funding.

Free aftercare services

If a person has been previously detained in hospital under certain sections of MHA 1983, a care home placement may be provided as an aftercare service under s.117 of that Act. Local authorities cannot charge for aftercare provided under s.117 (see **8.2.3**).

Continuing NHS healthcare

If the primary need of a person is for health services, the NHS is responsible for paying for the cost of care (see **Chapter 10**). Some people receive what is known as 'continuing care at home', i.e. nursing services delivered at the person's own home.

Although NHS funded, these arrangements do not define the client as an NHS in-patient so reductions in benefits made for NHS patients do not apply in these circumstances.

Registered nursing care contribution

A fixed amount is paid by the CCG in England or the Health Board in Wales towards the element of care in a nursing home provided by a registered nurse (see **Chapter 10** and **www.moneyadviceservice.org.uk/en/articles/registered-nursing-care-contribution**).

Intermediate care

Intermediate care in a care home can be arranged either as part of discharge arrangements from hospital or to avoid readmission to hospital. It does not normally last longer than six weeks and services are provided free of charge.

Respite care

Periods of respite care arranged by the local authority may be charged either a flat-rate charge or by application of the means test. If the means test is used, then the value of the person's main or only home is ignored.

War pensioners

Veterans UK (**www.gov.uk/government/organisations/veterans-uk**) can pay towards the cost of care for people injured while on military service, including civilians injured in wartime activity.

Local authority

An assessment of need, stating that care in a care home is needed, is required before the local authority will pay or contribute to the care home fees (see **Chapter 8**). In cases where the local authority disagrees that care is required, or regarding the level of care, a copy of the needs assessment should be obtained and relevant evidence of needs gathered.

The authority may either pay the full fee to the home and collect the resident's contribution or pay its share while the resident (and any third party) pays the balance. A contract with the authority or the home should state what is included in the charge and what are extras (see **Chapter 9**).

Those who enter a care home through an arrangement made by the local authority must pay or contribute to the cost, whether the authority provides or buys in the accommodation. Whether the home is run by the local authority or is independently owned, the rate is set on a weekly basis. Residents must generally contribute in accordance with their resources up to the weekly charge, but no one will be required to pay more.

If a person is placed on a waiting list and alternative care arrangements are put in place in the meantime, contributions should not be any greater towards the alternative domiciliary or residential care than would be contributed for care required in the person's preferred care home.

Where a care home increases its fees above the rate paid by the local authority, the resident should:

- ask for reassessment by social services that staying in the home is part of required needs and obtain an assessment of the risk of any move;
- seek a third party to top up;
- ask social services to negotiate with the home to charge only what social services will pay;
- move to another home.

14.2.3 Means testing

When the resident cannot afford the full charge, an assessment is made of their ability to pay (means test). This is normally reviewed annually but a resident should ask for reassessment at any time if this would be beneficial. Once the amount to be paid by the resident is determined, then unless agreed otherwise, this is paid to the local authority which in turn pays the full fee to the home.

Points to note:

- The assessment relates to both income and capital.
- Assessment relates only to the means of the resident.
- There is no power to oblige a spouse or civil partner to take part.
- Fifty per cent of occupational and private pensions of the resident can be re-routed back to the non-resident spouse or civil partner and so are not taken into account in the assessment. However, this transfer may affect the entitlement to means-tested benefits of the spouse or civil partner.
- All residents must be allowed to retain a personal expenses allowance of at least £24.90 per week for the period 2015–16, although £25.50 in Wales, to be used for expenditure of personal choice such as stationery, personal toiletries, treats (e.g. sweets, drinks, cigarettes) and presents. A variation may be considered to cover outgoings while selling the house. The authority has discretion to increase the amount, but it should not be used for top-up to provide more expensive accommodation, although it may be used for extra services at the care home that have not been contracted for.
- Local authorities should carry out a welfare benefits check because they have an incentive to ensure that people in homes are receiving maximum welfare benefits, such as pension credit. Some authorities may assume that a pension

credit claim would then be made, and charge against that additional income. This check should only be made with the informed consent of the resident.

Capital

In the period 2015–16, capital over £23,250 in England is assessed as a completely self-funded placement. Up to that figure tariff income of £1 for every £250 over £14,250 is applied. 'Tariff income' is not applied to capital under £14,250.

Wales has one capital sum of £24,000 (2015–16) under which full local authority support is provided. There is no assumed income if capital is below that figure.

Most assets, including any overseas assets (which can be realised), are counted as capital. Capital is valued at the amount a willing purchaser would pay to a willing seller or the surrender value. That figure may then be subject to any secured debts and a 10 per cent allowance for notional expenses of sale. Jointly owned assets are treated as divided equally unless otherwise evidenced.

Where the home is jointly owned a nil valuation may possibly be argued, as the current market value will be the price a willing buyer would pay to a willing seller. Some local authorities take that to mean half the actual value of the home, when the correct approach is to ascertain the interest in half a home (see *Chief Adjudication Officer* v. *Palfrey* [1995] 11 LS Gaz R 39).

Capital disregards

Disregards are listed in CSSG, Annex B in England and CRAG in Wales and include the following:

- The main or only home is disregarded indefinitely where it is occupied by:
  - a spouse or civil partner;
  - a relative who is over 60, or incapacitated, or under 16;
  - a child whom the resident is liable to maintain;
  - an estranged or divorced partner or civil partner who has a dependent child.

- There is a discretionary power to disregard where occupation is by others.
- The value of the home is disregarded for the first 12 weeks of a permanent stay, after which a deferred payments agreement may be entered into (or in Wales a legal charge applied against the property).
- The surrender value of life insurance policies or annuities.
- The value of personal injury funds held in trust or administered by a court.
- Personal possessions.
- The value of certain types of investment bond with a life assurance element.
- The £10,000 compensation payment made to Far East Prisoners of War on or after 1 February 2001.

This is not an exhaustive list.

Notional capital

Notional capital is assessed where:

- a person deliberately deprives themselves of capital to reduce the amount of charge to pay (known generally as a 'deliberate deprivation') (see **14.2.4**);
- a person fails to apply for capital otherwise available;
- capital is paid by someone else to a third party on a person's behalf.

Where notional capital is assessed it should also be diminished by the difference in each payment made. The local authority will apply diminishing notional capital rules to work out when eligibility for funding will arise. The notional capital is treated as diminishing each week by the difference between the amount the resident has to pay for the accommodation and the amount they would have paid if they were not being treated as having notional capital.

Income

All income is considered and is either included, fully disregarded or partly disregarded.

Disregarded income includes:

- the mobility element of either disability living allowance or personal independence payment (the care/daily living elements will stop after four weeks anyway), which falls within the 12-week period of the initial assessment;
- War Widows' special payments;
- Christmas bonus;
- income from savings;
- Supporting People payments;
- certain damages/compensation awards.

This is not an exhaustive list.

Partly disregarded income may include:

- £10 per week of a war pension.
- Fifty per cent of an occupational pension of a married person/civil partner where the other 50 per cent is paid to the spouse/civil partner.
- A partial disregard applies to council supported residents aged 65 and over who are receiving savings credit. In 2015–16, this is £5.75 for a single person (£8.60 for a couple who are both in care). Individuals whose income is such that it takes them above the pension credit savings credit level (£188.25 or £274.42 for a couple) are still entitled to this disregard.

Notional income

Notional income is income that is not actually received, as follows:

- income paid to social services as a third party top-up;
- income available if applied for;
- income due but not received;
- income deliberately deprived of to reduce or avoid charges.

Social services should only consider income that has been deliberately deprived if it would have normally been included in the financial assessment. Deliberate deprivation to reduce or avoid the charge does not have to be the main reason, only a significant reason for the deprivation. Where an income-producing asset is sold and thereby converted to a capital asset, any of the following may be taken into account:

- the former income;
- the difference between the former income and the tariff income;
- the increase in the tariff income.

Interim arrangements

Interim arrangements are available in cases that would be self-funding but where capital is not immediately available, for instance while a property is sold. During this period the charge will be based on income, with the full fee being payable and backdated once the capital is available. Attendance allowance should therefore remain in payment during interim arrangement periods.

The value of the property is disregarded for the first 12 weeks of a permanent stay in a care home. If the home is going to take a long time to sell a deferred payments scheme may be preferable.

Deferred payment

Deferred payment agreements are operated by social services who take a legal charge against the resident's main or only home instead of a contribution towards the cost of accommodation, so allowing the home to be retained. It delays actual payment until the property is sold. Such agreements:

- Must be in writing.
- Must last from the day the agreement is entered into until 56 days (in Wales) or 90 days (in England) after the resident's death or the property is sold, if earlier. (In Wales, interest is charged from 56 days after death or the property is sold; in England interest is charged on a compound basis from the date of the agreement, where the resident's assessment needs were deemed eligible after 1 April 2015.)
- Cannot include legal expenses.

- Cannot be terminated by social services in Wales, but in England an agreement can be terminated if the deferred sum has reached the maximum sum the local authority is prepared to lend.

Social services in Wales have discretion whether or not to agree to a deferred payments agreement, but in England it must be offered to those who have eligible needs, a property and insufficient financial resources to fund their care. From April 2016, Wales will operate an identical system to England.

Reasons for a refusal should be put in writing. All of the following must apply in order to qualify:

- a property disregard does not apply;
- capital apart from the home is below the maximum prescribed limit;
- cost of care cannot be met in full from income.

Legal charge

Social services cannot force the sale of land. However, as an alternative to a deferred payment agreement, a Welsh local authority may create a legal charge under HASSASSA 1983, s.22 to cover any unpaid care costs. This provision was repealed in England, following the introduction of the Care Act 2014. The Welsh legislation retains this power (s.70). The amount of the debt will take into account the capital limits. Interest will only be charged from the date of death. Where property is jointly owned, a caution only may be registered, but consider the possibility of a nil value (see above). If there is a disagreement with the valuation of property a complaint should be made. Any attempt to pass on the cost of creating the charge can be challenged.

14.2.4 Enforcement

New recovery powers are provided in England under the Care Act 2014, s.69 and in Wales in the Social Services and Well-being (Wales) Act 2014, s.70, for the recovery of any debt accrued in respect of care and support in the County Court; and/or under s.70 (in England) or s.72 (in Wales), they can recover charges from a third party where a person has transferred assets to them in order to avoid paying charges for care and support. These enforcement measures apply irrespective of where the care is or was being provided. In the case of a claim against a third party there is no time limit which applies to the transfer.

A debt which arose after the Care Act 2014 came into force must be recovered within six years of the date when the sum became due to the local authority. This is an extension to the previous limits for a debt that arose before the commencement of the Care Act 2014, which had to be recovered within three years of the date when it became due.

See Annexes D and E of CSSG about enforcement of debts.

HASSASSA 1983 was revoked in England from April 2015 and no new debts can be recovered under that provision. Until the new Welsh legislation is in force in April 2016, HASSASSA 1983 still applies in Wales, although the ability to recover a debt by placing a charge over the person's property is contained in Social Services and Well-being (Wales) Act 2014, s.71. Until the Welsh legislation is in force, the local authority is also expressly empowered to recover sums due from the resident as a civil debt through the magistrates' court, although in practice this is rare (National Assistance Act 1948, s.56).

Disputes as to charges that cannot be resolved by informal methods such as mediation or negotiation should initially be dealt with under the social services complaints procedure and there is no separate appeal procedure, although decisions can then be challenged by making a complaint to the Ombudsman or judicial review (see **Chapter 8**).

This is 'without prejudice to any other method of recovery' so does not preclude a debt claim in the County Court or bankruptcy proceedings under the Insolvency Act 1986.

Deliberate deprivation of assets

Where a person has deliberately deprived themselves of income or capital to reduce the amount of charge they would have to pay, the local authority will treat this as a 'deliberate deprivation' and charge the person as if they still had that income or capital.

The term 'deprivation' covers a broad range of ways in which an asset might be disposed of. The following are examples:

- a lump sum payment such as a gift or to pay off a debt;
- transferring the title deeds of a property to someone else;
- putting money into a trust that cannot be revoked;
- converting money into another form that has to be disregarded from the means test, e.g. personal possessions, investment bonds with life insurance;
- reducing capital through substantial expenditure on items such as expensive holidays or by extravagant living;
- selling an asset for less than its true value.

This is not an exhaustive list – see Annex E of CSSG.

Where a local authority believes deprivation has occurred, it may either charge the person as if they still possessed the asset or, if the asset has been transferred to someone else, seek to recover the assessed charges from that person. However, the local authority cannot recover more than the person gained from the transfer.

Establishing the purpose

To establish whether the transfer (whether a gift or a transaction at an undervalue) is a deliberate deprivation, the authority must consider the purpose of the transfer. The assessed person provides information for the means test to the local authority from which the authority can conclude whether he or she has available funds to pay the assessed charge. Deprivation of income or capital should only be considered where the income or capital would have been included in the financial assessment if possessed.

Avoiding the charge need not be the main purpose but must have been a significant one. Whether there is intention to reduce or avoid charges is established by a subjective test. In *R (on the application of Beeson)* v. *Dorset CC* [2001] EWHC Admin 986, it was shown that the council misdirected itself in failing to apply the subjective test. Furthermore, on appeal the court held its systems were not in breach of a right to a fair hearing under art.6(1) of the European Convention on Human Rights ([2003] HRLR 11).

The authority will endeavour to establish whether there is any link between the person making the gift and their needing care and support. If the person is unable to provide a reason for the gift the authority may conclude, in all the circumstances, that it must have been made to avoid future care costs.

Yule v. *South Lanarkshire Council (No. 2)* 2001 SC 203 confirmed there is no time limit on local authorities when deciding whether a person had deprived themselves of assets for the purposes of avoiding residential care fees.

The timing of the disposal of the asset will be taken into account in establishing purpose. It would be unreasonable to decide that a person had disposed of an asset in order to reduce the level of charges for their care and support needs if at the time the disposal took place they were fit and healthy and could not have foreseen the need for care and support (CSSG, para.12 Annex E; CRAG, para.6.064). Any gift made immediately before (or after) admission to a care home is vulnerable even if a further purpose can be established. There is no time limit but the longer it is since a gift was made the more difficult it will be to establish that the purpose was to avoid financial assessment.

An adviser must consider whether the elderly resident or donee is able to give evidence and face cross-examination.

The Law Society has issued good practice guidance on this subject in its Practice Note: Making Gifts of Assets (6 October 2011) where solicitors are advised at para.2.4:

> To protect yourself in the event of a subsequent dispute or a professional negligence claim, you must retain evidence of the advice you give your client. Your file notes and correspondence will normally be covered by legal professional privilege or the duty of confidentiality. A court will not usually order discovery of a solicitor's file unless there is prima facie evidence of fraud, but has done so where there are public policy considerations – see *Barclays Bank plc* v. *Eustice* [1995] 1 WLR 1238. It is possible that a trustee in bankruptcy, or a local authority bringing proceedings under the Insolvency Act 1986, section 423–425, may persuade the court to override privilege.

Indeed, in *London Borough of Brent* v. *Kane* [2014] EWHC 4564 (Ch), the court ordered the disclosure of privileged documents on the basis of iniquity, in circumstances where the documents allegedly related to transactions at an undervalue, but before any such proceedings had been taken.

It is important to note that guidance available on confidentiality has been substantially reduced under the SRA Code of Conduct 2011. Chapter 4, outcome 4.1 requires that you keep the affairs of clients confidential unless disclosure is required or permitted by law or the client consents' (see also Law Society Practice Note: Financial Abuse (13 June 2013)).

14.2.5 Alternative recovery

The local authority is obliged to meet the continuing cost of care even if any assessed financial contribution is not paid. In addition to enforcement as set out in **14.2.4**, recovery may be possible in a limited timeframe, by making:

- the individual bankrupt;
- an application to set aside the gift (Insolvency Act 1986, ss.339–340).

Other provisions enable transactions at an undervalue to be set aside if there was an intention to defraud creditors at the time of the transaction, even if the transferor was then solvent, by a single application to the court without time limit and without bankruptcy. The court may then make orders to restore the position to what it would have been had the transaction not taken place (Insolvency Act 1986, ss.423–425).

It is sufficient if the purpose was to put the asset beyond the reach of a person who might at some time make a claim or otherwise prejudice the interests of such a person (*Midland Bank plc* v. *Wyatt* [1995] 1 FLR 697). It may be sufficient for this to be a substantial rather than a dominant purpose (a finding of purpose sufficient for the gift to be treated as notional capital would also appear to justify the subsequent setting aside procedure). A gift may be disregarded and set aside by a single application to the court.

However, local authorities should only take court action to recover a debt as a last resort, and they should act reasonably, discussing debt recovery with the person receiving care or their representatives (CSSG, Annex E).

The local authority should consider not recovering a debt where the debt is small and the costs of recovery would be disproportionate. In addition, if the impact of recovering the debt would the affect the client's well-being or they or their representative could not reasonably have known that the asset in question needed to be taken into account in the financial assessment, the threat of legal action should be reconsidered. A deferred payment agreement to meet the debt should also be considered.

14.2.6 Choice of care home

Within resource constraints, and where the cost to the local authority is no more than the amount specified in the adult's personal budget for accommodation of that type, residents are to be provided with their choice of home (preferred accommodation) (see **Chapter 9**). The local authority should provide information about homes in its area but the choice is not restricted to these and homes in other areas may be chosen, though fees will usually only be met to the local level and the personal budget. The chosen home must appear to the authority to be suitable for the assessed needs and the cost should not exceed what it would normally expect to pay for these needs. Where no suitable place is available at the price the local authority would usually expect to pay or above the personal budget level, it must pay a higher price if necessary. Choice cannot be restricted by the local authority to its own homes or those where it has block contracts (CSSG, Annex A).

Where a more expensive care home is chosen in another area this may be fully paid for by the local authority if being in the chosen area is part of assessed needs. There are protocols in place to deal with cross-border placements and disputes over ordinary residence (CSSG, Annex J).

Top-ups

Top-up of fees – also known as 'additional payments' – by relatives or others is permitted to enable more expensive accommodation to be chosen. Social services need assurance that the ability to pay will continue for the likely duration of stay. Failure to pay may result in the resident having to move to other accommodation. Arrangements are made through social services and not with the care home provider. Where social services decide to place a person in more expensive accommodation a third party top-up should not be sought. However, if the care home fees rise faster than the rise in the level social services pay then the difference may fall to the third party to pay.

The local authority cannot expect third party top-ups as a matter of course and must be able to show that there are homes that could provide the service required within the cost paid by social services (see CSSG, Annex A). An increase in the resident's income will not necessarily reduce the third party contribution. The resident may only pay if they have disregarded capital or income:

- during the 12-week property disregard (although the cash value represented by the house cannot be used during this period, neither should cash/assets where the total is less than the minimum prescribed threshold, i.e. ignoring disregarded assets);
- if a deferred payment agreement is in place.

The local authority has to allow the resident to retain a personal expenses allowance (PEA) of £24.90 per week in England and £25.50 per week in Wales (2015/16 rates), which cannot be used towards the basic cost of care (these levels are revised annually).

The PEA should not be spent on aspects of board, lodgings and care that have been contracted for by the local authority. This does not preclude residents buying extra services from the care home, where these are genuinely additional to services that have been contracted for by the council and/or assessed as necessary by the council or NHS.

14.2.7 Temporary stays

Admission to a care home may be for respite care or convalescence. In Wales, until April 2016, for stays of up to eight weeks the authority need not carry out a means test but may charge what is reasonable for the resident to pay. For longer stays in Wales and any stay in England, where the local authority is to charge, there must be a means test (as above) but the resident's home is disregarded if there is an intention to return and any income support (or the guarantee credit part of pension credit) or housing benefit for housing costs that is received is ignored.

Intermediate care should be paid for by the NHS or local authority for up to six weeks. This is for people who no longer need to be in hospital but may need extra support to help them recover in a care home setting for a maximum of six weeks.

A trial period in a care home is a temporary stay if it is because the need for permanent care is not ascertained. Different charging rules apply – in addition, housing benefit in respect of the person's own home will remain payable if applicable, as it is seen as a temporary absence. Alternatively, if the admission is to see if a particular home is suitable, and return home is not an option, then this will be treated as a permanent stay, and the resident assessed accordingly.

Attendance allowance

Attendance allowance, the daily living element of personal independence payment or the care component of disability living allowance, may continue indefinitely while the resident is privately fully funding his or her care but will cease after four weeks of receiving local authority or NHS financial support. This often creates some confusion. Firstly, the four weeks do not have to be continuous. Individual short stays are added together if less than 28 days apart, until the 28-day payment limit is reached. The benefit is then only paid for days spent in full or part at home, not days in care. A gap in the short-stay or hospital stay arrangements of more than 28 days winds the clock back to zero.

Secondly, some residents are retrospective self-funders. If they have a house to sell, for example, and go into care, the value of the house is ignored for 12 weeks. This means that the benefits listed above are payable during the first four weeks only. They would then stop. But after 12 weeks, they would start again because the local authority will be taking the value of the house into account, by levying a deferred payment if not already sold. So the resident (or his or her estate) will be paying full cost for care from the 13th week, even if the fees aren't actually paid until much later. They are still 'self-funding', so benefit is due. This baffles many residents and their representatives.

It may also be the case that a person was assessed at a lower rate of the above benefits while living at home but the deterioration in their health may mean a reconsideration is due, to achieve a higher rate of benefit and therefore increase their self-funding income.

Help for war pensioners

Veterans UK may pay towards the cost of a care home providing nursing care for war pensioners in specific circumstances.

14.2.8 Practitioners' problems

When considering means testing for services provided by local authorities and in particular admission to a care home, problem areas include:

- transfer of assets (see **Chapter 18**);
- limited availability of occupational or personal pensions;
- choice of care home, home closures and shortfall in fees;
- run-down in resources and refusal of the local authority to assess in advance;
- presence of a non-relative or carer in a home belonging to the individual which is being assessed (the authority but not the Department for Work and Pensions has a discretion in this situation);
- joint ownership of capital assets, especially property and joint bank accounts;
- local authority's available resources (there have been several appeal decisions concerning the implications of this).

CHAPTER 15

Other financial support

Caroline Coats

15.1 NATIONAL HEALTH SERVICE

Support for an individual who is ill, infirm or otherwise in need of medical or nursing services is available through NHS bodies and the provision of these services is considered in **Chapter 10**.

15.1.1 Charges

NHS healthcare is generally free for UK residents but there are charges for some services such as prescriptions, dental treatment, sight tests and glasses, wigs and fabric supports, and fares to hospital. An annual flu jab is free for those aged 65 or over.

There is exemption from charges if a person is:

- resident in a care home and in receipt of assistance with the fees from the local authority;
- a war disablement pensioner and the service is required because of war disability (contact the Service Personnel and Veterans Agency);
- on a low income or in receipt of e.g. income-based jobseeker's allowance; income-based employment and support allowance; universal credit; pension credit guarantee credit.

Low income scheme

To qualify for full or partial remission from NHS charges (form HC1) a person must be aged over 60 and with capital of less than £16,000 (£23,250 if resident at a care home, £24,000 in Wales). An HC2 certificate is issued to those qualifying for full help and extends to their partner. It lasts between six months and five years depending upon the individual's circumstances. It gives entitlement to the full cost of NHS dental treatment and vouchers towards the costs of glasses/contact lenses. Reasonable travel costs to receive NHS treatment from a consultant are also paid for. An HC3 certificate gives entitlement to partial help and states the maximum the individual is expected to pay. It lasts the same amount of time as the HC2 certificate.

If a charge is paid for an item or a service that could have been received free or at a reduced cost, a refund may be obtained within three months (form HC5). The form must be requested at the time of payment, as it is not available later. If an item/service is received free or at reduced cost when full charge should have been made a maximum penalty of £100 can be issued.

Prescriptions

Help with the cost of prescriptions is possible by purchasing a prepayment certificate lasting for three months or a year (form PPC). Medicines administered in hospital or at an NHS walk-in centre are free. Otherwise, free prescriptions are obtained by completing the declaration on the reverse of the prescription, if the person is aged 60 or over or suffering from or requiring any of the following (and holds a MedEx certificate obtained by form FP92A from their doctor and which lasts for five years):

- a permanent fistula (e.g. caecostomy, colostomy, laryngostomy or ileostomy) requiring an appliance or continuous surgical dressing;
- a form of hypoadrenalism (e.g. Addison's disease) for which specific substitution therapy is needed;
- diabetes insipidus or other forms of hypopituitarism;
- diabetes mellitus, except where treatment is by diet alone;
- hypoparathyroidism;
- myasthenia gravis;
- myxoedema (hypothyroidism requiring thyroid hormone replacement);
- epilepsy requiring continuous anticonvulsive therapy;
- continuing physical disability which means the person cannot go out without the help of another person;
- cancer treatments.

All patients registered with a Welsh GP, who get their prescriptions from a Welsh pharmacist, are entitled to free prescriptions. Welsh patients living in Wales but registered with a GP practice in England are able to apply to their Local Health Board for an entitlement card, to get their prescription dispensed for free providing they take it to a Welsh pharmacy to get it dispensed. Wigs and appliances are also free of charge.

Sight tests

To qualify for a free NHS sight test a person must:

- be aged 60 or over;
- be registered blind or partially sighted;
- have a complex lens prescription;
- suffer from diabetes or glaucoma;

- be aged 40 or over and the parent, brother, sister or child of someone with glaucoma; or
- be a patient of the Hospital Eye Service.

Dental examinations

Dental examinations carried out in Wales are free for those aged 60 and over living in Wales.

Glasses

A voucher is available to buy or repair glasses if the older person is in receipt of pension credit guarantee credit or has a valid HC2 certificate, entitling the recipient to help with their healthcare costs.

Healthcare travel costs scheme

The costs of travel to hospital for diagnostic services or treatment while under the care of a consultant working for the NHS or referral by a doctor or dentist for the same may be recovered by patients exempt from charges because they have a low income or are in receipt of a qualifying welfare benefit. The services received:

- must not be primary care medical services or dental services; and
- must not be provided during the same visit and on the same premises occupied by the doctor or dentist making the referral.

Claims should be submitted and will be reimbursed in cash on the day of the appointment. Payment in advance may be requested in cases of difficulty. Any questions should be raised with the hospital before travelling. The cheapest means of transport should be used at the time of travel, bearing in mind the journey required, age, medical condition and any other relevant factors. Options may include public transport, community transport, a voluntary car scheme or a private car. Taxis will be an exception and should be cleared by the hospital beforehand. Car parking and road tolls are also reimbursed. Those travelling by car to a London hospital within the congestion charge area should discuss this with the hospital before travelling.

If the consultant, doctor, dentist or other health professional involved believes that for medical reasons an escort is required on the journey, the escort's travel expenses may also be claimed. Ensure confirmation is obtained that an escort is necessary before travelling.

Travel costs for visiting a patient in hospital cannot be claimed.

Hospital services

No charge is made for NHS hospital services, whether or not as an in-patient, but social security benefits are affected while in hospital. This depends on the benefit and the length of stay. Means-tested benefits will be reassessed. Usually there is no change for the first four weeks, but then some benefits cease and others are reduced:

- Jobseeker's allowance – stops after two weeks.
- Attendance allowance, constant attendance allowance and disability living allowance stop after four weeks.
- Income support, pension credit and income-based jobseeker's allowance may be reduced after four weeks.
- Carer's allowance may stop as soon as a person goes into hospital, or may continue for up to 12 weeks.
- Disability premium, enhanced disability premium and higher pensioner premium paid with income support may stop after 52 weeks.
- Winter fuel payment – those aged 60 or over may still be eligible until they have been in hospital for more than 52 weeks.
- Housing benefit and council tax benefit – cease after 52 weeks.

Benefits are reinstated during temporary absences but there are linking provisions for successive hospital stays. After one year in hospital the benefit paid to a patient is reduced to a weekly sum fixed annually:

- further benefits may be paid to any dependants;
- a personal expenses allowance is retained and when the patient is mentally incapacitated this may be collected by the hospital authorities and held in a special account.

It is not always easy to determine whether a claimant is in hospital. The question is whether the individual is receiving free in-patient treatment in a hospital or similar institution.

15.1.2 Equipment

The integrated community equipment service buys, delivers, collects, maintains and decontaminates community loan equipment. It is provided on the request of a qualified health professional involved with the patient's care. The equipment provided is aimed at keeping people independent and safe in their own homes, such as:

- moving and handling equipment;
- transfer aids;
- walking aids;
- bathing aids;
- pressure relieving equipment;
- bed safety rails;

- chair raisers;
- alarms;
- ramps and grab rails;
- keysafe;
- special footwear.

Other items may be provided on prescription, such as:

- oxygen cylinders;
- diabetes equipment;
- elastic stockings;
- incontinence pads and related equipment.

15.1.3   Information

For health advice information including details of local health services contact the following helplines:

- 0300 330 1348 – dental services;
- 0300 330 1343 – Low Income Scheme;
- 0300 330 1341 – medical exemption certificates;
- 0300 330 1341 – prescription prepayment certificates (PPCs);
- 0300 330 1349 – prescription services;
- 0300 330 1347 – tax credit certificates;
- 0300 123 0849 – to order paper copy HC12, HC5 and HC1 (SC) forms;
- 0300 330 1343 – all other queries.

See **www.nhsbsa.nhs.uk**.

15.2   NHS DIRECT PAYMENTS

15.2.1   Sources of law

- Mental Capacity Act 2005.
- National Health Service Act 2006.
- Safeguarding Vulnerable Groups Act 2006.
- Local Authority, Social Services and National Health Service Complaints (England) Regulations 2009, SI 2009/309.
- National Health Service (Direct Payments) Regulations 2013, SI 2013/1617.
- Care and Support (Direct Payments) Regulations 2014, SI 2014/2871.

Personal health budgets are an amount of money to support the patient's identified health and well-being needs, planned and agreed between them and their local NHS team. This allows people with long-term conditions and disabilities more control over their care.

The agreed care plan sets out the patient's personal health and well-being needs, the health outcomes they want to achieve, the amount of money in the budget and how the money is planned to be spent. A personal health budget may be used to pay for a wide range of items, services, therapies, personal care and equipment.

Since October 2014 adults in England receiving NHS continuing healthcare have a right to a personal health budget. Clinical commissioning groups (CCGs) may offer a personal health budget to other people with long-term conditions, if they would benefit from it. There is no obligation for the patient to have a personal budget.

A personal health budget may be managed in three ways (or a combination):

- Notional budget – no money changes hands. The patient discusses with the NHS how the budget is to be spent and then the CCG arranges the agreed care and support.
- Real budget held by a third party – such as an organisation or trust, who then buys the agreed care and support.
- Direct payment – the patient gets the cash to buy the agreed care and support.

On 4 September 2014, NHS England launched the Integrated Personal Commissioning Programme. If the patient has a personal budget for care and support from social services, and their local NHS team agrees, they may also have a personal health budget. Both may be paid into the same account as a direct payment to buy the agreed care and support needed.

Recipients will:

- be required to notify the CCG or local authority if their conditions or circumstances change sufficiently to require a reassessment of their condition or their package of care;
- provide a distinct and secure means of receiving a direct payment;
- provide evidence of and information about their spending, through the provision of receipts or any other information as required;
- agree to ongoing review to ensure that the care plan is meeting their care needs.

15.3 GRANTS AND SUBSIDIES

15.3.1 Sources of law

- Housing Grants, Construction and Regeneration Act 1996.
- Housing Act 2004.
- Care Act 2014.
- Social Services and Well-being (Wales) Act 2014.
- Regulatory Reform (Housing Assistance) (England and Wales) Order 2002, SI 2002/1860.

15.3.2 Housing grants

Almost all housing grants are now payable at the discretion of the local authority, including renovation grants, and grants for works to common parts of a building and houses in multiple occupation. The Regulatory Reform (Housing Assistance) (England and Wales) Order 2002, SI 2002/1860 gives powers to the local authority to improve living conditions in its area in the way it considers the most appropriate.

A grant is only likely to be mandatory when it is for defined works to make the dwelling suitable for a disabled occupier. For example, an application might be made to meet part or all of the cost of works needed to facilitate access to the dwelling, but the authority must be satisfied that the works are both:

- necessary and appropriate to meet the need; and
- reasonable and practicable having regard to the age and condition of the dwelling.

Local housing authority assistance

The 2002 Order gives local housing authorities power to provide assistance for:

- repair, improvement and adaptation of housing;
- the demolition of living accommodation and assistance with rebuilding costs;
- the acquisition of new accommodation where the property has been either compulsorily or voluntarily purchased by the local authority or it considers it is not economic to adapt or improve the residence.

Each local housing authority has a published policy, which is also available in libraries and citizens' advice bureaux on how it uses the powers. The policy will set out such things as eligibility, timescales, conditions that may be attached and the type of assistance that is available. This may take any form including the giving of grants, loans, material and/or advice. The local authority is required to:

- provide written terms and conditions under which the assistance is given;
- ensure appropriate information is given about the extent of any obligation being taken on;
- consider ability to make repayment.

There is no limit on the amount of help and it may be in addition to a disabled facilities grant.

Disabled facilities grants

Under the Housing Grants, Construction and Regeneration Act 1996 a person is treated as disabled if they are registered disabled with social services or suffering from:

- substantially impaired sight, hearing or speech;

- a mental disorder or impairment;
- substantial physical disablement.

Mandatory grants (maximum £30,000 in England or £36,000 in Wales) are awarded to provide access to the home and basic amenities. Adaptations must be 'necessary and appropriate' and 'reasonable and possible', for example:

- improved access;
- installing ramps;
- widening doors;
- installing a stair lift;
- providing a downstairs bathroom;
- suitable kitchen or bathroom facilities (for independent use);
- home safety;
- improved lighting;
- heating and lighting controls (for independent use);
- improved heating;
- garden access.

Discretionary grants are also available. There is no restriction on the amount and they may be given in addition to the mandatory grant, for example:

- to provide adaptations not covered by the mandatory grant;
- to top up the grant because the work is particularly expensive;
- to assist a move to a more suitable property.

The means test is applied to the disabled person and his or her spouse or partner. Savings below £6,000 are ignored and tariff income applied to savings above that sum. There is also an assessment of basic needs. If income is less a contribution is not normally required; if it is more then there may be a partial or no award.

A certificate is required that the disabled person will live in the property for at least five years after the work is completed. If the property is sold within 10 years a maximum of £10,000 may be recouped by the local authority provided the work costs at least £5,000.

Application is made to the housing department although it may also be made via the social services department. Social services conduct a needs assessment and decide what adaptations are necessary and appropriate, and make recommendations. An environmental health officer will then assess whether the proposed works are reasonable and practical for the property. Decisions should be given within six months and work should be completed within 12 months. Grants are not normally awarded if work has started before local authority approval is obtained. If the works are assessed as eligible for a grant, the housing department cannot refuse to pay on the grounds of lack of funds (*R* v. *Birmingham City Council, ex p Mohammed* [1999] 1 WLR 33).

If the works are not eligible, but the person is assessed by social services under the Care Act 2014, s.9 or Social Services and Well-being (Wales) Act 2014, s.19, as needing assistance with adaptations to the home, then social services may still be under a duty to make such arrangements (see **Chapter 8**).

Minor adaptations

All adaptations costing £1,000 or less are provided free of charge. In Wales there is a Rapid Response Adaptations Programme to provide small-scale adaptations quickly.

Home improvement agencies

These are not-for-profit organisations. They provide support for vulnerable people to help them undertake adaptations, repairs and improvements to their home. They will provide guidance through the financial assessment, planning and checking the accreditation of builders/suppliers. They may also provide services and guidance in connection with gardening, decorating, security and energy efficiency. They are also able to assist in privately funded cases.

Home Energy Efficiency Scheme (Green Deal)

The Green Deal helps householders make energy-saving improvements, for example:

- draught proofing;
- double glazing;
- insulation;
- heating;
- solar panels or heat pumps.

Grants are available for insulation, draught-proofing and energy efficiency advice to those who own or privately rent their home. The landlord's consent is required for improvements to rented accommodation and there are restrictions on resulting rent increases. The claimant's property must be assessed first, and they may have to pay for the assessment. The document, called a Green Deal advice report, is valid for 10 years and contains:

- An Energy Performance Certificate, that rates the claimant's home for energy efficiency.
- An occupancy assessment measuring how much energy each occupier uses.
- Recommended improvements.
- Estimate of potential money saved.

A Green Deal finance plan may be arranged to pay for the improvements. Green Deal repayments are automatically added to the person's electricity bill and the obligation to pay stays with the property.

The Green Deal Home Improvement Fund

It may be possible to claim back money from the government if energy-saving home improvements are made.

Up to £1,250 towards the cost of installing any two of the following may be claimed back:

- a condensing gas boiler on mains gas;
- double or triple glazing as a replacement for single glazing;
- secondary glazing;
- energy efficient replacement external doors;
- cavity wall insulation;
- floor insulation;
- flat-roof insulation;
- insulation for a room in the roof;
- a replacement warm air unit;
- fan-assisted storage heaters;
- a waste water heat recovery system.

Up to £500 more can be claimed if the person applies within 12 months of buying a home.

Energy company obligation

Energy companies may help to improve the homes of those receiving certain benefits, or living in hard-to-treat properties.

Warm home discount scheme

A one-off discount on the person's electricity bill may be automatically paid where the supplier is part of the 'warm home discount scheme' and the claimant is in receipt of the guarantee credit element of pension credit. Some suppliers extend the scheme to vulnerable people on a low income. The Warm Home Discount Team can be contacted on Tel: 0345 603 9439 or by writing to Pink Zone, 1st Floor, Peel Park, Brunel Way, Blackpool, FY4 5ES.

15.3.3 Subsidies

Travel concessions

BLUE BADGE PARKING

This entitles the holder to parking concessions because they are blind or have severe walking difficulties. It allows parking near shops, public buildings and other places for extended periods without charge. Those entitled to attendance allowance or the mobility component of disability living allowance qualify for a blue badge. It can be obtained from local authority social services departments.

DISABLED PERSON'S RAILCARD

This gives entitlement to a one-third reduction in the cost of most train journeys. Adult companions also get a one-third reduction. It can be obtained from train operators who may provide details of other assistance and concessions. The cost is £20 for a one-year card and £54 for a three-year card.

ROAD TAX EXEMPTION

One hundred per cent qualification for this concession depends on receipt of the higher rate mobility component of the disability living allowance, enhanced mobility personal independence payment or war pensioners' mobility supplement. Fifty per cent exemption is available for those in receipt of standard mobility personal independence payment. It can be obtained from the Driver and Vehicle Licensing Agency (DVLA, Swansea SA99 1DZ) for one car used for the benefit of that person. It cannot be backdated.

Mobility scooters, powered wheelchairs and invalid carriages must be limited to 4mph on footpaths and a maximum speed of 8mph on the road to be exempt.

MOTABILITY SCHEME

Qualification depends on receipt of the mobility component of disability living allowance, enhanced rate of mobility component of personal independence payment or war pensioners' mobility supplement. The benefit is paid direct to Motability, a registered charity, which arranges concessionary rates for hire, purchase, adaptation, insurance and service costs of a suitable vehicle.

OTHER ASSISTANCE

Local authorities may operate differing schemes, for example:

- dial-a-ride;
- bus pass;
- taxi tokens;
- vouchers.

Gas and electricity

Those who meet the age criterion (which changes every year) automatically receive the winter fuel payment) provided they meet the qualifying conditions. Those that do not receive it need to apply by 30 March (tel: 08459 151515, Mon–Fri,

8am–6pm). Cold weather payments per qualifying week (average temperature 0° Celsius for seven consecutive days) may be paid in addition.

Suppliers will give general advice on efficient appliances and will assess heating systems and advise on improvements. Suppliers have codes of practice which should be referred to if problems arise and payment schemes include prepayment, monthly budget and flexible payments. They may offer capped or fixed price tariffs but check that these are not higher than the standard tariff. Some suppliers offer social tariffs which are equal to their cheapest rates. Eligibility criteria vary. Payment by direct debit is usually cheaper. Consumers receiving income support or the guarantee credit part of pension credit may arrange direct payments.

Protection against disconnection is given to customers of pensionable age as they will not be disconnected between 1 October and 31 March if they cannot pay. Licence conditions 12A (British Gas) and 19 (public electricity companies) set out procedures to be followed. Prepayment meters may be offered or payment arrangements made for paying off arrears. Suppliers must have published codes of practice they will follow when dealing with those in arrears and setting out when they will disconnect.

If payments are made to a landlord for gas or electricity there is a maximum price they may charge called the maximum resale price. If threatened with disconnection inform the local authority and the supplier. Consumer Focus (020 7799 7900) and Consumer Direct (08454 040506) may also be able to assist.

Telephone

A range of door phones, intercoms and doorbells are widely available. Assistive telephones with tracking devices/man down technology are designed for ease of use by the elderly. Help may also be available from:

- the social services department of the local authority under the Care Act 2014, s.9 or Social Services and Well-being (Wales) Act 2014, s.19;
- BT, which operates rebate schemes and a protected services scheme: **http://btplc.com/Inclusion/ProductsAndServices/ServicesfromBT/ Otherservices.**

Television licence

Concessions are available to retired people of pensionable age who live in certain types of accommodation (care homes and some sheltered accommodation). A 50 per cent concession is available if the person is blind/severely sight impaired (partially sighted people do not qualify). Contact: TV Licensing, Blind Concession Group, Darlington, DL98 1TL.

Free licences are available for all those aged over 75 years (Communications (Television Licensing) Regulations 2004, SI 2004/692). Contact the Concessionary Licensing Centre, TV Licensing, Barton House, Bond Street, Bristol BS19 1TL

(Tel: 01272 230130). A free over-75 licence covers only the person's main address. People with another property must buy an additional licence.

Water

Protection is afforded against disconnection in certain circumstances and it is unlawful to arrange automatic disconnection on non-payment.

Council tax reduction

If the person needs extra space for a wheelchair or if their bed is in the main room downstairs, they may qualify for a reduction by one band of council tax. Discounts may also be available if they have a live-in carer. See **13.7** for more detail.

Other

Private businesses are often willing to make home visits to provide their services and may offer discounted rates, for example hairdressers, chiropodists, chiropractors, beauticians and therapists. However, many concessions for the elderly are little more than marketing tactics.

15.4 FAMILY AND CHARITIES

15.4.1 Family

Financial support may also be given to an older person by members of the family, normally on an informal basis without any legal commitment:

- care should be taken to ensure that support does not result in the reduction or loss of means-tested funding or increased charges for local authority services;
- informal carers should claim all financial benefits that are available as of right either in respect of the person cared for or for themselves as carers.

In case means testing applies it may be better to buy useful items and give these, rather than to make gifts of money. Another way may be to carry out tasks such as gardening or shopping.

15.4.2 Charities

Many charities, national and local, exist for the purpose of giving support to elderly or disabled people and this may include help with long-term care costs. They do not normally pay for services that should be paid for by the local authority.

See Charity Search (**www.charitysearch.org.uk**) to locate a suitable charity and also check with charities assisting the professions or the elderly.

419

15.5   PRIVATE AND VOLUNTARY CARE AGENCIES

Social services may be able to provide details of private and voluntary care agencies in your area. Agencies are required to register with the Care Quality Commission (CQC) in England or the Care and Social Services Inspectorate for Wales (CSSIW) and adopt the relevant essential standards of care.

Care agencies in Wales are obliged (whereas in England the obligation has been removed) to provide to prospective users a service user's guide which includes:

- the aims and objectives of the agency;
- the nature of the services provided, including specialist services;
- people for whom the service is provided;
- an overview of the process for the delivery of care and support from initial referral, through needs and risk assessment and development of the service user plan, to review of the care and reassessment of need;
- key contract terms and conditions;
- the complaints procedure;
- the quality assurance process;
- specific information on key policies and procedures: how to contact the CQC or CSSIW, social services, healthcare authorities and the Health and Care Professions Council or the Care Council for Wales;
- hours of operation;
- details of insurance cover.

The care requirements of service users, their personal or family carers when appropriate, should be individually assessed before they are offered a personal domiciliary care service and a care plan is written.

The contract between the service user and the service provider should specify the following, unless these appear in the service user's guide and care plan:

- name, address and telephone number of agency;
- contact number for out-of-hours and details of how to access the service;
- contact number for the office of regular care workers and their manager;
- areas of activity which care or support workers will and will not undertake and the degree of flexibility in the provision of personal care;
- circumstances in which the service may be cancelled or withdrawn including temporary cancellation by the service user;
- fees payable for the service, and by whom;
- rights and responsibilities of both parties (including insurance) and liability if there is a breach of contract or any damage occurring in the home;
- arrangements for monitoring and review of needs and for updating the assessment and the individual service user plan;
- process for assuring the quality of the service, monitoring and supervision of staff;

- supplies and/or equipment to be made available by the service user and by the agency;
- respective responsibilities of the service user and of the agency in relation to health and safety matters and arrangements to cover holidays and sickness;
- key holding and other arrangements agreed for entering or leaving the home.

When interviewing applicants, it may help to have someone else present to assist and to take up references.

CHAPTER 16

Financial matters

Julia Abrey and Imogen Davies

16.1 INVESTMENT ADVICE

Reference should be made to the following chapters:

- **Chapter 3** for the practice rules relating to investment business; for rules relating to the giving of financial advice; and for information in relation to financial services.
- **Chapter 4** where the client is incapable of dealing with financial affairs.
- **Chapter 13** for claims and payments relating to benefits.

Age UK's website **www.ageuk.org/money-matters** has a section on income and tax containing detailed information (which also covers council tax and equity release), links to factsheets and a tax calculator. There are also useful factsheets, in particular Factsheet 19: *State Pension*; Factsheet 48: *Pension Credit*; Factsheet 12: *Planning for Retirement: Money and Tax*.

16.2 PENSIONS

Most older clients will be at the stage where they are drawing (or entitled to draw) such pensions as they have. However, do not overlook the tax advantages of making further pension contributions, when permitted, and the potential growth in a pension or pension fund, if the pension is deferred.

There are tax incentives for individuals to provide for their own pensions:

- Private pension contributions are tax free up to certain limits. Tax will be paid at the highest income tax rate if contributions exceed the lower of 100 per cent of earnings in a year or the annual allowance of £40,000 (the annual allowance reduces to £10,000 a year if certain types of withdrawal from the pension have started). There is also a lifetime contribution allowance of £1.25 million.
- Pension funds are exempt from income tax and capital gains tax.
- Part of the pension can be taken as a tax-free lump sum.

New rules since April 2015 provide a greater level of flexibility for those aged over 55 with a defined contribution pension scheme as to how they can access and use their pension.

16.2.1   State retirement pension

It is no longer necessary to be fully retired from work before drawing the state pension. A taxable pension is paid on attaining state pension age but the claimant must have an adequate national insurance (NI) contributions record. An inadequate record means entitlement to a reduced pension or none at all. A claim can be based on the claimant's own contributions or on a spouse's/former spouse's or civil partner's/former civil partner's record. The state pension age (which was 65 for men and 60 for women) has been undergoing change since April 2010. The changes will see the state pension age rise to 65 for women between April 2016 and November 2018 and then to 66, 67 and 68 for both men and women. See the calculator at **www.gov.uk/calculate-state-pension**. There are plans to change state pension ages further.

Since April 2010 the age for entitlement to a number of benefits and social security provisions, previously linked to age 60, has increased as the state pension age for women has risen. These changes affect both men and women; however, men who were 60 or over on 5 April 2010 have not lost any benefits they were already receiving.

The state pension system is changing from 6 April 2016. Different rules will apply to those who reach state pension age before 6 April 2016 and those who will do so after that date.

Those living abroad should contact the International Pension Centre tvp.internationalqueries@dwp.gsi.gov.uk and look at **www.gov.uk/state-pension-if-you-retire-abroad/how-to-claim**. See also **www.gov.uk/browse/working/state-pension**.

Amount

THOSE WHO REACH STATE PENSION AGE BEFORE 6 APRIL 2016

These individuals will not be affected by the new rules even if they defer taking their state pension.

The state pension can be made up of a combination of different types of pension or addition. Each has separate entitlement criteria which have to be met. The types of pension are:

- **Basic state pension**. The full rate of basic pension will be received if NI contributions have been paid or credited for most years of working life. If not enough contributions have been made a partial pension may be paid. A basic pension may be received or increased using the NI contributions of a spouse or civil partner but these is a limit on how much this entitlement or increase can be. A weekly age addition is paid on reaching 80 years. Before April 2010, additions could be paid for dependants (e.g. a spouse/civil partner) unless they received some other benefits or had earnings above certain limits. It is no longer possible to claim this increase after April 2010, though if it was claimed prior to this date it can be kept until either the conditions for the increase are no longer met, or until April 2020, whichever occurs first.

- **Graduated retirement benefit**. This is based on graduated contributions paid on earnings between April 1961 and April 1975 and will be received when the basic pension is claimed. An individual may also be entitled to a graduated pension even if they do not qualify for a basic pension. The amounts are usually very small and are often paid as a lump sum rather than weekly payments.
- **Additional state pension**. This is not a fixed amount but is based on contributions from April 1978 until April 2002 (State Earnings Related Pension Scheme – SERPS) and after this date the State Second Pension (S2P). S2P also provides extra pension to certain carers, disabled people and others (who may not be earning) and low paid workers. The government website, **www.gov.uk/additional-state-pension/overview** gives more details about the additional state pension. It is possible instead of paying into the additional state pension to join a 'contracted out' occupational scheme (if available) or to take out a personal pension. Professional financial advice should be taken when considering these options.
- **Over 80s pension**. Those aged 80 or over, who have little or no basic state pension, can claim a pension even if they have not paid NI contributions, but there is a residence qualification (which in some circumstances may be satisfied by residence in another EU country).
- **Pension credit** is a benefit designed to provide pensioners with a minimum level of income and rewards those who have saved during their working life (see **13.2.2**).

THOSE WHO REACH STATE PENSION AGE AFTER 6 APRIL 2016

The new state pension system will be simpler than the pre-April 2016 system. All the elements of the state pension will be consolidated into a single amount called the 'Foundation Amount', the starting value of which will be set above the basic level of means-tested support. Qualification for the full state pension will require 35 years of contracted-in NI contributions or credits. No contracted-out benefits in either a workplace pension scheme and/or a personal pension are permitted to receive the full state pension. Those who do not have the full 35 years will be entitled to a pro rata amount, providing that they meet the new 10-year minimum qualifying period.

The pension will be reduced for those who have contracted out of the additional state pension, to reflect their lower NI contributions.

There are transitional provisions for those who have built up qualifying years or credits before 6 April 2016 to ensure that they will not receive a lower pension amount than they would have received under the previous system although they will have to meet the new 10-year minimum qualifying period. The calculations may be complex in the early years of the new system to take into account individuals with differing pension entitlements – i.e. those contracting out of the additional state pension and those with fewer qualifying years. As time goes by, however, the complexities will fall away. Those aged over 55 can request a pension statement under the new rules. The statement will give individuals an estimate of how much they will get under the new state pension based on their current NI record. The statement is an estimate, rather than a guarantee as it is based on current information and the position may change as further contributions are made. The state pension statement service is planned to be extended until everyone of working age will be able to request one.

Widows, widowers and surviving civil partners

A widow, widower or surviving civil partner who has reached pension age but does not qualify for their own full pension may use their spouse's/partner's contribution record to qualify for a full basic state pension.

A widow, widower or civil partner can inherit half of their spouse's/partner's graduated retirement benefit if both are over pension age at death. On the death of a spouse or civil partner, the survivor (if they reached state pension age after 6 April 2010) may be able to inherit up to 50 per cent of the deceased spouse's or civil partner's additional state pension. The amount which can be inherited depends on the NI contributions and age of the deceased spouse or civil partner.

Separation, divorce and dissolution of civil partnership

PRE-2016 RULES

It may be possible to rely upon a spouse's/civil partner's or ex-spouse's/ex-civil partner's contributions record:

- In certain situations, a separated wife may be able to claim the married woman's retirement pension on her husband's record but only from the date that he draws his pension.
- Following divorce either spouse may, on reaching pensionable age before 6 April 2016, use their former spouse's record during the marriage (or from the start of working life to the divorce) to get a better pension than on their own record. The rules for divorced couples also apply to a dissolved civil partnership. Those divorced before state pension age may need to pay further contributions after divorce to qualify for a full basic pension. The effect of remarriage or entering into a new civil partnership on the ability to claim a pension based on a

former spouse's/partner's contributions will depend on whether the spouse/partner who is remarrying is over state pension age. If they are under age, the right will be lost.

- Divorced or separated people or those whose civil partnership has been dissolved may have had their additional state pension considered as a financial asset which can be shared in a settlement through a pension sharing order.

POST-2016 RULES

It may be possible to claim a share of an ex-spouse's or ex-partner's protected pension through a pension sharing order. For most people reaching state pension age on or after 6 April 2016, the amount of state pension calculated under the current rules will be the least they will receive.

Deferral

Once people reach state pension age they can draw their state pension even if they are still working. People who have reached the state pension age can, if they wish, defer drawing their pension so as to receive a higher pension or lump sum payment at a later date. People who have started to draw their pension can choose to defer it, though they can only do so once.

Before April 2005 if a person deferred his or her state pension it was increased by 7.5 per cent for each year of deferment.

From 6 April 2005, an individual's pension increases by about 10.4 per cent for each year that it is not drawn. If an individual chooses a lump sum payment instead of receiving a higher pension, there will be interest of at least 2 per cent above the Bank of England base rate. If the pension is deferred for at least five weeks, it will increase by 1 per cent for every five weeks. There cannot be any increases to an addition a person receives for a dependent husband, wife or civil partner.

The deferral rules will change after 6 April 2016. Deferral will still be possible but the deferred payment will not be able to be paid as a lump sum and an increased pension once it is claimed will be the only option. The increase will reduce from 10.4 per cent to about 5.8 per cent.

16.2.2 Workplace pensions

Workplace pensions are arranged by employers (e.g. occupational or company pension schemes) and may be contributory or non-contributory. A separate trust fund is set up and employees receive a booklet setting out the terms. In general, benefits normally include:

- a pension at a specified age;
- a death benefit for those who die before retirement;
- a widow's, widower's or surviving civil partner's pension.

There are HMRC restrictions on:

- the maximum pension;
- the amount of the lump sum;
- the size of any widow's, widower's or surviving civil partner's pension following death.

Types of scheme

The available types of scheme include:

- **Defined benefit** – where pension is a proportion of salary for the last year (or average of the last few years) and is based on years worked multiplied by a set fraction (e.g. 30/60ths); the pension may be contracted into or out of the additional state pension. Many employers have closed or are closing this kind of scheme.
- **Average earnings** – where pension is based upon average earnings over the period of participation with a set calculation being applied for the pension.
- **Flat rate pension** – which is based on the number of years employed.
- **Defined contribution pension** – which depends upon the size of the employee's contribution to an investment fund and the growth in that fund; such pension may be contracted into the additional state pension. From April 2012, the additional state pension cannot be contracted out of on a defined contribution basis.
- **Automatic enrolment** – older employees who are under state pension age but not already in a workplace pension scheme may benefit from the introduction in 2012 of auto-enrolment into a workplace pension scheme. The scheme is being introduced incrementally, but by 2018 all employers must have automatically enrolled all their eligible workers into a scheme unless the employee opts out. Eligible employees earn over £10,000 per year (2015–16) but can work full or part time.

See **www.gov.uk/browse/working/workplace-personal-pensions** for more information.

Additional voluntary contributions

Additional voluntary contributions (AVCs) are a way of saving for retirement through a workplace pension scheme. Full tax relief is available on additional contributions (subject to limits) and free-standing AVCs (FSAVCs) can also be made to personal pension plans.

AVC schemes are mainly either a defined contribution or defined benefit scheme. There is more flexibility including early retirement or withdrawal, preserved rights after two years in a scheme and transfer to another company scheme or to a personal pension.

The benefits of AVCs are:

- lower administration charges in most cases than if invested into a separate pension scheme;
- the opportunity to stop or vary the amount paid;
- tax relief on contributions up to certain limits.

Some companies no longer offer AVCs as there are a range of options for topping up a company pension by other means.

16.2.3 Personal pensions

Self-employed people and employees may contribute to personal pensions:

- for employees this may be instead of the additional state pension, stakeholder pension or a workplace scheme;
- the rules about how much an employer has to pay into a workplace scheme is changing under auto-enrolment (see **16.2.2**);
- there are HMRC restrictions on contributions, retirement age and benefits.

Section 226 pension policies (introduced by the Income and Corporation Taxes Act 1970) were available solely for the self-employed until July 1988 and those then in existence may continue, be increased or reinstated if frozen, but the HMRC restrictions were slightly different from the later personal pensions.

From April 2010 the earliest age a pension can be taken is 55 though there are certain circumstances allowing it to be drawn before. It is possible to pay into a personal pension plan on someone else's behalf to help with their contributions.

Options

It is important to take independent financial advice on pension options, but be aware that:

- Up to 25 per cent of the fund can be taken as a tax-free lump sum and there is then a six-month period to start taking the remaining 75 per cent.
- The options are usually either to buy an annuity or invest in a fund which allows withdrawals (drawdown).
- Pension rule changes from April 2015 mean that it is no longer compulsory to buy an annuity by age 75.
- A range of drawdown funds exist – capped and flexi access are two available types.
- Treating the pension pot as a bank account is a new option, withdrawing funds as needed. It is not yet clear how these schemes (especially their taxation) will work in practice and their operation is subject to the restriction of the lifetime allowance of £1.25 million.

16.2.4   Stakeholder pensions

Stakeholder pensions are designed for people without access to employer-sponsored pension arrangements. They are a kind of personal pension but have to meet some minimum standards set by government in respect of management charges, the need for independent trustees and auditors and the ability for members to start and stop payments and switch providers.

The rules about this kind of pension changed on 1 October 2012. The introduction of auto-enrolment means that employers now do not have to offer the scheme to new or returning employees. Employers must continue to pay contributions from employees' income into any scheme they have set up before 1 October 2012 until employees request them to stop, cease contributing or leave. Funds in the stakeholder pension pot can be transferred to another pension provider.

16.3   TAXATION

16.3.1   Income tax

Allowances for elderly people

There are some allowances and reliefs with particular relevance for older taxpayers:

- The system of giving higher allowances to older people has almost disappeared. Since 5 April 2015 everyone receives the same personal allowance of £10,600 except for those born before 6 April 1938 who will receive £10,660. Those who qualify for the additional allowance but who have income of more than £27,700 will have their allowance reduced slightly but not to below the standard personal allowance.
- A widow, widower or surviving civil partner aged between 45 and state pension age at the date of bereavement may claim a bereavement allowance for the 52 weeks following the death of their spouse/civil partner (subject to various conditions including the level of the deceased spouse's civil partner's NI contribution; the allowance will be paid at the full rate if the applicant is over the age of 55 when their spouse/civil partner dies).
- A blind person's allowance may be available for those registered as blind with the local authority and any unused part may be transferred to the spouse/civil partner.
- Married couple's allowance can be claimed by a married couple or civil partners, where one of whom was born before 6 April 1935. The allowance is only worth 10 per cent of its face value in actual tax saving.
- Relief is available on gross rent (subject to a limit) from furnished rooms in the home: for information about tax on rental income generally and the 'Rent a Room' scheme, see **www.gov.uk/rent-room-in-your-home**.

Planning

Advisers must not forget the impact of self-assessment on the elderly client, particularly the dates for submission of a return and payment of tax, which should be proactively managed.

Simple steps may reduce the annual tax bill for a married couple/civil partners or assist with cash flow:

- Obtain and complete a Tax Claim Form R40 if in doubt at the end of the year. For more details and conditions which apply see **www.gov.uk/apply-tax-free-interest-on-savings/tax-free-savings**.
- Ensure that any Notice of Coding for PAYE on employment or pension income is correct; taxed income relief should be given if appropriate to secure the lower rate of tax on investment income (see **www.gov.uk/tax-codes**); reduce or increase income if 'caught in the margin': higher allowances reduce proportionately if income is more than a certain sum and this means that a high effective rate of tax is paid until the allowance is lost.
- Rearrange investments so that income is received gross (without deduction of tax) where a repayment claim would otherwise be necessary; non-taxpayers can apply to receive gross interest on bank/building society accounts (Form R85) (see **www.gov.uk/apply-tax-free-interest-on-savings/tax-free-savings**).
- Save tax free in an Individual Savings Account (ISA). ISAs can be cash or stocks and shares and an investment into one of each can be made annually. On the death of a spouse or civil partner on or after 3 December 2014, the survivor can inherit their ISA allowance.
- Transfer investments between spouses and civil partners to equalise income so that both gain the benefit of their personal allowances and the reduced rate band, any higher rate liability is minimised and neither party is caught in the margin as regards higher allowances.
- HMRC has a policy of taking individuals out of the self-assessment system where their tax can be collect by other means (i.e. PAYE or deducting at source) and there is no reason why HMRC needs to see an annual return. HMRC can be asked to remove a taxpayer from the PAYE system and if it refuses, it can be asked to justify its decision under its guidelines.
- HMRC guidance indicates that a tax return will not be required where gross income of less than £2,500 per year is received. For more details and additional conditions, see **www.gov.uk/self-assessment-tax-returns/who-must-send-a-tax-return**.
- Consider transferring allowances between spouses or civil partners in appropriate cases. The whole of any unused allowance (married couple's allowance or blind person's allowance) may be transferred or if both parties agree up to the whole of the minimum married couple's allowance or blind person's allowance may be transferred from one spouse or civil partner to the other (see **www.gov.uk/income-tax-rates**).

- As dividend tax credits are not repayable, consider a review of investments as a change to those which attract a refundable tax credit (e.g. gilt edged securities) may be beneficial and may reduce the need to complete a return (but be aware of potential capital gains tax on any change).
- Consider completing tax returns online to speed up any refund due; paper tax returns must be submitted by 31 October following the end of the tax year in question; the deadline for filing returns online is 31 January.
- Ensure that all eligible allowances have been claimed.
- Use HMRC's tax checker to estimate how much income tax should be paid: **www.gov.uk/check-income-tax**.

Information

Generally, see HM Revenue and Customs' website (**www.gov.uk/government/ organisations/hm-revenue-customs/services-information**).

The following sections/publications may be of particular use:

- Income tax and pensions (**www.gov.uk/tax-on-pension**).
- Living or retiring abroad (**www.gov.uk/tax-right-retire-abroad-return-to-uk**).
- What to do about tax and benefits after a death of a spouse (**www.gov.uk/ death-spouse-benefits-tax-pension/tax-national-insurance**).
- Employment and support allowance leaflet (**www.gov.uk/employment-support-allowance**).
- Blind person's allowance (see **www.gov.uk/blind-persons-allowance**). The number for the claiming this allowance is 0300 200 3301.
- Individual Savings Accounts (**www.gov.uk/individual-savings-accounts/ overview**).
- Self-assessment section generally (**www.gov.uk/browse/tax/self-assessment**).
- Dealing with HMRC (**www.gov.uk/browse/tax/dealing-with-hmrc**).
- Age UK Factsheet 15: *Income Tax* (**www.ageuk.org.uk**).

16.3.2 Capital gains tax

The gain in the value of an asset during the taxpayer's ownership is taxed on disposal by way of a sale or gift (transfers between spouses/civil partners are not treated as disposals). Capital gains tax (CGT) is payable on 31 January following the tax year of the disposal.

The expenses of acquiring, improving and disposing of the asset are deducted from the net sale proceeds or value to ascertain the gain.

Certain assets are exempt, e.g. an owner-occupied dwelling-house, but there is a restriction on the relief if the house is surrounded by a significant amount of land.

There is currently rebasing to March 1982, which means that only gains or losses since that date are taken into account. See **www.gov.uk/capital-gains-tax/ overview**.

Entrepreneurs' relief is available on disposals of assets used in a business or partnership, an interest in a business or partnership or shares in a trading company for which an individual worked and in which he owned at least 5 per cent of the ordinary shares which gave him at least 5 per cent of the voting rights. See **www.gov.uk/entrepreneurs-relief/eligibility**.

The net gains (after losses) of the taxpayer in the tax year are taxed at the rate of 18 per cent for a basic rate taxpayer and 28 per cent for a higher and additional rate taxpayer. But an annual exemption reduces or eliminates the taxable gain.

Independent taxation applies so each spouse or civil partner has the benefit of an annual exemption, although the losses of one spouse/civil partner cannot be set against the gains of the other.

Planning

The following strategies may be adopted to reduce potential CGT bills (the first two being for married couples and civil partners):

- ensure that realisations that produce gains are by the spouse/partner with the lower rate of tax;
- consider transferring assets into joint names before disposal to ensure utilisation of both persons' annual exemptions and/or lower rates of tax;
- review assets annually to consider disposals to use the annual exemption;
- when cash is needed dispose of assets that do not create a gain;
- realise losses prior to 5 April when a net taxable gain would arise;
- avoid making disposals that would produce a large gain shortly before death (all assets are revalued on death but CGT is not then charged);
- ensure that wills and investments are neutral for CGT purposes.

Many older people contemplate moving abroad on retirement and the implications of a change of residence or domicile upon capital taxation in this country should be first considered.

16.3.3   Inheritance tax

The capital value of all net assets held at death above a threshold (the nil rate band) (£325,000 in 2015–16) is taxed at a fixed rate (40 per cent):

- This includes lifetime gifts unless exempted (see **18.3.2**).
- The capital value of trusts may be aggregated.
- Certain types of asset are exempt or valued on a beneficial basis (e.g. business assets, agricultural property and woodlands) although conditions apply to the reliefs.

- Assets passing on death to a spouse or a charity are exempt.
- On the death of a surviving spouse or civil partner on or after 9 October 2007 where the first spouse or civil partner to die (whenever that death occurred) did not use the whole or part of the nil rate band on their death a claim may be made for the transfer of the percentage of the unused nil rate band to the estate of the second spouse. The amount transferred is the percentage of the nil rate band applicable at the time of the second death.
- From April 2017, the nil rate band threshold for the family home will increase until it reaches £500,000 in 2020. A married couple or civil partners will be able to pass on assets, including a family home, worth up to £1 million without paying any IHT. There are restrictions on the availability of the residence nil rate band; it is only available where the family home is passed to children (including adopted, step and foster children) and grandchildren. If the overall estate exceeds £2 million, the relief is reduced proportionately.

Information

See **www.gov.uk/inheritance-tax/overview**, which provides basic information and links to other specialised inheritance tax topics.

Planning

Possibilities include:

- Married couples/civil partners considering severing any joint tenancy in the matrimonial home by will leaving his or her share as tenant in common to the children either outright or in trust (but be careful to consider occupation issues between the surviving spouse/civil partner and children).
- Making gifts within the annual exemption or the small gift exemption.
- Making large gifts sooner rather than later to start the seven-year period running.
- Reviewing income to see if regular gifts from surplus income could be made which are immediately exempt (Inheritance Tax Act 1984, s.21).
- Considering investments which offer tax benefits: shares listed on the Alternative Investment Market are free of inheritance tax, subject to conditions, once owned for two years. Such investments can, however, be volatile and may not pay a dividend.

See **Chapter 18** for more detail on making gifts.

Trusts for disabled/vulnerable beneficiaries

There are special dispensations in respect of income tax, CGT and inheritance tax (IHT) for certain trusts for the benefit of disabled or vulnerable beneficiaries; see:

- Finance Act 2005, ss.23–45.
- Inheritance Tax Act 1984, ss.3A(1), (1A) and (3) and 89.

On this topic generally refer to **Chapter 19**.

CHAPTER 17

Housing

David Foster with Serdar Celebi

17.1 INTRODUCTION

Older clients normally occupy their homes as owners or as tenants. However, they may only have a licence to occupy. They may also share another person's home or allow another person to occupy or share their home. This chapter considers, in brief, the main issues which may arise in these contexts and where advice may be required and outlines some of the relevant law. Details of housing grants and subsidies are covered at **15.3** and issues on making a gift of the home at **18.4.4**.

17.2 THE ELDERLY CLIENT AT HOME

17.2.1 Choice of home or location: practical issues

People do not automatically wish to move home on reaching retirement age, but it is a good time to take stock and think ahead. The starting point is whether the client is happy and comfortable in the present home and able to cope physically and financially. Then consider how long this situation is likely to continue: putting things off may reduce the options, but a move can seldom be reversed. It may be wise to anticipate future needs by applying to go on a council or private registered provider of social housing (housing association) waiting list.

17.2.2 Contemplating moving checklist

- Will the client cope physically in the new home, e.g. access, stairs, convenience of layout, garden, security?
- Will the client cope financially in the new home, e.g. heating, maintenance and repairs?
- Is there room for all the client's personal possessions that are to be kept?
- Is the location suitable in terms of adequate facilities, e.g. shops, transport, library, post office?
- Is the location suitable in terms of necessary services, e.g. doctor, dentist, social services assistance?

- Is there enough to do in the area?
- Is it a safe and congenial environment at all times of the day and night?
- Will friends and acquaintances be lost who cannot be replaced?
- Can the client afford the costs of the move, e.g. removals, estate agent, solicitor's fees, stamp duty?
- If the client is moving nearer relatives is there a risk that those relatives will need to move?
- Is the move too hasty, e.g. after a bereavement?
- In the case of a couple, would the survivor wish to remain in the new home?

17.3   OWNER OCCUPATION

Always examine the implications as regards means-tested benefits when the sale or purchase of a dwelling for personal occupation is being considered. For more information and detail in this respect see **Chapter 13**.

17.3.1   Sole ownership

The sole owner may leave the home by will or it will pass to the next of kin on an intestacy. If the owner becomes mentally incapable and it is desired to dispose of the home or some interest in it, at present in the absence of a registered enduring power of attorney (EPA) or a lasting power of attorney (LPA) there is no alternative but to apply to the Court of Protection for the appointment of a deputy. See generally **Chapter 4**.

17.3.2   Joint ownership

Often a home will be owned jointly by husband and wife or an unmarried couple. A home may also be owned jointly by a couple of the same sex who have registered a civil partnership under the Civil Partnership Act 2004. All jointly owned property is held by the owners on trust, i.e. the joint owner will be a trustee or at least have an interest in the trust property.

Where a property is purchased or otherwise put in joint names it is important for there to be a precise statement as to how the beneficial interests are held, i.e. whether as joint tenants or tenants in common. Under a joint tenancy the survivor will automatically inherit on death. Under a tenancy in common the share as tenant in common may be left by will or pass under an intestacy and the precise shares should be agreed and recorded.

The statement is usually made in the appropriate section of the transfer deed by placing an 'X' in the relevant box (a copy should be retained) or in a separate deed of trust, but the statement to the Land Registry as to whether the survivor can give a valid receipt for capital money is not sufficient.

Upon a divorce (or judicial separation) the court may make a property adjustment between the parties and similar powers are available under the Civil Partnership Act 2004, but in the case of unmarried or unregistered same sex joint owners there are no similar procedures and the courts can only give effect to the intention and contribution of the parties.

An equitable interest in a house or flat belonging to another may arise where a person makes a financial contribution towards the cost of buying the property or pays for or contributes towards the cost of extending or improving the property.

This is likely to be of particular significance where the incentive for the financial input was the prospect of living in or sharing the home and that expectation is not fulfilled. Ideally, the expectations of the parties should be clarified and confirmed in a legal document before the arrangement is entered into, although this seldom happens within families.

An elderly client who decides to contribute a substantial sum towards the cost of purchase or improvement of a home with the intention of residing there with a member of the family will need to decide whether to do so by way of shared ownership, loan or gift. Factors to take into account, depending on circumstances, are:

- a gift has potential inheritance tax advantages, but the money may not be recoverable if needed (if a gift is to be made the sooner this is done the better as regards both inheritance tax and means testing);
- a loan or joint ownership creates vulnerability to means testing if residential care is needed at a later date;
- a loan or joint ownership protects the elderly individual in the event that the relationship breaks down but may leave the other joint owner vulnerable to having to move house;
- testamentary provision may need to be changed to compensate for a gift.

If the money is spent on building a bungalow in the grounds or providing a self-contained flat it may be best for this to be conveyed into the name of the elderly client rather than establish joint ownership in the entire property, but in that event you must ensure that the deeds are properly split and independent legal advice would be indicated.

See Law Society Practice Note: Making Gifts of Assets (6 October 2011) and **18.4.4**.

Disputes

Disputes relating to joint ownership of property may now be resolved under the Trusts of Land and Appointment of Trustees Act 1996. This overcomes various difficulties that arose under Law of Property Act 1925, s.30, although previous case law may still be relevant.

Anyone who is a trustee or who has an interest in trust property may make an application to the court which is then required to have regard to the following matters in determining the application:

- the intention of the person or persons who created the trust;
- the purpose for which the property subject to the trust is held;
- the welfare of any minor who occupies or might reasonably be expected to occupy any property subject to the trust as his or her home;
- the interests of any secured creditor of any beneficiary.

17.3.3   Incapacity of joint owner

A trustee may not generally delegate his or her powers so must act personally in any sale or other transaction. There are exceptions to this.

Under Trustee Act 1925, s.25 a trustee can delegate his or her functions by a power of attorney. This can only be for limited periods and is subject to specific safeguards.

Such a power cannot be an EPA or an LPA.

EPAs created before 1 October 2007 continue to have effect. An EPA is not revoked by the donor's mental incapacity. The attorney must apply to register the power with the Public Guardian if they believe the donor lacks or is beginning to lack capacity. EPAs dated after 29 February 2000 and earlier powers used in transactions dated after 28 February 2000 made by one of joint proprietors may only be used if:

- the donor has a beneficial interest in the land;
- there is no indication in the power that the donor did not intend the attorney to exercise trustee functions.

EPAs dated before 1 March 2000 may be used if:

- the power is registered with the Court of Protection (then the registration authority) following an application to the court before 1 March 2001; or
- an application made to the court for registration of the power before 1 March 2001 has not been finally refused.

LPAs have replaced EPAs as the principal way of choosing a decision-maker to act in the event of loss of capacity.

An EPA or LPA dated after 29 February 2000 may be used in relation to trust property if at the time it is used, the donor of the power owns a beneficial interest in that property unless contrary intention is shown in the power (Trustee Delegation Act (TDA) 1999, s.1).

A written statement by the attorney given within three months of the date of the document confirming that the donor had a beneficial interest in the property will be conclusive evidence of that fact (TDA 1999, s.2).

It will not be sufficient if the joint owner (e.g. spouse) is the sole attorney, because a capital receipt by trustees needs two signatures (TDA 1999, s.7), i.e. it cannot be signed by one person both as proprietor and as attorney for the other proprietor.

See generally Land Registry Practice Guide 9.

In the absence of an attorney with power to act as trustee, if a joint legal owner of freehold property becomes incapable by reason of mental disorder of exercising his or her functions as a trustee, a new trustee may have to be appointed before the legal estate can be dealt with.

17.3.4 Mortgages

There is no age bar to taking on a loan secured by a mortgage or charge and many lenders have become willing to consider applications from those at or near retirement. An interest-only mortgage may be available from a bank or building society under a special scheme for those who need capital (see **17.9**).

For a cautionary tale where a mother charged her home as security for her son's borrowing and the same solicitors acted for both parties, see *Clark Boyce* v. *Mouat* [1994] 1 AC 428.

17.3.5 Possession proceedings

When monthly repayments under a mortgage fall into arrears, the lender may claim possession in the local County Court and the possession order may be enforced by the bailiff under a warrant for possession.

However, since 19 November 2008 the lender must first follow the Pre-Action Protocol for Possession Claims based on Mortgage or Home Purchase Plan Arrears in Respect of Residential Property. This protocol was revised and re-issued with effect from 6 April 2015.

Under the Administration of Justice Acts 1970 and 1973 the court may adjourn the possession proceedings or suspend any possession order if the arrears and future payments which will fall due are likely to be paid within a reasonable period. In determining the reasonable period, the court should take as its starting point the full term of the mortgage: *Cheltenham and Gloucester Building Society* v. *Norgan* [1996] 1 WLR 343.

The court may use the same powers if the borrower is attempting to sell the property to give the borrower a reasonable time to complete the sale. The existence of equity in the security will be a significant factor when the court is deciding whether to exercise its discretion in the borrower's favour.

Loans taken out for consumer purposes and secured on the borrower's home are covered by the Consumer Credit Act 1974 rather than the Administration of Justice Acts mentioned and the court has wider powers to give the borrower more time to pay.

17.3.6   Grants

Under the Housing Grants, Construction and Regeneration Act 1996 various discretionary grants may be applied for from local authorities.

Mandatory disabled facility grants can be applied for under the 1996 Act currently for up to £30,000 (£36,000 in Wales). For more information, see **Chapter 15**.

17.4   LONG RESIDENTIAL LEASES

Many older clients own their homes under a long lease, in particular owners of flats, those who have a shared ownership lease and former council tenants or housing association tenants who have exercised the right to buy or acquire a flat.

17.4.1   Relevant legislation

After examining the terms of the lease and establishing for how long it is to run and the identity of the landlord, the following legislation may need to be considered. In the event of disputes the First-tier Tribunal (Property Chamber) which replaced the Leasehold Valuation Tribunal (LVT) from 1 July 2013 may have jurisdiction rather than the County Court or there may be concurrent jurisdiction. The LVT was part of the Residential Property Tribunal Service:

- Leasehold Reform Act 1967: this gives leaseholders of houses the right to buy the freehold (and in some cases the right to extend the lease).
- Landlord and Tenant Act 1985: service charges and administration charges are a common source of conflict between leaseholder and landlord. This provides that service charges are only recoverable to the extent they are reasonable and disputes may be determined by the First-tier Tribunal (Property Chamber).
- Landlord and Tenant Act 1987: this contains the right of first refusal, the right to apply for a manager to be appointed, the right to apply for the terms of a lease to be varied and related matters.
- Landlord and Tenant Act 1954, Part I: this gives security of tenure to residential tenants who hold under long leases at low rents. This is achieved by extending the leases on expiry and providing for the creation of new statutory tenancies within the Rent Act at fair rents.
- Leasehold Reform, Housing and Urban Development Act 1993: this gives most owners of long leases of flats a right as one of a group of flat owners to acquire the freehold (collective enfranchisement) or as an individual flat owner to acquire a new lease. It also gives the right to have an audit of the management of the block carried out.
- Housing Act 1996: this extends the rights of long leaseholders in relation to service charges, bad management by freeholders and the right of first refusal including a new right to appoint a surveyor to advise on service charges. It also

extends the enfranchisement and collective enfranchisement rights under the 1967 and 1993 Acts respectively.

- Commonhold and Leasehold Reform Act 2002: Part 1 of the Act introduces a new type of freehold ownership of buildings divided into flats – commonhold. Conversion of existing leasehold blocks into commonhold units will depend on the consent of every person with an interest in the land. Part 2 of the Act introduces the 'right to manage': the right to set up a company to manage without acquiring the freehold. The Act also introduced similar controls for administration charges as for service charges.

17.4.2   Shared ownership

Some councils and registered social landlords operate shared ownership schemes under which homes are part purchased and part rented on a long lease. There may be an option to purchase a greater share at a later date.

These schemes enable those with limited capital to enjoy the benefits of home ownership without borrowing, and investing available capital in this way may have advantages in regard to means-tested benefits, but increasing rents could become a problem.

Other arrangements for sheltered housing include:

- flexible tenure: option to buy, lease or share ownership;
- leasehold schemes for the elderly: buy at 70 per cent of the normal price and receive 70 per cent of value when the property is sold;
- loan stock schemes: 'buy' housing by making an interest-free loan to the trust or charity;
- buying at a discount: usually involves selling at a discount;
- a 'life share' in the property (or a part of it), usually organised through a finance company with the price depending on age, sex, marital status and the property value: there will be no return on death, but an annuity (or capital sum) may be paid to those who stop living in the property.

Ensure that the scheme is suitable for the client and that there are no restrictions which would inhibit resale. Most schemes are marketed for first-time buyers but some are designed for retired people.

17.4.3   Enfranchisement

Enfranchisement is a convenient word to describe the right to acquire the freehold, extend the lease or be granted a fresh lease. Long residential leaseholders have been given statutory rights. There is a distinction between houses and flats. The primary Act in respect of houses is the Leasehold Reform Act 1967 and that for flats the Leasehold Reform, Housing and Urban Development Act 1993.

In the case of houses, since 26 July 2002 the leaseholder has the right to acquire on fair terms the freehold or an extended lease where the following basic conditions are met:

- the original term of the lease must be at least 21 years;
- when giving notice exercising the right the leaseholder must have been the tenant of the house for the last two years.

In the case of flats, with effect from 1 November 1993, most long leaseholders paying a low rent in a predominantly residential building have the right to purchase collectively, at market value, the freehold of the building, where:

- at least two-thirds of the building is let on long leases;
- at least two-thirds of those leaseholders give notice of their wish to purchase.

Since 26 July 2002 a condition that half of the leaseholders giving notice must be resident has been abolished. In addition, most long leaseholders paying a low rent have the individual right to acquire an extended lease for a period of 90 years plus the outstanding period of the old lease.

17.5 TENANCIES

Some older clients will hold their properties under tenancies which are not long leases. Such tenants will be concerned about security of tenure, the amount of rent payable, succession to the tenancy and repairing obligations. The statutory rights in these areas vary according to the type of landlord and to some extent the date when the tenancy commenced.

The three main types of landlord are local authority type, private registered provider of social housing and private landlords. Local authorities are accountable to the local electorate and private registered providers were accountable to the Tenant Services Authority (TSA). The remit of the TSA was then expanded to regulate local authority, arm's length management organisations (ALMOs) and housing co-operatives from April 2010. The TSA then closed after the Homes and Communities Agency took over responsibility for regulation of social housing from 1 April 2012.

Government policy since 1979 has included:

- a shift from full protection of the tenant of the private landlord in terms of security of tenure and rent control to dependence on market forces: this is not retrospective so tenants do not lose any existing rights and should seek to retain earlier protected tenancies wherever possible;
- encouraging council tenants to purchase their properties through 'right to buy' legislation offering large discounts;
- encouraging privatisation of local authority housing by the transfer of council housing stock to housing associations: any tenant of a local authority whose

home is so transferred ceases to be a secure tenant and becomes an assured tenant (with a preserved right to buy);

- increasing control of public sector tenants' behaviour by the introduction of probationary tenancies and extending landlords' powers to deal with anti-social behaviour;
- moving from lifetime tenancies for public sector tenants and sustainable communities to 'flexible' fixed term tenancies.

17.5.1 Local authority type landlords

Tenants of a local authority, an urban development corporation, a housing action trust and certain other authorities will usually have the status of a secure tenant. The tenant (including most licensees) is a secure tenant provided the tenant condition is met. This condition is that the tenant resides in the dwelling as his only or principal home. (Problems arise where a tenant is absent from the dwelling for a significant period but absence for medical treatment should not affect rights as a secure tenant.)

The Housing Act 1985 (as amended) gives secure tenants long-term security of tenure and rights such as:

- the right to take in a lodger;
- the right to exchange tenancies;
- the right to buy.

However, local authorities now have the power to decide to grant probationary tenancies known as 'introductory tenancies' to all new tenants and this power is increasingly being exercised. For the first year of the tenancy the tenant in effect has no security of tenure. During this period, subject to the service of a written notice containing certain information including the reasons for bringing proceedings and the right to request an internal review, the landlord can recover possession for breaches of the tenancy agreement. After one year such tenancies automatically become secure.

In addition, since 1 April 2012, flexible tenancies have been available. Flexible tenancies should usually last for at least five years. If there is a good reason for the tenancy to be shorter, it could be for two years. A flexible tenant has the same rights as a secure council tenant. A flexible tenant has the right to request a review of the length of the tenancy being offered.

At the end of the flexible tenancy, the council may give another flexible tenancy, offer a secure tenancy or end the flexible tenancy. In the last event, the tenant must be given at least six months' notice of non-renewal before the tenancy expires and the reasons for non-renewal must be set out. The tenant has the right to request a review within 21 days.

A council tenant might be asked to consider a transfer to a private landlord (usually a housing association) and the local authority and the relevant government department may be considering a large-scale voluntary transfer. The tenant may be asked to consider agreeing to the creation of an ALMO to manage their property and others in the same area. Tenants must be consulted and are entitled to be balloted and vote on the proposed transfer/ALMO. Following transfer, such a tenant ceases to be a secure tenant and becomes an assured tenant. If the transfer is to a housing association the tenants in practice will be granted a tenancy agreement which contains terms which attempt in some areas to preserve the additional/better rights given to secure tenants. Under an ALMO the tenant remains a secure tenant of the local authority but the property is managed by the ALMO.

Notice to quit is not required to terminate the contractual period of a secure tenancy but a 'notice seeking possession' is required before possession proceedings can be brought. Where a flexible tenancy is not being renewed in addition to the six months' notice of non-renewal the tenant must also be given two months' notice saying the council requires possession before possession proceedings can be brought.

17.5.2   Private registered provider of social housing – housing association

A tenancy of permanent accommodation granted by a housing association after 14 January 1989 will be either an assured tenancy or an assured shorthold tenancy for a fixed term. However, existing tenancies granted before that date remain secure tenancies (see **17.5.1**).

In theory, registered social landlords should follow Homes and Community Agency regulatory standards.

The Housing Act 1988 (as amended) gives assured tenants long-term security of tenure. Assured tenants of housing associations may have the right to acquire their property under the Housing Act 1996. Housing associations cannot grant introductory tenancies. However, they can give a probationary or trial tenancy sometimes known as a 'starter' tenancy to all their new tenants. The trial period is usually one year. At the end of the trial period either an assured tenancy is granted or a fixed term tenancy usually for at least five years. When not giving assured tenancies they grant assured shorthold tenancies and thus in effect are then more akin to private landlords (see **17.5.3**).

Notice to quit is not required to terminate the contractual period of an assured tenancy but a notice seeking possession is required before possession proceedings can be brought.

17.5.3   Private landlords

Protected tenancies

Tenancies granted by private landlords before 15 January 1989 will generally be protected tenancies governed by the Rent Act 1977. Protected tenancies may be either contractual tenancies or statutory tenancies. Until the original tenancy agreement terminates they are contractual tenancies. After termination they become statutory tenancies. A contractual tenancy terminates on the expiry of a notice to quit or following the registration of a new fair rent by the rent officer and the service of a notice of increase by the landlord.

Protected tenancies represented the 'high water mark' for the protection of private tenants in a civilised society. The protected tenant generally has long-term security of tenure. There is rent control through the regime of fair rents and registration by the rent officer. Succession rights are the most favourable. Consequently, the elderly client still with a protected tenancy and faced with a landlord, for instance, wanting vacant possession may have a strong bargaining position.

Assured and assured shorthold tenancies

Tenancies granted by private landlords after 14 January 1989 will be either an assured tenancy or an assured shorthold tenancy under Part I of the Housing Act 1988. There are some exceptions. The most important are tenancies granted by resident landlords.

Before 28 February 1997 the landlord had to take the initiative and serve a notice in prescribed form before the tenancy started to create an assured shorthold tenancy. In addition, the tenancy had to be for an initial fixed term of not less than six months. From 28 February 1997 the position was reversed by the Housing Act 1996. Consequently, any new tenancies granted after that date are automatically assured shorthold tenancies unless notice is given that the tenancy is to be an assured tenancy. Housing associations do this but there is obviously no incentive for private landlords to do so.

A tenant who holds an assured tenancy and agrees with the same landlord to take a tenancy of a different dwelling will become an assured tenant under the new tenancy and not an assured shorthold tenant. The assured tenant generally has long-term security of tenure. However, there is little rent control and market rather than fair rents. There are some succession rights.

The assured shorthold tenant has no long-term security of tenure. There is little rent control and market rather than fair rents. There are no succession rights.

Where a long lease of a flat (or possibly a house) expires, until 14 January 1999 the tenant would have been entitled to a statutory tenancy under the Rent Act 1977: see Landlord and Tenant Act 1954, Part I. After 14 January 1999 the occupying tenant will be entitled to an assured tenancy: see the Local Government and Housing Act 1989.

17.5.4 Right to buy

Part V of the Housing Act 1985 gave the right to buy to secure tenants. This right to acquire was given to tenants of some housing associations by Housing Act 1996, s.16. The government in the Queen's Speech in May 2015 announced its intention to introduce legislation to extend the right to buy to housing association tenants.

Local authority type tenants have the right to buy at a discount after two years if a tenancy was given prior to 18 January 2005, otherwise after three years. There are different rules in Wales. The tenant may nominate certain family co-residents to purchase jointly. A council tenant whose dwelling is transferred to a private registered social provider or private sector landlord has a 'preserved right to buy'. Certain types of property or tenancy may be excluded (sheltered housing and properties particularly suitable for older people and most housing provided by charitable bodies).

The discount depends upon the duration of the tenancy and can be up to 60 per cent for houses and 70 per cent for flats. However, the maximum discount varies depending on the location of the property. From April 2015, the maximum discount in London is £103,900 and £77,900 in other areas.

The amount of discount awarded depends on:

- how long the person has been a council tenant;
- if the property is a house or a flat;
- the age and condition of the property.

Housing Act 1996, s.17 extended the right to buy – confusingly called the right to acquire – to assured tenants of housing associations and other registered social landlords. However, the dwelling must have been provided by public money and have remained in the social rented sector and have been built or acquired after 1 April 1997. Regulations cover the amount of discount.

There is no longer a right to a mortgage. Mortgages in practice can be obtained to cover the cost, possibly on an interest-only basis. If family members offer to underwrite the mortgage and repair costs, consider whether they will be able to do so and what will happen if they do not.

Whether to buy

It is not always advantageous for an elderly tenant to purchase. When comparing outgoings take into account that:

- the owner will be responsible for additional, uncertain outgoings (property insurance and repairing obligations);
- any service charges continue even though rent ceases;
- housing benefit will no longer be available (mortgage interest is covered by income support within limits).

17.5.5 Allocation

See the Housing Act 1996, Part VI (as last amended last by the Localism Act 2011) and *Allocation of Accommodation: Guidance for Local Housing Authorities in England* (June 2012).

From January 2003 there was a new statutory framework for the allocation of tenancies by a local authority. Allocation means the selection of a person to be a secure or introductory tenant, including an existing council tenant applying for a transfer, or the nomination of an applicant for the grant of a tenancy of permanent accommodation by a private registered provider of social housing.

In England, the provisions were changed again by the Localism Act 2011, primarily by re-introducing the right for local authorities to determine for themselves who qualifies for an allocation, subject to any regulations which require them to include or exclude specified classes of person.

Increasingly, local authorities operate choice-based lettings schemes under which applicants with sufficient priority bid online for available properties. Priority is based in practice on points schemes or banding schemes.

Successive governments have failed to build new public sector housing resulting in massive waiting lists for public sector permanent accommodation or for transfers to more suitable accommodation.

Authorities have considerable discretion in the manner in which they allocate, subject to a certain degree of central government control through the Guidance mentioned above. In addition, the applicant for housing in this context has a number of statutory rights.

Local housing authorities must have and publish an allocations scheme for determining priorities. They can only allocate accommodation in accordance with this scheme. Allocations may not be made to ineligible persons.

In determining priority between different applicants the local authority must give reasonable preference to a number of groups. The groups are now based on social need and include homeless people and are set out in Housing Act 1996, s.167(2). The local authority may give additional preference to sub-groups within those groups, provided they can be identified as having urgent housing needs.

When deciding how to award preference within these groups the local authority may take into account:

- the financial resources open to an applicant to meet his or her housing costs;
- any behaviour of an applicant (or household member) which affects his or her suitability to be a tenant;
- any local connection between the applicant and the local authority's area.

Subject to the reasonable preference groups mentioned, the allocations scheme may cover specific applicants or groups not within those groups. An applicant for an allocation of housing accommodation has the right to general information including likely priority and if an offer is likely to be made, how long before the offer. In addition, there is the right to be informed of any decision about the facts of his or her case affecting the treatment of his or her application: Housing Act 1996, s.166A(9).

Reviewing or challenging the decision

An applicant has the right to request an internal review of any decision of ineligibility for immigration type reasons or disqualifying him or her and any decision about the facts of his or her case affecting the treatment of the application.

Decisions of local housing authorities on housing allocation or failure to comply with statutory duties in this area can be challenged by judicial review.

Private registered providers of social housing in addition to nominations by local housing authorities allocate accommodation direct to applicants and have to deal with existing tenants applying for transfers. Under the Housing Act 1985, s.106 they too are required to publish their rules governing in effect their waiting list and transfer scheme and to supply details of the particulars which they have recorded as relevant to the application for accommodation.

The courts now regard housing associations as public bodies open to judicial review or having to act in a way compliant with the Human Rights Act 1998 – see *R (on the application of Weaver)* v. *London and Quadrant Housing Trust* [2009] EWCA Civ 587.

17.5.6 Security of tenure

A court order is generally needed before a home is repossessed (see below for sanctions). In cases involving the discretionary grounds for possession under the Rent Act 1977 (protected tenants), the Housing Act 1985 (secure tenants) or the Housing Act 1988 (assured tenants) the court has a wide discretion to adjourn the proceedings or to suspend or postpone the possession order. However, when doing so the court may impose conditions. The court must impose conditions with respect to payment of rent and arrears unless this would cause exceptional hardship or would otherwise be unreasonable. In other cases, possession orders against tenants must take effect not later than 14 days after the making of the order unless it would cause exceptional hardship, in which case the order can be postponed for up to six weeks (Housing Act 1980, s.89).

Secure tenancies and flexible tenancies before the end of the flexible tenancy

Security of tenure is achieved by the landlord only being able to obtain a possession order against the tenant on at least one of the 16 grounds set out in the Housing Act 1985. In addition to establishing the ground the landlord must also satisfy the court that it is reasonable to make a possession order. On four of the grounds the landlord must also satisfy the court that suitable alternative accommodation is available at the date of the hearing.

Security may be affected by an assignment or a sub-letting to the extent that this will often involve a breach of an express obligation of the tenancy which is covered in one of the grounds for possession.

The landlord must serve a preliminary warning notice, known as a notice seeking possession, before starting possession proceedings, specifying the ground on which possession may be sought and the date (at least 28 days ahead) after which proceedings may start. However, in the case of alleged anti-social behaviour the latter period may be shortened or even the notice itself dispensed with.

From 21 October 2014, a new absolute ground for possession was introduced in relation to serious criminal offences and anti-social behaviour (Housing Act 1985, s.84A). Here a preliminary notice is required and the tenant has the right to request a review within seven days.

Non-renewed flexible tenancies after the end of the flexible tenancy

The council must give two written notices.

A notice of 'non-renewal' must be given before the tenancy expires. This should:

- give at least six months' notice;
- notify non-renewal;
- set out reasons for non-renewal;
- inform of right to request review within 21 days.

The tenant must also be given two months' notice saying that the council requires possession.

If the council has served these notices and carried out a proper review if requested, a possession order must be made unless it would be disproportionate to do so.

Protected tenancies

The tenant has a high degree of security of tenure. If the protected tenancy is a contractual tenancy the landlord must first terminate this by notice to quit before bringing possession proceedings.

Security of tenure is achieved by the landlord only being able to obtain a possession order where:

- the court is satisfied that it is reasonable to make a possession order and suitable alternative accommodation is available or will be so;
- the court is satisfied that it is reasonable to make a possession order and at least one of the first 10 grounds (called cases, discretionary grounds) set out in the Rent Act 1977 is proved;
- at least one of the 10 remaining cases (mandatory grounds) is proved.

Security may be affected by an assignment or a sub-letting to the extent that this will often involve a breach of an express obligation of the tenancy which is covered in one of the discretionary grounds for possession. Where the claim for possession is based on suitable alternative accommodation being available, the court may direct that the new tenancy should be a protected rather than an assured tenancy. However, where there is statutory overcrowding or where a prohibition order has been made the tenant cannot rely on the protection given by the Rent Act 1977. However, in the latter case the local authority has a statutory duty to re-house the tenant under the Land Compensation Act 1973 which is more extensive than any duty owed under subsequent homelessness legislation.

See Rent Act 1977, s.98 and Sched.15 for the grounds for obtaining possession.

Assured tenancies

The tenant has a lesser degree of security of tenure. Security of tenure is achieved by the landlord only being able to obtain a possession order against the tenant on the grounds set out in the Housing Act 1988. In addition to establishing the ground the landlord must also satisfy the court that it is reasonable to make a possession order in most cases. However, in respect of rent arrears there is a mandatory ground for possession open to the landlord for arrears exceeding eight weeks or two months depending on whether the tenancy is weekly or monthly.

The landlord must serve a preliminary warning notice, known as a notice of intention to seek possession, before starting possession proceedings, specifying the ground on which possession may be sought and the date (usually at least 14 days ahead) after which proceedings may start. However, in the case of alleged anti-social behaviour the latter period may be shortened.

See Housing Act 1988, Scheds.1 and 2 for grounds.

17.5.7 Unlawful eviction

All tenants (apart from excluded tenants) are given protection from eviction by the Protection from Eviction Act 1977 in the following two ways. These protections also apply to licensees (apart from excluded licensees) (see **17.6**).

First, at least four weeks' written notice in prescribed form is required to terminate a tenancy where notice to quit is required and to terminate a licence. Notice to quit is required to terminate in particular protected tenancies which are contractual tenancies and non-secure council tenancies, e.g. a homeless applicant in temporary council accommodation.

Second, a court order is required before any eviction (s.3). Breach of this section is an actionable tort. Excluded tenancies and licences are as follows:

- accommodation is shared with a resident landlord;
- accommodation is shared with a member of a resident landlord's family;
- tenancies or licences granted as a temporary expedient to a trespasser;
- holiday accommodation;
- tenancies or licences granted other than for money or money's worth;
- tenancies or licences to asylum-seekers;
- licence to occupy a public sector hostel.

In addition, under Protection from Eviction Act 1977, s.1 criminal offences are created where the landlord or any other person unlawfully evicts or harasses any residential occupier. Offences are investigated and prosecuted by local authorities rather than the police and the CPS.

An injunction can be sought from the local County Court to prevent harassment or eviction. Damages can also be claimed for various torts and also for breach of covenant for quiet enjoyment. Under ss.27 and 28 of the Housing Act 1988 damages are available for the difference between the value of the property with and without a tenant. Claims for general, special, aggravated and exemplary damages can be considered.

17.5.8 Succession

Secure tenancy

The spouse of a deceased secure tenant, or another member of the family can qualify to succeed to a secure tenancy.

Civil Partnership Act 2004, Sched.8, para.20 amended Housing Act 1985, s.87 to ensure that a civil partner has the same rights to succeed to a secure tenancy as a spouse. Schedule 8, para.27 has amended the definition of 'member of a person's family' in Housing Act 1985, Part IV to include references to a civil partner or civil partnership alongside references to spouse or to marriage. The amendment also extends the definition to couples who are living together as if they were civil partners as well as people who are living together as husband and wife.

A cohabitee not married or in a civil partnership, but living with the tenant who died as though they were, can qualify to succeed if the tenancy started before 1 April 2012 and the property was the potential successor's principal or only home and they lived with the tenant for at least 12 months immediately prior to the death. If the tenancy started on or after 1 April 2012, then they qualify to succeed if it was their only or principal home at the date of the death.

Succession rights of relatives depend on when the tenancy began.

A relative can only succeed where the tenancy started on or after 1 April 2012, if the tenancy agreement expressly provides for this. If the tenancy started before 1 April 2012, a relative can succeed if the tenancy was his or her only or principal home at the date of death and he or she was living with the tenant for at least 12 months before the death.

A relative is a member of the family and potentially qualified to succeed if any of the following:

- parent or grandparent;
- child or grandchild;
- brother or sister;
- uncle, aunt, nephew or niece.

Step-relations, half-relations and in-laws are also included. Foster children are not.

There can be only one succession and where more than one person is qualified to succeed the spouse takes preference. If there is no spouse the potential successors may agree who succeeds. In the absence of agreement, the landlord selects.

Protected tenancy

A protected tenancy may be succeeded to twice where the first successor is a spouse including a person living with the tenant as the tenant's husband or wife. It may be succeeded to only once where the first successor is a member of the family. The spouse succeeds to a protected tenancy and must have been residing in the property immediately before the death. A member of the family only succeeds to an assured tenancy. The member of the family must have been residing with the deceased at the time of death and for the two years immediately before the death.

Following the requirement not to discriminate under the European Convention on Human Rights and the Human Rights Act 1998 and *Mendoza* v. *Ghaidan* [2002] EWCA Civ 1533, one surviving partner of same sex couple succeeds as a spouse rather than a member of the family.

See Rent Act 1977, s.2 and Sched.1 (amended by the Housing Act 1988).

Assured tenancy

Succession rights to an assured tenancy are more limited than those which apply to secure and protected tenancies. Only a spouse, which includes a common law husband or wife, may succeed and there can only be one succession. A joint tenant will automatically succeed to the tenancy but there can then be no further transmission. Another family member cannot succeed to the assured tenancy.

Similar amendments have been made to the Housing Act 1988 as to the Housing Act 1985 to allow for succession to civil partners and survivors of same sex couples.

17.5.9 Assignment and sub-letting

The general position at common law is that a tenant may assign or sub-let a tenancy unless the tenancy agreement provides otherwise. This basic position may be altered by statute.

Section 19 of the Landlord and Tenant Act 1927 provides that there is an implied proviso in any term allowing assignment with the landlord's consent that such consent shall not be unreasonably withheld. However, the Housing Acts 1985 and 1988 change the position for secure and assured tenants respectively.

Secure tenancies

Assignment in general is prohibited unless:

- the assignment is made in a financial settlement following divorce;
- the assignment was to a person qualified to succeed (see above) although this need not be the person next entitled (this option could be used to ensure that a child rather than a spouse succeeds);
- there has been a mutual exchange with landlord's consent (Housing Act 1985, s.92).

Sub-letting of part requires written agreement of the landlord and failure to obtain agreement could be a ground for possession. But consent must not be unreasonably withheld and if so withheld is treated as given. There is a right to take in lodgers but if the tenant sub-lets the whole, the tenancy ceases to be secure and cannot subsequently become a secure tenancy.

Assured tenancies

It is an implied term of every assured tenancy which is a periodic tenancy that the tenant, except with the consent of the landlord, shall not assign or sub-let the whole or part. However, the landlord has an absolute discretion as to whether or not to give consent.

17.5.10 Rent control

Local authorities may make such reasonable charges as they determine. They are under a duty to review rents periodically and may alter rents generally in their locality or alter particular rents as circumstances allow. They have complete discretion as to the setting of rents but are influenced by government decisions as to the payment of subsidy to housing revenue accounts and must not act irrationally or in bad faith or take irrelevant factors into account. Before varying the rent of a secure tenancy they must secure the agreement of the tenant or serve a notice of variation.

Housing association secure tenants have access to the fair rent regime under the Rent Act 1977. Either party can refer a proposed rent increase to a rent officer at the Valuation Office Agency, using the fair rent machinery of the Rent Act 1977, and there is a further appeal to the First-tier Tribunal.

A system of 'fair rents' applies to protected tenancies (notwithstanding any agreement to the contrary). Rent officers fix the rent with an appeal to the First-tier Tribunal. The rent ignores the scarcity value of accommodation, so is artificially low.

The rent for assured tenancies can be at market levels. Housing associations in practice set rents at affordable levels. Rent rises can be examined by the First-tier Tribunal if they are above market levels but not if in accordance with rent review provisions in the original agreement.

The rent for assured shorthold tenancies can also be at market levels. A tenant has the right to refer the rent to the First-tier Tribunal on the basis that the rent is artificially high but now only during the first six months of the tenancy.

Older people may be eligible for means-tested housing benefit to meet part or all of their rent. However, in the case of private landlords, if the claim for housing benefit was made after 6 April 2008 a new system of local housing allowances (LHAs) is in force nationally. The maximum rent covered by housing benefit is based on a flat rate allowance. LHAs are set and published locally. LHAs are based on the area in which the claimant lives and the size of property. The number of people in the claimant's household determines the size of property to which the claimant is entitled. For a continuous claim for housing benefit before 7 April 2008 a rent stop may be applied restricting the amount of rent covered by housing benefit.

Working-age council or housing association tenants with 'spare' bedrooms are subject to a housing benefit reduction called the under-occupancy charge but more commonly known as the bedroom tax.

The number of bedrooms that can be claimed for is based on the number of people living in the home.

The amount of rent for which housing benefit can be claimed is reduced by:

- 14 per cent where there is one 'spare' bedroom;
- 25 per cent where there are two or more 'spare' bedrooms.

From April 2013 to 2017, universal credit will gradually replace housing benefit. Help with the cost of rent will have to be claimed as part of a universal credit claim.

17.5.11 Service charges

Tenants of flats (including those of housing associations but not local authorities) have some statutory protection in respect of service charges:

- only reasonably incurred amounts are payable for services;
- any work must be carried out to a reasonable standard;
- a written summary of relevant costs may be required and accounts inspected.

See the Landlord and Tenant Act 1985 (and Housing Act 1985 for houses disposed of by the public sector).

17.5.12 Repairs and maintenance

A landlord is usually under an obligation to repair and maintain a dwelling which is let as such.

Contract: covenant to repair

In addition to any express term of the tenancy the landlord will normally be subject to a term implied by Landlord and Tenant Act 1985, s.11. Section 11 applies to tenancies granted after 23 October 1961 for a term of less than seven years. Under this term the landlord is responsible for repairs to the structure and exterior of the dwelling and the installations for the supply of heating, hot water, gas, water and electricity.

On a tenancy of a flat granted after 14 January 1989, these repairing obligations extend to common parts of a building or other parts which are controlled by a landlord. The courts may imply similar obligations into older tenancy agreements in order to give business efficacy to them. However, a landlord is not liable for breach of an express or implied term to repair unless he had notice of the defect.

Tort

Liability may also arise in tort. This arises primarily under Defective Premises Act 1972, s.4. The liability is similar to that under Landlord and Tenant Act 1985, s.11 but restricted to damage to contents and/or personal injury. However, the notice requirement is less strict. The landlord must know or ought to have known about the relevant defect. Consequently, failure to maintain reasonable arrangements for inspection when such defects would have come to light may result in liability.

Remedies

A number of different direct legal remedies are available to enforce repairing obligations:

- A tenant who suffers distress and inconvenience, injury or loss because of the landlord's failure to carry out repairs may seek compensation by a damages claim in the County Court and/or apply for an order of specific performance or injunction including an interim injunction for urgent repairs in some circumstances.
- An aggrieved person (not necessarily a tenant) can bring a private prosecution in the magistrates' court under Environmental Protection Act 1990, s.82 for an order to deal with a statutory nuisance – health risk. A 21-day statutory warning must first be given.
- Under Housing Act 2004, s.4 a complaint about the condition of the property indicating that a Category 1 or 2 hazard exists can be made to a local magistrate who can then compel the local Environmental Health Department to inspect and report to the relevant council committee.
- A claim for judicial review may be possible against a local authority which is failing to exercise its statutory duties or to consider properly the exercise of its powers to deal in particular with hazards and statutory nuisances in properties not in its own ownership.

Alternatively, the local Environmental Health Department may be asked to take action.

The local authority may issue an improvement notice requiring the owner to carry out works in accordance with those specified in the notice and failure to do so is an offence (a right of appeal lies to the First-tier Tribunal). Alternatively, it may issue a hazard awareness notice specifying the nature of the hazard and giving details of any remedial action it considers practicable and appropriate. The concept of hazards has replaced fitness and substantial disrepair as the trigger for local authority action. Local authorities must assess whether there are serious hazards (Category 1 hazards) and/or less serious hazards (Category 2 hazards). They have a duty to take enforcement action in relation to Category 1 hazards and a power to do so in relation to Category 2 hazards. The local authority has power to carry out the works itself and charge the person responsible. Enforcement action could also extend to the service of a prohibition notice.

Local authority environmental health officers have general powers in relation to a property which is a statutory nuisance (as defined in Environmental Protection Act 1990, s.79). The officer may serve a notice on the person responsible for the nuisance (e.g. the landlord or owner occupier) requiring the nuisance to be abated (appeal is to the magistrates' court within 21 days). If a notice is not complied with proceedings may be taken in the magistrates' court which can order the person responsible to abate the nuisance, impose a daily fine for as long as the nuisance continues and order compensation to anyone who has suffered injury or loss (such as a tenant).

17.6 LICENCES

17.6.1 Licence or tenancy?

The distinction between a licensee (e.g. a lodger) and a tenant is based upon control over the property and the degree of integration into the household (see *Street* v. *Mountford* [1985] 2 All ER 289).

An occupier who under the contractual arrangements has exclusive possession of a dwelling for a term and pays rent will usually be a tenant regardless of how he is described in the agreement. However, there will merely be a licence where there is a genuine service occupancy or there is no intention to create a legal relationship. In many situations the individual merely has a licence to occupy which may be:

- an exclusive licence where the accommodation is self-contained;
- a licence to occupy a private room where other essential facilities are shared;
- a licence to share a room and other facilities.

The distinction between a tenancy and a licence is important because only a tenant can have security of tenure and protection as to repair and maintenance.

17.6.2 Informal licence

When the individual is living with relatives or friends there will usually be merely an informal (or bare) licence to occupy a room or facilities, but:

- if regular payments are made there may be a contract and reasonable notice must then be given to terminate: this could include a contribution to household expenses;
- a 'licence coupled with an interest' may arise where the occupier contributes towards the cost of buying, altering or improving the home: someone who contributes towards the costs of acquiring a property will usually acquire an equitable interest in it.

If a court is asked to exclude an informal licensee from a property it may postpone any order to allow reasonable notice for alternative arrangements to be made, but if care services are being provided as well as the accommodation it may be difficult to ensure that these continue.

17.6.3   Contractual licence

When money is paid for the facility there will be a contract (e.g. a lodger or a room in a hotel or care home) and the terms should be complied with:

- the terms may have been published in advance (e.g. in an advertisement, letter or brochure) and will then be incorporated into the contract but some of the terms may need to be implied;
- a contract may arise even if the resident lacks mental capacity but any agreement should then be in simple terms and carefully explained to the resident (the contract will usually be entered into by the person managing his or her financial affairs, e.g. an attorney or a deputy).

17.7   HOMELESS PERSONS

A homeless person or a person threatened with homelessness may apply to the local authority for accommodation. A person in inadequate accommodation may possibly be considered homeless if it is no longer reasonable for him or her to continue to occupy the existing home.

When exercising their functions under Part VII of the Housing Act 1996, local housing authorities are bound to have regard to Homelessness: Code of Guidance for Local Authorities 2006, the Supplementary Guidance on Intentional Homelessness (August 2009), and the Supplementary Guidance on the homelessness changes in the Localism Act 2011 and on the Homelessness (Suitability of Accommodation) (England) Order 2012 (November 2012). If such an application is made then the local authority must under Housing Act 1996, s.184 make inquiries as to whether the applicant is eligible for assistance and, if so, what legal duty (if any) is owed in relation to re-housing. Broadly a person is eligible for assistance unless he or she is a person from abroad within certain categories or an asylum-seeker.

17.7.1   Priority need and unintentionally homeless

The local authority, when making the inquiries mentioned must establish in particular whether the applicant has a priority need for accommodation and whether or not he or she is homeless intentionally. The categories of person in priority need are defined in Housing Act 1996, s.189 and include a person who is vulnerable as a result of old age. This includes an applicant who has such a person living with him or her, or who might reasonably be expected to have such a person live with him or her.

The Code suggests that authorities should consider whether old age is a factor which makes it hard for applicants to fend for themselves, and that all applications from people aged 60 or over should be considered carefully.

An act or omission that led to homelessness must have been deliberate for a person to become homeless intentionally. The Code provides that it should not be considered deliberate if the applicant was incapable of managing his or her affairs for example because of old age.

17.7.2   No priority need and not intentionally homeless

If the local authority is satisfied that an applicant does not have a priority need and is not intentionally homeless, then it only owes a limited duty to give advice and assistance. In addition, the local authority has the power to secure accommodation or to prevent the threatened homelessness.

17.7.3   Priority need but intentionally homeless

If the local authority is satisfied that an applicant became homeless intentionally but is in priority need, then it only owes a limited housing duty to secure accommodation to give the applicant a reasonable opportunity of securing accommodation him or herself. In addition, there is a duty to provide advice and assistance in this context, but the local authority must now first assess the applicant's individual needs before giving such advice and assistance.

17.7.4   Duties to those with priority need and not intentionally homeless

While the local authority is making inquiries it has a legal duty to ensure that suitable temporary accommodation is available for the applicant pending the completion of the inquiries. Once the local authority has completed its inquiries and if it is satisfied that the applicant both has a priority need and did not become homeless intentionally, then it may refer the applicant to another local authority but only if there is a local connection with that other authority. In that event the local authority to which the applicant is referred completes the re-housing process and discharges the remaining legal duties owed in this respect.

If it does not so refer, its remaining legal duty at that stage is to secure suitable accommodation for the applicant. This is the full re-housing duty. In practice this often will be either temporary private rented or council or housing association accommodation. In the second case the tenancy would not be a secure council tenancy and in the last case not an assured housing association tenancy.

The Code of Guidance provides that housing authorities will need to be sensitive to the importance of pets to elderly people who may rely on pets for companionship and recommends careful consideration to this aspect where applicants wish to retain their pet.

17.7.5 Termination of the duty

Such accommodation must be secured indefinitely until one of the following events occurs:

- the refusal of an offer of suitable accommodation;
- ceasing to be eligible for assistance;
- becoming homeless intentionally from such accommodation;
- voluntarily ceasing to occupy such accommodation as an only or principal home;
- accepting an offer of permanent accommodation under the local authority's allocations scheme;
- refusing an offer of suitable permanent accommodation under the local authority's allocations scheme;
- accepting but not rejecting an offer of an assured shorthold tenancy from a private landlord.

Since 9 November 2012, the Council can also end such a duty by offering private rented accommodation (in this context private includes housing association rented) and an assured shorthold tenancy for at least one year.

Throughout the homelessness process, the homeless applicant may be allocated permanent council or housing association accommodation through the local authority's allocations scheme. The allocations scheme is the only route to permanent council accommodation. In that event the tenancy will be a secure or flexible or an assured tenancy or an assured shorthold tenancy for a fixed term of generally at least five years, as appropriate.

17.7.6 Challenging a homelessness decision

A homeless applicant has a legal right under Housing Act 1996, s.202 to challenge any of the following decisions made by the local authority by requesting a review within 21 days of being notified of the relevant decision:

- any decision on eligibility for assistance;
- any decision on what duty (if any) in relation to re-housing the local authority has towards the applicant;
- decisions concerning local connection referrals;
- decisions concerning the suitability of accommodation offered to the applicant, including private accommodation offers.

There is also a statutory right of appeal to the County Court in respect of the decision on review if this is adverse but only on a point of law and the appeal must be made within 21 days of notification of the adverse decision.

The only method of legal challenge of other decisions by the local authority in relation to a homelessness application is by an application to the Administrative Court for judicial review.

As a last resort an older person who is homeless may be entitled to accommodation being provided by social services under the provisions for adult care contained in the Care Act 2014 and Social Services and Well-being (Wales) Act 2014.

17.8 SPECIAL SITUATIONS

17.8.1 Shared occupation

Either financial circumstances or care needs may dictate that an elderly individual shares a home. This could involve:

- moving into and sharing the home of a relative or friend;
- a relative or friend moving into the elderly individual's home;
- taking a lodger;
- employing a resident housekeeper or carer;
- living in the home of a paid carer.

Family arrangements

Arrangements within the family sometimes prove unsatisfactory to one side or the other so ensure that all relevant factors are considered before it is too late. Experience shows that there may be an unacceptable loss of independence and privacy by the elderly individual or of freedom and privacy for the sharing family.

The arrangement should be the choice of the elderly person rather than the family (though it may be suggested by the family) and hasty decisions should not be made following bereavement or any period of ill health. While a legal document cannot provide for personal relationships, a clear enforceable agreement is desirable if either party commits capital to the arrangement (see **17.3.2**). It may be necessary to unscramble the financial arrangements in order to separate the personal relationships and it is better to discuss this before the parties are committed rather than after things have gone wrong – when the parties may not be talking anyway! If the arrangement does not work it is seldom possible for the previous situation to be restored.

Frequently shared occupation arises without any planning where a son or (more often) a daughter remains at home with parent(s). Often the parties rely on assumptions and fail to discuss their hopes and wishes, so you can perform a valuable service by encouraging them to do so in an open way in your presence. A mother may actually desire to move into a residential care home but not wish to leave her daughter alone, while the daughter may yearn for freedom yet not wish to desert her mother by putting her in a home.

Checklist for parties where family considering sharing arrangements

Considerations include:

- how well they get on now and are likely to get on living in close proximity (taking into account the effect upon any marriage and the existence of children in the household);
- whether the home is physically suitable and provides sufficient privacy;
- the effect on state benefits and community care provision;
- the implications of a decline in health and the need to provide care.

Commercial arrangements

Where the arrangement is with a stranger for payment it is essential to identify the understandings and assumptions on which it is based, from both points of view, and these should be recorded in writing. A formal document is not necessary and may be off-putting, but an exchange of letters is a minimum requirement.

Taking a lodger may produce an additional income and, if the relationship works out, provide company. The notice period and weekly or other payment to be made should be confirmed in advance and also what it covers (e.g. meals, laundry, telephone). The effect of this income on state benefits should not be overlooked (similar principles apply if the client proposes to become a boarder). There are tax concessions for income from letting one room.

If a housekeeper or carer is to live in, this will be an employment situation, but living in the home of a carer may be classed as being a boarder. In either event income tax, NI contributions and the effect on state benefits should be taken into account by both parties.

17.8.2   Sheltered housing

Housing restricted to and designed so as to be suitable for elderly people may be available and this is an option for those who want to live an independent life in their own home without all the responsibilities of home ownership. Most are apartments or bungalows, physical disabilities may be catered for and alarm systems are often installed.

Schemes include:

- purpose-built or converted housing without a warden;
- warden-assisted or warden-controlled housing;
- supportive housing where residents have their own room but use communal facilities and perhaps receive a cooked daily meal (e.g. Abbeyfield);
- housing with care (meals and care services are usually provided).

Tenure

The basis on which the property is held may be:

- freehold or long lease at a premium with service charge rent (enfranchisement may be possible for leasehold sheltered housing schemes);

- tenancy at a rent: those in the public sector will be secure or flexible or assured tenancies or assured shorthold tenancies but private sector rent control may not apply if 'attendance' is included;
- shared ownership or shared equity arrangement;
- licensee only.

Checklist for sheltered housing when considering the lease/other contractual arrangement

- Check for any restrictions on occupation, resale or assignment (problems have arisen over disposal of some homes following death).
- Can younger carers live in?
- Check the effect of the owner or spouse becoming a Court of Protection patient.
- Can the surviving spouse remain there (especially if younger)?
- Check what services are provided.
- What are the warden's duties?
- Check the service charge liability.
- Check whether there is a 'sinking fund' for property repairs.
- Check the identity of the managers of the scheme.
- Are they members of the Association of Retirement Housing Managers?
- Is there a residents' association and is it recognised by the managers?

NHBC

Registered house builders selling sheltered housing must comply with the NHBC Sheltered Housing Code of Practice (1990):

- The Purchaser's Information Pack contains useful information.
- Legally binding management agreements are required to a specified standard.

Age UK

Age UK produces useful Factsheets in this area (see **www.ageuk.org.uk/ publications**):

- Factsheet 2: *Buying Retirement Housing*.
- Factsheet 8: *Council and Housing Association Housing*.
- Factsheet 13: *Funding for Home Improvements*.
- Factsheet 35: *Tenants Rights: Rent*.
- Factsheet 64: *Specialist Housing for Older People*.

17.8.3   Homes for disabled people

From 1980 the role of local authorities changed to that of strategic planner rather than direct provider. A duty is imposed on local housing authorities to consider the housing needs of their district (Housing Act 1985, s.8). Under the Care Act 2014, s.1, or the Social Services and Well-Being (Wales) Act 2014, ss.1 and 2(2), local authorities have the general duty in the case of an individual to promote that individual's well-being and well-being means inter alia suitability of living accommodation.

Adaptations

Frequently an overlapping responsibility for the provision of adaptations exists between the social services authority and the local housing authority.

Under the Care Act 2014 or Social Services and Well-being (Wales) Act 2014, social services are under a duty to assess adults with care and support needs and if the relevant eligibility criteria are met to provide care and support, which would include assistance for adaptations. In this area unfortunately there is a problem in some areas caused by the shortage of occupational therapists used in practice in the assessment process. This can result in delay. See **Chapter 8**.

The duty of the local housing authority arises under Housing Grants, Construction and Regeneration Act 1996, Part I to provide disabled facilities grants subject to a means test (see also **17.3.6**).

VAT

Building alterations are subject to VAT, but many alterations for people with disabilities are zero-rated.

17.8.4 Park homes

'Park homes' is a new name for mobile home parks. A fully equipped caravan (or chalet designed so as to be classed as a caravan) may be purchased but a serviced site must be rented and security of tenure may be limited.

The Mobile Homes Act 1983 requires the park owner to enter into a legal agreement with each individual occupier dealing with rights and responsibilities regarding:

- increases in the site fees and any other charges that are made;
- the basis on which a caravan on a site may be sold or transferred (including commission charged and approval of the new occupier by the park owner);
- termination of the agreement.

References

The following may be useful:

- *Mobile Homes: A Guide to Residents and Site Owners* (Office of the Deputy Prime Minister, 2003).

- **http://england.shelter.org.uk/get_advice/
  other_types_of_accommodation/mobile_homes**.
- National Association of Park Home Residents (**www.naphr.org**).

17.8.5 Second homes and timeshare

Increased leisure may make second homes or timeshares attractive for those with
the energy and sufficient capital, but it is necessary to take into account:

- the expenses involved, which will continue until disposal even if continuing
  use cannot be made of the property;
- the problems of management or maintenance, especially if other people must
  be relied upon due to a decline in mental capacity;
- the difficulty of disposing of the property (especially timeshare);
- the capital tied up in the investment (which may still be included in any means
  testing for benefits or services);
- the capital gains tax implications.

17.8.6 Foreign properties

When acting for a client who wishes to purchase a home (or second home) abroad
you must encourage the client to consult a qualified lawyer practising in the country
concerned (unless you have the expertise in your own firm), because if you fail to do
so you could be liable if anything goes wrong. Each country has its own conveyancing procedures and the inheritance laws of the particular country may apply with
surprising consequences.

The Law Society of England and Wales maintains a register of its members with
recognised expertise in foreign jurisdictions.

Checklist for client before moving abroad

- Check pension and state benefits entitlement with the DWP.
- Check availability of healthcare and reciprocal arrangements.
- Check the income and capital taxes situation.
- Check ways to delegate powers, such as managing finances and affairs in the
  country of destination.
- Check the effect of a change of residence or domicile (e.g. on testamentary
  provision).
- Check the position if the person returns to the United Kingdom.

17.9   EQUITY RELEASE

Older homeowners may wish to release income or capital from their home and as it is not suitable for everyone other options should be considered initially:

- An independent financial adviser may be able to advise if the older person's investments or assets could produce a better return.
- Check if the older person is entitled to any welfare benefits, particularly as not all are means tested. See **Chapter 13**.
- If the older person is in debt, they may need advice on managing the debt.
- It may be appropriate to downsize and release equity in this way.
- If the aim of the release is specifically to pay for repairs, improvements or adaptations, the local home improvement agency, sometimes called Care and Repairs or Staying Put, may assist. Home improvement agencies (HIAs) help elderly people, disabled and other vulnerable people make adaptations to the homes they own. They are supported by government and local authorities, and are not-for-profit organisations. They will give information, advice and support to older homeowners who need repairs or improvements to their homes, or the assistance of a handyperson for decorating or gardening. The HIA will assess an elderly homeowner's needs and advise on practical financial and legal matters related to adapting the home, repairing or insulating it. Their main purpose is to help elderly people continue to live as independently as possible.

17.9.1   Conditions

Conditions which must be satisfied to obtain an equity release vary from company to company but include:

- a minimum age, usually 60, although some schemes are open to those over 55 while others are only available to people over 80;
- a maximum amount to loan, for example 75 per cent of the property value;
- the applicant's home must be owned by them and worth at least £40,000;
- there is significant equity in the property;
- some providers may require a minimum amount of money to borrow.

17.9.2   Types of schemes

The home reversion scheme involves selling the whole or part of the home to a reversion company. The price will not be the same as if the owner sold the property on the open market. In return the owner receives either a cash lump sum or a monthly income. The older person can remain in the home rent-free or for a nominal monthly rent, for the rest of their life. When the property is eventually sold the reversion company receives the proceeds from the sale, depending on what proportion of the home was sold.

Home income plans, also known as a mortgage annuity scheme, enable the older person to receive a monthly income for life while still owning and living in the property. A mortgage loan is taken out against the home usually up to a maximum of 75 per cent of its value. The money is used to buy an annuity which pays a regular income each month for the older person's life. The interest payments on the loan are deducted from this income. Limited tax relief applies to plans taken out before 9 March 1999 but for new plans there is no such advantage.

Roll-up (mortgage) loans involve the older person taking out a loan against the value of their home. Either capital or monthly income (or both) are paid. No repayments are made until the house is eventually sold, where the interest is rolled up and added to the total loan. These schemes were a problem in the early 1990s when the housing market was depressed and many people ended up in negative equity. These schemes are now regulated by the Financial Conduct Authority.

Interest-only loans allow the older person to obtain a capital sum and they have to repay the interest from their assets. Some banks and building societies provide these types of loans.

17.9.3 Other considerations

Consideration needs to be given to the cost of entering the scheme, such as valuation and legal fees and the commission payable to the financial adviser. The client should also consider if they are ever likely to want to move and in what circumstances, as not all schemes allow the plan to be transferred. The older person remains responsible for the repair, insurance and usual outgoings as a homeowner and they need to be sure they can afford to take out the plan in the long term.

For more information, see Age UK Factsheet 65: *Equity Release*.

PART D

Inheritance and death

CHAPTER 18

Gifts

Martin Terrell

18.1 INTRODUCTION

A solicitor advising in connection with a significant lifetime gift must proceed with a fair degree of caution. Large gifts should only be considered when the money or asset involved is surplus to the client's present or anticipated requirements. Even though the proposed gift might technically be affordable, care needs to be taken over issues of capacity, conflicts of interest and undue influence as well as any tax implications. The gift is not a simple matter of arranging a transfer of property or money. It needs to be considered in a much wider context, taking into account matters such as the donor's future requirements, past gifts, proposed future gifts, family relationships and the contents of the donor's will. Advice cannot be hurried and there will be a cost implication, although any legal costs should be a small price to pay for the reassurance (for both parties) of knowing that the transaction is a proper one and avoiding the infinitely greater costs involved if the transaction were to unravel.

Concerns often arise when the prospective donee is involved in the transaction. The donee may make the arrangements asking the solicitor to complete the formalities for a gift or the donor may initiate the transaction but clearly at the suggestion of the proposed donee. The solicitor needs to be act carefully and tactfully, ensuring that the donor is properly advised without giving the impression that he or she is being interrogated and family members presumed to be unscrupulous when they are more likely than not to be acting honestly and in good faith.

Before any advice is given, it is essential at the very outset of the matter to establish who the client is, who is receiving advice and whether there is a conflict of interest. In every case the prospective donor must be the client or, if there is a potential conflict of interest because the solicitor is acting for the donee, the donor must have independent legal advice.

When taking instructions, it is essential that the client is seen alone, except in the case of a couple where a joint approach might be appropriate (although care still needs to be taken as there may be different levels of capacity or different interests to consider, especially where there is a second marriage involved). If the client insists that the donee is present when instructions are taken, it is prudent to record this in writing as part of the instruction records. Often an anxious client may want the donee to be present at the first meeting or at the start of a meeting and there is no reason why the client cannot then be seen alone (or with someone else who is independent of the transaction).

When assisting a client in making a gift, it is essential to establish, and carefully record, the reason for making the gift. It is surprising how often clients believe (or are led to believe) that a gift should be made to avoid inheritance tax or assessment for care costs. On closer examination, these concerns may be unnecessary. The client's estate may be below or only marginally over the inheritance tax threshold; a gift may give rise to a capital gains tax charge which the client does not want to pay; care fees might be affordable especially if the client's property were sold or used as security for a loan to release funds to pay for fees. A desired gift may also be caught by anti-avoidance measures, such as reservation of benefit rules for inheritance tax and anti-deprivation rules where means-tested benefits are in issue. The client should be able to enjoy the security of knowing that the estate is there for the duration of his or her lifetime, and therefore has a right not to make gifts as much as a right to make gifts.

If a solicitor is not satisfied that the client has capacity to make the gift or feels that undue influence might have been brought to bear then it is best practice for medical evidence to be obtained addressing the client's capacity or obtain background information, which may clarify whether there is such influence. The delay while obtaining evidence also provides a natural pause in the transaction during which the client's rationale for making the gift can be considered more carefully. If this is resisted or there is still pressure for the gift to be completed, then the solicitor must decline to act, while being aware of the consequent danger of financial abuse or fraud taking place. It is then important that the solicitor addresses these matters promptly and transparently.

For further details, see:

- **Chapter 1** for capacity to make lifetime gifts.
- **Chapter 2** for taking instructions from elderly clients.
- **Chapter 4** for gifts under the Mental Capacity Act 2005.
- **Chapter 14** for the potential implications of means testing for local authority services.
- **Chapter 16** for tax planning issues.
- Law Society Practice Note: Making Gifts of Assets (6 October 2011).

18.2   VALIDITY OF GIFT

18.2.1   Capacity of donor

A gift is only valid if the donor had capacity to make the gift at the time it was made. Capacity is therefore time and function specific. Whether the common law test for capacity to make a gift has been superseded by the MCA 2005 test was considered by the court in *Kicks* v. *Leigh* [2014] EWHC 3926 (Ch), which concluded that the common law remains the correct test (see also **1.5.4**). The Court of Protection's approach to the test of capacity as set out in MCA 2005, ss.2 and 3 is to apply the common law test, as described in *Re Beaney* [1978] 2 All ER 595, to identify the relevant information, which a donor must understand to make a gift (*A CC* v. *MS and RS* [2014] EWHC B14 (COP)). The extent of the information that must be understood depends on the nature of the gift relative to the extent of the donor's estate. Thus, a lower degree of capacity is required if the donor is handing over a trinket which represents a small portion of the estate compared to transferring a valuable property which represents the greater part of the estate.

The making of a gift depends on a decision which is specific to the time and nature of the matter in question. Therefore, a donor may have capacity to make a simple gift while lacking capacity to manage and administer his or her property and affairs. An attorney acting under a power of attorney or a deputy appointed under the Court of Protection may need to take particular care when acting on the donor's express authority. The donor has the legal right to make the decision in question, and the attorney or deputy may be called upon to advise or assist with the transaction. A solicitor may be called on to advise in the same way as if advising any other elderly client whose capacity is in issue. If the attorney or deputy or their adviser is in any doubt as to the capacity of the donor or the probity of the transaction further medical or legal advice should be obtained. As a last resort an application may be made to the Court of Protection under MCA 2005, s.15 for a declaration that the donor has the requisite capacity.

Undue influence and capacity

Not only must the donor have the requisite capacity, there must be no undue influence. Reported cases involving issues of capacity, such as *Re Beaney* referred to above, also involve questions of undue influence as it is unusual for a donor who lacks capacity to make a gift without some form of assistance, whether from the donee or other individual such as a solicitor.

The case of *Hammond* v. *Osborn* [2002] EWCA Civ 885 involved a gift of assets worth just under £300,000 by a retired teacher to a very helpful neighbour. Although the gift had been prompted by the donor, it would leave his estate significantly depleted and his liquid assets insufficient to meet the tax liability created by the gift. The Court of Appeal held that even though the donee was not guilty of any 'reprehensible conduct' the nature of the gift created a relationship of trust and confidence and therefore gave rise to a presumption of undue influence. The tax liability, the irrational nature of the gift, the lack of any form of independent or objective advice and the fact that the donor did not appreciate the scale of the gift together ensured that the presumption could not be rebutted.

See also *Gorjat* v. *Gorjat* [2010] EWHC 1537 (Ch), which involved a transfer of assets to a joint account (where assets would pass by survivorship to the donor's second wife) in which it was held that there was no undue influence.

18.2.2 Acting for a donor who lacks capacity

Where the donor lacks capacity to make a valid gift, it may be possible for the gift to be made on the donor's behalf by an attorney acting under an enduring power of attorney (EPA) or lasting power of attorney (LPA) or by a deputy appointed by the Court of Protection. However, the authority of an attorney or a deputy is limited and needs to be exercised with great care and in the best interests of the donor. For a more detailed account of an attorney's or deputy's authority to make gifts or maintain another person, see **4.10**. See also Public Guardian Practice Note 02/2012 (**www.gov.uk/government/publications/public-guardian-practice-note-gifts**).

EPAs and gifts

An attorney under an EPA may pursuant to MCA 2005, Sched.4, para.3(1) and (2) (without obtaining any consent and subject to any restriction contained in the instrument) act under the power so as to benefit himself or persons other than the donor to the following extent but no further:

- in relation to himself or in relation to any other person if the donor might be expected to provide for his or that person's needs respectively; and
- do whatever the donor might be expected to do to meet those needs.

An attorney may furthermore dispose of property of the donor by way of gift to the following extent but no further and may make gifts:

- of a seasonal nature or at a time, or on an anniversary, of a birth, a marriage or the formation of a civil partnership, to persons (including himself) who are related to or connected with the donor; and
- to any charity to which the donor made or might be expected to make gifts,

provided that the value of each such gift is not unreasonable having regard to all the circumstances and in particular the size of the donor's estate.

Gifts made by an attorney should generally be quite modest, but more leeway may be allowed to an attorney providing for the needs of another person. For example, an attorney might be able to make gifts of £3,000 to the donor's children but may also be able to pay the donor's wife's care costs which may be several times greater.

LPAs and gifts

A donee of an LPA has similar but not identical authority under MCA 2005, s.12 but only in respect of the making of gifts (s.12(2)):

(a) on customary occasions to persons (including himself) who are related to or connected with the donor, or

(b) to any charity to whom the donor made or might have been expected to make gifts.

Customary occasion is defined in s.12(3) as:

(a)   the occasion or anniversary of a birth, a marriage or the formation of a civil partnership, or

(b)   any other occasion on which presents are customarily given within families or among friends or associates.

There is no equivalent authority for the donee of an LPA to maintain or provide for someone whom the donor might be expected to provide for.

Deputy and gifts

Most orders appointing a deputy are set out in similar terms to the statutory authority given to an attorney acting under an EPA. Where a person lacks capacity and a deputy is appointed, then a deputy may, if it is appropriate, make small gifts of a seasonal or anniversary nature or provide for an individual or a charity which that person may have been expected to provide for.

Gifts which cannot be made by attorney or deputy

An attorney acting under a registered EPA or an LPA, or a deputy may only make further gifts if expressly authorised by the Court of Protection under MCA 2005, s.18(1)(b). The attorney acting under an EPA may also apply for authority under Sched.4, para.16(2)(e) for the court to 'authorise the attorney to act so as to benefit himself or other persons than the donor otherwise than in accordance with paragraph 3(2) and (3)'.

For applications to the Court of Protection generally, see **4.7**.

18.2.3   Perfected gift

It is essential for a solicitor advising a party to a gift of property to make sure that the title to any gifted property is legally vested in the donee as a promise to make a gift is not enforceable: according to the maxim, 'there is no equity to perfect an imperfect gift'. The donor must have done everything that he needs to do to effect the transfer but it does not matter that something remains to be done by a third party:

* chattels and cash are transferable by delivery if there is an intention to give: a signed letter is useful to confirm the intention and fix the date;
* a gift by cheque is not completed until the cheque is cleared;
* waiver of a debt must be by deed (unless there is consideration);
* a transfer of land or an interest in land must be by deed;
* in the case of securities, it may be sufficient to hand over the certificates together with a signed transfer.

For tax purposes it is good practice to record any large gifts, especially those which may rely on a tax exemption or which constitute a potentially exempt transfer for inheritance tax purposes.

18.2.4 *Donatio mortis causa*

An exception to the rule that a gift must be perfected applies where the donor:

- is contemplating his impending death, in the near future from an identified cause (although it need not be inevitable);
- makes a gift which will only take effect if his contemplated death occurs. Until that time the donor can revoke the gift. In any event the gift will lapse automatically if the donor does not die soon enough;
- delivers 'dominion' over the subject matter of the gift to the donee. 'Dominion' is defined as physical possession of:
  - the subject matter; or
  - some means of accessing the subject matter (such as the key to a box); or
  - documents evidencing entitlement to possession of the subject matter (*King* v. *Chilton Dog Rescue* [2015] EWCA Civ 581).

Thus, if a man on his deathbed tells his housekeeper that he wishes her to have some specific shares on his death and hands her the key to a safe containing the certificates, this may constitute a valid gift of those shares (provided there is proof of this). It now seems that even freehold property is capable of being the subject matter of such a gift (*Sen* v. *Headley* [1991] Ch 425).

18.3 TAXATION

A solicitor advising a client in respect of any lifetime gift should take account of the taxation consequences. Unless the solicitor clearly excludes tax advice from his retainer, which may well be appropriate where specialist advice is required, the solicitor could be negligent (*Hurlingham Estates Ltd* v. *Wilde & Partners* [1997] STC 627).

If the client is acting without advice and fails to take account of the tax consequences of a gift, this may be relevant in determining whether the client actually had capacity to make that gift, as in *Hammond* v. *Osborn* [2002] EWCA Civ 885 (see **18.2.1**).

18.3.1 Capital gains tax

A gift may be a chargeable transfer for CGT (see **Chapter 16** generally), but in regard to gifts the following should be considered.

Hold-over relief

The donee takes the gifted property at the donor's acquisition value and there is no charge to tax on the transfer. Relief is not available if the transferee is not resident or ordinarily resident in United Kingdom. Hold-over relief now only applies:

- as between spouses or civil partners (where there is no tax);
- on disposal of a business asset (including agricultural property);
- on transfers immediately chargeable to inheritance tax (e.g. transfers into and out of a discretionary trust).

Timing and payment

If a client intends to make a gift of an asset with a fluctuating value, it is advantageous to do so when it has a relatively low value; appreciating assets should be given sooner rather than later. However, a client should also bear in mind the loss of the main residence exemption if gifting a property and the loss of the CGT uplift available to his assets on death. This is a particular issue for older clients who have often held investments for many years and face a considerable CGT liability if those investments are disposed of by way of gift. The necessity and importance of the gift needs to be weighed carefully against a potential charge to IHT if the gift becomes chargeable on the death of the donor.

There is a right to pay by instalments over 10 years for certain types of gift.

18.3.2   Inheritance tax

The value of lifetime gifts may be included in the estate of the donor (see **Chapter 16** generally) but in respect of lifetime gifts the following should be considered.

A gift to a spouse or civil partner is exempt from IHT (so is any inheritance by the spouse or civil partner) but there are restrictions where one is not UK domiciled. Other things being equal, a transfer of assets to a spouse or civil partner is useful to equalise the estates.

There are specific exemptions:

- small gifts (now £250 per donee) and normal, regular giving out of income;
- an annual exemption per donor (£3,000, or more on the donee's marriage or civil partnership);
- payments for the maintenance of certain members of the family.

Certain gifts with no benefit reserved will be potentially exempt transfers (PETs) and become exempt if the donor survives seven years, with taper relief between three and seven years, but gifts must equal or exceed the nil rate band at the time the gift is made. For a gift to be a PET, it must be in favour of an individual or a trust for a disabled person (see **16.3.3**). A gift to a trust constitutes an immediate chargeable transfer, although IHT is only payable where the value of the gift (taking account of the transferor's cumulative total) exceeds the available nil rate band.

The primary liability for IHT on gifts falls on the donee but there is a secondary liability on the estate of the deceased donor. Any gift which is neither exempt nor a PET is a chargeable transfer liable to IHT immediately at one-half of the rate applicable on death, taking into account all chargeable transfers during the past seven years. If the donor dies within seven years the full rate is charged, subject to taper relief and less any tax paid on lifetime gifts which is brought into account.

A gift between spouses (or civil partners) does not usually involve any liability to IHT and may be beneficial in tax planning. However, any such planning should involve a careful consideration of both wills to ensure that it is clear where assets will pass on the death of the donee. See *Gorjat* v. *Gorjat* referred to at **18.2.1**.

Practical points

- For those who choose to make a gift but retain a benefit, the advice should include the relevance and application of the reservation of benefit rule. There are several pitfalls to effective gifting of the donor's property or a share of the property, unless the donee occupies the property (so that the gift is for consideration). Even if the donee occupies the property, there is no guarantee that the donee will continue to occupy or that the donor will not need to raise capital from the property.
- Consider the rules against deprivation of assets for assessing entitlement to means-tested benefits (see **18.4.4** and **14.2.3**).
- Consider arranging life assurance for the donee on the donor's life to cover the potential tax liability on a gift.
- Take care with timing (the nil rate band benefits earlier gifts first). If the client wishes to make a PET as well as create a discretionary trust, do the latter first to ensure that the annual exemption is used (and for other technical reasons).
- Establish the value of gifted property at the time and obtain a formal valuation.
- Obtain specialist tax advice from a colleague within your own firm or from another firm, a tax consultant, an accountant or a barrister. The cost of giving incorrect advice is much greater than the cost of taking such advice.

18.4 CHARITIES

Giving to charities is tax effective if done in the correct way and properly recorded.

18.4.1 Income tax

Under the Gift Aid scheme, tax paid on any donation to charity can be recovered by the charity provided the donor confirms that he or she is a taxpayer. The amount of tax recovered by the charity is the basic rate of tax applicable to the net donation grossed up at the basic rate. Thus a gift by the donor of £100 is grossed up to £128.21, allowing the charity to recover £28.21. There is no longer any limit on the amount that can be given in this way, although individual charities may not accept gifts below a certain amount in view of the administrative work involved.

A higher rate taxpayer can also recover the difference between the higher rate tax paid on his income and the basic rate tax recovered by the charity.

18.4.2   Reliefs from capital taxes

There is no CGT on the transfer of an asset to a charity either by way of gift or at an undervalue and the charity will not pay CGT on a subsequent disposal. However, that relief only applies on a sale by the charity. If therefore a potential donor wants to sell an asset to make a gift to charity, he should consider transferring the asset to the charity before it can be sold.

A gift or legacy to a charity is exempt from IHT and the amount is not aggregated with the donor's estate. A beneficiary under a will may (possibly) be able to get the best of all worlds by:

* entering into a deed of variation in favour of a charity, thereby avoiding IHT on the amount transferred;
* also claiming income tax relief under Gift Aid on the same amount.

18.4.3   Bargain-bounty rule

A charity is in danger of losing its charitable status (and tax relief on gifts) if it repeatedly, or on a substantial scale, contracts in return for gifts to provide that which it would normally provide as part of its charitable activities:

* a charity cannot legally bind itself to provide a service for a particular person in return for a gift;
* nevertheless, having received a gift, the charity may have regard to the wishes of the donor (especially if more gifts may be made).

18.4.4   Gifts of the home

Advising the client checklist

Elderly people often contemplate transferring their home to their children even though they still intend to live there, and it may be a son or daughter who puts the idea into their heads and seeks to give instructions. Advisers should have detailed knowledge of the implications on the possible future liability to pay for care and the social care funding rules, as the local authority may seek to treat the client as still owning the asset, charge them accordingly and seek to recover those charges. In addition, advisers should understand what care is provided free from the NHS (see **Chapter 10**).

The following matters should be considered before acting in such a transaction. They are not exhaustive and reference should be made to the Law Society Practice Note: Making Gifts of Assets (6 October 2011).

* Who is the client? If it is the elderly person you must act in that person's best interests but if it is a donee then the elderly person should be advised (and expected) to take independent legal advice to avoid conflict of interest issues.

- How well do you know the client? It may be necessary to spend some time with the client and talk about wider issues on their own before giving relevant advice to satisfy yourself as to capacity and undue influence issues.
- Has another solicitor previously acted for the client? If so, should you speak to that solicitor in case there are factors to be taken into account which are not apparent (and which the donee seeks to avoid)?
- Does the client have capacity to make the gift? (See **18.2.1** and, for more detail, **Chapter 1** for tests of capacity.)
- Why is the gift to be made and will the purpose be achieved?
- What other financial resources does the client have and can the client raise alternative funds?
- Does the client understand the effect of the gift (that it passes ownership) and recognise and accept the vulnerability that the gift creates?
- What previous gifts have been made, how much and to whom?
- Does the client understand the impact of the gift on the will or intestacy?
- Does the client actually want and intend to make a gift or expect that some rights or benefits will be reserved?

Reasons for making a transfer

There may be compelling reasons for the transfer by an elderly person of the home, or an interest in that home, to another member of the family or even an outsider. The legal title may not have been vested in the appropriate person in the first place, or the title may not reflect the true beneficial interests in the home. This may be the case where another person has:

- made substantial financial contributions to the home;
- provided care services over many years in reliance upon assurances that the home would become theirs after the death of the present owner.

In these (and other) situations it may be desirable to give effect to the transfer while the elderly owner can still make the decision so as to establish legal rights which all would wish to be acknowledged. This is of particular importance where the recipient is already a joint occupier of the home.

Of most concern are gifts made to preserve the home for the next generation with vague assurances as to future occupation and provision of care if needed. Before the client decides to make the gift the factors to be taken into account should be explained on a benefits versus risks basis.

Potential benefits

- Assumed certainty as to the future ownership of the property.
- Saving of probate fees and administrative costs and (depending on the circumstances and asset) inheritance tax following death.
- Minimising delays on incapacity or death.

- Avoiding the stress of selling a property.
- Avoidance of means-tested contributions towards the cost of residential or nursing home care or other services arranged or provided by the local authority.
- The release of income from maintaining and insuring the property (if the donee will meet these expenses).
- Peace of mind where moral obligations are fulfilled.

Potential risks

- Disputes within the family as to the validity of the gift.
- The value of the home may still be taken into account under means-testing rules (see **14.2.3**); the donor could be deprived of funding even though lacking personal resources and without any redress against the donee; the home would not in any event be taken into account if still occupied by a partner or by a relative who is incapacitated or has attained 60 years.
- Effect on capital gains tax liabilities: the owner-occupier exemption may be available for the gift but lost thereafter; there will be no revaluation of the home on the donor's death.
- Effect on IHT liabilities: there could be a liability if the donee dies before the donor; there will be no saving while the donor continues to live in the home because of the 'reservation of benefit' rules (different schemes exist to mitigate this but HMRC has challenged some of these).
- The donee may fail to support the donor or seek to release the value in the home by moving the donor prematurely into a care home; die without making any suitable provision for the donor; become ill, divorced or insolvent and unable to support the donor.
- The home may be put at risk or lost on the divorce of the donee; its use by the donee as security for a loan; the insolvency or bankruptcy of the donee.

The risk of circumstances changing is illustrated by *Thomson* v. *Foy* [2009] EWHC 1076 (Ch), where the elderly donor wished to recover a gift of a share of a property made in different circumstances. The well-advised donor should at the very least consider all possible alternatives to an absolute gift which preserve some flexibility and control for the donor.

Some of these pitfalls could be avoided by creating a tenancy or settlement of the home to secure a parent's right to continued occupation, although this may not assist the usually desired benefit of avoiding a means-tested contribution towards the cost of care provision. Nevertheless, the significance of proper legal documentation should not be overlooked in inter-generational arrangements.

CHAPTER 19

Testamentary dispositions and trusts

Amanda King-Jones and Stewart Stretton-Hill

19.1 SUCCESSION

An individual may state by will who is to inherit any assets owned at death and appoint executors to administer the estate. The Court of Protection may make a statutory will for a person who lacks testamentary capacity. In the absence of a will, the intestacy rules specify who is entitled to inherit and the order of priority for administrators. Such outcome may be changed in a number of ways:

- any beneficiary may disclaim a legacy;
- beneficiaries may enter into a deed of family arrangement and in effect rewrite a will or the effects of intestacy;
- the court has power to provide for dependants under the Inheritance (Provision for Family and Dependants) Act 1975;
- foreign laws relating to foreign assets may override UK law and a UK will;
- a person who causes the death of another is usually prevented from benefiting from the death of his victim, whether under a will, intestacy or gift, although there is discretion in the case of manslaughter under the Forfeiture Act 1982.

The succession rights of a descendant of a beneficiary who disclaims or forfeits his entitlement are preserved by the Estates of Deceased Persons (Forfeiture Rule and Law of Succession) Act 2011 which came into force on 1 February 2012.

It is possible that unmarried partners may acquire certain rights under the Cohabitation Rights Bill 2015–16, which proposes certain protections for persons who live together as a couple and for cohabitants. This is subject to it being enacted.

19.1.1 Reasons for making a will: intestacy

It is very important to ensure the devolution of a client's estate in a way that they wish, and not as the law decrees it under the intestacy rules (see **19.3**). Where there is no valid will, an estate is administered according to the intestacy rules and this can lead to unexpected consequences. In many cases this will actually prejudice the surviving spouse, may distribute the estate to relatives who would not have been in the thoughts of the testator (e.g. brothers or sisters) or can create an unequal distribution between issue.

19.1.2   Reasons for making a will: other

These include:

- to include appropriate administrative powers;
- to take advantage of inheritance tax (IHT) planning;
- to appoint executors of the testator's choice to administer the estate and provide for substitution of executors;
- to protect assets and beneficiaries;
- to protect against potential claims under the Inheritance (Provision for Family and Dependants) Act 1975, particularly where insufficient provision would be made under the intestacy rules;
- to record funeral requests and arrangements;
- to provide appropriate authority to individuals to arrange the funeral;
- to protect against the future bankruptcy of a beneficiary;
- to protect against future financial claims on divorce;
- to overcome indecision of a testator as to how the estate is divided, giving executors guidance in a separate letter of wishes;
- to protect mentally/physically incapacitated beneficiaries and to preserve assets;
- to postpone the age of entitlement of beneficiaries.

These issues are addressed in more detail throughout the remainder of this chapter and **Chapter 20**.

19.1.3   Foreign assets and domicile

It is very important to establish domicile of a deceased at the outset of taking instructions. This has an impact on:

- validity of the will;
- liability to IHT and other taxes (and particularly the application of Inheritance Tax Act 1984, s.18 (spouse exemption));
- the acceptance of appointment of executor and trustees and the right to a grant to representation;
- succession to the estate and assets;
- deemed domicile provisions (Inheritance Tax Act 1984, s.267) (a person may be domiciled outside England and Wales for other purposes but be deemed domiciled in England and Wales for IHT).

Many people assume if they own assets abroad these will not be taken into account for IHT on their death. If the client is domiciled in England and Wales (broadly, this is their home and where their assets are based) they will be liable for IHT on their worldwide assets.

Even assuming an England and Wales will has been made, it is advisable for there to be a will covering the assets in the foreign jurisdiction, particularly as many

European countries have laws which require particular proportions of an estate to go to certain 'reserved beneficiaries', generally the testator's children rather than their spouse.

It should be noted that the EU Succession Regulations (Brussels IV) (Regulation (EU) 650/2012) came into force on 17 August 2015 and are binding on all member states, except the UK, Ireland and Denmark. The Regulations will enable testators to make an express choice of law under their will on jurisdiction, applicable law, recognition and enforcement of decisions and acceptance and enforcement of testamentary documents.

Although the UK has opted out of the Regulations, the rules may impact on individuals making wills in England and Wales. If the testator does not make an election in their will, the Regulations will apply the law of the country where they are habitually resident. Further, if the testator already has a will in another EU state, this could imply an election and might result in rules of forced heirship being applied.

Steps should be taken at the outset to determine the client's habitual residence and great care must be taken in deciding whether to make an election under the Regulations.

While it may not be appropriate to determine domicile in advance of death, it is vital that the issues of evidence concerning domicile are addressed prior to death and should wherever possible be recorded including:

- nationality of the deceased (and if appropriate their surviving spouse) and where they were born;
- an outline of their education and employment history;
- the date they left England and Wales and set up their main home abroad;
- the dates of return to England and Wales;
- how long they stayed in England and Wales;
- the purpose of the stay;
- a statement as to why the deceased did not intend to remain in or return to England and Wales with details of the evidence to support this;
- details of citizenship and passports held by the testator during his or her lifetime.

To provide certainty of domicile in England and Wales, a non-UK domiciled individual can elect to be treated as domiciled in the UK for the purposes of claiming spouse exemption. Provided certain conditions are satisfied, the election can be made during the lifetime of the couple (Inheritance Tax Act 1984, s.267ZA(3)) or within two years after the date of death of one of the couple (Inheritance Tax Act 1984, s.267ZA(4)).

It is important to note that a client's habitual residence for the purposes of the Succession Regulations may not necessarily be the same as their domicile as different tests apply. Habitual residence requires a close and stable connection with the particular state. When determining habitual residence, the practitioner should consider, among other factors, how often an individual visited and how long they spent in the state concerned together with the purpose of the visits.

19.1.4 The 'estate' and joint property

Schedules IHT404 (Jointly owned Assets), IHT418 (Assets held in Trust), IHT409 (Pensions) and IHT410 (Life Assurance and Annuities) accompanying the IHT400 form raise pertinent and searching questions of personal representatives on the death of a testator. Provision of records by clients in advance of death could save considerable time and costs if the information is available and in order.

Establishment of ownership is vital because it has an impact on:

- devolution of assets;
- the 'estate' available under Inheritance (Provision for Family and Dependants) Act 1975 claims;
- the burden of IHT and personal representatives' liability: they are liable to the extent of the 'estate' of the deceased and they are personally liable for the incorrect distribution of assets;
- intestacy;
- the gross and net estate for probate;
- IHT;
- survivorship and commorientes.

The basic assumption is that the client's name on the title or other documentation is evidence of beneficial ownership, but if that is not to be treated as the correct ownership then further documentation must be in place. Declarations of trust must be made by deed or document to establish ownership as tenants in common or joint tenants, which in relation to land must be recorded by formal notice of severance and/or a restriction placed on the Land Registry title.

Assets that are not in sole or joint beneficial ownership, e.g. held as nominee, trustee, attorney, must be documented. Assets written in trust particularly for tax planning purposes, e.g. insurance proceeds, pension death benefits, must be recorded through proper documentation, normally in the form either of specially prepared declarations of trust or in standard printed forms produced by insurance companies. These need to be submitted to the insurance companies or placed with the will.

Any property or savings in joint names normally passes to the surviving joint owner(s) beneficially unless they are trustees, although land can be held in undivided shares (i.e. as tenants in common) which pass to the personal representatives on death.

Although unusual, it is possible for individuals to hold savings as tenants in common but this can result in great difficulty determining the value of the account attributable to each co-owner and may depend on their contributions to the savings during their lifetime.

19.1.5 Severance by will

It is well known that under Law of Property Act 1925, s.36(2) the joint tenancy of a property can be severed. However, in *Re Woolnough; Perkins* v. *Borden* [2002] WTLR 595 it was determined that it was possible for severance of the joint tenancy of a property to take place by will even though the wills were not sufficient to be mutual wills. It was held that the way in which the property was to be dealt with under the wills of each of the brother and sister was sufficient to infer that a severance of the joint tenancy of a property owned by the brother and sister had taken place on the execution of their wills. However, both wills contained an express reference to the property and both of them had given instructions to the same solicitors at the same time.

Conversely, in *Carr* v. *Isard* [2006] EWHC 2095 (Ch) it was held that the joint tenancy was not severed by the wills of the husband and wife because there was not enough evidence to demonstrate an intention to sever the joint tenancy. This was based on the findings that it was not clear what one of the parties had intended to achieve in their will. As a result, it was not certain that the provisions of the will were inconsistent with a joint tenancy and the couple had not communicated the terms of their wills to each other.

These decisions emphasise the need to ensure clients understand the devolution of their assets and clear steps are required to evidence an individual's intention to sever a joint tenancy.

19.1.6 Professional risks

Solicitors may also be negligent if they do not advise on or prepare a notice of severance for a client where the terms of the will would make the devolution of the property go in the contrary direction intended if held one way or the other (*Carr-Glynn* v. *Frearsons* [1999] Ch 326).

19.1.7 Nominations

Certain assets may be disposed of on death by a written nomination which may be statutory or non-statutory but will be of no effect if the nominee dies first:

- these may include industrial and provident society accounts;
- pension schemes may also include provision for nominations;
- those for National Savings Certificates and National Savings Bank accounts were discontinued in 1981 but any then in existence may still take effect.

19.2 WILLS

19.2.1 Testamentary capacity

For information on the capacity for making a will, see **1.4.3**, **1.5.3** and **4.10.2** in respect of statutory wills.

Testamentary capacity checklist

Keep a record of where the points below are evidenced (e.g. letter to client/ attendance note/will commentary).

1. **Does the testator understand the nature of the act (of making a will or making a different will) and its effects?** Meaning that the testator should understand:

   (a)   they will die;
   (b)   the will shall come into operation on their death, but not before;
   (c)   they can change or revoke the will at any time before their death, provided they have capacity to do so;
   (d)   who should be appointed as executors and why;
   (e)   who gets what under the will;
   (f)   whether a beneficiary's gift is outright or conditional;
   (g)   if they spend their money, give away or sell their property during their lifetime, the beneficiaries may lose out;
   (h)   the likely effects of making or not making a will or deciding to change their will.

2. **Does the testator understand the extent of the property being disposed of?** Meaning that the testator should understand:

   (a)   the extent of all the property solely owned by them;
   (b)   that certain types of jointly owned property might pass automatically to the other joint owner regardless of what the will says;
   (c)   whether there are benefits payable on their death which might be unaffected by the terms of their new will;
   (d)   the scope of their property might change during their lifetime.

3. **Does the testator comprehend and appreciate the claims to which they ought to give effect?** Meaning that the testator should understand:

   (a)   their reasons for wishing to benefit some people and not others;
   (b)   that possible beneficiaries may have already received adequate provision from them, may be financially better off than others, may have been more attentive or caring than others, or may be in greater need of assistance due to their age, gender, physical or mental problems.

4. **Does the testator have a disorder of the mind that poisons his affections,**

perverts his sense of right, or prevents the exercise of his natural faculties to bring about a disposal of property which, if the mind had been sound, would not have been made?

It is important to remember here that you are assessing the testator's ability to make a decision, not their ability to make a sensible or wise decision. If the answer is yes, move to question 5. If the answer is no, move straight to question 6 below.

The test of capacity, above, was originally set down in *Banks* v. *Goodfellow* (1870) LR 5 QB 549. It has been unclear whether the statutory test of capacity set out in the Mental Capacity Act 2005 superseded the common law *Banks* v. *Goodfellow* test. The rulings in *Kicks* v. *Leigh* [2014] EWHC 3926 (Ch) and *Walker* v. *Badmin* [2014] All ER (D) 258 (Nov) held that the common law test still applies in relation to testamentary capacity, although it may take a decision in a higher court for the debate to be put to rest.

5. **Decision-making and reasoning.** If it is considered that an unusual decision has been made by the testator, ask why the will is being made in this way, record the answer and assess whether the testator's answer is satisfactory in light of their capacity. Consider also the possibility of undue influence.

This is an exercise to establish whether the testator can justify their decision.

It is advisable to be fully conversant with the Law Society Practice Note: Financial Abuse (13 June 2013) which sets out potential forms and signs of financial abuse to help identify the possibility of undue influence.

6. **Timing and testamentary capacity.** If the answers to the above questions are all satisfactory, have they been consistently satisfactory:

(a)   on taking initial instructions; and
(b)   on executing the document.

Prior to execution of the will, remind the testator about the nature and effect of the will that has been drafted and where the assets are going.

If capacity on execution has changed since taking initial instructions, move to question 7 below.

7. **Further analysis of capacity at the time of executing the will.** Does the testator:

(a)   Remember and understand their initial instructions given in order to prepare the new will?
(b)   Understand each clause of the new will when explained?
(c)   Understand that they are executing a will for which they have previously given instructions to us?

The test, above, was established in *Parker* v. *Felgate* (1883) 8 PD 171 and was confirmed in *Perrins* v. *Holland* [2010] EWCA Civ 840.

Importantly, where the testator is considered elderly or seriously ill, it is good practice for the will to be witnessed or approved by a medical practitioner (*Re Simpson; Schaniel* v. *Simpson* (1977) 121 Sol Jo 224). If there is doubt as to the testator's capacity, it is advisable that an opinion from an appropriately qualified medical practitioner is obtained. The importance of this is enshrined in Principle 3 of the STEP Code for the Preparation of Wills in England and Wales. However, it is vital that the medical report is obtained promptly otherwise the individual preparing the will may find themselves at risk of a negligence claim, see *Feltham* v. *Bouskell* [2013] EWHC 1952 (Ch), in which the medical report was not received for five weeks after the doctor received instructions. On the facts the court found that the solicitor should have chased for the report after 10 days. This decision could cause practical problems for practitioners given the pressures under which doctors are often placed.

8.   **Does the testator satisfy the requirements of MCA 2005, s.3?** Meaning do they:

(a)   understand the information relevant to the decision;

(b)   retain that information;

(c)   use or weigh that information as part of the process of making the decision;

(d)   communicate their decision (whether by talking/using sign language or other means).

19.2.2   Fees and confirmation of instructions

The cost of the will and any supplemental services should be discussed with the client at this stage in accordance with the SRA Code of Conduct 2011, Chapter 1, in particular outcome 1.13 which requires that clients receive the best possible information, both at the time of engagement and when appropriate as the matter progresses, about the likely overall cost of the matter. The solicitor should also discuss with them how they will pay the costs in accordance with outcome 1.6.

19.2.3   Taking instructions

The Law Society Practice Note: Initial Interviews (6 October 2011) provides guidance on the information to be obtained from the client, and on the initial information to be given to the client and the main areas to be covered in the interviews.

SRA Code of Conduct 2011, outcome 1.12 requires that clients are put in a position to make informed decisions about the services they need so the solicitor should obtain all necessary information (especially if they are to be an executor) and this generally comprises:

- personal and family details, including domicile and foreign assets; marital status; whether a cohabitee (same sex or heterosexual relationship); prospects or intentions; and issues involving second marriages and any possible claimants on the estate;
- the general nature and size of the estate including the extent of debts and liabilities (e.g. mortgages); personal chattels; jointly owned assets (joint tenants or tenants in common); life assurance provision and continuing pensions (and any nominations and declarations of trust); any business interests;
- any interests in a trust or settlement (or power of appointment);
- any substantial gifts made or to be made during lifetime;
- the persons for whom the client wishes to (or should) provide, including any cohabitee or dependent person and any particular problem situations (e.g. a mentally incapacitated beneficiary);
- any relevant special wishes: the importance to the client of tax planning; any beneficiary for whom provision is to be made in priority to all others;
- any changes that may occur before death in any of the foregoing matters.

At the same time as taking instructions the opportunity should be taken to consider whether the client also requires or needs:

- a lasting power of attorney (financial decisions or health and care decisions) (see **Chapter 4**);
- an advance statement (see **11.8**);
- an advance decision to refuse medical treatment (see **11.8**);
- assistance with tax affairs or investment or tax planning advice.

Particular care should be taken to identify potential tax implications and to refer the matter to a specialist if the advice is outside the practitioner's specialism. Although successfully appealed, *Mehjoo* v. *Harben Barker (a firm)* [2014] EWCA Civ 358 illustrates the risk to professionals of failing to clearly establish the extent of the matters on which they are retained to advise.

For interviews in a client's own home there must also be compliance with the Consumer Contracts (Information, Cancellation and Additional Charges) Regulations 2013, SI 2013/3134. These regulations are relevant to all contracts.

When a contract is not made in the client's home or business premises, at the time the contract is made the client must be given notice of his/her right to cancel the contract and work should not be undertaken during the cancellation period unless authorised in writing, email or by a similar medium.

In addition the specific requirements, in relation to contracts made in a client's home or business premises are:

- Information must be provided in a clear and comprehensible format on paper or, if the client agrees, on another 'durable medium' (e.g. by email) in relation to the:

    - main characteristics of the services;

- identity (name, address, telephone number, email and fax number) of the practice;
- total price of the services, including all taxes;
- timescale for provision of the service;
- arrangements for payment;
- complaints handling policy including the address to which complaints should be sent;
- conditions, time limit and procedure for cancelling the contract;
- reasonable costs the client will be required to pay if authorised to start work within the cancellation period;
- availability and how to obtain a copy of the SRA Handbook; and
- complaints handling role of the Legal Ombudsman.

See also the Law Society Practice Note: Consumer Contracts Regulations 2013 (18 September 2014).

19.2.4 SRA guidance

The SRA has published useful guidance (SRA Ethics Guidance: Drafting and Preparation of Wills, 11 July 2014) on will writing which highlights specific points of compliance and good practice.

When preparing wills for clients the solicitor must have regard to SRA Code of Conduct 2011, Chapter 1: outcomes 1.2, 1.4, 1.5 and 1.12 and Chapter 7: outcomes 7.2, 7.3, 7.6 and 7.8.

Note in particular the following.

Appointment of solicitor as executor

It is not improper for a client to appoint a solicitor personally or the solicitor's practice as an executor of the will. However, the client must not be led to believe that the appointment of a solicitor is essential or the usual practice. The client must not be encouraged to appoint a solicitor or their practice as an executor unless it is in the client's best interests, which might be the case if their affairs are complex, there may be potential disputes in the family or all the beneficiaries are minors. All the options available including the fact that it is not necessary to appoint a professional must be explained to the client and that advice documented.

Gifts to connected parties

If the client wishes to leave a significant gift to the solicitor preparing the will, or a member of their family, the client must be advised to seek independent legal advice. The solicitor must cease acting until the client has taken such advice. The gift does not necessarily have to be of significant size in relation to the client's estate but simply significant in value itself. Further guidance can be found in the Law Society

Practice Note: Preparing a Will When Your Client is Leaving a Gift for You, Your Family or Colleagues (20 January 2015).

Retention of the will

Finally, it must be explained to the client that it is important for the executors to know where the will is kept and that they should keep a copy of the will at home. Options other than keeping the will at home or with the solicitor's practice must be explained to the client such as the Probate Service storage facility which may be more convenient for executors.

19.2.5   Law Society Wills and Inheritance Protocol

In 2013 the Law Society launched the 'Wills and Inheritance Quality Scheme' (WIQS). The purpose of the scheme is to provide a quality mark showing that accredited practices have the necessary expertise to deliver wills and inheritance advice, reassuring clients that they will receive the best quality advice. The Scheme is referred to by the SRA as 'guidance on best practice in taking instructions for and drafting wills'. The principles in WIQS are, therefore, important for any practitioner involved in preparing wills whether or not the practice has signed up to the Scheme.

WIQS is designed for practices authorised by the SRA offering both wills and estate administration services. It is voluntary and practices applying for accreditation must demonstrate compliance with the Wills and Inheritance Protocol.

The Protocol sets out obligations on the accredited practice to ensure transparency in process, costs and communications. Among other things the Protocol requires the practice to:

- explain to the client the issues raised and options for dealing with them;
- explain to the client the processes involved;
- set out for the client a likely timeframe for dealing with the matter;
- acknowledge client correspondence within 48 hours;
- consider whether the client requires advice on matters beyond the expertise of the practice (e.g. tax advice) and to make a record of the client's refusal to take such advice, if applicable;
- keep accurate attendance notes particularly in relation to instructions received from elderly or ill clients;
- take full details of assets including life insurance policies, trust interests and death benefits, liabilities, family, dependants, ownership of assets, and priorities for estate;
- be alert to the signs of undue influence and financial abuse;
- identify and advise on assets passing independently of the will;
- consider and advise on inheritance tax including potential reliefs available on certain assets;

- consider and advise on the use of trusts;
- consider and advise on the choice of executors.

The application process and full details of the Protocol can be found on the Law Society website.

19.2.6 Recording instructions

After a death there is often a need for information about the circumstances in which a will was made. The Law Society Practice Note: Disputed Wills (6 October 2011) provides guidance for solicitors preparing testamentary instruments to record the circumstances relating to the preparation of these instruments.

Following the testator's death, professional advisers acting for a potential claimant in relation to a claim on the validity of a will should consider whether it is appropriate to seek information from the solicitors who prepared the will. A letter requesting this information has come to be known as a *Larke* v. *Nugus* letter ([2000] WTLR 1033). This type of letter may request some or all of the following information:

- How long had you known the deceased?
- Who introduced you to the deceased?
- The date you received instructions from the deceased.
- Contemporaneous notes of all meetings and telephone calls including an indication of where the meeting took place and who else was present at the meeting.
- How the instructions were expressed.
- What indication the deceased gave that he knew he was making a will.
- Whether the deceased exhibited any signs of confusion or loss of memory.
- Whether and to what extent earlier wills were discussed and what attempts were made to discuss departures from the deceased's earlier will-making pattern; what reasons the testator gave for making any such departures.
- How the provisions of the will were explained to the deceased.
- Who, apart from the attesting witnesses, was present at the execution of the will and where, when and how this took place.

This information can only be obtained from the original file. It is very important that files are retained in accordance with the Law Society Practice Note: File Retention: Wills and Probate (6 October 2011).

19.2.7 Contents and form of will

A simple will may (and usually should) contain clauses dealing with:

- revocation of previous testamentary dispositions;
- appointment of executors (and guardians and trustees for any infant children);
- any specific legacies (of realty and of personalty) and pecuniary legacies;

- disposal of the residue of the estate;
- any wishes as to burial or cremation.

In less straightforward situations, especially where there are infant beneficiaries or continuing provision is intended, further clauses may need to deal with:

- the terms of any trust;
- any additional powers of the trustees;
- administrative provisions;
- survivorship provisions;
- gifts to charities.

19.2.8 Execution

A will must be in writing and the testator must sign or make his mark:

- The testator's signature need not be at the end of the will provided it was intended to give effect to the will.
- A person may sign on behalf and by the direction of the testator in his presence (Wills Act 1837, s.9, as substituted by Administration of Justice Act 1982, s.17).
- The signature (or mark) must be witnessed by, or acknowledged to, two people present at the same time who sign as witnesses.
- An incomplete signature is only sufficient if the signatory is unable to finish for physical reasons and not because of a change of mind.
- A testator who cannot read needs to have known the contents of the will before signing and the attestation clause must make this clear. Include 'with knowledge of the contents thereof' in the attestation clause where the testator is blind or partially sighted. This is also desirable where the testator's signature appears doubtful.

You could be liable in a negligence claim to disappointed beneficiaries if you accept instructions for a will but delay in its preparation or fail to ensure that the will is valid (see *White* v. *Jones* [1995] 2 WLR 187 and *Esterhuizen* v. *Allied Dunbar Assurance plc* [1998] 2 FLR 668). In the latter case Longmore J said:

> It is in my judgment not enough just to leave written instructions with the testator. In ordinary circumstances just to leave written instructions and to do no more will not only be contrary to good practice but also in my view negligent.

To protect themselves solicitors should have in writing an offer in the following terms:

- the client can visit the solicitor's office to sign his will and have it attested; or
- if the client prefers, the solicitor will visit the client's house with a member of staff to sign the will and have it attested; or
- if the client prefers, the client can make his or her own arrangements.

If the client makes his own arrangements, the solicitor should follow up within a reasonable time to ensure that the client has executed the will and the will should be checked to ensure it has been signed correctly.

19.2.9   Revocation

A will may only be revoked by a testator, e.g. by a later will or physical destruction with intent to revoke. A will is revoked by subsequent marriage but not by supervening incapacity. The capacity required for revocation is the same as for execution of a will.

19.2.10   Mutual wills

In some situations the equitable doctrine of mutual wills may impose a trust on property to frustrate the effect of the revocation of a will.

If two (or more) people make complementary wills and agree not to revoke their wills without the others' consent and the first to die has kept to that agreement, the survivor's property will be subject to a trust on the terms of the mutual wills. There are three requirements which must all be satisfied for there to be valid mutual wills:

1.   The testators must agree to make their wills in agreed terms.
2.   They must agree not to amend them unilaterally.
3.   On the death of the first testator to die that person must have continued to have carried out the agreement: *Re Goodchild (Deceased); Goodchild* v. *Goodchild* [1997] 1 WLR 1216.

19.2.11   Precedents

Reference should be made to the following published works:

Angus T., Clarke A., Hewitt P. and Reed P. (2006) *Inheritance Act Claims: A Practical Guide*, Law Society.
Barlow R. *et al.* (2014) *Williams on Wills*, 10th revised edn, LexisNexis.
Kessler J. (2014) *Drafting Trusts and Will Trusts: A Modern Approach*, 12th edn, Sweet & Maxwell.
King L. (2015) *Probate Practitioner's Handbook*, 7th edn, Law Society.
Law Society (2013) *Wills and Inheritance Protocol*, Law Society.
Whitehouse C. and King L. (eds) (looseleaf) *Administration of Estates*, LexisNexis.

19.3   INTESTACY

19.3.1   Legislation

See the Administration of Estates Act 1925 and Inheritance and Trustees' Powers Act 2014 in relation to the estates of persons dying on or after 1 October 2014. In relation to deaths between 1 February 2009 and 30 September 2014 the Family

Provision (Intestate Succession) Order 2009, SI 2009/135 applies and for deaths before 1 February 2009 the Family Provision (Intestate Succession) Order 1993, SI 1993/2906 applies. Since the Civil Partnership Act 2004 came into effect on 5 December 2005, same sex couples that have registered their partnerships have broadly the same rights as married couples under the intestacy rules.

19.3.2 Entitlement

The rules relating to entitlement under the intestacy rules changed on 1 October 2014. On an intestacy a surviving spouse or civil partner receives the following, but can make certain elections, including taking the matrimonial home at valuation as part of his or her share (or making up any shortfall):

1. For deaths on or after 1 October 2014 and the deceased left no surviving issue: the entire estate.

2. For deaths on or after 1 October 2014 and the deceased left surviving issue:

    - a statutory legacy (with interest) of £250,000; and
    - a life interest in half the residue.

3. For all deaths before 1 October 2014:

    - all personal chattels (as defined);
    - a statutory legacy (with interest) which:
        - for deaths from 1 December 1993 to 1 February 2009 is £125,000 when there are issue and £200,000 when there are no issue but there is a specified relative surviving; or
        - for deaths on or after 1 February 2009 is £250,000 when there are issue and £450,000 when there are no issue but there is a specified relative surviving;
    - when there are issue, a life interest in half the residue;
    - when there are no issue but there is a specified relative surviving, half the residue absolutely;
    - when there are no issue and there are no specified relatives surviving, the entire estate absolutely.

'Specified relatives' who may inherit apart from a spouse or civil partner are a parent, brother or sister of the whole blood or the issue of such persons.

Issue receive all that the surviving spouse or civil partner does not receive, and this is on the statutory trusts which means equally between those who attain 18 years or marry before then, with children of a deceased child taking that child's share on the same basis.

Others

If there is no surviving spouse or civil partner or issue the estate goes to a surviving parent or brothers and sisters of the whole blood on the statutory trusts, whom failing to remoter relatives (and ultimately to the Crown, though ex gratia payments may then be made to persons whom the deceased would have been likely to benefit).

Only a spouse or civil partner or blood relatives (or adopted persons) can benefit, and a cohabitee has no rights under an intestacy.

19.4 STATUTORY WILLS

The Court of Protection has jurisdiction to authorise the execution, for a person who lacks capacity to do so, of a will making any provision which could be made in a will executed by that person if he had capacity to make it (see MCA 2005, ss.16, 18 and Sched.2, para.2).

A statutory will is particularly useful where wills may be out of date or may not carry out the intentions of a testator. For details of the procedure and considerations see **4.10**.

There is a helpful Court of Protection Practice Direction on how to start statutory wills proceedings. This is Practice Direction 9F: *Applications Relating to Statutory Wills, Codicils, Settlements and Other Dealings with P's Property*.

19.5 INHERITANCE PROVISION

19.5.1 Claimants

Under the Inheritance (Provision for Family and Dependants) Act 1975 (as amended by the Inheritance and Trustees' Powers Act 2014), certain persons may apply to the court for financial provision out of the estate of a deceased person:

- a spouse or civil partner of the deceased;
- a former spouse or former civil partner of the deceased, but not one who has formed a subsequent marriage or civil partnership, unless the claim is prevented by a court order made on the financial settlement following divorce or dissolution of a civil partnership;
- any person if, during the whole of the period of two years ending immediately before the date when the deceased died, the person was living:

  - in the same household as the deceased; and
  - as the spouse or civil partner of the deceased;

- a child of the deceased, whether or not a dependant;

- any person (not being a child of the deceased) who, in the case of any marriage or civil partnership to which the deceased was at any time a party, was treated by the deceased as a child of the family in relation to that marriage or civil partnership;
- any person who immediately before the death of the deceased was being maintained, either wholly or partly by the deceased.

A person may qualify as being maintained by the deceased if they can show that the deceased made a substantial contribution to their reasonable needs other than for valuable consideration.

19.5.2 Relevant matters

The application is made on the basis that the disposition of the deceased's estate effected by his will or the law relating to intestacy, or a combination of both, is not such as to make reasonable financial provision for the applicant. In deciding whether to make an order the court takes into account all the circumstances. When determining whether reasonable financial provision has been made the court must have regard to the following matters (Inheritance (Provision for Family and Dependants) Act 1975, s.3):

- the financial resources and financial needs which in the foreseeable future the applicant, any other applicant or any beneficiary of the estate has or is likely to have;
- any obligation and responsibilities which the deceased had towards any applicant or beneficiary;
- the size and nature of the net estate;
- any physical or mental disability of any applicant or beneficiary;
- any other matter, including the conduct of the applicant or any other person, which in the circumstances of the case the court may consider relevant;
- (on an application by a spouse or former spouse) the age of and contribution made by the applicant, and duration of the marriage (s.3(2));
- (on an application by a child or person treated as a child of the deceased) the manner in which the applicant was being (or might be expected to be) educated or trained and, if treated as a child, the extent to which the deceased had assumed responsibility for maintenance and whether any other person was liable;
- the standard of living enjoyed by the applicant during the lifetime of the deceased and the extent to which the deceased contributed to that standard.

It is not clear when and to what extent the financial resources of the applicant include any means-tested state benefits or support that could be received.

19.5.3 Objective test

The facts as known to the court and the claimant's circumstances at the date of the hearing are relevant, rather than those at the date of the will or the death.

The question is whether, in all the circumstances, the disposition of the deceased's estate makes reasonable financial provision for the applicant, not whether the deceased has acted reasonably in making no or only limited provision. The deceased's moral obligation, if any, may be a relevant factor, though again this must be balanced against all the other factors. The deceased's reasons and wishes comprise only part of the circumstances of the case and may be outweighed by other factors. A statement made by the deceased, whether or not in writing or signed, is admissible as evidence of any fact stated therein (Civil Evidence Act 1995).

19.5.4 Court's powers

The court may make an order in favour of the applicant for periodical payments, a lump sum, transfer of property or acquisition and transfer or settlement of property. It may also:

- treat a joint tenancy in any property as severed and the deceased's beneficial share as part of the net estate to such extent as appears just in all the circumstances;
- set aside dispositions made by the deceased within six years prior to the death with the intention of defeating an application for financial provision;
- vary the trusts on which the deceased's estate is held, whether under a will or intestacy.

19.5.5 Procedure

An application must be made within six months from the date of the grant of representation to the estate, unless the court in its discretion gives leave to extend time.

Applications are made in the County Court for the district in which the deceased resided at the date of death and there are criteria under the Courts and Legal Services Act 1990 for determining whether a case should be moved up to the High Court (Chancery Division or Family Division). Rules and Practice Directions set out the detailed procedure to be followed.

19.5.6 Tax implications

Where an order is made (including a consent order) the estate is treated for IHT purposes as if the deceased's property devolved subject to the provisions of the order (Inheritance Tax Act 1984, s.146). Unlike variations (see below) there is no time limit and an election is not required. If agreement is reached within two years this can be dealt with by a deed of variation rather than a consent order through the court.

19.5.7 Other claims

Consideration now also needs to be given to claims concerning proprietary estoppel. Where a person has relied on a promise to his detriment, that person may be entitled to an interest in any property concerned although he may not be entitled to claim under the Inheritance (Provision for Family and Dependants) Act 1975. *Gillett* v. *Holt* [2001] Ch 210 set out prerequisites for a claim. The claimant succeeded in receiving a share of an estate. A promise had been made that a benefit in property would be received on a person's death and the claimant changed his situation and acted to his detriment based on that assurance or promise.

19.6   POST-DEATH TAX PLANNING

It is not too late to change the provisions of a will or the outcome of intestacy after the death. An individual beneficiary may disclaim a benefit or the beneficiaries may agree to vary the distribution of the estate, and the testator can even provide for this by leaving the estate (or part of it) on a discretionary trust.

19.6.1   Variations and disclaimers

Inheritance Tax Act 1984, s.142 provides that if, within two years of death, any dispositions are varied or benefits disclaimed, such variation or disclaimer is not a transfer of value and tax is charged as if the variation had been made by the deceased or the disclaimed benefit had never been conferred.

The variation or disclaimer:

- Must be in writing.
- Must not be made for any consideration in money or money's worth.
- Must be entered into by the person 'whose interest is affected'. This can cause problems if there are owners whose interests are affected. If a beneficiary does not have mental capacity to agree to a variation, a Court of Protection order will be required to effect a variation which reduces or affects that beneficiary's interest under the will or intestacy. The same procedure is followed as for statutory wills (see **19.4**).
- Can be made even if the property involved has been distributed and the estate administered.
- May result in a repayment of IHT or additional IHT having to be paid.

There are differences between a variation and a disclaimer:

- A variation of the property can be given to anyone whereas a disclaimer is merely a refusal to accept the property and it passes to the next in line which could give rise to an intestacy in relation to the disclaimed assets.
- Receipt of a benefit prevents disclaimer but not a variation, and part disclaimer may not be allowed (but one of two gifts could be disclaimed).
- A variation will only be read back to the date of death if a written election is made in the instrument of variation, whereas this is automatic for a disclaimer.
- A variation is not retrospective for income tax purposes, whereas in the case of a disclaimer the beneficiary is deemed never to have had an interest.

HM Revenue and Customs provides advice relating to deeds of variation on the Gov.uk website together with an Instrument of Variation Checklist (IOV2).

19.6.2 Capital gains tax

Similar provisions exist in Taxation of Chargeable Gains Act 1992, s.62(6)–(10), whereby the variation or disclaimer need not be treated as a disposal. For capital gains tax (CGT) a separate election is made for a variation, but none is needed for a disclaimer.

19.6.3 Practical planning

Consideration should be given to the use of a variation to achieve inheritance tax advantages not only in the estate of the deceased but, potentially, on the death of the deceased's spouse. This can be achieved by careful structuring and allocation of assets to utilise the nil rate band.

If an individual was widowed and remarried it is possible, if unused, to utilise the previous deceased spouse's nil rate band by placing this into a relevant property trust, preserving the current deceased's nil rate band to claim on their widow's subsequent death. This, in effect, enables the value of three or four (if both spouses were previously widowed) nil rate bands to be used against the estates.

If a valuable property becomes worth very little within two years of death, vary the will so that it passes to charity (the value at death is then exempt).

If a beneficiary dies within two years of the testator's death, consider a variation (it can still be done) to achieve more advantageous overall IHT treatment: there are several possibilities.

If the deceased left significant legacies to charity, it is worth considering whether a variation to increase those legacies may result in the rest of the estate benefiting from a reduced rate of inheritance tax (Inheritance Tax Act 1984, s.7 and Sched.1A). In certain circumstances this can result in the chargeable beneficiaries receiving a larger net amount. For example, if a gift of £10,000 is left to charity from an estate worth £575,000 it is worth increasing the gift up to £25,000 to achieve the reduced rate with no effect on the amount the residuary beneficiaries would receive:

	£	£
Estate	575,000.00	575,000.00
Less nil rate band	(325,000.00)	(325,000.00)
Taxable balance	250,000.00	250,000.00
Charitable gift	(10,000.00)	(25,000.00)
Tax due	(96,000.00)	(81,000.00)
Balance for residuary beneficiaries	469,000.00	469,000.00

19.6.4 Discretionary provision

Where flexibility is required, possibly for tax reasons, the testator may avoid the need for all beneficiaries to agree to a variation by giving a power of appointment to the executors or trustees and requiring them to exercise this within two years (see Inheritance Tax Act 1984, s.144):

- there should be a default trust at the end of the two-year period in case an appointment is not made;
- IHT is ultimately paid as if the will had provided for the outcome effected under the appointment;
- if there is an initial discretionary trust, IHT will be charged on the basis thereof on application for a grant;
- distributions made outside the two-year period will be subject to the normal IHT exit charge.

There are no corresponding CGT provisions.

19.6.5 Precatory gifts

Where a testator expresses a wish that property bequeathed by the will be transferred by the legatee to other persons and the wish is complied with within two years of death, that disposition takes effect for IHT as if the property had been originally bequeathed to the transferee (see Inheritance Tax Act 1984, s.143). No particular formality is required.

19.7 DISABLED PERSONS' TRUSTS

An elderly testator may wish to make long-term provision for a relative who is infirm or disabled. This commonly arises in the following situations, although the principles involved may be applied by anyone wishing to make financial provision for someone suffering from a disability:

- a parent seeks to make provision for a disabled son or daughter;
- a son or daughter seeks to make provision for an infirm parent;

- one spouse seeks to provide for the other who has become frail, infirm or mentally incapacitated;
- unmarried brothers or sisters or friends seek to provide for each other.

19.7.1 Key points

The beneficiary may be unable to handle his or her own financial affairs but quite apart from this there will often be:

- uncertainty as to what the needs of the beneficiary will be and the need to take into account the high cost of care and services and any provision under community care policies;
- uncertainty as to what provision will actually benefit the beneficiary due to the loss of Department for Work and Pensions (DWP) or local authority funding and means testing in respect of the cost of services provided;
- a desire to provide tax-effective support by utilising normal tax planning principles and the tax concessions available in respect of disabled beneficiaries under trusts;
- concern about potential inheritance claims by (or on behalf of) the disabled beneficiary and others.

There is no simple solution and each case must be dealt with taking into account all the likely circumstances as best as these can be ascertained, including the wishes and priorities of the testator.

19.7.2 Care provision

The personal circumstances of the beneficiary will depend upon:

- the resources (both personal and financial) of the individual;
- the nature and degree of the disability or infirmity;
- availability of personal carers or care provision;
- outside funding available, whether from a trust or from the DWP or a local authority.

The beneficiary may, either at present or at some time in the future:

- be provided with a basic income and left to cope;
- live in his or her own home with some support;
- be cared for by another member of the family or friend;
- live in a supervised home or hostel with other disabled or infirm people;
- be looked after in a care home;
- be in need of full-time nursing care in hospital.

In many cases the testator is seeking to replace the care and support already being provided on a personal basis by financial support, and this will be for an uncertain period of time. Whatever the circumstances at the time when the provision is discussed, these are likely to change.

19.7.3   Funding and means tests

The financial resources available for the support of this beneficiary are likely to come from:

- personal income, including pensions, interests on savings and the return from any investments;
- personal capital resources, including savings and investments;
- the individual's home, if owned in full or in part;
- any trust provision available (including that now being contemplated);
- voluntary financial support from family and friends (or charities);
- support from society through the DWP, local authorities or NHS bodies.

Means tests are likely to be applied on a formal or an informal basis as a prerequisite to any support provided, and these may take into account the income and capital resources of the individual. Means tests regulate:

- pension credit paid by the DWP to those whose income from other sources is insufficient for their needs (see **Chapter 13**);
- housing benefit (to cover rent) paid by the local authority (see **Chapter 13**);
- housing or disabled facilities grants from local authorities (see **Chapter 15**);
- the cost of residential, day and domiciliary services provided or funded by the local authority (see **Chapter 14**).

Any financial provision that is made on a legal basis could result in reduction or withdrawal of a significant source of income, or a charge for services.

19.7.4   Objectives and strategy for financial provision

The testator is likely to have conflicting objectives:

- to provide for the disabled or infirm beneficiary to the extent necessary;
- to ensure that funds that are not needed pass ultimately to other beneficiaries;
- to avoid loss of other sources of funding but fill gaps in care provision.

Testators must decide their priorities as they often cannot achieve all objectives.

Trust provision may last for many years but the means-testing rules, circumstances of the beneficiary and services needed constantly change so flexibility is desirable in the provision made. The following are key points to have in mind:

- the terms of the trust will depend upon whether the beneficiary is likely to be self-reliant or dependent upon others, though many fall between these extremes;

- the beneficiary's own resources and all other sources of funding, actual and potential, should be taken into account;
- the means-testing rules and particularly those assets which are disregarded for assessment which include trust assets subject to certain conditions (see **Chapter 14**).

19.7.5   Options

The testator has the following options when seeking to make provision for a disabled or infirm beneficiary, and these may apply to the entire estate, a share thereof, or a specified sum set aside for the purpose.

Leaving money

Money may be left to:

- the beneficiary absolutely and ignoring means-testing implications;
- other relatives in the hope that they will support the disabled beneficiary on a voluntary basis;
- a charity on one of the special schemes available.

Creating a trust

A trust could be created:

- with the disabled beneficiary having a (protected) life interest;
- which is discretionary as regards income and/or capital and includes the disabled beneficiary;
- for charitable purposes (perhaps limited to charities with specific objectives);
- using a two-year discretionary trust to create a 'wait and see' period so that the changed needs of the beneficiary can be ascertained before the trustees choose between the above options.

If substantial funds are available a combination of money and trusts designed to fit the particular circumstances may be best.

19.7.6   Information required to create a trust

Before advising on the terms of a will or any trust provision you need to know in respect of the ultimate beneficiary:

- name and age;
- present capital and income and any changes that may arise;
- the nature and implications of any incapacity;
- present residence and extent of care, and any changes to be anticipated;
- present funding arrangements and any changes that may take place;

- any other financial provision that has been or may be made;
- help likely to be provided by charitable organisations or others.

You must determine and take into account the potential size of the fund available for this beneficiary (is it to be a share of the estate or a fixed sum?).

19.7.7 Practical points

Disabled persons' trusts

Try to avoid identifying the trust fund too closely with the disabled beneficiary (to the extent that the testator will tolerate this). It may be better to:

- have a discretionary fund identifying many potential beneficiaries including this specific beneficiary;
- adopt a trust period other than the life of this beneficiary;
- ensure that the class of potential beneficiaries includes persons who may care for or support this beneficiary (the trustees can even be given a restricted power to enlarge the class).

Providing financial assistance to a carer often benefits the person cared for. If money can be paid to other people, they may provide voluntary support (thereby avoiding means-testing issues).

Take care over the inclusion of any power to advance or appoint capital to the disabled beneficiary:

- restrict it to specific purposes;
- restrict it to specific situations.

Include adequate discretionary powers for the trustees, such as power to:

- invest in chattels and residential accommodation;
- make loans and permit occupation and use of trust assets (a power to appoint capital may not then be necessary);
- benefit those who may help the disabled beneficiary;
- benefit or support charities (they may help the disabled beneficiary);
- pay funeral expenses for the disabled beneficiary.

Tax dispensations are available under the provisions below in respect of certain trusts for the benefit of disabled persons, but utilising these may have adverse consequences in respect of means-tested support and benefits:

- Taxation of Chargeable Gains Act 1992, Sched.1, para.1.
- Inheritance Tax Act 1984, s.3A(1) and (3) and s.89.

It may be a question of tax benefits or state benefits as the testator is seldom able to achieve the best of both worlds.

19.7.8 Challenges to the provision

An application may be made to the court under the Inheritance (Provision for Family and Dependants) Act 1975 by or on behalf of the dependent beneficiary on the ground that the will does not make reasonable provision:

- the court has wide powers to redistribute the estate;
- for the matters taken into account see **19.5.2**;
- the financial resources of the potential beneficiary will be taken into account but the extent to which these include means-tested state benefits or local authority provision that would otherwise be available is not clear.

The question is not 'did the testator act reasonably?' but rather 'has reasonable financial provision been made for this person?'.

19.8 DISCRETIONARY TRUSTS

These trusts are where trust income and capital are held at the discretion of the trustees among a class of beneficiaries. Income may be distributed or accumulated. These trusts are used where the testator wishes to leave assets in favour of a number of beneficiaries, leaving the trustees to determine who should benefit.

19.9 INTEREST IN POSSESSION TRUSTS (OR LIFE INTEREST TRUSTS)

The trustees are directed to pay trust income to a particular beneficiary and then the capital to someone else. These are used, for example:

- to protect assets for children following a second marriage;
- to protect assets of a beneficiary whose assets may be vulnerable to claim by creditors, insolvency or divorce;
- for tax planning purposes.

19.10 ACCUMULATION AND MAINTENANCE TRUSTS

Prior to 22 March 2006 it was possible to create accumulation and maintenance trusts which benefited from favourable inheritance tax treatment provided three conditions imposed by Inheritance Tax Act 1984, s.71 were complied with. The basic form of these trusts was a trust for a class of beneficiaries who had a common grandparent giving the beneficiary the right to income and capital at 18 years old. Sometimes the beneficiary's age could be postponed to 25 years.

Although no new accumulation and maintenance trusts can be created, those that were in existence before 22 March 2006 continue to exist and the trustees have been able to exercise one of three options:

1. Before 6 April 2006 they could have amended the terms of the trust so that the beneficiaries would have become absolutely entitled to the property on or before the age of 18. The trust would then continue to be able to enjoy the exemptions previously available to accumulation and maintenance trusts.
2. The trustees could have rewritten the rules of the trust before 6 April 2008 so that the beneficiaries become absolutely entitled to the trust assets on or before their 25th birthdays. The trust would therefore have become an 18 to 25 trust so that exit charges apply both to any distributions made to the beneficiaries and when the beneficiary is entitled to the trust property at the age of 25.
3. The trustees could have done nothing so that the accumulation and maintenance trust would become a relevant property trust and it would be subject to the normal charges that apply to relevant property trusts including 10-year anniversary charges.

19.11 BARE TRUSTS

Bare trusts are included in wills, for example, where smaller legacies are gifted to minors but directed not to be paid to them until they reach 18. The money belongs to the minor but he or she cannot give a discharge until attaining the age of 18. Grandparents may also use bare trusts to settle smaller sums of money while control of the money is retained until the child reaches 18. The income and capital is treated as the child's own with the ability to use their personal income tax and CGT annual allowances.

19.12 CHARITABLE TRUSTS

Charitable trusts might be created where a testator does not want to be committed in advance to identifying specific charities or charitable objects or where they wish to leave their assets for the benefit of charitable causes generally but with trustees of their choice making the determination which organisations should benefit.

19.13 LIFE POLICY AND DEATH BENEFIT TRUSTS

The proceeds of a life policy (death in service benefit or pension policy) may have been written in trust so that they do not form part of the deceased's estate and may not be subject to IHT. There are detailed rules relating to these (see **Chapter 16**) for IHT purposes under Inheritance Tax Act 1984, ss.3, 4 and 5. Careful consideration should be given to this at the time of taking out the policy but also when taking instructions for a will (see **19.2.3**) to establish what will comprise the 'estate' of the testator to pass under the terms of the will (see also **Chapter 16**).

19.14 LETTERS OF WISHES, STATEMENT OR MEMORANDUM

Instead of revealing in the will their wishes and intentions in regard to the administration of their trust fund, testators should prepare and sign a suitable letter addressed to the trustees setting these out, which will reassure not only the testator but also the trustees when they consider the exercise of their powers in future years.

Unless the words in the will (or trust deed) direct the executors/trustees to take a particular action or refer to a letter already in existence, this type of letter is not a document incorporated in the will and is not legally binding. It should be noted that letters of wishes are inherently confidential (see *Breakspear* v. *Ackland* [2008] EWHC 220 (Ch)).

These are vital papers giving testators opportunities to record and have in place their written record regarding:

- funeral arrangements and wishes, remembering that the executors of the will have legal authority over these, not the next of kin;
- requests for distribution of chattels (with timescale and mechanism for selection) enabling these to be dealt with by executors without large lists being made in the will or a testator having to make decisions on making the will and enabling the use of Inheritance Tax Act 1984, s.143 (precatory trust);
- guidance to trustees of discretionary trusts (of the nil rate band or residue) which a testator might not otherwise be able to, or wish to, put on the face of a will, taking care not to fetter their discretion;
- guidance to the trustees for the advancement of capital or any other matters;
- reasons of a testator (if appropriate) as to why provision has or has not been made to seek to prevent claims on death for greater provision.

A letter of wishes should be signed and dated by the testator but not witnessed if it is not to be incorporated in the will. The basic rule of incorporation is that a document is deemed to be incorporated in a will (even though a document is not itself executed as a testamentary disposition) if:

- the document is in existence at the time of the will;
- the will refers to the document as an existing document;
- the reference in the will or other available evidence is sufficient to identify the document.

19.15 LIFETIME SETTLEMENTS OR BY WILL

It may be advantageous to establish the desired trusts under a lifetime settlement:

- the settlor's will (and that of a spouse) can leave money to the trustees and thus be kept simple;

- other people (e.g. grandparents of a disabled child or children of an infirm parent) can also leave money to the trustees of the settlement and avoid having to set out their own trusts;
- life insurance and pension benefits may be held on these trusts.

The administration costs of a settlement may make it an inadvisable option if the trust fund is too small, although a nominal sum may be settled initially in anticipation of substantial sums being added under the will of the settlor or other persons.

19.16   PRACTICAL POINTS

19.16.1   Information required to create a trust

Basic information required:

- trustees;
- beneficiaries;
- trustees' powers of appointment or advancement;
- default terms and beneficiaries;
- administrative powers;
- indemnity provisions;
- taxation considerations;
- restrictions on trustee powers;
- trust period;
- type of trust;
- trust fund.

19.16.2   Publications

On this topic generally, reference should be made to the following published works:

Clutton O. and Jennings S. (eds) (looseleaf) *Administration of Trusts*, LexisNexis.
Kessler J. (2014) *Drafting Trusts and Will Trusts: A Modern Approach*, 12th revised edn, Sweet & Maxwell.
Steel G. (2012) *Trust Practitioner's Handbook*, 3rd edn, Law Society.
Tucker L., Le Poidevin N. and Brightwell J. (2015) *Lewin on Trusts*, 19th edn, Sweet & Maxwell.
Thurston J. (2013) *Practitioner's Guide to Trusts*, 10th revised edn, Bloomsbury Professional.
Withers LLP (looseleaf) *Practical Trust Precedents*, Sweet & Maxwell.

CHAPTER 20

Death

Amanda King-Jones and Stewart Stretton-Hill

20.1 REGISTRATION OF DEATH

20.1.1 Sources of law

- Births and Deaths Registration Act 1953.
- Coroners and Justice Act 2009.
- Registration of Overseas Births and Deaths Regulations 2014, SI 2014/511.
- Registration of Births and Deaths Regulations 1987, SI 1987/2088.
- Registration of Births and Deaths (Welsh Language) Regulations 1987, SI 1987/2089.

20.1.2 Deaths in England and Wales

The occurrence and cause of every death in England and Wales must be entered on the register by the Registrar of Births and Deaths for the sub-district in which the death occurred or in which the body was found (Births and Deaths Registration Act (BDRA) 1953, s.15).

The Registrar will receive information about a death from a 'qualified informant' or from a coroner; he will also receive a certificate stating the cause of death completed by a registered medical practitioner or by a coroner.

20.1.3 The qualified informant

Where a death occurs in a house, the qualified informant with a duty under BDRA 1953, s.16 to attend the Registrar and give the Registrar information about the death is, in descending order:

1. the nearest relative of the deceased person present at the death or in attendance during his or her last illness;
2. any other relative of the deceased residing or being in the sub-district where the death occurred;
3. a person present at the death or the occupier of the house if he or she knew of the happening of the death;

4.   each inmate of the house who knew of the happening of the death or the person causing the disposal of the body.

The 'nearest relative' includes relative by marriage and civil partner; and 'house' includes public institutions such as 'a prison, lock-up or hospital, and such other public or charitable institution as may be prescribed' (BDRA 1953, s.41).

In circumstances where a person dies elsewhere, the qualified informant with a duty under BDRA 1953, s.17 to attend the Registrar and give the Registrar information about the death is, in descending order:

1.   any relative of the deceased with knowledge of any of the particulars required to be registered concerning the death;
2.   any person present at the death;
3.   any person finding or taking charge of the body;
4.   any person causing the disposal of the body.

20.1.4   Duties of the qualified informant

Qualified informants have a duty under ss.16(3) and 17(3) to attend the Registrar and to give to the Registrar the particulars concerning the death they possess as set out in the regulations (see below). It is an offence wilfully to give any false information upon registration.

Where the deceased has been attended by a registered medical practitioner (RMP) during his or her last illness the RMP will give the qualified informant a notice in the prescribed form that a medical certificate of cause of death (MCCD) has been written and signed. The qualified informant must deliver this notice to the Registrar. The notice will often include printed instructions to help the qualified informant to discharge his or her duty.

Rather than send the MCCD directly to the Registrar it is common for the RMP to also give to the informant a sealed envelope containing the MCCD, which the informant must also deliver to the Registrar.

Qualified informants must carry out their duty within five days of the death or of finding the body. Although if, within five days, written notice is given to the Registrar of the occurrence of the death (or of finding of the body) accompanied by a written notice from the RMP that the MCCD has been signed, this period is extended to 14 days after the death or of finding the body (BDRA 1953, s.18).

The qualified informant can find the address of the Registrar for the relevant sub-district by using the search tool at **www.gov.uk**, or in the local telephone directory, or from the hospital, doctor, police, local council or post office.

A qualified informant is discharged from his or her duty to attend the Registrar and provide information about the death to the Registrar if:

- another qualified informant has already provided information to the Registrar; or
- the death is referred to a coroner and the coroner opens an inquest.

If a death is referred to the coroner but the coroner does not open an inquest, instead completing Form 100A or 100B, the qualified informant will remain under a duty to attend the Registrar and provide information about the death.

Where after expiration of the statutory time limits the Registrar has not registered a death owing to default of the qualified person, the Registrar can require the attendance of, and information from an informant (BDRA 1953, s.19).

Particulars to be supplied by the qualified informant

The particulars concerning the death that must be given by the qualified informant to the Registrar at the relevant sub-district are set out in the particulars of death form: Registration of Births and Deaths Regulations 1987, SI 1987/2088 (as amended by SI 2006/2827), Sched.2, Form 13:

- date and place of death;
- name and surname of the deceased;
- sex of the deceased;
- if the deceased is a woman who has been married, her maiden surname;
- date and place of birth of the deceased;
- date of birth of any surviving spouse or civil partner;
- occupation and usual address of the deceased and name and occupation of any deceased spouse;
- name and surname of the informant;
- qualification of the informant (see **20.1.3**);
- usual address of the informant;
- cause of death.

The Registrar will first make a draft entry of these particulars and show or read them to the qualified informant, whereupon the Registrar shall correct any errors or omissions.

The corrected particulars will be recorded by the Registrar in the presence of the qualified informant on the particulars of death form: Registration of Births and Deaths Regulations 1987 (as amended by SI 2006/2827), Sched.2, Form 13.

The cause of death will be given in the form of the MCCD from a registered medical practitioner. The Registrar will record on the particulars of death form the cause of death and the name, surname and qualification of the RMP: Registration of Births and Deaths Regulations 1987 (as amended by SI 2006/2827), reg.42.

The informant will sign or make his or her mark on the particulars of death form to certify that the particulars given by them are true to the best of his or her knowledge and belief and the Registrar will sign and enter the date of the registration.

The other non-obligatory information the Registrar may request from the qualified person includes:

- the deceased's birth certificate;

- the deceased's marriage or civil partnership certificates;
- the deceased's national insurance number and confirmation of any state benefits in payment;
- the deceased's NHS number and medical card.

20.1.5 Duties of the registered medical practitioner

Medical certificate of cause of death (MCCD)

Where the deceased has been attended by a registered medical practitioner (RMP) during his or her last illness, the RMP is required to complete a MCCD in the prescribed form and 'shall forthwith deliver that certificate to the registrar' (BDRA 1953, s.22(1)). The form of certificate is prescribed in Registration of Births and Deaths Regulations 1987 (as amended by SI 2006/2827), Sched.2, Form 14.

The RMP is responsible for the delivery of the MCCD to the Registrar. The RMP may deliver the MCCD personally or send it by post to the Registrar, or he may give it to the qualified informant in a sealed envelope for delivery to the Registrar.

The RMP must also give to the qualified informant written notice in the prescribed form that a MCCD has been written and signed. The RMP's notice is prescribed in Registration of Births and Deaths Regulations 1987 (as amended by SI 2006/2827), Sched.2, Form 16.

If there is no doctor who attended the deceased available to certify, or if the certifying doctor did attend the deceased, but has not seen them either within 14 days before death, or after death, the doctor will seek advice from the coroner.

Doctor's referral of death to the coroner

There is no statutory duty on the RMP to report a death to a coroner. However, the *Guidance for Doctors Completing Medical Certificates of Cause of Death in England and Wales* (Office for National Statistics and the Home Office, July 2010: **www.gro.gov.uk/images/medcert_july_2010.pdf**) suggests that doctors usually report the following deaths to the coroner:

- a death that may be due to:
    - accident;
    - suicide;
    - violence;
    - neglect (by self or others);
    - industrial disease;

- a death with an unknown cause;
- a death occurring before an operation;
- a death before full recovery from an anaesthetic;
- a death occurring in or shortly after release from police or prison custody;

- if there is no doctor who attended the deceased available to certify, or if the certifying doctor did attend the deceased, but has not seen them either within 14 days before death, or after death.

Where a doctor does refer a death to the coroner the ONS *Guidance* recommends that the doctor 'explain to the family why the death is being referred, as well as how and when they will learn the outcome of the referral'.

20.1.6 Documents issued by the Registrar

Deaths notified by the qualified informant

Where a death is registered following attendance by the qualified informant and the supply of the MCCD, the Registrar will issue to the informant:

- a certificate for burial or cremation ('Green Form') giving the permission required by the undertaker for a burial or for an application for cremation to be made (unless the coroner has issued an order for burial in Form 101 or Form CR6 coroner's certificate for cremations);
- a certificate of registration of death (containing Form BD8 for benefit claims).

On request and payment of the appropriate fee, the Registrar will also issue a certified copy of the entry on the register (a death certificate).

Duplicates of the death certificate are cheaper if requested at the time of registration. To avoid the cost of duplicate death certificates, the Law Society has agreed a protocol with the British Bankers Association, the Building Societies Association and the Association of British Insurers allowing solicitors to send a death certificate verification form that guarantees to asset holders that the solicitor has a death certificate in their possession and has inspected an original.

The Registrar may also give to the qualified informant leaflets about bereavement benefits (see **20.5**) as appropriate.

Deaths referred to the coroner

In cases where the death has been referred to the coroner, the Registrar cannot proceed with registration until he receives from the coroner:

- Form 100A (and the MCCD from the RMP); or
- Form 100B following a post-mortem examination; or
- a coroner's certificate following the conclusion of an inquest (Form 99); or
- a coroner's certificate following an inquest not restarted stating the result of criminal proceedings.

After an inquest has been opened by the coroner, and in place of the Registrar's certificate for burial or cremation, the coroner may provide an order for burial on Form 101 or on request complete Form CR6 (certificate of coroner authorising cremation) (previously Form E). The coroner may also issue an interim death certificate to assist the bereaved with the administration of the deceased's estate. These certificates will only be issued after the coroner has received the results of all post-mortem and special examinations.

20.1.7 Registration of overseas deaths

If a person dies overseas the death must be registered according to the practice and relevant legislation in force in that country. Among the information that will be needed to register a death abroad will be the deceased's full name, date of birth, details of next of kin, passport number and the place and date of issue.

In addition to registering the death locally the bereaved may also register the death at the relevant British Consulate. Registering with the Consulate allows the bereaved to purchase a UK-style death certificate and the record will be sent by the Consulate to the General Register Office in the UK, so that further certificates may be purchased in the future.

See **20.3.6** for more information about arranging repatriation and burial or cremation in England and Wales.

20.2 CORONERS AND INQUESTS

Relevant legislation is:

- Coroners and Justice Act 2009.
- Removal of Bodies Regulations 1954, SI 1954/448.
- Coroners Rules 1984, SI 1984/552.
- Coroners Allowances, Fees and Expenses Regulations 2013, SI 2013/1615.
- Coroners (Inquests) Rules 2013, SI 2013/1616 (Inquests Rules).
- Coroners (Investigations) Regulations 2013, SI 2013/1629 (Investigations Regs).

20.2.1 Reporting a death to the coroner

Coroners are independent judicial officers who are appointed by the local authority. They are either doctors or lawyers but, all new coroners appointed must be lawyers.

The Coroners and Justice Act 2009 introduced the Office of the Chief Coroner. The first Chief Coroner was appointed in September 2012. The role of the Chief Coroner is to have overall responsibility for the coroner system and coroners in England and Wales. A useful *Guide to Coroner Service* was published by the Ministry of Justice, in February 2014 and is available from **www.gov.uk**.

There is a general duty on a person to report a death to the coroner where the person is aware of circumstances that would require an inquest into the death to be held.

There is also a statutory duty, under Registration of Births and Deaths Regulations 1987, SI 1987/2088, reg.41, for the Registrar to report a death to the coroner on Form 52 when (among other things):

(a)   the deceased was not attended during his or her last illness by a registered medical practitioner;

(b)   he is unable to obtain a duly completed MCCD;

(c)   it appears to the Registrar, from the MCCD, that the deceased was not seen by the certifying RMP either after death or within 14 days before death;

(d)   the cause of death appears to be unknown;

(e)   he has reason to believe the death to have been unnatural or caused by violence or neglect or to have been attended by suspicious circumstances;

(f)   it appears to have occurred during an operation or before recovery from the effect of anaesthetic;

(g)   it appears from the contents of any MCCD to have been due to industrial disease or industrial poisoning.

A prison governor also has a duty to report the death of an inmate to the coroner.

In practice, deaths are most commonly reported to the coroner by medical practitioners and by the police.

20.2.2   Coroner's duty to inquire

Where a coroner is informed that the body of a deceased person is within that coroner's area, the coroner has a duty (as soon as is practicable) under the Coroners and Justice Act (CJA) 2009, s.1 to conduct an investigation into the person's death if the coroner has reason to suspect that:

(a)   the deceased died a violent or unnatural death;

(b)   the cause of death is unknown; or

(c)   the deceased died in custody or otherwise in state detention (such cases will automatically be referred to the coroner for an inquest to held in the presence of a jury).

The Chief Coroner issued guidance in December 2014 (No. 16), which opined, that a person dying subject to a deprivation of liberty safeguards authorisation (or a relevant Court of Protection order) should be the subject of a coroner investigation because that person was in 'state detention' within the meaning of s.1.

The coroner may make whatever inquiries seem necessary in order to determine whether a duty to investigate exists. Under the Coroners (Investigations) Regulations 2013, the coroner is no longer restricted to holding inquests within his own district. The coroner has the option to relocate the inquest if it is in the interests of the bereaved family.

Should the coroner decide that he does not have reasonable cause to suspect, the coroner will notify the Registrar (usually using Form 100A), and advise the RMP to complete the MCCD and deliver it to the Registrar. Instructions on the back of the form request the Registrar to enter the cause of death as given on the MCCD.

If the death is subject to a Form 100A procedure, the coroner may not need to take possession of the body.

20.2.3 Coroner's possession of the body

The coroner will take possession of the body until any inquest is concluded, but will release it after he has received the results of all post-mortem and special examinations. A burial order can only be made when the coroner is satisfied that the body is no longer required for the purposes of the investigation (Investigations Regs, reg.21).

A coroner must release the body for burial or cremation as soon as is reasonably practicable. Where a coroner cannot release the body within 28 days of being informed that the body is within his area, the coroner must provide the reason for the delay to the next of kin or personal representatives of the deceased (reg.20).

The coroner may have to retain possession of the body where a second post-mortem is requested or when a second post-mortem may be required in criminal proceedings.

The coroner must complete all investigations within six months of notification or as soon as practicable after that (Inquests Rules, rule 8). Once 12 months have elapsed since notification, the coroner must provide the reason for the delay to the Chief Coroner.

Any person intending to remove a body out of the country must first give notice to the coroner within whose jurisdiction the body is and certain formalities must then be complied with (see Removal of Bodies Regulations 1954, SI 1954/448).

Guidance from the Ministry of Justice states that bereaved people may also 'ask the coroner, via the funeral director, for reasonable access to see the body before it is released for the funeral' (see *A Guide to Coroners and Inquests* (Ministry of Justice, 2010: **www.leics.gov.uk/moj_coroners_and_inquests.pdf**) para.29.2).

20.2.4 Post-mortem examination

CJA 2009, s.14 sets out the arrangements for ordering post-mortem examinations. The term 'post-mortem' is purposefully not defined in order to include other forms of examination other than an intrusive autopsy (for example, cross-sectional imaging by way of a CT scan or an MRI scan). Once the post-mortem has been concluded, the coroner must decide whether to continue the investigation and, if so, how it should continue. The coroner has the following three main options:

1. If the post-mortem reveals that the deceased died of natural causes and the coroner thinks that it is not necessary to continue the investigation, then the coroner must:

    (a) discontinue the investigation (CJA 2009, s.4(1));

    (b)   provide an interested person, on request, with a written explanation of his decision (CJA 2009, s.4(4));

    (c)   complete Form 100B and take no further action (Investigations Regs, reg.17).

2.   If the post-mortem reveals that the deceased died of natural causes but the coroner considers that it is necessary to continue the investigation, then the coroner must:

    (a)   hold an inquest (CJA 2009, s.6); and

    (b)   open the inquest as soon as practicable (Inquests Rules, rule 5).

3.   If, after the post-mortem, the coroner still has reason to suspect that the deceased died a violent or unnatural death, or the cause of death is unknown, or the deceased died in custody or some form of state detention, then the coroner must:

    (a)   hold an inquest (CJA 2009, s.6); and

    (b)   open the inquest as soon as practicable (Inquests Rules, rule 5).

The Chief Coroner has subsequently emphasised that pre-signed Forms 100A and 100B should not be used.

The coroner has a duty to notify certain parties of the time, date and place of the post-mortem examination (Investigations Regs, reg.13). These parties include, but are not limited to:

(a)   any relative of the deceased who has notified the coroner of his desire to attend, or be represented at, the post-mortem examination;

(b)   the deceased's regular medical attendant;

(c)   if the deceased died in a hospital, the hospital.

Unless a notified party is a medical practitioner they cannot attend the post-mortem, but they have the right to be represented at the post-mortem examination by a medical practitioner.

The deceased's GP must inform the coroner if he or she wishes to attend the post-mortem.

A person with a proper interest may request to view the results of the post-mortem examination or request a copy of the results. The bereaved are also entitled to request a further post-mortem examination at their own cost.

20.2.5 Inquests

The purpose of an inquest is to decide who the deceased was and how, when and where he or she came by his or her death. The decision must be reported using Form 1 entitled 'Coroner's certificate of fact of death' (Investigations Regs, Schedule, Form 1).

Rule 11 of the Inquests Rules requires coroners to hold all inquest hearings in public. However, the coroner may direct that the public be excluded from all or part of an inquest hearing if the coroner considers it to be in the interests of national security to do so (rule 11(4)).

The coroner decides where and when an inquest is to be held, and it must be formally opened, adjourned and closed. A jury (of at least seven people) is only required in certain circumstances, but the coroner has a discretion to summon a jury. The coroner must report to the Registrar within five days of closing an inquest.

A person with a proper interest may request to see the notes of the inquest written by the coroner or may apply for a copy of these notes, on payment of an appropriate fee.

20.2.6 Evidence at inquests

Witnesses give evidence on oath but as it is an inquisitorial process it is for the coroner to decide which witnesses to summon. The coroner must examine anyone with knowledge of the facts whom he thinks it expedient to examine and anyone who wishes to give evidence. Medical witnesses may be called, including to express an opinion as to the cause of death. Certain classes of person and any person who in the opinion of the coroner has a proper interest may also examine any witness either personally or by a solicitor (Inquests Rules, rule 19).

Legal aid for bereaved families wanting legal representation is not normally available (except in exceptional circumstances and when the death occurred in prison or in police custody and financial eligibility criteria are met).

Strict laws of evidence do not apply, but the coroner takes notes of the evidence.

20.2.7 Coroner's certificates

1. **Form 100A.** Form 100A 'Notification to the Registrar by the Coroner that he does not consider it necessary to hold an inquest – No post-mortem held' is not prescribed by regulations and there is no legal requirement to issue it. The form was created by the Registrar General. It is used by coroners to give notice to the Registrar that a death has been reported and that the coroner has decided not to open an inquest or direct a post-mortem.
2. **Form 100B.** Form 100B 'Notification to the Registrar by the Coroner that he does not consider it necessary to hold an inquest'. The form was created by the Registrar General. It is used by coroners to give notice to the Registrar that a death has been reported, that the coroner has ordered a post-mortem examination, and that the coroner has decided not to open an inquest.
3. Statutory forms under the Investigations Regs:

    - **Form 1.** Coroner's certificate of fact of death.
    - **Form 2.** Notice of discontinuance.
    - **Form 3.** Order for burial.

- **Form 4.** Direction to exhume.

4. Statutory forms under the Inquests Rules:

   - **Form 1.** Juror summons.
   - **Form 2.** Record of an inquest.

5. **Form 99.** When the inquest is complete the coroner will issue the registrar with Form 99.

6. **Form 101: order for burial.** Where an inquest has been opened and the deceased is to be buried a coroner will issue an order for burial on Form 101. It is issued in place of the Registrar's 'Green Form'.

7. **Form CR6: certificate of coroner.** Where a post-mortem examination has been carried out on direction of the coroner or an inquest has been opened, and the deceased is to be cremated, the coroner will complete Form CR6 certificate of coroner.

8. **Interim certificate of the fact of death.** The coroner will adjourn an inquest until any relevant criminal proceedings have been concluded and supply the Registrar with an interim certificate of the fact of death. The interim certificate gives the name and address of the deceased, the date of death, and if known, the precise medical cause of death. If an adjourned inquest is not resumed, the coroner must issue a signed certificate to the registrar stating the result of the criminal proceedings.

20.3 FUNERAL ARRANGEMENTS

Relevant legislation includes:

- Cremation Act 1902.
- Human Tissue Act 2004.
- Removal of Bodies Regulations 1954, SI 1954/448.
- Cremation (England and Wales) Regulations 2008, SI 2008/2841.

20.3.1 Authority required before burial or cremation

In circumstances where a qualified informant has attended the Registrar to give information concerning a death, the Registrar will give the qualified informant a certificate for burial or cremation 'Green Form' and this must be handed to the person effecting the disposal of the body.

If after 14 days of issuing a certificate for burial or cremation the Registrar has not received notification from the person effecting disposal of the body of the date, place and means of disposal, the Registrar must make an enquiry of the person to whom the certificate was issued and that person will have a duty to supply this information (BDRA 1953, s.24(5)).

Alternatively, if a coroner has opened an inquest and has received the results of all post-mortem and special examinations, the coroner will issue an order for burial (Form 101), or if the body is to be cremated, the coroner will complete Form CR6 certificate of coroner.

Where the deceased is to be cremated and the coroner has not opened an inquest, but has carried out a post-mortem and completed Form 100B, the coroner will need to complete Form CR6 coroner's certificate in place of the Registrar's certificate.

There are different procedures which apply for deaths that occurred overseas (see **20.3.6**).

The coroner will have jurisdiction to hold an inquest into a death that has occurred abroad where the body has been repatriated for funeral in England or Wales and the coroner has reason to believe the death meets the criteria for an inquest (see **20.2.2**).

There is no ownership of a body after somebody has died in the normal sense of the word. Possession of the body will belong to the executors if the deceased died leaving a valid will appointing executors. In all other cases, possession will pass on to the next of kin.

If there is a disagreement, the court is reluctant to interfere on the application of a relative with the executors' decision as to funeral arrangements. In the case of an administrator the court may make a decision which it did in *Hartshorne* v. *Gardner* [2008] EWHC B3 (Ch).

20.3.2 Donations of body or organs

The executors can decide to donate the body for medical research and would usually follow any request of this nature in the will but are not obliged to do so. Organs can be removed soon after death if the deceased has indicated in writing a wish to be a donor (e.g. by carrying a donor card) or if no objections are raised by relatives when inquiries are made (see the Human Tissue Act 2004).

If a death will be reportable to the coroner it will be necessary to gain the coroner's consent before removing organs from a transplant donor.

20.3.3 Financial responsibility

The person who instructs the undertaker may become personally responsible for the cost but will normally be entitled to an indemnity from the estate. The deceased's bank may release funds to an undertaker direct before probate, on production of the death certificate (or interim death certificate or death certificate verification form: see **20.1.6**) and funeral account.

If the deceased leaves no money, arrangements will be made by those prepared to pay, but assistance may be available from public funds.

Pre-paid funeral plans

Individuals may arrange directly with an undertaker or a plan provider for the payment of funeral costs in advance.

Other available payments

Other payments on death may be available from insurance schemes and pension schemes.

Funeral payments

A funeral payment may be obtained from the Social Fund using Form SF200 subject to certain eligibility criteria:

- the applicant or applicant's partner must be in receipt of a state benefit, e.g. pension credit, housing benefit, council tax benefit (see **www.gov.uk** for the full list of qualifying benefits);
- the applicant is a partner of the deceased, or parent of the deceased, or close relative or friend of the deceased (who may be reasonably expected to accept responsibility of funeral costs);
- the deceased must ordinarily be a UK resident and the funeral must be in the UK;
- there are further restrictions on eligibility for close friends or relatives where the deceased has a partner, parent, child or other close relatives (**www.gov.uk**).

Funeral payments can be claimed to cover: necessary burial or cremation fees, certain other specified expenses and up to £700 for any other funeral expenses, such as the funeral director's fees, the coffin or flowers. The funeral payment is repaid from the estate of the deceased.

An applicant may be eligible for a funeral payment even where there is a funeral plan, although any such funeral payment will only be available to cover costs not covered by the funeral plan.

Funeral costs paid by local authority or health authority

The local authority (usually Environmental Health Department) must arrange and pay for a funeral where the deceased has no relatives or friends willing to do so and has not made advance arrangements. The cost can be claimed from the estate, if there is one, or from any person liable to maintain the deceased.

The person's local clinical commissioning group/Health Board will make the arrangements if the death was in a hospital.

20.3.4 Funeral directors

It is not obligatory to use a funeral director, but there are two trade associations that regulate their activities: National Association of Funeral Directors (**www.nafd. org.uk**) and National Society of Allied and Independent Funeral Directors (**www- .saif.org.uk**). Both associations have a code of practice which members should follow and both operate a complaints procedure. Quotes may be obtained and a basic funeral can be requested.

20.3.5 Procedures for burial or cremation

The decision about disposal of the body is strictly that of the executors or, in the absence of a will, the next of kin who will be the potential administrators. Directions may be in or with the will and it is prudent to check in all cases. Although these are not legally binding they will invariably be followed where possible and will be compelling where there is disagreement between executors. It is wise to consult the next of kin (and tactful to consult any cohabitee) and professional executors will usually follow their wishes unless in conflict with the will or each other.

Always ascertain whether the deceased has already made arrangements: a grave space may have been reserved or there may be funeral insurance.

Burial

In England and Wales everyone is entitled to be buried, or have their ashes interred, in the churchyard of the parish where:

- they died in the parish; or
- they lived at the time of their death; or
- they were on the church electoral roll at the time of their death;

provided there is a churchyard and there is space in the churchyard.

The permission of the local clergy is required elsewhere but grave space may have been bought in advance.

There are also cemeteries owned by local authorities or privately, and widely varying fees are charged.

The authority of a coroner is required if a body is to be removed from England and Wales, whether or not the person died from natural causes (see the Removal of Bodies Regulations 1954, SI 1954/448).

Cremation

Several prescribed forms must be completed and delivered to the medical referee at the cremation authority before a cremation can be carried out:

- **CR1:** application for cremation of the body of a person who has died (completed by the next of kin or other suitable person authorising the cremation authority to carry out the cremation).
- **CR4:** medical certificate (completed by the doctor who attended the deceased in the last illness certifying the cause of death and sent in a sealed envelope to the doctor who will sign Form CR5).
- **CR5:** confirmatory medical certificate (a confirmatory certificate by another doctor certifying the fact and cause of death who must also have seen the body).
- **CR6:** certificate of the coroner (in circumstances where a post-mortem has been carried out or an inquest has been opened CR6 will replace the need for CR4 and CR5).

A fee is payable to each doctor completing Forms CR4 and CR5. The British Medical Association has agreed with various associations a fee of £82.00 for each form. The fee will usually be paid by the funeral director and passed to their client. There is no fee payable for the coroner's Form CR6.

If the deceased died in a hospital at which they were an in-patient and a post-mortem was carried out at the hospital, there is no requirement for a confirmatory certificate in Form CR5.

The forms are submitted to the medical referee of the cremation authority who will complete Form CR10 (authorisation of cremation of deceased person by medical referee). The medical referee will also charge a fee.

The applicant is informed of the right to attend the cremation authority to inspect the medical certificates (Forms CR4 and CR5) by guidance available with Form CR1 and by advice from the funeral director.

If an applicant has completed Form CR1 and requested the right to view the medical certificates on their own or with a nominated representative, the cremation authority must make all reasonable efforts to contact the applicant and their nominated representative (if appropriate) as soon as the medical certificates are received. The applicant and their nominated representative have 48 hours from the time that they are notified to view the medical certificates and to make any representations to the medical referee as a result of viewing the certificates.

The forms and guidance on the regulations are available online (see **www.gov.uk/government/organisations/ministry-of-justice**).

20.3.6   Funeral arrangements after death overseas

If a citizen of England or Wales dies abroad, the deceased may be buried or, if possible, cremated locally.

Alternatively, the bereaved may wish to repatriate the deceased for burial. Before a body can be transported back to England and Wales, the following are commonly required:

- a certified translation of a foreign death certificate (which may indicate the cause of death);

- a certificate of embalming; and
- a certificate from the foreign coroner or other authority giving permission to transfer the body to the UK.

The British Consulate can advise on what is required. The costs of repatriation can be met by the deceased's travel insurance provider or by the bereaved.

If the deceased is brought back to England or Wales to be buried, the bereaved will need to take the foreign death certificate to the Registrar in the area where the burial is to take place. The Registrar will need to issue a 'certificate of no liability to register'.

If the deceased is brought back to England or Wales to be cremated, the Home Office or the Coroner will need to first issue a certificate.

20.3.7　Headstones and memorial stones

There may be regulations restricting the shape or style and wording of headstones. Advice should be sought from the incumbent or priest in charge of the parish where the burial or interment of ashes is to take place.

20.4　PRESUMPTION OF DEATH

Relevant legislation is:

- Presumption of Death Act (PDA) 2013.

20.4.1　The presumption of death

The Presumption of Death Act 2013 came into force on 1 October 2014 and provides a single procedure for obtaining a declaration from the court that a missing person is presumed dead. The benefit for the applicant is that PDA 2013 now avoids the need to make different applications for the various aspects of the missing person's life and estate.

The court has jurisdiction when either:

- the missing person was domiciled in England and Wales on the day on which he or she was last known to be alive;
- the missing person had been habitually resident in England and Wales throughout the period of one year ending with that day; or
- the application is made by the spouse or civil partner of the missing person and the applicant is domiciled in England and Wales on the day on which he or she was last known to be alive, or has been habitually resident in England and Wales throughout the period of one year ending with that day.

20.4.2 Making the declaration

PDA 2013, s.2 provides that, on an application to it under s.1, the court must make a declaration of presumed death if it is satisfied that the missing person:

- has died; or
- has not been known to be alive for a period of at least seven years.

The declaration must include a finding as to the date and time of the missing person's death.

PDA 2013, s.2 goes on to set out how the date of death must be calculated. If the court is satisfied that the missing person has died but is uncertain as to which moment death occurred during a specific period, the date of presumed death is the final day of the period in which the missing person is believed to have died (PDA 2013, s.2(3)).

If the court is not satisfied that the missing person has died but is satisfied that the missing person has not been known to be alive for a period of at least seven years, the date of presumed death is seven years starting from the day after the date the missing person was last known to be alive (PDA 2013, s.2(4)).

20.4.3 Who can apply for a declaration?

The following persons (as so related to the missing person) have an automatic right for his/her application to be heard by the court:

- spouse;
- civil partner;
- parent;
- child; or
- sibling (which s.20(1) defines as including a sibling of the half-blood).

Any other person may make an application but, for the application to be heard by the court, the court must satisfy itself that the applicant has a sufficient interest.

20.4.4 Procedure

Applications must be made to the High Court. The procedure for making an application is governed by Part V of rule 57 of the Civil Procedure Rules (CPR), which states that a claim for a declaration of presumed death (or variation order, for which further details are set out below) must be made by issuing a claim form in accordance with CPR rule 8. Applicants must also consult Practice Direction 57B, which sets out in full the specific information required by the court and the steps that the applicant must follow.

An application must be advertised within seven days in at least one newspaper with a circulation near the last known address of the missing person. A copy of the newspaper page must and the date of the advertisement must be filed with the court at least five days before the hearing.

The applicant must also serve notice (by way of a copy of the application, plus any other information required by the court) on the following persons within seven days of issuing the claim:

- the missing person's spouse, civil partner, parent, children and siblings (both full and half-blood);
- the missing person's closest living relative known to the applicant (if none of the above);
- any other person who appears to the applicant to have an interest in the making of a declaration; and/or
- (if the application is for a variation order) the applicant for the declaration of presumed death.

Any spouse, civil partner, parent, child or sibling (both full and half-blood) has a right to intervene in proceedings for a declaration of presumed death (or for a variation order). The Attorney General, or any other person, also has a right to intervene subject to obtaining the prior permission of the court. The court can send papers to the Attorney General during any such application and the parties can be ordered to pay the Attorney General's costs.

20.4.5   Effect of a declaration

A declaration made by the court under PDA 2013 is conclusive of both the presumed death of the missing person and the date and time of such death.

The declaration is effective against all persons and for all purposes, including for the purposes of ending a marriage or civil partnership or for the purposes of acquiring an interest in property.

It should be noted that the declaration has the above effect only once the period of appeal (as determined by the Part 2 of the Civil Procedure Rules) has lapsed with no appeal or, if an appeal was lodged within the permitted time limited, where that appeal has been unsuccessful.

The court will send a copy of the declaration to the Registrar General to be entered on the Register of Presumed Deaths and only a certified copy of the entry will serve as proof of death (for example, for the purposes of applying for a grant of representation).

20.4.6   Varying a declaration (variation order)

Any person may apply to the High Court for a variation order to vary or revoke a declaration of presumed death. However, the court must refuse to hear an application for a variation order if it considers that the applicant lacks a sufficient interest.

The original declaration can be varied as to the time and/or date of the presumed death. The original order can be revoked if the court is satisfied that the missing person is alive and no longer missing.

Unless the court considers that there are exceptional circumstances which make it appropriate to do so, the court must not make an order in relation to any interest in property acquired as a result of the original declaration if the application for the variation order was made more than five years after the date of the original declaration.

Any marriage or civil partnership which is brought to an end as a result of a declaration remains unaffected by a variation order. The court does retain, however, a power to determine any question that relates to an interest in property which arises as a consequence of the variation order (PDA 2013, s.7(1)) and it must make any orders it considers reasonable in relation to any interest in property acquired as a result of the declaration that the applicant wishes to vary (PDA 2013, s.7(2)). When deciding what order to make under PDA 2013, s.7(2), the court is obliged to take into account principles of trust and capital sum payments made by insurers (PDA 2013, s.8).

It is possible for trustees of a trust that is created or affected by a declaration to take out insurance to protect themselves from the consequences of any variations orders made in the future. The insurance premium(s) can be paid from the trust fund itself.

20.5 INFORMATION FOR CLIENTS

Information for clients can be found in:

- Age UK guide: *When Someone Dies* (**www.ageuk.org.uk**).
- Age UK Factsheet 27: *Planning for a Funeral* (**www.ageuk.org.uk**).
- 'What to Do After Someone Dies' (**www.gov.uk/after-a-death**).
- The Coroners' Society (**www.coronersociety.org.uk**) has useful information – also available in Welsh, Polish and Portuguese.
- Ministry of Justice's *Guide to Coroner Services* **www.gov.uk/government/publications**.
- *The Inquest Handbook* (**www.inquest.org.uk/help/the-inquest-handbook**).

Useful information about the procedures when a person dies outside England and Wales can be found by contacting the local British Consulate and from resources such as:

- Foreign and Commonwealth Office leaflet *Deaths Overseas* (**www.gov.uk/government/publications/coping-with-death-abroad**).
- **www.gov.uk/register-a-death**.

- 'Registering an overseas death' (**www.bereavementadvice.org/topics/ registering-a-death-and-informing-others/registering-an-overseas- death**).

Addresses and contact details

Abbeyfield Society

St Peter's House
2 Bricket Road
St Albans
Hertfordshire AL1 3JW
Tel: 01727 857536
www.abbeyfield.com

Action on Elder Abuse

PO Box 60001
Streatham
London SW16 9BY
Tel: 020 8835 9280
Tel: 080 8808 8141 (helpline)
www.elderabuse.org.uk

Action on Hearing Loss

19–23 Featherstone Street
London EC1Y 8SL
Tel: 0808 808 0123 (helpline)
Textphone: 0808 808 9000
Email: informationline@hearingloss.org.uk
www.actiononhearingloss.org.uk

Administrative Court

Administrative Court Office
Royal Courts of Justice
Strand
London WC2A 2LL
Tel: 020 7947 6655
DX: 44457 Strand

Age UK

Tavis House
1–6 Tavistock Square
London WC1H 9NA
Tel: 0800 169 2081 (advice or information)
Tel: 0800 169 8787 (other enquiries)
www.ageuk.org.uk

Alzheimer's Society

Devon House
58 St Katharine's Way
London E1W 1LB
Tel: 0300 222 11 22 (helpline)
Tel: 0330 333 0804 (customer care)
www.alzheimers.org.uk

Arthritis Care

Floor 4
Linen Court
10 East Road
London N1 6AD
Tel: 020 7380 6500 (switchboard)
Tel: 0808 800 4050 (helpline)
www.arthritiscare.org.uk

Arthritis Research UK

Copeman House
St Mary's Gate
Chesterfield
Derbyshire S41 7TD
Tel: 0300 790 0400
www.arthritisresearchuk.org

Brendoncare Foundation

The Old Malthouse
Victoria Road
Winchester
Hampshire SO23 7DU
Tel: 01962 852133
www.brendoncare.org.uk

British Heart Foundation

Lyndon Place
2096 Coventry Road
Sheldon
Birmingham B26 3YU
Tel: 0300 330 3311 (helpline)
Tel: 020 7554 0000 (Head Office)
www.bhf.org.uk

British Red Cross

UK Office
44 Moorfields
London EC2Y 9AL
Tel: 0344 871 11 11
Textphone: 020 7562 2050
www.redcross.org.uk

Business Disability Forum

Nutmeg House
60 Gainsford Street
London SE1 2NY
Tel: 020 7403 3020
Textphone: 020 7403 0040
www.businessdisabilityforum.org.uk

Care Quality Commission

Citygate
Gallowgate
Newcastle upon Tyne NE1 4PA
Tel: 03000 616161
www.cqc.org.uk

Care and Social Services Inspectorate for Wales (CSSIW)

Welsh Government Office
Rhydycar Business Park

Merthyr Tydfil CF48 1UZ
Tel: 0300 7900 126
Email: cssiw@wales.gsi.gov.uk
www.cssiw.org.uk

Carers Trust

32–36 Loman Street
London SE1 0EH
Tel: 0844 800 4361
www.carers.org

Carers UK

20 Great Dover Street
London SE1 4LX
Tel: 020 7378 4999
Email: advice@carersuk.org
www.carersuk.org

Carillion Energy Services Ltd

Carillion House
84 Salop Street
Wolverhampton WV3 0SR
Tel: 0191 676 3000
Email: greendeal@carillionplc.com
www.carillionenergy.com

Centre for Policy on Ageing

Tavis House
1–6 Tavistock Square
London WC1H 9NA
Tel: 020 7553 6500
Email: cpa@cpa.org.uk
www.cpa.org.uk

Citizens' Advice

3rd Floor North
200 Aldersgate Street
London EC1A 4HD
Tel: 03444 111 444 (England advice line)
Tel: 03444 77 20 20 (Wales advice line)
www.citizensadvice.org.uk

Contact the Elderly

2 Grosvenor Gardens
London SW1W 0DH
Tel: 020 7240 0630
Tel: 0800 716 543 (Freephone)
www.contact-the-elderly.org.uk

Court of Protection

First Avenue House
42–49 High Holborn
London WC1A 9JA
Tel: 0300 456 4600
DX: 160013 Kingsway 7
www.gov.uk/court-of-protection

Cruse Bereavement Care

PO Box 800
Richmond
Surrey TW9 1RG
Tel: 020 8939 9530
Email: info@cruse.org.uk
www.cruse.org.uk

Department of Health

Customer Service Centre
Richmond House
79 Whitehall
London SW1A 2NS
Tel: 020 7210 4850
Textphone: 0203 741 8449
www.gov.uk/government/organisations/
department-of-health

Department for Work and Pensions

Attendance Allowance

Tel: 0345 605 6055
Textphone: 0345 604 5312
Monday to Friday, 8am to 6pm
www.gov.uk/government/organisations
department-for-work-and-pensions

Postal address for Attendance Allowance

Attendance Allowance Service Centre
Warbreck House
Warbreck Hill
Blackpool
Lancashire FY2 0YE

Disability Benefits Centre

www.gov.uk/disability-benefits-helpline

Disability Living Allowance (DLA)

Born on or before 8 April 1948:
Tel: 0345 605 6055
Textphone: 0345 604 5312
Monday to Friday, 8am to 6pm

Born after 8 April 1948:
Tel: 0345 712 3456
Textphone: 0345 722 4433
Monday to Friday, 8am to 6pm

Postal address for DLA Adult (aged 16 and over):
Disability Benefits Centre
Warbreck House
Warbreck Hill
Blackpool
Lancashire FY2 0YE

Make sure you include your date of birth to confirm you're 16 or over.

Postal address for DLA Child (under 16):
Disability Benefit Centre 4
Post Handling Site B
Wolverhampton WV99 1BY

Personal Independence Payment (PIP)

Tel: 0345 850 3322
Textphone: 0345 601 6677
Monday to Friday, 8am to 6pm

The Pension Service

www.gov.uk/contact-pension-service

Pension claim line
Tel: 0800 731 7898
Textphone: 0800 731 7339
www.gov.uk/find-lost-pension

Pension credit
Tel: 0800 99 1234
www.gov.uk/pension-credit/how-to-claim

Winter Fuel Payments Helpline
Tel: 0345 915 1515
Textphone: 0345 606 0285
www.gov.uk/winter-fuel-payment/
how-to-claim

International Pension Centre

Tel: 0191 218 7777
Textphone: 0 191 218 7280
www.gov.uk/international-pension-centre

Disability Rights UK

Ground Floor
CAN Mezzanine
49–51 East Rd
London N1 6AH
Tel: 020 7250 8181 (office)
Tel: 0808 800 0082 (Equality Advisory and
Support Service)
Tel: 0300 555 1525 (personal budgets hel-
pline)
www.disabilityrightsuk.org

Elderly Accommodation Council (EAC)

EAC FirstStop Advice
3rd Floor
89 Albert Embankment
London SE1 7PT
Tel: 0800 377 7070
Email: info@firststopadvice.org.uk
www.housingcare.org

Equality and Human Rights Commission

FREEPOST
Equality Advisory Support Service
FPN4431
Tel: 0808 800 0082 (helpline)
Email:
correspondence@equalityhumanrights.com
www.equalityhumanrights.com

Financial Assistance Scheme

PO Box 234
Mowden Hall
Darlington DL1 9GL
Tel: 0345 604 4585
Textphone: 0845 604 4139
www.pensionprotectionfund.org.uk/FAS/

Financial Conduct Authority

25 The North Colonnade
London E14 5HS
Tel: 0800 111 6768 (helpline)
Tel: 020 7066 1000 (switchboard)
www.fca.org.uk/consumers

Financial Ombudsman Service

Exchange Tower
London E14 9SR
Tel: 020 7964 1000 (switchboard)
Tel: 0800 023 4 567 (helpline)
Textphone: 07860 027 586
www.financial-ombudsman.org.uk

First-tier Tribunal (Care Standards)

HM Courts and Tribunals Service
1st Floor
Darlington Magistrates' Court
Parkgate DL1 1RU
Tel: 01325 289 350
www.gov.uk/guidance/appeal-to-the-care-
standards-tribunal

First-tier Tribunal (Primary Health Lists)

HM Courts and Tribunals Service
Darlington Magistrates' Court
Parkgate
Darlington DL1 1RU
Tel: 01325 289 350
www.gov.uk/guidance/
appeal-to-the-primary-health-lists-tribunal

The Forum of Mobility Centres

c/o Providence Chapel
Warehorne
Ashford
Kent TN26 2JX
Tel: 0800 559 3636
www.mobility-centres.org.uk

HM Revenue and Customs

Inheritance Tax payments by post

HMRC Banking
St Mungo's Road
Cumbernauld
Glasgow G70 5WY
DX: 550100 Cumbernauld 2

National Insurance Contributions and Employer Office

Tel: 0300 200 3500 (general enquiries)
www.gov.uk/topic/personal-tax/
national-insurance

Probate and Inheritance Tax Helpline

Tel: 0300 123 1072

Savings helpline

Tel: 0300 200 3312

Shares and Assets Valuation Helpline

Tel: 0845 601 5693

Trusts and Deceased Estates Helpline

Tel: 0300 123 1072

Hospice UK

34–44 Britannia Street
London WC1X 9JG
Tel: 020 7520 8200
Email: info@hospiceuk.org
www.hospiceuk.org

Independent Age

18 Avonmore Road
London W14 8RR
Tel: 020 7605 4200
Email: charity@independentage.org
www.independentage.org

The Law Society

113 Chancery Lane
London WC2A 1PL
Tel: 020 7242 1222
DX: 56 Lond/Chancery Ln
www.lawsociety.org.uk

Law Society Practice Advice Service

Tel: 0207 320 5675
Email: practiceadvice@lawsociety.org.uk

Lawyerline

Tel: 0207 320 5720
Email: lawyerline@lawsociety.org.uk

PII helpline

Tel: 0207 320 9545

Legal Ombudsman

PO Box 6806
Wolverhampton WV1 9WJ
Tel: 0300 555 0333
Email: enquiries@legalombudsman.org.uk
www.legalombudsman.org.uk

Local Government Ombudsman

PO Box 4771
Coventry CV4 0EH
Tel: 0300 061 0614
www.lgo.org.uk

Macmillan Cancer Support

89 Albert Embankment
London SE1 7UQ
Tel: 020 7840 7840 (switchboard)
Tel: 0808 808 00 00 (support line)
www.macmillan.org.uk

Mind

15–19 Broadway
London E15 4BQ
Tel: 020 8519 2122
Email: contact@mind.org.uk (general enquiries)
Email: legal@mind.org.uk (legal line)
Email: info@mind.org.uk (infoline)
www.mind.org.uk

Mind Cymru

3rd Floor, Quebec House, Castlebridge
5–19 Cowbridge Road East
Cardiff CF11 9AB
Tel: 029 2039 5123

Motability

Tel: 0300 456 4566
www.motability.co.uk

Multiple Sclerosis (MS) Society

MS National Centre
372 Edgware Road
London NW2 6ND
Tel: 020 8438 0700
Tel: 0808 800 8000 (helpline)
Email: helpline@mssociety.org.uk
www.mssociety.org.uk

National Association of Funeral Directors

618 Warwick Road
Solihull B91 1AA
Tel: 0121 711 1343
Email: info@nafd.org.uk
www.nafd.org.uk

National Society of Allied and Independent Funeral Directors

SAIF Business Centre
3 Bullfields
Sawbridgeworth
Herts CM21 9DB
Tel: 0345 230 6777
Email: info@saif.org.uk
www.saif.org.uk

NNS Business Services Authority

Helplines

0300 330 1348 – dental services
0300 330 1343 – Low Income Scheme
0300 330 1341 – medical exemption certificates
0300 330 1341 – PPCs
0300 330 1349 – prescription services
0300 330 1347 – tax credit certificates
0300 123 0849 – to order paper copy HC12, HC5 and HC1 (SC) forms
0300 330 1343 – all other queries
www.nhsbsa.nhs.uk

Office of the Public Guardian

PO Box 16185
Birmingham B2 2WH
Tel: 0300 456 0300
Email: customerservices@publicguardian.gsi.gov.uk
www.gov.uk/government/organisations/office-of-the-public-guardian

Offices of Court Funds, Official Solicitor and Public Trustee

Court Funds Office

Glasgow G58 1AB
Tel: 0300 0200 199
Email: enquiries@cfo.gsi.gov.uk
www.gov.uk/contact-court-funds-office

Official Solicitor and Public Trustee

Victory House
30–34 Kingsway
London WC2B 6EX
Email: enquiries@offsol.gsi.gov.uk
DX 141423 Bloomsbury 7
Tel: 020 3681 2751 (Court of Protection – Healthcare and Welfare)
Tel: 020 3681 2759 (Trust and Deputy Services)
www.gov.uk/government/organisations/official-solicitor-and-public-trustee

Parkinson's UK

215 Vauxhall Bridge Road
London SW1V 1EJ
Tel: 0808 800 0303 (helpline)
Email: hello@parkinsons.org.uk
www.parkinsons.org.uk

Parliamentary and Health Service Ombudsman

Tel: 0345 015 4033
Textphone: 0300 061 4298
www.ombudsman.org.uk

Patients Association

PO Box 935
Harrow
Middlesex HA1 3YJ
Tel: 020 8423 9111 (administration)
Tel: 0845 608 4455 (helpline)
www.patients-association.com

Pensions Advisory Service

11 Belgrave Road
London SW1V 1RB
Tel: 0300 123 1047 (helpline)
www.pensionsadvisoryservice.org.uk

Pensions Ombudsman

11 Belgrave Road
London SW1V 1RB
Tel: 020 7630 2200
www.pensions-ombudsman.org.uk

Public Services Ombudsman for Wales

1 Ffordd yr Hen Gae
Pencoed CF35 5LJ
Tel: 0300 790 0203
www.ombudsman-wales.org.uk

Registered Nursing Home Association

Derek Whittaker House
Tunnel Lane
Off Lifford Lane
Kings Norton
Birmingham B30 3JN
Tel: 0121 451 1088
Email: frankursell@rnha.co.uk
www.rnha.co.uk

Relatives and Residents Association

1 The Ivories
6–18 Northampton Street
London N1 2HY
Tel: 020 7359 8148
Email: info@relres.org
www.relres.org

Royal National Institute of Blind People (RNIB)

105 Judd Street
London WC1H 9NE
Tel: 0303 123 9999 (helpline)
www.rnib.org.uk

Scope

6 Market Road
London N7 9PW
Tel: 0808 800 3333 (helpline)
Email: helpline@scope.org.uk
www.scope.org.uk

Senior Courts Costs Office

Thomas More Building
Royal Courts of Justice
Strand
London WC2A 2LL
Tel: 020 7947 6000
Email: scco@hmcts.gsi.gov.uk
www.gov.uk/courts-tribunals/
senior-courts-costs-office

Shelter

88 Old Street
London EC1V 9HU
Tel: 0808 800 4444 (helpline)
Tel: 0344 515 2000 (switchboard)
Email: info@shelter.org.uk
www.shelter.org.uk

Society of Pension Professionals

St Bartholomew House
92 Fleet Street
London EC4Y 1DG
Tel: 020 7353 1688
Email: info@the-spp.co.uk
http://the-spp.co.uk

**Society of Trust and Estate
Practitioners (STEP)**

Artillery House (South)
11–19 Artillery Row
London SW1P 1RT
Tel: 020 3752 3700
Email: step@step.org
www.step.org

Solicitors for the Elderly

Studio 209
Mill Studio Business Centre
Crane Mead
Ware
Hertfordshire SG12 9PY
Tel: 0844 567 6173 (public line)
Tel: 0844 800 9710 (members line)
Email: admin@sfe.legal
www.sfe.legal

Solicitors Regulation Authority

The Cube
199 Wharfside Street
Birmingham B1 1RN
Tel: 0370 606 2555
DX: 720293 Birmingham 47
www.sra.org.uk

Professional Ethics Team

Tel: 0370 606 2577

Stroke Association

Stroke Association House
240 City Road
London EC1V 2PR
Tel: 020 7566 0300
Tel: 0303 3033 100 (helpline)
Textphone: 18001 0303 3033 100
Email: info@stroke.org.uk
www.stroke.org.uk

Veterans UK

Ministry of Defence
Norcross
Thornton Cleveleys
Blackpool FY5 3WP
Tel: 0808 1914 2 18
Email: veterans-uk@mod.uk
www.gov.uk/government/organisations/
veterans-uk

APPENDIX B

Further reading

GUIDANCE

Age UK

See **www.ageuk.org.uk/publications** for information guides and factsheets.

Codes of Practice

- Department for Constitutional Affairs (2007) Mental Capacity Act 2005: Code of Practice (**www.gov.uk/government/publications/mental-capacity-act-code-of-practice**).
- Department of Health (2015) Mental Health Act 1983: Code of Practice (**www.gov.uk/government/publications/code-of-practice-mental-health-act-1983**).

Law Society Practice Notes

See **www.lawsociety.org.uk**.

- Anti-Money Laundering (22 October 2013).
- Appointment of a Professional Executor (6 October 2011).
- Client Care Information (26 March 2013).
- Compliance Officers (9 October 2013).
- Conflict of Interests (3 March 2015).
- Consumer Contracts Regulations 2013 (18 September 2014).
- Data Protection (6 October 2011).
- Disputed Wills (6 October 2011).
- Equality Act 2010 (2 May 2012).
- Estate Administration: Banking Protocols (28 January 2013).
- File Closure Management (2 June 2014).
- File Retention: Wills and Probate (6 October 2011).
- Financial Abuse (13 June 2013)
- Holding Client Funds (29 April 2015).
- In-House Practice: Regulatory Requirements (28 February 2013).
- Information on Letterheads, Emails and Websites (24 August 2015).
- Information Security (11 October 2011).
- Initial Interviews (6 October 2011).
- Lasting Powers of Attorney (8 December 2011).
- Making Gifts of Assets (6 October 2011).
- Meeting the Needs of Vulnerable Clients (2 July 2015).
- Outcomes-Focused Regulation: Overview (18 June 2015).
- Outsourcing (29 April 2015).
- Powers of Attorney for Banking (6 October 2011).

- Preparing a Will When Your Client is Leaving a Gift for You, Your Family or Colleagues (20 January 2015).
- Provision of Services Regulations 2009 (22 August 2013).
- Publicising Solicitors' Charges (15 September 2015).
- Redundancy (19 December 2008).
- Representation before Mental Health Tribunals (22 January 2015)
- Setting Up a Practice: Regulatory Requirements (21 February 2013).
- Supervision (6 October 2011).

BOOKS

Law for the elderly

Ashton G. and Bielanska C. (2014) *Elderly People and the Law*, 2nd edn, Jordan Publishing.
Bielanska C. (2013) *Elderly Clients: A Precedent Manual*, Jordan Publishing.

Benefits

Child Poverty Action Group (2014) *Fuel Rights Handbook*, 17th edn, CPAG.
Child Poverty Action Group (2015) *Welfare Benefits and Tax Credits Handbook 2015/16*, CPAG.
Ennals S. and Wall C. (looseleaf) *Tolley's Social Security and State Benefits*, LexisNexis.
Greaves I. (2015) *Disability Rights Handbook: A Guide to Benefits and Services for All Disabled People, Their Families, Carers and Advisers*, 40th edn, Disability Rights UK.

Community care law

Butler J. (2015) *Community Care Law and Local Authority Handbook*, Jordan Publishing.
Clements L. and Thompson P. (2011) *Community Care and the Law*, 5th edn, Legal Action Group.

Court of Protection

Ashton G. (ed) (2015) *Court of Protection Practice 2015*, Jordan Publishing.
Lush D. and Rees D. (ed) (looseleaf) *Heywood & Massey: Court of Protection Practice*, Sweet & Maxwell.
Pearce N. and Jackson S. (2014) *Urgent Applications in the Court of Protection*, 2nd revised edn, Jordan Publishing.

Employment

Barnett D., Gore K. and Scrope H. (2014) *Employment Law Handbook*, 6th edn, Law Society.
Mansfield G., Bannerjee L. *et al.* (2014) *Blackstone's Employment Law Practice*, 8th revised edn, Oxford University Press.
Slade E. and Jones S. (2015) *Tolley's Employment Handbook*, 29th edn, LexisNexis.
Wallington P. (2015) *Butterworths Employment Law Handbook*, 23rd edn, LexisNexis.

Equality and human rights

Duggan M. (2010) *Equality Act 2010: A Guide to the New Law*, Law Society.
Kapoor S. (2006) *Age Discrimination: A Guide to the New Law*, Law Society.

O'Dempsey D. *et al.* (2013) *Discrimination in Employment: A Claims Handbook*, Legal Action Group.

Wadham J. *et al.* (2012) *Blackstone's Guide to the Equality Act 2010*, 2nd edn, Oxford University Press.

Housing

Arden A., Orme E. and Vanhegan T. (2012) *Homelessness and Allocations*, 9th revised edn, Legal Action Group.

Astin D. (2015) *Housing Law Handbook*, 3rd revised edn, Legal Action Group.

Cottle S. (2009) *Housing Law Handbook: A Practical Guide*, Law Society.

Luba J. *et al.* (2010) *Repairs: Tenants' Rights*, 4th edn, Legal Action Group.

Mental capacity and health law

Bartlett P. and Sandland R. (2013) *Mental Health Law: Policy and Practice*, 4th edn, Oxford University Press.

British Medical Association and the Law Society (2015) *Assessment of Mental Capacity: A Practical Guide for Doctors and Lawyers*, 4th edn, Law Society.

Butler J. (2013) *Mental Health Tribunals: Law, Practice and Procedure*, 2nd edn, Jordan Publishing.

English V. (2007) *Withholding and Withdrawing Life-prolonging Medical Treatment*, 3rd edn, Wiley-Blackwell.

Fennell, P. (2011) *Mental Health: Law and Practice*, 2nd edn, Jordan Publishing.

Greaney N., Morris F. and Taylor B. (2008) *Mental Capacity: A Guide to the New Law*, 2nd edn, Law Society.

Johnston C. (2010) *Medical Treatment: Decisions and the Law: The Mental Capacity Act in Action*, 2nd edn, Bloomsbury Professional.

Jones R. (2015) *Mental Health Act Manual*, 18th revised edn, Sweet & Maxwell.

Powers of attorney

Lush D. (2013) *Cretney and Lush on Lasting and Enduring Powers of Attorney*, 7th edn, Jordan Publishing.

Thurston J. (2012) *A Practitioner's Guide to Powers of Attorney*, 8th revised edn, Bloomsbury Professional.

Ward C. (2011) *Lasting Powers of Attorney: A Practical Guide*, 2nd edn, Law Society.

Tax

Angus T., Clarke A., Hewitt P. and Reed P. (2006) *Inheritance Act Claims: A Practical Guide*, Law Society.

Grant Thornton LLP (2012) *Capital Gains Tax Planning 2011–2012*, Bloomsbury Professional.

Homer R., Burrows R. and Goodall A. (2010) *Tolley's Tax Guide 2010–2011*, LexisNexis.

McLaughlin M. *et al.* (2015) *Ray and McLaughlin's Practical Inheritance Tax Planning*, 12th revised edn, Bloomsbury Professional.

Schwartz J. (2014) *Booth and Schwarz: Residence, Domicile and UK Taxation*, 18th edn, Bloomsbury Professional.

Wills, trusts and probate

Barlow R. *et al.* (2014) *Williams on Wills*, 10th revised edn, LexisNexis.

Clutton O. and Jennings S. (eds) (looseleaf) *Administration of Trusts*, LexisNexis.

Kessler J. (2014) *Drafting Trusts and Will Trusts: A Modern Approach*, 12th revised edn, Sweet & Maxwell.

King L. (2015) *Probate Practitioner's Handbook*, 7th edn, Law Society.

Law Society (2013) *Wills and Inheritance Protocol*, Law Society.

Steel G. (2012) *Trust Practitioner's Handbook*, 3rd edn, Law Society.

Thurston J. (2013) *A Practitioner's Guide to Trusts*, 10th revised edn, Bloomsbury Professional.

Tucker L., Le Poidevin N. and Brightwell J. (2015) *Lewin on Trusts*, 19th edn, Sweet & Maxwell.

Whitehouse C. and King L. (eds) (looseleaf) *Administration of Estates*, LexisNexis.

Withers LLP (looseleaf) *Practical Trust Precedents*, Sweet & Maxwell.

Index